The
SLOOP OF WAR
1650–1763

... an experiment for Sailing
is a good vessel but Did not Sail so well as some
the others —— byett in the Year 1732

Stewards Cabbins

Doters Cabbin

passage to the Magazine

Magazine

Fishroom

Master Cabbin

Lieutenants Cabbin

11 10 9 0 7

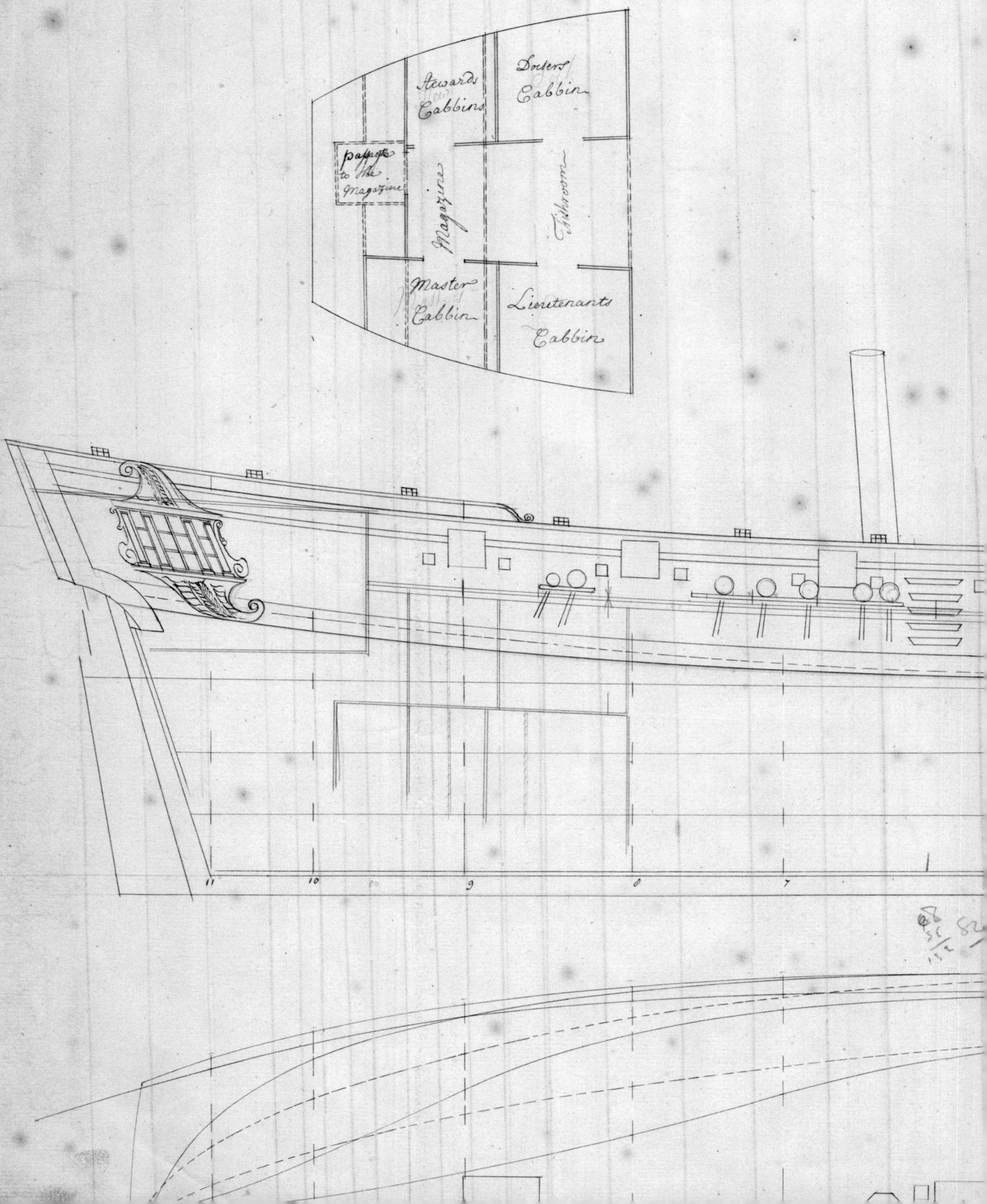

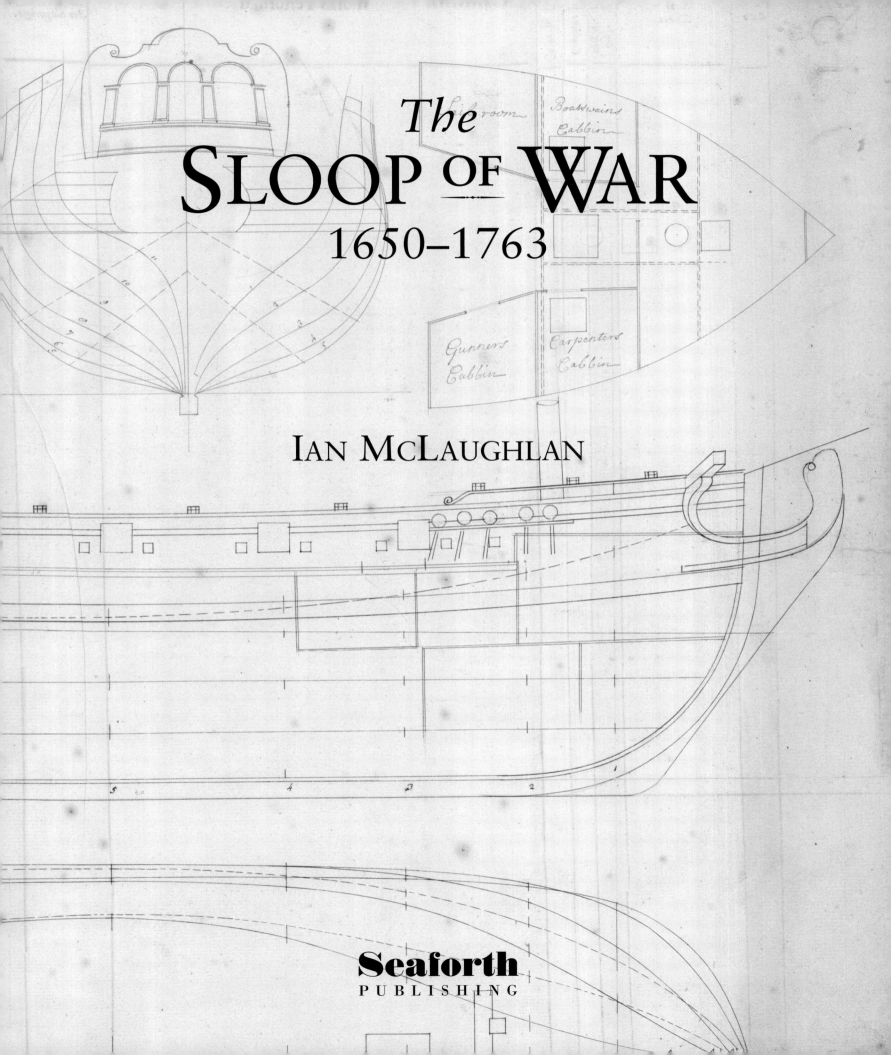

The
SLOOP OF WAR
1650–1763

Ian McLaughlan

Seaforth
PUBLISHING

FRONTISPIECE: Original Admiralty draught of HM Sloop *Spy*, 1732.
National Maritime Museum J0138

This book is dedicated to Derek Andrews without whose years of painstaking research at the Public Records Office, this book could not have been written.

Copyright © Ian McLaughlan 2014

First published in Great Britain in 2014 by
Seaforth Publishing
An imprint of Pen & Sword Books Ltd
47 Church Street, Barnsley
S Yorkshire S70 2AS

www.seaforthpublishing.com
Email info@seaforthpublishing.com

British Library Cataloguing in Publication Data
A CIP data record for this book is available from the British Library

ISBN 978 1 84832 187 8

Typeset and designed by Stephen Dent
Printed and bound in China through Printworks International Ltd.

CONTENTS

PREFACE

Many books have been written out of a mild sense of anger or frustration and this is certainly true of this one. Over the years, particularly during the last three decades, there have been countless volumes written – many in the greatest detail – on the ship of the line and other rated ships down to the Sixth Rate frigates. Very little has been said about the sloop of war or her counterpart, the French corvette. This is astonishing since this class of warship became, by the end of the Napoleonic wars, the most numerous of all in the Royal Navy. Other nations had their equivalents though only the French and the Spanish, and the Dutch with their yachts, came anywhere near to matching the breadth of their use by the Royal Navy. The nation to come closest to this position was France: that is until the United States of America declared for independence, but that is beyond the period of this book. The classification 'sloop' would remain in the Royal Navy right up to the end of the Second World War, which also saw the reintroduction of the word 'corvette', albeit without much regard for historical precedent.

The inspiration for this work came many years ago from a book called *The Line of Battle*, a misleading title since it covered all classes of warship, rated and unrated over a period of 200 years. The chapter that caught my eye was on the Sloop of War and was written by Robert Gardiner. For me this short account was a delight and fortunately, shortly after buying the book, I had made the precaution of taking it with me to hospital knowing that I would be stuck there for a few days. I thus had the opportunity to read and re-read this chapter. It dawned on me that the subject would be an excellent one for a new study since there seemed to be no book yet written that was specifically devoted to the Sloop of War. There was clear scope for amplification which, together with copious use of illustrations, would bring these trim and attractive fast-sailing warships to the notice of the maritime reader and modelmaker.

My original intention was to cover the period 1650 to 1950, but I felt that this would produce a colossal volume and cover too many differing interests. I decided therefore to consider three separate works, one to cover the origins (and birth) of the early sloops from 1650 to 1763, one to cover the great age of the sailing sloop from 1763 to 1815 and one to cover the end of sail and the transition to steel and steam from 1815 to 1950. Whether these latter two will ever be written I cannot say: much will depend on the success or otherwise of this first volume and whether I will still have the mental facilities to research and write a sequel!

In this first volume I have spent much time on the origins of this class of vessel as I feel that without such an exploration a true understanding of the Sloop of War and its work cannot be achieved. Like their larger cousins, the frigates (Fifth and Sixth Rates), they were maids of all work, though with a slightly different emphasis in the types of role. Also like the frigates they were designed to be fast-sailers and to 'point high' into the wind. In fact they were probably the most weatherly and manoeuvrable of all naval square-rigged warships except in extremely rough conditions. And like frigates they would not normally form part of a fleet in battle but be employed in support for reconnaissance and communication. And for these two tasks they had to sail well. For this reason I have given some time to a consideration of their rig since this is elemental to fulfilling these two tasks.

There are three people without whose encouragement and support I could not have written this book. First, as you will have surmised, is Robert Gardiner, whose earlier work on sloops in *Line of Battle* was the inspiration for this book. Beyond this he has acted as my mentor throughout its preparation. One critical piece of support was his recommendation that I should contact Derek Andrews, a man who is probably the greatest expert in this country on the sailing sloop of war. Derek Andrews was a teacher of English at a grammar school just outside Birmingham. He has never lived near the sea and has no experience of sailing or seafaring in his background. Yet for some inexplicable reason he developed an almost obsessive interest in these tiny warships.

It may be that he was struck by their form and beauty. Whatever the reason, it led him into years of work at the then Public Record Office researching old, crumbling Admiralty documents, unearthing a mass of detail which he would then analyse to draw comparisons and develop arguments as to the shape, form and rig of these vessels. Sadly, because of ill health, he did not feel able to bring his researches together into a book and unselfishly agreed to pass his notes on to me. This is more the shame since, with his great knowledge and his command of English, he would have no doubt furnished you with a better and more lucid account than I have been able to relate. For him this has been a lifetime's work and therefore this book is quite rightly dedicated to him.

Although I could probably have written the book without him, the support of John Garnish, a co-member of the Society of Model Shipwrights, has made my task immeasurably easier. Not only has he read all my work, but with similar interests to me, and with a scientist's brain, he has questioned some of my more outlandish assertions! Moreover, having the computer skills that I lack he has made much of the illustrative material more presentable. He has in short provided a pre-editing service which has reduced the scale of Robert Gardiner's nightmare on receiving my drafts!

There are then two institutions, if that is what they should be called, without which much of the detail in this book could not have been obtained. The National Archives hold the vast majority of Admiralty and Navy Board documents. They also have a computerised system to help the reader identify the documents he requires that even I can understand. This is backed up by really helpful staff, many of whom appear to be as interested in the reader's subject as this reader himself! The National Maritime Museum has four departments holding four great collections that have so much to offer the researcher into warship types: The Brass Foundry, which houses the Museum's vast array of ships' plans; the Caird Library, in which is probably the greatest collection of nautical literature in the world; the picture gallery, whose critical contribution to this book is its huge folio of works by the Van de Veldes, father and son; and finally the ship model department, housed partly in the Museum and partly at the Historic Dockyard at Chatham. In all cases, the staffs at these departments have been most helpful in meeting my requests but I would like to mention three in particular. Jeremy Michell and Andrew Cheung at the Brass foundry were most generous in allowing me to trawl through their computer records to identify plans that would support this book. It has to be said that in many ways, and certainly from the beginning of the eighteenth century, it is these plans that form the essential visual ingredient of the work. I am very grateful for the considerable assistance they provided for me. The third is David Lindridge who looks after the Museum's reserve collection of models at Chatham. These models are stored in climatically controlled compartments in tiers and it requires some effort to find and extract any model. On my visit I required several to be brought out for examination. I have to thank him for laying out a range of models in ideal conditions for research.

Finally there are a quartet of books which form the foundation of any study of this subject, two English and two French. The earliest is David Lyon's *The Sailing Navy List*. In it the combination of plans and text in chronological order was invaluable in forming an overview of the subject. Following it, Rif Winfield's volumes *British Warships in the Age of Sail* expanded on David Lyon's work, giving the career details of every sloop in my interest. Those could then be used in conjunction with Admiralty documents from the National Archives. The third and fourth books are in French and are both specialised and focused. They are the monographs on *La Creole – Corvette* and on *La Belle – Barque* by Jean Boudriot. These books give us a well argued and illustrated account of the development of the French equivalents to British sloops which, when combined with plans held by the National Maritime Museum at Greenwich and the comments of other writers, give us a fascinating insight into the differing requirements of our two seafaring nations. I am most grateful to Jean Boudriot for allowing me to incorporate much of the information in their pages into my chapters on the small French warships that provide such a useful comparison to our own. His contribution has been augmented by Gerard Delacroix whose monograph on *L'Amarante* further displays the design of the French corvette. The French contribution to the design of British sloops in this period was considerable. Therefore, I would advise any serious student or modelmaker to consult two online sites: ANCRE – Collections Archaeologiques, developed by Jean Boudriot and the late Hubert Berti, and Modellisme Arsenale, an online forum for members building models from the monographs by Jean Boudriot and the site developer Gerard Delacroix.

The last 'thank you' is to my partner Michela, who gave up her desk, computer, printer and office for my use in preparing this book. For months she has run her office from a small chair-side table, mobile telephone and a laptop computer. For her the thought of a sequel to this book is not an entirely happy one!

ABBREVIATIONS
The following abbreviations are used throughout the text, tables and appendices.

BDR	Breadth to depth (ratio)
BU	Broken up
DoH	Depth in hold
Dyd	Dockyard [Royal]
LBR	Length to breadth (ratio)
LGD	Length on the gundeck
LoK	Length on the keel
NMM	National Maritime Museum
pdr	pounder
RB	Rebuild, Rebuilt

INTRODUCTION AND DEFINITION

The expression 'sloop of war' belongs to the eighteenth century. It came into use in the twenty years following the end of the War of the Spanish Succession in 1714. Yet its history begins in 1650, when England was a republic and politically isolated in a Europe of monarchies. Its origins can be traced to this time because it was here that England, and later Britain, began its long passage to the mastery of the seas. The sea-wars this policy created inevitably affected the security of the waters around these islands. Fishermen lying to their nets and the crews of coal ships plying the coast now looked out on a sea that at times swarmed with enemy privateers or, to use the Dutch expression, 'capers'.

In response to this a plethora of small warships joined the fleet during the latter half of the seventeenth century, having been ordered by the Council of State or by the Admiralty to meet a number of tasks, including surveillance and patrol – sometimes as a preventative to smuggling – advice (reconnaissance) and communication, convoy and the guarding of the fisheries, and the provision of a sea-borne taxi service for VIPs. All these were later subsumed into the broad category of 'cruising' tasks. More specialised work involved shore bombardment and attendance on the fleet as tugs to support and rescue larger ships in battle.

In time of war many vessels found that they were employed on duties for which they were not specifically designed. This was particularly so for those acquired for particular short-term activities such as fleet actions and shore bombardment. When not in their primary role they were deployed to some of the other tasks above, and although not ideally suited to these, their contribution was clearly of great assistance. The little ships providing these services tended to be built rapidly during hostilities, almost as a result of a panic attack, and to disappear with equal rapidity when the emergency had passed. This phenomenon has occurred repeatedly over the centuries. These small ships were designed and built mainly in Royal Dockyards, but they were also acquired as prizes or hired or purchased from commercial sources. They had differing hulls, rigs, armaments and crews; and they were variously categorised as ketches, brigantines, sloops, advice boats, pinks, yachts and bomb ketches. In this era there was also one particular type of specialised vessel, the fireship, which, though usually classified for seniority purposes as a Fifth Rate, was occasionally employed to act in some of the roles described above.

The French had a good expression for these ancillary warships: *bâtiments interrompus*, meaning literally interrupted or incomplete vessels – incomplete in the sense that they did not have the attributes to fit them to be rated with the larger warships of their navy. The British equivalent of this expression was 'unrated': that is, not included in the formal establishment that divided the Royal Navy's fighting ships into six rates. However, in practice unrated also meant unregulated, and it is the retention of this status that is one of the great assets of the sloop of war since it permitted a high degree of experimentation – mainly through trial and error.

The amalgamation, in the early eighteenth century, of all the operational roles applicable to unrated vessels in the closing years of the seventeenth century into the one category of 'sloop of war' meant that it was difficult to lay down a precise establishment that would satisfy the broad sweep of duties required of these small

A small Pepysian sloop with a Biscay rig runs before the wind. *Author*

vessels. An attempt was made to do this in 1732 but the matter was left open, though from it emerged in essence an unregulated seventh rate of which the first and best example is the *Alderney* of 1734: part cruising sloop, part bomb ketch. Up to this point the hulls of bomb vessels had been very different from those of cruising sloops, though this did not stop them being used as cruisers when required. The divergence in design was to occur again in the middle of the eighteenth century with a new class of bomb vessel, some of which now had a ship rig. Again, much of their time was spent in the cruising role despite their more cumbersome hulls.

This failure to lay down a precise establishment for the building and rigging of the sloop of war was indeed fortunate in that it allowed evaluation of variants in hull design and in the modification of rigging and sail plans. To this end the Admiralty directed trials to compare the effect of differing rigs and hull forms, augmenting these with the demand for captains to report on the sailing qualities of their commands.

At this point it is important to come to terms with the protean word 'sloop'. In the understanding of most people, a sloop was a vessel used for commercial or leisure purposes with but one mast and carrying a fore-and-aft rig or sail plan. Though this idea remains with us in the form of the racing yacht, in earlier times the concept was much more elusive. The expression is largely accepted as deriving from the word 'shallop' which, in the early seventeenth century and before, was used to signify a shallow-draught coastal boat, equipped to row or to be sailed, with one or two masts, the after one, if in use, being the mainmast. That description fits neatly the rig and form of the early naval sloops of the 1670s. These sloops were two-masted vessels whose role was to attend the fleet to tow off damaged or endangered ships. Little used in this role, they were quickly deployed onto other coastal duties.

It is no accident of history that it was their name that came to describe all the small ships, whatever their rig, still in use at the beginning of the eighteenth century: rather it was these vessels that carried the sail plan that was to form the basis of the sloop of war rig in the first half of that century – that of 'snow'. One other rig, that of 'ketch', continued to be carried by

some sloops of war, but it was not common enough to be used as a designator for a distinct class of vessel, except when applied to the 'bomb ketch', which itself came under the generic category of 'sloop'. To this must be added the fact that by 1719 the only small unrated warships still in service in the Royal Navy amounted to four sloops for general duties and four ketch-rigged bomb vessels. The growth in the number of sloops was to outstrip by a long way the increase in the number of bomb ketches, hence the spread of the term 'sloop of war'.

All the foregoing considerations may lead us to see the expression 'sloop of war' as a way of describing a concept of operations, or a role, as well as a method of describing a particular group of vessels.

But there is another, rather perverse influence on the classification 'sloop of war' that is almost comical from today's perspective. This concerns the rank of their commanders. In the eighteenth century officers appointed to be captains of sloops, of whatever variety, were given the rank of 'master and commander'. Above the sloop, all rated vessels had, in addition to their captain, a sailing master whose duties included responsibility for the navigation of the vessel. Sloops were considered small enough to dispense with this individual, his work being assumed by the officer appointed as captain: hence 'master and commander'. The *rank* of Captain, as opposed to the honorific title applied to any officer in command of a ship, was reserved for those officers appointed to the command of a rated ship – of the Sixth or higher rate.

The smallest ships of the Sixth Rate at the beginning of the eighteenth century were armed with 24–26 guns, 20 on the upper deck and 4 or 6 on the quarterdeck. By 1720 the smallest Sixth Rate had been established at 20 guns. These eventually became known as post ships: that is, commanded by an officer who had been 'posted' on the Navy's list of captains. From this it follows that a vessel in the sloop category could be armed with up to 18 guns, but in fact very few in our period had more than 14, although by the middle of the eighteenth century most ship-rigged sloops carried 16 or 18 guns. Although many of the Sixth Rates in the late seventeenth century had less than 20 guns, all had been sold, lost or taken by the end of the century so did not have to suffer the indignity of being expelled from the Sixth Rate. The shape and layout of these small Sixth Rates do, however, contribute to the design of the sloops in the early eighteenth century. On the other hand, during the eighteenth century small frigates that were temporarily reduced to less than 20 guns in order to carry extra stores or troops (described by the French term *en flûte*) would be re-rated as sloops with a new captain in the rank of Master and Commander. Conversely, such was the importance of the royal yachts that, despite having only 8-10 guns, they were commanded by Post Captains.

This account starts by looking at the Biscay double shallop, a large open rowing and whaling boat with two masts. It then unfolds the development of the sloop of war through an examination of individual seventeenth century types or classes of vessel, both French and English. In doing so, and because the class of sloop of war came to incorporate vessels with differing operational functions, this study is confined to craft expressly built for the duties listed at the beginning of this chapter. The development of the fireship is covered only briefly, in Chapter 8. They were rated as sloops by dint of the captain holding a master and commander rank. However, the typical fireship was the conversion of an old Fifth or Sixth Rate ship and even the few purpose-built fireships were larger than other unrated warships; ideally, they required a complete lower deck for the 'fireworks', so the design of their hull and rig did not play a part in the development of the sloop during the period covered by this book.

This study will cover the French naval *barque longue* and corvette since these and the privateers and prizes that were captured from the French had an influence on the design of British sloops, mainly from the middle of the eighteenth century onwards. Descriptions of these and their British counterparts are partly technical but are primarily designed to give a feel for what the ship was like and how she was sailed, rigged, armed and manned.

A 200-ton sloop of 1732, with a brig rig, very close in pattern to the snow rig, achieved by giving the vessel an enlarged snow sail which is then laced to the mast and boomed out. This is discussed in Chapter 12.
Author

A ship-rigged sloop of about 1760. *Author*

No account of the operational status and roles of a class of warship should be separated from the historical context in which it served. To provide that context chapters will outline the broader issues of the period and their influence on naval strategy and tactics. These can then be related to the demand (and sometimes, surprisingly, the lack of demand) for minor warships. That demand can in turn be illustrated by reference to the number and type of vessels acquired, showing dates of ordering, launching and subsequent operational activities.

In most accounts of sailing warships their rig is dealt with last, as they usually carry the standard three-masted rig. To avoid endless repetition later, and because the form of rig is fundamental to these vessels, this volume will start with an outline description of the various rigs adopted by these small ships. Unlike the rated vessels, sloops of war and their predecessors were mainly associated with a variety of two-masted rigs, although by the 1750s some were beginning to be altered to the three-masted square rig that was so much the norm that it was simply known as the 'ship rig'; by 1756 they were being designed for this sail plan. Furthermore, the rigs of individual vessels were frequently altered throughout their service to meet either their commander's wishes or the requirements of the Admiralty, such as a change to a special operational role like shore bombardment or exploration.

Another topic that recurs frequently throughout the book is the choice of hull design for these vessels, since it did vary significantly between groups and even between individual vessels within one group or class. This account is therefore supported by plans and by photographs of models. Appendix 3 offers a select list of sloop plans at the National Maritime Museum (NMM) and advice on how these plans can be interpreted. Contemporary paintings and the author's impressions are used to show what these small fighting ships looked like in their environment and to illustrate the contexts in which they served. In some cases it has been possible to acquire detailed specifications and dimensions that will be of particular interest to modelmakers.

Confusion can occur over the names of individual vessels, since the Admiralty were in the habit of re-using names on a rapid basis. Indeed, it is possible to find instances where two sloops launched in the same year have the same name, because the first had been taken or sunk by the time the second was ready to be launched; instantly reusing the name was a way of both commemorating the previous vessel and replacing it on the Navy List. In Appendix 1 is an alphabetical list of all sloops purpose-built or otherwise acquired between 1650 and 1763 showing their periods in service. In this appendix, and in the text where confusion might arise, ships of the same name are distinguished by Roman numerals after their names – I, II, III etc – indicating that they are the first, second, third, etc of that name covered in this book (not the first, second or third time the name was used by the Navy).

A volume covering the work and design of the sloop of war through the run of maritime history from 1650 to 1763 can only be of a general nature. It is nearly true to say that each sloop was an individual – certainly this would apply to their rigs – so this book is not an exhaustive study, nor does it aspire to reveal in depth the anatomy of these ships. To do so, the book would have to be so lengthy, and so detailed, as to be indigestible. Its main purpose is to outline the development of a class of warship that has yet to be given a dedicated study of its own, particularly since that class came to be the largest in the Royal Navy.

Chapter 1

THE RIGGING OF SLOOPS

INTRODUCTION
The purpose of this chapter is to provide an introduction to the different types of rig fitted to sloops over the period 1650 to 1763. The chapter falls into three parts. The first deals with the different types of sail (by no means exclusive to sloops) that went to make up the various rigs, and the nomenclature involved with their rigging. The second attempts to show how these sails were combined to produce the desired rigs. Those readers familiar with the general arrangement of sails and their control can skip to the second part of this chapter. The third discusses the management of sloops under these rigs and deals with the questions of both directional and vertical stability.

The subjects of rigging and the arrangement of sails are normally left to the last when a large ship is being described but, because rig can be a defining issue when it comes to a discussion on sloops, it is sensible to describe the rigging of these small warships at the beginning of the story. A rig is relatively easy to describe in outline, but the methods of setting up the standing and running rigging of a vessel are complex and changed over the centuries to a degree that makes it impossible to incorporate the high level of detail this subject engenders within the compass of an outline history of sloops in general. Indeed, such is the variety of rigs that were used by sloops that a complete book could be written on this topic alone. The problem is compounded, particularly in the case of the early sloops, by the habit of making customised changes to rig and to the dimensions of spars and masts within the lifetime of many of these small ships. It follows that this chapter can only be an overview of the subject and will therefore confine itself to a consideration of the basic arrangements for masts and spars and the

types of sails deployed on them. Examples of the dimensions of mast and spars will be found in Appendix 2. Those readers who wish to plunge into greater detail are referred to some excellent authorities and publications in the Bibliography.

Because the sloop was an unrated vessel, there was a degree of anarchy in the matters of rigging and of hull design. Thomas Riley Blanckley in his work of 1732 entitled *A Naval Expositor* wrote:

> Sloops – Are Sail'd & Masted as Mens fancys leads them sometimes wth One Mast, wth Two and wth Three, wth Burmudoes, Shoulder of Mutton, Square Lug & Smack Sails, they are in Figure either Square or Round Stern'd.[1]

Possibly the main confusion arises from the modern understanding that a sloop is, and indeed was, a vessel with a single mast rigged fore-and-aft, broadly similar to the present day sailing yacht.[2] However, this book is concerned with the word 'sloop' as applied to a great fleet of small warships with differing rigs, hull shapes and operational tasks. Unlike the rated classes above them, which were normally ship-rigged with three masts, sloops carried a variety of sail plans, usually set on two masts, occasionally on three, and very seldom on a single mast.

TYPES OF SAIL AND THEIR CONTROL LINES
There are two terms applying to rig that will be referred to repeatedly throughout the book: 'fore-and-aft' and 'square'. A fore-and-aft sail is one that is attached in some way to a mast or a stay by its forward edge and lies, at rest, along the centreline of the vessel. Such sails can be used, when hauled in tight, to cleave the wind.

They can be eased and allowed to lie across the ship, when the wind is from behind. Square sails lie across the ship but can be canted and trained round so that they can also cleave the wind, though they will not allow the ship to point as high (as near to the wind direction) as the fore-and-aft-rigged version.

Under ideal circumstances, both types of sail will assume an aerofoil shape, with the forward-most curve of the aerofoil directly in line with the incoming airflow. It is necessary at this point to distinguish between the 'true' wind (ie the direction in which the wind is blowing over the sea surface) and the 'apparent' wind, which is the direction of the wind as perceived from the ship. When the ship is head to wind or sailing downwind, these directions coincide; in every other situation, when the ship is travelling forwards at an angle to the true wind direction, the apparent wind direction will be closer to the direction of travel than the true wind. The triangle of velocities in Fig 1-1 illustrates the effect.

It is easy to see that as the boat speed increases relative to the true wind speed, the apparent wind moves more and more ahead. If the sails were already set to their optimum angle, then it will be necessary to bear away

even further from the true wind direction. Any attempt to avoid this by sheeting the sail in beyond the optimum will increase the sideways forces (and hence leeway), again moving the vessel away from the true wind direction.

Obviously, the exact performance of a vessel depends on many factors, both inherent (hull shape and resistance, sail orientation, etc) and external (eg wind direction and boat speed), but as a rule of thumb a square-rigged ship could rarely get closer than 75 degrees to the true wind. A typical fore-and-aft rig, by contrast, could usually achieve about 50 degrees off the true wind. Such a difference is critical; with the additional influence of leeway, a square-rigger could often tack backwards and forwards repeatedly without making any ground to windward, while the fore-and-aft rig could usually progress. This distinction is vital to understanding the evolution of sloop rigs.

The importance of windward ability cannot be over-emphasised, particularly for ships such as sloops working close to a coast on surveillance, reconnaissance and communications. The need to round headlands and beat out of bays was their lot. In the wide ocean it is of less importance, unless there is a need to close with or run from an enemy. In single-ship engagements the ship with the best windward ability would have a clear advantage.

Square sails are ideally suited to a following wind as they present a large well-controlled area to the wind. Fore-and-aft sails can be inefficient downwind, particularly if they have no boom along their foot. If the sail can be held out by a boom then it can be made to present a satisfactory face to the wind but few fore-and-aft sails are suitably rigged to accept a boom along their foot, in which case they will stall and cease to pull the vessel through the water. Many of the examples shown below carry sails of both varieties within their sail plan and can use both, simultaneously or separately, to achieve the optimum arrangement for any particular direction of wind.

In rigging their ships, the nations facing the Atlantic, the North Sea or English Channel initially favoured square rig alone, although well before the time of our interest a fore-and-aft sail, the lateen or settee sail, originating in the Eastern Mediterranean, was in use on the mizzen mast of ships with three masts and on

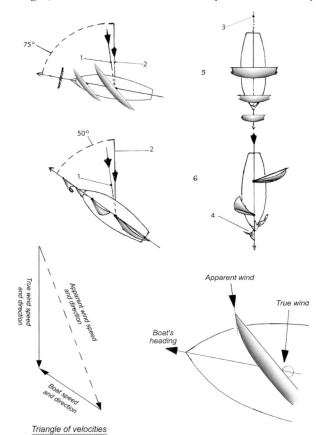

Fig 1-1. True and apparent wind close-hauled and running
1. Direction of apparent wind
2. Direction of true wind
3. Following wind where true and apparent are the same
4. Fore and aft head sails will not draw properly
5. Square rig
6. Fore-and-aft rig

Triangle of velocities

ketches with two masts. Therefore it is logical to start with square sails and leave the lateen sail to the fore-and-aft section later.

Standing rigging is relatively simple to describe. Masts could be a one-part or 'pole' mast or a mast built up of two or more sections (Fig 1-2). In the latter's case, each section except the uppermost would have at its head a construction capable of receiving and securing the lower part of the mast above into a housing comprising a cap, crosstrees and trestletrees. Masts were secured against lateral forces using shrouds, against fore-and-aft forces using stays, and against quartering forces using backstays, which could be supplemented in extremis by additional backstays set up on a temporary basis. All these items of standing rigging could be adjusted using deadeyes and lanyards or blocks and tackles.

The lowest square sails just above the deck were the main and fore courses. They were set from a spar or yard lying at right angles to their masts and across the centreline of the vessel (Fig 1-3). The yard on the mainmast would be just over twice the ship's beam and the sail a little less. The sail could be trimmed using bridles on its luff (the windward edge of the sail) leading to bowlines, which led through some firm point forward of the sail, thus permitting the crew to set the leading edge of the sail taught in order to cleave the wind. This was important to give the vessel any chance of working into the wind. The area of the sail could be reduced by removing a 'bonnet', which was laced to the foot or 'skirt' of the sail. Alternatively, a reduction could be had by gathering up a portion of the sail to the yard using reefing lines already let into the sail in a band across it. In the seventeenth century the method of reducing the courses was by lowering the yard and stripping off the bonnet. This practice had disappeared by the eighteenth century (together with the bonnet) in favour of reefing the sail to the yard. The other lines that helped this operation were the reefing pendants. These brought the sides of the sail in line with the desired band of reef points up towards the yardarm thus creating slack in the sail for those topmen gathering in the sail before securing it with reefing ties.

The other lines controlling these sails were the sheets and tacks from the clews (loops fashioned into the bottom corners of the sail) to set

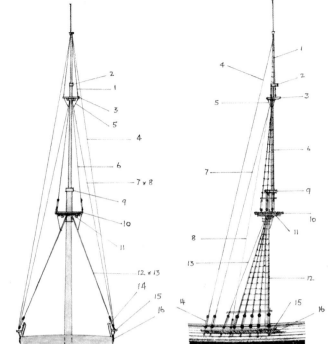

Fig 1-2. Standing L.C. rigging
1. Topgallant shrouds
2. Topmast cap
3. Crosstrees
4. Topgallant backstay
5. Futtock shrouds
6. Topmast shrouds
7. Topmast backstay
8. Topmast running backstay
9. Mainmast cap
10. Main top platform
11. Trestletrees
12. Mainmast shrouds
13. Mainmast backstay
14. Deadeyes and lanyards
15. Channels
16. Chain plates

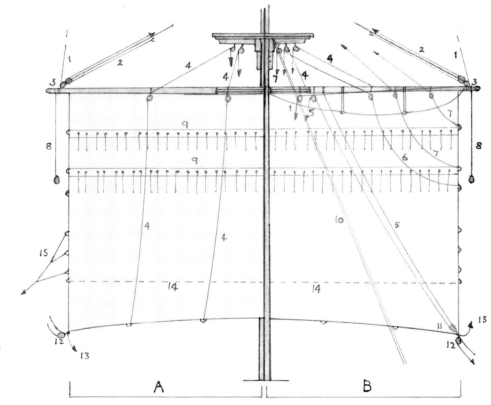

Fig 1-3. Main and fore course
A. Fore side of sail
B. Aft side of sail
1. Topsail sheet
2. Main yard lifts
3. Topsail sheet block
4. Buntlines
5. Clewline
6. Leechline
7. Reefing pendants
8. Brace pendants
9. Reefing bands
10. Main shrouds
11. Clew block
12. Main sheet block
13. Tack
14. Bonnet line (seventeenth century only)
15. Bowline and bridle

the luff (the leading edge of the sail) and the leech (the trailing edge of the sail), the clewlines to hoist the clew up to the yard amidships and the buntlines, set on the front of the sail to assist in gathering up and collapsing the sail. Attachment of the head of the sail to the yard was by a set of rovings – short pieces of rope passing through grommets let into the head of the sail and tied over the yard.

The yard itself was controlled by halyards to hoist the spar and its sail up into its working position, by lifts which – being attached to the outer extremities of the yard from a point above it – could alter its horizontal angle to the mast, and by braces also attached to its outer ends and led forward or aft, through blocks to some belaying point. These latter lines could alter its position relative to the centreline of the sloop thus playing a key role in trimming the sail to the wind. Using all these lines a crew could achieve any angle best suited to the wind conditions and the desired course of the vessel.

Above the courses, topsails could be set (Fig 1-4). Broadly similar to the courses and controlled and trimmed in the same way, they differed from them in three aspects. Unlike the lower courses, whose sides were close to perpen-

dicular, their sides tapered markedly towards the head, particularly in early vessels. They had no bonnets at their skirts and they were equipped with more reefing bands; sometimes as many as three. Their sheets did not lead directly to the deck; rather they were led through blocks at the outboard end of the yard below them, then to the mast and down to the deck. It may be noted that this method of controlling the clews obviated the need for separate tacks on all top- and topgallant sails. In those vessels possessing three masts and in those equipped with the ketch rig (of which more later), the aftermost or mizzen mast could also be equipped with a topsail. However, in its case there would be no lower course beneath it other than the lateen sail already mentioned or later the snow or gaff sail. To control the clews a crossjack (pronounced and usually spelt cro'jack) yard was hoist below the topsail to take its sheets. This yard had braces and lifts as did all the other yards. In the interests of clarity the topsail yard lifts have been omitted from Fig 1-4.

The topgallant sails, which are set above the topsails, were not in use by sloops until the early eighteenth century. Previously, captains of sloops were generally more interested in reducing sail area rather than adding canvas to vessels that were already hard-pressed. The large increase in burthen of sloops from 1702 provided the base from which to introduce topgallant sails. These sails were in essence the same as the topsails but without reef points, the thinking being that if this sail needed to be reefed it probably needed to be struck (ie brought down). It is unlikely that the topgallant yard would have had any footropes. There would have been no leechline since these sails were small. Therefore, it is unlikely that they would have had buntlines; relying simply on the clewlines to collapse and control the sail.

There were three other square sails in the inventory: the spritsail (Fig 1-5), the sprit topsail and the buss sail. The first two of these sails could only be used effectively when the vessel was headed away from the wind, since the control of the weather sheets would be particularly difficult on the wind and there was no way of controlling the luff through bowlines. The topmast spritsail was an un-seamanlike abomination and was seldom, if ever, used on sloops, though amazingly it was popular in the

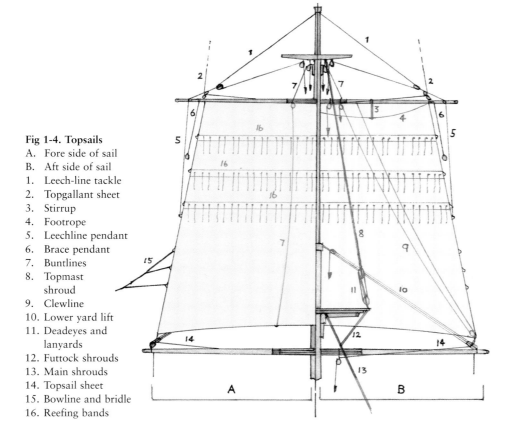

Fig 1-4. Topsails
A. Fore side of sail
B. Aft side of sail
1. Leech-line tackle
2. Topgallant sheet
3. Stirrup
4. Footrope
5. Leechline pendant
6. Brace pendant
7. Buntlines
8. Topmast shroud
9. Clewline
10. Lower yard lift
11. Deadeyes and lanyards
12. Futtock shrouds
13. Main shrouds
14. Topsail sheet
15. Bowline and bridle
16. Reefing bands

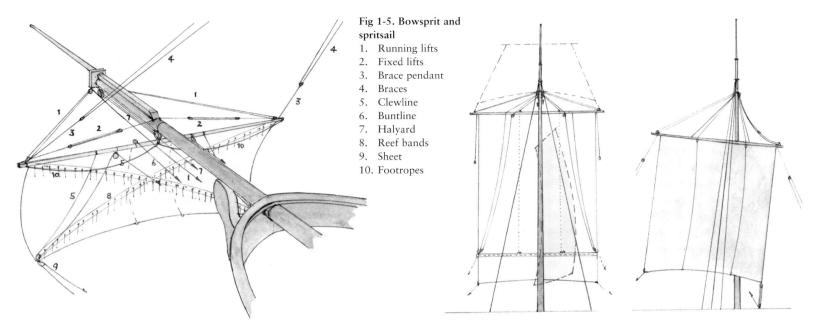

Fig 1-5. Bowsprit and spritsail
1. Running lifts
2. Fixed lifts
3. Brace pendant
4. Braces
5. Clewline
6. Buntline
7. Halyard
8. Reef bands
9. Sheet
10. Footropes

larger rated classes, possibly because these ships, being low at the head and high at the stern had considerable windage aft and needed canvas far forward to give downwind stability. Some sloops built at the beginning of the eighteenth century were rumoured to have had such a sail but this cannot be confirmed.

The third sail, the buss sail, (Fig 1-6) was, in naval usage, peculiar to sloops and ketches. In the case of sloops it was hoisted on the main and aftermost mast, which was often a high pole mast; it was taller and narrower than the conventional course and did not always carry a main topsail above it. Its shape and its correspondingly shorter yard gave it the advantage of being able to be set inside the shrouds, being hoist either from its centre as normal or from a point one-third along the yard as for a lug sail.

Additions to the square rig sail plan were available in the shape of studding sails, often referred to by seamen as stunsails (Fig 1-7). These were set from small yards which could be run out from above the lower and topsail yards in order to extend the coverage of the courses and topsails. The example shown does not use a topgallant studding sail, hence no topmast studding sail boom is shown. They could be used for long passages in the right weather or as part of cramming on all sail to escape from or close with a foe. They were not the sort of sail to have flying as you closed for combat.

Turning to the fore-and-aft pattern of sails, these can be divided into three types: those bent to yards, those bent to the stays of the standing

rigging, and those set flying – that is, raised without their luffs being attached to any stay. Those bent to yards will be covered first.

The earliest fore-and-aft sail set on a yard, the settee or lateen sail, came from the Eastern Mediterranean (Fig 1-8). Its origins are unclear. During the period when the Romans dominated that sea, the bulk of passage was under square canvas. Whether the square sail was re-cut to a triangular shape and set at an angle so that its head and yard cleaved the wind or whether

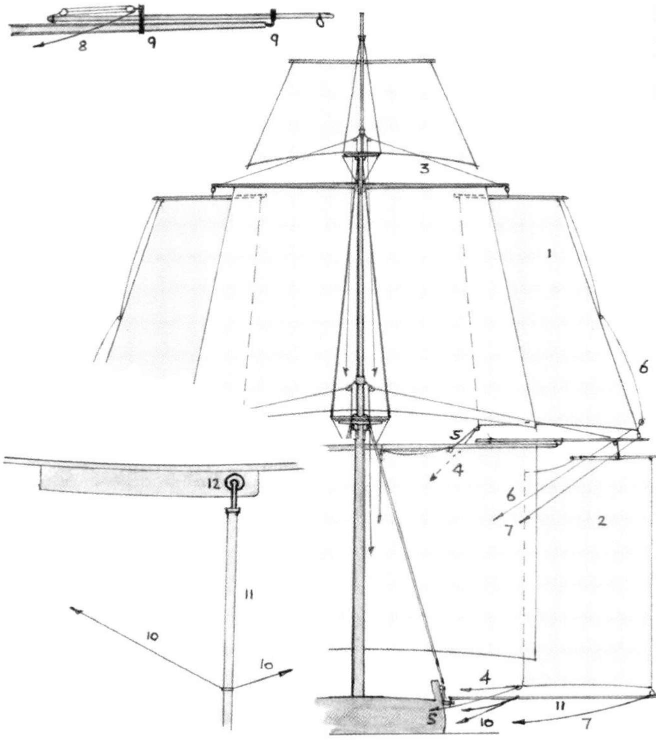

Fig 1-6. The buss sail
This diagram attempts to show the use of a buss sail in a fore-and-aft posture and hoist inside the shrouds. For this to work the lifts would either have to be led below the shrouds or, if in the conventional position above the shrouds, they would have to be eased. Operating as a lug sail, the buss sail would not need the use of lifts. Hoisting a yard at a point one-third along its length was an established practice, but probably more frequently so outside the shrouds. The sail's bonnet has been removed in the fore-and-aft setting.

Fig 1-7. Studding sails
1. Topmast studding sail
2. Lower studding sail
3. Halyard
4. Fore sheet
5. Aft sheet
6. Downhaul
7. Tack
8. Studding sail boom outhaul
9. Boom iron
10. Forward and aft boom guys
11. Lower studding sail boom
12. Boom pivot

Fig 1-8. The lateen sail
1. Mizzen topsail
2. Mizzen topsail braces
3. Peak or leech brailing lines
4. Foot brailing lines
5. Aftermost main shroud
6. Mizzen bowline or tack
7. Peak halyard
8. Throat halyard
9. Mizzen sheet
10. Lateen mizzen course
11. Reef band

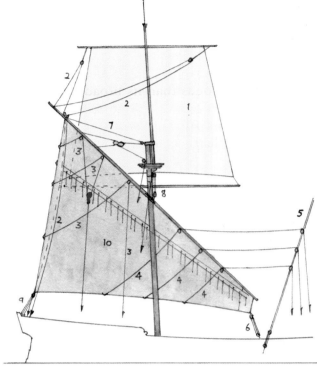

Fig 1-9 Fore-and-aft sails on main and mizzen masts
A. Mainmast with bilander sail
B. Mizzen mast with loose-footed smack sail
C. Mizzen mast with gaff-headed spanker
1. Main topmast
2. Mizzen topmast
3. Main square topsail
4. Mizzen square topsail
5. Bilander main course
6. Mizzen loose-footed smack sail
7. Mizzen gaff-headed boomed-out spanker
8. Main lower mast
9. Mizzen lower mast
10. Foremast aftermost shroud
11. Tack
12. Sheet
13. Vang

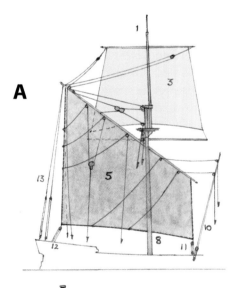

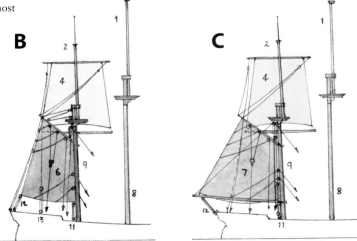

other influences caused the change is not known, but the arrival of Islam on the eastern and southern shores of the Mediterranean sea coincided with the demise of Roman sea power and the emergence of this new sail, so its source may well be Arabian. That said, recent research suggests that small craft in Late Antiquity carried a variety of fore-and-aft rigs, so there may be a connection between 'lateen' and 'Latin', which would suggest that the lateen sail might have been a Roman innovation.

This sail was still in use on small trading vessels on the eastern seaboard of Africa and in the Arabian Gulf in the early 1960s, and is still in use to this day on the feluccas plying the River Nile. One interesting feature is that this sail is reefed to the yard unlike all other fore-and-aft sails, which reef up the foot of the sail. This sail came to be used in the Atlantic as an addition to the square rig in the form of a mizzen or balancing sail. It was still employed like this on large warships until the mid-eighteenth century. It rarely featured as part of a sloop's rig except in the seventeenth-century ketches, though it may have been used as a temporary balancing sail in other early versions of the sloop class when it was unlikely to have had a mizzen topsail above it. The sloops, possibly because of the nature of their two-masted rig, used other types of fore-and-aft sail (Fig 1-9).

However, the lateen did spawn a similar sail in the form of the bilander sail that came into frequent use by sloops at the end of the seventeenth century (Fig 1-9A). This trapezoid sail was in effect a lateen sail with its front end removed. The spar was hoist from near its centre and rode at an angle close to 45 degrees. The difficulty with this sail – and with the lateen for that matter – was the necessity of lowering it and then raising it on the other side of the mast during every tack. This problem was solved early in the eighteenth century by removing that part of the sail in front of the mast and bending the portion aft of the mast to a short spar, called a gaff yard, secured behind the mast, again at an angle of 45 degrees or less (Fig 1-9B). The resultant type of sail, known as a smack sail, had of course been in use in small vessels for many years before the end of the seventeenth century, most noticeably in the Stuart yachts and also in the hoys used as harbour craft, which needed this sort of sail to facilitate easy manoeuvring in confined spaces.

This sail underwent improvement in the early eighteenth century. The outer end of its foot or skirt was extended by a boom pivoting on the mast from which the sail flew (Fig 1-9C). This led to a lengthening of the foot of the sail and to far better control of its fore-and-aft setting. Where no boom was employed, the trim of the sail was adjusted by vangs attached to the outer end of the gaff yard and led down to the quarters of the vessel. This system made it difficult to generate the twist in the sail so important to fore-and-aft sailing. The gaff-headed boomed-out sail was also used by sloops as a main course, considerably enhancing their windward performance.

Somewhere between the square sail and the truly fore-and-aft rig came the lug sail. This presented a problem for the captains of sloops: it was less handy than a square sail and less effective off the wind but it could provide vastly improved windward performance provided progress did not rely on rapid tacking. As with the lateen, the origin of the lug sail is unclear. Some regard it as a development of the lateen, though the leading edge of that sail was attached to a steeply set yard, which is conceptually very different to the principles of the lug sail. Others saw it as a new way of using a square sail. Before its adoption, and beginning in the later Viking period, there had been attempts to improve the windward ability of the square sail, particularly in vessels like merchantmen that did not have a large crew capable of rowing to windward.

Two methods were used. The earliest was the use of a bowline and bridle (Number 15 at Fig 1-3), whereby the leading edge of the sail was held steady and prevented from flapping (which would spoil the airflow over the sail). This required a point forward to which the bowline could be led and hence the need for a beak or bowsprit. The other method was to rig a spar in the bow, which reaching beyond the stem hooked into a cringle on the sail's leading edge holding it steady. Evidence of this will be seen later. But even with these aids, there was a limit to how far the yard carrying the sail could be trained round towards a fore-and-aft position; the shrouds limited the angle. Canting the yard down at its leading end helped to gain a

few extra degrees but only when the yard was raised inside the shrouds could a true fore-and-aft posture be achieved.

The tall thin buss sail (Fig 1-6), often set on a pole mast, presented a better opportunity for use inside the shrouds than its broader cousin, the main course. Unlike a conventional rig, the shrouds for a buss sail went nearly to the masthead, leaving plenty of scope for a narrow square sail to be raised inside them. Furthermore, the practice of raising a square sail a third out from one of its ends and virtually making it a lug sail, rather than as normal at its centre point, was current before the end of the seventeenth century; but by then the lug was already in use.

For fishing boats the lug was set up on a freestanding mast with its halyard acting as the shroud and backstay. For sloops it would have been used in place of the main course or as a balancing sail on a small mizzen mast (Fig 1-10). In such positions there would have been ample fixtures on deck and in the rigging to control its leading edge, but the yard and sail would have been inside the shrouds, which, whilst giving excellent windward performance, would be less than ideal downwind. The lug was more suited to the buss-rigged mast as this arrangement provided more space inside the shrouds. There are instances of sloops having their lug sails altered to a square pattern and vice-versa; also of changing from a lug sail to a square sail on

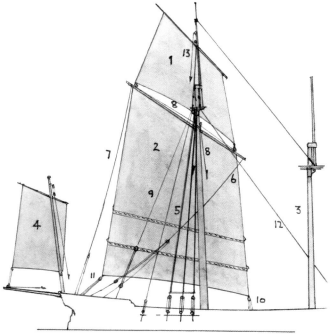

Fig 1-10. Lug sails
1. Main topsail
2. Main course
3. Foremast
4. Mizzen
5. Main shrouds
6. Dipping line or brace
7. Brace or vang
8. Topsail sheets
9. Main halyard
10. Main tack
11. Main sheet
12. Main stay
13. Topsail halyard

passage, which would suggest the same yard was used for both sails, albeit hoist in different positions along its length.

The connection between lugs and square sails is supported further by the fact that in the sixteenth and seventeenth centuries lug sails were set with their yards virtually horizontal. These sails were of two types: the dipping lug with the tack of the sail secured to the deck ahead of the mast on the centreline of the vessel; and the standing lug with the tack secured to the foot of the mast as shown on the mizzen sail in Fig 1-10. Sloops used the former variety on their mainmasts between approximately 1690 and 1710 when the sail was replaced with a gaff-headed boomed-out sail (Fig 1-9C) or by a conventional main course with a fore-and-aft snow sail immediately abaft the mast (Fig 1-11). These systems got rid of the complications of tacking a lug sail, which involved releasing the tack and hauling the yard aft round the mast to take up the opposite tack. The lug sail could be augmented by a topsail of a similar pattern controlled just by its halyard and sheets which led through blocks on the extremities of the main yard.

Before leaving fore-and-aft sails set from yards, other than the lateen sail, a word is necessary on the subject of brailing. This is an operation that in principle is similar to the collapsing and furling of a square sail using clew- and buntlines. Brailing lines were led from a number of blocks positioned on the yard and sometimes the mast, round the leech of the sail, back to a block close to the point of origin but on the other side of the sail, thence down to the deck. This could be done even with a boom controlling the clew of the sail, provided the line holding the outhaul clew was released. Once sails ceased to be loose-footed and were attached to the boom along their foot, then brailing was impossible and the gaff yard had then to be lowered and the sail secured to the boom. This latter arrangement did not arrive until well into the nineteenth century.

Fig 1-11 shows the brailing of a snow sail or trysail. Sloops made extensive use of this sail and the wing sail from the beginning of the eighteenth century (Fig 1-12). The snow sail was virtually the same as the smack sail but, instead of using the mast as its pivotal base, it used a vertical spar (a trysail mast) or, for Royal Navy purposes, a hawser (stout cable) with its upper end secured to the platform top abaft the

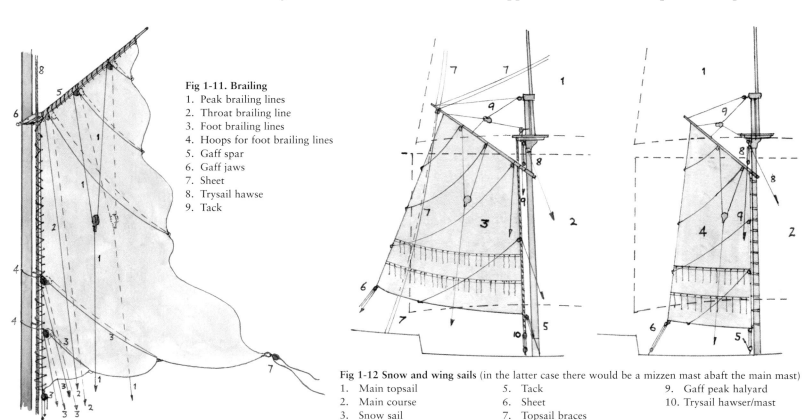

Fig 1-11. Brailing
1. Peak brailing lines
2. Throat brailing line
3. Foot brailing lines
4. Hoops for foot brailing lines
5. Gaff spar
6. Gaff jaws
7. Sheet
8. Trysail hawse
9. Tack

Fig 1-12 Snow and wing sails (in the latter case there would be a mizzen mast abaft the main mast)

1. Main topsail	5. Tack	9. Gaff peak halyard
2. Main course	6. Sheet	10. Trysail hawser/mast
3. Snow sail	7. Topsail braces	
4. Wing sail	8. Gaff throat halyard	

mast and its lower end secured to the deck beneath. The sail was laced to a gaff spar by a roving set up through grommets woven into its head. The jaws of this gaff spar pivoted on the trysail mast. Where a hawser was in use in place of the trysail mast, the jaws of the gaff spar would have had to be modified to avoid chaff. The aim of the arrangement was to prevent the gaff jaws from fouling the parrel beads holding the main yard to the mast. The sail's luff was laced or ringed to the trysail mast or hawser, whilst its foot was set loose without a boom, in the manner of the 'hoy rig'. This meant that the mainmast of a two-masted ship could carry a main course and a fore-and-aft course simultaneously. Ships so rigged came to be known as snows. The wing sail, which not surprisingly looks like a sea-bird's wing, was also like the smack sail but with a particularly short gaff. It could be set up behind any mast and was loose-footed and without a boom to extend its foot. This sail was in use at the end of the seventeenth century and was set up when conditions were so bad that the main course could not be used.

Next for consideration are those sails set from stays leading forward from the masts (Fig 1-13). Known as staysails, they were given the name of the stay to which they were hanked: for example, the main topmast staysail or the mizzen topmast staysail. These sails could be triangular with their luff running parallel to the stay, or trapezoid, with their head attached to the stay, in which case their luff would be vertical with the tack secured to a line leading down to the deck. Their heads would be held taut with lines running from those points to blocks forward and aft secured to the mast or rigging close to where the stay was fastened. Those staysails that led forwards from the foremast were all triangular, with their tacks all secured to either the stem of the vessel or to a point on the bowsprit. Their sheets were all led down to the deck and usually involved some form of tackle to give the necessary purchase. Certainly the fore(mast) staysail could be reefed along its foot but the fore topmast staysail, whose tack would be secured to a line led to a block well out on the bowsprit, would be struck rather than reefed. By the early eighteenth century, the old square sprit topsail had disappeared, certainly on the smaller ships, with its role taken on by a fore-and-aft sail. Riggers and

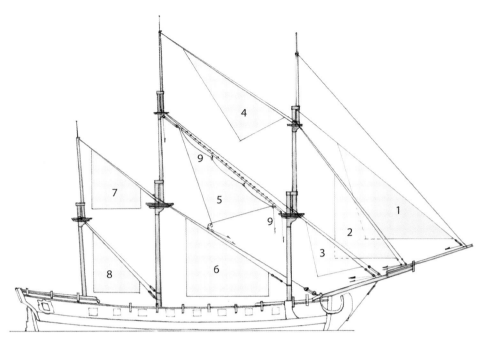

Fig 1-13. Staysails and jibs
1. Jib
2. Fore topmast staysail
3. Foremast staysail
4. Main topgallant staysail
5. Main topmast staysail
6. Main staysail
7. Mizzen topmast staysail
8. Mizzen staysail
9. Example of a downhaul

shipwrights had realised that a moveable extension could be made to the bowsprit by the addition of a jib boom, which could extend the length of the bowsprit (see Fig 1-5 and 1-13). The new sail was called a jib and the line from its tack led through a block secured at the outer end of the jib boom. In all other respects it was treated just like a fore topmast staysail.

TYPES OF RIGS FOR SLOOPS

Each type described briefly here will be discussed in much greater detail in the later chapters, but this summary provides the essential context to their development.

With the inventory and use of sails in mind, it is time to look at how they were combined for the purposes of the sloop class. In the main, the class espoused the two-mast rig so the origins of this rig form the natural starting point. Here there are two possible sources leading to two rather different rigs. In Fig 1-14 the profile on the left has its mainmast in the centre and a similar, smaller foremast forward. The profile on the right again has its mainmast in the centre but with a smaller mizzen mast aft. The former will be discussed first.

Whilst the single mast with square sail became the rig favoured by the Atlantic and Scandinavian countries from the end of the Roman Empire in the north until the fifteenth century,[3] the pattern was different in the Mediterranean Sea. Here the most common vessel, until the arrival of large lateen-rigged

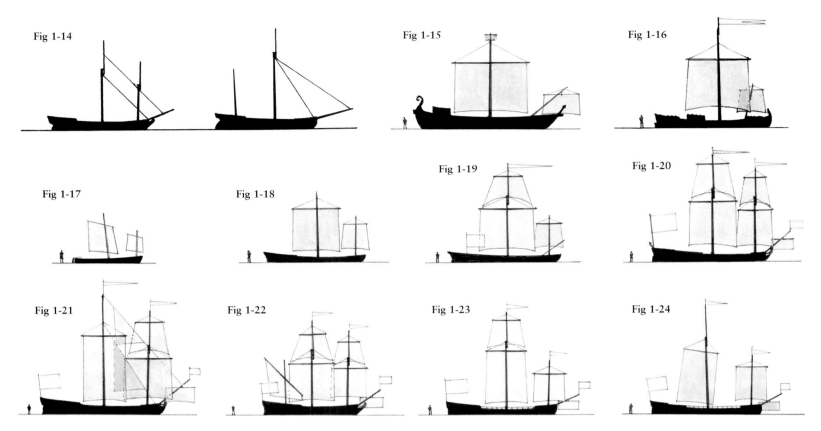

Fig 1-14 Fig 1-15 Fig 1-16

Fig 1-17 Fig 1-18 Fig 1-19 Fig 1-20

Fig 1-21 Fig 1-22 Fig 1-23 Fig 1-24

vessels around 500-600 AD, was the Roman merchant trader (Fig 1-15). This ship had, in effect, two masts, both carrying square sails. Its foremast was raked forwards at an angle of 45 degrees and carried a sail half the size of the mainsail. In many ways it was an arrangement half way between a foremast with foresail and a bowsprit with spritsail.

An early equivalent of this rig was recorded by Rear Admiral Joao de Oliveira as a Portuguese *barcha* in his volume on the ships of exploration (Fig 1-16).[4] One such vessel, small as it was, managed in 1434 to prove the route round what is now called the Cape of Good Hope. Whilst for normal coastwise trade this little ship would have had but one mast, a second smaller mast could be set up well forward in the bows to give downwind stability and to act as an alternative main if the sail area had to be dramatically reduced.

The same can be said for the Basque sailing whaleboats of the sixteenth century (Fig 1-17) but these were, like many of the earliest naval sloops, set up to row as well as sail. They were not only excellent sea-boats but also proved ideal for exploration and coastwise travel. Their sails were not square, but lug sails, hoist with their yards horizontal and with their halyards

close to the centre points. In this way they could be used in the manner of a square sail across the boat and in the style of a lug sail, using the fore-and-aft form. The boats being small, at about 28ft in length, and with a low aspect rig, it was possible to set up their masts to be freestanding except for the support given by the halyards, which were led down to the weather rail.

The temporary foremast became a permanent one in the seventeenth century, confirming this form of the two-mast rig. In England it came to be referred to as the basic 'Biscay' rig. It was this rig (Fig 1-18) that was used on what is known as the Biscay double shallop and subsequently on many of the small naval vessels of France and England in the last quarter of the seventeenth century.[5]

In the latter half of the seventeenth century, French designers used the hull and rig of the Biscay double shallop in developing the *barque longue*. The boundary between the Biscay double shallop and the *barque longue* can probably be defined by the introduction of a full weather deck to carry carriage guns. The rig at Fig 1-19 is that which could be applied to a large naval shallop, though it is possible that the early *barques longues* used this basic Biscay rig enhanced by the addition of a main topmast on which could be set a topsail, probably flying.[6] It provided the additional advantage of a means of signalling from a decent height. However, this rig was also in use before 1600. It is recorded in a depiction of the port of Amsterdam in about 1600, when that city was ruled by Spain. It can also be seen in an engraving of English shipping in the time of Elizabeth I,[7] and it formed one of the rigs used by many of the Dutch and English herring busses in the first half of the century. Therefore, it would be unwise to accept that the Biscay double shallop was the only type of craft to dictate the rigs of the *barques longues* or through them, for that matter, the early English sloops. However, its fine lines and the fact that it could be rowed were to play an important role in their development.

The hull of the *barque longue* was substantially different from that of the double shallop. Because of the requirement to carry guns in the waist of the vessel, their hulls became more like that of a miniature frigate: the *frégat légère*, a ship-rigged vessel similar to the small 20-gun Sixth Rates of Queen Anne's navy. At the same time, 1676, the classification *barque longue* was replaced for official purposes by the all-embracing phrase *barque longue ou corvette*, and so it would remain until the middle of the eighteenth century when only the name *corvette* would survive. But for the present the rig was developed into a permanent two-mast arrangement (Fig 1-20) with courses and topsails on both.[8] At this stage a bowsprit was added with a spritsail. This was in effect what the English would call the early snow rig – of which more later.

A modification was made to this sail plan, probably at the end of the seventeenth century.[9] Whilst still retaining two masts, the main is now a pole mast carrying one large, tall sail. It is in effect a 'buss' sail, so called, at least in England, because of its use on herring busses. The foremast retains the conventional course and topsail. Staysails are rigged between the main and foremasts and possibly between the foremast and the stem and bowsprit (Fig 1-21). A small flying topsail could be set above the buss sail. This is similar to the rig that was given to the English brigantines in the 1690s.

Given the popularity of the two-mast rig for fishermen and for inshore traffic and the fact that the first sloop on Pepys's list of the navy taken from the French in 1656 would have had a two-masted rig, it seems odd that the first group of sloops actually to be called 'sloop' and commissioned in England in 1667 were given a three-mast rig with topsails on the fore- and mainmasts and a lateen sail on the mizzen – and this despite their small size.[10] They measured barely 40ft on the keel, therefore being little larger than the Biscay double shallops (Fig 1-19).

At the outset of the Third Dutch War, 1672, another much larger batch of sloops was ordered as fleet tenders and as tugs for line-of-battle ships. In this case they were given a two-mast rig (Fig 1-23). Contemporary illustrations show both variants, some using the tall narrow buss sail on their mainmasts with a one-part foremast for a small square sail, others equipped with a two-part foremast to carry two square sails. Being equipped with a tall buss sail, these sloops could have adopted the practice of lowering it and hoisting it inside the shrouds, attaching its halyard to a point on the yard one-third from either end, thereby converting it to a fore-and-aft sail (Fig 1-24). This practice is also a possibility for other small warships such as the brigantines described below.

No sooner had these sloops been launched than the war was over so they were scarcely employed in their intended role and by 1683, after ten years of peace, almost all had gone. Their task was to be required again, which leads into a consideration of the next programme of vessels built for this role some ten years later: confusingly, they were to be classed as brigantines.

Amongst his manuscripts, Pepys includes a list of sloops, just one of which, *Whipster*, is annotated 'brigantine'.[11] The brigantine or *brigantin* was a type of vessel hailing from the Eastern Mediterranean. Equipped with oars and usually two masts carrying lateen sails, they were deemed hybrids, being able to perform equally well under either means of propulsion. There are three possible explanations for *Whipster* being described as such a vessel: either she was rigged as a brigantine, or she was equipped with oars to an extent that she was a hybrid, or both. However, her complement of guns and crew and her dimensions were the same as those for any of the other Pepysian sloops so, on the face of it, it would appear that it was her rig that caused her to be classified as 'brigantine'. On the other hand, it is possible that, when required to use oar-power, she would have taken on board supernumeraries to do the job, as was certainly the intention with those built in the 1690s. Her rig is unknown so the basis for the classification remains a mystery, but it may have had nothing to do with her rig, simply indicating her intended role: that of being a tug.

Some twenty-five years later, in King William's navy, the term brigantine had come to define this role, rather than rig. This definition reflected the hybrid nature of the craft's propulsion as these brigantines, of a novel design, were given a large complement of crew as well as adequate sailing arrangements, the latter in a variety of configurations. However, by the 1720s the term brigantine had come to mean the rig, and this provides a salutary warning: in describing any vessel the date of classification must be taken into account because the same term can change its meaning as time passes. Whilst all this will be discussed in detail later, the possibilities need to be illustrated now.

The example of the brigantine *Shark* shows the flexible approach to rig. She was commissioned in 1691 with a two-masted fore-and-aft rig. Her builder Fisher Harding had recommended bermudan sails (Fig 1-25) and whilst it is by no means certain that she was given these sails, the fact that within six months she had her sail plan changed to lug sails would tend to support the contention (Fig 1-26). These diagrams also show the reduction of the bulwark in the vessel's waist to allow the use of an outrigger for the oarsmen – what in

Mediterranean galleys was termed an *apostis*. Her lug rig was later changed to square rig and this rig was given to all the other eight brigantines. This does tend to bear out Blanckley's remarks about sloops.

The square rig would, according to some commentators, have been a fully rigged two-part foremast equipped with a proper top and trestletrees carrying a course and topsail. The mainmast would have been a pole mast carrying a tall thin buss sail (Fig 1.27). This rig is very similar to that on the French corvette of about 1700 (Fig 1.21), with the exception of the construction of the foremast. In both cases it would have been a two-part mast, but where the English brigantine would have had a full top with trestletrees and cap, the French equivalent would have had its lower and upper foremasts banded together at the doubling, relying on crosstrees to steady the topmast.

At least one of this class had been equipped with a third, or mizzen, mast before she was sold in 1712, as were a number of the new sloops built in 1699. Unfortunately it is not clear what sail was set on the mizzens of these vessels. The French were also in the habit of adding a mizzen or balancing sail to their two-masted vessels when the occasion demanded.

Before leaving the seventeenth century it is necessary to consider the steps being taken to develop a more weatherly rig for these small warships, in an attempt to improve their windward performance. The flexibility of using the buss mainsail in a fore-and-aft fashion, thereby converting it into something similar to a lug sail,

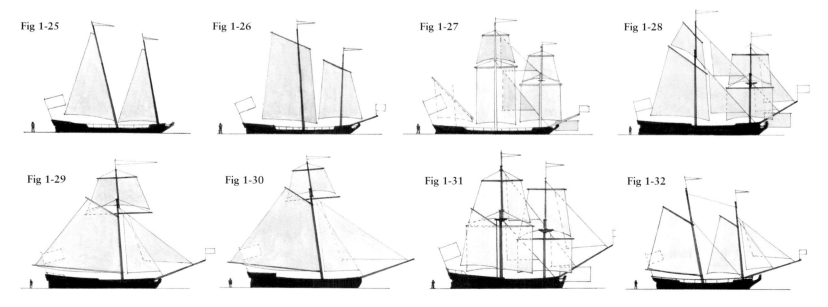

Fig 1-25 Fig 1-26 Fig 1-27 Fig 1-28

Fig 1-29 Fig 1-30 Fig 1-31 Fig 1-32

has been described earlier. This practice may have contributed to the adoption of the lug sail as a main course for use on brigantines and on the sloops of 1699 (Fig 1-28). It was certainly to be used on packet boats and was possibly also fitted to the Navy's advice boats of the 1690s and to sloops built between 1702 and 1710.

The other sail that could be used to improve windward performance was the bilander sail (Fig 1-9A); indeed, some of the captains' logs indicate that it was preferable to the lug. There was another aid that was being developed to improve windward performance. As will be seen from the rigging and sail plan diagrams, towards the end of the seventeenth century the brigantine and snow rigs began to include staysails set between the main and foremast. Fore staysails were flown from the foremast and its topmast and anchored to points on the stem and bowsprit. All these sails made a major improvement to a vessel's ability to sail into the wind.

In 1710–1711 two groups of sloops were constructed that were unusual in their rig, being given only one mast. The plan of one of them, *Ferret*, is still available in the NMM collection (see Appendix 3). Speculative attempts have been made to redraw their rig. They could have been given the 'hoy' rig as were the royal and naval yachts, but this is unlikely.[12] By this date a boomed-out, loose-footed mainsail would have been more effective (Fig 1-29), but they have also been shown with a rather different profile based on pictorial evidence from America (Fig 1-30). The difference in the degree of rake to the mast in these two examples is very marked, leading to different handling characteristics. It is unlikely that the rake of *Ferret*'s mast would have been so extreme, and her plan, which shows the deadeyes and chain plates, tends to support this contention. By 1716 all had been given the two-masted snow rig. The single-mast rig may have been considered a risk since its loss would have rendered the sloop defenceless. Moreover, the fore-and-aft course was enormous, making it difficult to tame and reef in a blow. This may have contributed to the decision to distribute its force over two masts.

In the closing years of the seventeenth century, the two-masted square rig, where the courses and topsails were of conventional proportions, developed into the 'snow' rig. Initially this rig was composed of a course on each mast, the main course being square in shape, not the tall buss sail. Each mast, which was properly constructed with platform top and trestletrees, had a topsail, again of square proportions. A bowsprit with spritsail completed the suit. At some point very early in the eighteenth century a short ancillary mast was added immediately abaft the mainmast with its head secured to the mainmast top platform and its base to the deck. This amounted to bringing a notional mizzen mast forward to a point just behind the mainmast. Onto this 'trysail' or 'snow' mast was set a gaff-headed sail (Fig 1-31). The practice in the Royal Navy was to replace the trysail mast with a stout rope, which would have been easier to repair in combat and adjustable as to tension.

Following the end of the War of the Spanish Succession in 1713, apart from lingering hostilities with Spain until 1718 and operations in the Baltic Sea, a period of relative peace persisted until 1739. This slowed down the demand for sloops so that few were launched in the next two decades. The main preoccupation for small vessels became the suppression of smuggling, so new designs in the 1720s were of small size and displacement and only lightly armed.[13] Their sail plan could have been the snow rig above or possibly the schooner rig, a rig developed by the Dutch in the mid-seventeenth century (Fig 1-32). Another possibility would have been a rig similar in principle to that which was to be proposed for some of the long, low and much larger sloops of the 1730s. This proposal consisted of a fully set up, two-part foremast with course and topsail. The mainmast, also two-part, would have had either a lug or bilander sail. This sail is trapezoid in outline and is similar to a lateen sail with the front third removed (Fig 1-33).

By the end of the 1720s when new larger sloops were ordered, the bilander sail would have been largely replaced by a fore-and-aft boomed-out mainsail above which there would have flown a square topsail with its own sheets, braces and lifts (Fig 1-34). This is what came to be understood by 'brigantine' rig in the eighteenth century, with square-rigged foremast and main topmast and topgallant, and a fore-and-aft main course. Eventually, in the nineteenth century, the square main topsail was to be altered to a fore-and-aft one, making a brigantine as it is understood today, now identified by rig rather than role: square-rigged on the fore-mast and fore-and-aft rigged on the mainmast.

One final point that needs clarification is the difference between the brig rig (the term itself possibly a shortened form of 'brigantine), which was introduced in the 1770s and the earlier brigantine rig. Whilst the brigantine had a tall lower mainmast or even a pole mast carrying a fore-and-aft main course with a long luff, and with possibly a small topsail added above it, the brig rig used a shorter lower mainmast with a proper top and platform, above which were fidded top- and topgallant masts, the whole mast being fully square-rigged. Additionally, in most conditions instead of a square main course, there was a short-luffed, gaff-headed, boomed-out fore-and-aft sail abaft the lower mainmast; this sail had proportionally a much shorter luff than that of the true brigantine.

At this point it is necessary to backtrack to the mid-seventeenth century and to the other source of two-mast rig. Well before these sloops and brigantines were built, there was in use another well established two-masted rig allied to a robust and well balanced hull: the ketch. Indeed, the ketch was the first vessel that could be regarded as a sloop in terms of its opera-tional role in support of the Commonwealth Navy. Its rig had developed from the three-masted herring buss rig, with the foremast having been removed for operational reasons, the missing square sails being replaced with large fore-and-aft staysails (Fig 1-35).

This semi-square rig also existed on the conti-nent. The French used it for their *galiote à bombe* of the 1680s, the forerunner to the English bomb ketch. The Dutch employed it, albeit in a fore-and-aft configuration, on their galliots and doggers, vessels employed in the carrying and fishing trades. It was also used by English royal yachts in the late seventeenth century when they forsook their fore-and-aft single-masted 'hoy' rig.[14] This two-mast rig was to remain one of the two principal rigs of sloops until 1753, when the last ketches were delivered.

Although the sail plan was relatively simple, in its initial form the ketch's rig, particularly the running rigging, was complex. Not surprisingly, the main resembles the tall buss sail as fitted to fishing boats; a small topsail could be set above it. The mizzen was invariably a lateen sail at this stage, above which, again, a topsail could be set. This rig was well suited to the early bomb vessels since the disposition of the masts provided a space forward of the mainmast from which mortars could be fired without setting fire to the rigging. The rig was substantially modified in the eighteenth century in order to improve the sailing performance of the bomb ketch.

By the 1730s the design of the bomb ketch was moving towards that of the sloop, at least in terms of hull shape and conventional arma-ment. This trend proceeded to a point where the two types of vessel became almost interchange-able. Ketches ordered as bombs were commis-sioned as sloops, reverted to ketches and were then transferred back to the sloop role, depending on the threat at the time. It was also possible to convert a sloop to a bomb. The hull structures of the two were obviously very different, but the improvements to the ketch rig were such that it could be used effectively for cruising and convoy duties.

The precise positions of the masts had altered from those favoured on the seventeenth century ketches to accommodate the mortar beds more comfortably and to provide a better sailing ability. The introduction of traversing mount-ings for the mortars in the 1690s meant that the two main weapons were no longer fitted side-by-side forward of the foremast. Both were now on the centreline, with one amidships, allowing both the main and mizzen masts to be moved forward. Whilst the mainsail was a square sail, it had behind it a fore-and-aft gaff-headed smack sail pivoting on the mainmast. The mizzen course was also a gaff-headed sail. The rig was further improved with square topsails on both masts as well as mizzen and main stay-sails (Fig 1-36). However, the search for even better performance under sail meant that by 1757 bomb vessels had become ship-rigged.

The ketch rig continued to be fitted to sloops, sometimes to assess its comparative perform-ance relative to their snow-rigged sister ships, so it would not be right to say that the ketches were poor sailers as such, but we may have to accept that the ship rig did have advantages, particularly when sailing with the fleet. The last ketches ordered for the Royal Navy were launched in 1759 and were destined for a shore bombardment role.

In the 1740s, when sloop production quick-

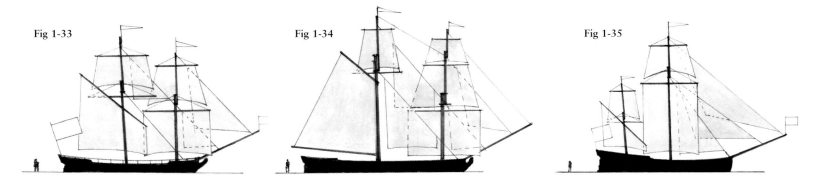

Fig 1-33   Fig 1-34   Fig 1-35

ened in response to the wars against Spain and France (1739–1748), not only were the existing rigs of snow and ketch modified, but also a few of the snow-rigged sloops were altered to accommodate a third, mizzen mast, thus becoming ship-rigged (Fig 1-37). The first such alteration of this period was to provide for a voyage of exploration.

By 1746 in France the term *barque longue*, as part of the family of unrated warships, had disappeared leaving only the *corvette* as a representative of the old class. By now the corvette had the three-mast ship rig similar to that in Fig 1-37. However, the two-mast arrangement in the form of the snow rig continued in service in the British navy until the end of the Seven Years War (1757–1763) and, in its final form, employed three-part masts as in the example of a light sloop of only 12 guns shown in Fig 1-38. Whilst many of these sloops had a mizzen mast added during their careers, the majority of sloops ordered after the start of this war were designed from the outset to carry ship rig; in fact they were initially referred to as 'frigates', simply because they had three masts, despite the fact that they never mounted more than 18 guns (Fig 1-39).

A comparison between these sloops and those two-masted sloops converted to ship rig shows the slightly different relative positions of the three-mast layout as shown at (Fig 1-37). The converted snows tended to display a mizzen unusually close abaft the mainmast, since the main on a two-masted vessel lies well behind the deck's mid-point, whereas those sloops designed as ships, where the mainmast is closer to the mid-point of the deck, exhibit proportional distances between their masts that are more normal for the ship rig.

To summarise: before 1700 minor warships that could be said loosely to belong to the sloop family might be classified by rig, hull type or role. In his 'State of the Royal Navy in 1688', published in 1690,[15] Pepys listed a number of unrated vessels below the Sixth Rate. The first of these were three described as 'bombers' (bomb vessels), which would have been ketch-rigged; and 'fireships', of which he listed twenty-six. These would usually have been ship-rigged. With the coming of a new administration in 1688, fireships would be grouped with the Fifth Rate and some would be purpose-built.[16] This may seem sensible since the majority would have been modified for this role from old Fifth

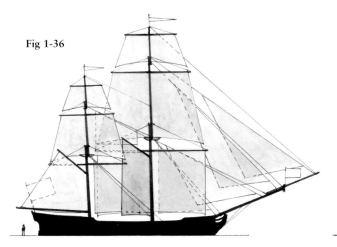

Fig 1-36

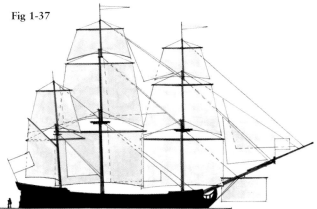

Fig 1-37

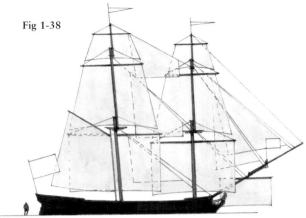

Fig 1-38

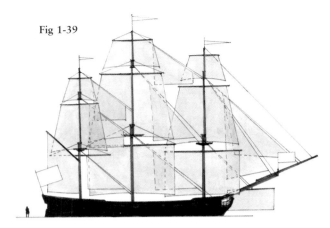

Fig 1-39

and Sixth Rate prizes or from merchant ships of similar size. There were also six 'hoys', single-masted vessels for harbour work; their rig was employed by yachts as well. In addition to the bombs, there were three armed 'ketches' for general service, thirteen 'yachts' for royal and navy use, and finally five 'smacks', probably used for communication. Notably, there were no 'sloops'; these had almost all been lost in action or at sea or sold as useless in 1683 and were not replaced as a class until 1699.[17]

When Pepys was preparing his *Memoires* England had been at peace with the world for fifteen years, so it is understandable that the large numbers of minor warships in service had declined steeply since the end of the Dutch Wars in 1674. At the beginning of King William's War against Louis XIV, following the Revolution of 1688, the fleet of minor warships expanded again to include more ketches as well as brigantines and advice boats, but nothing called a sloop was added until the war was over in 1698. The sloops that were ordered between 1699 and 1701 were small, carried either 2 or 4 guns, and were given the two-masted rig as before. They were used to enforce the ban on the export of wool. Those launched after 1702 were far heavier and armed with 8 to 14 guns: the War of the Spanish Succession had started.

By 1710 there had been some rationalisation of typology, in that the Navy started to classify their minor warships as sloops and bomb ketches, but both coming under the generic heading of sloops. In fact, had the expression 'bomb ketch' been replaced by 'bomb sloop' there might have been less confusion. This is similar to more recent arrangements where the Navy has deployed convoy and minesweeping sloops in two world wars. The eighteenth-

century classification remained unaltered until the divergence of the class into ship-sloops and brig-sloops in the 1770s. The bomb vessel was by then a three-masted ship-rigged vessel and still capable of being deployed as a cruiser or convoy sloop. By the end of our period, that is 1763, the sloop was to reach a burthen of 316 tons – nearly six times that of the Pepysian sloops of 1660s.[18]

MANAGEMENT UNDER SAIL

The foregoing discussion of sail plans shows that until the 1740s the majority of sloops had two masts. As will be seen later, these rigs were inherited from fishing and whaling boats of the late sixteenth century. The English navy was to face difficulties with two-masted rigs from their adoption in the middle seventeenth century until the 1720s. These problems were more pronounced in the sloop rig than with the ketch, but both rigs needed improvement in order to get the best out of the hulls they served. The common rig for sea-going vessels in north-west Europe up to the early fifteenth century was one mast with one square sail set upon it. This was then followed by three masts, allowing a fore and aft balance to be retained. The two-masted ketch, which carried enormous fore and aft foresails, was able to maintain this balance by the use of a mizzen sail aft but the sloop, whose second mast was placed in the bows, found great difficulty in maintaining directional stability unless off the wind.

This lack of balance in the sloop rig can be seen as having developed from the simple fact that early sloops were essentially single-masted vessels with a small foremast and sail added purely for downwind stability. The mainsail on the aftermost mast was centrally positioned and was used to drive the sloop to windward without the assistance of the small, square sail set on the foremast. The development of the rig placed two square sails on each of the masts and, for off-wind sailing, a sail forward of the bow on a sprit, thereby compounding the problem and making the vessel exceedingly difficult to handle if working to windward. This can be illustrated (Fig 1-40) by considering the relative positions of the centre of lateral resistance (CLR) in the sloop's hull against the water and the centre of effort (CE) applied by the force of the wind in the sails. In working to windward the sails pull the hull through the water and it is the centre point of this pull that is important, for if it is aft of the CLR, as in the case of CE3, the vessel will tend to turn into the wind and this tendency, which is referred to as 'weather helm', will increase as the vessel heels. This then destroys the airflow over the sails and reduces their power to drive the ship forward. If the CE is too far forward of the CLR, as in the case of CE1, the vessel will fall off the wind and finish up running downwind. A small lead is required for the CE forward of the CLR, as shown at CE2, to compensate for the onset of weather helm as the vessel heels and to reduce the possibility of the vessel broaching broadside on to the following seas when running, thereby testing her stability to the limit (see Fig 4-20 in Chapter 4). But if this lead is too great it can make the vessel unmanageable and virtually impossible to sail to windward. This is an extremely dangerous condition as it can reduce a ship's ability to claw its way off a lee shore, putting it in danger of being wrecked. It called 'lee helm'. It is generally considered preferable for a vessel to carry a small amount of weather helm.

There were a number of things that could be done about this lack of directional balance, some structural, others connected to sail handling and the trim of the hull. The main challenge was to ensure that the sloops retained weather helm. For this to happen the CLR had to be moved forward or the CE drawn further aft. There were two methods of achieving the first of these. As shown by the dotted lines in Fig 1-40, the vessel's gripe could be extended forwards at the foot of the stem because many of the early sloops had a forward rake of 45 degrees to their stems, a design not helpful for sailing to windward. Alternatively the captain

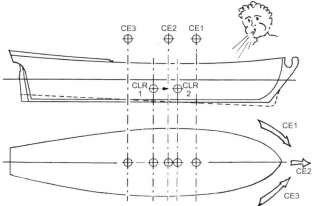

Fig 1-40.

could trim his ship down by the head. These two measures would tend to move CLR1 to CLR2. In dockyards, builders resorted to moving the whole mainmast back or increasing its rake or both, thereby bring the CE of the sail plan further aft from CE1 to CE2. To modify the relative position of CE3 would require the reverse of these processes to achieve balance. Another practice was to move the main shrouds further aft, allowing the mainsail yard to be braced round at a greater angle, improving its windward capability though not altering the CE to a great degree; if anything it moved it forward. The real answer, in a structural form, was to add a mizzen mast, and this was done in the Restoration Navy (Fig 1-41), but a short cut to this solution lay in the setting up of the trysail mast or rope horse immediately abaft the mainmast on which was set a fore-and-aft wing sail. This brought balance back to the two-mast rig without the need for a mizzen mast and all its attendant rigging and extra crew. This measure was not introduced into the Royal Navy until 1716 with the refitting of some single-masted sloops with the snow rig. The other improvement that becomes increasingly evident as the eighteenth century progresses is that sloops are rigged at the outset with their mainmast set well back from the midpoint between stem and sternpost. From 1730 onwards there was little evidence of sloops lacking directional stability.

The captains could also do much to help themselves. Indeed, most of the pressure for modification came from captains complaining, through the Admiralty, to a Navy Board that was not always sympathetic to their requests. Topmasts could be set either before or aft of the lower masts. In the latter position they would certainly bring the CE backwards. Judicious use

Fig 1-41.

of staysails, when they came into use at the end of the seventeenth century, could improve windward performance and balance. The removal of the foretopsail when making to windward would help prevent lee helm. But possibly the greatest help was to use the main course as a fore-and-aft sail, improving its angle to the wind by canting the yard (heaving down the luff thus raising the leech) or by attaching the main halyard one-third along the yard's length. In this way the main course was converted into a lug sail, which would have a marked effect for the better on the handling of the sloop both by moving the CE aft and by allowing it to sail closer to the wind. There is some evidence that within this arrangement there was the possibility of raising the sail inside the shrouds like a true lug sail. It was also possible for sloops to hold two types of main course: lug and square. Perfection did not come to the sloops' two-masted rig until the 1770s when a radical change was made with the formal introduction of a gaff-headed, boomed-out fore-and-aft main course. This was the brig. However, there were instances of this arrangement occurring in the 1720s and 1730s, usually as a result of captains trying to improve the performance of their sloops.

The other main problem besetting the sloops was stability. Once again it applies mainly to the sloop-rigged vessels rather than ketches, which when first introduced had deeper, fuller hulls. The sloops were designed to be fast under sail and oars and as such were descended from shallow and often narrow coastal craft. Their mean draught was 5-7 feet in the seventeenth century rising to 8-9 feet in the early eighteenth. By 1700 their length-to-breadth ratio was about 3.65 (it had been as high as 6.0 in the Restoration Navy) and their breadth-to-depth ratio 1.9. Their sail plans invariably turned out to be too large, and there were instances of yard officers being asked to shorten masts, even before commissioning, sometimes by as much as 10 feet. Requests also came in from captains to have the size of their sails reduced, which implies that when fully reefed there was still too much canvas. There are two separate issues here. The first concerns the proportional rate of reduction between two- and three-dimensional objects, in this instance a sail plan and a hull. Ship constructors at the end of the seventeenth century were accustomed to building and

rigging rated ships and may have unwittingly applied sail proportions applicable to such vessels to the hulls of sloops. The effect of so doing can best be shown by considering a cube with a side of 100 feet. Each face is 10,000 square feet and its volume is 1,000,000 cubic feet. If its dimensions are reduced by 60 per cent then with a side of 40 feet each face will be 1600 square feet and the volume 64,000 cubic feet. The proportional reduction of the square is 0.16 whereas that of the cubic volume is 0.064, *ie* the cube has reduced at 2.5 times the rate of the square. The failure to allow for this may form part of the early sloops' stability problem at the design stage.

An oversized sail plan can be compensated for by giving a vessel a high ballast ratio (*ie* making her 'stiff') – that is the ratio of the weight of the ballast alone to that of the whole craft including its rig, armament, equipment, crew, hull and ballast. The ratio on a modern racing yacht might be as much as 0.5, but the modern yacht also has a feature not possible to apply to the sloop: external ballast. It is not just this ratio that is important; it is also the distance of the ballast below a vessel's centre of buoyancy. In extreme cases external ballast can pull a yacht's centre of gravity down to a point almost below and outside the hull. The sloop, with its ballast laid out internally, has only a small distance between the centre of gravity and the centre of buoyancy; indeed they may be at the same point. Once fully loaded it is highly likely that the centre of gravity will be well above the centre of buoyancy, particularly in sloops of shallow draught and narrow beam. From a sailing point of view this makes them very 'tender' and therefore easy to force over to a dangerous angle of heel – hence the complaints of captains that their lee rail was often under water. This condition obtains when the vessel heels because the righting lever between the centre of downward effort due to gravity and the centre of upward pressure caused by buoyancy is very small. The value of external ballast is that it provides a low centre of gravity thus creating a larger righting lever which actually increases as the vessel heels.

These arrangements are illustrated at Fig 1-42 where a cruiser-racer yacht of about 1980 is compared with a sloop of around 1700 and a Thames barge of approximately 1900. The drawings are not to scale with each other but the sections are true to shape and proportion. Two points are of interest: first the centre of gravity of the vessel when ballasted and loaded (G), and second the centre of buoyancy (B). B can be taken as being in the same position as the centre of gravity of the immersed portion of the hull. Unlike the centre of gravity of the whole hull, rig, equipment and armament, which is normally in a fixed position unless the ballast shifts or the load is altered in size or position, the centre of buoyancy/centre of immersed gravity moves sideways as the vessel heels and its underwater shape changes.

Both the forces of gravity and buoyancy act in a vertical plane, that of gravity working downwards, that of buoyancy working upwards. The righting lever, which is represented by the distance between these two vertical forces, is labelled G-Z. If this righting lever reduces to zero the vessel will capsize and founder. In this example the sloop at 30 degrees of heel is close to the point of capsize.

In the case of the yacht as she heels to leeward at 15 degrees, B also moves out in that direction, whilst G, because it lies below B when the yacht is upright, moves in the opposite direction to windward, opening up a consider-

able distance G-Z between the vertical planes. Further heeling to 30 degrees produces an even larger righting lever. So the more the yacht heels the greater the righting moment and therefore the 'stiffer' she becomes. This is achieved because G is well below B when the yacht is upright. In the case of the sloop, G is above B and the heavier the load the higher G will rise above B; and the higher that G is above B, the quicker the righting lever G-Z will reduce, and this spells danger. Were G above the waterline the sloop would capsize at a negligible angle of heel. At an angle of heel of 30 degrees, B moves to leeward. The way in which it moves depends on the precise underwater shape of the hull, but in round-bottomed hulls, such as those on a sloop, this move is not all that marked (in the extreme case of a cylindrical cross-section, there is no movement of B at all). This makes the sloop very 'tender'. By contrast, in the Thames barge, thanks to its mighty beam, B is able to move well outboard, creating a large righting lever and thus a strong resistance to heeling, making her 'stiff'. It follows that severe loading of the sloop, which would give her a high centre of gravity, means that she has only a small righting lever at this angle of sailing. Lightly loaded, with a lower centre of gravity, she

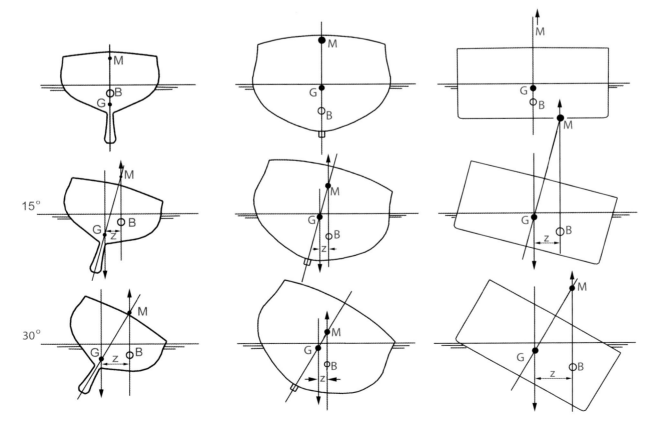

15°

30°

Fig 1-42.

would be in a far safer position. Were the sloop to be forced over to 45 degrees, G would be close to directly overhead of B and she would be in imminent danger of capsize.

Measures that could be taken to mitigate this problem of 'tenderness' – commonly referred to at this time as being 'crank' – included reducing the weight of armament and equipment on deck and stowing the hold with great care. Lead was sometimes recommended for ballast, to be carried in the lowest place possible, between the floor timbers; in some cases it was shaped to this purpose. Breadth might be increased marginally to improve stability by 'girdling' (adding an extra layer of planking). There was even the instance of the sloop *Tryall* in 1711 which was ordered to have the space between her wales filled up (they had double wales in those days) and an extra strake laid along the ship beneath them.

From the sailing point of view, sloops required a well-trained crew able to reduce sail speedily at a moment's notice. Sloops had to be capable of sailing fast, so they had to accept a generous sail plan for a light and relatively shallow hull. These small ships would not have behaved like the large steady line-of-battle ship but would have been much more sensitive to any change in the prevailing conditions. This required of their captains and crews the ability to sail these vessels as if they were yachts and to be constantly alert to the weather and sea state and therefore to the trim and control of their sails and the security of their guns, equipment and stores. Sailing a sloop in rough conditions was not for the faint-hearted.

There is one other point on Fig 1-42 that becomes important as the vessel heels: point M, the metacentre. It is a measure of the initial stability of the vessel when it is upright. It is not the point itself that is important but its distance from B and, once the vessel is heeled, G. The speed at which this distance reduces gives a measure of the vessel's stability. There is not the space here to go into the detail of how the meta-centric height BM is calculated, save to point out that it is akin to the cube of the beam divided by the displaced volume of the vessel, where the greater the beam and the smaller the displacement the greater the metacentric height will be. In effect the metacentric height denotes the vessel's resistance to heeling. Once heeled its

location is found when a vertical line from B is extended to cross the vessel's centre line at M and the metacentric height is then read as G-M. It can be seen that the height of M is determined by the position of B. A long metacentric height, created by B moving well to leeward, as in the case of the Thames barge, means that the vessel is stiff and will exhibit short shallow rolls, often very uncomfortable. If the metacentric height is short as in the case of the sloop when heeled, due to the small movement of B in this type of hull, it means that she will roll slowly but deeply putting her stability in question. This can become very dangerous when sailing down-wind when the rolling arc becomes wider and wider to a point where the vessel becomes unstable and capsizes.

An idea of some of these sailing difficulties can be gleaned from the sailing reports that captains were required to make on their sloops from time to time. They are of course subjective and not suitable as a form of measurement but they do give a fair idea of how sloops might behave in given conditions of sea and wind. Some examples are discussed at Appendix 4.

CONCLUSION

Rigging is an art which relies on science. In the period covered by this book, the understanding of the precise effect of a wind across a sail was in its infancy. This applied particularly to the sail in fore-and-aft mode. Ideas were introduced on the basis of chance discovery and trial and error. Small ships, particularly if they were not regulated by rating, provided good platforms for experimentation and adjustment as sea officers and designers learnt more about the behaviour of sails. Therefore, a great array of rigs was fitted to sloops, but even this catalogue does not include all the minor amendments to rig made by individual captains, such as altering the position of the shrouds or transferring a topmast from in front to abaft its mainmast or having the Navy Board approve alterations to the dimensions of their sails, masts or spars. The practice of rigging was to become more regulated by the middle of the eighteenth century, but up until that time there was a high degree of individuality to how any particular sloop was rigged. Therefore all this chapter has been able to do is give an approximation of the rigs and sail plans that were achieved.

Chapter 2

THE FISHING BOAT LEGACY

For monarchs of countries with a substantial coastline, the acquisition of a fleet was normally a priority concern because not only was a fleet a tool to prevent invasion, but it was also an essential force to support the invasion of another. These fleets could not operate effectively without the help of small vessels for communication and intelligence and for the many small commissions a commander might require that would be inappropriate or wasteful for a larger vessel to undertake. There was also another less prominent though equally important role for small vessels, which related to the protection of the shoreline and coastal fishing grounds from small raiders.

The origins of these small vessels lay with the fishing and whaling fleets of those countries facing the Atlantic Ocean and the North Sea. Here there was a division leading to two separate lines of development. The requirements of whaling with a harpoon spawned the creation of a small fast undecked craft propelled by oars and sail. The function of fishing, particularly for herring, demanded a stouter craft, decked and relying principally on sail. How these contrasting types both developed into craft for military use in a coastal setting is the theme of this chapter.

THE BISCAY DOUBLE SHALLOP
The inspiration for these small craft came from two directions. The first, and influencing a rather specialised craft, originated in the Mediterranean. Here could be found the fast, low, narrow galleys and their smaller cousins, the brigantines. Whilst they were not well suited to the boisterous seas and hard winds of the Atlantic coasts, their use of oars and their sleek hull meant that they could be employed for communication and raiding or protecting coastwise trade. It is important to remember

Fig 2-1. (Left) A Biscay double shallop under oars. Note the method of securing the yards when the sails are not in use. *Author*

Fig 2-2. (Left) A Biscay double shallop running before the wind. *Author*

Fig 2-3. (Right) Basque whaling boat of about 1540. *Author*

that both France and Spain had Mediterranean as well as Atlantic and Channel coasts and were thus more influenced by Mediterranean practices than the countries of the North. The part these influences played will become a recurring theme in this and later chapters. The second source of influence is the Basque whaling boat.

In the development of ships there is never an example of design that is entirely produced from scratch. New designs evolve, in response to a demand, from a convergence of earlier designs with modifications and some experimental innovation, so it is always difficult to determine a precise starting point for a particular class of vessel. Therefore, rather than look at a design, it is more useful to consider an operational concept. Looking at the increase in maritime warfare in the late sixteenth and seventeenth century, including piracy and privateering, and its threat to coastal commercial shipping on either side of the Atlantic, it is possible to discern the evolving need for some method of protecting that trade. The requirement was for a fast, lightly armed vessel with shallow draught capable of working under sail

Fig 2-4. This view is included by courtesy of the National Parks of Canada and shows the Red Bay Biscay shallop, whose sweet lines are those of a vessel that would not be out of place had it been designed today. Note the two large strakes that form the sheer, fastened clinker style, and the slender sawn frames. The stem is higher than the stern, which was necessary for whaling operations.

and oars. The Spanish and French were the first to identify such a model, one that with enlargement and modification could meet the need.

In the sixteenth century the Basque region, astride the Atlantic coasts of France and Spain, was the base for a prodigious whaling industry. To support that industry the Basques had developed a sleek *txalupa* (shallop), fast enough to be able to close with a whale and allow the use of a harpoon. The shape of the boat then had to ride easy as the whale dragged it through the water at high speed. The shape of this boat was possibly the main influence on the later design of the Biscay double shallop.

In his book *Sloops & Shallops*[1] William A Baker collates a number of references dating from 1607–1611 to describe the Biscay shallop as follows:

These few references are sufficient to indicate the existence of a well-known small craft, whose home waters were in the Bay of Biscay, but which was probably employed generally around the Iberian Peninsula. It was a fairly sizeable craft with enough distinguishing features to take it out of the plain 'boat' category. Its distinguishing features were also such as to make it particularly desirable for exploring expeditions and for fishing operations.[2] It was admired and widely adopted along the Atlantic coast of France, in Cornwall through connections with Brittany, and in the Netherlands.

He also mentions that it was used as a whale-boat.

When he wrote this book, he did not have the advantage of having an example to hand. We do. The wreck, dating from 1565, was found, underwater at Red Bay on the Labrador coast in 1978 (Fig 2-4).[3] Although today its shape would not excite attention, the fact that it is over 400 years old certainly does. Its lines were far in advance of its time in shape and it met the demands of lightness, strength and speed that applied to hunting whales. Unusually, it was of both carvel (flush planked) and clinker construction with overlapping strakes, which disproves the contention that this latter method was only known to the northern countries. The sheer strake and its partner beneath were

Fig 2-5. These two images of a replica of the Red Bay whaleboat have been offered for inclusion by the Albaola Association based at Pasaia on the coast of the Pays du Basques. This replica was built from plans made of the actual sixteenth-century boat. To prove the original's capability, a 2000-kilometre passage was made down the St Lawrence river and up the Labrador coast to Red Bay.

fastened clinker-style whilst the remaining strakes were set up in carvel fashion. This would have given it strength at the gunwale, important in whaling.

The craft was about 26ft long with a beam of around 6ft 6in, giving a length to breadth ratio (LBR) of 4. Its draught was of little account, 2ft at the maximum. It was an open boat with a crew of seven including the harpoonist and the helm/skipper. It was set up for two masts, the foremast being right in the bow (Fig 2-5).

It was not only the hull that was to influence a later generation of coastal craft, but also the rig. This may be one of the exponents of the two-mast rig whose particular interpretation of that rig was to become so influential for the English sloop and the French *barque longue* in the closing decades of the seventeenth century and beyond (but see Chapter 1, Fig 1-17/18/19). Like most fishing craft this whaleboat carried lug sails. In many ways this was a hybrid sail, capable of being set either fore-and-aft for sailing into the wind or square for downwind work. In these Basque whaleboats, the lug spar was set almost horizontal and for the most part was used downwind in the fashion of a square sail. The small foresail was primarily there to give downwind stability but could also be used to replace the mainsail in heavy weather. Whilst this sail was popular with fishermen, it did not gain the affection of the navies of France and

England where the square sail remained predominant in small vessels other than yachts and hoys, in which windward ability was important, though even they did not use the lug, but rather the smack sail.

The images of the Red Bay replica demonstrate the hybrid approach to propulsion: sail and oar. This approach was manifest in the small warships of Britain and France, in one form or another, right up to the middle of the eighteenth century, even though the navies had to cope with the additional problem of working oars and armament together.

Fig 2-6. This is another view, looking aft, of the replica of the Red Bay whaleboat built by the Albaola Maritime Heritage Association at the Ontziola Traditional Vessel Research and Construction Centre in Pasaia. She proved to be an excellent sailer. Note the position of the mast partners between thwarts four and five. These partners were designed to allow the mainmast to be raked to a significant degree. Steering was by rudder or oar; see the pegs for the steering oar on the port quarter right aft. All her masts and spars could be stowed within the length of the boat.

The Basque whaling *txalupa* may also be responsible for the word 'shallop', since 'tx' is the same sound as 'sh'. And the word shallop leads naturally to sloop. Possibly the first English contact with this vessel was in 1615, when the Muscovy Company decided to set up a whaling expedition in northern waters and hired four Basque harpoonists with their *txalupas* in order to learn how to catch whales with the harpoon. This prompts the question of how these 26ft long boats were carried. Specifications by whaling captains normally included the requirement that *txalupas* should be carried inside the *nao* or mother ship. This was certainly not possible with the Biscay

double shallop that was developed from these smaller boats.

Moving on to the Biscay double shallop, though inspired by the *txalupa*, this vessel was considerably larger, in many cases was half decked, and had square sails but on the same pattern of rig. On the subject of shallops, Blaise Ollivier, master shipwright at Brest,[4] in his *Traité de Construction* writes:

These shallops are larger than those carried onboard vessels and are either half or fully decked. They are intended to guard the coast and to protect commerce. Their length from stem to stern is 40-50 feet, their beam is in the order of 3¼ inches per foot of their length and their depth of hold is 4½ inches for every foot of their beam. Their bottoms/hulls are like those of ship-borne shallops, but they have above and around their deck or half deck bulwarks of 18 inches height forward and amidships and 2–2½ feet aft. When the double shallops were deployed to fight, they would be equipped with a number of small or swivel guns on each side. Their rig would be similar to ship-borne shallops were they to be equipped with lateen sails, but otherwise they would be rigged with a mainmast, with a large square course and topsail, a foremast which carries only one sail and a bowsprit on which could be set a jib. Most double shallops, particularly those that are square-rigged, have a head similar to that of a ship.

The illustration at Fig 2-7, based as it is on an engraving by Guéroult du Pas (see Fig 10-4), provides a fair representation of Ollivier's description. This is a much longer and more powerful vessel than the small whaleboat; also, it has a square, high-position transom, allowing a wider space at the quarters, necessary for a small fighting vessel. The rig is also more powerful, with standing rigging and square sails. One interesting feature is the use of a spar to extend the foresail beyond the stem, being secured to a strong point inboard and with its outer end engaged with the clew or tack of the foresail, thereby holding the luff taut. (This was used on Viking longships and is best described by the Norse term *vargord*.) The bowsprit here

Fig 2-7. This drawing has been developed from a contemporary engraving by Guéroult du Pas. His caption to this illustration reads 'A double shallop used for the protection of coastal commerce and as a scout for a naval force'.[5] *Author*

not only provides the same facility as the *vargord* but also allows the edges of the sail to be fitted with bridles and bowlines to improve the set of the luff. These vessels were also equipped with mainstays, as was the *txalupa*, but in this case the fore yard braces lead onto that stay, whereas in the *txalupa* they lead straight down to the deck. Therefore, in broad terms this is a more sophisticated rig, though it is probably not as flexible as the *txalupa*'s.

Whilst the hull retains a degree of the original's boat-like shape, it is made more formal in appearance by the addition of a head, as in a large ship (not shown here but see Fig 10-4), and by the provision of a screen or netting arranged above the bulwarks. The vessel's small high transom, being well above the waterline, avoids spoiling the perfect canoe shape of the underwater body.

In calm conditions and when requiring progress to windward, these vessels – and similar ones into the next century – would normally be rowed using at least eight sweeps a side. The engraving at Fig 2-8a shows that the crew, at this time, sat on thwarts to row. This practice would have become difficult in later classes of vessel, particularly those that were fully decked and equipped with carriage guns. The thwarts, unless removable, would have hampered the use of such guns. To solve the problem, armed double shallops may have carried their guns right aft on swivels, or on a low short quarterdeck if using carriages, leaving the main part of the boat clear for the oarsmen. This became the practice on similar vessels in England at about this time.

There are two other illustrations of a double shallop, this time by Jouve.[6] They are dated 1670 and purport to be of *barques longues*. For reasons that will be expounded in a later chapter, these are unlikely to be *barques longues* but rather large naval double shallops. They differ somewhat from Ollivier's description. They have a shape that is closer to the Mediterranean galley or brigantine and it is a reasonable assumption that these vessels have been built for use on the Mediterranean coast of France and not the Atlantic coast to which the earlier example seems applicable.

Were the square sails to be exchanged for lateen sails then the craft would begin to look like those from the Levant. The shape of the bow is totally different from that on vessels built on the Atlantic coasts and the rake of the stern reflects Mediterranean practice. This shallop is armed with two patereroes (or swivel guns) of about 1½-pounder calibre at the forward end of the quarterdeck. The yards appear to have no lifts, there is no mainstay and both yards are braced directly to the deck.

It is worth comparing these vessels to the one at Fig 2-9, which is a Mediterranean vessel. The proportions of the masts are similar as is the run of the sheer strake. The small square, high transom is not present but that may demonstrate how design features can be modified from one sea to the next. Another feature shared by both these examples and the brigantine at Fig 2-10 is the position of the ensign staff, placed well into the quarterdeck rather than on the taffrail. The oarsmen on the brigantine are seated for the main part, pulling their oars, with the leading three pairs in the bow seemingly seated but pushing their oars. It is reasonable to

Fig 2-8a and b. A large naval double shallop under oars and under sail based on originals in the Jouve Album. Note the swivel gun on the port quarter of the vessel under sail. *Musée de la Marine*

Fig 2-9. (Left) A
Mediterranean two-masted
lateener. *Author*

Fig 2-10. (Right) A
Mediterranean brigantine
under sail and oar. In the
original on which this is
based (see Fig 6-2), the crew
in the bow appear either to
be rowing by pushing as
opposed to pulling their oars,
although it is more likely that
they are equipped with long
paddles to assist in the
steering of the long, slender
vessel. *Author*

Fig 2-9. (Left) A
Mediterranean two-masted
lateener. *Author*

Fig 2-10. (Right) A
Mediterranean brigantine
under sail and oar. In the
original on which this is
based (see Fig 6-2), the crew
in the bow appear either to
be rowing by pushing as
opposed to pulling their oars,
although it is more likely that
they are equipped with long
paddles to assist in the
steering of the long, slender
vessel. *Author*

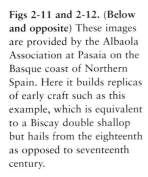

**Figs 2-11 and 2-12. (Below
and opposite)** These images
are provided by the Albaola
Association at Pasaia on the
Basque coast of Northern
Spain. Here it builds replicas
of early craft such as this
example, which is equivalent
to a Biscay double shallop
but hails from the eighteenth
as opposed to seventeenth
century.

conclude that in vessels of this size (less than
60ft) oarsmen were generally seated to row.

As a final note on the double shallop, the two
images at Fig 2-11 and 2-12 are of a reconstruction by the Albaola Association. They show a
craft of about 30ft overall bearing a close similarity to the double shallop. The rig is the classic
Biscay rig and proportionally close to the
masting of the shallop but with lug sails. The
craft represents one from the early eighteenth

century. The form of the hull is beautiful.

This examination of the double shallop
reveals that because the sea is a highway for
multi-directional movement of ideas, influences
on design and rig can travel anywhere; from this
it follows that any particular vessel or class of
vessel may show arrangements and features that
do not originate in its home country. At the
same time there appears to be a dominant gene
that can determine the general concept of a

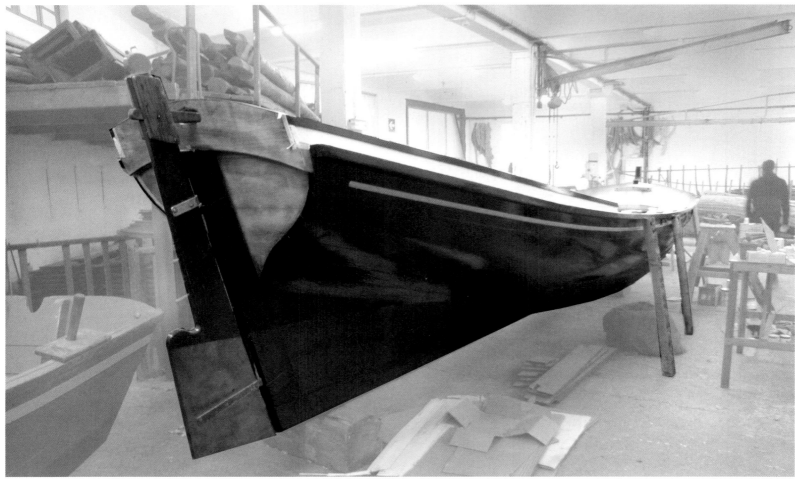

family of vessels over a considerable period of time and for that a good example is the little *txalupa*, which gave its shape and possibly, with others, its rig to a line of small vessels that remained in that style until the end of the seventeenth century.

THE HERRING BUSS AND KETCH

These represent a totally different type of fishing craft. The ketch or 'cache' is first mentioned in the Howard Household Books in 1481 as a cargo carrier in the Thames estuary and its approaches. This suggests that it had a seaworthy design and rig that enabled it to cope with the often turbulent seas of that coast and the intricate passages of its estuarine shore.[7] To carry a valuable cargo ketches would have had a weather deck and a full, round shape. This is confirmed much later in 1625 by Glanville in his *Voyage to Cadiz* where he remarks that

'Catches being short and round built, be verie apt to turne up and downe and useful to goe to and fro and to carry messages between ship and ship, almost with any wind.' His references here are to the ketch's ability to go up- and downwind and to tack with ease, which suggests a certain type of rig. If Glanville's comments are added to Boteler's assessment that ketches 'will endure and live in any sea whatsoever', the value to a navy of such a craft for coastal operations is clear.[8] This leaves the crucial question: is it a type of boat or a type of rig? It may be both but it was the rig description that endured in naval usage for nearly a century.

The ketch, possibly a corruption of the word 'cache' or 'catch', suggests a connection with fishing, though there is a view that it is connected to the Dutch word 'jacht'. Its rig is unusual, often described as that of a ship without a foremast, but in terms of suitability for a fishing vessel it did have certain advantages and the design of its rig may have come from another contemporary vessel.

The most common offshore fishing vessel between the fifteenth and eighteenth centuries was the herring buss (Fig 2-15). This round,

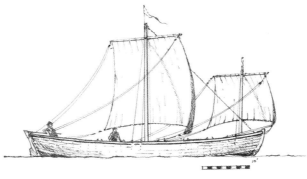

Fig 2-13. A simple Biscay double shallop. This rig served a great variety of different hulls, ranging from English fishing boats, where the square sails were replaced by lug sails, to bluff-bowed Dutch craft, again mainly used for fishing. *Author*

Fig 2-14. A ketch of the Commonwealth Navy checking traffic on the English west coast. *Author*

Fig 2-15. A model of an
English herring buss of the
mid-sixteenth century. Note
the use of a *vargord* to extend
the luff of the foresail. This
Viking-derived device played
a part in the mutation of the
square sail into a lug sail in
the seventeenth century. Note
also the setting of the
shrouds, well aft from the
masts, allowing a more fore-
and-aft trim to the square sail
yards. The model is in the
Science Museum, London.

heavy and robust vessel could be found with
two or three masts, but in both versions the
mizzen mast was critical since it allowed the
vessel to lie to her nets in safety, head to wind.
At the other end of the vessel, the heel of the
foremast was housed in a tabernacle, which
allowed the mast to be lowered backwards onto
the deck, thereby reducing windage forward
and providing space for the crew to handle their
nets, which led forwards from the stem.

Fig 2-16. A Dutch ketch-
rigged herring buss.

This model in London's Science Museum [9] is
instructive, not just for its portrayal of the
three-masted buss rig but also of the rig used
by the Pepysian sloops of 1672–1673, in that
their rig was as shown here but without the
mizzen sail. The foresail has a *vargord* holding
the luff, necessary since there is no bowsprit to
take bowlines from that sail. Neither it nor the
main topsail have lifts, the latter being set
'flying' with no yardarm braces. The mizzen
also appears to have neither braces nor lifts.
The foremast was considered to be a disadvantage. It carried only a small square sail and had
to be lowered whenever the vessel shot its nets.

In the two-masted versions (Fig 2-16) the
mizzen had to be retained for the reasons
explained, but the foremast was discarded,
making it easier to handle the nets on the foredeck.[10] However, there remained a need to have
canvas forward otherwise the vessel would be
completely unmanageable. This was arranged
by the use of a striking (retractable) bowsprit,
which could take the tack of a jib flown from
the central mainmast. The mainstay was now
brought forward to the stem providing a large
area in which to set a fore staysail. The mizzen
had to be placed far enough forward so that it
could carry a sail of sufficient size to contribute
to driving the vessel, whilst still providing the
ability to lie to the sea and wind. The square
mizzen was replaced by a fore-and-aft sail,
which was better able to help the vessel lie to
the wind. Drive would also have been provided
by the substantial staysail and jib forward of
the mainmast. Note how both versions have
their shrouds placed well aft of the main and
mizzen masts, allowing them to brace round
these sails to improve the windward performance of the vessel.

There is a view that the ketch rig was created
through a deliberate modification of the three-
masted herring buss, but it is not entirely clear
which came first; but given the remarks in the
Howard Household books above it would seem
that this rig was already in being before the
change to the rig of herring busses was made.
As a general rule, across all Atlantic rigs, one
mast preceded three masts, which in turn came
before two masts. The two-mast rig, with its
origins in the Mediterranean, probably found
its way into the Atlantic via Spain and Portugal
and therefore contributing to the rig of the

Basque whaleboats and through them the Biscay double shallop. On the other hand, the adoption of the two-masted ketch rig may have been brought about in a rather different way. What is known is that in the seventeenth century the three-masted, square-rigged herring buss disappeared in favour of the two-masted ketch for operational reasons. But three masts would reappear in eighteenth-century fishing boats with the arrival of the lug sail.

At this point it is necessary to consider the relevance of this two-masted fishing boat to the work of a small coastal warship. They are first listed in the Commonwealth Navy, some as prizes and some ordered for specific roles such as advice boat. Many are referred to as 'pinks' and this usually means that a foremast has been added to their rig (Fig 2-17). However, this was often done as a temporary measure to cover a long passage or transatlantic voyage. The basic rig contained five sails: a jib, a fore staysail, a main course, a main topsail and a lateen mizzen. A mizzen topsail was not long in being added to the wardrobe and was certainly a normal addition in the Restoration Navy. The rig underwent few changes until the end of the seventeenth century, when the ketch fell out of favour in the Royal Navy, with the notable exception of the bomb ketch. However, the ketch rig was to be revived between 1732 and

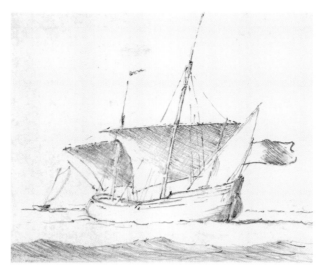

Fig 2-17. A pink, after a sketch by Van de Velde the younger. *Author*

1759, not just for bomb ketches but for a minority of the smaller cruising sloops.

The hull and rig of the ketch made it admirably suitable for coastal tasks and its robustness meant it could carry a reasonable armament. It had proved itself in the blustery conditions round Britain and it could be seen as a readily available answer to the needs of coastal security and communication. Unlike the *txalupa*, it did not lend itself to a long line of development but rather it filled a gap, and quite a sizeable gap, until the coming of the more powerful sloops at the beginning of the eighteenth century. Thereafter it was only its rig, much modified, that was to survive.

Chapter 3

THE SEA-WARS BETWEEN ENGLAND, HOLLAND, FRANCE AND SPAIN
1651–1678

The underlying causes of the Anglo-Dutch sea-wars (1652–1674) were greed, envy and humiliation: greed on the part of the Dutch, envy in the hearts of the English, and humiliation in the breasts of the kings of France and England. The underlying theme of all three wars lay in the question of who was to have control over the use of the sea and therefore the trade upon it and the lands beyond it; but the reasons that sparked the outbreak of each war were different. The wars were short and, as far as England was concerned, they were fought entirely at sea at squadron or fleet level or by small ships amongst the shoals of the southern North Sea.

In 1648 the Dutch eventually won their independence from the Spanish. It had taken them 80 years to remove this yoke from what was then part of the Spanish Netherlands. Spain's enormous empire in the Americas was beginning to show signs of wilting by this time and at sea

the Dutch had been making life uncomfortable for them, encroaching on their trade and supporting this with strong and effective warships. Whilst Spain had become the leading overseas trading nation of the sixteenth century, the Dutch were to capture that crown from them in the closing years of the century and establish, for a while, hegemony in maritime power.

At home the Republic was governed by a merchant class during the Stadtholderless period (1650–1672),[1] although the House of Orange held the titular position of Stadtholder. Whilst the Stadtholder had the allegiance of many, particularly from the inland southern provinces, the financial and maritime power rested with the northern provinces, particularly those on the seaboard: Holland with Amsterdam and Zeeland.

WAR BETWEEN ENGLAND AND SPAIN 1654–1660

Spain did not enter into the first Anglo-Dutch War but was challenged separately by Cromwell's Protectorate in 1654 as a result of commercial rivalry between the two countries. This second war was to last until 1660, when the restored English monarchy made peace with Spain. Whilst the first Anglo-Dutch war had been a success for England, the Spanish war was disastrous. The only clear advantages – but they were considerable ones – were the capture and holding of Jamaica and the demonstration of ubiquitous English naval power. But this diversion of interest and the fact that England lost between 1500 and 2000 merchant ships in

Fig 3.1. A royal yacht of the Restoration Navy acting as a tender to the fleet in battle being used mainly for communication purposes and as a fast taxi service for key officers and civilians. *Author*.

this war enabled the Dutch to recoup their position as the prime trading country of Europe.

By far the largest loss to English merchant shipping occurred in the North Sea and the Channel and this was due, almost entirely, to the efforts of Spanish-backed privateers, based in the port of Dunkirk. This made its capture a matter of political urgency for Cromwell. In 1657 Cromwell was able to establish a year's alliance with France in its war with Spain, thus allowing him to bully the French, aided by English regiments, into attacking and occupying the harbours from Gravelines to Ostend, including Dunkirk, in what had been the Spanish Netherlands. English troops played a key part in the capture of Dunkirk, including standing fast against two attacks by the future King James II of England.[2]

If the first Anglo-Dutch sea-war (1652–1654) had not raised the need for the coastal security of commercial activity in the narrow seas, the war with Spain most certainly did. England had been fortunate in capturing 1200 commercial vessels in the war against the Dutch but was to lose far more to Spanish privateers between 1654 and 1658.[3] It is no surprise, therefore, that the first employment of small unrated warships by England at this time had nothing to do with the Anglo-Dutch War, but was driven by the threat posed by Spain to commercial shipping in the Channel, in the North Sea and, following England's capture of Jamaica, in the Caribbean.

Dunkirk, still under the control of Spain, was notorious for producing privateers that could outsail any other vessels. Light, with a large crew and powered by oar and sail, they could do as they wished. No English ship could catch them. It is important to remember that there was a strong link between the harbours of the

Fig 3-2. Early ketch rig. *Author.*

Spanish Netherlands and the Basque ports in northwest Spain, which were noted for the production of fast vessels under sail and oar. This was not a new problem to the English, or the Dutch for that matter; both countries had tried to produce vessels capable of dealing with them since Tudor times, even to the point where dockyards were directed to build small warships in the 'Dunkirk fashion'. In time this threat was considerably reduced by the capture of Dunkirk and its subsequent garrisoning by Cromwell's troops in 1658. The problem would then disappear following the Restoration of the monarchy in 1660 when Charles II, almost immediately, made peace with Spain. Nevertheless, in the mid-1650s there was an urgent need for small unrated warships, able to keep the sea and sail well, in order to provide advice to commercial shipping of the imminent presence of predators.

The vessels ordered for this work were ketches, and it is of interest that not one of them was taken during this war. They – and others built after the Restoration – continued to serve throughout the remaining wars of this period.

Table 3-1: ACQUISITIONS OF KETCHES, 1651–1660

Launch	No.	Rig	Burthen	Guns	Men	Fate	Remarks
1651	1	Ketch	47	6	30	Survived beyond 1660	First Commonwealth ketch. Eventually sold to start Hudson's Bay company
1655–1656	4	Ketch	55	6–8	35	All survived beyond 1660	All built by contract, 'Ketch fashion'
1656	2	Ketch/pink	88	14–16	40–50	Both survived beyond 1660	Dockyard-built as pinks with three masts.
1657–1658	6	Ketch	55	4	30	One taken 1657	All, less *Lilly* (63 tons), shallow draught
Total	13						

Notes:

Details here have been averaged. Fuller accounts can be found in *The Sailing Navy List*, David Lyon (Conway 1990), pp31–33; and *British Warships in the Age of Sail, 1603–1714*, Rif Winfield (Seaforth Publishing 2012), pp223–227.

Fig 3-3. Samuel Pepys, Clerk
of the Acts to the Navy Board
1660–1674, then Secretary to
the Admiralty until 1688. Oil
painting by Godfrey Kneller,
1689. *National Maritime
Museum BHC2947*

Fig 3-4. Charles II, King of
England 1660–1685.
Watercolour miniature by
Samuel Cooper, dating from
the early years of the king's
reign. *National Maritime
Museum C9422*

The table below gives an outline of the Cromwellian programme. Dimensions and statistics have been averaged to give a simple outline of the programmes.

THE RESTORATION AND THE SECOND ANGLO-DUTCH WAR

In his diary for 25 May 1660 Samuel Pepys made the following entry:

> About noon (though the brigantine that Beale made was there ready to carry him) yet he would go in my Lord's barge with the two Dukes. Our Captn. steered, and my Lord went along bare with him. I went and Mr. Mansell, and one of the King's footmen, and a dog that the King loved, in a boat by ourselves, and so got on shore when the King did, who was received by General Monk with all imaginable love and respect at his entrance upon the land of Dover.[4]

The defining experiences that Charles brought with him to the government of his kingdom consisted for the most part of the trauma of civil war, the execution of his father in 1649, and a decade of exile, defeat and the indignity of powerless dependence on foreign courts. It is not surprising, therefore, that on his restoration

he would seek to re-establish that governing autonomy that had been taken from his father by force of arms. Indeed, throughout his reign many of his actions were directed to this end, not least the treaty with his autocratic cousin Louis XIV, made without consulting Parliament and signed in secret at Dover in 1670. He had also endured poverty and this was to have an effect on his financial dealings with Parliament, particularly after the Second Anglo-Dutch War. Both these issues were to hamstring his country since they prevented it from reaching its full potential and ultimately turned the public and Parliament against him.[5] His brother James, Duke of York, who succeeded him as king in 1686, was an even more ardent exponent of arbitrary and absolute power, but he also made the gravest of mistakes by seeking to re-establish Roman Catholicism as the religion of his realm; an action unacceptable to his people, who ultimately rejected him.

Charles arrived in England with a good knowledge of the sea and ships. He was known to display an understanding of the form and construction of a ship that amazed those who later had to brief him, his education in the shipwright's trade no doubt coming from his time spent in the Isles of Scilly and the Channel Islands. His brother, whom he appointed Admiral of England – although it may have been James himself who decided that this was to be his new role – had little knowledge of the sea and ships at this time, but was to develop into an effective naval administrator and fighting admiral, acquiring a deep grasp of the nature, opportunities and limitations of sea power.[6] Their cousin Prince Rupert had, during the interregnum, commanded the Royalist squadron formed of those officers and men who had remained loyal to the crown. With no fixed base from which to sortie and seemingly impossible difficulties with ships, armament, manpower and finance, Rupert still managed to pose a severe threat to the trade and security of the Commonwealth in the Atlantic and Mediterranean until finally exhausted by Blake's operations against him. Thus the arrival at Dover brought with it a fund of naval knowledge and, more importantly, interest, which was to be used to good effect if not always for the right purposes over the next fourteen years in the struggles with the Dutch Republic.

Charles's arrival at Dover also brought a more tangible asset to England. On his departure from his exile in Holland, the Dutch had given him a yacht, the *Mary*, named after his mother, the sister of Louis XIII. Yachting was going to become a royal sport in the first decade of his reign and through that sport contribute to the design of small warships thereafter. English master shipwrights were to improve this class of vessel, making it lower and with more draught and finer lines. The rig would concentrate the English mind on the advantages of fore-and-aft sail and fine underwater lines.

At the approach of the Second Anglo-Dutch War, many in the mercantile and naval fraternity had severe doubts as to its long-term effects. In view of the fact that yet again the opportunities for English trade had been enhanced by a revised Navigation Act in 1661, which included the protection of the fishing grounds, Parliament took some persuading to support the war, which was promoted on the basis that its successful outcome, which was largely taken for granted, would lead to an expansion of English overseas trade. This, it transpired, was largely an illusion and in many respects maritime trade suffered badly, particularly from the attacks of Dutch privateers, which had not been so effective in the first war. The catalyst for the war was the acquisitive

Fig 3-5. James, Duke of York; King of England 1685–1688. Watercolour miniature by Samuel Cooper, dating from around 1671. *National Maritime Museum 9281*

drive of a group of merchant adventurers, naval officers, members of Parliament and junior ministers, headed by James, Duke of York. This faction, gathered around the court, had substantial sums invested in overseas mercantile projects, many in competition with the Dutch, and were in a position to use the Royal Navy for their own vested interests. Thus the Second

Fig 3-6. This miniature model by Donald McNarry of the Dutch-built royal yacht *Mary* shows the high poop deck, which the English constructors reduced to produce a clean sheer-line. *By courtesy of Pauline Chard*

Dutch War was fought not for the professed broader aim, which had won the support of Parliament, but for the narrower interests of those in power and government.

At this point the story of small warships branches out in two directions to face the separate threats faced in fleet actions, and those in coastal convoy and fishery protection. The Dutch had developed some expertise in the use of the fireship, which was a potent weapon system to use in the shoal waters of the southern North Sea, particularly along the coasts of Flanders and the Dutch Republic, where large warships could be trapped and placed at the mercy of the fireships. As the war came closer, James, as Lord High Admiral of England, recognised this threat and directed the Admiralty to order the building of sloops to 'attend the fleet for the towing off of ships', whether they be endangered English warships or Dutch fireships.

This demand was inadequately met by a programme that produced only three purpose-built sloops for this role. However, there is much pictorial evidence to show that the fleet was attended in battle by a host of ketches and yachts. Not only were they there for the provision of that key element in any battle, communication, but they could also be assigned to capital ships for a host of other tasks, which might include assisting a crippled ship.

Charles II had inherited a powerful navy from Cromwell. Partly through the fame of Pepys (he was always his own best publicist), and partly due to the flamboyance of the times combined with a strong interest in naval affairs

from the top, the Restoration period has come to be regarded as a high point in English naval history. It is generally forgotten that it was the Commonwealth/Protectorate that created the powerful navy that Parliament failed to succour after 1660. Had it not been for a king who cared deeply about his navy and a secretary who gripped its administration, then it is doubtful whether England would have developed a maritime empire in the face of stiff competition from other European states.

In the realm of small warships, Charles inherited only eleven ketches from the Commonwealth Navy; two were given to the Irish packet service but the remainder all survived the second war with the Dutch. To these were added seven new ketches, three built by contract, two in dockyards and two bought as built. Again, all these served in, and survived, the second war. The sloop programme was minuscule – only three were built, two by dockyards and one by contract. Their role was to attend the fleet but they may have been used to keep the coast clear of privateers when not engaged with the fleet. All survived the war, partly because they were delivered close to its end.

The Second Anglo-Dutch War answered nothing. The promised improvement in trading possibilities failed to materialise and, following the Dutch raid on the Medway, the Dutch had achieved the upper hand at sea. Morale in England was low, and at this point Charles may have found the results of his efforts rather humiliating. Frustrated by Parliament's refusal to give him a budget to continue against the Dutch, he moved towards a secret and underhand treaty with his cousin, Louis XIV.

THE THIRD ANGLO-DUTCH WAR, 1672–1674

The royal ambition of war against the Dutch Republic remained unchanged, but it was now piqued by the humiliation Charles had received at the hands of the Dutch with their destruction of his ships in the Medway; nevertheless, the means of achieving that ambition was outrageous. Through the mechanism of a secret treaty between Charles and Louis XIV, an unprovoked joint attack would be made against the Dutch Republic.[7] Whilst on the surface this could look like (and was) another attempt at

Fig 3-7. Detail from an ink painting by Van de Velde the elder shows two ketches, near and far left, and a yacht, right, at the successful Battle of Lowestoft in 1665. *National Maritime Museum PY3903*

Table 3-2: ACQUISITION OF KETCHES, SLOOPS AND YACHTS, 1660–1667

Launch	No.	Type	Burthen	Guns	Men	Fate	Remarks
1655	11	Ketch	55–88	8	35	All survived the Second war. Two given to Irish Packet Service 1661	Inherited from Commonwealth Navy
1661	2	Ketch	48, 54	2, 6	40	Both survived the war	Purchased
1664–1665	5	Ketch	72–100	8–10	45	All survived the war	Three contract-built, two by dockyard
1666–1667	3	Sloop	28, 39, 43	4	28–30	All survived the war	Two dockyard-built, one contract
1660	2	Yacht	54, 92	0, 4	30	Both survived the war	Gift from the Dutch. Probably did not attend the fleet
1660	2	Yacht	91, 94	8	30	Both survived the war	Built for Charles and James to race
1662	2	Yacht	31, 35	4, 6	4 and 10	Both survived the war	Probably did not attend the fleet
1663–1666	4	Yacht	106	8	30	All survived the war	Yacht *Navy* 74 tons
Total	31						

Notes:

Details here have been averaged. Fuller accounts can be found in *The Sailing Navy List*, David Lyon (Conway 1990), pp31–33; and *British Warships in the Age of Sail, 1603–1714*, Rif Winfield (Seaforth Publishing 2012), pp223–227.

The sloops were all commissioned right at the end of the war or just after it, so it is most unlikely that any attended the fleet in action. *Spy*, built at Harwich in 1666 was, according to her builder Anthony Deane, meant for the purpose of coping with privateers in the vicinity of that port.

Navy was an Admiralty yacht, the others were all royal commissions.

reducing Holland's maritime hegemony and trade, from Charles's position it was another stepping stone on his way to achieving absolute power and avoiding the frustration of going cap-in-hand to Parliament for funds that it was not anxious to offer. By agreeing to this venture against the Dutch, Charles was to be financially supported by Louis, thereby easing his dependence on Parliament.

The outcome of the war, thanks to the superb seamanship and superior naval tactics of the Dutch, was that no invasion of the Netherlands took place from the sea. So once again, apart from Louis' advances into the southern provinces of the Republic, this was to be a war conducted entirely at sea by an English fleet supported by a French squadron. Charles's duplicity, whilst not officially 'discovered' until after the war, was strongly suspected and he was forced to change course and dismantle his pro-French policy and, for a while, his crusade for absolutism.[8] There followed a period after his withdrawal from the Dutch war when England was at peace with the world whilst internally being deeply divided against itself. This did not stop the expansion of English seaborne trade. Rather England's neutral position allowed the 'carrying' trades to flourish whilst the navy shrank, until James, on becoming king, began its restoration.

THE CONSEQUENCES FOR THE COMMERCIAL USE OF THE SEA

All three wars were premeditated and yet their side effects may have been inadequately thought through, possibly because of over-

Table 3-3: ACQUISITIONS OF KETCHES, SLOOPS AND YACHTS, 1672–1674

Launch	No.	Type	Burthen	Guns	Men	Fates	Remarks
N/A	5	Ketch	Various	8–10	30–45	Survived the war	Already acquired: 3 from Commonwealth, 2 from Restoration
N/A	3	Sloop	Various	4	10	Survived the war	All from Restoration
N/A	13	Yacht	Various	8	30	1 taken, 1 sunk in action	4 acquired since end of second war
1671–1673	2	Ketch	90	10	50		Both purchases, one: no details
1672–1673	17	Sloop	48–68, 19 and 22	2 or 4	10–36	4 lost, 1 taken, 1 sunk in action	
Total	40						

Notes:

Details here have been averaged. Fuller accounts can be found in *The Sailing Navy List*, David Lyon (Conway 1990), pp31–33; and *British Warships in the Age of Sail, 1603–1714*, Rif Winfield (Seaforth Publishing 2012), pp223–227.

The sloops were all commissioned during the war. Full details of these are in Chapter 5.

Fig 3-8. This drawing by Van de Velde the elder shows the Dutch herring fleet under the watchful eyes of two guardships fishing possibly within sight of villages and towns on the East Anglian coast. The busses appear to be ship-rigged and have lowered their mainmasts onto the deck. Note that they appear to gather their nets in over the side, not the bow. *National Maritime Museum PY1711*

confidence in a quick and victorious outcome or, in the Third War, the need for secrecy. There was always the myth that a successful war would provide an increase in maritime trade. This may have been true of the first war, in which the Commonwealth Navy captured some 1200 Dutch merchant ships through naval and privateering action, whilst losing few of their own. The Navy also attacked, destroyed and dispersed the Dutch fishing fleet operating off the English East Coast. However, similar successes did not attend the Second War when the odds were even. In the Third War the Dutch had the best in this sector of operations. One of the reasons for this growth in the Dutch privateering war against trade (and fishing) was the decision by the Dutch State to curtail commercial shipping operations during the summer months. Their reasoning was that their navy could either fight the English or protect trade but not do both simultaneously. It also needed the trained manpower of the merchant fleets to man the fleet in battle. The side effect was to deflect investment from supporting trade into the financing of privateering syndicates, until the winter brought back commercial maritime activity.

The North Sea provided many opportunities for prize-taking on both sides, but the coast between the Scottish border and the approaches to the Thames was the landward 'front line' in any war against the Dutch. The southern North Sea had become a 'no-man's land'. Down it came coal from Newcastle; into its harbours came the hauls of the fishing fleets.[9] It also contained the principal shipyards that built the fleet; and it faced the Dutch seaboard. Its waters were shallow and its countryside largely flat and open, similar to that of Holland and Zeeland. All this made a desirable and easy target for capers (the name for Dutch privateers). The capers came in all shapes and sizes but a feature common to most of them was shallow draught, suiting them to inshore operations.

In 1660 the English capacity to protect coastal trade and fishing was minimal. Charles inherited a navy that had an impressive battle fleet, albeit a bankrupt one. Unfortunately, it contained only a few of the smaller ships of shallow draught that would be ideal for protecting coastal commercial activity.[10] Of Sixth Rates there were seventeen, but two were converted to fireships before the Second War and seven were either lost, sold or broken up, leaving eight for operations in 1665.[11] Unrated vessels with shallow draught suitable for coastal convoy amounted to twelve, of which one was abroad and remained so, one was sold and one lost. Those nine available for hostilities in 1665 were all ketch-rigged. The total of small Sixth Rates and unrated armed vessels suitable for coastal trade protection therefore amounted to a mere seventeen.

With the possibility of war, there seems to have been some recognition that there was a need to increase the stock of small warships providing coastal convoy. One purchase in 1661 and three programmes between 1664 and 1666 were ordered, bringing a further thirteen new vessels to the business of convoy, making a total of thirty. This figure does not include a number of small prizes taken during the course of the war which augmented the stock of purpose-built ships and sloops. The last programme was for sloops, with the construction actually carried out during the conflict in what would now be called an emergency war programme.[12] The sloops were different from

the Sixth Rates and ketches in certain important respects. They were ordered as fleet tenders, which would include the ability to tow crippled ships out of the line or away from fire-ships. They were completed late in the war and when not employed with the fleet, which was most of the time, their ability to operate in shallow water helped in the fight against Dutch capers, who would lurk in the shoal water along the English East Coast. The problem was that they were lightly built, under-gunned and under-complemented, but all survived the war.[13]

Preparations in this respect for the Third War were negligible. The 'private' nature of this war, in the sense that Parliament was not consulted, may have had a bearing on the lack of overt preparation in this sphere, as may the concept that this was to be a war of invasion and that all the action would be on the Dutch coast: a very naive assessment if true. The existing total of Sixth Rates, ketches and sloops was thirteen. Two Sixth Rates had been launched by Anthony Deane at Portsmouth in 1669 and 1672,

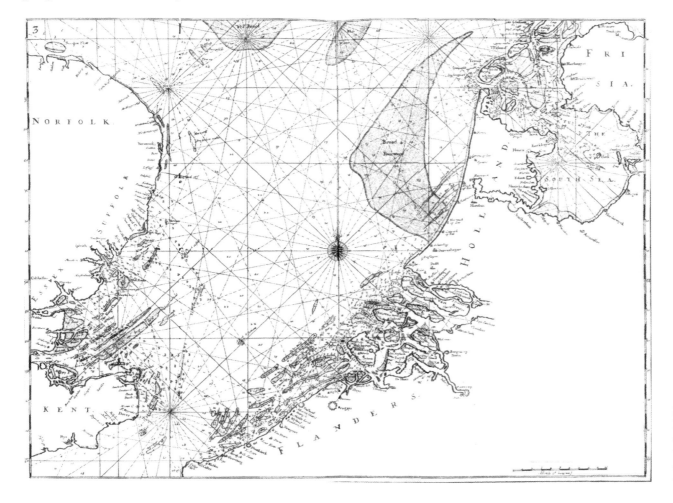

Fig 3-9. The 'narrow seas'. Note the large amount of extremely shallow water which could be both a help and hindrance to naval operations.

included in the thirteen above, but they were the only recent additions.[14]

At the outset of the war, in order to assist the fleet (of which more below), an emergency programme was ordered for seventeen sloops. These were all produced in a rush in the Royal Dockyards, six in 1672 and eleven in 1673. The work, design, structure, armament and complement of these sloops will be discussed in a later chapter, but it would seem that they were a quick answer to an urgent operational need. Although they were required for a fleet role in battle, the nature of their deployments when not so tasked indicate that all these small vessels, Sixth Rates included, were acting in what was to become in the eighteenth century the classic 'sloop' roles of convoy, surveillance and communication.

Before going any further, it would be wise to consider the theatre of war. Unlike later campaigns, the bulk of the action took place in a relatively small area, which ran like a great sickle from southern Norway in the north to the Channel Soundings in the southwest. Its southern boundary was the coast of the Low Countries and France, from the Frisian Islands in the north to the western end of the Channel. Its outer boundary ran from Shetland in the north to Land's End, but the bulk of the coast-

wise trade that needed protection plied from the Tyne to the Thames. This coast is bounded by shoals through which the tide can run fast. Its shallowness quickly creates short sharp seas when a fresh breeze sets in, particularly if that breeze is against the tide. The coastwise trade was dense, with a preponderance of colliers plodding down the coast, heavy laden for a coal-hungry London, and small merchantmen bustling north carrying corn; adding to this the ubiquitous fishing industry made an excellent field for prize-taking.

The Dutch shared the same type of coastline but they enjoyed the further advantage of knowing the English coast well, having fished it for decades during the inter-war years, even selling their catches in England at competitive prices. In war, English fishermen were vulnerable to being disrupted by capers; the shoals were up for grabs. Many of Pepys's notes to captains of sloops exhorted them to return with all speed to the fisheries 'the season of the year greatly requiring it',[15] so in addition to providing coastwise convoy to colliers and merchantmen, the sloops, under the wing of a Sixth Rate, would be tasked to protect the fisheries in season.

In respect to the protection of trade, there is one other topic that bears mention and that is

Fig 3-10. This pen and wash sketch by Van de Velde the elder shows a sloop centre stage in the foreground. Beyond are another two sloops and four, possibly five, royal or naval yachts. Ideally they keep to windward of the action so that they can render assistance quickly. *National Maritime Museum PT2529*

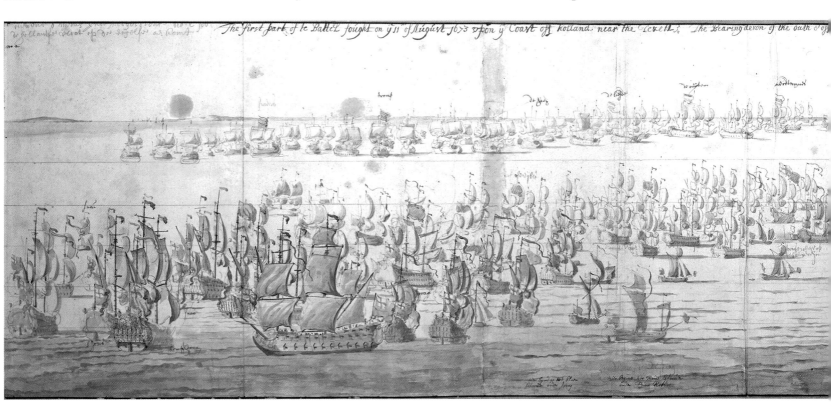

the possession of Dunkirk. As has already been noted, this port was a serious menace to the security of commercial shipping in the 'narrow seas'. It was inherited by Charles, thanks to Cromwell's acquisition of it in 1658, but Charles sold it to France in 1662 for reasons of cost and doubts over the loyalty of the ex-Commonwealth garrison.[16] Though this loss would not cause problems in the wars against the Dutch, it was to pose severe difficulties from 1688 onwards in the long struggle with France.

FLEET SUPPORT

Fleet support was an entirely different type of operation. One of the facts that bedevilled the direction of battle at sea at this time was the inability of admirals to communicate with their captains or, indeed, with other admirals. Apart from flags, which were rudimentary in what they could express and were often obscured by smoke, ship commanders used their longboats to seek out their admirals to discover their intentions.

The paintings of battles in the Third War portray not only the longboat movement but an abundance of small armed sailing vessels – ketches, yachts and sloops – closing on line-of-battle ships, or standing out to a flank, waiting. These would have been used for communica-

Fig 3-11. A sketch of *Fan Fan*, a sloop which became a royal yacht, developed by the author from a painting of the *Prince*, a First Rate ship, whom she was attending at the Battle of Solebay. Following that battle she was ordered to convey Lord Sandwich's body to London. *Author*

tion and, because they could be rowed effectively, for towing fireships clear of stricken ships or vice-versa. In some of the paintings the sloops seem to form a screen. One possible explanation may stem from the fact that the English captains were understandably wary of running aground on the shoals off the Dutch coast and therefore would want to know what depth lay ahead of them; a task for which a sloop, with its shallow draught and good manoeuvrability, would be ideal.

Throughout the Restoration period of twenty-eight years, the total time when England was at war with the Dutch Republic was only five years; but there were other threats, such as those in the Mediterranean, and ketches and sloops were attached to squadrons in the 'Straits' and even in the Caribbean. Their roles continued to be coastal convoy, communication, surveillance and ferrying VIPs, but following the Third War there were no more acquisitions until after the Glorious Revolution of 1688; indeed, many of the small escort craft were 'sold as useless' in 1683. By 1688 all that was left of a coastal convoy fleet were three ketches. All the sloops had come and gone, except one who, because she had been a privateer/yacht for Prince Rupert, was classified as a Sixth Rate: she was the *Fan Fan* (or *Phan Phan*), no doubt the nickname of one of Prince Rupert's mistresses.[17]

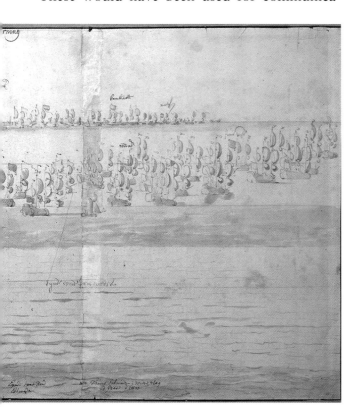

Chapter 4

THE SMALL WARSHIPS OF THE COMMONWEALTH AND THE RESTORATION NAVIES 1651–1688

THE COMMONWEALTH AND RESTORATION KETCHES

The ketch was well represented in the Commonwealth Navy. As war with the Dutch

Fig 4-1. Drawing by the author of a 10-gun ketch of about 90 tons burthen and with a crew of around 35 men. Note the 'pink' stern, common to ketches, and the use of a square mizzen topsail. The main is a two-part mast, although it might equally have been a one-piece, or 'pole', mast. *Author*

Fig 4-2. The 'pink' stern and the 'ketch' bow. *Author*.

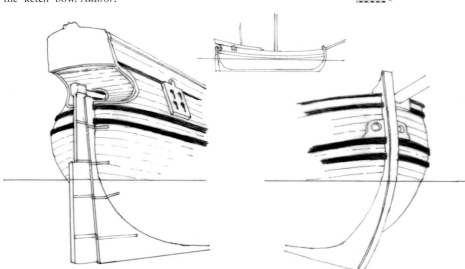

Republic loomed ever closer, it was the only type of small sailing vessel capable of being out in all weathers and robust enough to carry a respectable armament – usually between eight and ten 3pdrs. For this reason it would be reasonable to say that the ketch was the first class of vessel to be specifically ordered for one of the sloop's operational tasks: the 'advice' boat. In the seventeenth century 'advice' was synonymous with 'intelligence' or 'information', and these boats were essential to the Commonwealth Navy to give advance warning of the presence of privateers and warships from the Spanish Netherlands.

The prototype naval ketch was *Nonsuch*, which in 1651 became the State's first acquisition of such a craft. She passed in and out of state commission throughout her long life, becoming well known in the process. Originally built at Wivenhoe in Essex in 1650 for commercial purposes by Robert Page, who was famous for building good ketches, she was hired, with her owner/captain, shortly after completion 'to work amongst the sands'; this was a phrase that was to return to Admiralty specifications time and again when concern arose about the security of English coastal waters, particularly on the East Coast. In 1652 *Nonsuch* was transferred to fishery protection, remaining in the North Sea until purchased outright by the State. Under a restored monarchy, she was in a fleet support role at the Battle of Lowestoft in 1665, eventually being sold to Prince Rupert and others for their trading expedition to Hudson's

Fig 4-3. These two photographs of a model of the *Nonsuch* by John Garnish show an exact copy of the reconstruction made of the vessel for the Hudson's Bay Company. Unlike many of the naval ketches she does not have a buss sail: indeed, her sail plan is like that on the main and mizzen masts of an earlier reconstruction, the *Mayflower*. Her stern work resembles that of a yacht whereas most ketches had pink sterns. It may be that alterations were made when the original was sold out of the service. Note the substantial deadeye arrangement for securing the mainstay to the stem head.[1]

Bay in 1668. Her roles in the North Sea and in fleet support were the same as those of a naval sloop in the eighteenth-century sense of the word. She was, in effect, the first of a most numerous type of small warship because the Commonwealth Navy commissioned no less than twelve similar vessels between 1655 and 1658. This was backed up by the acquisition of a further seven by the Restoration Navy.

The ketch was to change very little in form and general pattern of rig until well into the eighteenth century. The hull shape was commodious – after all, they came from a background of the carrying trades and of offshore fishing. Most ketches of the mid-seventeenth century were built with what was called a pink stern, which meant that the shape and framing aft was nearly identical to that of its bow and therefore strong. In order to place a more spacious, square-ended quarterdeck above this narrowing stern, an attractive linkage was

contrived above the upper wale, but there was a limit to how broad such a quarterdeck could be so most pink-sterned vessels had rather narrow decks aft. The arrangement can be seen in profile in Fig 4-1 and in three dimensions in Fig 4-2. Although some ketches ordered later for the Restoration Navy may have had broader taffrails (and by the 1680s yachts were being equipped with the ketch rig whilst maintaining their ornate square sterns), it is unusual to see an early ketch such as *Nonsuch* with a broad square stern.

Another variant of the pink stern was developed at much the same time, but not necessarily for the ketch. The stern waterlines of the ketch were very bluff, but other designs produced a rather sharper plan as they neared the stern. The conversion of this pointed shape into a square one above the upper wale was called a 'cat' stern, as shown in Fig 4-4. This type of stern will be seen later on other vessels; indeed, if this drawing is correctly dated to 1700, it is probably not on a naval ketch, since there were very few left at that date. It may well represent the stern of a small Sixth Rate or sloop. Examples of both types of stern were to be used on the bomb ketches introduced into the Royal Navy in the 1680s.[2]

The bows of naval ketches, other than yachts, had a plain stem and no head was added (Fig 4-2). They shared this feature with the sloops/shallops that were to be ordered for the Second and Third Anglo-Dutch wars. This feature can be seen in the excellent grisaille by Van de Velde the elder at Fig 4-5. The other feature that can be seen here is that the bowsprit lies alongside, rather than over, the stemhead, so it is probable that it could be drawn in over the deck in port or in rough weather when a jib would not be set on it. This picture portrays a largish ketch pierced for 12 guns.[3] Her rig is of interest in that it is very different from that set up on the *Nonsuch* replica above. Her mainmast is far taller and the structure about the doubling is much lighter. Indeed, she appears not to have a platform top but just crosstrees to spread her standing rigging. Her mainsail is colossal but is not similar to a buss sail, which would be narrower. The tacks and sheets for her mainsail are well shown, as are the braces, which fall to a rail on the quarterdeck. She has a mizzen

topmast stay that runs to the mid part of her mainmast, another indicator of how tall that mast is. On her mizzen is a crossjack yard for taking the clews of the mizzen topsail, which can just be seen above it. Her stern is of interest since it is not of the pink pattern: her quarters are too slender for that. It could be a cat stern or even a square stern, though the latter is unlikely. Rather like *Nonsuch*, her quarters are well decorated.

One of the ketches ordered by the Restoration Admiralty was the *Roe*. Most unusually, there was already a Cromwellian ketch in the Navy with the same name, although she had been 'made a kitchen' in 1661 so was probably not regarded as a commissioned warship. The *Roe* at Fig 4-6 acquired some fame from her involvement in the *Mary Rose* action in December 1669. While escorting a group of merchantmen the *Mary Rose* was set upon by seven Algerian corsairs, her only support being the *Roe*. This shows that ketches were not only used for coastal convoy. The rig of the *Roe* is very similar to that of the previous example, which raises a question mark over the rig of the *Nonsuch* replica. Also like the earlier example, she is flying a long pennant from the masthead. However, her main dissimilarity is her stern, which is of a classic pink form. She also shows signs of having a well-developed gripe at the bottom of her stem to counteract any tendency to develop lee helm.[4]

A similar vessel to the *Roe* is shown in a detail from a drawing by Van de Velde the elder (Fig 4-7a). It depicts the unsuccessful English

attack on the Dutch East India Company's convoy sheltering in Bergen in 1666.[5] Sensibly the artist has left out all the standing rigging from his work, which allows a better view of the shipping. The pink stern, fulsome body and ten guns of the ketch are well shown. Elsewhere in the drawing is a much smaller ketch (Fig 4-7b) with the typical ketch hull but only four guns, which are carried on the quarterdeck. Most noticeable is the rig, which is fore-and-aft in the manner of a Dutch galliot. This vessel does not match any of the listed naval ketches, so she may be a Dutch prize, such as a dogger or flyboat, or she may be an English hoy with a small mizzen mast added to its smack rig. This is another reminder of Blankley's 'definition'.

Whilst tables outlining the ketch-building programmes are given in Chapter 3, some more details are worth recording. During the Commonwealth, and after *Nonsuch* had been acquired in 1651, three programmes were ordered. The first in 1655 was for four vessels of 40ft–42ft on the keel, 16ft breadth with a draught of 7ft–8ft 7in and displacing between 54 and 56 tons. All were meant to carry 35 crew and 8 guns, probably 5pdr sakers. These were long guns but the broad decks of the ketches could manage them.

In the following year (1656) the second programme provided two rather larger ketches.

Fig 4-6 This detail from a sketch by Van de Velde the younger shows the *Roe* ketch under topsail and jib as she supports the *Mary Rose* in her fight with no less than seven Barbary corsairs whilst escorting a convoy. *National Maritime Museum PY3905*

Figs 4-7a & 4-7b. Two details from a panorama of the English attack at Bergen in 1665 by Van de Velde the elder. They show a pink-sterned square-rigged ketch, and a small 4-gun ketch with a smack mainsail and a pink stern. This vessel may have been a harbour craft or other utility vessel armed for this occasion. Many of the small sloops were indeed merchant vessels co-opted to help the war effort.

Fig 4-8. Sloops of the 1672–1673 programme on and off the wind in the shallow waters off the East Anglian coast. Although ordered as fleet tenders for the Third Anglo-Dutch War, they were subsequently used for the many coastal duties that required small ships of shallow draught. These duties were mainly concerned with security and communication. *Oil painting by the author*

These were ordered for overseas service with a length on the keel of 45ft–47ft, a draught of 8ft 4in–9ft and a burthen of 87–90 tons. Both were given what was called a 'pink rig' by the addition of a foremast to the usual ketch sail plan. The two rigs were easily interchanged and it was considered prudent to provide the three-masted pink rig for long distance passages. The pink rig is essentially a three-mast 'ship' rig, but in the confusing maritime nomenclature of the period, the word 'pink' referred to the stern shape of the vessel as well as to the type of rig.

The third and largest programme, this time for six ketches, was ordered in 1657. The Council of State specified that they should be crewed by 30 men, armed with 4 guns and draw no more than five feet of water. In fact they turned out to be of slightly larger dimensions. Nevertheless, this is a similar specification to that for the sloops of 1672–1673. The shallow draught gives an indication of where they were required to work, and the only records of their service show that they were used in the Channel and North Sea and in one case in the 'Sound' (the entrance to the Baltic). Circumstantial evidence suggests that their purpose was to warn and protect coastwise trade and fishing. The only one lost was *Parrot*, captured by two Spanish privateers and taken into Flushing.[6]

In 1660, all but the *Parrot* of the Commonwealth ketches entered what at the Restoration became the Royal Navy. Two were given in 1661 to the Irish Packet Service, so they cannot have been slow sailers; moreover a good windward ability is a help on that crossing. The choice of the ketch as a useful minor warship continued in the Restoration period. Having just given away two ketches, the Navy promptly purchased another two of nearly the same displacement but slightly increased draught. It then followed this by a programme of five in 1664–1665. The most famous of this group was the *Roe* (as pointed out above, for the heroic part in the *Mary Rose* action), but the *Deptford* was also well known, enjoying a fine, wide-ranging career that only ended in a capsize during a squall off Virginia in 1689. Three of these ketches were built by contract, two of them by Page at Wivenhoe, the leading specialist who had built *Nonsuch*. The other two were built in the Royal Dockyards. These were all larger than most of the Commonwealth ketches: not much longer on the keel but between 72 and 100 tons displacement. They thus had a greater draught and were similar in size to the *Blackamore* group which had been designed in 1656 for foreign service. Their career records show that they were used for convoy, fishery protection and coastal patrol. Most saw overseas service, in the 'Straits' (the Mediterranean) and in the Americas. Two were converted to a three-masted pink rig. Such were the times that only two lasted beyond the Third Anglo-Dutch War, those being *Deptford*, built at Deptford by Shish, and *Wivenhoe*, built at Wivenhoe by Page.

During the Commonwealth and Restoration periods, the ketch had proved to be a versatile small warship, handy and seaworthy in almost any weather and capable of carrying an armament that could defeat the smaller privateers. As such it was used for convoy, fishery protection, coastal patrol, expedition, and as an advice boat. Unlike the sloops, which came on the scene at the time of the Third Dutch War, they did not have the ability to enter really shallow water and they appear not to have been set up for rowing. But despite that they were a better choice for most of the above tasks than the sloops. For these reasons they are most rightly one of the principal forerunners, in an operational sense, of the sloop classes of the eighteenth century.

THE PEPYSIAN SLOOPS 1656–1687

It would be wrong to assume, simply because of its 'sloop' designation, that the seventeenth-century Pepysian sloop had a greater influence on the design and role of the eighteenth-century sloop of war than any of the other small warships of the time. In fact, the design of the early sloops of war at the beginning of the eighteenth century bore a closer relationship in hull design to the model of the Stuart royal yachts and the smaller Sixth Rate ships than to any other vessels. Later in that century, a return to the Pepysian sloop hull form would be seen for a time in the sloops of the 1730s. However, these small warships are significant in the sloop story for a number of reasons. They were not planned far in advance but built during wartime to meet an urgent operational requirement. In 1665 James, Duke of York had requested the 'speedy building of a convenient number of shallops to carry 10–20 men such as may be useful to attend on the great ships for preventing of the enemy fireships from coming onboard them'.[7] A large number were built over a very short space of time: three rather late in 1666–1667 when the second war was virtually over and seventeen in 1672–1673 for the third war. They were all, save *Emsworth*, constructed in Royal Dockyards by the leading master shipwrights of the time: the first group by Deane, Tippets and Smith; the second group by Pett II and III, Deane, and Shish.[8]

Nowadays such a massive order would have been built to a standard design, but before mass-production there were no real economies of scale. As a result of the seventeenth-century hand-crafted, one-off approach, the burthen, dimensions and crew complement of these sloops were all different. Only armament, with one exception, was constant, with the first group equipped with 4 guns and the second group with a mixture of 2 and 4, but mainly the latter. The only guide to the labyrinth of these programmes is Pepys's 'Register of Ships' that were in the Royal Navy from May 1660 to March 1686, in other words during the reign of Charles II.[9] The sloops are listed in alphabetical order, which is unhelpful, so the document has been rearranged at Table 4-1 partly in chronological order by group and partly by sub-groups based on designer/builder.

The first sloop on Pepys's list was *Dunkirk*.

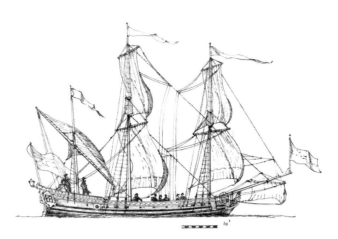

Fig 4-9. Unlike the sloops of the 1672–1673 programmes, the earlier sloops, such as *Fan Fan* shown here, were ship-rigged with topsails on fore- and mainmasts. *Fan Fan* is reputed to have carried a mizzen topsail. *Author* [11]

Little is known about this vessel, except that she was captured from the port she was named after in 1656, and it is probable that she was built there. She was small, being only 40ft on the keel with a beam of 12ft 6in, drawing 4ft 6in and measuring 33 tons, with a crew of 20.[10] There is a tendency to think of fast vessels hailing from Dunkirk as being French; this is true after 1662, but not in 1656 when Dunkirk was under the loose suzerainty of Spain. Therefore, any influence on the design of this vessel is more likely to have come from the Basque coast of Spain so she may have been based on the Biscay double shallop; she was certainly reputed to be fast under sails and oars.

The first group of purpose-built sloops resembled her in burthen and dimensions, although it is not sure that her model played a part in their design. However, within the English naval establishment for decades there had been great respect for Dunkirk-built vessels due to their ruthless ability to destroy English coastwise commercial traffic and their gift for escaping retribution. Indeed, yards had been directed to build 'in the manner of Dunkirk' [the town], so it is likely that *Dunkirk*'s design was at least considered.

Rig. The first group consisted of four sloops, one of which, *Fan Fan*, was employed by Prince Rupert as a privateer and accorded the status of 'yacht' shortly after launch, and thereby officially became a Sixth Rate. Unlike those of the second group, certainly three of these sloops, including *Fan Fan*, were ship-rigged with topmasts on fore and main and a lateen sail on the mizzen. The illustrations at Fig 4-9 and Fig 4-10 show that the sail proportions are conven-

Fig 4-10. Unlike all the other sloops built for the Second Anglo-Dutch War, *Emsworth*, if this is she, was not built by one of the master shipwrights at the Royal Dockyards. Note the use of staysails at this early stage and the tiny size of the vessel demonstrated by the size of her crew. Developed by the author from a sketch by Van de Velde the younger in the possession of the British Museum *(ref 1940-1214.15)*.

Fig 4-11. Two sloops attending the fleet at the First Battle of Schooneveld. This detail from a grisaille by Van de Velde the elder is one of the best depictions of these vessels. Note the oar ports along the topsides and the fact that these small warships did not have a head at this stage. They were very much part of an emergency war programme. *National Maritime Museum BHC0305*

Fig 4-12. Detail from a sketch by the younger Van de Velde of the departure of Mary of Modena from Calais, bound for England to become James, Duke of York's second wife. Note that this tiny sloop has raised her yards 'by the third' making them equivalent to lug sails. *National Maritime Museum PT2537*

tional and particularly the shape of the main course, which is not like the tall, thin buss sail that was used in the second group.[12] The other notable feature in Fig 4-10 is the use of a main staysail, here shown furled; this was a feature not seen on the models of 1672–1673. Therefore, to some extent the first group contradict the contention that the design of the sloops followed that of the Biscay double shallop, at least as far as rig is concerned. If Van de Velde's illustration is accurate, it seems that their hull was different as well, so this is worth examining in detail.

This tubby little sloop in Fig 4-10 is possibly *Emsworth*, the smallest of the first group and built at Emsworth by John Smith. She could not be less like the sleek Biscay double shallop, but her rig and other details are of interest, notably:

1. The main course is conventional and not like a tall narrow buss sail.
2. The top and lower masts are banded together.
3. There are topsails on both fore- and main-masts; the main topsail and yard has been brought to deck level.
4. The spritsail yard has been brought in.
5. No oar ports have been drawn, though they may exist.
6. The bulwarks appear to be 2ft 6in high.
7. Crew and guns on deck, therefore possibly fully decked at the sheer strake.
8. Crutch stowage for oars; possibly these were used over the rail with crew standing to row.
9. A main staysail, furled.
10. No mizzen topmast.

The second group, built in 1672–1673, appear to be more uniform in rig, most using the basic Biscay sail plan on two masts. This was a popular rig and can be seen in many of the contemporary prints and paintings throughout the seventeenth century and into the early eighteenth. The rig in action can be seen in Fig 4-11 in Van de Velde the elder's paintings of the Battles of Schooneveld and Texel in the summer of 1673. In Fig 4-12, a small sloop is part of the convoy for Mary of Modena's passage across the Channel in December 1673 to her marriage with James. Even within these two figures there is a variance in the sail plan.

The main courses shown on both the sloops in Fig 4-11 are square in proportion. Neither vessel has a main topsail, though both carry fore topsails furled. Both vessels seem to have a large crew on board, possibly supernumeraries added for the battle. The nearest sloop may be *Woolwich*, *Bonetta*'s sister, which was present at the Battle of Texel. The oar ports can be seen along their sides. In Fig 4-12, the rig is totally different with a tall thin main buss sail, rigged in the fashion of a lug sail complete with a topsail. The foresail is very small. This vessel is

tiny and may be the *Dove* of 19 tons. She is smaller with far less top hamper than the big sloops in Fig 4-11.[13]

Though these sloops were set up for two masts, there is a distinct possibility that they carried a mizzen mast, on a temporary basis at least. The evidence for this is not strong but the sketch in Fig 4-13, which is of *Bonetta* from the starboard quarter, shows what may be a mizzen.[14] It is worth remembering that these sloops were also used for fishery protection, when they would have been required to lie-to when the fishing fleets were lying to their nets. The best way to do this is to hoist a mizzen sail, which need not be large, and stream a sea anchor. The type of sail could have been a lateen, although a gaff-headed wing sail would have been handier (see Fig 4-14).

Looking further at the rig of these sloops, the Dutch herring buss in Fig 4-14 carries a mizzen sail on a short gaff or half-sprit, where the normal sail was either a square one or possibly a lateen sail.[15] The other interesting point about this herring buss which is laying a close-hauled course is the hoisting of its square sails inside the leeward shrouds, thus using them as lug sails and giving the vessel an ability to come much closer to the wind. There is no reason why the

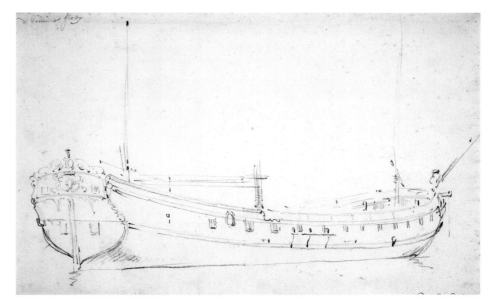

Pepysian sloops could not have managed their sails in precisely the same way. The small yacht at Fig 4-15 also has a fore-and-aft sail as a mizzen but this time it has been boomed-out.[16] The square foresail has been hoisted in the manner of a lug sail (of which more later).

Before leaving the subject of rig, there is one more variation to cover. The sloop *Whipster* was alone in Pepys's Register in being classified as a brigantine, yet she had the same dimensions as the other large sloops with a similar arma-ment and small crew. Therefore, it might be reasonable to consider her as being a brigantine-rigged sloop. However, at this time brigantines were associated with rowing as their prime method of propulsion so she may have had the basic Biscay rig but have been set up for rowing to a greater degree than her sisters. A develop-ment of this arrangement is shown in Chapter 6.

Fig 4-13. A sketch by Van de Velde the younger inscribed on the reverse with the words 'die bonettie'. Thought to have been made around 1675, it indicates only one gun port whilst, according to Pepys, *Bonetta* had two per side. There is also the tantalising question of whether a mizzen mast is shown and what the horizontal spars abaft the main may indicate. *National Maritime Museum PY1865*

Fig 4-14. (**Left**) This drawing is based on a painting by the elder Van de Velde describd as 'A Buss and other Dutch craft in a light breeze' (Robinson oil paintings catalogue, Plate 645). The square sails are trimmed fore and aft and appear to be set inside the lee shrouds; somewhat similar to lug sails. *Author*

Fig 4-15. (**Right**) Detail from 'A Prospect of the Bay, Towne of St Hillary, Castle of Elizabeth and Tower of St Aubin' (Jersey) made as part of a military survey of the Channel Islands in 1680. This small private yacht has three masts, the mizzen having a gaff-headed and boomed-out sail. This might seem unusual for the seventeenth century, but the draughtsman was Thomas Phillips, whose work was technically accurate. *National Maritime Museum L4403*

Fig 4-16. The simple rig of the sloops of 1672–1673, similar to that of the Biscay double shallop. Note the oar ports along the length of the deck. *Author*

Fig 4-16. The simple rig of the sloops of 1672–1673, similar to that of the Biscay double shallop. Note the oar ports along the length of the deck. *Author*

Hull design. These sloops are best presented by way of sub-groups according to the designer-builder. The bulk of sloops produced in 1672 were by Jonas Shish at Deptford. A perplexing group of eight sloops, they varied from 40ft to 58ft on the keel and measured 19 to 68 tons burthen (one might be forgiven for thinking that he was building according to the material he had available). The average length to beam ratio (LBR) for his designs was 3.5. The individual sloops in the other groups in most cases conformed to given dimensions and burthen. Sir Anthony Deane at Portsmouth built three of 60ft on the keel with a displacement of 46 tons and one smaller at 44ft on the keel. Longer and comparably lighter than those by Shish, the

larger ones had a LBR of 5.0. Phineas Pett III built two, the *Bonetta* group at 61ft on the keel and of 57 tons displacement with a LBR of 4.0. His father, Phineas Pett II, built the Chatham group of three at 57ft 6in on the keel with a displacement of 50 tons and a LBR of 4.5. The specification must have been rather loose, simply giving some general parameters. The only known clear images of the second group are in the illustrations above.

The diagrams in Figs 4-17 and 4-18 have been developed from the sketch of *Bonetta* above in order to better understand the shape. Built with *Woolwich* by Phineas Pett III, she was one of the larger sloops with a length on the keel of 61ft and a breadth of 15ft, giving a LBR of 4.0. Her draught was 4ft 6in, with a depth in hold of 5ft, which implies she was fully decked. Considering her draught of 4ft 6in and allowing for a keel height of 6in and her depth in hold, it is likely that the deck would have been approximately 18in above the load waterline. From these dimensions and those of the human frame it is possible to construct, with the help of the Van de Velde sketch, a possible longitudinal profile and half-breadth plan for this vessel.

These draughts are drawn in perspective so no measurements can be taken from them. Interestingly, the bow sections do accord with the drawing of sloops at the Battle of Schoonevelde. See Fig 4-11.

Fig 4-17. (Upper) Perspective projection of *Bonetta* from starboard quarter. *Author*

Fig 4-18. (Middle) Perspective projection of *Bonetta* from starboard bow. *Author*

Fig 4-19. (Lower) This draught, by the author, has been drawn to scale from the dimensions given for the *Bonetta* group. Were the sloop to be cut down to a line between the oar ports and the wale, the remaining profile would be that of a very large rowing boat. Although bluff-bowed at the rail, the entry at the waterline is fine and the conclusion of the hull at the sternpost leaves the flat transom well clear of the waterline; this ensures that eddies produced by movement through the water are minimal. Here a resemblance to the Biscay double shallop is very clear. Note the shallow draught depicted in all these diagrams.

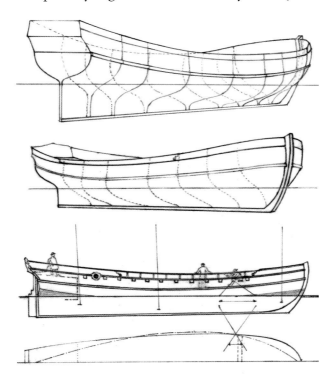

Armament and manpower. With few exceptions, all sloops of the second group had 4 guns. Of these, two would have been placed on the quarterdeck and two possibly forward to maintain trim. In some cases ports for two guns side by side were cut in the after part of the vessel, which might have affected trim. From these considerations there now comes the main question: were these vessels rowed sitting or standing? By far the most efficient way to row is sitting, but with a line of thwarts in the body of the vessel it would have been impossible to position any guns in the waist, hence their being kept at the ends of the vessel. These craft had the foremasts in the extreme bow with the windlass possibly aft of the mast, hence room for a gun there would be confined, which led to the side by side arrangement aft.

Although there are twelve oar ports each

Table 4-1: LIST OF THE PEPYSIAN SLOOPS, 1656–1693

Sloop	Builder	Launch	Length keel	Beam	LBR	Depth in hold	Draught	Tons burthen	Gun	Men[1]	Fate
Dunkirk	Spanish, Dunkirk	Prize	40ft 0in	12ft 6in	3.2	4ft 6in		35	2	10, 10, 20	Captured 1656 Sold 1660
Spy	Deane, Harwich	1666	44ft 0in	12ft 0in	3.7	4ft 0in	4ft 4in	28	4	10	Sold as useless 1683[4]
Fan Fan	Deane, Harwich	1666	44ft 0in	12ft 0in	3.7	5ft 8in	5ft 6in	33	4	18, 25, 30	Converted to yacht 1666; pitch boat 1693
Emsworth	Smith, Emsworth	1667	40ft 0in	13ft 7in	2.9	4ft 9in	5ft 0in	39	4	10, 10, 10	Sold as useless 1683[4]
Portsmouth	Tippets, Portsmouth	1667	40ft 0in	14ft 0in	2.8	7ft 0in	5ft 10in	43	4	18, 24, 28	Taken by Dutch caper off East Coast 1672
Dove	Shish, Deptford[2]	1672	40ft 0in	9ft 10in	4.0	4ft 0in	4ft 0in	19	4	10, 10, 10	Sold as useless 1683[4]
Lilly	Shish, Deptford[2]	1672	52ft 0in	14ft 6in	3.6	5ft 6in	5ft 0in	58	6	12, 18, 23	Cast away at sea 1674
Swallow	Shish, Deptford[2]	1672	50ft 0in	16ft 0in	3.1	6ft 0in	5ft 0in	68	2	15, 20, 25	Cast away at sea 1673
Tulip	Shish, Deptford[2]	1672	43ft 0in	10ft 0in	4.3	6ft 0in	5ft 0in	22	2	15, 20, 25	Cast away at sea 1673
Whipster Brigantine	Shish, Deptford[2]	1672	58ft 0in	14ft 6in	4.0	5ft 0in	4ft 6in	64	4	10,10, 10	Sold as useless 1683[4]
Dolphin	Shish, Deptford[2]	1673	54ft 0in	14ft 6in	3.7	5ft 6in	5ft 0in	60	2	10, 10, 36	Sunk at Battle of Texel 1673
Lizard	Shish Deptford[2]	1673	47ft 0in	12ft 6in	3.8	4ft 9in	5ft 0in	39	4	15, 25, 30	Taken by privateer off Berry Head Feb 1674
Vulture	Shish, Deptford[2]	1673	50ft 0in	16ft 0in	3.1	6ft 0in	5ft 0in	68	4	10, 10, 10	Sold 1686
Prevention	Deane, Portsmouth	1672	60ft 0in	12ft 0in	5.0	5ft 0in	4ft 6in	46	4	10, 10, 10	Sold as useless 1683[4]
Cutter	Deane, Portsmouth	1673	60ft 0in	12ft 0in	5.0	5ft 0in	4ft 6in	46	2	10, 10, 12	Cast away at Deal 1673
Hunter	Deane, Portsmouth	1673	60ft 0in	12ft 0in	5.0	5ft 0in	4ft 6in	46	4	10, 10, 10	Sold as useless 1683[4]
Invention[3]	Deane, Portsmouth	1673	44ft 0in	11ft 0in	4.0	5ft 0in	4ft 0in	28	4	10, 10, 10	Sold as useless 1683[4]
Chatham	Pett II, Chatham	1673	57ft 6in	12ft 10	4.5	5ft 0in	4ft 0in	50	4	10, 10, 10	Run ashore by slaves to avoid capture 1677
Chatham Double	Pett II, Chatham	1673	57ft 6in	12ft 10	4.5	5ft 0in	4ft 0in	50	4	10, 10, 10	Sold as useless 1683[4]
Hound	Pett II, Chatham	1673	57ft 6in	12ft 10	4.5	5ft 0in	4ft 0in	50	4	10, 10, 10	Sold as useless 1683[4]
Bonetta	Pett III, Woolwich	1673	61ft 0in	13ft 0in	4.7	5ft 0in	4ft 6in	57	4	10, 10, 10	Sold 1687
Woolwich	Pett III, Woolwich	1673	61ft 0in	13ft 0in	4.7	5ft 0in	4ft 6in	57	4	10, 10, 10	Wrecked Barbados 1678
Experiment	Lawrence, Greenwich	1677	35ft 0in	11ft 6in	3.0	6ft 4in	5ft 0in	24	4	10, 10, 10	Given to Sir Thomas Allin 1680

Notes:
1 The figures under the heading 'men' represent the complements for peace, war overseas and war in home waters.
2 Shish-built sloops are of varying shapes and sizes, pointing to construction based on what material was available.
3 Deane's sloop Invention is smaller than the others whilst built at the same time; again possibly a lack of materials.
4 Nine sloops were sold as useless in 1683.

Fig 4-20. Watercolour by the author of a sloop of about 1672–1673 in danger of broaching in storm conditions. Some of these small semi-open vessels were lost at sea, though the number was not as large as might have been expected. Note that just the foresail is used here to maintain downwind stability, essential if the vessel is not to broach side on to the waves.

roles that are described for the *barque longue*, their French equivalent.[17] On the other hand, they were invaluable in shallow waters so that an inshore security and policing role would make sense.

Five sloops were 'cast away' during 1673 or shortly thereafter. Unlike the ketches and yachts, whose presence is noteworthy at all the battles and which were fully decked, robust and more powerfully armed, these sloops were narrow and of low freeboard and could founder in stormy weather (Fig 4-20). Another three were taken or sunk by the Dutch, principally because they lacked firepower even though all had large crews.[18] In 1674 Charles withdrew from his war against the Dutch Republic and England then enjoyed a period of relative peace. During this time the sloops were employed overseas and around the English coast. Slowly their numbers reduced until the big disposal of 1683 when most, including two of the first group, were 'sold as useless'. Four survived the disposal, two being sold in 1686, leaving only *Bonetta* and *Fan Fan*; *Bonetta* was sold in December 1687 and *Fan Fan* became a pitch boat in 1693.

side, *Bonetta* had a complement of only 10 crew, as did most sloops. Five of the eight Shish-designed sloops had large crews ranging between 23 and 36, so size of crew may reflect the role each sloop was intended for. A large crew would certainly indicate ability under oars but beyond that a high likelihood of engagement with the enemy may have influenced complementing. For the other sloops, a complement of only 10 suggests an extra-fleet role where their main duties might involve communications, surveillance, reconnaissance or possibly fishery protection. These are the

THE STUART ROYAL YACHTS 1660–1688
The iconic vessel of the Stuart Restoration,[20] the 'royal yacht', started a long-running and close connection between the monarch and the sea. These small vessels need little introduction.

Fig 4-21. This painting, from about 1700, by the younger Van de Velde, depicts two schooner yachts beating to windward. The single-masted yacht on the left seems to be sailing under a wind direction that is different to that being used by the schooners! The schooner rig will be discussed later at Chapter 7, but it must be considered as a possibility for some of the Pepysian sloops since the rig was in use by the Dutch early in the seventeenth century. The flag at the head of the bowsprit may well be the Stuart ensign. By 1700, Mary, the Stuart wife and queen to William of Orange, was dead, but when William died in 1702, Mary's sister Anne ascended the throne. *The Parker Gallery*[19]

Repeatedly the subject of contemporary marine paintings and also portrayed in model form, they represent possibly the prettiest of all ships of the Stuart period – and it was a time of good-looking ships! Their value to shipbuilding and design generally was that they were used by the king and his brother to race (with large sums staked on the results), which encouraged the

Fig 4-22. A sketch by the author of a Pepysian sloop, but in this case with a head at its stem. These may have been fitted postwar. The brigantines of the 1690s were fitted with a head despite their small size.

Fig 4-23. Possibly the Stuart royal yacht *Katherine*, the second of that name and built in 1674 following the capture of the first *Katherine* at the Battle of Texel.
National Maritime Museum F9318-001.

Fig 4-24. The yacht *Mary*, gifted to Charles II by the Dutch Republic on his restoration to the throne of England. *National Maritime Museum F9231-003*

leading shipwrights to consider the question of speed and handiness to the benefit of naval architecture generally. Like much of the maritime innovation of the time, the yacht originated in Holland. However, the Dutch concept of the 'jacht' was rather different from that which developed in England. Derived from the word for hunting (although the English notion of 'the chase' might be more appropriate) the term encompassed all small, fast-sailing boats, whether used for communications, state business, commercial transport, leisure or war. The Dutch employed many yachts, to various designs, whereas in England they were, at least initially, solely for the pleasure of the king and his brother, although they saw naval service in times of crisis. Both private and government yachts came to be built later, but the breadth of

their employment never matched that of the Dutch.

It is well known that Charles II was introduced to yachting by the Dutch, towards the end of his exile. He was so impressed by the performance and the broader leisure possibilities of these small ships that a yacht, which had been built for the Dutch East India Company (VOC), was gifted to him by Amsterdam: the yacht *Mary*. This was followed shortly by another, smaller one, the *Bezan*. These gifts inspired English imitations, but because English coastal waters were to a degree different from those of Holland, particularly when away from the Thames and its approaches, the Dutch design was altered to give English yachts a better windward ability, without resort to the cumbersome Dutch leeboards. The dimensions,

Figs 4-25. A Van de Velde portrait of the *Prince's Yacht*, built for the House of Orange. Apart from the elaborate decoration, the general bulkiness of the vessel, its fulsome buttocks and superstructure, plus the use of leeboards, form a marked contrast to the yacht style soon developed in England. *National Maritime Museum PY3835*

Fig 4-26. A sketch by the author developed from a painting by Van de Velde the elder, assisted by his brother Adriaen, showing the *Mary* surrounded by a host of smaller vessels. Most of the painting was done by Adriaen, as evidenced on the original by the initials 'AVV 1661' inscribed on the ensign of one of the yachts. Note the Union flag being flown from every possible position.

burthen and rig were nearly identical, but the improvement was to be found in the underwater lines of the yacht and in the treatment of her topsides. In the first *Katherine*, for example, the English version probably had softer sections and finer lines at bow and stern. The English yachts were to be designed and built by the finest naval shipwrights of the time, who are likely to have imported some aspects of the design of their Sixth Rates into the form of the new yachts. It is also worth noting that as a design inspiration the *Mary* was not like the majority of private, business and state yachts in Holland, but was a deep-sea yacht designed to accompany the VOC on oceanic passages.

Royal yachts were some 60–70ft long with a beam of 18–21ft and displaced between 90 and

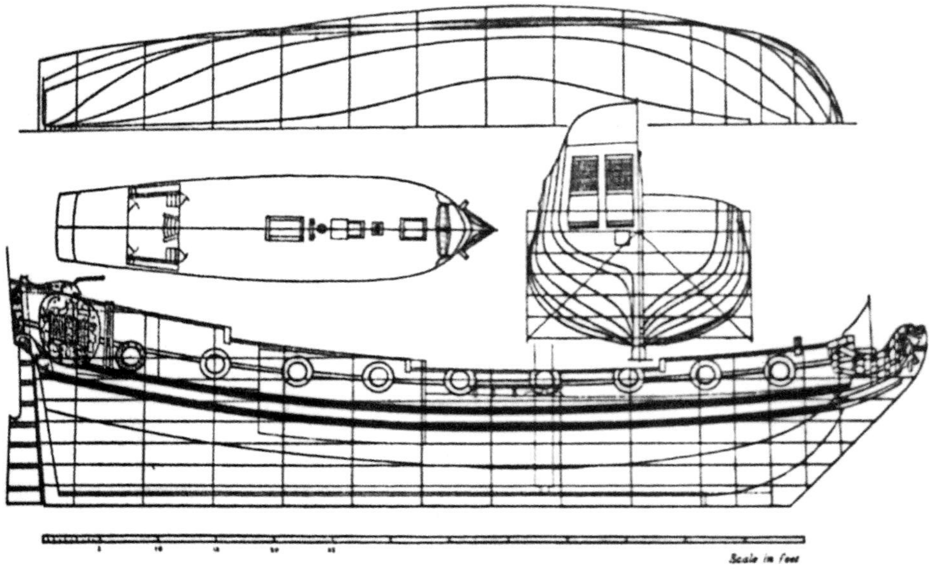

Fig 4-27. Plan of the royal yacht *Katherine* II of 1674, based on a model that was in the Science Museum.

100 tons initially, but in the 1680s, with the gradual switch to ketch rig, they increased to 140 tons or more and were armed with 8–10 guns, although often giving the appearance of being armed with 16. They were heavily decorated, particularly at the stern. The guns were carried on deck forward of the mast, with the remainder of the deck modified to provide quarters and standing headroom for the king's party. This was done without disrupting the sweet sheer line of the vessel by having the deck step down to the royal stateroom in the aft cabin, with the bunk, probably a double one, situated so that the king could gaze at the sea through the large glazed ports.

Hull form. Looking at the *Mary* in Fig 4-26, the similarities are evident between her and the second *Katherine* (Fig 4-27) built in 1674 and probably very similar in shape to the first yacht of that name built in 1661. Whilst *Mary* has similar dimensions to *Katherine* II, she has far more top hamper as well as a greater freeboard. Her high sides would have made much windage, pushing her to leeward when on the wind.

The English model appears lower in the water than *Mary* and has a clean low sheer line. Apart from the sharp rise to her poop deck, her hull is similar to a small Sixth Rate ship. Indeed, the royal yachts were so rated no matter what their size. But there is one significant difference and that is in the 'run' (the shape of the after waterlines). 'Cod's head and mackerel tail' was considered the right form for a fast hull, giving lean, tapering lines to the sternpost, but if this narrowing were pronounced, it could affect buoyancy aft, reducing the Sixth Rate's ability to carry guns on her quarters. However, with the yacht's armament concentrated forward of the mast with blanked-off ports aft in the way of the cabins, the designers had a free hand with the waterlines aft of midships. Note that the point of maximum breadth is about 5ft forward of midships in the way of the mast. In profile, the English yacht has a more compact and upright stem and a clean sheer line to the taffrail, whereas the Dutchman has a long beak forward and a tall built-up cabin at the poop.

Rig. Whilst sharing the fore-and-aft rig, these two yachts had a different method of extending the fore-and-aft mainsail from the earlier and smaller Dutch yachts, which normally used a full sprit running from the base of the mast, out and up to the sail's peak to hold it in place. This does not seem to be the case with the *Mary*, which is another reason for suggesting that she was built for oceanic passages, where a long sprit could be clumsy. The gaff or half-sprit shown at Fig 4-28 was used by the English for all fore-and-aft rigged yachts. This latter arrangement allowed for a more successful reduction of sail, the gaff being partially lowered whilst the bonnet, the lowest section of sail, was removed. By contrast, this single-masted sail plan was only used once on naval sloops, which were normally two-masted vessels. That one exception was for a group of six sloops built in 1710–1711, and then it only lasted for four to nine years before being replaced with a two-mast rig. In their case the main course was boomed-out.

By the end of the Second Anglo-Dutch War, ending in the bold raid on the Medway and the embarrassing removal of the First Rate *Royal Charles*, the novelty of yacht-racing in royal circles seems to have waned, even though others continued in the sport. By the 1680s the royal yachts were beginning to be rigged ketch-fashion, a non-competitive rig, but one that was good for cruising. This was to remain the preferred rig for royal yachts for decades until replaced by the ship rig.

The ketch-rigged royal yacht at Fig 4-29 is thought to be *Isabella*, built at Greenwich in 1683 by Phineas Pett, the last yacht he built. Beyond her, on her starboard side is another yacht but with the 'old' smack rig. Her main topsail is aback and her fore-and-aft canvas is flogging. She may just have come to anchor. On the *Isabella* the rig is very similar to the naval ketches, except that the main course has a conventional shape compared to their tall high buss sail. Her fore staysail has been neatly furled onto the forestay and the jib is being gathered in. The main topsail clew garnets can be seen but the main yard lifts appear to run up to blocks on the topsail yard, an interesting configuration.

Role. As mentioned above, the royal yachts had a dual role. Normally provided for the king's personal use, they were regarded as commissioned ships in the king's navy in times of war.

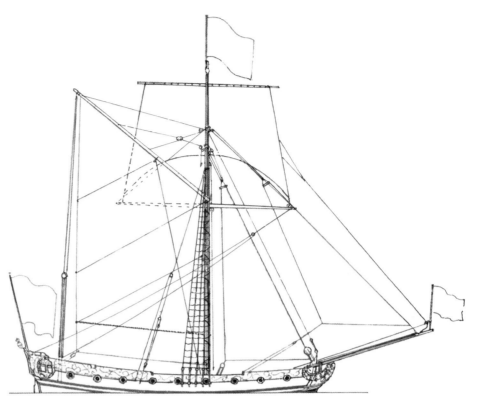

Fig 4-28. This sail and rigging plan, made from the Science Museum model, shows the tall narrow gaff-headed or 'smack' sail and its bonnet. Note the vangs aft used to control the peak of the gaff. The cro'jack yard is braced but not the topsail yard. Note also the bowlines from the topsail to the head of the bowsprit. The angle they take on does not look very effective.

Together with the sloops and ketches they provided communication between ships and particularly between admirals and their captains in battle. The Dutch also used yachts for this purpose; at the Battle of Texel, de Ruyter had no fewer than fourteen supporting his fleet. The Royal Navy also had its own yachts but they were generally smaller and more lightly armed and used for administrative rather than operational communication.

The yacht *Katherine* II, whose lines are shown in Fig 4-27, would have been similar to *Katherine* I which was captured by the Dutch whilst trying to join the fleet at sea off the Texel. She was caught by two large Dutch frigates and forced towards the shore.[21] She was taken into Amsterdam, an event recorded by the Burgomaster of that city in the second edition of his work on Dutch shipbuilding.[22]

On the 4th of September 1673, there was to be seen at Amsterdam in front of the palisades a very costly yacht of his Majesty the King of England. It is low in the water, carries 10 brass guns, and is so shaped and built that it can keep the sea. Sail, mast and gaff of the shape that is usual in this country [Holland]. The stem is upright, after the new fashion, formed

of a strong piece. Has a fine yellow-painted head supported by sea-nymphs and goddesses; it spreads out wide but below it is sharp and of a good shape, very proper to cut the water and make good speed. All round on the outside for two feet below the rails it is covered with costly sculpture and gold-painted carvings of grotesque figures and plants. It has no leeboards; is also not tarred outside, as one is accustomed to do to ships here, and this is very elegant, for the Irish timber of which it is made shows all the better its nature and its ruddy colour which is agreeable to the sight; to tar this wood or to preserve it with paint or otherwise is not necessary, for it is the finest wood to be found in Europe, and resists all worm and rot. It is true this wood is not so flexible as the oak that is used for ship-building in this country, and therefore this yacht is not of such a curved shape as they are built in this country, but more straight sided, which nevertheless does not look bad, though many masters consider this the important feature of a ship. It has low bulwarks. The mast is stepped in such a way that it can be moved to and fro to seek sailing power, from the truck flies a silk streamer which in a calm hangs down to the water; and it is on all sides proudly decked with flags. The lower part of the stern is round, and spreads out high and broad (after the English fashion).

Table 4-2: ROYAL YACHTS, 1660–1674

Detail	Mary, 1660	Katherine I, 1661	Katherine II, 1674
Length overall	66ft 6in		
Length on the keel	50ft 0in	49ft 0in	56ft 0in
Breadth	18ft 6in	19ft 0in	21ft 1in
Depth in hold	7ft 4in	7ft 0in	8ft 4in
Displacement	92 tons	94 tons	132 tons
Draught	7ft 0in	7ft 0in	8ft 4in
Guns	8 x 3pdr	8 x 3pdr	8 x 3pdrs
Crew	30	30	30

Royal yachts were rated as Sixth Rates requiring that they should be commanded by an officer of captain's rank, although this may be more accurately expressed by suggesting that only an officer of such rank was deemed acceptable and of adequate experience to be in charge with the sovereign aboard. It gave unmatched opportunities to garner royal favour, so the post inevitably went to the best-connected officers.

To illustrate the arbitrary nature of naval classification of unrated vessels in the seventeenth century, there is no better example than the sloop *Fan Fan*. She originated with three others as one of the first group of Pepysian sloops, and was designed by Sir Anthony Deane, a close friend of Pepys. She was built at Harwich in 1665, according to Sir Anthony, for the purpose of 'clearing the sands before this harbour so much infested with small Dutch picaroons'.[23] However, *Fan Fan* quickly became Prince Rupert's yacht and in that role, with magnificent cheek, fired the first shots at the

Fig 4-29. (Opposite) This painting by Monamy, a replacement for the original by the younger Van de Velde, is of the ketch-rigged yacht *Isabella*. Note the unusal lead of the main yard lifts onto the topsail yard!

Fig 4-30. The experience gained by master shipwrights in building fast yachts for competitive racing was of great benefit to the design of the smaller warships. Indeed, a perfect example of the close relationship is the *Saudadoes*, seen here in a Van de Velde sketch. Built as a yacht in 1670 – the ship's Portuguese name was a compliment to Charles II's queen, Katherine of Braganza – the yacht was converted into a Sixth Rate three years later. *National Maritime Museum PZ7691*

Dutch flagship, *Eendracht*, at the opening of the battle off Lowestoft in 1665.

In the records describing her arrival with the fleet off the mouth of the Thames, she is hailed as a shallop; by the next day she is described as a sloop and following her attack on the Dutch flagship, as a yacht. She had a busy career. Like many royal yachts she was placed under naval orders for operational use. Following the St James's Day Battle in 1666, she was lent to Sir Robert Holmes as a command ship for his assault on the Dutch merchant fleet in the Vlie estuary, her shallow draught being an asset to this operation. She became a 'fetch and carry vessel' for Pepys and spent time working with the revenue service as well as providing convoy along the East Coast. She had the honour of transporting the body of the Earl of Sandwich to London, following his death at the Battle of Sole Bay. She lasted until 1693, a long time for a yacht/sloop, when she was turned over to become a pitch boat.

In all some 39 royal or naval yachts were built before the death of the last Stuart monarch, Queen Anne in 1714. Thereafter the royal yacht became larger and adopted the three-masted ship rig. The *Peregrine Galley* originally rigged with two masts in 1700 was converted to a ship-rigged yacht, the first such instance, in 1703 and renamed *Carolina* in 1716. By this time the close connection between the yacht and the sloop of war had parted. From 1711 the sloop of war, although retaining the influence and, in particular, the hull shape of the royal yachts, was being designed for specific purposes assessed to meet specific threats. However, the importance of the Stuart yachts to the subsequent design of small warships should not be underestimated, a theme to be taken up in a later chapter on the early Sixth Rates (Fig 4-30).

Chapter 5

THE WARS AGAINST FRANCE
1688–1714

The period 1688–1714, which runs from the 'Glorious Revolution' to the end of the War of the Spanish Succession, is pivotal in the story of the sloop. At its outset, what was to become the 'sloop' class was merely a collection of minor warships of varying shapes, rigs, dimensions and with different armaments and functions. At its close the concept of a single minor war vessel, capable of independent action, had emerged. There were two main branches: firstly, vessels for the general duties of communication, surveillance and the provision of coastal convoy; and secondly vessels which, whilst designed for the specific role of shore bombardment, could be co-opted to assist in the other activities above. In order to understand the factors driving this development, it is helpful

to look briefly at the strategic background to the naval aspects of the two wars that took up most of this period.

The arrival of William of Orange, Stadtholder of Holland, at Torbay on 5 November 1688, followed by the flight of James II to France in December, set in train a series of events that would cause a bloodless revolution within England and a major change to her foreign relations with the continental powers of mainland Europe. Some take the view that William was invited to England to replace James II as king (William's wife Mary was James's daughter, which lent a veneer of legitimacy to what was otherwise a coup d'etat). It was true that a body of the English political elite conspired to this end, acting on more widely felt

Fig 5-1. William III of Orange, Stadtholder of the Dutch Republic and the third of his family to hold this position. Born 1650, he married Mary, his first cousin, in 1677 and they became joint King and Queen of England, Scotland and Ireland in 1689. Died 1702. Oil painting by Godfrey Kneller of the King in his coronation robes. *National Maritime Museum BHC3094*

Fig 5-2. Mary Stuart, eldest surviving daughter of James II of England, born 1662, died 1694. She ruled jointly with her husband William III and was a firm governor during his frequent absences on the Continent. Oil painting by Godfrey Kneller of the Queen in her coronation robes. *National Maritime Museum BHC2853*

fears that James would seek a close alliance with Louis XIV, thereby strengthening his own drive towards absolutism at home and promoting the return of Roman Catholicism as the 'official' religion of the country. However, there were also many within the Dutch Republic who strongly desired the removal of James. For the Dutch, the inability to create an Anglo-Dutch Alliance would place them in peril of invasion by France, possibly supported by a catholic England under James, which would dash William's hopes of strengthening the overstretched coalition of European states already engaged against Louis XIV and his expansionist aims.[1]

THE WAR OF THE LEAGUE OF AUGSBURG

The birthplace of this coalition was Augsburg, a small town about 40 miles northwest of modern-day Munich. It was here, in 1686, on the advice of William III of Orange, that Leopold I, Emperor of the Holy Roman Empire, brought together an alliance of Western European states to contain the territorial ambitions of Louis. Joining this alliance were the Netherlands, Austria, the Holy Roman Empire, Bavaria, most of the German states, and Spain. Its principal aim was to protect the Palatinate, lying immediately to the east of the Rhine, from French occupation. But William also feared for his own country, which had been at war with France and England from 1672 to 1674 and with France alone until 1679.[2]

Fig 5-3. A map of Europe about 1700 showing the French incursion into the Rhineland and the threat to Savoy Turin.

The opportunity to grasp the English crown, made feasible by his marriage ten years earlier to James's daughter Mary, must have seemed to William like a gift from God, since if he were successful in that enterprise he would have the chance to secure his real aim: to save his country, the Dutch Republic, from extinction.[3] Once William had succeeded in taking the crown of England, thereby adding her power to the League, it was decided that thereafter it would be called the Grand Alliance. Under that title it fought two major wars on land and at sea against Louis: the War of the League of Augsburg, 1688–1698 and the War of the Spanish Succession, 1702–1714.

For England, her maritime perspective now shifted to meet a broader scheme of hostilities. Whereas the Dutch Wars had produced a highly localised area of engagement between two well-matched antagonists with similar strategic aims, the War of the League of Augsburg would introduce the French and, to a lesser extent, the Spanish into the maritime equation. In effect, this enlarged the area of operations to include the western approaches to the Channel, and the French and Spanish seaboards facing both the Mediterranean Sea and the Atlantic Ocean. As if this was not enough, because of Louis XIV's intent to return the catholic James to the English throne, using as a springboard the catholic nation of Ireland and the latent Jacobite sympathies in Scotland, the waters round these regions became the focus of English and French naval operations.[4]

A brief account of William's opening naval arrangements is helpful. Following his landing at Torbay and before his arrival in London, he was already in contact with Lord Dartmouth, James's naval commander-in-chief. Additionally, his own fleet and transports were still in the West Country, mainly based on Plymouth and commanded by the English Admiral Herbert. With his continental background, and probably a lack of understanding of the nature of sea power, his initial intention was to place Dartmouth's command into a winter stand-down. He was quickly advised of the folly of such a move by Dartmouth, Herbert and Pepys. As a result, both fleets were kept ready, and Allied (Anglo-Dutch) deployments comprising mixtures of Third, Fourth and Sixth Rates supported by fireships, were set up for the

Straits of Gibraltar,[5] the Channel and the Irish Sea. A reserve of rated ships was kept in the dockyards in readiness, the task of guarding the Channel Islands being assigned to that portion of it at Portsmouth. At this point England possessed no sloops, so for communication and surveillance she had to rely on yachts, a few ketches and smaller Sixth Rates, together with a hastily assembled force of hired small craft.

These dispositions reflect the two require-ments of protecting Dutch and English trade, and securing home waters. Unfortunately, there was sluggishness in activating these deploy-ments, probably due to the need to set up a new and therefore inexperienced Board of Admiralty. This led to the Allies' failure to forestall some of Louis' opening naval moves. An attempt by France to secure Ireland for James in 1689–1690 nearly succeeded because of the inadequacy of the English response.[6] For a slightly different reason, mainly over-commitment elsewhere, the Allies suffered a defeat off Beachy Head in 1690 and for a time the French controlled the Channel but did virtually nothing to exploit their domi-nant position.[7] However, Louis' preparation of an invasion fleet and its escort in 1692 was met with decisive action. It is well to remember that between 1688 and 1692 Louis' fleets had to cover both the Mediterranean and Atlantic theatres, but when opportunities allowed these fleets to be combined, he could deploy the most powerful sea-force in Europe.

Although the naval operations off the coast of Ireland and Scotland could have benefited from the assistance of minor war vessels, in view of the scarcity of such shipping, only four were deployed. Two bomb vessels[8] accompa-nied a large squadron to Bantry Bay in south-west Ireland in 1689 to contest a French landing. Later in that year a Sixth Rate of 16 guns, a yacht (8 guns) and a ketch (4 guns) formed part of a small squadron operating in the North Channel between Scotland and Ireland in support of the operation to relieve Londonderry. Minor war vessels could also have benefited the Allied fleet off Beachy Head in 1690. For the outnumbered Anglo-Dutch fleet the battle was essentially a fighting retreat, with disabled ships left behind, so had such vessels been present it might have been possible to avoid their capture. This appreciation may have led directly to the ordering of a new batch

of sloops, this time to be called brigantines, for towing ships out of the line of battle. The later French move in 1692 that the Allies were able to defeat was no less than a full-blown attempt at the invasion of England – and the chance of its success was far greater than the German threat in 1940, so the importance of this action cannot be over-emphasised.[9]

Having recovered from Beachy Head, the Allied fleet took station off the Cherbourg peninsula where the invasion forces were assem-bled. Although smaller, the French fleet intended to escort the invasion flotilla gave battle off Cap Barfleur on the Cotentin penin-sula on 29 May 1692. In the ensuing engage-ment over six days, the French fleet was dispersed, resulting in the destruction of twelve French capital ships, including the great fleet flagship *Soleil Royal*, off St-Vaast-la-Hougue and three at Cherbourg, without the loss of any Allied vessels. In its final phase the action involved small boats closing with the French ships sheltering inshore and burning them. A newly built brigantine called *Shark*, the first of nine such vessels, led the attack at La Hougue, which was hideously successful. It was witnessed by James from the shore: it must have been a supreme irony for him to watch the fleet he had restored as King of England destroy the one that had been prepared by Louis to return

Fig 5-4. The *Soleil Royal* and other French line-of-battle ships, seeking shelter off St-Vaast-la-Hougue after the inconclusive battle off Cape Barfleur in May 1692, are burnt by ships' boats from the Anglo-Dutch fleet, seen in this painting by Adraen van Diest. This attack was led by the brigantine *Shark*, at the time operating as a tender to Admiral Russsell's flagship. *National Maritime Museum* BHC0337

him to that kingdom. Nevertheless, legend has it that he could not resist telling his French allies with real pride that only his 'brave English tars' could have accomplished such a deed. It is one of the most tactless comments in history.

Whilst this defeat finally dashed James's hopes of recovering his kingdom, thereby thwarting Louis' intention to weaken the Grand Alliance, it did leave the Allies with a difficult problem. La Hogue (as the battle is always known in the Royal Navy) was a strategic victory with a significant impact on the eventual outcome of the war. From this point onwards the Allied fleets were to retain command of the sea, allowing them to influence activities on land along the coasts of France and Spain to the considerable advantage of the Grand Alliance. The down side was that it drove the French from disputing command of the sea to a war on trade, an area in which the Allies were to suffer significant casualties at the hands of French state-sponsored privateering.

Following La Hogue, there were four separate demands on the Admiralty. The first priority was to maintain a fleet ready to meet any sortie by the French battle fleet, which was still a potent force, particularly if they could join their Mediterranean and Atlantic squadrons. Second, it had to provide for the security of the coasts of England, Ireland and Scotland against a Jacobite landing.[10] Third, there was rightly much pres-

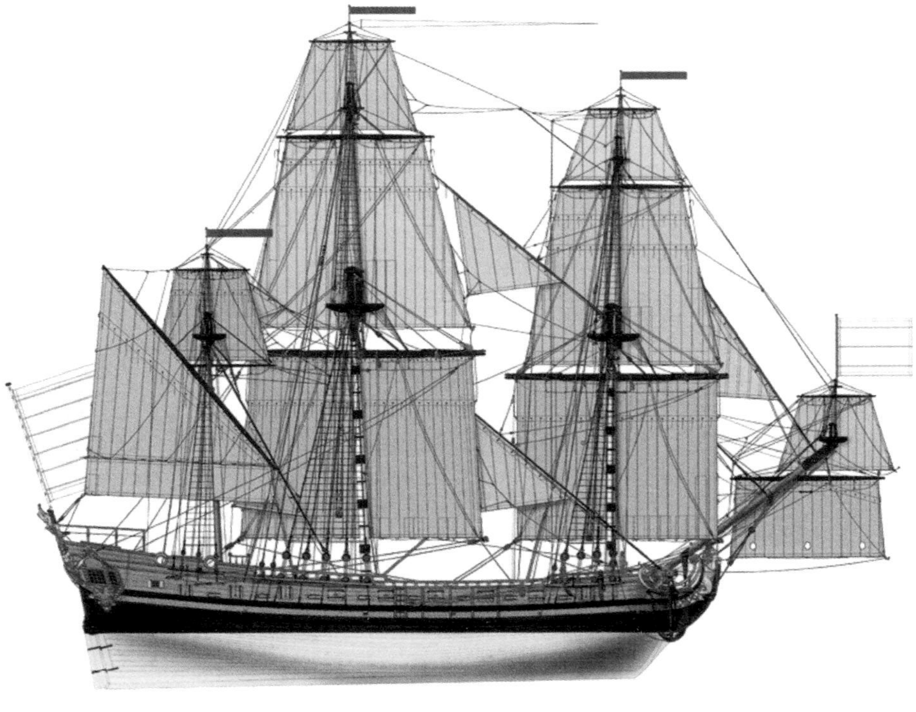

Fig 5-5. This representation of a French *frégat légère* equates in terms of size and armament (eighteen 4pdrs) to some of the privately owned vessels employed in the *guerre de course*. Clearly the small English ketches and brigantines were no match for this type of vessel, being significantly smaller in size and armament. *By courtesy of Editions ANCRE*

sure from Parliament for the proper protection of convoys and trade. Fourth and finally, King William wanted to use his fleet to contribute to the containment of France on the Continent. This last demand was directed at turning back the advances of Louis into Catalonia and this required English sea power to be brought to bear on the Mediterranean coasts of Spain and France. Indeed, so important did William regard this policy that he directed Admiral Russell, his commander-in-chief at sea, to retain the fleet at Cadiz over the winter of 1694–1695 to maintain pressure against this area of French expansion. The Royal Navy succeeded in delivering on three of these satisfactorily; on one it failed deplorably. England was to lose close on 4000 commercial vessels in this war and a minimum of 2000 in the next,[11] despite a concerted effort to destroy privateering bases in 1694–1696.[12] This latter stratagem involved shore bombardment and minor amphibious operations at St Malo, Dieppe, Calais and Dunkirk. The bomb vessels used in these attacks were part of the 'sloop' class and by the next century could be used in a cruiser role to supplement the efforts of the sloops.

In terms of resources and geographical position, which included a Mediterranean coast with a fleet at Toulon, France was well placed to prosecute this sea-raiding war. A substantial part of her battle fleet had remained intact and with no strategic need to carry out fleet actions, she could afford to deploy both men and ships to harass her enemy's trade. Not only was she able to sponsor privateering syndicates, she also lent small line-of-battle ships and their crews to these organisations, benefiting financially from the prizes taken. This meant that powerful privateering squadrons based on Dunkirk, St Malo and Brest were able to capture prizes at both ends of the Channel, in the North and Irish Seas and in the Bay of Biscay. France could do this with virtual impunity since, unlike the maritime powers, she was not so heavily reliant on overseas trade. But France realised that this privateering war would only work effectively if she were able to show also that she still possessed a fleet in being that could threaten those of the Alliance. This, she hoped, would force the Allies to split and therefore weaken their forces in order to cover more than one threat simultaneously.

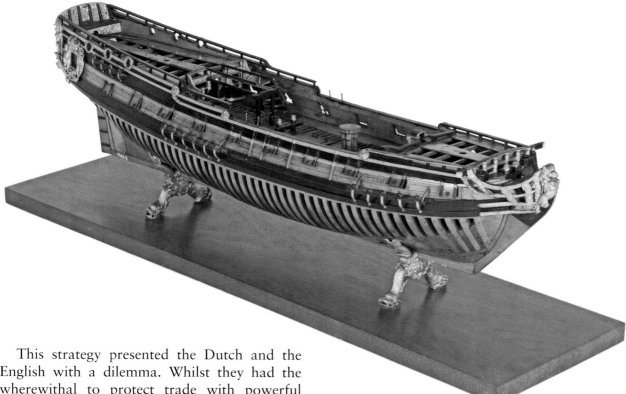

Fig 5-6. This model of a 20/24-gun Sixth Rate is dated by the inscription 'AR 1706' on one of the supporting crutches. This reference to Queen Anne's reign is mirrored by the initials 'BR' on the other crutch, thought to refer to Benjamin Rosewell, who became master shipwright at Chatham in this year. It is possible that he was the builder of this model, or that it was presented to him. The model does not match exactly the dimensions of the Sixth Rates of this decade but is very similar to some of those designed in the 1690s. Carrying twenty 6pdrs on their flush gun decks, these ships also had four 4pdrs on their quarterdecks, an armament well capable of dealing with the average French privateer. *National Maritime Museum L2356-002*

This strategy presented the Dutch and the English with a dilemma. Whilst they had the wherewithal to protect trade with powerful convoys, they could not detach the bulk of their battle fleets to this purpose in case the French fleet should sortie, in the worst-case scenario in support of an invasion. By keeping a fleet in being, the French were able to ensure that Allied convoys were often inadequately protected. That protection had to be provided by fleet units in numbers strong enough to beat off French raiding squadrons. Convoy also required the provision of escorts, Fifth and Sixth Rates, to face the smaller privateers travelling in the train of the main French privateering squadron and ready to pounce on unprotected merchantmen. Unrated vessels had no part to play in this business. The smallest viable weapon in this situation was a 20/24-gun ship (Fig 5-6). This ruled out the use of any minor, unrated warship in the convoy escort role, at least at oceanic level, but possibly not in home waters.

Whilst both the Dutch and English had a keen regard to the importance of their sea-borne commerce and its security, there seems to have been a neglect of the protection required for coastal and inshore traffic, which demanded ships of shallower draught. At the outset of this war the meagre inventory of vessels that could provide this support included only three ketches and nine yachts.[13] As the war progressed, more ketches were added, as were prizes that had

been taken from the French. After La Hogue, it was possible to add the brigantines to this force since the Allied victory had left the brigantines without a pressing fleet role. They had been ordered and designed originally as fleet tenders and tugs so, on the assumption that a fleet engagement was unlikely without good warning, they were pressed into service as coastal escorts, there being so few suitable craft available, apart from the swiftly diminishing stock of ketches.

As far as coastal trade was concerned there appears to have been a failure to recognise the strides that France had taken in strengthening her privateering arm. As a result the provision of suitably armed protecting warships fell far short of the requirement. This was to be addressed in the next war by a programme of building larger and well-armed coastal escorts.

The failure to do so for this first war is illustrated by the fates of five of the eight ketches built in 1691 (Table 5-1), all taken by pairs of French privateers equipped with 18 guns or more, ships generally similar to the *frégat légère* (Fig 5-5). The same fate befell a later pair of ketches built in 1694–1695, and it was to happen yet again in the next war with the small,

Table 5-1: ADDITIONS TO THE SLOOP CATEGORY OF WARSHIP, 1689–1697

Launch	No.	Type	Burthen	Guns	Men	Fate	Remarks
1691	8	Ketch	91–99	10	50	5 taken, 2 stranded	
1691–1693	5	Brigantine	74–79	6 + 8*	35	3 sold, 2 broken up	First (*Shark*) was only 58 tons
1694	4	Advice boat	71	4 + 6*	40	2 taken, 2 lost	
1694	2	Ketch	99–104	10	50	Both taken	
1692–1696	4	French prizes	Various	4–8	20/30		
1695–1696	4	Brigantine	70–79	6 + 2*	35	2 lost, 1 taken, 1 sold	
1695	2	Advice boat	76	4 + 6*	40	1 sold, 1 taken	
1696	2	Advice boat	152–154	4 + 6*	40	Both lost	For trans-oceanic use

Notes.

Details here have been averaged. Fuller accounts can be found in *The Sailing Navy List*, David Lyon (Conway 1990); and
British Warships in the Age of Sail, 1603-1714, Rif Winfield (Seaforth Publishing 2012).
One very small advice boat has not been included; it operated only in the Solent.
* Signifies swivel guns.

under-armed, peacetime sloops built in 1699. The advice boats were rather a different matter. They were designed for intelligence and communication work and to sail fast; they were sent in harm's way and 50 per cent were lost to the French. Of the six built for European waters, three were taken and two were lost. Fortunately, their function could be performed as effectively by prizes taken from the French. The oceanic advice boats had short careers, being lost in heavy weather on either side of the Atlantic. All this provides the lesson, which seems not to have been understood at the time, that 'making do will not do'. This was not a happy tale and some rethinking was necessary as this war drew to its close. The conclusion to be drawn from this is that, while the unrated warships of the Royal Navy had been relatively effective cruising during the localised Anglo-Dutch wars, they were too weak to survive in these later wars of William and Anne on a wider stage against the might of France.

The last word on this war should be that of the great American historian of sea power A T Mahan who, in discussing the competing strategies of fleet battle and the war against trade concluded that: 'The results of the war of 1689–1697 do not therefore vitiate the general conclusion that a cruising, commerce-destroying warfare, to be destructive, must be seconded by a squadron warfare, and by divisions of ships-of-the-line, which, forcing the enemy to unite his forces, permit the cruisers to make fortunate attempts upon his trade. Without such backing the results will be simply the capture of the cruisers.'[14]

THE WAR OF THE SPANISH SUCCESSION

If the War of the League of Augsburg had been about the containment of France's eastern border and the survival of England under a protestant house, the War of the Spanish Succession, four years later, not only returned to these issues but added new ones about the future governance of the Spanish empire and the immense and looming question of the demarcation of boundaries in the New World. The inability of the Hapsburg King Charles II of Spain to produce an heir posed the question of which state, or dynasty, was to inherit the sprawling Spanish possessions. The contenders to thus become the supreme power in continental Europe were the Austrian House of Hapsburg and the French House of Bourbon. The situation outside Europe was more complex since the maritime powers of Holland and England were better placed than the continental powers to challenge for the overseas territories of the slowly dying maritime power of the Spanish Hapsburgs.

The same pressures surfaced as in the earlier war. On the landward side France was forced to fight on two fronts: one from the outset in 1702 against Holland, and therefore England, Austria, and the Palatinate states bordering the Rhine, and the other from 1703 against Portugal, Spain and Savoy. The land war again drew most of England's attention, not least because the command of the land battle along France's eastern border fell in large part to John Churchill, Duke of Marlborough. Not only was he a remarkable general but also a consummate diplomat and one who wielded very strong influence at the court of Queen Anne.

The War of the Spanish Succession further enlarged the maritime horizon to include the whole of the western Mediterranean and the seaways amongst and along the far-flung possessions of the European states on the other side of the Atlantic. The main naval protagonists were the allied Dutch and English (after the 1707 Union with Scotland more accurately described as the British), both maritime powers and heavily dependent on oceanic and coastwise trade for the welfare of their economies, and France, a continental power, not reliant on overseas trade but nevertheless aspiring to a transoceanic empire.

The navies on either side reflected the difference in the nature of their power and political aims, leading to two distinct and differing strategies. For the Allies, the war at sea was largely one of sea-control; for France it was one of sea-raiding. Thus it was the Allies who saw the value of sea power in support of land operations, though they were to have problems with the other great task of a maritime power, the safe passage of mercantile trade. The French, by contrast, sought to disrupt their opponents' naval contribution to the land-battle and to attack their maritime commerce in order to undermine their economic strength. This in turn

led to differences in the choice of warships, and in their design and construction.

In the previous war, because William was also Stadtholder of the Dutch Republic, the land campaigns to contain France tended to receive most of his attention, but two maritime issues continued to engage his concern. The first was an opportunity: William could see the advantage of using naval power to support the Spanish and Savoyards against France in the Mediterranean, thereby drawing off French pressure against his allies in the north and east. He had already done this in 1695 in support of the Spanish. The second was a vulnerability: the French understood that maritime trade was vital to the English and Dutch economies, so they would make plans to destroy it their highest naval priority. In the event, William would die within a year of the start of the war but the government of his successor Queen Anne continued to fight the war in the same manner.

These two strategic demands were in competition with each other since supporting one could possibly leave the other open to failure. England had sent a fleet to the Mediterranean in the previous war, but for the next conflict, not only was the main fleet deployed to that sea, but it remained there for most of the duration,

Fig 5-7. (**Left**) Queen Anne. Born 1665, a daughter to James II and younger sister to Mary, Anne succeeded to the throne in 1702 on the death of William of Orange. Her husband, Prince George of Denmark, was Lord High Admiral. Her reign spanned the War of the Spanish Succession. She died in 1714. Oil painting by Michael Dahl, about 1714. *National Maritime Museum BHC2515*

Fig 5-8. (**Right**) John Churchill, 1st Duke of Marlborough, was born in 1650, the same year as William of Orange. In his early career he had experience of fighting at sea and was present at the Battle of Solebay. Chiefly remembered for his outstanding victories against the French in the War of the Spanish Succession, he lost favour in 1711–1712 and died in 1722. Oil painting by John Closterman. *National Portrait Gallery*

capturing Gibraltar, engaging the French fleet off Velez Malaga (albeit with an inconclusive result), blockading the French naval base of Toulon and supporting Savoy and Spain. This Mediterranean campaign drew heavily on resources and this impacted on the Allies' ability to provide adequate protection to trade, both oceanic and coastal. This situation in turn forced vigorous debate in Parliament leading to the introduction of the Convoy and Cruisers Act in 1708, whereby a set number of warships of the Third to Sixth Rates were allocated to specific sea areas for the protection of trade.[15]

As in the earlier war, many of the skirmishes resulting from French attacks on ocean-going allied trade were no place for the small unrated warships, but this was not always the case in home waters. There were actions where French privateering squadrons would have in their train relatively small vessels, corvettes or *barques longues*, which would attempt to board the merchantmen whilst the squadron engaged the escort. These would have been suitable targets for sloops armed with 10 or 12 guns. No provision was made for this level of threat by the Admiralty until the third year of the war. A programme to build 20/24-gun Sixth Rate ships was ordered rather belatedly (1710–1712). Whilst these vessels might deal effectively with the larger corvettes or *frégats légères*, they were not suitable for inshore and coastal work, even if they could be spared, so the focus turns to what these strategies meant for the small unrated warships on both sides of this struggle.[16]

On the Allied side the roles of minor war

vessels had remained largely the same: communication, surveillance, shore bombardment, the provision of convoy in a coastal setting, the protection of the fishing grounds, and attendance on the fleet for a number of tasks, one of which remained as towing. For the French it meant the attack on coastal trade – a strategy in which they were becoming increasingly effective – and the defence of their own coastal traffic. Through the privatisation of this form of warfare, in which they continued to use fleet assets in association with privateers, all of which could sortie from strategically placed and well protected havens, the French could dictate the time, point of contact and the level of force required.

However, throughout the war there were areas that only suited smaller escorts, namely the coastal reaches of the Channel and the Irish and North Seas. For these the Admiralty ordered three building programmes to supplement the meagre stocks available at the outset of this second war. This inventory amounted to 2 ketches, 2 advice boats, 6 brigantines, 12 bomb vessels and 10 sloops. All these would have drawn less than 10ft, enabling them to work close inshore. The brigantines were particularly fortunate in being well set up for rowing, helpful to navigating amongst the sands. Table 5-2 includes ten sloops that were built before the war to enforce the ban on the export of wool. They were lightly armed and only a little larger than the Restoration sloops of 1673. Some had their armament increased to 6 guns but even so they were no match for the French

Fig 5-9. This drawing by the author is derived from the draught of *Ferret* of 1710–1711 in the National Maritime Museum and a model of the sloop built by Dana MacCalip. The model is unrigged, and was based on a reconstruction by Howard I Chapelle, the American naval architect and ship historian. The deck detail has been altered slightly from that reconstruction with both the pumps and the galley relocated. Note the single-masted rig and the fact that although there are six gun ports a side there are only five guns (the established number). She is totally different from the sloops of 1699 but may be closer to the larger sloops of 1704.[17]
Author

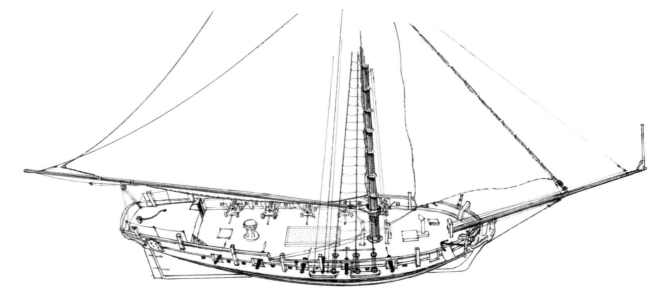

Table 5-2: ACQUISITION OF SLOOPS AND SMALLER SIXTH RATES, 1699–1712

Date	No.	Type	Burthen	Guns	Men	Fates	Remarks
1699	8	Sloop	64–66	2 x 1½pdr	50/35	4 taken, 1 wrecked, 3 sold postwar	Ordered in peacetime to enforce the ban on the export of wool
1699	2	Sloop	83	4 x 1½pdr	50/35	1 taken, 1 wrecked	Took transatlantic advice boat role post-1703
1704	4	Sloop	125	12 x 3pdr	80	1 taken, 2 sold and 1 BU for RB in 1729	First sloops of war. *Drake*, 175 tons, 14 guns
1709	8	Small Sixth Rate	164	14 x 4pdrs	70	2 wrecked, 6 sold postwar	*Lively* 125 tons
1710–1711	4	Sloop	114	10 x 3pdr	80	*Jamaica* foundered 1715, *Trial* broken up for rebuilding 1719, *Ferret* taken 1718, *Shark* broken up for rebuilding 1722	All survived the war
1711	2	Sloop	114	6 x 3pdrs	80	*Hazard* wrecked 1714, *Happy* rebuilt 1724	Complement reduced to 40 at end of war in 1712
Total	28						

Notes.

Details here have been averaged. Fuller accounts can be found in *The Sailing Navy List*, David Lyon (Conway 1990); and *British Warships in the Age of Sail, 1603-1714*, Rif Winfield (Seaforth Publishing 2012).

privateers. Two of their number, which were slightly larger and equipped with 4 guns, were to be used to replace two transatlantic advice boats that had been wrecked in 1698 and 1703. Five of the ten were taken during this war.

In 1704 the situation seems to have been addressed by the building of four sloops specifically ordered for use along the coasts of England and Wales. Much larger than the earlier sloops, they had a broadside of six 3pdr guns, capable of contending with the smaller privateers that would be lurking inshore. These were the first sloops that could be deemed capable of independent action. They were joined five years later by eight Sixth Rates built by different yards, all at slightly different dimensions. Their names, size and armament, though not their rigs, were very similar to the sloops that were to follow them in 1710–1711.

The *Jamaica* group, ordered in 1710, was intended for employment in the West Indies. This suggests that the Admiralty was beginning to realise the contribution a small warship might make to the security of overseas possessions. There were four sloops in this group but only two of them were sent to the West Indies during the war, though a third did deploy there in 1718. A two-vessel group built a year later to the same dimensions were used in home waters initially, but eventually made their way to the Americas, one to be wrecked in 1714 off Massachusetts Bay and the other to complete a tour in Jamaican waters. The reign of Queen Anne saw the birth of what may be considered the genuine sloop of war concept. A clearer definition of the vessel was to be set in 1719 with the introduction of the first full Establishment, which laid down that all Sixth Rates would have a minimum of 20 guns, which implies that sloops could be given no more than 18. At the end of hostilities with France in 1712 (the war was to continue until 1714 elsewhere) the Royal Navy had twenty sloop-type vessels, which included the small Sixth Rates and two of the old brigantine class.

By 1713 all the remaining Sixth Rates had been sold, as had the three remaining sloops from 1699 and the brigantines. Of the 1704 group of sloops, only three remained, one of which would be rebuilt, but all the sloops of 1710–1711 continued to serve. Their fates post-1713 will be dealt with later. In the main, these small warships were built for an emergency and discarded once that emergency had passed, so by the end of 1713, apart from the bomb vessels, the Royal Navy possessed only nine sloops remaining out of the twenty-eight that had been constructed just before or during the war.

The war left the Allies in a strong position at sea, which was enhanced by the possession of bases at Gibraltar and Port Mahon (Menorca) in the Mediterranean and others in the Caribbean and along the North American seaboard. Britain was beginning to realise that it had a maritime empire which it needed to protect and administer. This would become a consideration in the debate as to the number of sloops the Navy would require in the following decades.

Chapter 6

KETCHES, BRIGANTINES, ADVICE BOATS AND SLOOPS, 1689–1702

The cumbersome title of this chapter serves to underline the profusion of small warships of various types that accumulated and developed during the reign of William and Mary, and later that of Anne. However, this chapter will cover only those types ordered during the lifetime of William III.

Each of the types above was ordered for a specific purpose, but such is the nature of conflict that circumstances forced them to adapt to sharing each other's roles. For example, the sloops designed for anti-smuggling purposes in 1699 would later be used as small cruisers; or brigantines, ordered for the purpose of towing crippled ships out of danger in battle, could act as advice boats, albeit rather slow ones, and did act as cruisers for the purposes of enforcing the ban on the export of wool until replaced by sloops specially built for the purpose. Ketches could be prepared to accommodate mortars or be converted to fireships in a matter of days and, if really necessary, could be tasked as escorts. This chapter will look at each type in turn, but, because of their specialised nature, bomb ketches and fireships will be dealt with separately later.

KETCHES OF THE 1690s

At the outset of King William's War against France (1689–1697), the Admiralty ordered eight 10-gun ketches to be built to virtually the same specifications as their Restoration predecessors. These were all built by contract, possibly because the Admiralty had habitually ordered this old design, based on commercial/fishing boat practice, from specialist private yards.[1] There is little to add here to the description in Chapter 4, except that, like the Restoration ketches, they were twice the displacement of the Commonwealth ketches. Their dimensions were similar to the largest of the Restoration ketches, their burthen being between 91 and 99 tons. In average dimension, compared with the Restoration ketches, they were generally six inches larger in all respects and measured 2.7 tons more. Armament was similar at 10 guns instead of 8–10. Herein lies the problem for the Admiralty, in that they had replicated a vessel that had met the requirement in the 1670s to good effect, but could not do so in the more demanding 1690s. This order reeks of a quick answer to an old problem and of trying to fight the new war with the last war's weapons.

The Royal Navy now faced the French and their sponsorship of fast, well-armed privateers carrying 18 or more guns. Often hunting in pairs, they were more than a match for these steady, less well armed ketches. There is a view that the sailing ability of these ketches was not that good, but this was relative, the result of an unfortunate comparison with newer French opponents. There had been much progress across the Channel in the production of fast sailing types that had evolved from the *barque longue*, corvette and *frégat légère*. Such development had not been made with the English ketch. More lightly armed and unable to run away from superior firepower, it is not surprising that several of these Williamite ketches were taken by French privateers. Their fates were:

Aldborough, 1691 – Blew up 1696.

Eaglet, 1691 – Taken 1693 by two large French
    privateers.

Harp, 1691 – Taken 1693 by two French priva-
    teers.

Hart, 1691 – Taken 1692 by two 18-gun French
    privateers.

Hind, 1691 – Taken 1697 by two French priva-
    teers.

Roe, 1691 – Stranded 1697.

Scarborough, 1691– Taken 1692 by two 18/20-
    gun French privateers.

Martin, 1694 – Taken 1702 by two French
    privateers.

Wren, 1694 (pink-rigged) – Taken 1697 by two
    French privateers.

This order does not reflect credit on Admiralty
planning in the early days of William's reign.
The Board of Admiralty was a new institution
and there had been personnel changes at the
Navy Board; it would take time for them to
comprehend the dangers faced by coastwise
commercial traffic. The acquisition of these
ketches compares badly with the large order for
escorts of the Sixth Rate in July 1693, when the
level of threat had been clearly recognised,
certainly as far as offshore and oceanic trade
was concerned, following the adoption of the
guerre de course by France in 1692. As a result
of this new order, Sixth Rates mounting 20–24
guns took many privateers, although they were
themselves vulnerable to attack by the small
ships of the line that were now (1693–1694) in
the ruthless and effective hands of the privateering syndicates. The old, round-hulled ketch
in the seventeenth-century style would not
appear again as a cruiser, but its rig, albeit
modified and on a very different hull, would
return in the middle decades of the eighteenth
century for the bomb vessel and some of the
cruising sloops.

THE BRIGANTINE

This class of vessel had not appeared in the
naval lists, with one exception, since the time of
Elizabeth I. The exception was the Pepysian
sloop *Whipster* which, unlike all the other
sloops, had been specifically classified as a brigantine.[2] In fact the operational role for which
the Pepysian sloops were ordered, within the
Restoration navy, was the same as that planned

for the brigantines of the Williamite navy. This
role involved attendance on the fleet to tow off
ships, to remove or divert enemy fireships and
to provide rapid inter-ship communication.
Both these early sloops and the later brigantines
found themselves, from time to time, in the
other roles of surveillance, fishery protection
and coastal convoy. Both classes were also built
in Royal Dockyards by master shipwrights of
the Royal Navy.

By 1689 not one of the earlier sloops
remained in naval service, so to a degree the
brigantines were a replacement for them and in
some operational respects they resembled
them. The brigantines were out-of-the-ordi-
nary craft, and further interesting because at a
time when some of the smaller ship types had
begun to be associated with a particular rig,
the naval brigantines exemplified the opposite
process;[3] sails that had been characteristic of
them in Tudor times were discarded, and they
were tried, at least at the introduction of the
class, with a variety of rigs. Thus for the lifetime of this group their name implied a certain
build and function, in the old manner of classi-
fying ships, and it is not until well into the
eighteenth century that an acknowledged 'brigantine rig' in naval service is referred to, but by
then it is on a sloop.

Fig 6-1. Just one of the rigs
applied to brigantines, which
were vessels which had
originally been intended
primarily for rowing. Note
the apostis in the waist,
designed to improve the
leverage of the oars. Some
were equipped with square
sails throughout their careers,
as shown here, while some
had their main course
converted to lug. Eventually
some were given mizzen
masts. *Author*

Fig 6-2 A brigantine (on the right) in hot pursuit, under sail and oar. Note that it is low in the water, that the oarsmen sit to row and that the leading three oars are pushed rather than pulled (although they may be paddles). These vessels were fast and were handled superbly. The prey is a Christian felucca, where the oarsmen appear to be standing and pushing their oars. *National Maritime Museum PZ4898*

Fig 6-3. This is a Dutch pleasure boat of about 25ft length overall, from the middle of the seventeenth century. It is an early example of what was to become the 'schooner' rig. It carries unsupported masts and bermudan sails and can do so because it would be for use on sheltered inland waters. This sail plan applied to a brigantine would require the masts to be supported to cope with the rigours of the open sea. It would appear that neither sail has a boomed out foot. Although not shown, this craft would have had some provision for rowing, although it is primarily a sailing boat. Drawn by Douglas Phillips-Birt From a painting dated 1629 by Adam Willaerts.

The Williamite brigantines were the brain-child of Edmund Dummer, the Assistant Surveyor, who was one of the most innovative ship designers of the period. A formative experience of his career was a voyage he undertook to the Mediterranean in 1683 from which he brought back the first technical intelligence about the new French naval weapon, the bomb vessel. However, he also collected information on anything he found of potential naval interest, and must have been inspired by a kind of half-galley or *galiote à rames* that was in widespread use by Mediterranean naval forces. These were of light construction, probably narrow and equally at home under oars or lateen sails (Fig 6-2). They were usually referred to as brigantines.

Notwithstanding the Pepysian brigantine *Whipster*, Dummer obviously felt his concept was unusual enough to require the support of

Edward Russell, William III's fleet commander and the senior naval lord at the Admiralty, if it were to be accepted by the notoriously conservative Navy Board. Its commissioners were summoned to a joint meeting with the Admiralty in January 1691 at which Russell presented Dummer's proposal, along with the 'draught of a vessel to be built for rowing to attend the fleet for the towing off ships, and cutting off fireships'. Although the junior board was told to consider and report, the patronage of Russell ensured a favourable response.[4]

Despite their apparent originality, it is difficult to know what these brigantines looked like since, although Van de Velde the younger was still alive in the 1690s, he has left no drawings of them. Therefore, it has to be accepted that any attempt to portray their appearance is riddled with conjecture; nevertheless, their characteristics are so elusive that it is worth making an attempt.

The first of the Williamite brigantines was *Shark*. Her name struck a more predatory note than usual in small ship names, and appears a surprising choice if she was to be little more than a salvage tug. She was, at 57ft 10in on the deck, not twice the length of a 60-gun ship's longboat; indeed, her proportions were not unlike those of the longboat, for she was lean and shallow, her 4ft 8in draught of water being suited to inshore operations. As the vessel neared completion at the Royal Dockyard, Deptford, in April 1691 the Navy Board consulted her builder, Fisher Harding, on his views on masting this novel craft. In response he recommended the use of galley sails and proceeded to list the lengths and diameters of the main and foremasts and main and fore yards, together with yards for carrying square sails on both masts. Fisher Harding seems to have had in mind a larger version of Fig 6-2 when he made these recommendations.[5] This suggests that to William and Mary's navy a brigantine was in essence a small two-masted galley rigged with lateen sails, which were supplemented or replaced by two square sails for use when running before the wind. Such a vessel could be found then in foreign navies, preserving as they did an unbroken tradition of galleys.[6]

However, Fisher Harding concluded that in his judgement bermudan sails would be far

better because they had no shrouds or yards to encumber the oarsmen and were much easier to handle. This recommendation is sensible (but see the comment at Fig 6-3) since wearing round a heavy lateen spar in a choppy sea would be an alarming evolution, but the recommendation of freestanding masts would preclude the use of square sails for downwind work. This is quite an unexpected proposal from Harding. To find that he gives priority to the business of rowing rather than sailing causes no surprise, and his reasons are valid, but here he advocates a markedly lighter rig than was standard for the type. Bermudan sails ('bermoodee' in contemporary spelling) were triangular and resembled a narrow lateen sail in reverse, with the longest cloth at the leech. But they differed from it in having the luff bent to the mast instead of to a yard. In spite of such a departure from the norm as this rig presented, it is almost certain that the Navy Board gave it their approval and that *Shark* was fitted in the manner that Harding recommended.[7] When it came to deciding her guns and complement, she was given the eight 'patereros'[8] and 30 crew that he proposed. Nevertheless, on 24 October – barely six months after *Shark*'s launch – Harding wrote briefly to the Board asking its permission to alter the sails to lug sails. (See Chapter 1, Fig 1-26.)

It is only possible to guess at the reason for the change, but the request itself seems to confirm that bermudan sails had been tried. If so, they were found wanting, perhaps because they proved to be less convenient than expected;

more probably because, having neither a yard above nor, unlike the modern version, a boom below, they could not be effectively spread to develop the desired speed, particularly downwind.[9] Two lug sails, unless of the standing sort, might have the disadvantage of making more work than bermudan sails for the crew, besides calling for some lateral support for the masts that made no concessions to the oarsmen, but they would be powerful when on the wind and adequate before it; moreover they could be augmented with topsails.[10] One curiosity of the discussion about the rig is that Dummer does not seem to have been involved at all, which may simply reflect the fact that his brigantine concept was essentially a hull form that could be driven by any one of a number of rigs.

Not many explicit details are known of *Shark*'s design or of the eight that followed her. Three of them were built at Deptford Dockyard, to enlarged dimensions as suggested by Harding in order to make them heavier in the water and render them more serviceable for towing off heavy ships. These 'new Sloops' as he at first calls them would be 'of the same shape as before' – presumably referring to the *Shark* rather than the Pepysian sloops of 1672–1673. Their length to breadth ratio (LBR) is much lower than those of the more slender Pepysian sloops; as for size, whereas *Shark* was 58 tons burthen, her successors ranged from 70 to 80 tons, an increase reflected in their armament of 6 carriage guns and 4 swivels, though the latter were reduced to 2 for those built in 1695–1696. An important feature on their hull was the

Figs 6-4a and 6-4b.
Although the righthand print shows Amsterdam in the first decade of the seventeenth century, the brigantine represented is instructive. First it carries the basic Biscay square rig rather than the lateen rig as on the left, but with a two-part mainmast capable of carrying a topsail. The vessels have similar hulls. There appear to be no guns unless swivels are carried for mounting when required. Both examples have a Mediterranean style awning on the quarterdeck and an apostis supported by hanging knees. The engraving on the right from about 1600 is by by Johannes Saenredam of Zandam, whilst on the left is a detail from a painitng by Van Wieringen of Heemskirk's defeat of the Spanish off Gibraltar in 1607. *Fig 6-4a National Maritime Museum BHC0265*

Fig 6-5. This drawing is based on an engraving of around 1710 by Guéroult du Pas entitled 'A small naval galley, serving in the fleet of an English Admiral'. There were no vessels classified as galleys in the Royal Navy at this time, so this may well be a brigantine; if so it is the only known illustration of the type. Du Pas' engravings are generally accurate although proportions and curves are sometimes exaggerated. He would not make a mistake about the number of masts and yards for example. Note the apostis, which appears to be planked up, the three-mast ship rig, the main staysail and the size of the crew. *Author*

Fig 6-6. The author's interpretation of a small sketch by Van de Velde the younger that is useful for its depiction of rig. The hull does not give the impression of a craft low in the water as the brigantines were reputed to be. Note that the foresails have been furled aloft and that the buss mainsail has been lowered for furling and is lying inside the shrouds. The vessel on the right is lying to the tide. The article accompanying the orginal publication of this sketch in *The Mariner's Mirror* (Vol VII/3, p203) regards the main course as a square sail. It may well be a lug sail or a square buss sail which could be hoised in a fore-and-aft configuration. Given the likely date of 1690–1710 then either of these two possibilities can apply.

outrigger – what on a Mediterranean galley was called the *apostis*, (Fig 6-4) – positioned along each side to take a total of 24–30 oars, and substantial enough to justify an extra item sometimes when main dimensions were listed.[11]

Because *Shark* carried only light portable guns, it would have been possible for her to have planked-up bulwarks, rather than open rails. And it would have been desirable for the others too, as they had to be provided with gunports above a very limited freeboard. However, in order to row these craft using an apostis, it is most likely that planking up the bulwarks would prevent the sweep of the oars, so open rails may have been one option. Another would have been to plank-in the apostis top, bottom and side. But the sea would have impacted on this structure and with considerable force in bad weather, which would have stressed the hull and at worst damaged the apostis. It would also have added to the topside

weight. Were the first option used, sailing in the open sea would have been both uncomfortable and dangerous. The commander of *Dispatch*, built in the year after *Shark*, states in his journal that during a hard gale her lee gunwales were continually under water, which again suggests that she had open rails.

Apart from dimensions and displacement, there was another major difference between *Shark* and the other eight craft. Whilst *Shark* with her smaller size and Harding's mildly experimental approach to rig, was set up with a fore-and-aft sail plan, certainly two of the larger brigantines were square-rigged; in fact, by the end of their service, it is probable that all had square rig except for the main course. There are reasons for proposing that they were all square-rigged on two masts with courses and topsails. The square rig, if well handled could be reasonably effective at going to windward, particularly if it was combined with staysails, which would have been the case on brigantines. It was also probably the best rig for manoeuvring and turning ship. The Navy was confident in the rig and was cautious about new ideas – although this was to change.

There is a view that the main course was a buss sail (Fig 6-6) and not a normal square course as shown in Fig 6-5, and that it would be possible to set a small topsail above it. At Fig 6-6 the indication of crosstrees on the mainmast above would support this contention. Some argue that the foremast of a brigantine was like that of a ship, with a fidded topmast complete with platform top and all the associated standing rigging, whilst the mainmast was a tall pole mast as drawn in Fig 6-6.[12] This may not have always been the case and the alternative of a two-part mast with crosstrees could well have been used. The examples under discussion were built in the period when the meaning of the word 'brigantine' was changing from describing a vessel and its purpose to describing a rig. Fig 6-5 follows the former premise as it is fitted with an apostis, is equipped with oars and is ship-rigged, whilst Fig 6-6 follows the latter in suggesting a brigantine rig. This is shown more clearly in Fig 6-7.

To further underline the variability of rig on these unrated and, one might add, 'unregulated' warships, the example of *Fly* will serve. Lug sails, requested for *Shark* in 1691, possibly replacing bermudan sails, found favour else-where when five years later at least one of this design was in use on board *Fly*, which had recently been built at Portsmouth. Yet only months after *Fly*'s launch, Deal Yard was ordered by the Navy Board to alter it into a square sail.[13] Whilst this change would have reduced her windward ability, it would have certainly made a difference to her progress downwind. The resultant rig would have been very like that of *Dispatch*, which is known to have had square courses and topsails on fore- and mainmasts, a main staysail and a flying jib, together with a wing sail. A spritsail under the bowsprit might also be expected.

On the evidence culled from her captain's logs, it was long assumed that these features constituted the Navy's 'brigantine rig'.[14] As already demonstrated by reference to only three of the nine vessels concerned, that assumption is an over-simplification, but it does focus attention on three other possibilities for a two-masted rig. As has been shown before, certain craft were able to use their square sails in a fore-and-aft configuration and so, in this case, even with a square-cut main course, there remained the possibility, particularly if the course was a buss sail, of converting it temporarily to a lug sail by hoisting the yard off-centre and inside the shrouds.[15] To control the resulting sail there would need to be some carefully positioned cringles woven into the bolt-rope for the tack and clew. Another possi-bility, on a two-masted rig that appeared at the turn of the century, was the bilander main course; half way between a lateen sail and a lug sail, it was trapezoidal rather than triangular in shape. It would give a brigantine a strong wind-ward ability (Fig1-10).[16]

The third option was a rig prominent in both navy and merchant service for something like a century, if not longer: the snow rig. As such it needs to be examined more closely, but later in the story, since the evidence would seem to point to its introduction – into the Navy at least – towards the end of the first decade of the eigh-teenth century, when some of these brigantines were still afloat. But before that there is at least one more, unsuspected, guise to be recorded for certain vessels of this group.

In June 1702 the storekeeper at Deptford submitted sail estimates to the Navy Board for

ships from Fourth Rates downwards, including those for two brigantines. This list showed principal sails only and in the case of the brig-antines, as one would expect, no demand was made for mizzen course or topsail. In July a revised estimate was issued which included sails for four brigantines, but this time including a mizzen course, a mizzen topsail and, surpris-ingly, a spritsail topsail – producing something similar to the vessel in Fig 6-5. Whether the intention to re-rig brigantines as ships was ever carried out is uncertain, but the logs of *Dispatch* up to early 1709 give no hint that she might have been one of those converted. Nevertheless, after surviving longer than all the others, when put up for sale in 1712 she was definitely three-masted.[17]

In that year *Fly* was also sold, described as

Fig 6-7. This drawing of a brigantine is from the early eighteenth century and is possibly of an East India Company vessel. The hull certainly looks mercantile, but its rig is illustrative of that which could have been used by *Fly* in the preceeding decade. Note the use of staysails on the main and what appear to be two jibs, both set flying. *National Maritime Museum BHC 0978*

Fig 6-8. The author's interpretation of a drawing in the Wallace Collection by Francis Swaine (1720–1783), which is of the period but probably depicts earlier practice. The small ship on the left shows what may be a square or lug sail yard hoist inside the shrouds.
A close inspection of the sail shows that it is not a lateen sail. This rig may be a similar rig to that of *Fly*. It is also worth comparison with the Van de Velde sketch at Fig 6-6 which shows a spar lowered to the deck and lying inside the shrouds.

lacking topgallant yards. Topgallant sails were no part of a brigantine's clothing at this time, whereas some vessels of similar tonnage could boast full ship's rig. If both *Dispatch* and *Fly* had undergone a recent conversion it was possibly in January 1711, when, after a report on the latter's dilapidation, the Admiralty ordered them to be refitted at Chatham, cleaned and put in a condition to lie as guard vessels in the River Medway.

A few points gleaned from letters bearing on repairs, together with details from the captains' journals, give some indication of the appearance of these small ships. For example, in answering a criticism as to the leakiness of *Dispatch* above the waterline, her builder (Harding) assured the Board that her top-timbers and upperwork had been renewed on both sides from the fore bulk-head to the cabin. This reveals a little about the structure at her bow and the form of her cabin. For her sister *Diligence*, when she had suffered damage to her head by collision with a foreign ship, the list of repairs included taking off the old broken knee of the head, fairing and bolting on a new one, repairing the figure, making and fastening two new rails and a crosspiece and the production and stepping of a new bowsprit. Even for these times of elaborate ornament it is a surprise to find a figurehead on so small a vessel; in other respects these details could

equally have been applied to the sloops of twenty years later.

Another detail about the structure can be inferred when, in 1699, the then captain, having taken on board 30 brigantine oars, decided a month later to put 14 of them ashore because they had made the ship 'crank' – unstable and inclined to tip sideways very quickly. The physical situation here is that the centre of gravity is moving too far above the centre of buoyancy, meaning that the vessel has little inclination to right itself when heeling, so it is always in danger of capsizing. In this case the weight of the oars made the centre of gravity rise, and because these vessels had a very shallow draught and were quite slender, the ballast had little in the way of leverage to keep the hull upright. For similar reasons, captains of small craft were to complain frequently of too much sail and masts that were over-long.[18]

Based on *Dispatch*'s dimensions and the details from her captains' journals, Fig 6-9 is a conjectural reconstruction of her hull. This raises a number of problems! From her known main dimensions, it is assumed that her shape would have been similar to, though broader and deeper than that of the earlier sloops, with possibly a greater rake to her sternpost. Her LBR was 4.07. Using the same criteria for measurements, *Bonetta*'s LBR would have been 4.20. Depth in hold was 5ft 0in for *Bonetta* and 6ft 2in for *Dispatch* with respective estimated draughts of 4ft 6in and 5ft 8in.

The rig has already been discussed and only the positions of the masts are shown here. The main area of conjecture revolves round the business of rowing. Her captain's log reveals that on occasion he took on men for rowing and once had an additional complement of 60 over and above his normal establishment of 35. However, the number of sweeps that could be pulled is limited by the space available. In his book on oared fighting ships Anderson gives a recommended minimum space between oarsmen of 3ft 4in. On this basis, *Dispatch* could only have deployed a bank of 12 oars. Thus a team of 24 oarsmen would have sufficed, unless each oar was pulled by two men. However, the geometry of doubling up becomes difficult.

The log refers to taking on 'brigantine' oars; this may describe their length, which would have been at least 17ft 6in, the maximum

Fig 6-9. Conjectional reconstruction of *Dispatch*. Length on the keel 53ft 0in; breadth moulded 16ft 9in; depth in hold 6ft 2in; freeboard 1ft 10in; LBR 4.07; BDR 2.58. *Author.*

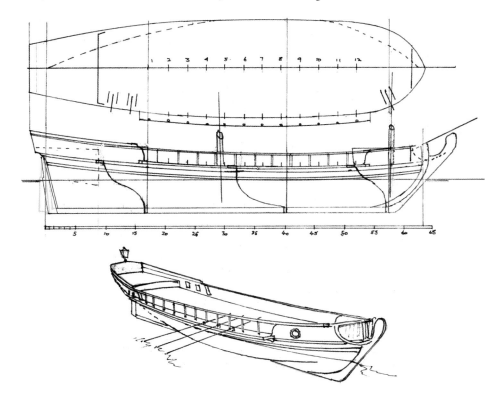

recommended length for a one-man pull. The diagram at Fig 6-10 uses this length and places the oarsman 5ft from the sweep's pivot point. This gives his 'pull' a 3ft span. Whilst this is manageable, another oarsman inboard would have a pull of 4ft 6in, which is not, unless he were able to stand. The other explanation of the large 'pulling' crew could be the need of a 'reserve team' since towing a large warship for any distance would be an exhausting labour.

The adoption of a rail and stanchions enclosing the weather deck may appear questionable, but planked up topsides would have prevented the movement of the oars, although a spirketting board would not have obstructed them. With the deck open to the sea, it is therefore not surprising that the captain was concerned about his lee gunwales being constantly awash. An example of this arrangement is at Fig 6-11, though from an earlier period (around 1600) and in a galley. Another aspect of rowing is the weight of oars on deck when not in use. As mentioned above, the captain had to unload some oars because they were making the vessel unstable or 'crank'. The implication is that beneath the waterline her hull was narrow with a fine entry and run and of little depth of water. She was therefore very tender.

The life on board these small vessels was tough and, unfortunately for the crew, respite might not be found for months on end. Captain Robert Jackson, who was given command of the Sixth Rate *Squirrel* in November 1704, writes of his last crew in *Fly*, 'The men belonging to the Brigantine after two years venturing their lives ... are very desirous to

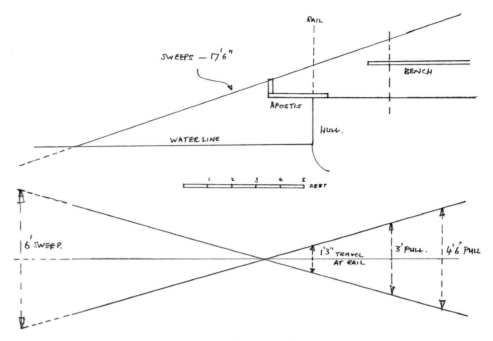

Fig 6-10. The geometry of rowing for a brigantine if the crew were seated. *Author.*

remove [with me].'[19] Another officer, Commander John Jeffcott, who heard he was appointed to one of the 'new sloops' (1699), asked that he might be considered for the ship *Queenborough*, because his last command had been the *Basilisk* Bomb, 'where the lowness has occasioned my being often wet and [I have] contracted a lameness in my limbs.' He had been seventeen years in the Service; he was given *Queenborough*.

As has already been mentioned, the task for which these vessels were ordered was not necessarily the work they ended up performing. Certainly the log of *Dispatch* talks of the role they were designed for – towing – but in the main they would have been used for scouting, dispatch, fishery protection and providing coastal convoy. This design was not a great

Fig 6-11. A detail from a painting of the battle on Haarlem lake, 1572. The galley illustrates the use of an apostis and a waist cloth to give the oarsmen some protection from the elements.

Fig 6-12. Brigantines at anchor and under sail. *Author*.

success and was not repeated. However, they were optimised for their prime role, that of a tug for crippled ships in the line of battle, but thanks to the defeat of the French fleet at La Hogue in 1692, this was rarely required. The design did not suit them to escort work where they were expected to chase off French privateers. During her whole career *Dispatch* only caught one privateer and it took her 24 hours to do so. The lesson must be that designing specifically for a single role generally does not produce a flexible warship.

ADVICE BOATS

Whilst the French were using their *barques longues* for a clutch of coastal roles including 'advice', the English elected to design a specific vessel for this purpose and then use it for many different tasks. In the context of King William's war, the advice boats were primarily needed for

Fig 6-13. An advice boat gives advance warning of enemy activity. These fast light craft were also used to gather intelligence and to carry government communications. They were built in two sizes, the larger ones being for transatlantic use. *Author*

reconnaissance – on a tactical level to scout for the main fleets and at the strategic level to monitor activities in enemy ports, especially the principal centres of privateering. They were occasionally used for what modern forces call 'covert operations', playing a part in the cross-Channel war of subversion and intelligence-gathering. Given these activities, it is not surprising that in the correspondence of senior naval officers of the day the terms 'spy boat' and 'advice boat' are interchangeable. They also carried official dispatches, so the design requirements may have been similar to civilian packet boats, whose task was to make fast passages between ports with the mails and passengers. The Navy built two types: those employed on short offshore and coastal passages and those for trans-oceanic work. The intention was that they should be lighter and faster than the brigantines which, whilst used in this role, had not been designed for it. Indeed, brigantines had been given a greater draught and displacement following experimentation with the prototype and this made them too heavy for the purposes of 'advice'.

Only nine advice boats were built. The first two groups, totalling four vessels, were launched in 1694 and were designed and built in the Royal Dockyards at Portsmouth and Plymouth, two by William Stigant and two by Elias Waffe. They were set up at approximately 61ft on the range of the deck with a beam of 16ft (this gave them a LBR of 3.8) and a depth in hold of 6ft, measuring 73 tons. They can be compared with the brigantine *Dispatch* of 80 tons outlined at Fig 6-9 and with the larger advice boats required for oceanic passages.

The intention to make them faster and lighter than the 'heavy and slow' brigantines does not seem to have amounted to much. Only seven tons separated *Mercury* from the brigantine *Dispatch* and the latter was 1ft 9in longer on the length of the deck and 4in less on the length of the keel. It would therefore be reasonable to assume that they were very similar craft with the exception that *Mercury*, as a sloop, did not have an apostis and possibly drew rather less water. Groups three and four, amounting to three craft, were all designed by Stigant and launched in 1695. Two were very slightly larger than his first group and indeed larger than *Dispatch*. The third was a small boat of 38ft LGD used to keep an eye on shipping in the Solent; it was so insignificant it is not even clear if it had a name being variously referred to as the Scout Boat or the Solent Advice Boat. Discounting this boat, three of the others were taken by the French during the course of the two wars, two were lost at sea and one was wrecked, leaving only one survivor to be sold in 1713.

Setting aside a crude comparison of dimension and displacement, it may have been that the advice boats had a distinctly different shape from the brigantines. Nevertheless, the relationship between burthen (as calculated from the dimensions) and true displacement in such small vessels must have been similar, so roughly the same bulk of vessel had to be dragged through the water even if the advice boats had a sharper hull form. Two large advice boats, the *Eagle* and the *Swift*, were constructed by commercial yards at Arundel and launched in 1696. Their displacement was over twice that of those in the earlier groups. Both were lost, one being wrecked off Virginia, the other on the Sussex coast during the Great Gale of 1703.

In the United States Naval Academy Museum at Annapolis there is an unusual, and in many ways unique, contemporary model; although it came originally from the collection of Charles Sergison, Pepys's successor as Clerk of the Acts, it is as yet unidentified (Fig 6-15).[20] This model will be analysed in detail later, but for the present the question is whether it might represent one or other of the two large advice boats. The design portrayed in this model displays many of the principles espoused by Edmund Dummer, the Surveyor of the Navy in the 1690s,[21] and its proportions do match closely those of the *Swift* II built by Moore in Arundel in 1696–1697. Dummer happened to be the MP for Arundel and it is possible that he was able to help one of his constituents on his way to a Navy Board contract (the other large advice boat was also built at Arundel, but by a different shipbuilder). The other possible connection with Dummer is that after he was dismissed from the Navy Board for alleged corruption in 1698, he set up his own yard and became an expert on packet boats, not dissimilar to advice boats; indeed he was instrumental in starting the transatlantic packet service in 1702.[22]

Another way in which the Royal Navy

managed to acquire small ships, other than through purchase, was by the capture of enemy vessels. Because an illustration exists, a good example for this period is a small ship-rigged craft, a privateer called *Brillant* (Fig 6-16). She was taken early in 1696 and commissioned into the Royal Navy in March of that year as *Brilliant*. She was used for clandestine operations on the French coast, where her Gallic looks helped her disguise. She was light at an estimated 60 tons, yet she carried 6 carriage guns.

In 1710 another small French-built vessel was taken which, being only three years old, was surveyed and recommended for use as an advice boat. The yard reported that she had a

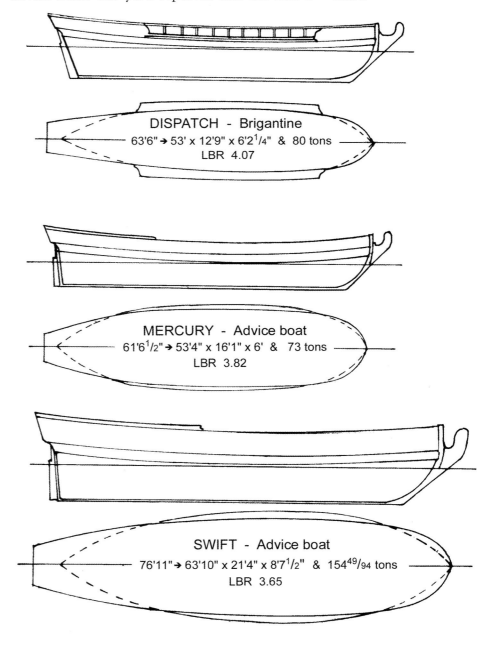

Fig 6-14. A comparison of a brigantine and two advice boats of different sizes. *Author*

DISPATCH - Brigantine
63'6" → 53' x 12'9" x 6'2¹/4" & 80 tons
LBR 4.07

MERCURY - Advice boat
61'6¹/2" → 53'4" x 16'1" x 6' & 73 tons
LBR 3.82

SWIFT - Advice boat
76'11" → 63'10" x 21'4" x 8'7¹/2" & 154⁴⁹/94 tons
LBR 3.65

Fig 6-15. This model, part of the Henry Huddleston Rogers Collection at the United States Naval Academy, was once part of the Sergison Collection. Sergison was Pepys's successor and built up a large collection of models covering all classes of warship. There has been much argument as to what this one represents, but one of the main confusions is its rig which is seemingly so unbalanced. *By courtesy of Grant Walker*

promising body for sailing (which qualified her for an advice boat), being of the dimensions and burthen following: length by the deck 53ft 6in, length of the keel 43ft 4½in, extreme breadth 16ft 10in, depth in hold 7ft 1in, burthen $65^{35}\!/_{94}$ tons. Her LBR would have been 3.73. This ship could carry a crew of 50 and was armed with eight 2pdrs and two swivels.

Before leaving the advice boats, a word is necessary on their rig. It has been suggested that they may have had some early form of schooner rig. However, it is known that they were equipped with topmasts, which is unlikely in the schooner rig of that time; it was normally set up on pole masts as portrayed by Van de Velde the younger in Fig 4-20. Nevertheless, a two-masted rig would have been used based on a

square rig with topsails on both masts and stay-sails to improve windward performance. However, there is one piece of evidence for an unusual variation of this rig in the contemporary manual *Britain's Glory or Shipbuilding Unvail'd*, published in 1717 by William Sutherland.[23] The frontispiece shows graphically all the vessels in the Royal Navy in October 1714. One item is labelled '10 Advice Boats' and they are depicted with what appears to be a square main course rigged fore-and-aft on the mainmast (Fig 6-18). Whether this is supposed to show the square course re-rigged as a lug sail or a proper lug sail is uncertain, but this does flag up a variation on the rig that points the way to the fore-and-aft main course of the sloops of the late 1720s. A similar arrangement can be seen on the Harwich packet boat of around 1700–1710 at Fig 6-19, but in this case the main course is a fore-and-aft lug sail and the square main course has been dispensed with. These packet boats were very fast and as part of an essential service to the Continent would have been noticed by Edmund Dummer in his capacity as Surveyor of the Navy; indeed, there is a resemblance between this vessel and the model at Fig 6-15.

THE SLOOPS OF 1699

King William's War, or the War of the League of Augsburg, was concluded by the Treaty of Ryswick in 1698, although the possibility of another loomed ominously in the corridors of the country palace where agreement was finally reached. So, on the basis that when war stops, smuggling begins, the Navy Board's minute of 3 June 1699 to the Admiralty is no surprise. This proposed the employment of advice boats and brigantines to cruise upon the coast of Ireland against the 'owlers' (night-time smugglers) 'until proper vessels can be built'. In response the Admiralty directed the Navy Board to 'lay before us draughts of proper vessels to be built'. The result was a batch of eight sloops armed with only two guns and some patereroes. By 15 August captains had been nominated and by 1 September the first was ready to be launched, a reflection of both the small size of the vessels and the urgency of the problem. This

Fig 6-16. This sketch is based on a drawing by Van de Velde the younger of the French prize *Brillant* that shows the slender nature of this small ship. Her rig is very tall and she sensibly has a mizzen to balance her sail plan when clawing to windward. She is not unlike the *barques longues* of this period and she will therefore be discussed later. Her construction is likely to have been far lighter than the English advice boats. Her mission as a privateer would have been to close fast with her prey and put her crew aboard him and when outfaced by superior force to run faster than her opponent. She was taken into English service as an advice boat. *Author*

was the illegal export of wool, and the frequent recurrence of this issue well into the next century would require more 'light' sloops to be built. Initially these sloops were deployed to Irish and Scottish waters, both in the Irish Sea and Atlantic, but later, with a new war looming, some were transferred to the North Sea and the Channel in other roles.

In form and rig these sloops were very unlike the earlier sloops of the Restoration navy (Fig 6-19). Apart from the difference in their intended roles, the main variations lay in the

Fig 6-17. A very large scale model, 1:24, catalogued as a recreational vessel or yacht of about 1705, but very much the sort of small ship that could be co-opted for service as an advice boat. *National Maritime Museum F2855-004*

Fig 6-18. An enlarged detail from the frontispiece of Sutherland's *Shipbuilding Unvail'd* of 1715. The item is labelled as an advice boat but its main interest is the rig, which shows a square sail yard being hoisted, not in its centre but one third out from one end, turning the square main course into a lug sail. It is this arrangement that would make sense of the mast positions on the model at Fig 6-15.

Fig 6-19. A detail from a Johannes Kip engraving of Harwich from the early 1700s. This is identified in the key as a packet boat, which would have run the service to the Low Countries. These were very fast and had a fore-and-aft main course to allow them to sail better to windward. Note the similarity in layout to the Annapolis model in Fig 6-15. *National Maritime Museum PY9672*

length to beam ratio and in the draught of water. When this new batch was ordered, there had been no so-called sloops in the Royal Navy since 1687, the year when the first *Bonetta* was sold. She had been designed and built in time of war by Phineas Pett as a fleet tender, though she later ran the usual gamut of sloop errands. The remainder had all been sold in 1683 except *Fan Fan*, which was a general-purpose yacht, although originally designed for use in a sloop role. The concept of a long lean easily driven hull, as typified by *Bonetta* I, had vanished and

the dimensions of the new sloops present the distinct possibility that their designers were simply returning a miniature version of a Fifth or Sixth Rate. As with the Restoration sloops these new ones were all designed and built in Royal Dockyards by master shipwrights. Two further sloops were built in 1700 of slightly larger dimensions with a three-masted ship rig. They were equipped with 4 swivels and 4 carriage guns as opposed to the 2 allocated to the six earlier and lighter sloops. They too were for Irish waters.

These small ships had to cope with rather different seas from those facing the Restoration sloops. The St George's Channel between Carnsore Point on the southeast tip of Ireland and Milford Haven in Wales, and its cousin, the North Channel between the Mull of Kintyre and the Antrim coast, are some of the nastiest stretches of sea around the British Isles. Similarly, the west coast of Ireland is exposed to 3000 miles of Atlantic fetch. It is small wonder that these designs displayed a more robust appearance than the slender sloops of 1672–1673. With the coming of the War of the Spanish Succession these sloops were re-tasked to the warlike duties of surveillance, coastal convoy and fishery protection, where their opponent was no longer the smuggler of wool in a leaky craft that had seen better days but the well-armed French privateer against which the sloop was woefully under-armed. In two cases they became transatlantic packet ships, replacing the two advice boats built at Arundel that may have been designed by Edmund Dummer when he was Surveyor of the Navy.

The main areas of interest are the rig, armament and ballasting of these sloops, since these aspects were of the greatest concern to their captains. There has been speculation about how these vessels were rigged, possibilities including one mast as in the mercantile version of a sloop, or possibly two masts with schooner rig. However, their logs show that they had two if not three masts and that these carried square sails.[24] In almost all cases, substantial changes had to be made to the dimensions of their designed rigs and in some cases to the positioning of the masts or shrouds. For example, in the case of *Merlin*, even before her first commission, the yard officers at Woolwich had reduced the height of her mainmast by 10ft, making

proportional reductions in her other mast and spars. Within one month of her launch her captain had the mainmast moved 2ft further aft, possibly to counteract lee helm. Not surprisingly, less than a year later requests came for her courses to be shortened; they were chaffing the shrouds. For once the Navy Board agreed with the captain's request and he was able to report that 'the sloop doth sail the better for it'. It is also clear that she could carry a wing sail on her mainmast. Another modification by her captain was to move her shrouds further aft, thus allowing her lower yards to be braced round to a more acute angle to improve windward performance.[25] She was probably two-masted at this point (April 1702) but, when sold, part of her inventory included a horse for the mizzen sheet; so by then she had three masts.[26]

The captain of *Bonetta* II fared less well when, having had to cut away his main and mizzen masts in a gale in Brancaster Bay, he had written to their Lordships to ask that she be given a sloop sail (*ie* a fore-and-aft sail) as she would sail more weatherly and be stiffer. There are two interesting points to this request: first, that she had three masts, a fact which can be verified from a log entry for September 1699 that mentions striking the mizzen topmast;[27] second, that her captain must have had knowledge of small ships rigged in bilander – or better, brigantine – fashion, as in the case of the packet boats. However, the Navy Board laid down that 'she would have to go with the sails she had', despite the fact that there were already instances of sloops being issued with bilander sails. Later that year, while acting as escort to four corn vessels bound for Newcastle, the captain had to report an incident in which his command was in danger of foundering.

The stability of these sloops seems to have been a problem not only because their initial sail plans appear to have been over-ambitious but because their shallow draught gave insufficient moment to allow the ballast to counter effectively the heeling forces on the hull. Indeed, at the launch of *Merlin*, her designer, Fisher Harding, advocated 10 tons of lead ballast since it would take up least room in her hold, which already afforded little space. Moreover, he directed that the pigs should be moulded to fit, so they could lie as low as possible to exert the greatest effect.

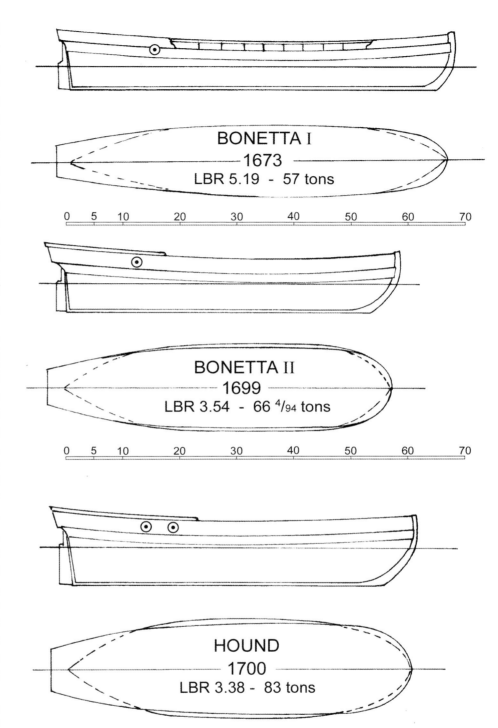

Fig 6-20. A comparison of sloop proportions 1673–1700. *Author*

The other gripe of captains concerned armament. These sloops were designed to apprehend smugglers, not to fight off French privateers. Their broadside consisted of one carriage gun and four patereroes, anti-personnel pieces. However, *Merlin* had had her complement of carriage guns increased to six by 1705, giving three each side; though the captain could cross them over to provide a broadside of five guns using the spare gun ports. Nevertheless, following a partial engagement with four priva-

Fig 6-21. Watercolour by the author depicting a brigantine towing a disabled warship out of the line of battle. In this circumstance it was intended that extra crewmen to help with the rowing would be added temporarily to the brigantine's complement from the warship she was attending.

teers of four to six guns each, he put in a request for 'two carriage guns of five hundred weight each, he having but six, whilst he could fight five a side'.[28] The year before, the captain of *Bonetta* II had requested four falconet carriage guns in lieu of four patereroes which were unserviceable. A similar request came from a sister sloop, the *Wolf*, in the same year.

As with the ketches built at the outset of the King William's War, these sloops, when committed to the next war in 1702, proved unable to cope with the power of French privateers, and in some cases, rated ships from their navy. They could not fight and they could not run. Of the ten sloops launched in 1699–1700, six were taken by the French, but only one was lost at sea, which says something for the seaworthiness of their design. Three were eventually sold on the conclusion of the war in 1712 and 1714. Any future design intended for a fighting role would have to incorporate far more force.

During William's reign, 1689–1702, the Admiralty ordered thirty-five unrated vessels, excluding the very small advice boat commissioned to work in the Solent. These were all launched between 1691 and 1700. None of them had particularly successful careers, which in the main can be put down to a failure to recognise that if a ship is designed for a specific purpose it should fulfil that role satisfactorily, but if it is expected to cover a multitude of other tasks then frequently these will be less well performed. The other major failure of this period was strategic: the Admiralty never devised a method of coping with the attack on trade, including designing small craft specifically for the task, so existing vessels of little strength were often deployed where they were likely to succumb to superior force, without having the speed to escape. Of the 35 vessels built, 16 were taken but only 4 were lost to non-military causes. By 1714 all remaining slooptype craft had been sold.

Chapter 7

EARLY SMALL SIXTH RATES AND THE DEVELOPMENT OF FORE-AND-AFT RIG AND OARED PROPULSION

It may seem surprising to combine a review of small Sixth Rates with a discussion on the management and design of rigs, armament and oared propulsion generally, but the vessels described here display a number of features that were important in the design of sloops during the first half of the eighteenth century. Even the *Drake* (Fig 7-1), built and launched by Pett in 1652, exhibited a flush deck with 18 guns, a ship rig and a raised quarterdeck, all of which were to be incorporated into the design of ship-rigged sloops from 1757 onwards.

The rating of a warship, a classification that goes back to the time of the Commonwealth, depended primarily on the number of guns carried, but by the beginning of the eighteenth century a division of labour had grown up between the six rates. The First, Second, Third and some of the Fourth rates were considered suitable for the line of battle. Although the number of guns varied slightly, depending on specific date and ship, in broad terms these classes were armed with 100, 90, 70–80 and 60–64 guns respectively. However, the Fourth Rate also included the 50-gun ship, which by Queen Anne's reign was no longer considered suitable for the line of battle and was therefore deployed as a cruiser and as a capital ship on minor foreign stations. Down the scale, it was followed by the Fifth Rate ship, which at this time was armed with anything from 44 guns down to 28.[1] These ships were designed primarily for cruising duties and, together with other smaller classes, for convoy protection.

The same role applied to the Sixth Rate, which can conveniently be split into two levels:

ships of between 20 and 26 guns, and those with fewer than 20 guns. It is this latter group which contribute to the development of the sloop category in the first half of the eighteenth century. At the time of the Glorious Revolution in 1688, the only small Sixth Rates to survive from the Restoration Navy were those designed and built by possibly the greatest naval architect of the era, Sir Anthony Deane: *Saudadoes*, *Greyhound* and *Lark* (together with the *Drake* already mentioned, built by Pett).[2] Their average dimensions were about 75ft on the keel, 88ft LGD (by calculation), 22ft on the beam and 9ft draught of water; the burthen was around 195 tons. This gives them an LBR of 4, which is quite slender, and a BDR of 2.4. They

Fig 7-1. Small Sixth Rates like *Drake*, built by Pett in 1652, were ordered to 'ply among the sands and flats to prevent pirates', foreshadowing one of the classic sloop roles. *National Maritime Museum VV0600*

Fig 7-2. A model of the *Peregrine Galley* as first built. The ship was designed by Peregrine Osborne, the Marquis of Carmarthen, as a replacement for one of his earlier creations, the yacht *Royal Transport*, which was given to the Tsar as a gift from England. Note how far forward the main channels are on this two-masted vessel. *National Maritime Museum F5849-002*

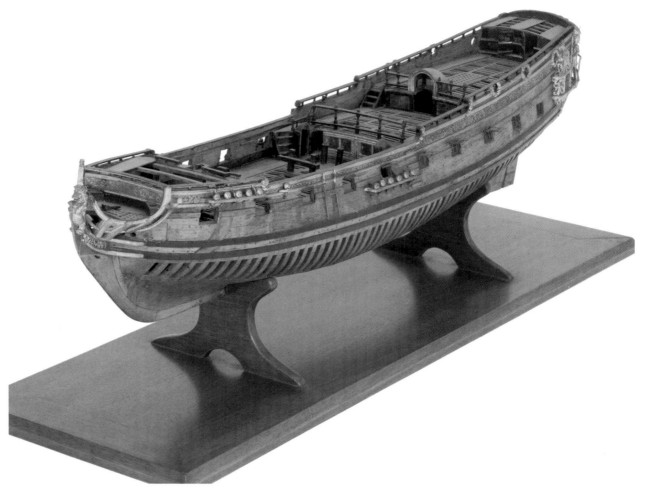

carried variously 14, 16 and 18 guns. Whilst sloops would not reach these dimensions and armaments until the 1730s, the classic roles of these small Sixth Rates (until 1698, by which time they had all been sold) and the later sloops of Queen Anne's reign were the same: coastal convoy, communication, surveillance and fishery protection. In design they were essentially smaller versions of larger rates, though one of their major features prefigured that of the eighteenth-century sloops and frigates: the single flush gun deck.[3]

Before looking further at ships with fewer than 20 guns, there is one vessel, not strictly a Sixth Rate, that demands close attention, because her lines were to have a major influence on sloop and frigate design during the eighteenth century. This vessel was the *Peregrine Galley* (Fig 7-2), designed by Peregrine Osborne, at that time the Marquis of Carmarthen.[4] A serving flag officer and a gifted amateur ship designer, Peregrine Osborne's flamboyant personality and style harked back to the licentious and carefree court of Charles II,

yet he retained influence, certainly in naval circles, in the more austere court of William and Mary. His father, who eventually became the Duke of Leeds, was a leading figure in the revolution that installed William and became an influential figure in the politics of the 1690s, which undoubtedly opened doors to his son's advancement. Despite the often-fraught relationship with his father, in his younger days Peregrine seems to have persuaded him to fund his nautical enthusiasms.

Peregrine's genius as a designer was well recognised in particular for three vessels. One was the *Bridget Galley*, which Osborne employed nominally as the tender to his flagship the *Resolution* (at the state's expense) but actually ran as a very successful privateer (for his private profit). *Bridget* was well-known in the fleet and described as 'an incomparable sailer' by Admiral Sir Cloudesley Shovell, when he strongly urged that the ship be taken as a model for the first advice boats; his suggestion was rejected on the grounds of cost (Osborne was never one for austere or cheap solutions).

The other two, the *Royal Transport* and the *Peregrine Galley*, are discussed here. His speciality was small fast-sailing craft, and these are the largest, and best-known, examples of his expertise. The *Royal Transport* is as much a description as a name, having been built specially for the task of conveying King William to and from his continental campaigns every year. As the king's entourage was vulnerable to both the enemy and the weather while on passage, a nervous government was willing to pay for a particularly fast and well-armed yacht to minimise this risk. The result was judged a great success – so much so that the yacht took the fancy of Peter the Great during his visit in 1698 and the king judged it good diplomacy to gift the vessel to the Tsar.

Although chronologically the *Royal Transport* came first, Osborne's ideas are better understood by starting a more detailed analysis with the *Peregrine Galley*, about which far more is known. The ship's origin was as eccentric and unlikely as her designer, being a form of compensation for a royal debt. Osborne petitioned the king for a pension he was allegedly owed, but persuaded William to let him build another yacht in lieu of payment, perhaps as a replacement for the *Royal Transport*. Not only did Osborne produce the draught, but he was also allowed to oversee its construction in a Royal Dockyard, directing every detail of fitting out, which, as he was not spending his own money, became an acute source of friction with the Navy Board, producing an adventitious dividend of information in the resulting correspondence.

Designed in 1699, the yacht's frames were made up at Chatham before being delivered to Sheerness for assembly and completion by the master shipwright William Lee (he had also built the *Royal Transport* so may have enjoyed a special relationship with Osborne). The new vessel was launched in September 1700 and with no show of false modesty was named after her devisor. Planned as a yacht, she was formally listed as a Sixth Rate and armed like a small cruiser. Originally pierced for 20 guns on her main deck, she was equipped with twenty sakers (5pdrs), sixteen on her gun deck and four on her quarterdeck. Her dimensions were 86ft 6in on the gun deck, 71ft on the keel, 22ft 10in on the beam and with 10ft 7in depth in the

hold. This would have given her a draught of about 9ft 6in; burthen was 196 84/94 tons. Her LBR would have been 3.78 and her BDR 2.54.

Like Osborne's previous yacht, she was renowned as a fast sailer and with the outbreak of the War of the Spanish Succession in 1702 she came to be used as a taxi by VIPs, including Marlborough, needing travel to and from the Continent. Subsequently, she conveyed George I to England following the death of Queen Anne in 1714, and in 1716 was renamed *Carolina* after George's wife, whom she had also brought to England. At this time she was refitted and listed as a yacht. In 1733 she was rebuilt and lengthened by Richard Stacey – to all intents and purposes a new ship – to fit her for duties as the principal royal yacht, being renamed *Royal Caroline*. In 1739 she was re-rated as a Sixth Rate, but was actually refitted for naval service in 1748 as a sloop and renamed *Peregrine*. She was lost at sea in the Western Approaches over the winter of 1761–1762 in storm-force winds.

Her rig is of particular interest because it demonstrates the experimental approach to design so prevalent at the turn of the century, particularly in small warships. Experiments, for the purposes of evaluation and trial, could be more readily applied to small ships rather than

Fig 7-3. The *Pergrine Galley* and a rig that may have been the original intention of her designer. Note the figure standing on the forecastle as an indication of scale. *Author*

those of the larger rates. There is a model in the National Maritime Museum which has been identified as the *Peregrine Galley* as built (Fig 7-2). This model exhibits one very unusual feature, in the positioning of the channels for the mainmast, which is well forward of the midpoint of the hull. This was unusual at this date for a two-masted vessel, but there is no suggestion of a mizzen mast.[5] If the masts were intended to carry square sails this would have created a sail plan that would have made it well nigh impossible for the vessel to make any progress to windward; indeed, such would have been her lee helm that her points of sailing would have been confined to the downwind quadrant. Any sailor who has tried to make headway out of a bay against the wind will know that this sort of weakness can be fatal.

In January 1703 the Deptford yard officers planned to replace her original two-masted rig with a conventional ship rig, listing both her original and proposed mast and spar dimensions.[6] From these it can be seen that she appears to have carried the conventional snow rig but without the snow sail abaft the mainmast. What cannot be determined from the dimensions is whether her yards, or more likely just her main yard, were set up to carry a square or fore-and-aft sails. Peregrine Osborne had a wealth of experience with yachts and had designed, built, rigged and sailed some fast vessels. It is unlikely that he would have designed a rig that was demonstrably so dangerous and unworkable. Therefore, his intention may have been for something other than a conventional square sail plan: perhaps one that included at least a fore-and-aft main course (Fig 7-3).

This is perhaps the right moment to return to the earlier *Royal Transport*, eventually given to Peter the Great in 1698. This small ship, listed as a Sixth Rate, was reputed to be the fastest vessel in the Royal Navy at the time. The Tsar's particular interest in her was supposedly her superior ability to sail into the wind, with the obvious advantage that would confer on a small vessel attempting to evade a larger one. It is most likely that she would have had been partly rigged fore-and-aft to enable her to do this.

Although there is a model that purports to represent this vessel in the St Petersburg Naval Museum, the identification was only made in the nineteenth century and its hull does not conform to what is known about the internal layout of the vessel, so any conclusions to be drawn from its rig and sail plan must be very tentative (Fig 7-4). For example, there is a probability that the foremast was square-rigged, not fore-and-aft as shown in the model. Although at this time the word 'schooner' had not been invented, this is the best description of the rig of the St Petersburg model. The position of the foot of the mainmast is, like that of the *Peregrine Galley*, forward of a midpoint between her stem and sternpost. The other important fact is that she has a boom to her mainsail, which means that the sail can be set to be effective downwind as well as upwind. It would also do much to improve the upwind performance. The use of a boomed-out mainsail for fore-and-aft rigged craft is evident from Dutch paintings as early as 1620.[7] Her dimensions were slightly larger than those of the *Peregrine Galley*, except for her depth in hold, which was less at 7ft 9in as opposed to 10ft 7in. At 90ft on LGD, 75ft on the keel, 23ft 6in on

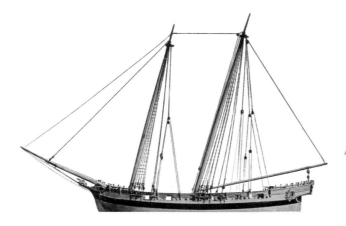 

Fig 7-4. The model in the Central Naval Museum at St Petersburg said to be of the *Royal Transport*. The model is schooner-rigged and is shown here beside an alternative and more plausible rig and stem profile for this vessel. *Author*

the beam and with a draught of water in the order of 7ft, her burthen was $220^{29}\!\!/\!_{94}$ tons.

Whilst the schooner rig for sloops at this period should not be entirely discounted – for example it would be a helpful rig for an advice boat – it was not popular with a conventionally minded navy, which seemed to be in love with square rig. One good reason for this was the ability to back square canvas, which gave fighting ships a manoeuvring advantage in combat, even if it restricted their sailing ability to windward. The Dutch were greater exponents of fore-and aft rig, but they had to be in order to sail up canals and narrow estuaries.

There is an illustration by Van de Velde the younger of this type of rig, seen already in Chapter 4 (depicted here in Fig 7-5). Although the rake of the masts seen in this is considerably less than on the St Petersburg model, the position of the mainmast on both vessels is similar: well forward of midships. However, the lengths of the yards here and on the St Petersburg model are smaller than those recorded for *Peregrine*. Also these examples have no topmasts.

There is one other possible rig that Peregrine Osborne may have had in mind. The illustration at Fig 7-6 contains, at point 'L', a drawing of a packet boat from about the same time as the *Peregrine Galley* was being commissioned. This vessel has a square rig on her foremast and what appears to be a yard, its heel running slightly forward of the mainmast, able to carry a large lug sail as a main course (see enlargement in Fig 6-19). Again, the mainmast is well forward in the hull. The picture is of further interest in that in the right foreground is a small armed vessel running with what by 1700 might be called a brigantine rig (Fig 7-7). This may be a merchant vessel as she carries no commissioning pennant. In the left foreground is another small vessel this time carrying a naval jack and setting the basic Biscay rig. Her yards are well braced round to almost a fore-and-aft posture. This could possibly be a sloop if the drawing is post 1702 since before that time all the English sloops were in Irish waters.

The demands on the *Peregrine Galley* were to be similar to those on a packet boat, requiring an ability to make fast passages often against the wind. Here may be an explanation for this seemingly odd arrangement of masts on the model. Nevertheless, the fact that a year and a

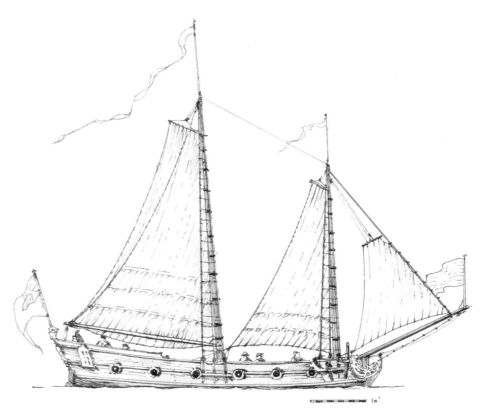

Fig 7-5. Schooner rig was used on large yachts not much smaller than the *Peregrine Galley*. *Author*

half after launch she had to be given ship rig points to a mistaken conception of her initial rigging and its balance. It is also worth noting that the yachts in the Van de Velde painting are possibly of 140–150 tons displacement, therefore not all that much smaller than the *Peregrine*'s 195 tons.

Returning now to the *Peregrine Galley*'s hull, (Fig 7-8) there are some differences between the surviving plan and the model above. The plan shows Stacey's modifications for the 1733 rebuild. The ship is now 79ft on the keel and 91ft overall. The channels now accept a conventional ship rig, although she would already have had ship rig at the time of the alteration. The stem has been re-cut to a concave as opposed straight profile presenting a better gripe, but this was normal for the early Georgian navy. There is an extra pair of gun ports shown on the draught, but those aft of midships contain glazed lights to the accommodation spaces, as is the case in the original model. The quarter-light has been enlarged. The quarterdeck carriage guns have been replaced by swivels as the deck here has largely been removed. However, these alterations only affect habitability and did not change the all-important shape of her hull. She was noted as a fast sailer so it is instructive to consider why.

Fig 7-6. (Right) This excellent
panorama of Harwich by
Johannes Kip gives a clear
picture of two-masted rigs as
they were around 1700, but
the vessel of particular
interest is the packet boat
(marked 'L') anchored just
above the town (see Fig
6-19). *National Maritime
Museum PY9672*

She starts with a LBR, using the length on the
gun deck, of 3.96. Although this is not as
extreme as some of the sloops of 1672–1673, it
is nevertheless a slender hull. Her run and
entrance are hollow and because of her high
LBR they do not cause sharp curves in the
waterlines, which would create eddies. In fact,
her run is so fine that she could have had difficulty with the positioning of guns in her quarters unless they were very light, such as 500lb
falconets. Her midship section is comfortable
and sea-kindly. The hull is a blend of the lines of
the Stuart royal yachts and the Restoration
Sixth Rates rather than the Pepysian sloops,
which had a very small draught of water and a
LBR of between 5 and 6. Until the influence of
French design began to affect that of British
sloops in the 1750s, the shape of the majority of
sloops constructed from 1728 onwards are
broadly similar to this galley/yacht/sloop.

The term 'galley' leads us to consider another
feature of early Sixth Rates that bears on the
design and general arrangement of the early
eighteenth-century sloops. This concerns the
age-old problem of how to manage the often-
simultaneous needs of rowing, operating the
guns and managing the sails. In the galley fleets
of the Mediterranean this had not been a
problem since the main armament was ranged
across the vessels at the bow and stern leaving
the sides completely free for oars. Also, with a
lateen rig the demands and complexity of sail-
handling were significantly reduced. Whilst
these narrow vessels fought under oars and had

Fig 7-7. Detail from Kip's
prospect of Harwich,
showing a small vessel
carrying what might have
been described at the time as
a brigantine rig.

A Prospect of the Towne & ?
Bullingbrook one of her Maj. Prince
A. The Queens Yard & Store house B. the Queens Key C. S.
W the Harbour behind the Towne & the River leading to Man
old by Tho. Taylor at the Golden Lyon near the Horn Tave

HARWICH

r of HARWICH.   Humbly Dedicated to the Right Hon.ble Henry Lord Viscount
retaries of State Lord   Lieutennant of y.e County of Essex & Recorder of y.e Towne of Harwich

ch D. the Towne hall E. the Gate   Leading to London & the Fire Light house over it F. the Candle Light house G. Landguard Fort
ll Haven K. the River leading to   Ipswich L. the Pacquett Boats M. the Breakers N. West street O. Shotley Gate house P. Shotley Church.
t, and by Rob.t Hulton at the   Corner of Pall mall over against the Hay market S.t James

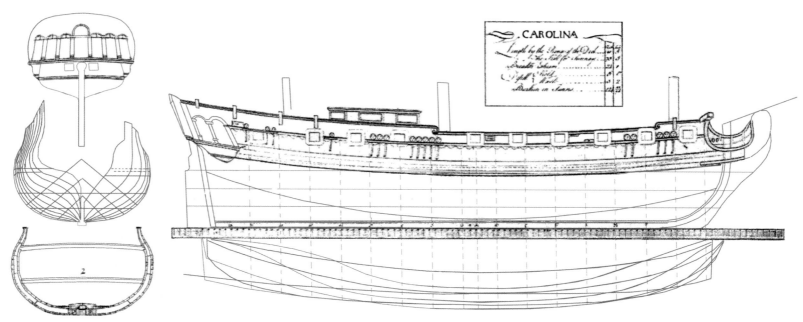

Fig 7-8. A draught showing the lines of the *Carolina*, redrawn for the 1733 rebuild by Richard Stacey. Although the hull was enlarged, the form does not seem to have been altered substantially. The draught from which this plan was taken is not available online and has not been scanned. *National Maritime Museum*

tactics to suit their armament and propulsion, a later creation, the more beamy galleass, was designed to fight under sail and oar and had some difficulty in managing these three operations simultaneously.

This problem had been addressed in England as early as 1515 in the design of Henry VIII's *Great Galley* and later in 1546 in a smaller craft called the *Bull*. Both these ships deployed oarsmen on the main deck with a gun deck above. Interestingly, the *Bull* was similar in deck layout and displacement to a sloop design of 1730. A proposal of 1625 (Fig 7-9) also illustrates this arrangement and shows a single bank of well-spaced sweeps, each worked by four men, all standing. A similar arrangement was provided for the *Charles Galley*.

Built for the primary purpose of defending English trade against the Barbary pirates, they proved to be too slow despite having three men to each sweep. They may have been too heavily built, whereas the pirates possibly favoured a lighter construction.[8] This arrangement for rowing was to surface again in 1689 for a radical new type of Fifth Rate which carried a few guns at either end of what was essentially a deck cleared for rowing. In a cut-down form, this layout was the basis for the 20-gun ships of the 1719 Establishment and from them developed the classic frigate form of the later eighteenth century.

Except in one instance, which will be discussed later, this arrangement of the oar banks below the gun deck could not work for

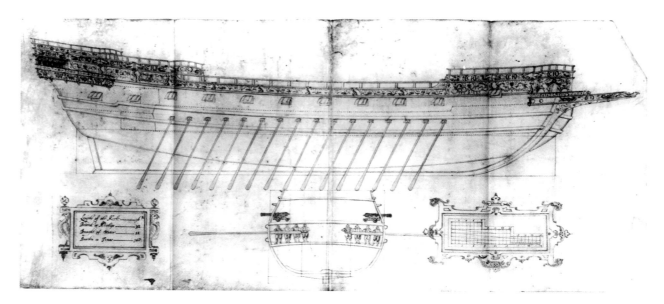

Fig 7-9. This early draught of a projected vessel from around 1625 shows that the separation of sweeps from guns was a preoccupation in the early days of the Stuart dynasty. Note the cross section and the lack of headroom for the standing oarsmen. *National Maritime Museum F3026*

the sloops, mainly because they were low and small, which would mean that 'tween deck space would have been severely limited unless the oarsmen sat to row. Indeed the *Peregrine Galley* would have been unable to use this arrangement since the deck under her weather deck was below the waterline. Her model at Fig 7-2 has no oarports shown, but her name suggests she was intended to be rowed. In later usage, oar scuttles were easily cut (and stopped up with equal facility), but there are also examples of smaller ships deploying sweeps from the gun ports.

On the early sloops of the Restoration and on the brigantines of the Williamite navy, the separation of armament and oarsmen was horizontal. Their ordnance was either placed on their quarters or on the forecastle, with oarsmen, probably seated, taking up the waist of the vessel. This could not be done on a small Sixth Rate as it would preclude the use of a proper full-length broadside. Therefore a compromise was made whereby guns and oarsmen were placed on the main deck with the guns being positioned towards the bow and the stern providing a short waist for the oarsmen and, over both, a weather deck with its own armament on its quarterdeck. The weather deck also allowed for the unimpeded handling of the sails whilst rowing was in progress in addition to providing some shelter for the oarsmen and gunners when in action.

This alternative to vertical separation is demonstrated in a controversial model, briefly mentioned earlier (Fig 7-11), from the Henry Huddleston Rogers Collection at the United States Naval Academy Museum at Annapolis. The identification and rig of this model has perplexed nautical scholars for a century. The model originally formed part of the collection of Charles Sergison, Clerk of Acts to the Navy Board from 1690 to 1719. His collection seems to have formed a representative cross-section of the various rates and classes of ships within the navy he administered.

R C Anderson, one of the earliest experts on sailing warships, inspected this model before it left England, together with the rest of the Sergison collection, for the United States of America in the 1920s. He suggested that the model was probably built to the usual 'official' scale of 1:48, which would give the proposed

ship 80ft on the gun deck, 64ft on the keel and a beam of 21ft 6in. This would give her a LBR of 3.72, which is slender.[9] He also made a sketch-plan of the model, which shows the covered waist in which the oarsmen would have sat (Fig 7-12).[10] The broadside of nine gun positions, including two each side of the quarterdeck, makes this an 18-gun vessel, which would be well into the Sixth Rate category at this date. The waist of the vessel has seats – not shown – for 40 men, thus two per sweep. Whether both oarsmen sat to row is not known, but the seats would indicate that there was space for them to do so.[11]

An earlier chapter raised the possibility that this model might perhaps represent an advice boat, but there is another candidate. The dimensions are close to those of an early Sixth Rate, the *Hind*, designed and built by the ex-Surveyor

Fig 7-10. This magnificent modern model at 1:48th scale of the *Charles Galley* by Keith Smith demonstrates how the rowing and fighting was separated on the galley-frigates of the late seventeenth century, which carried their main armament above a deck principally devoted to working the sweeps. However, even on this lower deck there were gun ports right forward and aft for chase guns in a form of horizontal separation imitated in the early sloops. *Keith Smith*

Fig 7-11. This view of Model No 2 in the Henry Huddleston Rogers Collection illustrates the separation of oars from guns in the horizontal plane. The battery is disposed before and abaft the rowing deck, which is only just lower than that of the gun deck – presumably to give the oarsmen some headroom or to bring their oars closer to the water level. There is a spar deck over the gun and rowing decks. *By courtesy of Grant Walker*

Fig 7-12. Anderson's sketch plan of the model at Fig 7-11. Note the spar deck as a dotted line. Like the deck below, it is not flush. From *The Mariner's Mirror*, Vol VIII/2.

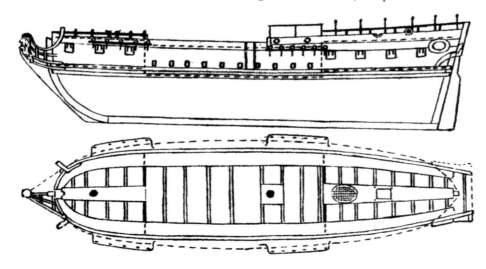

of the Navy Edmund Dummer. She was launched in 1709 and wrecked in the same year.[12] Although there is much of Dummer's thinking reflected in this model, both in rig and hull design, particularly in the use of a 'pink' or 'cat' stern which gave more strength and in the removal of the glazed window from the quarter badge, which became purely decorative, it is unlikely that it represents the *Hind*. The degree of decoration is too lavish for 1709, which is when the *Hind* was launched, and the gripe, the forefoot of the stem, is cut to a point as opposed to a small curve, tending to place the ship represented into the seventeenth century. Finally, there is strong evidence that, despite their small

size, the Sixth Rates acquired at this time were ship-rigged, or at least originally intended to be. Be she Sixth Rate or advice boat, the vessel portrayed is unusual in her layout. This concept was not lost, however, because in 1730 master shipwright Richard Stacey designed a sloop using the same arrangement – except that in her case she was to be rowed from both the weather and the main decks simultaneously.

When the model came to be restored it was in very poor condition and devoid of any rigging so all that the restorer had to go by were the mast steps inside the hull and the number and position of the deadeyes for the shrouds. R C Anderson, from whom he requested advice, suggested the rig might 'probably be that of a brigantine'.[13] This may have been an ingenious guess and Anderson may have realised that to make sense the rig had to be able to set a fore-and-aft sail on the mainmast for reasons already outlined. To reiterate: this ability was available to the small brigantines of the 1690s, by the conversion of their tall buss sail main course into a lug sail. Indeed some were issued with lug sails for use in summer. This arrangement was to carry the word 'brigantine' forward, not as a class of warship but as a form of rig, so that the fore-and-aft rigged mainmast was to become the identifying characteristic of the brigantine of the eighteenth century. Unfortunately the restorer of this model placed a conventional square course on the mainmast instead of the more flexible and taller 'buss' sail, producing a rig that would be downright dangerous if used in a full-size version.

Although not of an early Sixth Rate, there is a delightful portrait by John Cleveley senior of a 10-gun sloop of about 1750 that shows her with a brigantine rig using a lug or bilander sail as the main course (the lug sail arrangement was usually referred to as bilander rig). Strictly speaking, by this date a brigantine rig usually incorporated a fore-and-aft main course suspended from a gaff spar.[14] Note the fall of sail cloth at the fore end of the lug yard, which prevents one confusing this with a lateen sail: no lateen sail could be furled in such a way (Fig 7-13).

As a closing comment to this chapter it is worth pointing out that the majority of sloops in the first half of the eighteenth century did not use the arrangements discussed above, preferring to place oar ports between the gun positions, an arrangement that had been used for small Sixth Rates in the Restoration navy. To operate the sails, guns and oars simultaneously in this fashion would have been particularly difficult and it perhaps accounts for the declining priority given to oared propulsion as a design requirement as the eighteenth century unfolded.

Many take the view that the naval administration of William III's government, and to an extent that of his successor Anne, was less competent in matters of warship design and construction than the administration run by Pepys and James II. In fact, as far as the smaller warships were concerned, its record is one of willingness to try a wide range of innovation and experiment, probably driven by the novel challenges of war with France. There was continuity in the influence on hull design of the royal

Fig 7-13. A close-up from a perfectly detailed painting of a sloop of about 1740 by John Cleveley the elder. She is rigged as a bilander or hollander, *ie* one of those ships that ran the packet service to Holland. She may carry a main course in addition to her large fore-and-aft bilander sail. *National Maritime Museum BHC1043*

yachts introduced in the Restoration period whose sleek lines moulded the design of Fifth and Sixth Rates and eventually the sloop of war; but there was also an exploration of new options for managing oars, guns and sails that was to last well into the otherwise-conservative eighteenth century. For the sloop of war class this was to include flexibility and variety in the design of sail plans both for operational and purely experimental reasons.

Chapter 8

THE BOMB VESSEL AND FIRESHIP
1683–1712

Whether or not bomb vessels and fireships should be included in the 'sloop' family is open to question. In the case of fireships, their claim to be a sloop comes only from their occasional use in the cruising role. They do not share any intrinsic feature with the sloop, since for the most part they were conversions of old, small warships, usually Fifth or Sixth Rates or they were suitably altered merchant vessels or prizes (Fig 8-1). Ideally two full decks were required, the lower deck with ports that would fall open, thereby creating a draught to fan the

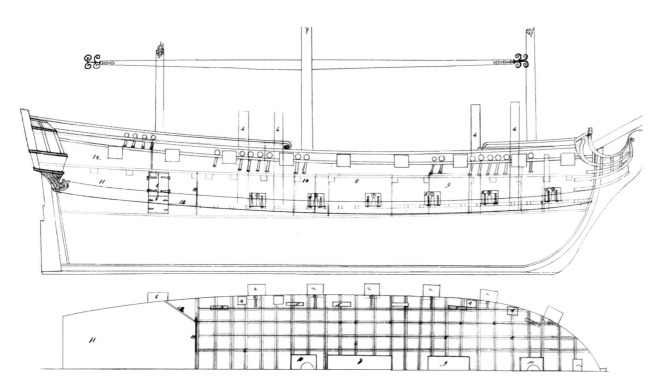

Fig 8-2. Plan of a fireship showing the detailed preparation needed for the 'tween decks fire-room. Note the yard with grappling hooks at its ends. *Rigsarkivet, Copenhagen*

fire. This same deck would also be compart-mentalised for the containment of combustibles (Fig 8-2). So from the point of view of form they were very different, in the majority of cases, from the sloop, where one of the main features in many of them was just one flush gun deck. Furthermore, fireships usually had three masts, again a contrast to the sloops of this period, which generally had two.

There were only two occasions in their history when fireships were purpose-built. Those constructed in 1689–1694 were similar in layout to the smaller rated vessels and were ship-rigged. However, in the second instance (1781–1802) they resembled a contemporary ship-sloop, with hull lines derived from a French prize captured forty years earlier. They were consciously designed for fast sailing – primarily to enhance their effectiveness in fire-ship attack – but their qualities would have made them effective cruisers; in practice they were generally employed in sloop roles. Using a fast and handy sloop form makes sense since these attributes would assists in positioning itself for a fireship attack, which was usually best made downwind and down tide.[1]

In fact, the closest connection between the sloop and the fireship is as opponents. As explained earlier, the naval sloops of 1672–1673 were built specifically to deal with the fireship threat, either by towing the target

vessel away from the fireship's course or by attempting to divert the fireship itself; an heroic duty indeed.

Fireship successes are well recorded, but even when they were unsuccessful they could have a significant impact. In 1588, when the Elizabethan navy wished to force the Armada further eastwards from its anchorage in Calais roads, Drake proposed the use of the weapon, knowing that the likelihood of burning any Spanish vessels was slight, but that the terror they would induce in the Spanish would cause them to cut and run, which is what they did. This tactical use of the weapon was not lost on either the English or the Dutch, who both strove to employ it in the Anglo-Dutch wars, the Dutch with the greater success. In 1639 the Dutch had also deployed it with effect against the Spaniards, who had unwisely anchored in the Downs in a position from which escape was difficult. And it was this factor, the inability of a target to move, that was the prerequisite for the successful expenditure of a fireship. This ideal situation may not have occurred all that frequently. Of the twenty-five fireships acquired between 1689 and 1694 only six were expended, of which only three reached their targets.

Three stark examples of the requisite situa-tion are the burning of 170 Dutch merchantmen off the island of Vlie in 1666 by Sir Robert

Holmes; the destruction of the crippled and un-supported English flagship *Royal James* at the Battle of Solebay in 1672 (Fig 8-3); and the disposal, by the English, of fifteen French line-of-battle ships at La Hogue and at Cherbourg following the Battle of Barfleur in 1692. In the last case only three fireships were used, two meeting their target. At la Hogue, because the French ships had been grounded and for the most part abandoned, the alternative of ships' boats, crammed with the necessary materials, was used in conjunction with one fireship. From all this it is obvious that a degree of helplessness is required of the target for this method of engagement to be successful.

Both bomb vessels and fireships were specialised warships, which meant that they could only be used on specific missions, so their use 'in role' was spasmodic. Therefore, in a navy that was perennially short of small warships for the mass of minor but essential tasks, these two ship types were readily co-opted to cruising roles. In both cases the re-conversion to a general duties vessel could be effected quickly and, most importantly, did not

require the vessel to be hauled out of the water.[2] So this was an attractive proposition in that these precious assets, whose designed function was rarely required, were not left lying idle and were able to contribute to the security of offshore and coastal trade.

The claim for the bomb vessel to be part of the sloop family is rather stronger than that of the fireship. Not only were the first bomb vessels based on the form and rig of the ketch – a member of the sloop family and possibly what might be regarded as the eldest – but the roles of the vessels were interchangeable. This was particularly so after 1730, when an improved rig that gave better sailing ability for general work, and a finer shape of hull, meant that bomb vessels could be commissioned as sloops and later fitted out for shore bombardment, and vice-versa. But this same arrangement was applied in many cases during the wars of the League of Augsburg and the Spanish Succession.

The story of the bomb vessel starts in France towards the end of the seventeenth century, possibly as a result of frustration. For decades the Christian countries of northern Europe and

Fig 8-3. The *Royal James* engaged with a Dutch fireship at the Battle of Solebay. This attack was successful and the English three-decker was destroyed. *National Maritime Museum BHC0302*

their Mediterranean-bound mercantile trade had been plagued by the piratical policies of the Barbary states lining the North African littoral. Unfortunately, most of these states fielded very fast ships and galleys which were adept at taking prizes and were particularly difficult to catch. They also had a ready refuge in heavily fortified Barbary ports. One solution to this problem was to reduce their port defences and then destroy their shipping. For a conventional navy using naval guns this was a difficult task as elevation, which gave range and height to a trajectory, was impossible to achieve when firing through a gun port and from a conventional carriage. The solution was provided by a French engineer from the Basque country, Bernard Renau d'Elicagary. He applied one of the weapons developed on land to reduce fortifications, the mortar, for use at sea. It was first used against Algiers and, shortly after, Genoa.

The mortar is an 'area weapon', meaning that it is not particularly accurate or consistent in its fall of shot. However, its salient characteristics are an ability to fire over the top of high cover (Fig 8-4), to deliver an explosive munition rather than a solid shot, and to achieve a range of fire sufficient to keep the mortar itself out of danger from enemy counter-measures. There were four difficulties in using it on board a small warship. First was the damage to the vessel's rigging that might be caused by the blast of the departing projectile. This was solved by using a ketch rig for the bomb vessel, allowing the mortar to fire over the bows, the fore rigging having been drawn back to the main and leading mast situated behind the mortar.[3] Second was the enormous shock to the structure of the vessel resulting from the discharge of the mortar. Initially various methods were used, including laying the mortar on an earth bed which in turn would be positioned and supported by a timber framework and the use of chain or, better, heavy rope cable underneath the mortar's emplacement to cushion the force. Subsequently, a strong structure was built up underneath the deck to take the force of the discharge and the weight of the mortar. Third was the question of coping with the sea and wind, and finally there was the problem of finding the right range with a weapon that had a fixed elevation. These last two points will be dealt with later.

Fig 8-4. Watercolour of an early bomb ketch, modelled on the *Serpent* class of 1695, on the point of discharging one of its mortars, which by this stage, 1695, could be traversed. *Author.*

The ketch was a well-known type in England, but not so in France. The French introduced a vessel based on the Dutch galliot, a strong, beamy vessel usually associated with fishing, but it also had a ketch rig. The French modified the hull to include a square stern, as opposed to the more prevalent pink stern used by the Dutch and the English. The Dutch rig for a galliot was often a fore-and-aft one but the French set up a square rig for their model, which was more often found on the 'dogger', a heavy round-hulled fishing buss. The French called their new vessel a *galiote à bombe*. This beamy vessel and its rig gave them the opportunity to install two mortars side by side ahead of the mainmast. By chance or design (it is uncertain which), the earliest operations of this weapon system were observed by a man whose name is already familiar: Edmund Dummer. At the time, 1683,

Fig 8-5. This clever cut-away sketch of a French bomb ketch was made by Edmund Dummer during his visit to the Mediterranean in 1682. From his manuscript book *A Voyage into the Mediterranean* in The British Library.

his talents as a naval draughtsman had already been recognised, and he was engaged on a tour to inspect Mediterranean shipping.[4] It is unlikely that he was able to get on board one of the new vessels, but the information he gleaned is impressive in its detail, and included an analysis of the effects of the French bombardment of Genoa in 1684. Dummer employed his excellent drawing skills to record his intelligence of these vessels in a sketch and a draught to illustrate their design.

From his drawing at Fig 8-5, it can be seen that the mortars are fixed, side by side, in the waist of the ketch and protected by a high forecastle and bulwarks. The mainstay and associated rigging has been drawn aft to the mainmast. A defensive broadside of three small guns is in place under the quarterdeck and finally the vessel appears to be moored by both its stem and stern. This last observation points to the third main difficulty facing those using this sort of artillery at sea: the sea itself and the wind.

Provided an admiral chose his weather carefully, he would have little difficulty in causing a high degree of destruction at cities such as Algiers or Genoa, both ports bombed by Louis' new weapons. The Mediterranean would be calm, there would be little wind to make the bomb vessel sheer around at her mooring, and no tide to force the vessel into an alignment that

took it off target. The French mortars were fixed in their emplacements, therefore the only way that the target could be engaged was by pointing the bow of the vessel straight at it. By contrast, consider the target to be St Malo, where the tide rips in and out at high speed and where the weather can be unreliable: success and accuracy under these conditions would have been hard to achieve unless some other method of alignment was used. In due course this was to be worked out by the English.

Dummer presented his findings to his king, but it would be three years before England was to start the production of these vessels in 1687–1688. The shape of the hull and the type of rig was broadly the same as used by the French, along with two side-by-side mortars, but the craft was given a larger complement of guns for self-defence (Fig 8-6). The first construction programme was ordered in 1687 for two ketches, *Salamander* and *Firedrake*, each to carry two 12¼in mortars. As with the French method, these were fixed in elevation and traverse, so the positioning of the vessel itself was going to be critical to success. Unlike the French *galiotes*, which were all built to similar dimensions, these two vessels were very different from one another, with *Firedrake* having twice the burthen of *Salamander*. This should not surprise us as the new vessels were in the experimental stage, and it may have been an attempt to discover a workable minimum size.

Joining this programme in 1688 was the sloop *Portsmouth*. She was one of the royal yachts, built by Phineas Pett in 1674 and she had already been in service as a cruiser. Her burthen of 144 tons, and her force, far exceeded that of any sloop at that time; indeed, there were very few sloops left in the 1680s, particularly after the big disposal of 1683. Her rebuilding was extensive in that apart from the timber framework to support the mortars, changes were made to her conventional armament. Additionally her rig had to be altered from the single mast, fore-and-aft rig of a yacht to that of a two-masted square-rigged ketch. She was recommissioned as a sloop of 16 guns in 1689 and then returned once again to being a bomb vessel in 1694. She and all her crew were lost in the great gale of 1703. The group was joined in 1692 by a smaller yacht of only 103 tons, the *Kitchen* (Fig 8-7), so named because

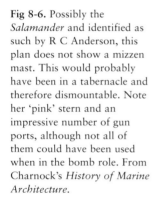

Fig 8-6. Possibly the *Salamander* and identified as such by R C Anderson, this plan does not show a mizzen mast. This would probably have been in a tabernacle and therefore dismountable. Note her 'pink' stern and an impressive number of gun ports, although not all of them could have been used when in the bomb role. From Charnock's *History of Marine Architecture*.

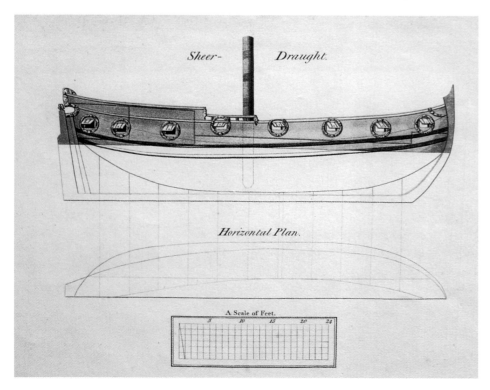

Sheer-   *Draught.*

Horizontal Plan.

A Scale of Feet.
5   10   15   20   24

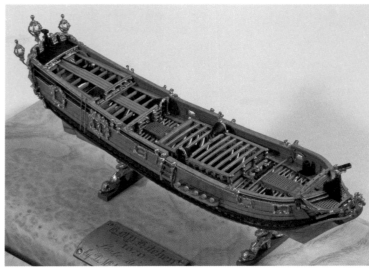

she was fitted to provide food for the royal yachting excursions of the preceding monarchies. Being small, it is probable that she carried only one mortar. She replaced *Firedrake*, one of the purpose-built ketches, which had been taken by the French in 1689.[5]

This group was attended by a support ship, an old Fifth Rate prize, the *Helderenburg*. This opens the question of the logistical support to bomb vessels. The beds and framework for the mortars took up much of the space that would normally have been available for accommodation and stores, including ammunition. This was doubly important when the English started to place mortars in column rather than abreast. Furthermore, the weight of the mortars if carried at sea could make the vessel crank in rough conditions. So a vessel was needed to carry stores, ammunition and occasionally the mortars themselves. The support vessel also acted as a 'dormitory' for the artillerymen, seconded from the army, to operate the mortars.[7]

Although the bomb vessels were to be ordered and commissioned whilst James was still king, they would not see action until William III had replaced him in 1688. Both the purpose-built bomb ketches sailed with Admiral Herbert to Bantry Bay on the southwest tip of Ireland in 1689 to contest the landing of French troops and material in support of James's invasion. The engagement could have been more successful but one surprise did come out of it. Captain John Leake of *Firedrake*, the son of the Master Gunner of England, managed at some point in the engagement off Bantry Bay to blow

up the poop of a French 54-gun ship, *Le Diamant*; she did not sink but she was severely damaged. If this was done with a mortar shell, fired from a mounting with no ability to traverse or elevate, this success must have owed something to luck![8] Following this battle the bomb vessels returned to the Channel, thereby missing an opportunity. Had Herbert attached them to the small squadron that Captain Rooke took north to support the relief of Londonderry, they could have made a substantial difference to that operation.

Apart from the difficulty of setting the trajectory and direction of the bomb, the Royal Navy wrestled with another problem, namely the inability of the ketches to sail sufficiently well to keep up with the fleet and to be able to make oceanic passages when required. Part of the difficulty arose from the need to accommodate the weight of the mortars and their emplacements amidships, which meant that the main (and leading) mast had to be further aft than ideal. This would have made them unhandy and slow, particularly off the wind. As a result for the next generation of bombs in 1693 a decision was made to choose ship rig. By this time Edmund Dummer had become Surveyor of the Navy and was insistent that the new vessels should have a foremast, mainly due to the size of the vessels. To prepare these ship-rigged vessels to fire, the foremast, its rigging and the mainstays would all have had to be dismantled, which would have taken an age and was probably impractical in an actual combat situation. Dummer therefore argued logically that the foremast should be a pole mast with but one sail

Fig 8-7. Two views of the Stuart yacht *Kitchen*. These give some idea of the amount of work that would be required to re-rig and refit the vessel for use as a bomb. The mortar would have fired from a point in the vessel's waist. The mainmast would be well aft of this point with the mizzen at the fore end of, what is here, the poop deck. This model was built by Donald McNarry to a scale of 1/16th of an inch to the foot (1:192). It is only five and a quarter inches long![6] *By courtesy of Pauline Chard*

Fig 8-8. This early draught of
the ship-rigged bomb vessel
Mortar looks very much like
a Sixth Rate of the time.
Much larger than the earlier
vessels, she was of 270 tons
burthen. Her mortars and
those of the other three in her
class were originally arranged
side by side ahead of the
mainmast, as shown here. At
this time her mortars would
have been fixed and were
designed to fire ahead. The
foremast was probably some
form of pole mast with
minimal rigging to dismantle
before opening fire.
Rigsarkivet Copenhagen

set on it and that to be a buss sail. To speed up
preparations for firing, the mast would have to
be lowered, so Dummer advised some sort of
tabernacle arrangement whereby the mast was
to be folded forwards onto the bowsprit, as was
the practice with hoys 'when they went under
bridges'. Bomb vessels were an early example of
a 'joint-service' weapons system, and the preparation of the bombs was under the overall
control of a military engineer, Colonel Thomas
Phillips. After trials with two of the new bomb
vessels he worked out a way of firing the
mortars without dismantling the fore rigging.
Unfortunately, he is not specific about how it
was achieved, but it may imply that Dummer's
proposed pole mast (but stepped on the deck,
not folding) was adopted.[9]

Mortar was a member of the *Firedrake* group

ordered in 1693. *Firedrake* had been taken in
the Channel in 1689, so the first vessel of this
group was named in commemoration of her.
The group comprised four vessels, all of similar
dimensions and close to those of the original
Firedrake, whose builder, Fisher Harding, seems
to have taken the lead with the design of the
new class. Because the first two, somewhat
experimental bomb ketches had not been satisfactory, the Navy Board enlisted the aid of a
Frenchman named Jean Fournier. Presumably
one of the many Huguenot refugees fleeing
persecution in France, Fournier had been
involved in the construction of such vessels for
Louis' navy at Toulon. A new position with the
impressive title of Master Builder of Bomb
Vessels was created for him, but whilst his experience of mounting mortars in a hull was

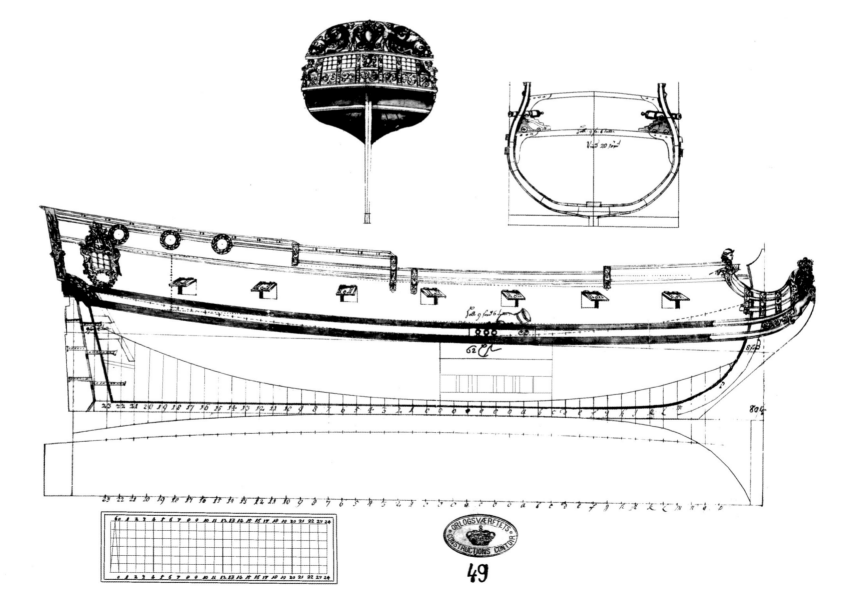

helpful, his views on the type of hull were not. Wisely the Board declined his recommendation for a broad and flat-bottomed hull on the grounds that whilst such a shape might work in the Mediterranean, the sailing ability of such a craft would not be up to the requirements of the Royal Navy, which specified long-distance passage-making, often in hard weather.[10]

In the event Harding came up with a design (Fig 8-8) closer to a Sixth Rate cruiser than to a beamy, slow galliot. This group were rather larger than all but one of the earlier group with an average burthen of 270 tons. These new vessels were first deployed by Admiral Benbow and Colonel Phillips in an attack on St Malo in 1693, but although they may have sailed better than the first bombs, their poor performance at shore bombardment highlighted a more pressing shortcoming. The main contributor to the failure of the attack was the vicious tidal current in the approaches to the port, the third problem referred to earlier. Bombardments were carried out at anchor and the only time that these vessels could be pointed at their targets was at slack water, which does not last for long in that area. No amount of effort with a spring on the mooring line would allow the bombs to traverse onto target across the tidal flow. The upshot of this was that the English were to design a traversing mounting for the sea mortar, allowing bombs to be anchored in the most favourable position in relation to the tide while the mortars were swivelled on to the required firing line. This was the idea of another artilleryman, Colonel Jacob Richards, who had long been a leading exponent of the use of mortars on land. His invention would make a significant change in the design of the future bomb ketches. In the meantime the enthusiasm for this new weapon system did not falter.

The adoption of a traversing mortar rendered redundant the arguments about rig, and it is perhaps surprising that this did not lead to the retention of ship rig. This would have been perfectly workable, as was shown later in the 1750s and beyond, and indeed in the refitted *Mortar* – the impressive sketch (Fig 8-9) by her captain shows her in 1702, with a full three-part fidded foremast. Nevertheless, it was to a class of new ketches that the improved equipment was to be delivered. Ten new ketches of the *Blast* or *Serpent* class were ordered and

Fig 8-9. The bomb vessel *Mortar* as she was at Vigo in 1702 (drawn by her captain), now with a proper fidded three-part foremast. This was presumably allowed by the new traversing mortar mountings, but it is not known how they were disposed at this time, side by side or fore and aft on the centreline. Note the small openings below the line of gun ports; these are too small for sweep ports and probably represent ventilation scuttles.

launched in 1695. They were smaller, at 143 tons average burthen, than the preceding *Firedrake* group. The adjustable mortars now permitted one mortar to be placed in front of the mainmast and one behind it. Whilst this afforded the possibility of reducing beam, thereby allowing for a smaller vessel, it did mean that the aftermost mortar had a restricted arc of fire between the main and mizzen shrouds. On the other hand, dispensing with the ship rig meant that the forward mortar now had an arc of fire that must have approached 220 degrees if the mainstay was removed.

With the exception of the prototype, the sloops of this new class were built by commercial contractors. At the same time a number of merchant vessels were purchased to add to the bombardment force.[11] Commercial building and purchase of merchant hulls for conversion are indicative of the operational urgency for this weapon. The strategic aim was to attack the Channel ports of France to divert the efforts of Louis' army from their action against William's forces in the Low Countries. It also satisfied the purpose of attacking the French privateers, which were causing such havoc amongst the English and Dutch commercial shipping, by rendering their bases untenable. The campaign was waged mainly in 1694 and 1695 and was a great disappointment; certainly as far as the damage wrought on the French ports and shipping was concerned. The merchant ship conversions were all sold by 1698 and one as early as 1695. They would have been less useful as sloops than the purpose-built models, five of which survived both wars to be broken up or sold between 1713 and 1725.

Fig 8-10 provides a general arrangement of the *Blast* class of bomb vessels. It illustrates the

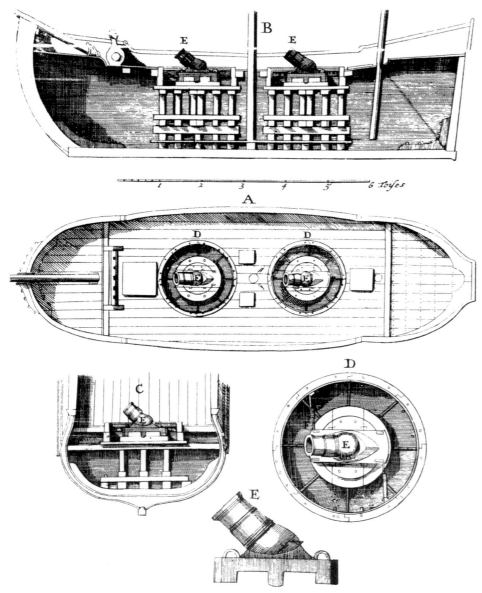

this model is that there are no gun ports. All the bombs of 1694–1695 were armed with a minimum of six guns. There appears to be little room available for guns on this model and it is possible that when set up for shore bombardment, the vessels carried a reduced, or no, defensive armament; they were employed as part of a fleet so could rely on escorts to protect them. The capstan at the aft end of the vessel is there not for mooring purposes, but rather to control the spring used to adjust the vessel's alignment. This may have been an English arrangement since the Navy's craft were used in the Channel tides. In the tide-less Mediterranean the French method of relying on warps from the stern as well as the bow may have been sufficient to achieve the desired heading. See Fig 8-5 above.

this model is that there are no gun ports. All the bombs of 1694–1695 were armed with a minimum of six guns. There appears to be little room available for guns on this model and it is possible that when set up for shore bombardment, the vessels carried a reduced, or no, defensive armament; they were employed as part of a fleet so could rely on escorts to protect them. The capstan at the aft end of the vessel is there not for mooring purposes, but rather to control the spring used to adjust the vessel's alignment. This may have been an English arrangement since the Navy's craft were used in the Channel tides. In the tide-less Mediterranean the French method of relying on warps from the stern as well as the bow may have been sufficient to achieve the desired heading. See Fig 8-5 above.

The arrangement at Fig 8-12 allows the force of the tide to be used to good effect. By trimming the spring, a fine adjustment could be made, although given that by 1695 the English had mortars that could be traversed, the fine adjustment of the ketch's heading may no longer have been so important. The direction of the anchor is where the tide is coming from or the resultant combination of wind and tide.

Fig 8-13 is of the quarterdeck of a rigged model of a bomb ketch of about 1695. Made by Bob Lightley, it is based on the drawing of *Thunder* above at Fig 8-10, on the lost model from the Science Museum at Fig 8-11, and on sketches made by the captain of the *Blast*, a bomb from the same class. This model raises a number of issues. The restricted arc of fire for the aft mortar is shown by the position of the portside shrouds. The stepping for the mizzen mast appears not to be a tabernacle, which would allow the foot of the mast to pivot, thereby aiding its erection, but a rather simple casing with straps to hold the mast in place. If it were taken down before going into action, how this was done is hard to fathom; if it were not, the capstan might be hard to turn given that the mizzen mast and mortar emplacement are likely to block the passage of the capstan's bars, and there is no evidence of where a spring might enter the hull through a turning block. The other mystery is that there is no space for any guns for self-defence, which is backed by the drawings of *Blast* that show no gunports, only a quarter-badge being represented (Fig 8-14).

Fig 8-10. Although this drawing is from a French publication, it is thought to be of *Thunder*, which was captured by them in 1696. It shows the first of many British improvements to the effectiveness of bomb vessels – the traversing mountings on the centreline that allowed two mortars to be carried in narrower, and therefore smaller and cheaper, vessels. The elevation was still fixed. From Pierre Suriry de Saint Remy, *Memoires d'Artillerie*, 1698.

large amount of space required for the timber framework supporting the mortar beds, and shows the design for the traversing emplacements and the method of setting up the timber supports. Point E shows the fixed mounting for the mortar placed on its moveable bed. The windlass on the forecastle was for the mooring cable, but as shown at Fig 8-11, there should be a capstan aft to allow for the use of a spring attached to the anchor cable. This would allow the crew to veer the vessel in order to bring the mortars' arcs of fire onto the target. The mizzen here is indicated by its deadeyes and channels, but it is not clear how it was stepped, whereas on the plan at Fig 8-10 it is stepped on the keel. The advantage of being able to dismount the mizzen mast is that it increases vastly the arc of fire for the aft mortar. The surprising feature of

Fig 8-11. This model formerly in the Science Museum is now lost. It demonstrates the traversing emplacements for the mortars, although the aft mortar is missing. Note the tabernacle for the mizzen, the capstan and the windlass.

The established defensive armament was only four tiny 2pdrs, so these may have fired over the bulwarks.

The English had solved the problem of traversing the mortar, though the French continued to use fixed emplacements until well into the eighteenth century. There remained the fourth problem: that of trajectory. Colonel Richards developed a method of varying the charges to alter the range of shot but a mortar for sea service and with a variable elevation would not be developed until 1726. This is covered in a later chapter.

This discussion can be brought to a close by considering the strategic background to the use of the bomb vessel. To be able to bombard an enemy's coast required the attacker to have command of the sea, at least for the duration of the operation. By 1694 the French had largely surrendered that command, partly through the destruction wrought upon their Atlantic fleet at Barfleur and La Hogue and partly because the bulk of state finances were being directed at the army, leaving little for the improvement or repair of the fleet. But behind that lay the lack of will on the part of Louis, whose mind was directed to the continent rather than the oceans. It is ironic to see the country that invented the bomb vessel unable to use it because it did not have command of the sea, whilst its opponent

could choose when and where he wished to attack and could do so with impunity. This was not lost on 'Dutch William' who now realised that because he had mastery of the seas, he could use his navies to influence the war on land by supporting operations in Spain and by attacking the French coasts.

The War of the League of Augsburg was a high point in the use of the bomb vessel. England had taken a French invention, improved it considerably and then turned it against its inventor. Yet the invention had not been particularly successful in the level of damage it caused. Despite this it may have helped to support William's strategy in the Low

Fig 8-12. This diagram shows the use of a spring laid onto the mooring cable to veer the vessel and adjust its heading. The forces would be considerable, hence the positioning of a capstan towards the stern of the vessel in addition to the windlass in the bow. *Author*.

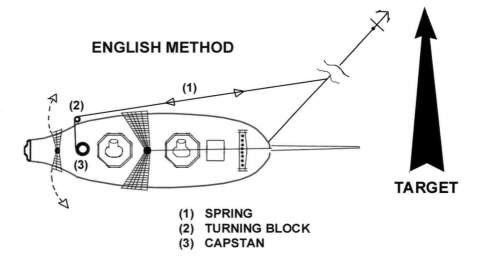

ENGLISH METHOD

(1) **SPRING**
(2) **TURNING BLOCK**
(3) **CAPSTAN**

TARGET

Table 8-1: THE PRELIMINARY GROUP OF PURPOSE-BUILT BOMB KETCHES, 1688–1692

Name	*Salamander*	*Firedrake*	*Portsmouth*	*Kitchen*
Ordered	1687	1687	1688 conversion	1692 conversion
Launched	1688	1688	1688	1692
LGD	64ft 4in	85ft 9in	71ft 0in	59ft 0in
LoK	54ft 6in	68ft 0in	59ft 0in	49ft 6in
Beam	21ft 6in	27ft 0in	21ft 4in	19ft 6in
LBR	2.99	3.18	3.32	3.02
Depth in hold	8ft 4in	9ft 10in	9ft 0in	8ft 0in
Burthen	134 tons	279 tons	143 tons	100 tons
Mortars	2 x 12¼in	2 x 12¼in	2 x 12¼in	1 x 12¼in
Guns	10	12 + 6 swivels	10	8
Men	35	50, later 65	50	30
Rig	Ketch	Ketch	Ketch	Ketch
Fate	Rebuilt 1703, sold 1713	Taken 1689 in Channel	Lost 1703	Sold 1698
Builder	Lee, Woolwich Dyd	Harding, Deptford Dyd	Pett, Woolwich Dyd	Castle, Rotherhithe

Fig 8-13. This drawing by the author is based on a model of the *Serpent* class bomb ketch *Thunder* by Bob Lightley. It illustrates the position of the capstan but on the model there is no indication of where a fairlead block might be for the spring, so this is suggested in the drawing.

Fig 8-14. A drawing by Captain Martin of his bomb ketch *Blast* showing her dismasted and under jury rig during a voyage from Newfoundland in November 1697. He went on to command the ship-rigged *Mortar* of whom he also made an engraving, Fig 8-9.

Countries and in the Mediterranean. Its use in the next war was to be concentrated in the latter theatre with attacks on Barcelona and Toulon and in the defence of Gibraltar.

In 1698 England possessed eleven bomb vessels. By the end of 1703, one year into the War of the Spanish Succession, three had been lost at sea and one taken. The three lost were all from the 1693 group of ship-rigged vessels. *Salamander*, the prototype bomb of 1688, was rebuilt in 1703 so England had eight vessels on hand for the rest of the war. All the commercial vessels hired for the previous war had been sold between 1695 and 1698, the last year of the war. No new vessels were ordered throughout the second war and a much reduced use of bomb vessels was evident. The attacks on the privateering bases in 1694 and 1695 had not reduced the commerce-raiders' activity and the Admiralty chose to deal with that threat by building Sixth Rate cruisers to escort merchant convoys. This in turn was not entirely successful and had to be supported by the Cruisers and Convoy act of 1708 which allocated naval shipping to fixed sea areas, a policy almost certainly not to the liking of senior naval officers. However attacks were made on Ostend in 1706 and on St Valéry at which bomb ketches were present.

During the War of the Spanish Succession, John Churchill, Duke of Marlborough, did not need diversionary attacks on the coast to assist the land battle, as he and Prince Eugene of Savoy were proving more than a match for the French armies. But naval pressure was helpful in the Mediterranean. The main effort in this theatre was the attack on the French naval base at Toulon. This was a joint operation by an army approaching from the east supported and, in some aspects, transported by the Allied fleet. Five bomb ketches were involved in the actions at Toulon against the French fleet. The land assault faltered, but the bombardment achieved a limited success when the French sank most of their ships in shallow water to avoid this kind of attack, but aggressive French deployment of batteries forced the withdrawal of the ketches.[12] The Mediterranean continued to be the centre of attention for bomb vessels when, after the war, the British continued hostilities with Spain until Admiral Byng roundly defeated their fleet in 1718 at the Battle of Cape Passaro. To underline the long-range abilities of these craft, a pair of bomb ketches was attached to the St Lawrence expedition in 1711, and another pair was deployed to the Baltic in 1713 as soon as hostilities with France were over. Some of these deployments found the ketches acting in a cruiser role, but with the ability to resume their primary task if required.

No new bomb vessels were to be acquired until 1728, partly due to a long 'peace' that developed after the end of the War of the Spanish Succession. However, some strategic issues remained unresolved, the chief of which was the continuing competition between the Spanish and the British for domination of the Mediterranean and the western Atlantic and thereby the control of trade upon those waters.

DETAILS OF BOMB VESSELS, 1688–1695

Apart from the purpose-built bomb vessels listed, there were nine converted ex-merchant vessels during 1694–1698.[13] These are not detailed below since they were only used in the shore bombardment role and had little or nothing to do with the work of sloops. What

these lists also show is the extraordinary speed with which these vessels were built using commercial yards, particularly in the *Blast* class programme of 1695.

Table 8-2: THE SECOND *FIREDRAKE* GROUP OF PURPOSE-BUILT BOMB VESSELS, 1693

Name	*Firedrake* II	*Granado*	*Serpent*	*Mortar*
Ordered	1693	1693	1693	1693
Launched	1693	1693	1693	1693
LGD	85ft 2in	87ft 0in	86ft 0in	86ft 0in
LoK	66ft 0in	72ft 10in	69ft 9in	69ft 9in
Beam	24ft 1in	26ft 10in	26ft 6in	26ft 6in
LBR	3.53	3.24	3.23	3.23
Depth in hold	9ft 10in	——	9ft 9in	9ft 9in
Burthen	279 tons	279 tons	260 tons	260 tons
Mortars	2 x 13in	2 x 13in	2 x 13in	2 x 13in
Guns	12 sakers + 6 swivels	12 sakers + 6 swivels	12 sakers + 6 swivels	12 sakers + 6 swivels
Men	65	65	65	65
Rig	Topgallant ship	Topgallant ship	Topgallant ship	Topgallant ship
Fate	Foundered 1703	Blown up 1694	Wrecked 1694	Wrecked 1703
Builder	Harding, Deptford Dyd	Fowler, Rotherhithe	Lee, Chatham Dyd	Lee, Chatham Dyd

Table 8-3: *SERPENT* OR *BLAST* CLASS OF PURPOSE-BUILT BOMB KETCHES, 1695

Name	*Serpent*	*Thunder*	*Furnace*	*Granado*	*Carcass*	*Basilisk*	*Dreadful*	*Blast*	*Terror*	*Comet*
Ordered	1695	1695	1695	1695	1695	1695	1695	1695	1695	1695
Launched	1695	1695	1695	1695	1695	1695	1695	1695	1695	1695
LGD	65ft 6in	65ft 6in	65ft 6in	64ft 5in	66ft 6in	72ft 2in	66ft 10½in	66ft 1in	65ft 8in	66ft 1½in
LoK	49ft 8in	50ft 6in	50ft 6in	50ft 6in	50ft 6in	57ft 4in	50ft 6in	50ft 6in	50ft 6in	50ft 6in
Beam	23ft 0in	23ft 5in	23ft 2in	23ft 5½in	23ft 2in	23ft 2in	23ft 6in	23ft 1in	23ft 6in	23ft 2in
LBR	2.84	2.79	2.82	2.74	2.87	3.11	2.85	2.87	2.78	2.85
Depth in hold	10ft 0in	10ft 0in	10ft 0in	10ft 0in	10ft 0in	10ft 2in	10ft 11in	10ft 0in	10ft 2in	10ft 0in
Burthen	140 tons	147 tons	144 tons	148 tons	143 tons	164 tons	147 tons	143 tons	149 tons	143 tons
Mortars	2 x 12½in	2 x 12½in	2 x 12½in	2 x 12½in	2 x 12½in	2 x 12½in	2 x 12½in	2 x 12½in	2 x 12½in	2 x 12½in
Guns	4 x 2pdr	4 x 2pdr	4 x 2pdr	4 x 2pdr	4 x 2pdr	4 x 2pdr	4 x 2pdr	4 x 2pdr	4 x 2pdr	4 x 2pdr
Men	30	30	30	30	30	30	30	30	30	30
Rig	Ketch	Ketch	Ketch	Ketch	Ketch	Ketch	Ketch	Ketch	Ketch	Ketch
Fate	Taken 1703	Taken 1696	BU 1725	BU 1718	Sold 1713	BU 1729	Burnt 1695, St Malo	BU 1724	Taken 1704	Taken 1706
Builder	Lee, Chatham Dyd	Snelgrove, Limehouse	Wells, Bermondsey	Castle, Deptford	Taylor, Rotherhithe	Redding, Wapping	Graves, Limehouse	Johnson, Blackwall	Davis, Limehouse	Johnson, Blackwall

Chapter 9

THE FIRST SLOOPS OF WAR
1704 – 1719

Fig 9-1. The taking of HM Sloop *Ferret* in Cadiz bay in 1718 on her way to the Mediterranean as part of Admiral Byng's fleet, a deployment that was to result in the destruction of the Spanish fleet at Cape Passaro. *Ferret* was probably rigged with a single mast on commissioning, but by this date she had been refitted with a snow rig, as would be the survivors of the similar sloops built in 1710–1711. *Author*.

The war of the Spanish Succession formed a pivotal period in the development of the sloop. It would see the bringing together of the various sloop specialisations – advice boat, brigantine, escort, bomb ketch and even fireship – into one class and embodied in one vessel, generic in nature: the sloop of war. It is therefore the purpose of this chapter to examine the factors driving this amalgamation of roles. This involves taking stock of the position at the outset of the war, then looking at the threat posed by the French *guerre de course* as practised in waters adjacent to the British Isles, which will then lead naturally to the British response.

There is no doubt that for both of the wars against France, covering the turn of the century, England and her ally, the Dutch Republic, were poorly equipped to deal with the huge increase of French privateering activity. Following the

defeat of their Atlantic fleet, at Barfleur-La Hogue (1692), the French had turned to a war on trade – what they termed the *guerre de course* – as the best way of attacking their opponents' economies. The hiring or lending of what remained of that fleet to privateering syndicates produced squadrons that were often more powerful than the over-stretched Allied trade defences. The augmentation of this 'piratical' warfare affected both oceanic and coastal trade, including fishing and whaling activities. The Allies attempted to meet the problem first by attacking the privateering squadrons in their ports and then, when this proved to be ineffective, by increasing the stock of Sixth Rate escorts.[1] Whilst this was of some value to the business of oceanic convoy, it was an incomplete answer since it did not solve the problem of protecting the commercial use of inshore and shallow waters.

The answer did not lie in a return to the construction of outdated escort types. Such a response would inevitably lead to the loss of these vessels to powerful French privateers. In the interim, the Royal Navy transferred twelve of its tougher and better-armed bomb ketches, when available, into the cruising sloop role to supplement the meagre resources. However, they were less than ideal for this work and six were lost during the war. Additionally, without the prospect of a serious fleet battle with the French, the six brigantines, normally attending the fleet, could be switched to the provision of coastal convoy. To this force Britain was also able to add eight small sloops that had been built to prevent wool-smuggling in the short gap between the wars from 1698 to 1702.[2] As soon as the second war started they were re-tasked to

provide convoy. These little sloops were robust vessels and if they had been given a decent armament they might have made a worthwhile contribution to coastal escort work. Some attempt was made to increase their armament, usually in response to pleas from their captains, but this only brought them up to six guns.[3] Not being designed for this role, their gun ports often turned out to constrict the working of their guns, particularly in elevation. Early on in the war four of these little sloops would be captured, usually by French privateers of considerably greater force, leaving three to survive and be sold in 1712.

All the brigantines bar two had survived the previous war and it is noteworthy that in this new war only one was taken by the French.[4] Nevertheless, they were old and lacked seaworthiness. During the course of the war another two were broken up and one was sold. The remaining two were sold at the end of hostilities in 1712–1713. There were also two advice boats available. One, used for the transatlantic run, was wrecked in the Great Storm of 1703

and was replaced by two larger sloops; the other survived the war. Two old ketches entered the war but one was quickly taken and the other sold soon after.

This, then, was the starting position. It had become clear that British unrated warships were unsuited to the new levels of violence offered by the French and that a more powerful and better armed type was required for the protection of coastal trade and to fulfil duties outside home waters in the Mediterranean and in the Americas.

During this war the Royal Navy managed to augment its force of sloops with fifteen French prizes, mainly privateers, carrying between 10 and 18 guns, though one, *La Nymph* of Calais had only 4. On being brought into British service, they were all classified as small Sixth Rates, probably because they carried the three-masted ship rig and had up to 18 guns. Plans survive of two of these craft, *La Gracieuse* and *Le Saint-Sulphice*, captured early on in the war (1702 and 1703), and they show the form of French shipbuilding for small ships at the turn

Fig 9-2. *Rochester's Prize*, a French privateer taken in 1702 was very similar to this *frégat légère* designed by Cochois in 1697. *Musée de la Marine, Paris*

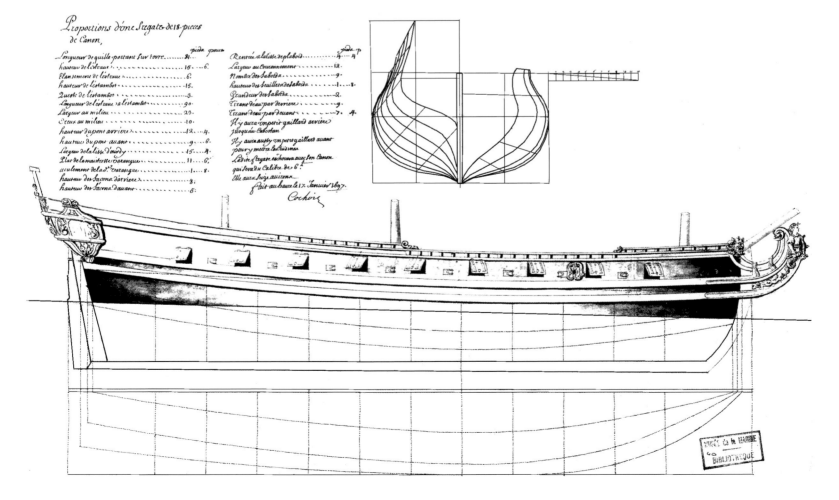

of the century. More importantly they were an example to the Admiralty that things had moved on since the War of the League of Augsburg. The first at Fig 9-2 is of limited value in that no waterlines are included. The lines shown are fairing lines but from them and from the body plan it seems that the vessel has a very fine run. The design portrayed here is of an 18-gun *frégat légère* for the French Navy by Phillipe Cochois at Le Havre, who also designed *La Gracieuse*, again of 18 guns, so it is a safe assumption that she was somewhat similar to this plan. What this plan does reveal is the type of vessel facing the small sloops and brigantines of the Royal Navy. In terms of force she falls between the 12-gun sloops and the 24-gun Sixth Rates. Perhaps significantly, she was taken by the far larger 50-gun ship *Rochester*.

The second plan at Fig 9-3 depicts another 18-gun ship, *Le Saint-Sulphice*, but this time a privateer. She has an additional armament on the quarterdeck and has a greater height of topside. Her hull form is rather different, displaying a body that is probably fuller than *La Gracieuse*. The waterlines show the intent to achieve fine lines at bow and stern but her midship section is very different – an early version of what would become a common French form, with short floors and a two-turn bilge, but a rounder overall shape and markedly less deadrise than later examples. The hull is also shorter and deeper, so whilst she may well be the better sea-boat, she is unlikely to be as fast as *La Gracieuse*. However, she did enjoy a

reputation as a fast sailer and, at a later point in this chapter, her lines will be compared with those of the smaller British sloops of 1710–1711. She was taken by *Advice*, another 50-gun ship.

The generally unsatisfactory state of affairs was eventually recognised in 1704, possibly prompted by the examples of the French privateers, by the placing of orders to build what might be seen as the first sloops of war capable of independent action. Once again, Edmund Dummer was the inspiration behind a new class of vessel. Having been dismissed from the Navy Board in 1698, he had set up his own yard to build packet boats for the transatlantic run. Dummer had probably been behind the design of their naval equivalents, the 'oceanic' advice boats of the 1690s, but he now proposed vessels to 'cruise on the coast of this Kingdom' and 'to row with oars'.[5] In March 1704, the Navy Board was instructed to contract with him for two such vessels and, by way of comparison, to have a third built to the same specification at Woolwich Dockyard by William Lee. All three, armed with twelve 3pdrs, were launched in the same year. *Drake*, a fourth and rather larger sloop of greater force, was launched in 1705, again at Woolwich, but by a different builder, John Poulter.

The specifications for these vessels point to a massive increase in dimensions, burthen and firepower in comparison to all the earlier purpose-built sloops of the seventeenth century, which were rarely of more than 60 tons burthen

Fig 9-3. *Advice Prize*, ex-French privateer *Le Saint-Sulphice*, a very powerful small warship of 26 guns. Note that her commander's cabin is on the quarterdeck rather than below as was more normal. *National Maritime Museum J6871*

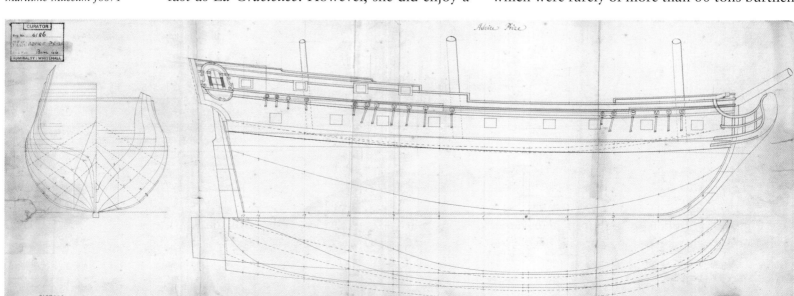

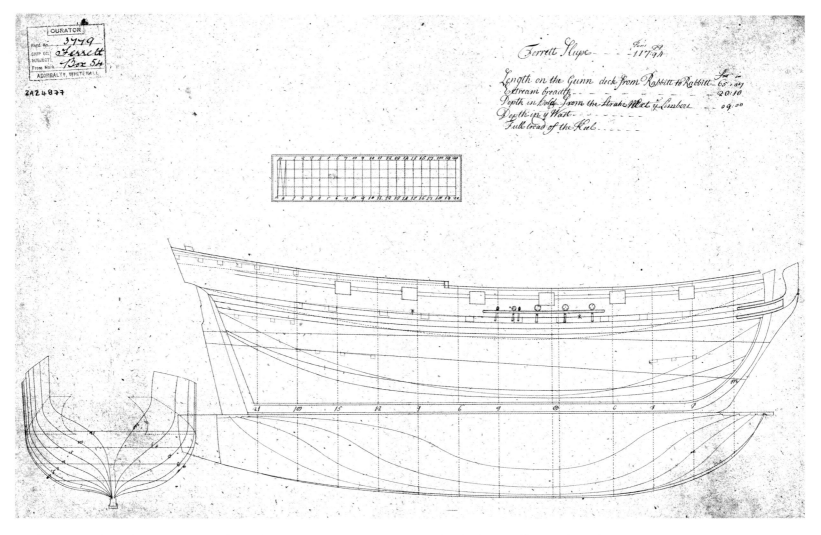

Ferrett Slupe — 1179 4

Length on the Gunn deck from Rabbitt to Rabbitt — 65:04
Extream breadth — 20:10
Depth in hold from the Strake Next y Limbers — 09:00
Depth in y Wast —
Full tread of the Keel —

and equipped with 2-4 guns. What these new vessels looked like is unknown but they probably resembled the large advice boats built at Arundel in the previous decade, a view prompted by Edmund Dummer's remark that they were 'to row with oars' since these vessels and the earlier advice boats were designed with that in mind. They had, however, a smaller armament and dimensions, particularly their depth in hold, which would suggest that they were designed to operate in shallow water.

Both of Dummer's sloops, *Ferret* and *Weazle*, were launched on the same day, 9 September 1704, having been ordered in March. The dockyard version, *Swift* II, by Lee was ordered in April and launched in October. *Ferret* did not last long, being taken by six French privateer galleys off the coast of Flanders in 1706, but *Weazle* and *Swift* II both survived the war. *Drake* also survived the war and had a successful career serving in the Mediterranean and Channel, taking two French privateers

towards the end of the conflict. After the war she served on one expedition to the Baltic and lasted until 1728 before being broken up for a rebuild at Deptford. She was more powerfully armed than the *Ferret* group, having fourteen 3pdr guns to their twelve.

Edmund Dummer's yard, now at Rotherhithe, was also to launch two small Sixth Rates as part of the response to the Admiralty's order of 1709 for three vessels, specifically required 'to free the coast of the enemy's privateers, which are daily lurking thereon'. A further two were then ordered, followed by another three of similar size purchased while building: a total of eight vessels. One of his small Sixth Rates was the *Swan*. She had dimensions that were very close to those of the *Swift*, the advice boat that had been built at Arundel in the 1690s, whilst Dummer was Surveyor of the Navy, and possibly modelled by HHR 2 (Fig 9-5). This vessel should not be confused with *Swift* II, the sloop built by Lee at Woolwich in

Fig 9-4. Original draught for the *Ferret* of 1711. Her lines make an instructive comparison with those of *Advice Prize*, 1703 (Fig 9-3). *Ferret* had an LBR of 3.1 which, in order to acquire a fine entry and run, meant introducing severe curvature to her lower waterlines – with attendant problems of turbulence. *Saint Sulphices*'s LBR was leaner, at 3.34, giving her gentler waterlines. Both have the midship bend well forward. *National Maritime Museum J0218*

1704. The fact that this group were all of a similar burthen and dimension to the *Swift* advice boat may suggest that Dummer's was the greatest single influence on the design of minor warships at this time, be they sloops or small Sixth Rates. It is arguable that this group of eight small Sixth Rates should have been classed as sloops, despite the fact that they are reputed to have had ship rig. Certainly their size, names and armament all lie more comfortably in the sloop category; besides which they were all commissioned under commanders, the appropriate rank for the captain of a sloop.

Before leaving this group, it is necessary to take one final look at HHR Model 2. This has been carefully re-measured by the historian of the Rogers Collection and has been shown to be close to both the advice boat *Swift* and the Sixth Rate *Swan* in dimensions and proportions. Were the model to have had a small mizzen mast with a lateen course and square topsail, she might well resemble these small Sixth Rates.

The model's hull is pierced for 14 guns, as was the *Swift*'s, and has 4 on the quarterdeck although she was credited with carrying only 10 with some swivels. On the other hand, the Sixth Rates of 1709 carried fourteen 4pdrs. The conclusion must therefore be that there is a high likelihood that these small Sixth Rates, or at least those by Dummer, would have been similar in appearance to this model.

The closing years of this war saw the emergence of a permanent role for the sloop of war – overseas. In 1710 the *Jamaica* group of two sloops was proposed by Sir Charles Wager specifically for deployment to the West Indies. They, and the four that followed them in 1711, were a departure from the practice of earlier sloops in that they had only one mast and a fore-and-aft rig. This may have been related to a rig popular amongst the islands of the Caribbean and parts of the North American coast.

The plan of *Advice Prize* at Fig 9-3 bears comparison with that of *Ferret* II at Fig 9-4. The comparison illustrates the problem of trying to set up fine lines for a small and short vessel. In narrowing the ends of the hull 'humps' are created in the waterlines which induce turbulence that disrupts the smooth flow of water around the hull and therefore impedes the speed of the vessel. Another interesting feature in the case of *Ferret* II is the complete absence of 'tumblehome', that is the narrowing-in of the hull side above the waterline. The French were keen exponents of extreme tumblehome, as can be seen in the plan of *La Gracieuse* and to a lesser extent that of *Advice Prize*. The reasoning behind this practice may be connected to stability, in that the closer the guns were to the centreline of the vessel the less tender or crank she would be. Whilst this may be so, the disadvantage would be an increase in rolling (it reduced the righting moment, the tendency to force a heeling ship upright) and made for a cramped deck for gun-handling. The Navy Board may have felt that a sloop carrying a large amount of fore-and-aft canvas – and therefore optimised for windward performance – needed to be as stiff as possible: hence a LBR of 3.1, a beamy vessel indeed, and no tumblehome. She would certainly have had spacious decks. This 'wall-sided' design was hardly ever repeated in the period covered by

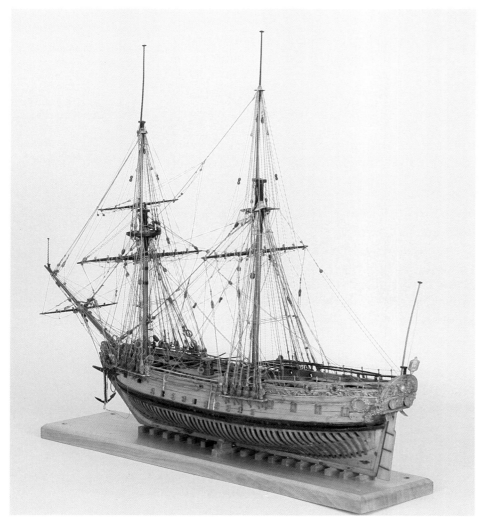

Fig 9-5. A view of Model No 2 in the Henry Huddleston Rogers Collection at the United States Naval Academy. It shows the inadequacy of the mainmast's sail plan. The model was in great disrepair when delivered to America and the restoration in the 1920s, which included much of the rigging, did not reflect the use of a large fore-and-aft main course. At a credible scale the model is close in measurement to the two small Sixth Rates launched by Edmund Dummer in 1709. Note the use of the cat stern shown in Fig 4-4. *By courtesy of Grant Walker*

this book, but there is another unusual feature in the 'drag' to the keel, which gives the vessel an appreciably greater draught aft than forward. Most sailing ships were set up to draw more water aft than forward, but up to this point in time it was rare to see such a pronounced form of the arrangement.

The reconstruction at Fig 9-6 has been developed from the information in the original draught. In the sheer plan here, the buttock–bow lines have been laid off from the body and half-breadth projections. These buttock–bow lines give a good idea of the shape of the hull if cut vertically. The gradient of these lines as they pass the designed waterline give an idea of how smooth will be the flow of water: the steeper the gradient the more turbulence will be created and thus the greater the drag on the hull. These lines are crossing the waterline aft at approximately 25–35 degrees, when an angle of near 13 degrees would be preferable. Nevertheless, her run appears, from these lines and the body plan, to be clean and straight, if albeit a bit steep. But that cannot be avoided on a short beamy hull. Returning to the plan of *La Gracieuse*, it should be noted that the length of the keel in relation to the length on the deck is much closer than on *Ferret* II. This allowed the French to draw out their lines, creating a smoother flow of water. Nevertheless, the *Jamaica* group must have been a success since, out of that group of four sloops and the two sloops of the *Happy* group, built to the same specification, no fewer than three were rebuilt between 1719 and 1724. Either their timbers must have been excellent or they had proved to be ideal for the task for which they were designed.

This group did have one design weakness – their rig (Fig 9-7). Apart from purchases or prizes, the Navy would never again use a single-masted sloop.[6] There could be a number of reasons for adopting this particular rig – and for getting rid of it. It may have been considered particularly suitable for passages amongst the islands of the West Indies and it would have certainly given the sloops better windward ability than most other vessels in that area, with the obvious tactical advantage that would offer. But there has to be a risk in that if the mast is lost in battle or as a result of severe weather, it leaves the sloop virtually helpless until some

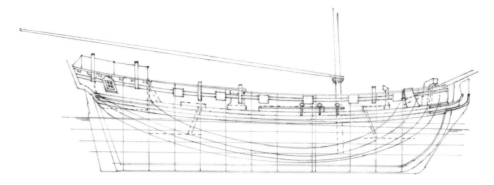

form of jury rig can be set. Other reasons may have been that the size of the main course meant that in some conditions, such as a tough squall, it could have become uncontrollable and that in a broadside engagement the rig would have offered less manoeuvrability than a two-masted square rig. In any event, all those that survived past 1717 are likely to have been given a snow rig.

A better understanding of the original rig of these sloops can be gained by examining the log of *Trial*, one of the first pair ordered by the Admiralty on the advice of Sir Charles Wager.[7] The log confirms her single mast rig but it also mentions the use of a jib boom. This must be an early manifestation of the spar onto which would have been set a flying jib; that is, one that did not run on a stay. However, it is unclear if the other sloops carried a jib boom. *Trial*

Fig 9-6. A reconstruction of *Ferret* by the author showing the buttock–bow lines plotted from the body plan and half-breadth plan on the original draught.

Fig 9-7. A possible single-mast rig for the *Jamaica* and *Happy* classes of sloop. Those not already lost had all been re-rigged as snows by 1719. Note the early use of a boomed-out main course. *Author*

Fig 9-8. A detail from a watercolour painting dated May 1747. The main picture is of the Sixth Rate *Sheerness* and this could be one of her French prizes, although it exhibits some of the characteristics of British sloops of the early eighteenth century. Intriguingly, in May 1746 *Sheerness* recaptured the sloop *Hazard* II which had been taken by Jacobites and turned over to the French. *National Maritime Museum PU8482*

retained a single-mast rig until 1719 when she was rebuilt and at the same time given a two-mast snow rig (see Chapter 1, Fig 1-34). Shortly after this her mast positions had to be brought further aft, presumably to balance her better. Eventually it was decided to give her a 'brigantine' rig.[8] Three further points are of interest in her rig. The log mentions the use of a cro'jack yard on her mainmast but at times it is also called a main yard, which would suggest the habit of setting a square mainsail on an occasional basis. In 1728 there is mention of a fore topgallant yard but there is never any suggestion of a main topgallant yard. It seems reasonable, therefore, to regard the mainmast as a tall mast with a small topmast secured by iron bands and supported by crosstrees.[9] Finally, in this latter half of her career she is recorded as having a fore gaff, which could suggest that she had a wing sail abaft her foremast and was therefore some sort of schooner. This is an incredible litany of rig alterations and it proves the point that to recreate a sloop's rig it has to be related to a specific vessel at a specific date, since many of them changed their rig frequently. The vessel at Fig 9-8 is possibly a French privateer, yet she has a rig that is the same as that described in *Trial*'s log, though this vessel appears to carry no boom for her gaff-headed sail.

These little sloops were well armed. *Ferret* II here (Fig 9-9) is pierced for 12 guns though she was equipped with only 10: eight 4pdr and two

Table 9-1: THE *FERRET* GROUP OF SLOOPS, 1704

Name	*Ferret*	*Weazle*	*Swift* III	*Drake* [1]
Ordered	1704	1704	1704	1705
Launched	1704	1704	1704	1705
LGD	72ft 0in	71ft 11in	73ft 5in	83ft 8in
LoK	60ft 0½in	59ft 11½in	60ft 6in	70ft 2½in
Beam	20ft 0½in	20ft 0¼in	19ft 7in	21ft 8¼in
LBR	3.59	3.59	3.73	3.84
Depth in hold	7ft 3in	7ft 1½in	7ft 6in	6ft 6in (from lower deck)
Burthen	128 tons	128 tons	123 tons	176 tons
Guns	12 x 3pdr	12 x 3pdr	12 x 3 pdr	14 x 3pdr
Men	80	80	80	85
Rig	Sloop	Sloop	Sloop	Sloop
Fate	Taken 1704	Sold 1712	Sold 1719	BU for RB 1728
Builder	Dummer, Blackwall	Dummer, Blackwall	Lee, Woolwich Dyd	Poulter, Woolwich Dyd

1 A one-off rather shallow vessel not part of *Ferret* group.

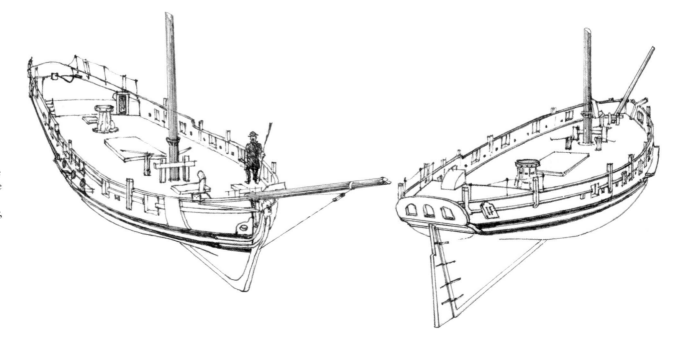

Fig 9-9. These two views of *Ferret*, constructed by the author, give some idea of the rearrangement that would be needed on conversion to a two-masted rig. In particular, the main mast would be repositioned where the capstan is shown here and a new foremast would be required well forward into the bows. Hatches and companion ways would all require relocation.

3pdr. She was also given four swivels; the stocks are shown at Fig 9-9 on the quarterdeck.[10] The groups had varied careers. They all served in the West Indies or on the North American seaboard except *Ferret* II, whose career in the Royal Navy ended in her capture by a Spanish 50-gun ship, the *Arminona*, off Cadiz in September 1718. Some also saw service in the Channel and in the Irish Sea. On this latter station they were there again to enforce the ban on the illegal export of wool.

Before leaving these sloops, it is worth considering a very similar vessel that appeared in a famous picture of 'A sloop off Boston Light', drawn around 1725. This engraving influenced Chapelle's reconstruction of *Ferret* II and her rig, which conforms closely to what is portrayed here. The original picture has the sails furled but the proportions used at Fig 9-10 are those used in the original. By the time the engraving was made all the remaining sloops of this group had been wrecked, taken or broken up for rebuilding; they had also been rigged with two masts. So whilst it is highly unlikely that this represents one of the *Ferret* group, it is possible that the rig of those vessels serving in the Americas was copied or modified to suit other similar craft. There are many examples of the diffusion of maritime information, concepts and ideas on the eastern side of the Atlantic, so a little of the same may be accepted in this case. There is also a significant difference in the rake

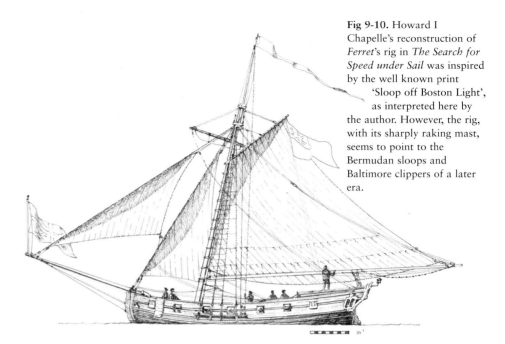

Fig 9-10. Howard I Chapelle's reconstruction of *Ferret*'s rig in *The Search for Speed under Sail* was inspired by the well known print 'Sloop off Boston Light', as interpreted here by the author. However, the rig, with its sharply raking mast, seems to point to the Bermudan sloops and Baltimore clippers of a later era.

of the mast since it is likely to be much greater than that of *Ferret* II. If the channels and chains depicted on the draught are examined closely (as in Fig 9-11), the direction of shrouds

Fig 9-11. *Ferret*'s deadeyes, channels and chain plates as depicted on the draught indicate a mast in a close to vertical position. *Author.*

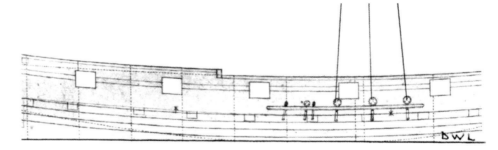

Table 9-2: THE *OTTER* GROUP OF SIXTH RATES/SLOOPS AND PURCHASED SLOOPS, 1709

Name	*Delight*	*Seahorse*	*Otter*	*Margate*	*Swan*	*Hind* [1]	*Jolly* [1]	*Lively* [1]
Ordered	1709	1709	1709	1709	1709	1709	1709	1709
Launched	1709	1709	1710	1709	1709	1709	1709	1709
LGD	77ft 8in	76ft 0½in	76ft 3¼in	77ft 2½in	78ft 4in	78ft 4in	75ft 4in calculated	68ft 9in calculated
LoK	63ft 0in	62ft 1in	62ft 3in	63ft 0in	63ft 6½in	63ft 5½in	61ft 10½in	56ft 5in
Beam	22ft 1in	22ft 1½in	22ft 6in	22ft 0¼in	21ft 10¾in	21ft 10in	22ft 7¼in	20ft 6in
LBR	3.52	3.43	3.39	3.51	3.58	3.59	3.32	3.35
Depth in hold	9ft 3in	9ft 3in	9ft 3in	9ft 3½in	10ft 0in	9ft 11in	10ft 1in	10ft 0in
Burthen	163 tons	163 tons	168 tons	163 tons	162 tons	161 tons	168 tons	126 tons
Guns	14 x 4pdr	14 x 4pdr	14 x 4pdr	14 x 4pdr	14 x 4pdr	12 x 4pdr	10 x 4pdr	12 x 3pdr
Men	70	70	70	70	70	60	70	60
Rig	Ship	Ship	Ship	Ship	Ship	Ship	Ship	Ship
Fate	Sold 1713	Wrecked 1711	Sold 1713	Sold 1712	Wrecked 1709	Sold 1714	Sold 1714	Sold 1712
Builder	Stacey, Woolwich Dyd	Yeames, Limehouse	Smith, Rotherhithe	Allin, Deptford Dyd	Dummer, Rotherhithe	Dummer, Rotherhithe	Johnson, Blackwall	Wicker, Deptford

1 Purchased on the stocks not ordered.

Fig 9-12. *Ferret* as she might have appeared at sea under all plain sail before conversion to the snow rig. *Author*

those remaining being bomb ketches. During the war she had acquired 15 prizes and built 18 new vessels; 16 of these new vessels survived the war but 7 were sold off after its close, along with all the prizes. By 1719, a year after the end of hostilities with Spain, the stock of sloops had been reduced to 4 cruisers and 4 bombs. This may seem an unlikely scenario for the recognition of the sloop of war as a distinctive class of warship, but the wars had shown that the various different categories of sloop could manage each other's roles effectively without too much time being spent on modification. The remainder of this story will attempt to show how this small cadre of cruising sloops and bomb ketches, cleared of all the other ancillary craft, was to multiply nine-fold within less than half a century and develop the flexibility of interchangeable roles.

From here on the Navy Board's surviving collection of plans is fairly complete, so that it will be possible to follow the development of the sloop category in some detail in terms of rig, hull shape and interior fitting.

leading to the hounds suggests a mast stepped near to the vertical. Of the six sloops from these two groups, two were wrecked, one was taken and three were to be rebuilt; this is not a bad record.

England had entered the war with 32 sloops of all kinds, of which 12 survived to its conclusion; 6 of these were disposed of immediately,

Table 9-3: THE *JAMAICA* AND *HAPPY* GROUPS OF SLOOPS, 1710–1711

Name	*Jamaica*	*Trial*	*Ferret* II	*Shark* III	*Happy* [2]	*Hazard* [2]
Ordered	1709	1709	1711	1711	1711	1711
Launched	1710	1710	1711[1]	1711[1]	1711[1]	1711[1]
LGD	64ft 7in	64ft 6in	64ft 7in	64ft 10in	62ft 7in	62ft 7in
LoK	50ft 1in	50ft 5in	50ft 5in	50ft 0in	50ft 2in	50ft 2in
Beam	20ft 8in	20ft 8in	20ft 8in	20ft 8in	20ft 8in	20ft 8in
LBR	3.13	3.12	3.13	3.14	3.03	3.03
Depth in hold	9ft 1in	9ft 1in	9ft 1in	9ft 1in	9ft 0in	9ft 0in
Burthen	114 tons	115 tons	115 tons	114 tons	114 tons	114 tons
Guns	8 x 4pdr + 2 x 3pdr + 4 swivels	8 x 4pdr + 2 x 3pdr + 4 swivels	8 x 4pdr + 2 x 3pdr + 4 swivels	8 x 4pdr + 2 x 3pdr + 4 swivels	8 x 4pdr + 2 x 3pdr + 4 swivels	8 x 4pdr + 2 x 3pdr + 4 swivels
Men	100/60[3]	100/60	100/60	100/60	100/60	100/60
Rig	One-mast sloop	One-mast sloop	One-mast sloop	One-mast sloop	One-mast sloop	One-mast sloop
Fate	Lost 1715	BU for RB 1719	Taken 1718	BU to RB 1722	BU to RB 1724	Wrecked 1714
Builder	Allin, Deptford Dyd	Allin, Deptford Dyd	Allin, Deptford Dyd	Allin, Deptford Dyd	Acworth, Woolwich Dyd	Acworth, Woolwich Dyd

1 It took only three months to build these craft.

2 *Happy* and *Hazard* were built to the same specification as the earlier four by a different master shipwright.

3 War/peace complements

Chapter 10

THE *BARQUE LONGUE* AND EARLY CORVETTE
1671–1714

Much has been written about the term *barque longue*, which is not surprising since it was used in many countries in slightly different cognate forms. Despite the literal translation, however, the one thing it definitely was not was a longboat.[1] Chapter 2 covered the development of an open or partly decked boat, which for convenience was called the Biscay double shallop. These boats were unarmed unless given two or four patereroes or swivel guns. They had a military use and could serve as a lookout or as an advice boat or be used for carrying dispatches. They were listed among other small naval craft as *bâtiments interrompus*,[2] the closest match in English being 'unrated vessels'. However, the French classified their ships into only five rates, unlike the British six. Their Fifth Rates were classified as Frigates of the 2nd Order and would have had guns on one deck with smaller weapons on the quarterdeck and possibly on the forecastle. Below this rate there was a specific class: the *frégat légère* armed with 10–20 guns. These warships were therefore similar in force to the small English Sixth Rates before 1700.

The classification *bâtiments interrompus* ranked below that of *frégat légère*. Within this overarching classification the development of the double shallop into the *barque longue* was first recognised in 1671. These small vessels were listed not by name but just by their total number. However, in 1676, with their development sufficiently complete and accepted, they were given their own distinct class in which at that time there were nine such vessels.[3]

Therefore, in broad terms they equated to an amalgamation of the English sloop (whether she be sloop- or ketch-rigged), brigantine and advice boat. It may also be reasonable to assume that their design was more cohesive than the disparate arrangements pertaining on the north side of the Channel. Whilst the English were laying down different specifications to perform particular roles, the French built one type of vessel to cover a variety of tasks. This is not to say that all *barques longues* were identical in size, but it is likely that some very rough guide was laid down, leaving the designers and builders to develop their own individual style suitable to their own coastal surroundings.

Fig 10-1. *Barques longues* from Dunkirk attack a merchant flute in the narrow seas. *Oil painting by the author*

Fig 10-2. One rig of the *bâtiments interrompus*, equivalent to English unrated vessels. This vessel and its rig lie between the Biscay double shallop and the *barque longue*. *Author*

Fig 10-3. The *frégat légère* of less than 20 guns was the smallest rated class in the French Navy. The development of the *barque longue* was an attempt to produce a much smaller version of this type. Eventually the corvette would be grouped with *barque longue* as an equal partner before increasing in size and replacing both the *frégat légère* and the *barque longue* in official lists. By the middle of the eighteenth century corvettes were to range in size from 6 to 18 guns. *Musée de la Marine, Paris*

Just how the Biscay double shallop at Fig 10-2 evolved into the *barque longue* is not entirely clear, but they must have been very different in shape and design. Whereas the shallop was essentially an open boat, lightly armed possibly with swivel guns on stanchions, the *barque longue* was armed with small carriage guns and therefore must have had a proper deck on which to handle them. Whether this deck was a full 'weather deck' – one laid above the sheer strake – is not entirely certain. In October 1673 the commissioner at Dunkirk, Hubert, wrote to Colbert, then French Minister of the Marine, pointing out that 'whilst all the *barques longues* would be able to serve *á la course* [as requested by Colbert], only three could operate in rough weather, the remainder needing to stay close to their home ports where

they could take refuge in bad conditions.' Unfortunately he does not say why, but some of the vessels may have been in poor repair or their design did not fit them for keeping the sea in all weathers. The latter proposition could mean that not all the *barques longues* were fitted with full weather decks at this stage in their evolution from the double shallop.[4]

In 1673 the English and the French were in alliance against the Dutch Republic. At that time the English were using fully-decked sloops armed normally with four guns, but these were all mounted on the quarterdeck and not in the waist of the vessel, probably to allow the craft to be rowed by men sitting with oars rather than standing with sweeps. The role for the English sloops was to attend the fleet to tow endangered ships out of the line, so they had to perform well under oars. The *barques longues* were not built for this purpose. The pictorial evidence available shows that by the 1690s the *barque longue* had its guns in the waist and that therefore the crew would have stood in between the guns to row. The other possibility is that the type evolved out of an application of the concept of the *frégat légère* (Fig 10-3) to the double shallop.

There are two revealing engravings by F V Guéroult du Pas, one of a double shallop and the other of a *barque longue*, which were published in 1710 but they illustrate vessels that would have been in use from the beginning of the century, if not before.[5] The similarity between the shallop at Fig 10-4 and the *barque longue* at Fig 10-5 is in the run of the sheer strake, the shape of the bow and stern and in the size of the figures relative to the length of the vessels.[6]

A large shallop would be as long as many of the *barques longues* though their freeboard appears to be less. Under the water the tale would be different. Shallops, like very large rowing boats, had a shallow draught that would be unsuited to carrying six or eight carriage guns. There are marked differences in the hull. Where the *barque longue* has ports for four or possibly five guns each side set in a fully planked-up bulwark, the shallop has a low gunwale surmounted by a waist cloth or some light latticework. The engravings further demonstrate that the shallop was intended and readily set up to be rowed by men pulling their

Double Chaloupe, Servant pour porter des avis, et de Vedette dans une Armée Navalle

Barque longue, Servant pour les decouvertes, a escorter les bat.^s March.^ds et faire le Commerce pendant la Guerre. F

oars and therefore seated, whereas in this *barque longue* there appears to be no provision for rowing at all, suggesting that its primary function was to sail.

The rig of the double shallops in Fig 10-4 is still the simple Biscay rig that was discussed in Chapter 2 except that the further vessel has a bowsprit whereas the nearer one uses a *vargord* to secure the luff of the foresail. The *barque longue* has a much-improved version of this basic Biscay rig but here again there is a difference in the sail plans. The vessel on the right in Fig 10-5 has an early form of the snow rig without the fore-and-aft snow sail abaft the mainmast but with a spritsail under the bowsprit. She also has a main staysail shown furled. Confusingly the main-course bowlines lead through blocks on the mainstay, as do the fore-course braces, thus fouling the hoist of that sail. The sail plan of the further vessel is reminiscent of one of the rigs for the brigantine and of HHR Model 2, although in contrast to that

model the main course is correctly a tall buss sail set on what appears to be a pole mast braced high up with crosstrees. These two rigs are further contrasted at Figs 10-6 and 10-7.

A final look at the work of F V Guéroult du Pas provides an introduction to the corvette. In 1674 a *barque longue* was launched at Rochefort on the French Biscay coast. Unlike all previous vessels of this description that had been armed with four guns, she had eight, even though she was not the largest in burthen. Her name was *La Corvette*.[7] In his portrayal of a corvette at Fig 10-8, du Pas points out that she was intended for the same employment as the *barque longue*. The only difference that can be discerned is that the vessel is considerably larger than the *barque longue*. It has the rig shown at Fig 10-7 with both main and topmast staysails. The mainmast is a two-part pole mast with the top section strapped to the main section by iron bands. It seems that the distinction between a *barque longue* and a corvette is very difficult to

Fig 10-4. (left) A naval Biscay double shallop, the forerunner of the *barque longue*, engraved here by Guéroult du Pas. Essentially a coastal, semi-decked boat used for inshore security, escort and advice and similar to the early English sloops. Note that in the distant vessel the crew seem to be sitting to row. *Musée de la Marine, Paris*

Fig 10-5. (Right) The *barque longue* (a radical step up from the double shallop), being required to mount carriage guns, must have had a rather different underwater form to her predecessor. She would most probably have been fully decked. Her role was as a lookout and an escort to coastwise traffic; also to carry stores in wartime. Note the furled main staysail and the lead of the bowlines. Another view by Guéroult du Pas. *Musée de la Marine, Paris*

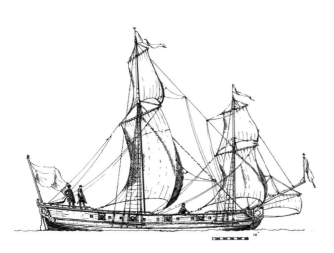

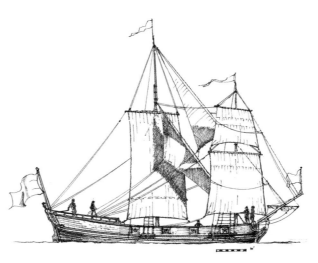

Figs 10-6 and 10-7. A comparison between the *barque longue* on the left and the corvette on the right. There was very little difference between these craft: indeed, they had the same roles and were later considered a joint class. From the scale in each drawing it can be seen that the corvette is the larger vessel but this may not have always been so. The different rig is of little importance since both types could carry either rig. *Author.*

define and that, for a short period at least, corresponding to the two wars at sea with England and the Dutch (1688–1714), they were one and the same type. In a list prepared by Jean Boudriot, the French maritime historian, there is a marked increase in the size and force of many of the *barques longues* in the last decade of the seventeenth century. It is at this time, 1696, that the class name was changed from '*barque longue*' to '*barque longue ou corvette*'.

In order to close on the relationship between the naval double shallop, the *barque longue* and the corvette it is worth noting du Pas' captions to his engravings. Of the shallop he says that it 'serves as an advice boat and as a lookout within a naval force'. Of the *barque longue* he says that it 'serves as a reconnaissance vessel, as an escort for merchant ships and as an armed store-ship'. For the corvette he simply points out that is for the same use as a *barque longue*. The subject of an armed store ship will be covered later in the chapter.

These *barques longues* and early corvettes exhibit the five characteristics of most of the small warships in the English and French navies up to the beginning of the eighteenth century: speed, light construction, shallow draught, two masts, and dual propulsion by oar or sail. Beyond this period other influences, mainly ever increasing armament, were to dilute some of these principles in their design to a point where they began to resemble miniature frigates. Therefore, it is reasonable to conclude that, whilst the *barques longues*, early corvettes and sloops were a development upwards of the original Biscay double shallop, their successors became increasingly influenced by the design of larger vessels.

When *La Corvette* was launched in 1674, she was fitted with an armament of eight guns, which would have ruled out any partial-deck arrangement. The increased weight of armament and its position in the waist of the vessel would have forced a change in design involving a full weather deck and probably an increase in beam to provide a better gun platform. From 1675 to 1690 the normal armament for this class was 6-8 guns, but thereafter there is an increasing frequency of 10-12-gun *barques longues*/corvettes. This suggests that full decking would have been provided from 1674 onwards and that gradually the *barque longue* began to change her shape to accommodate a more powerful and weighty armament. With guns in the waist of the vessel, oar ports would have been placed either side of them and it is probable that from this point onwards the crew stood to row.

By way of comparison, in the English Navy by 1673 the sloop *Bonetta* – similar to the English sloop at Fig 10-9, sailing under Dutch colours at the Battle of Texel 1673 – was fully decked above her wale, although she did not have guns in her waist and therefore could be rowed sitting.[8] There are other interesting comparisons. Boudriot gives a uniform crew complement of 28 for all vessels, be they *barque longue* or corvette. Some English sloops had this number but only on a war basis; usually there were far fewer. The sloop shown here is using the simple basic rig as used in the double shallop (see Fig 10-2). She may be the *Portsmouth*, taken by the Dutch in a fight off Ostend in 1672.

Returning to the introduction of the description 'corvette' in 1687, the most likely origin of this term is the Latin *corbis*, a basket. Roman trading vessels used to carry a basket for the lookout at the masthead and so came to be called *corbitas*. The sounds of the letters B and V can be confused, certainly in Spanish, allowing the corruption of *corbetta* into *corvette* in French. The old term *corbeta* of the fifteenth century is described as a *bâtiment de charge* (a cargo carrier). This is particularly interesting since under his illustration of a *barque longue*, Guéroult du Pas makes the point that this vessel was used for carrying merchandise in war. Regarding the load-carrying aspect, it is worth pointing out that in the eighteenth century French corvettes came to be listed in three categories: 'Corvettes *de Guerre*', 'Corvettes *Aviso*' and 'Corvettes *de Charge*'. These last were purpose-built naval transports, designed to keep up with a fleet, and could displace up to 800 tons.[9] As an informal classification, the term 'corvette' was to cover a variety of small ships in terms of size, armament and operational role for over three centuries – indeed, it is still in use – rather in the way that 'sloop' has been used as a catch-all term for a host of small British warships until the end of the Second World War.

The classification *barque longue* may have seemed inappropriate to the French authorities since, although these vessels were small, they were poorly described by this term.[10] *La Corvette* may have been a similar size to the other examples, but had double their armament, being equipped with eight 4pdr guns and the normal complement of 28 crew. Although her dimensions are unknown, a similarly equipped vessel of the same burthen of 36 tons is recorded as being 57ft 5in on the gun deck by 14ft 4in on the beam and of 5ft 9in depth of water. This makes them of similar size to the larger Pepysian sloops, though of considerably less burthen. For example, the sloop *Lilly* built by Shish in 1673 at Deptford was 52ft on the keel; therefore 60ft 8in, by calculation, on the gun deck, with a 14ft beam and 5ft depth of water. Her burthen was 58 tons.

It may seem unreasonable to argue that these French equivalents to the English sloops, although of lighter construction than the English sloops, were of a bulkier design.[11] *La Corvette* would have had a LBR of 4.01 and *Lilly,* built by Shish, one of 4.14. Shish's sloops normally had a lower LBR than those of Pett and Deane, who designed to ratios between 4.5 and 5. However, a low LBR does not necessarily indicate a full body. The French sensibly retained a good beam but by drawing the stem and sternpost as near as vertical as possible they could achieve a fine entry and run. Apart from this their midship sections were less full than those of their English equivalents. This is all evident at Fig 10-10. Apart from the engravings by Guéroult du Pas, there are only three examples of these small ships that can be used to illustrate this class. However, hereafter there is more objective evidence, including a plan, and tables of dimensions of hull, masts and spars. The first example (Fig 10-10) is illustrated by plans held in the Danish National Archives of a 50ft corvette together with masting dimensions for a 57ft vessel and the hull dimensions for *Volage*, which can be identified on a list of *barques longues*/corvettes.[12] These documents and the plan provide probably the best guide to shapes and dimensions, since no reconstruction is required. However, the information is limited to delineating the hull, masts and spars.

The second example is based on a rapid sketch of a known vessel, *Le Brillant*, which can only provide a general conception of such vessels. The third example is derived from the salvage and analysis of a wreck discovered on the Texas coast in 1995. The lines of the wreck, identified as *La Belle*, have had to be reconstructed after great care in excavation and in research.[13] What the wreck does provide is the evidence for the equipment and weapons, such as the guns and rigging items, that would have been on many of these small vessels. The other bonus is that the vessel corresponds in many ways to the plan of the first example as far as general layout is concerned, although this may be due to the use of the plan itself in interpreting the information from the wreck. However, the wreck is of further interest because the shape of hull is totally different from that of the first example.

This *barque longue* or corvette at Fig 10-10 must be one of the most attractive and extreme designs for a small ship at the end of the seventeenth century. The figure of a man, and the scale on the plan, shows how small the vessel is. A particular delight is the design of her quarter badge. Note the dotted line depicting the forward bulkhead of the captain's cabin. Her

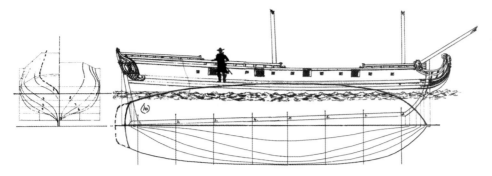

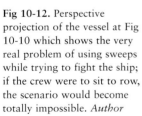

Fig 10-10. This plan of a small *barque longue* shows an advanced hull form. Note also the high degree of deadrise in her sections and the amount of drag to the keel, features that could be seen 80 years later in American fast designs. The figure has been added to show how tiny these vessels were. *Author after an original in the Rigsarkivert, Copenhagen*

Fig 10-11. In his great work *Architectura Navalis Mercatoria* of 1768 the Swedish naval architect F H Chapman includes this plan of a small frigate, the lines of which bear a close resemblance to the tiny *barque longue* in the previous illustration.

Fig 10-12. Perspective projection of the vessel at Fig 10-10 which shows the very real problem of using sweeps while trying to fight the ship; if the crew were to sit to row, the scenario would become totally impossible. *Author*

small size probably places her construction date into the early 1680s, if not earlier. She has a length on the gun deck of 48ft and a beam of 12ft 8in giving her a LBR of 3.89. Her depth of water is 5ft 5in. Another, built in 1689 at Dunkirk and carrying eight guns, measured 58ft 7in on the deck, had a beam of 13ft 9in, a LBR of 4.26, drew 5ft 4in and had a burthen of 30 tons. It is therefore likely that the example illustrated had a burthen of little more than 25 tons.

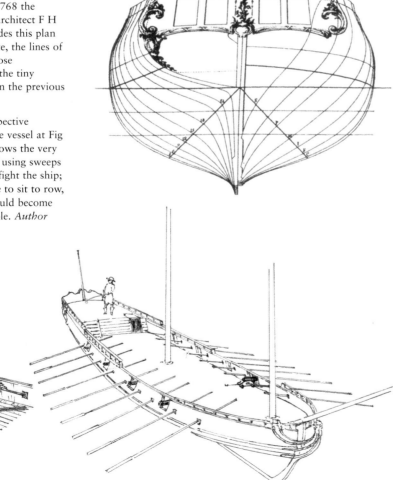

This points to light construction and fine lines as compared with equivalent vessels on the other side of the Channel. This example bears out the comparison of the vessels portrayed by Guéroult du Pas in that his *barque longue*, despite carrying carriage guns, appears to be smaller than the double shallop.

A vessel like this would have avoided any major gunnery duel and would have used her speed, under sail, oars or both, to escape encounter. She might well have been used as an *aviso* (advice boat), for reconnaissance and surveillance, or as a dispatch-carrier. The remarkably fine entry and run are testament to her light displacement. Her midship section seems to foreshadow those laid out by F H Chapman, the great Swedish naval architect, 70 years later[14] but also conforms to the same sort of section shown in a Danish sloop of about 1660, a good example of diffusion (Fig 10-11).

The difficulty of mixing seated oarsmen with carriage guns suggests that, on these vessels at least, the French stood to row. This beautiful little vessel retains the grace and style of a large open rowing boat (Fig 10-12). Her extreme lines may indicate that the plan represents a proposal, and it is possible that other vessels of this same category may have looked different. At the time she was built, if it was in the late 1680s, craft such as these no longer existed on the other side of the English Channel. England had been at peace since 1673 and had no need to spend on 'defence'. When in the 1690s the English government wished to acquire such vessels, they were built to heavier scantlings with more robust lines, even though they were similarly armed. Unfortunately they were slow. Not until the *Cruizer* class of 1732 did the British produce sloops of such an attractive appearance and boat-like proportions. No rig accompanies the Danish plan, but there is a table of spars for a similar but slightly larger vessel that provides a good idea of its layout. The plan does indicate that she had two masts and, true to the Biscay rig, her mainmast is just behind the mid-point between her stem and sternpost. Unlike the other examples she does not carry a third mast and in this respect she resembles the English sloops. Yet she may have raised a third mast on occasion as most probably was done with the English sloops, if required to make a long passage.[15]

Another and similar French vessel, *Le Brillant*, although slightly larger, was captured by the English in 1696 and was used by them as an advice boat until 1698 when she was sold. The rapid sketch of her by Van de Velde the younger (Fig 10-13) supplies some interesting information. First as to rig, points of note include the use of a balancing sail on the quarterdeck and the fact that the crosstrees on the main topmast and on the mizzen mast would seem to suggest that she might have been able to fly a mizzen topsail and a main topgallant sail, although these upper spars were generally reserved for flags. The foremast seems to have been shot away in action, but its relative size can be gauged from the three deadeyes on the fore channel compared with four on the main. There is a remarkable difference in the lengths of the yards for her main course and main topsail. Given the height of her rig this is perhaps not a bad thing.

Down on the deck, the use of gun ports lids on an open weather deck opening sideways is understandable but unusual. Not so unusual is the locating of the 'seats of ease' over her delightful lute stern rather than in the head of the vessel, a practice known to have existed in the Tudor navy. Her rails at the quarterdeck and at the foredeck are treated in a similar fashion to the example in the plan above. She appears to have a bulkhead, on deck, across her forecastle just aft of the stem, which is unusual for small craft. This does not appear in the Danish plan or in the reconstruction of *La Belle*. The marks where the scuppers are indicate the run of her weather deck and the hastily drawn figures about the deck give some indication of her size, though they do appear to be too small for the vessel described, which although there are no dimensions available, is reputed to have had a burthen of 60 tons and might therefore have been 60ft–70ft long.

The hulls of these two examples are extremely fine, with a marked narrow entry and a gently tapering run, giving them good agility and speed. This is evident in the plan above and also in the shape of the bow and transom as shown in the Van de Velde drawing. What cannot be seen in his sketch is the considerable drag to the keel and the swift rise of the floors illustrated in the plan. This style of hull is remarkably advanced for its date and fore-

shadows the designs of the small and fast American vessels of the mid-eighteenth century.

As already suggested, the terms *barque longue* and corvette appeared to cover a multitude of craft of different dimensions, burthen and armament. This conjecture is supported by the discovery in 1995 of a wreck lying off the coast of what is now Texas. The discovery provides us with a similar vessel but at the opposite end of the spectrum in relation to hull shape, almost to the point where it seems she came from an entirely different class and was

Fig 10-13. A drawing by Van de Velde the younger of *Le Brillant*, a French privateer taken by the English in 1696 and then used as an advice boat for clandestine operations on the French coast. Note the long overhanging counter and its similarity to the corvette at Fig 10-8. *National Maritime Museum PW6663*

Fig 10-14. This small exploration barque, *La Belle*, was stranded near the mouth of the Missisippi in 1686. Its remains were discovered in 1995. It has been described as a *barque longue* and even as a *frégat légère* but its shape does not accord with these types. The designer had specified broad floors which gave the vessel a good carrying capacity. The value of this wreck is that it gives insight into the methods of construction for small ships at the time as well as an opportunity to see the fittings and armament used. The information gained from the wreck has led to the construction of many models in the United States and in France. This lines plan has been developed by G Grieco directly from measurements of the wreck. *International Journal of Nautical Archaeology Vol 30, No 4*

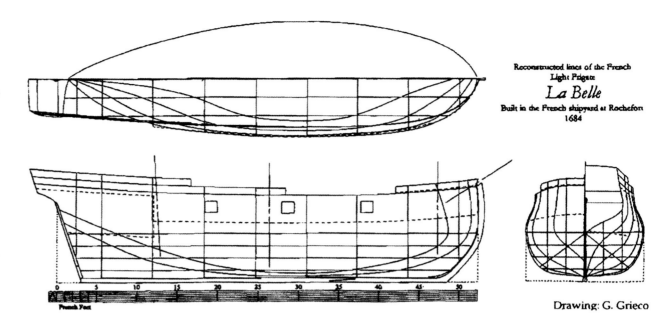

designed for a very different purpose. The remains of the vessel (Fig 10-14) included about three-quarters of the starboard side and a third of the port side, from which it was possible to build up a lines plan. When compared with the lines of the Danish example, this indicates that the vessel was designed to have good carrying capacity rather than speed and weatherliness. The wreck was identified as a vessel forming part of an ill-fated expedition, commanded by the French explorer La Salle, to establish a small colony close to the mouth of the Mississippi River in 1686. The vessel was thought to be *La Belle*, a *barque longue*/corvette built under the supervision of Honoré Mallet at the port of Rochefort on the French Biscay coast in 1684.[16] This identification led to the discovery at Rochefort of a list of measurements signed by the shipwrights and others involved in the construction of the vessel. It was these measure-

Fig 10-15. These drawings by the author are based on plans from a monograph on *La Belle* by Jean Boudriot. It shows the construction method and internal structure based on information gleaned from the wreck. *Monographie de La Belle. Barque – 1680*, published by Editions ANCRE[17]

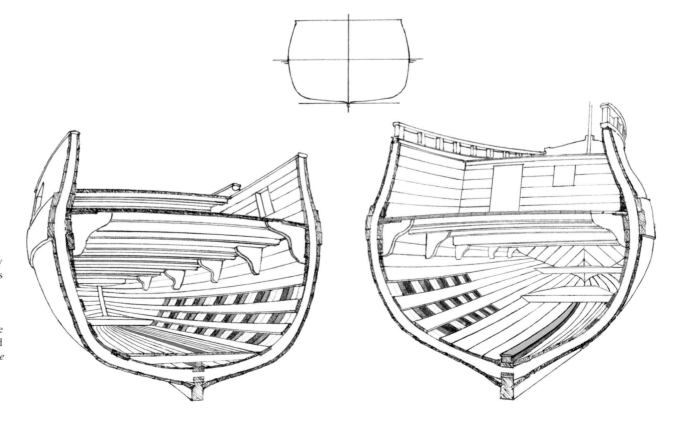

ments that together with the information from the wreck enabled the reconstruction of the lines plan and of the methods used in the building of *La Belle*.

The hull is recorded as being 45ft on the keel and 51ft on the length of the deck with a breadth of 14ft. This gives the vessel a LBR of 3.64, which should be compared with the examples above where the LBRs were 3.89 and 4.26. But it is not just the LBR that is so different. In the list of measurements the master shipwright has laid down that the flat of the master floor be 9ft 4in.[18] This imposes on the vessel a corpulent body, one that is designed for carrying capacity rather than speed (Fig 10-14).

What can be seen from the wreck is the system of framing and planking these vessels (Fig 10-15). The English practice, for ships of the Royal Navy, was to construct a heavily framed hull, leaving only a small gap between the frame pairs, designed to enhance structural strength. The English also tended to plank up the interior side of the frames leaving no gaps between planks. This is known to be true for rated vessels, at least, although there is little evidence about construction methods for unrated craft. However, English naval vessels had a reputation for strength, which would tend to point to larger scantlings and a more robust build but at a cost to the vessel's speed. The French practice seems to have been to place frame pairs at a distance from each other roughly equivalent to the sided thickness of the pair. At the same time, interior planking or ceiling was laid down with large spaces between strakes. These two measures made for a much lighter hull than the English equivalent.

The only official records refer to *La Belle* as a 'barque'. Although a century later, Falconer's description of a bark or barque is a vessel with three masts, having the fore and main square-rigged and the mizzen with only fore-and-aft canvas. So *La Belle* would have had a mizzen mast. Such a mast might well have seemed a good precaution on a transatlantic passage but the designation of barque would suggest that it was intended as a permanent feature.[19] *La Belle* was also described at the time of her demise as a *frégat légère*. But *frégat légère* she was not. The confusion may have arisen and persists to this day because she was equipped with a mizzen mast. The mere presence of this mast is

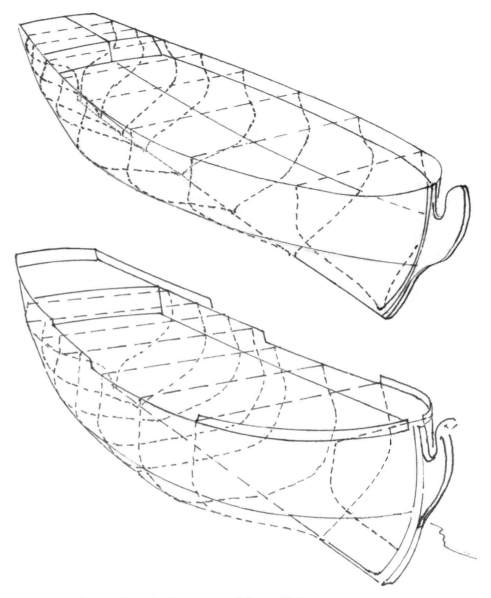

not enough to classify her as a *frégat légère* since those vessels had square as well as fore-and-aft canvas on their mizzen masts and carried a minimum of 10 guns (Fig 10-2). They equated broadly to the smaller English Sixth Rate ships.

As pointed out earlier, the classification *'barque longue ou corvette'* might embrace a wide variety of vessel types of different shapes and sizes. Whilst this little ship was officially recorded as a barque, she was also listed as one of four *barques longues* in Rochefort available at the time to support La Salle's expedition. This seems to relate to du Pas' statement that *barques longues* could be used for carrying merchandise and stores in time of war. These two images at Fig 10-16 and 10-17 show the difference in hull design between the first the

Figs 10-16 and 10-17. Perspectives showing a comparison between the *barque longue* and the barque *La Belle*, and in particular the far greater volume of the latter due to the width of floor specified by the designer. *Author*

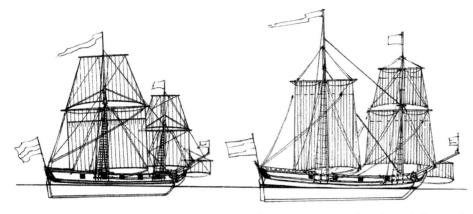

Fig 10-18. The *barque longue* (left) and corvette, a liaison that lasted from 1696 to 1746. *Author*

upper example (Fig 10-16), developed from the plan at Fig 10-10, and below, at Fig 10-17, from the lines of *La Belle* by G Grieco, informed by the work of Jean Boudriot.

To conclude this review of the French experience with vessels similar to the English sloops, it is necessary briefly to consider the future of the *barque longue*/corvette up until the end of the War of the Spanish Succession. It is not until well into the eighteenth century that the French 'Corvette de Guerre' develops into a larger vessel broadly equivalent to the British 20–24-gun ship, but this period can be summarised by a passage from *Archéologie Navale* compiled by Auguste Jal for King Louis Philippe in 1840.[20]

In 1698 [the end of the War of the League of Augsburg], the Royal Navy of France had twenty corvettes or *barques longues*.

Of these the most powerful was *La Paquebot*, constructed in England in 1689 with ten 4pdrs [possibly a commercial packet boat]. In 1716, [two years after the War of the Spanish Succession] the King had no more than seven corvettes or *barques longues* of which the most powerful was the *Immaculate Conception*, which originated in Majorca, and was armed with ten 6pdrs.

The remainder had either been taken by the British or Dutch or lay rotting in creeks along the French coast, their raison d'être gone.

In his article for the *Nautical Research Journal*, Jean Boudriot makes a telling statement – that no small vessels of 6-8 guns were built for the French Navy between 1718 and 1770, to the disadvantage of young naval officers. Lack of opportunity to command at an early age leads to problems later in the naval career in coping with the stresses and demands of command, without prior experience of that singular position. This dearth of minor warships in France contrasts sharply with the British experience where from about 1730 onwards, in order to protect their colonies and coastal and oceanic trade, the Admiralty set in train programmes to increase the stock of sloops, allowing young officers to cut their teeth as master and commander.

Chapter 11

THE HANOVERIAN SUCCESSION AND THE WARS FOR TRADE AND EMPIRE
1714–1763

The Hanoverian era, or more precisely the reigns of George I and II, began in a period of comparative peace, certainly in home waters, and finished with a global war. Although the War of the Spanish Succession did not end until 1714, the British Government had already begun to negotiate a cessation to hostilities with France in 1712. The support that the Duke of Marlborough had enjoyed for his land campaign on the Continent began to wane when a Tory administration came to power in 1710. With its increased influence on Queen Anne it was able to present her with arguments against the war's continuance, at least against France.[1] For politicians of a 'Blue Water' bent – those that believed Britain's true interests lay elsewhere and further afield – this was an understandable line to take, though one of the many factors in promoting this argument may have been that Marlborough's campaigns were not good value for money. Two years later, the death of Queen Anne in 1714 coincided with the Treaty of Utrecht, which brought the war to its official closure.

For Britain, the end of the war and the arrangements for Queen Anne's successor required some realignment. Queen Anne, whose children had all pre-deceased her, was to be the last of the Stuart dynasty, a fact ensured in advance by the Act of Settlement in 1701 prohibiting any Roman Catholic from ruling Great Britain.[2] Despite the fact that there were fourteen claimants who had a better right in blood to the throne of Britain, it was handed to George Frederick, Elector of Hanover, a distant Protestant relative of Anne. His succession was

Fig 11-1. George I in his coronation robes. During the reigns of George I and II, power in the land was to shift away from the king towards his prime minister – from 1721 Sir Robert Walpole – to a point where eventually the monarch retained only strong influence but not real power other than his choice of ministers and his command of the Armed Forces. Oil portrait by Godfrey Kneller. *National Maritime Museum BHC2709*

not universally popular in a country whose public still held with the continuance of a family line in its monarchy. Had Anne's half-brother, a potential James III, publicly espoused the Protestant faith, then with strong public pressure from the many Jacobites, the Hanoverian might never have been offered the throne.[3]

It might be asked what all this had to do with sloops. The answer is that the Royal Navy was the front line in the strategy of countering any potential rebellion against the Hanoverian succession. During the recent war, it had already had to forestall a French attempt to land James, the 'Old Pretender', in Scotland in 1708.[4] The

French squadron was commanded by a great exponent of the *guerre de course*, comte de Forbin, whose attempted landing failed after a chase up the North Sea in which Byng attempted to capture his squadron in the mouth of the Firth of Forth. However, James was eventually able to land in Scotland in 1715, but through inept planning and management by his lieutenant in Scotland, he found his supporters already defeated and was forced to flee in 1716. There was another attempt by Spaniards to raise a revolt in the Highlands in 1719 and a serious plot for a landing in the West Country in 1722. As a result naval planning had to allocate resources to detecting and if necessary neutralising this ongoing threat.[5] With Scotland the likely crucible for a Jacobite rebellion, this meant that the North Sea and Irish waters had to be kept under constant surveillance, for any pretender to the throne would have to sail through these seas. And in this connection it should be noted that 'home waters' was the priority station for those sloops still in commission after the end of the war. This threat continued until 1745 when James III's son 'Bonnie Prince Charlie' failed in his attempt to take the crown. Thereafter Scotland was to go through that unpleasant process called 'pacification'.

Apart from this nagging ongoing threat of insurgency, the reign of George I was to be relatively peaceful, not least due to the efforts of Walpole, his prime minister, to follow a policy of peace wherever possible. In broad terms, the naval activity during his regime (1714–1727) was further from home, covering the Baltic, the Mediterranean and the Caribbean.

Looking at the Baltic first, the Great Northern War was fought on and across this sea and in the states and provinces surrounding it. In the early seventeenth century Sweden had benefited from the disarray caused by the Thirty Years War in western and central Europe. It had been able to make encroachments into territories lying on the southern fringes of the Baltic, a situation that other states in the region could not accept. Therefore in 1700 an alliance of these states was formed, headed by an emerging Russia and including Denmark and Saxony. The aim was to return Sweden to her 'original' borders, divesting her of most of her southern Baltic conquests. Initially the Swedish armies were highly successful but by 1714 the struggle had begun to turn against them.

For most of this war, Britain was predominantly occupied with the War of the Spanish Succession and had neither the time nor resources to engage in a Baltic conflict. Nevertheless, although they had no territorial interest in the region, both Britain and the Dutch Republic had a massive incentive to ensure the safe passage of trade across the Baltic Sea and its approaches since that trade contained materials that were essential to the construction and maintenance of the ships within their navies. However, if the British Government had no territorial interests in this war, the British monarch did. One of the risks of importing a foreigner to be king is that he may have a different view of foreign policy from that of his government (although Charles II proved that this could also be true of a 'native' monarch). There was an earlier example in the workings of William of Orange, whose continental policy was at variance with some of his English government's maritime and mercantile priorities.

Whilst both George and his Whig government had a strong interest in the Baltic, the latter was primarily concerned to secure the safe passage of trade whereas the king did

Fig 11-2. Northwest Europe showing the Baltic Sea. Note the Swedish possessions (shown in dark grey) at the eastern and western end of that sea and those on the German North Sea coast, which George I was keen to annex to his own province of Hanover.

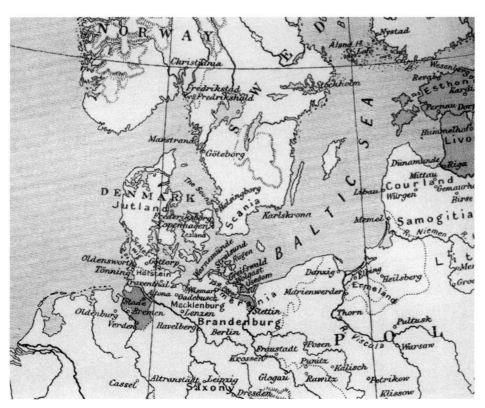

indeed have a territorial interest. His home-land, in what is now northern Germany, was a land-locked state and it was George's intention to take the opportunity this war afforded to negotiate with the Swedish to release the provinces of Bremen and Verden from their crumbling empire. This would give him access to the North Sea. To achieve such an aim might require a rather different naval deployment from that needed to secure safe passage through the Baltic Sea and its approaches. Indeed, it was George's wish, though one that Britain could not publicly espouse, that the Royal Navy, together with the Danish Navy, should attack Sweden's naval forces, thereby giving him more leverage in negotiating access to the sea for Hanover.[6] On the other hand, the threat to safe passage lay in the struggle between the Russian-led alliance and Sweden for domination in the lands adjacent to the Baltic Sea. The volatility in the area, caused by this contest, demanded that a British naval presence was necessary, on occasion, to provide a balance of naval power between the belliger-ents and thereby to secure that safe passage so essential for British trade.

This dichotomy could make life difficult for any admiral attempting to satisfy two masters: his government and his king. Fortunately, the flag officer selected to command Britain's Baltic squadron was both admiral and diplomat. Admiral Sir John Norris may be regarded as a particularly fine exponent of the use of a naval presence in promoting his country's purposes by diplomatic action. Ultimately the British naval presence in the Baltic was there to maintain a balance of power between Russia and her allies and the now much reduced Swedish empire. By the time the war had concluded in 1721, Admiral Norris, supported by excellent British diplomatic action, had managed to achieve the country's double aim of safe passage for trade in the Baltic and the addition of Bremen–Verden to the Electorate of Hanover.

Primarily due to their small overall numbers, only one sloop was deployed to the Baltic and that on the first expedition in 1715. This was the *Drake* of 14 guns. She had a shallow draught and would have suited operations amongst the islands and archipelagos off the coasts of Sweden and Finland. She was not included in any other expeditions, returning to home and Irish waters until the end of her career in 1728.[7]

Far away from the entanglements of the Baltic, the British Navy was still in action against Spain in the Mediterranean. One of the important outcomes of the War of the Spanish Succession was the development of a permanent British presence in the Mediterranean achieved by the capture of Gibraltar in 1702, the taking of Port Mahon on the Island of Menorca and the effect, although only temporary, of the disaster wrought upon the French Fleet at Toulon in 1707. Though Britain was at peace with France after 1712, this was not the case with Spain, which would not accept a treaty that gave the British Gibraltar and Mahon. Moreover, Spain had a new monarch, a Bourbon and a grandson of Louis XIV, who was also keen to acquire, on the basis of national inheritance, those dominions in Italy that had belonged to Spain's last king, Philip IV, a Hapsburg.[8] This policy might be considered a continuance of the War of the Spanish Succession and it ensured that Britain main-tained a strong presence in that theatre. Spain's resurgence was finally capped by a quadruple alliance (1718–1720) of France, the Dutch Republic, Austria and Britain, which largely removed the gains that Spain had made following the War of the Spanish Succession. As a result, the last six years of George I's reign were blessed with a near-total absence of foreign hostilities, although there was ever the need for the navy to keep an eye on the security of Britain's overseas possessions and the possi-bility of a Jacobite rebellion.

There was more at issue with Spain than Britain's conquests and activities in the Mediterranean. Spain regarded much of the South and Central American littoral as a mercantile as well as political monopoly. She did not appreciate the spread of what she saw as British predatory influence in that theatre and took steps to secure her position and the safe passage of her trade and bullion. This was seen by Britain as a potential threat to the develop-ment of its shipping and commerce and to the security of its Caribbean communities, particu-larly Jamaica (taken from Spain in 1655). Both the Mediterranean and the Caribbean were to become areas of increasing tension that required some form of naval presence, not simply to contain the threats from other European powers but to suppress that age-old activity, piracy.[9]

Finally, the Channel remained England's doorstep and had to be kept secure despite the fact that between 1712 and 1742 there was no threat from France other than its support for the Stuart cause. But there was another totally different issue that affected the Channel as well as the Celtic and Irish seas and that was the enforcement of the ban on the illegal export of wool, a material that formed a highly important part of the British economy. This trade was called 'owling', apparently because the smugglers used the cover of darkness to carry out their illegal trade.

A review of sloop and bomb vessel deployment in the nine years following the cessation of hostilities with France shows that the priority theatres for the sloops, such as were left, were: first, Home Waters; with the West Indies a close second; and third, 'owling'. As noted above, there was only one sloop deployed to the Baltic between 1712 and 1721, the *Drake* in 1715 during the latter stages of the Great Northern War. One sloop, the *Ferret*, was ordered to the Mediterranean, though she never reached it, being taken by the Spanish off Cadiz in 1718. One sloop was dispatched to Newfoundland for surveying. The bombs had a rather different pattern with their deployments being solely to the Mediterranean and Baltic.[10] By 1721 the

Royal Navy had only four cruising sloops, two of which were in the West Indies, one at Gibraltar and one in home waters. Therefore it is perhaps not surprising that the new construction in 1721–1722 was a programme of small vessels ordered principally to assist the Revenue, though their work would have included fishery protection and surveillance duties: not very glamorous roles, but demands would change in the next decade.

The year 1727 saw the death of George I and the coronation of his son who, like his father, would preside over a generally peaceful period, at least until 1739 when war would erupt again, this time with Spain in the Caribbean. This war later widened into the War of the Austrian Succession, which brought France into the conflict on the side of the Spanish. In the meantime the areas of tension affecting British possessions and trade overseas remained centred on the Caribbean and the Western Mediterranean. It was protection of these areas, particularly the Caribbean and the transatlantic trade, that was to result in the ever-increasing demand for sloops and small Sixth Rates.

The pivotal point in the history of the sloop of war was undoubtedly 1732, for it was in that year that the Admiralty and the Navy Board recognised a need to establish standard requirements in terms of measurement, burthen, armament and crew for general-purpose sloops. From this time onwards the size and number of cruising and bomb sloops in the Royal Navy was set to increase massively. Why this was so, during a period of comparative peace, is the central question: the answer, putting it broadly, was that the time was ripe. British naval capabilities and responsibilities were expanding, the transatlantic trade with the Caribbean was growing, the colonies themselves were becoming better established and the Mediterranean continued to be a region of potential instability. This all added up to an environment where a small, fast and handy vessel would be of great use, one that would work under the umbrella of British naval superiority and whose employment was economical but adequate for the job in hand. In broad terms the size was to remain close to 200 tons throughout the 1730s rising to 250 tons in the 1740s when there was an increase in gun calibre from 4pdrs with the introduction of the short

Fig 11-3. The *Ferret* and others of the *Jamaica* and *Happy* classes were originally given a single-masted rig, but this probably included a large square course set from the cro'jack yard in the right conditions, as well as the conventional gaff-headed fore-and-aft main. *Author*

6pdr. This weapon was to remain the preferred armament for the sloop until the coming of the carronade in the late eighteenth century. From the late 1740s onwards ship rig would be increasingly common, either by conversion or through new-building, and burthen would eventually rise to 350 tons.[11]

These increases in number and size reflect the nature of the wars that were about to engulf Europe and its overseas possessions. These started with the 'War of Jenkins' Ear' in 1739 between Britain and Spain. The unusual name for this war points up the root cause of the problem. Jenkins was the captain of a merchant ship which in 1731 was apprehended by the infamous Spanish *Guarda Costa* for dubious reasons relating to trade. In the ensuing fracas Jenkins had his ear cut off. Eight years later this incident was to become a retrospective 'last straw' in the British determination to harry and assault Spanish possessions and trade in the greater Caribbean.

It was essentially a war about trade and the licence that allowed Britain to provide slaves to the Spanish colonies of Central America. The conflict lasted until 1748, being subsumed in 1740 into the greater War of the Austrian Succession. Although France and Britain were engaged against each other on land from the outset, France did not declare war until 1744, following this with an attempted invasion that failed whilst still at sea. In 1740, the Royal Navy under Vernon was initially successful, capturing the small poorly defended Spanish port of Porto Bello in what is now Panama. But thereafter almost all the amphibious operations against Spanish possessions failed, not least due to the sickness and disease that invariably

Fig 11-4. George II in old age, after a painting by Robert Edge Pine. *National Maritime Museum BHC2710*

accompanied a long operation in the tropics, but also due to the difficulty of establishing harmonious inter-service relationships. Much of this was on the personal level.

The war in the Americas continued with the failure of British amphibious operations, largely through the afore-mentioned disease but also due to the well-defended nature of the Spanish ports. The element of surprise had been lost and the targets selected by Britain's admiral in the region proved to be too hard a nut to crack. At sea privateers on all sides, French, Spanish and British, attacked each other's trade, but only the

Fig 11-5. The growth in the size of sloops (drawings to the same scale). Many of the *Merlin* class sloops of 1745 were converted to ship rig in the 1750s, although this was under consideration in the 1740s. *Author*

1720 – 114 tons   1732 – 200 tons   1745 – 270 tons

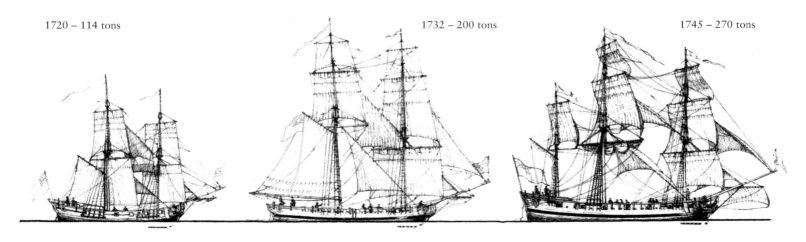

British regularly used naval ships to provide escort to commercial shipping. Once again the sloop of war had the opportunity to engage her arch-enemy, the privateer.

In the Mediterranean 1744 saw a combined Franco-Spanish fleet sail from Toulon. There followed an indecisive engagement with the British fleet, based at Mahon but with orders to blockade Toulon and prevent the Spanish, with French assistance, from reinforcing their forces on the Italian peninsular. Britain, although only minimally involved in the plethora of land battles that punctuated this war, was an ally of Austria and its Hapsburg rulers and therefore as part of that alliance was committed to using its power at sea to support the Austrian cause in Italy. The Spanish interest in Italy lay in their desire to repossess the inheritance of their last Hapsburg king. The question arose over the right of a woman, Maria Theresa, to succeed to the Hapsburg Austrian Empire, an outcome unacceptable to many and providing Spain with an opportunity to grab parts of Italy.

At home, a Channel fleet under old Admiral Norris kept an eye on French moves for an invasion across the Channel or through a Jacobite rebellion in the North. In the event the invasion failed at sea and the rebellion, initially successful with Prince Charles Edward's forces reaching Derby, turned into a rout at Culloden near Inverness.

The few naval successes in this period, apart from Porto Bello, came towards the end with the foundation of a new strategy that kept the British fleet at sea in the Western approaches when at war with France. From this position Britain could guard the Channel, since the seaborne element of any French invasion force must make use of Brest. It also allowed the British to attack French squadrons and convoys from an up-wind position; it also guarded any approach to Ireland and the Irish Sea, often a vulnerable point in the past. The difficulty was to sustain squadrons in waters that were habit-ually rough and gale-blown. However, Torbay, on the South Devon coast, offered a reasonable refuge in all winds except from east to south. The last major engagements of the war were fought off Finisterre, on the west coast of France, against French convoys, and both were successful. At the second Battle of Finisterre the British squadron was commanded by a young rear admiral named Edward Hawke. He destroyed the escort but the convoy escaped towards the West Indies, so immediately following the engagement he sent the fast-sailing sloop *Weazle* III to Jamaica to warn of the arrival of an unescorted French convoy. The necessary action was taken to 'welcome' them.

The series of engagements of this war – at home, in the Americas, the East Indies and in the Mediterranean – can be seen as providing the British Navy and Army with experience that they would put to good use in the Seven Years War of the following decade. They also supplied the incentives to establish defensible bases capable of sustaining a large naval force and a victualling and logistic system to keep those bases and their ships in a condition to dominate their region.

At times the Royal Navy had been severely overstretched but by the conclusion of this war some hard lessons had been learned, and it had just about re-affirmed its position as the most powerful in the World. This was to be challenged in the next conflict, the Seven Years War (1757–1763), by a revitalised French Navy. Spain elected to remain neutral for most of the war, but very unwisely decided to enter it in 1761 on the side of France, which allowed a British Navy, at the height of its success and confidence, to seize both Havana and Manila. In this war Britain was to secure a dominant position in the Indian subcontinent, in North America and Canada and in the greater Caribbean. It left Britain with a global empire to protect but it provided her navy with bases from which she could dominate the seas.

Chapter 12

THE 'PEACETIME' SLOOPS
1714–1728

Whilst the treaty of Utrecht brought the War of the Spanish Succession to a conclusion in 1714, it did not deliver a universal peace. However, the intensity of sea fighting between the southern North Sea and the Mediterranean did ease somewhat. For the sloops, it brought to a halt the incessant French privateering activity, at least around the coasts of Britain, though hostilities continued in the western Mediterranean, the West Indies and the Baltic. The count of sloops and bombs was to reach its lowest ebb in the years immediately following the end of this war. The number then rose again, partly though the building of new sloops (eight for use in home waters and one for use overseas), and partly through the rebuilding of three of the six 1710–1711 sloops, which again were for use overseas.[1]

THE REBUILT SLOOPS OF 1719–1725

In 1712 Britain had fifteen cruising sloops, including the small Sixth Rates of 1709, and six bomb sloops. By the end of 1714 that number had been reduced to six cruisers, shortly to be four, and four bombs, the latter old vessels from the 1690s. No further sloops of either type were built until 1721, with the exception of a rebuild, in 1719, for *Trial*, one of the 1711 *Jamaica* group. This decline in the stock of sloops was driven by two factors. The main one concerns the role of the cruising sloops. They were acquired during the War of the Spanish Succession to combat interference with Britain's coastal trade by small French privateers. To do this they had to be of light draught to be able to work in shallow water, amongst the sands and mud banks, and to be able to navigate in narrow estuaries. This could only be accom-

plished with the use of oars to provide the necessary manoeuvrability, something that a Sixth Rate, 120ft long on the gun deck and drawing well over 10ft, would find difficult. The need for the smaller vessel was therefore urgent during war with France, but its conclusion removed the privateering threat and encouraged a reduction in the number of sloops. The other factor, which is perhaps more speculative, is that the Admiralty and Navy Boards concentrated on the rated warships because they knew that they could procure sloops relatively quickly and easily by hiring, buying merchant ships under construction in commercial yards or by ordering a quick build in a naval dockyard. Nevertheless, there were peacetime tasks that required the continuing availability of sloops, such as anti-smuggling operations, coastal surveillance, fishery protection

Fig 12-1. HM Sloop *Spence*, built just after this period, with schooner rig inferred from the draught. This may have been an intention but it was never carried out and she was rigged as a snow on first commissioning. *Author*

and communication. For these tasks there would be a new building programme in 1721–1722, which will be covered in more detail later.

There was also the ongoing problem of the security of British settlements and trade in the West Indies, since not only did Britain have competitive commercial difficulties with Spanish interests in that region but there was also the ever-present threat of piracy, although this had been brought under a degree of control in the 1720s. Piracy was replaced by Spanish-sponsored privateering and the largely unregulated actions of their *Guarda Costa* (literally 'Coast Guard', but in effect a kind of privatised revenue-protection system). Two of the six sloops of the *Jamaica* and *Happy* groups, ordered for the West Indies in 1710–1711, remained on station there until 1719, when the *Trial* returned home to be broken up for a rebuild, subsequent to which she was in home waters before being sent to the Straits.[2] She was replaced on station by *Happy*. *Shark* III remained there until 1722 when she likewise returned home for rebuilding. By 1721, before the new-build programme had started, the stock of sloops was down to as few as four: the rebuilt *Trial* at home, *Shark* III and *Happy* in the West Indies and the old 14-gun *Drake* of 1705, by now in Irish waters. This number is in stark contrast to the situation a century later when the sloop class would account for nearly half the warships in the Royal Navy.

Shark III was rebuilt in 1722 and *Happy* in 1725; *Trial* had already been rebuilt in 1719. So by 1725, as far as cruising sloops were concerned, the Navy possessed eight new-built, light sloops, three rebuilt medium sloops, one old heavy cruising sloop (*Drake*), and one new-built medium sloop, *Spence*. Taking the rebuilds first, and regarding them for the present as medium sloops, the rebuild lengthened two of the three, the rebuilt *Trial* being the largest with burthen increased to 142 tons. They were all originally 113–115 tons. All eventually returned to the Americas or the West Indies. The rebuilding of a sloop seems an unusual measure and it is questionable whether it was good value for money, but it may have been an administrative fiction in which little more than the name was retained; this was certainly the case with larger warships, although timber in good condition was usually reused. The fact that there was one new addition to these three sloops, *Spence*, built in 1722–1723 to the 1711 specification at 113 tons, underlines the value of this design and specification (but not rig) for operations in the West Indies.[3]

Because there is a surviving plan of *Ferret* II of 1711 that shows deadeyes and channels for one mast only, there is a view that all six sloops of the *Jamaica* group were similarly rigged. However, there is no certainty that the design plan was followed, although it is supported by the log of the *Trial*.[4] In any case, between 1716 and 1719 all four remaining sloops of this group (two had been wrecked by this stage) had been re-rigged with two masts. The broad assumption follows that all sloops thereafter had two or more masts, but what is not quite so clear is what rig was placed on those two masts. The presumed rig is that of the snow, which in its most basic form consisted of two sails on each of two masts, but in the case of these sloops it would have included staysails, spritsails, jibs and the fore-and-aft, gaff-headed 'snow' or 'wing' sail immediately abaft the mainmast. This sail is sometimes called a trysail, whose traditional role was, and remains, a small fore-and-aft sail raised abaft a mast, for use in a storm.[5] The snow sail is rather larger than the trysail but is set on a gaff spar

Fig 12-2. HM Sloop *Ferret* and others of the *Jamaica* and *Happy* classes after conversion to snow rig. *Author*

bearing on a small 'trysail' mast standing immediately behind the mainmast and attached to the aft timbers of the main top (see Chapter 1 fig 1-11). The arrangement is shown at Fig 12-2 where, instead of the trysail mast, a hawser is used to carry the luff of the snow sail, as was naval practice.

On the model at Fig 12-3 the hawse is replaced with a wooden spar, a mercantile practice. This model was once in the collection of the Science Museum. It was allegedly a contemporary model with its original sails and rigging. However, there are some difficulties with this contention. The general arrangement of the hull, deck and armament does tally with what is known of these early sloops of war and indeed the model's measurements match to within less than six inches those of *Happy*.[6] But the rig appears to be a little more recent than '1710–1711', the date ascribed to the model. Topgallant sails are possible but unlikely at this date on a small sloop, although they were certainly in use by the 1720s, by which time *Happy* would have been rebuilt. The use of a spar to take the snow sail's luff, as noted earlier, was not naval practice. The model does display a jib boom, which was certainly in use when these vessels were plying their way through the Caribbean islands. Another interesting point is the presence of a capstan in the waist of the vessel, which would have made the stowage of the ship's boat difficult. In one instance the capstan on one of these sloops had to be moved to make space for a boat. The model also has a raised forecastle, a feature not seen on any earlier sloop but one that was to appear on the new built sloops of 1721–1722. Nevertheless, whilst this model has its ambiguities, it gives a good impression of an early sloop.

Returning to the matter of rig, whilst it seems that either before or during their rebuild these sloops were fitted as snows, the experiences of *Trial* show that this was not always the case. In July 1719 she had been given a main boom and two masts, which were immediately moved further aft. In September her captain reported breaking his fore gaff so her first rig after rebuilding seems to have been like that of a schooner with topmasts carrying square sails.[7] In October that year she entered the Lisbon River to be made into a brigantine, which would most likely give her two square topsails

Fig 12-3. This model, identified as being very close to the sloop *Happy* of 1711, shows her after her conversion from a single-mast rig to the two-masted snow rig. Unfortunately the model is no longer in the Science Museum, having been returned to its owner. There is a good description of the model in the Science Museum publication *Sailing Ships*, Part II, by G S Laird Clowes.

and naturally a square fore course. Before 1719, square sails and a wing or snow sail had been a very satisfactory alternative to the one-masted rig for the 1710–1711 survivors, but *Trial*'s increased length seems to have called for more sail aft than a snow rig could provide, although the positioning of her mainmast could have been a critical issue; yet by 1727 she had been given a snow rig. All this goes to show the volatility of sloop rig at this particular period. By 1740 a stable pattern would emerge, but the earlier decades represent a rather experimental environment, with rigs specific to ship and date.

During the rebuilds, *Happy* (Fig 12-3) retained her original dimensions. In the table of the rebuilds below it is worth noting that although the length and depth for *Shark* III were changed, her beam was left as originally built. This was not the case for *Trial*. Add to this the fact that the percentage addition to *Trial*'s

REBUILT SLOOPS 1719 AND 1722

Name	LGD	LoK	Beam	Depth in hold	Burthen
Trial original 1711	64ft 6in	50ft 5in	20ft 8in	9ft 1in	115 tons
Trial rebuild 1719	76ft 0in	59ft 3in	21ft 3in	9ft 6in	142 tons
Shark original 1711	64ft 10in	50ft 0in	20ft 8in	9ft 11in	114 tons
Shark rebuild 1722	69ft 2in	54ft 8in	20ft 8in	9ft 6in	124 tons

length on deck was greater than that applied to her keel and it becomes evident that she would have looked rather different from her original guise. In the case of *Shark* III, the proportional lengthening of keel and the length on deck are very close to each other and she retained the same beam. These measurements suggest that *Shark* was altered but that *Trial* was completely rebuilt with a new set of frames. It would therefore be more accurate to say that she was broken up so that her timber could be used to build an entirely new ship.

THE NEW-BUILT SLOOPS OF 1721 AND 1722

One of the recurring tasks for the Navy, more often in peacetime than during hostilities, arose from the demand to provide ships to prevent the illegal passage of goods. It was with this task in mind that the Admiralty Board ordered the building of three batches of small cruising sloops to be used in home waters. In their minutes of 11 January 1721 the members

resolved that the following sloops be appointed to cruise in the respective stations against their names expressed for preventing the running of goods, obliging ships and vessels coming within their reach to perform quarantine and seizing and carrying into the next port such as shall be suspected for carrying on a clandestine trade. And to correspond with the custom house officers and give constant accounts of their proceedings.[8]

Regrettably, these instructions were not always complied with in that several of these sloops were caught landing 'privately' those goods that they were charged with handing to the customs officials. Their cruising grounds ran from North Britain (Scotland), where *Weazle* was deployed under the aptly named Captain Chilly, down the East Coast, along the South Coast, including the Channel Islands, and up to Milford Haven.

These sloops, at least the *Otter* and *Cruizer* groups, turned out to be rather different from their predecessors, and their form was never repeated in the Navy. The first group, *Bonetta* II and *Ferret* III, were under 66 and 67 tons respectively and only 55ft long. This makes them of similar size and burthen to the sloops of 1699 ordered for the same purpose. There is evidence that they were initially rigged in a similar fashion, with two masts and topmasts. They also had a gaff for a snow sail and a jib boom for a flying jib; but when *Bonetta* III returned from the sea in 1731, the survey reported that she had a boom without a main yard. This would imply that she had disposed of her square main course, replacing it with a fore-and-aft course and thus adopting the brigantine rig.[9] Their hull shape and deck arrangement are unknown, although they had a fair beam with a LBR of just 3.24. Their armament was four 4pdrs, specified as 4ft 6in long, with four swivels 3ft long and they were allocated a crew of 40.

The accommodation must have been sparse on board as *Bonetta* III's captain had to request an awning to shelter the crew. Wisely, he pointed out that this would not impair his sailing as it would be stowed with the oars in their crutches when at sea. Their normal patrol area lay between the Downs and the Isle of Wight. The pair were sold in 1731, although *Bonetta* III's surveyor felt that she had four more year's life in her. These two and the other six often worked in company or in pairs with tasks such as 'to endeavour to procure men for the fleet' and 'to guard the herring fishery during the season'.[10]

The second group, *Otter* III and *Swift* V, were larger at 91 and 93 tons respectively. Fortunately, their appearance is known for there is a plan of *Swift* V at the NMM (Fig 12-5). Apart from the fact that she has a billet head, she looks like a small commercial vessel. She has a flush deck stepped down forward and aft with

Fig 12-4. Watercolour of HM Sloop *Swift* with brigantine rig. *Author.*

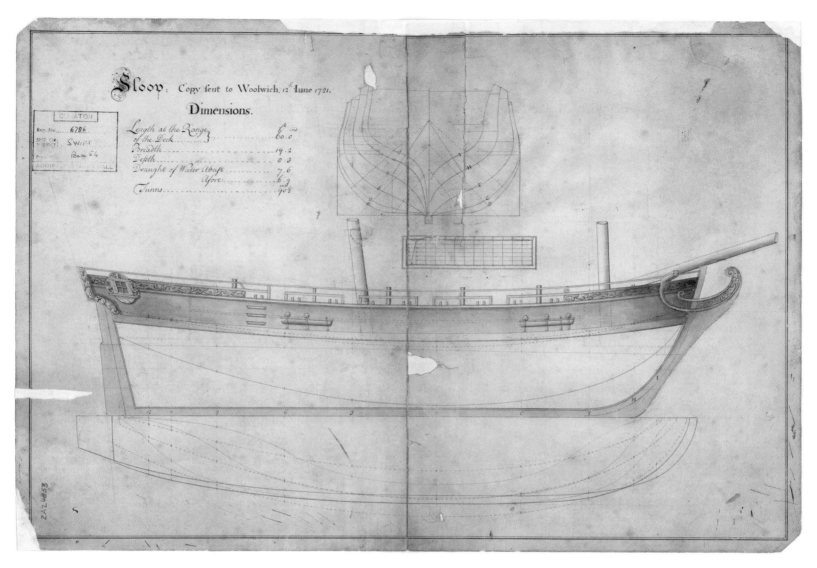

a low quarterdeck and forecastle above each drop, creating two small cabins. She appears to have shallow bulwarks with a fore-and-aft rail above running in a clean sweep from bow to stern. The interesting point on her sheer plan is the arrangement for deadeyes and channels. The fore channels might support a square foresail and topsail but the main channels, which appear to be set up to receive only two shrouds, would not, so she probably had a different rig on this mast. Karl Heinz Marquardt, an expert on eighteenth-century rigging and on the schooner rig in particular, suggested a schooner rig for *Swift* V, as shown in the author's interpretation at Fig 12-7. Yet her captain's log is evidence that she started with two masts and topmasts, both square-rigged.[11] However, in July 1722 he requested that she be rigged as a brigantine. It is worth quoting his report to the Navy Board following the granting of his earlier

request, since it is fundamental to the two-mast rig as applied to the smaller sloops, which were commonly regarded as being snow-rigged although very often they were not.

Since you were pleased to order the *Swift* sloop to be fitted with a 'shoulder of mutton' mainsail (which was in the beginning of May last) I have try'd all the experiments that I could think of to discover the difference of her sailing with that sail to what she did with a square mainsail, and find that she goes far better with it both 'by' and 'large', for sailing with the wind upon the quarter you cannot set a studdingsail to leeward whereas this sail naturally booms out upon the lee quarter and you may set the same studding sails to windward as you could do with a square sail. The main staysail likewise draws very

Fig 12-5. This plan of *Swift* is one of the earliest sloops in the collection of the National Maritime Museum. Note the rake of the masts which indicate that at least the main mast is likely to have carried a fore-and-aft main course. Note also that the mainmast is only supported with two shrouds per side, which would reinforce the possibility of a fore-and-aft sail here. It is also worth noting the drawn back position of the shrouds, indicating the desire to be able to haul any square sail as closely as possible into a fore-and aft trim. *National Maritime Museum J0151*

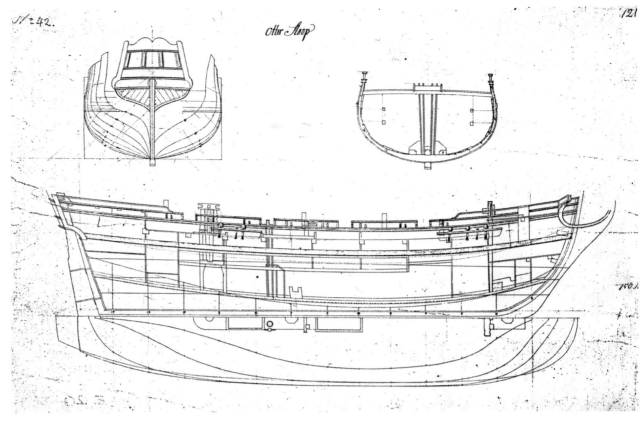

Fig 12-6. The Swedish War Archives (Krigsarkiv) in Stockholm preserves a draught of *Swift*'s sister ship *Otter*, which shows the internal layout, with the deck stepped down at bow and stern. Although the draughting style is entirely different, it confirms all the main features of the *Swift* design bar one – the body plan shows significantly more deadrise. Interestingly, although produced to the same specification, *Otter* was built by Richard Stacey, who was to become a highly regarded designer of sloops. *Krigsarkiv Stockholm*

well quartering; to windward she holds a better wind and works much better, but the mainmast is too short for a brigantine and the main topsail too large, which if it was altered I am of the opinion she would go yet better; I mean to have no square mainsail at all which would ease her of a great deal of top hamper, and I believe would be much for the advantage of the vessel's sailing.[12]

Later in the year, when she was in for refit, he reminded the Navy Board of his request for a

longer mainmast. There is also mention in the log of replacing a broken boom with the cross-jack yard, indicating that she retained square topsails. Therefore, weighing all the evidence, her final rig must have been similar to Fig 12-7 but with a square fore course in place of the fore-and-aft one shown here.

The *Otter* was virtually identical to the *Swift* in hull and rig and, like her, was ordered in March 1723 to have her rig altered to a brigantine. In her case her captain got agreement to apply more rake to her mainmast and shifted its head from 14in off plumb to four and a half feet![13] As with the smaller *Bonetta* and *Ferret* III, her captain had to ask for a waist cloth and an awning to protect his crew, which given the low-cut bulwarks does not come as a surprise. Life on these small sloops must have been hard. This pair of sloops was allocated an armament of four to six 3pdrs, four ½pdr swivels and a crew of 45.

A footnote to this pair of sloops: both were to be caught smuggling. It was reported that '...in 1729 the Southampton Customs sadly complained that every time the Admiralty sloop *Swift* went over to Guernsey on her preventive duties, she invariably returned with brandy and wine and dutiable provisions in

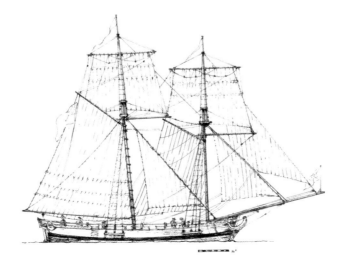

Fig 12-7. The schooner rig as may have been applied to *Swift* and other small sloops. *Swift* was given a brigantine rig, which would have been similar to that shown here, but without the fore wing sail and with a fore course added (see Fig 12-4). Her captain correctly pointed out that her mainmast needed to be longer (than shown here) and that he would dispense with a square main course. *Author*

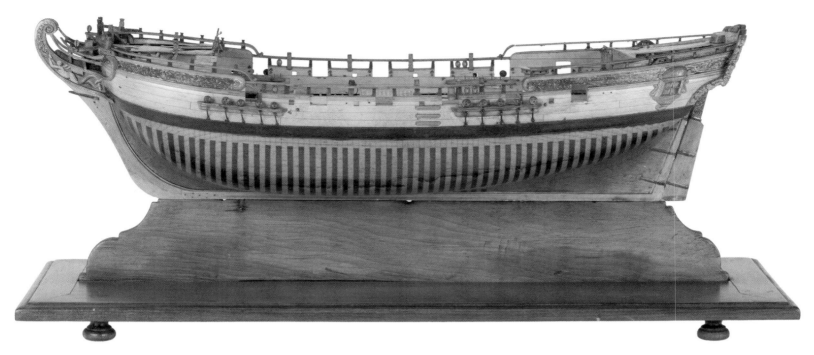

quantities so vast that, with the best will in the world, they could not be regarded as the legitimate "ship's stores" they were alleged to be.' It was a similar tale with another sloop, when in 1739 there was a seizure of tea and brandy on board 'HM Sloop *Otter*, lying at Harwich'.[14] *Hawk* was also to get a dishonourable mention in this respect.

An important piece of evidence is a detailed contemporary model of what is probably a sloop of the *Cruizer* class (Fig 12-8). The similarity to the form of *Swift* V is evident but there are some important differences. Her forecastle and quarterdecks are raised higher, as are her bulwarks, delineating more clearly the gun positions. Her quarterdeck is very exposed and although the helmsman can steer from this position with a tiller, there is an arrangement on the model (sadly damaged) that shows an alternative helming location, which would allow him to use a wheel immediately forward of the aft cabin bulkhead. This was quite unusual at this time on a small vessel. Like *Swift* she has a simple billet head and a round bow at deck level as did *Ferret* II. However, the difference here is that unlike *Ferret* II, she and *Swift* V have a raised forecastle deck, the first instance of a sloop having such a feature, though it may have been introduced to the rebuild of *Trial* in 1719. The evidence for this is on the model of her sister sloop *Happy* (Fig 12-3), rebuilt in 1724–1725, which shows a

ladder on the port-hand side that must lead up to a forecastle deck. The *Cruizer* class sloops had a flush deck stepped only at the stern to create a cabin for the captain.

Although on this model (Fig 12-9) the hull has been carved out of a solid block of wood, it has been hollowed out so that the deck construction is fully represented. This image and that at Fig 12-8 show the noticeably forward position of the midship section, giving these small sloops decidedly blunt bow sections which are not seen on earlier sloops, whose waterlines were hollow. It would seem that this shape was particular to this set of small sloops, which as compensation had a fine run aft. The other main difference to her sister *Swift* V lies in the deadeyes and channels. Those shown here are capable of holding up three-part square-rigged masts, which suggests that she was designed for snow rig. But of course changes would be made during their careers.

These sloops all started out with snow rig

Fig 12-8. A sloop of the *Cruizer* class of 1722. This model has not been made 'Navy Board fashion'; rather the rooms between the frames have been indicated by paint. This vessel is larger than *Swift* at 100 tons, and though she is similar in form and deck layout, she has more robust bulwarks and wheel steering. Possibly the main difference is the position of the deadeyes and channels which suggest a snow rig rather than the lighter brigantine and schoooner rigs. Small and lightly armed, most of these little vessels remained in home waters or in the Irish Sea for their entire careers. *National Maritime Museum L2622-001*

Fig 12-9. The NMM's model of a *Cruizer* class sloop showing beams and carlings, hatches and companion ways.

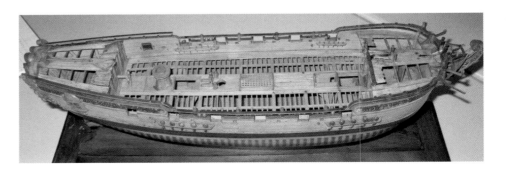

but, certainly in one case (that of *Spy* III), there was no snow sail abaft the main. Her captain requested one in July 1723, a year after her launch. His request was granted immediately and as a result he was able to report that the sloop sailed the better for it, particularly to windward. Unfortunately, having no trysail mast or hawse, he found that the jaws of the snow sail gaff continually fouled the parrels holding his main yard to the mast. Later, due to damage to her main cap, he re-rigged the shrouds around the topmast at the mainmast head, lengthened his snow sail and dispensed with the square main course. As a result he was able to report that the ship sailed better with this arrangement. However, there were some who felt that the large fore-and-aft main course was dangerous in heavy weather, possibly because of the risk of an involuntary gybe when sailing downwind. The Surveyor of the Navy at this time, Sir Jacob Acworth, in defending his earlier decision to agree to the captain's request, stressed the value of speed to these small ships and made the very valuable point that any modern yachtsman would understand: 'if they are designed to sail fast, they must have a quantity of canvas to assist them, and in a gale of wind care must be taken to hand or

shorten sail in time, and in my opinion such vessels, especially small ones, that do not sail fast, should not be employed, but laid up as quite useless.'[15] Like her sister *Swift* V, *Cruizer* also had her rig altered – and more than once, possibly suffering the greatest number of rig changes of any sloop. Starting as a snow in 1721, by 1726 she had been converted to brigantine rig and by 1729 to ketch rig, as can be seen from her sail inventory.[16]

These details demonstrate that it was the captains of these small sloops who were stumbling towards the brigantine rig and not the builders or designers. However, interest in such issues also came from the top, as shown in an account of a visit to Deptford in January 1729 by Lord Torrington, Admiral Sir John Norris, Admiral Sir Charles Wager (who had originally suggested the sloops for Jamaica), Commissioner Cleveland and Sir Jacob Acworth. They wanted to compare the sailing abilities of *Cruizer*, now with a ketch rig and using a square mainsail, with *Spy* III carrying a brigantine rig. Having inspected them alongside, they invited them to 'stand' up and down Greenwich Reach whilst they viewed them from the yard in order to assess their sailing qualities. These were the most senior members of both

Fig 12-10. Model of a schooner with a hull similar to that of the *Cruizer* class of 1722 but with a rig of around 1800! The model is in the collection of the Science Museum and was rigged in the museum in 1902, but based on a mistaken notion of what the hull represented. The model is described in the Science Museum publication *Sailing Ships*, Part II, by G S Laird Clowes.

Admiralty and Navy Boards and this gives a clear indication of how much importance was placed on the sailing ability of these sloops, as well as an understanding of their value as trial horses for new ideas.[17] This comparison between snow, brigantine and ketch rigs was to repeat itself right up to the arrival of ship-rigged sloops in the 1750s.

There was still no universally accepted formula for masting these ships. *Hawk* II, having been given a brigantine rig with a long pole mainmast, ended up with her fore-and-aft main course carrying a boom of 45ft. Her captain complained, not unreasonably, that this was putting a tremendous strain on the main-mast head when the boom had to be topped up to avoid it being plunged into the water whilst sailing large (well off the wind) in a heavy sea. The Navy Board had her returned to snow rig and her captain was very happy to agree to this. This seems to run counter to Acworth's view expressed above.[18]

Another aspect of rig, which repeated the experiences of earlier sloops, was the frequent demand for shortening masts. At her launch, *Cruizer* was to have 4ft and 3ft respectively removed from her fore- and mainmasts.[19] This prompts a consideration of the reason behind this recurring problem of too lofty or large a sail plan and its implications for the stability of sloops. The critical factor is the close proximity of the centre of gravity to the centre of buoyancy (see Chapter 1), and because they were of shallow draught, this meant that their ballast had limited leverage with which to counterbalance the sideways heeling force of the sails. In the case of *Spy* III and others, they had lead 'pigs' inserted between their timbers, held in place by the heels of the futtock frames. This is the lowest possible place for the densest weights to be installed and the position from which they could exert the greatest righting leverage. This also provides a clue to their construction in that they were not fully framed (with double 'framed bends' as were rated ships), but lightly built with significant 'rooms' between their frames. Indeed, lightness was a requirement for sloops at this time, as will be shown later. The four sloops of the *Cruizer* group were allocated six 4pdrs and six ½pdr swivels, with a crew of 50.[20]

As a footnote to this section, and to underline the general obscurity surrounding this subject, there are two examples of misleading information that need mentioning. Over the winter of 1726–1727, somewhere in the Celtic Sea, the *Cruizer*'s captain 'spoke with a schooner bound for Gibraltar'. Though no one doubts that the Americans were the great developers of this rig in all its forms and uses, this observation corrects the myth that at some point in the latter half of the eighteenth century, the Americans

Table 12-1: PROGRAMME OF REBUILDS, INCLUDING NEW-BUILT *SPENCE*, 1719–1725

Name	*Trial*	*Happy*	*Shark* III	*Spence*
Ordered	3-1719	9-1724	10-1722	11-1722
Launched	5-1719	8-1725	9-1723	3-1723
LGD	76ft 0in	62ft 7in	69ft 2in	64ft 6in
LoK	59ft 3in	50ft 2in	54ft 8in	50ft 1½in
Beam	21ft 3in	20ft 8in	20ft 8in	20ft 8in
LBR	3.58	3.01	3.35	3.12
Depth in hold	9ft 6in	9ft 0in	9ft 6in	9ft 6in
Burthen	142 tons	114 tons	124 tons	114 tons
Guns	10 x 4pdr + 4 swivels	10 x 3pdr + 4 swivels	10 x 3pdr + 4 swivels	8 x 3pdr + 4 swivels
Men	100	80	80	80
Rig	Schooner to Brigantine	Snow	Snow	Snow
Fate	BU Deptford 1731	Sold 1735	Sold 1732	BU Deptford 1730
Builder	Stacey, Deptford	Stacey, Deptford	Stacey, Deptford	Stacey, Deptford

Table 12-2: PROGRAMME OF NEW-BUILD *BONETTA* AND *OTTER* GROUPS, 1721

Name	*Bonetta* III	*Ferret* III	*Otter* III	*Swift* V
Ordered	3-1721	3-1721	6-1721	6-1721
Launched	4-1721[1]	5-1721	8-1721	8-1721
LGD	55ft 2in	55ft 5½in	64ft 6in	60ft 6in
LoK	42ft 11¼in	43ft 1in	51ft 5in	47ft 0in
Beam	17ft 0in	17ft 1½in	18ft 3in	19ft 3in
LBR	3.25	3.24	3.53	3.14
Depth in hold	7ft 6in	7ft 6in	8ft 3in	8ft 0½in
Burthen	66 tons	67 tons	91 tons	93 tons
Guns	4 x 3pdr + 4 swivels	4 x 3pdr + 4 swivels	4 x 3pdrs + 4 Swivels	4 x 3pdr + 4 swivels
Men	40	40	45	45
Rig	Snow to brigantine	Snow to brigantine	Snow to brigantine	Snow to brigantine
Fate	Sold 1731	Sold 1731	Wrecked Suffolk 1742	Sold 1741
Builder	Stacey, Deptford	Hayward, Woolwich	Stacey, Deptford	Hayward, Woolwich

1 Note the amazing speed with which a small sloop could be built.

Table 12-3: PROGRAMME OF NEW-BUILD *CRUIZER* GROUP, 1721

Name	*Cruizer*	*Weazle* II[1]	*Hawk* II	*Spy* III
Ordered	8-1721	8-1721	8-1721	8-1721
Launched[2]	10-1721	11-1721	11-1721	12-1721
LGD	62ft 0in	61ft 6in	62ft 0in	62ft 1in
LoK	47ft 10in	47ft 11in	47ft 9½in	48ft 6in
Beam	19ft 10in	20ft 0in	19ft 10in	20ft 0in
LBR	3.12	3.08	3.12	3.10
Depth in hold	9ft 0in	9ft 0in	9ft 0in	9ft 0in
Burthen	100	102	100	103
Guns[3]	6 x 4pdr + 6 swivels	6 x 4pdr + 6 swivels	6 x 4pdr + 6 swivels	6 x 4pdr + 6 swivels
Men	50	50	50	50
Rig	Snow to brigantine to ketch	Snow to ?brigantine	Snow to brigantine to snow	Snow to brigantine
Fate	BU Deptford 1732	Sold 1732	Lost Atlantic 1739	Sold 1731
Builder	Stacey, Deptford	Hayward, Woolwich	Rosewell, Chatham	Naish, Portsmouth

1 Commanded by Cmdr George Anson in 1723.
2 Note quick build time.
3 Generally 4pdrs were around 5ft long, but there were many different lengths at this time; ½pdr swivels were 3ft long.

invented the word for what was already an old-fashioned rig, first used in European waters by the Dutch in the seventeenth century. As pointed out earlier, it was a rig proposed for the sloop and indeed there is a model in the Science Museum's collection which is labelled as a 'Naval Schooner (1760-1780)'.[21] Whilst the style of schooner rig here is taken from Steele's treatise of 1780, the hull of the model, its shape and deck detail, bear an exact resemblance to the *Cruizer* class sloop discussed above; the model's rig and hull are both authentic, but they do not match each other. At the end of the eighteenth century the Navy started to make much use of schooners for communication purposes but apart from the outside possibility that this rig may occasionally have been used by these light sloops of the 1720s and also by the new *Spence* II and *Drake* II in 1728–1729, it is unlikely that any British sloop, as opposed to Navy schooner, was ever to be rigged in this fashion again except by way of experiment, trial or purchase. This was so in the case of the schooner *Barbadoes*, for example, acquired in the West Indies in November 1763, which on being taken into the Navy was classed as a sloop.

This chapter would not be complete without a brief consideration of life on board a small sloop in the boisterous conditions off the British coastline or the alternating calms and hurricanes of the West Indies. Activities that are regularly logged by captains are the repairing and adjustment of rigging and this includes scraping and blacking spars where appropriate, taking out and replacing masts, altering sails, repairing spars, securing to a wall so as to scrape and tallow the hull and the shifting and renewal of ballast. This list is far from exhaustive. The crews of these small ships were made up of regular sailors and some pressed men but they were remarkably resilient and could turn their hands to most tasks. Although not in home waters, the *Trial* lost her one and only mast in a minor hurricane in the Caribbean. The crew and the carpenter were sent ashore to cut down a tree to make a new, and probably temporary but perfectly serviceable, mast. Managing sails in a hard blow was more difficult than on a large, steady, rated ship and for much of the time the crew would be soaked. In calm, out would come the sweeps, normally stowed in crutches on the quarters or bound together and lashed to the quarterdeck stanchions, and the tedious and demanding business of rowing whilst standing would begin. The accommodation was negligible and once wet it would need a good run of fine weather to get dry again. The monotonous round of domestic activities would be punctuated by points of sheer terror such as a mast breaking just above the partners in a near hurricane or equipment and fittings being swept away by heavy, breaking seas. Engagement would be infrequent though readily met, as when *Trial*, on 3 December 1711 'exchanged broadsides with a French 32-gun ship', quite cheeky unless it was a mere formality. Later she 'took, by boarding, a ship of 16 guns'.[22] Then in 1726 Commodore St Lo, commanding the Jamaica station, was 'invited to keep the *Spence* and *Trial* with him for intercepting Spanish privateers...'[23] The one thing that can be said for these small ships was that, although their crews endured an incredibly hard life, they probably had more variety in their work than those on a large ship of the line stuck in port or on blockade.

Chapter 13

TOWARDS A SPECIFICATION
1728–1740

The year 1728 can be seen as one of the key points in the development of the sloop of war. Hitherto sloops had been ordered in differing dimensions and rigged with a variety of sail plans; from here on the requests by individual captains for variations to rig would decrease and the Admiralty would order the snow rig for most of the subsequent two-masted sloops. The addition of a third or mizzen mast would not appear until the 1740s. This does not mean to say that minor alterations did not occur by way of adjustment to sail area or spar and mast positions and dimensions, but the overall plan of snow rig would become standard. The other important feature of sloops built after this date was the substantial increase in dimensions and burthen for sloops ordered to replace those of 1719–1725, which rose from around 130 tons and 65ft LGD, to over 200 tons and 85ft LGD. The other key date was 1732, when the Admiralty ordered eight new sloops to be built to a common specification, which it laid down in some detail.

The old sloop *Drake* of 1705, who finished her life in Irish waters, was returned to Deptford in 1728 to be broken up and rebuilt. At 176 tons she was far bigger than the other sloops of her time. She was different from all the sloops built since 1710 in that she had two decks, her main or lower deck carrying eight 3pdr guns and her upper deck six similar pieces. She had two masts and was probably snow rigged.[1] In their minutes of 27 July, ordering her rebuild, the Admiralty directed the Navy Board that

> The *Drake* Sloop ... is to be taken to pieces and they are to be directed to build a vessel

Fig 13-1. HM Sloop *Spence* with schooner rig. Note the depiction of studding sails set from the fore and cro'jack yards, derived from what the captain of the *Swift* says of the advantage of having a fore-and-aft main course, as quoted in Chapter 12. *Author*

in her room proper for sailing and rowing and as light as conveniently may be, but a letter is to be written to them not to go in hand with her before they lay before us a block model of such a vessel.[2]

Subsequently the Admiralty approved the model in October of that year. The new vessel, which should be called *Drake* II because she was to a new design, was built by Richard Stacey, master shipwright at Deptford. His previous experience with sloops included the building of the small Sixth Rate or sloop *Delight* in 1709 and the rebuilding of all the three survivors of the *Jamaica* and *Hazard* groups of 1710–1711 (see Chapter 9). These facts are important since the new *Drake* II was to be snow-rigged like his earlier rebuilds, have two decks like the original *Drake* and hull lines similar to those of the extended *Jamaica* group. It is instructive to compare the lines of one of

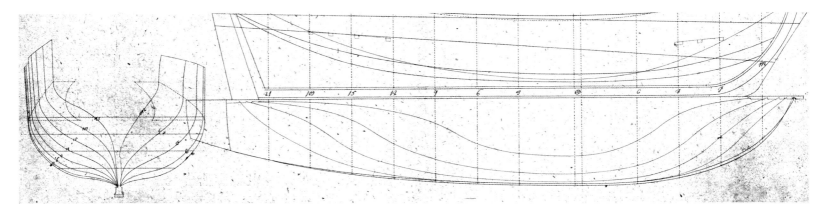

Fig 13-2. The form of *Ferret* shows some similarity to that of *Spence* at Fig 13-3. Richard Stacey had rebuilt three sloops of the *Jamaica* and *Happy* groups and these may have influenced his design for *Spence*. *National Maritime Museum J0218*

this group, *Ferret* (Fig 13-2), with Stacey's proposals for *Drake* as shown in the plan of her sister sloop *Spence* (Fig 13-3).

In June 1729, in order to replace *Spence* which was worn out after only seven years service, the Admiralty ordered the Navy Board 'to cause a sloop to be built at Deptford of the dimensions of *Drake* [II]', adding, in October, 'that the *Spence* [II] sloop was to be rebuilt in the same manner as the *Drake* sloop and if any improvements can be made, the Navy Board are to cause the same to be done.'[3] Stacey duly built both these sloops to identical dimensions and burthen and both were given the same complement of guns.

The salient features in both plans are the hollowed out entrance and run and the similarity apparent in the underwater shape of the transverse sections, though *Spence* would seem to have a larger breadth to depth ratio. Her sections, were they completed to the rail, would have shown that, like the sloops of 1710–1711, she had no tumblehome. Unfortunately, the waterlines on the two plans are struck at different levels, but the general shape of *Spence* does suggest a drawn-out *Ferret* II. There are some other interesting points on this plan. She has a pink stern as seen in the waterlines and in the aft cabin plan. From the plan it appears that both decks can be used for rowing, the lower deck for oarsmen, possibly seated, and the upper deck for rowing standing, though it has to be said that the lower deck is on or just below the designed load waterline, so only viable in a flat calm. There are also some strange inexplicable openings on the upper deck centreline; these are interpreted as gratings by Howard Chapelle in his reconstructed plan in *The Search for Speed under Sail*.

Possibly the most interesting feature is the

indication on the sheer draught for the mast positions and their rake, which is considerable. The rake and the position of both masts suggest schooner rig (see Fig 13-1), but her mast and sail dimensions prove that she was most definitely snow-rigged. It is, therefore, a reasonable conclusion that this was Stacey's original proposal for *Spence*, possibly coloured by his experience of *Trial*, which may have been schooner-rigged, but that the eventual sloop might not have been set up exactly as suggested by the draught. However, it is worth noting that on the plan the mainmast is positioned well

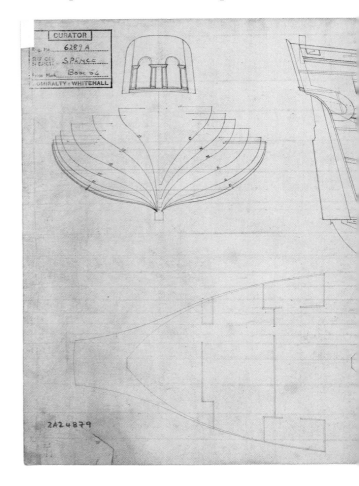

abaft the hull's mid-section and it is the thinking behind this that gives the snow rig its balance, in that the square course's centre of effort and that of the wing or snow sail are brought well aft.

From the plan, and from the advice given by the yard, it would appear that *Drake* II, and presumably *Spence,* were to be armed on both decks, the lower with two 6pdrs and the upper with four 4pdrs.[4] However, the *Spence* plan shows her as pierced on the lower deck for a demi-battery of four guns aft and two forward, with four aft and two forward on the upper deck. This does not match their eventual allocation, but it was common at this time to cut ports where space allowed, whatever the formal gun establishment, and this seems to have been extended to sloops; in action it allowed the guns to be moved to the most advantageous position (in this case, possibly moving them all to one broadside), and of course more guns could be added later if needed. She was also allocated twelve ½pdr swivels. Because both had a lower deck, they are recorded as having a small depth in hold of only 6ft, as was the case with their

predecessor *Drake,* who when taken in for breaking up, floated whilst still loaded at 9ft depth of water forward and 9ft 6in aft, which meant that her lower deck was below the load waterline.[5] The dimensions for *Drake* II and *Spence* are tabulated below.

A list of sails ordered for *Drake* II at Port Mahon in 1731 shows clearly that she was rigged as a snow with a square mainsail, that her wing sail had no boom and that she was therefore not brigantine-rigged.[6] There were minor changes made to this rig not only in the dimensions of masts, yards and sails, but also in the removal of her fore topgallant yard for a period. Unusually these changes generally followed a pattern of enlargement. Her sister *Spence,* at launch and whilst unloaded and probably un-ballasted, drew a mere 4ft 10in forward and 6ft 6in aft and swam exactly upright! She too had a snow rig and it is known that it was balanced and effective – her captain, in 1736, whilst demanding some stronger cordage, pointed out that there was 'nearly an accident by the shifting of the trysail sheet block, [on its horse] the sloop being so quick in

Fig 13-3. *Spence,* designed by Richard Stacey, can be seen as an elongated version of *Ferret.* She was given two decks and was at least considered for two banks of oars, hence the lower deck. Other sloops before and after *Spence* had lower decks and were – or could be – equipped with oars. Note that she has three gun ports a side on the lower deck (plus a bow-chase port), with the same number of positions immediately above them on the upper deck (indicated by half-round recesses in the gunwale). This arrangement harks back not only to her predecessor *Drake* but also to Model No 2 in the Henry Huddleston Rogers Collection. *National Maritime Museum J4688*

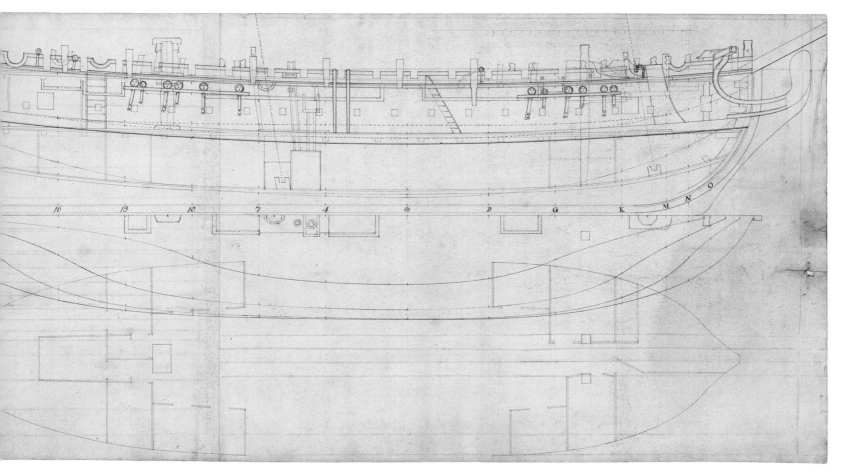

staying [tacking].'[7] His request for an iron horse was approved.

The members of the Admiralty Board had stressed the need for both these sloops to be as light as possible in both construction and rig and they had also insisted on the need for rowing to be effective. In following this direction, the design harked back, in principle, to the galleys of the Restoration, to the oceanic advice boats of King William's navy and to Edmund Dummer's proposals in 1704 for a small ship 'to cruise upon the coast of this kingdom and to row with oars'.

A brief look at the careers of these sloops indicates that on commissioning *Drake* II was deployed to the Mediterranean until 1734, when she returned for a great repair and refit at Deptford, as did *Spence*, though for only a middling repair. Thereafter both went to the West Indies: *Drake* for the remainder of her career until she returned home in 1740 as part of a convoy and was broken up at Deptford; *Spence* had a longer career which included a further two repairs, the first a middling one in 1736, after which she was deployed to the African coast and then to the West Indies. At the outbreak of the War of Jenkins' Ear against Spain and her possessions in the Caribbean, she was in operations off the coast of Georgia and then, in 1741, she joined Vernon's fleet before returning to Deptford for a great repair lasting five and a half months, after which she was considered 'almost new', which means she had a lot of new timber in her.[8] She was then sent to the Mediterranean and was at the second Battle of Toulon, then accompanied the convoy to Louisbourg (Canada) in 1745 before returning to the Mediterranean, where she took a Spanish privateer, the impressively named *Nuestra Senora de Buen Aires y San Juan Nepucemeno*. There is a possibility that after she had been sold in 1749, at the conclusion of the War, she herself became a privateer: one list of captures made in 1756 notes that the *Unicorn*, Captain Galbraith, took a privateer of '22 x 9pdrs and 190 men, formerly HM Sloop of War *Spence*'.[9] One wonders how she could have carried such a 'payload'. Her career shows the wide-ranging deployment of these small warships, particularly at a time of European war, which inevitably progressed to the colonies.

Two further sloops were built in 1731, both

with a two-deck system in the manner of *Drake* II and *Spence* II; both were snow-rigged. *Grampus* was smaller than the earlier pair at only 160 tons but *Wolf* (Fig 13-4), again built by Stacey, was of 244 tons burthen. This increase over *Drake* II at 207 tons was all in the beam. *Wolf* was the fastest of all four sloops. She was also Edward Hawke's first command in 1734. Unlike *Spence* II she could not be rowed from the lower deck; indeed one might question whether this facility was included on *Spence* II when she was built. It was certainly most unusual and, from the look of it, dangerous.

On 18 and 19 February 1732 *Wolf*, *Grampus*, *Otter*, *Hawk* and the 24-gun ship *Experiment* (106ft LGD and 375 tons) joined for sailing trials southeast of the Lizard. In these trials *Wolf* was fastest on all points of sailing, but this is not surprising because she was longer than the other sloops (*Otter* and *Hawk* were just over 60ft long and 90–100 tons displacement). With a quartering breeze she managed

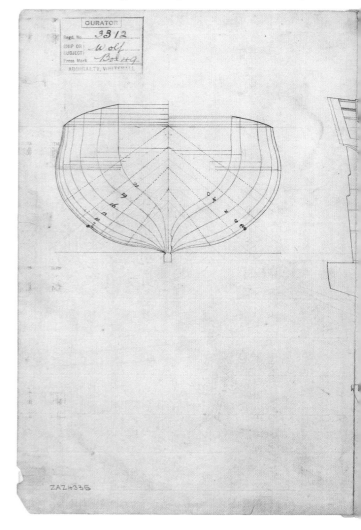

10 knots and, on the wind, 7 knots. She was also lighter than *Experiment*, size for size, and therefore had a greater power to weight ratio.[10] The surprising outcome of this competition was that *Experiment*, though considerably larger, could not beat either *Grampus* or *Wolf* on any point of sailing and on the wind and downwind she fell astern of all the sloops. Only with the wind on the beam could she beat the small *Otter* and *Hawk*. What this trial does show is the weatherly ability of these sloops and that despite their small size they could sail faster than a larger vessel, particularly to windward.

In 1719 the Admiralty laid down an establishment for rated warships, although it did not affect the sloops, which were able to develop in different ways both in hull and rig. With the possibility of setting up a new establishment in 1733, thought was given to the option of introducing some form of regulation to the category of 'sloop'. To this end, in 1732 the Navy Board invited the master shipwrights to consider indi-

vidually and recommend optimum dimensions for a cruising sloop. What parameters were given to the master shipwrights is not known but it would be hard for them to come up with an optimum design if they were not aware of the operational roles, level of threat and maritime environment the sloops were to face. Of the five invited, Ward had no views, not surprisingly since he had no experience of constructing sloops. Of the other four, only Stacey, possibly the most experienced builder, gave an indication of length on the keel and burthen. John Locke produced only beam and depth in hold. Their views are laid out in the table below.

Fig 13-4. HM Sloop *Wolf* designed by Stacey, longer and lower than *Spence* and with a lower deck but with very little headroom. *National Maritime Museum J4220*

PROPOSED SLOOP DIMENSIONS 1732

Master Shipwright	LGD	LoK	Beam	LBR	DoH	Burthen
Richard Stacey	87ft 6in	71ft 1in	23ft 0in	(3.80)	10ft 0in	200 tons
John Hayward	80ft 0in		24ft 0in	(3.33)	9ft 6in	
Joseph Allin	80ft 6in		24ft 6in	(3.26)	9ft 6in	
John Locke			23ft 4in		9ft 6in	

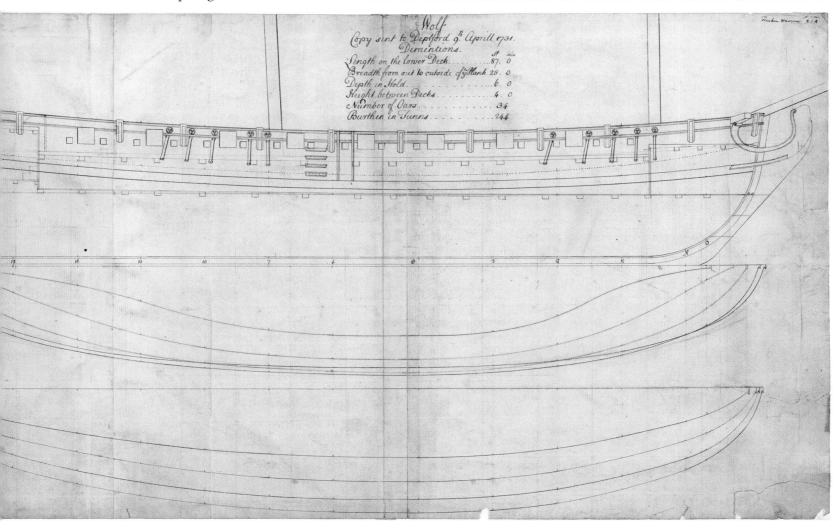

Wolf
Copy sent to Deptford 9th Aprill 1731.
Dimentions.
                                                    ft ins
Length on the lower Deck . . . . 87 . 0
Breadth from out to outside of ye Plank 25 . 0
Depth in Hold . . . . 6 . 0
Height between Decks . . . . 4 . 0
Number of Oars 34
Burthen in Tunns 244

As a result of this review, on 4 May 1732 the Admiralty ordered seven sloops to be built, all of 200 tons as Stacey had advised, one each by five of the leading master shipwrights and two by Richard Stacey; in July 1732 an eighth was added, again to be built by Stacey. This was to be the *Trial*, later to become famous on account of her hardships and scuttling during Anson's circumnavigation of 1740–1742. The warrant for one of these sloops, *Shark*, to be built in Portsmouth by Joseph Allin, is worth quoting *verbatim* as it shows how much detail was applied to these documents by the Navy Board at this time. The same warrant was sent to all yards.[11]

New Sloop, how to Build and Equip.

The Rt Honourable, the Lords Commissioners of the Admiralty having examined into the Models and Solids of the Sloops lately sent from the several yards, discoursed thereupon, and determined to have Eight Built in such manner, as an Experiment may be made of their Sailing; you are, in pursuance of an order from their lordships of the 28th Instant, hereby directed and required to cause a sloop to be Built at your Yard with all the dispatch that may be, agreeable to the model prepared and sent to us by the Master Shipwright, in the manner following Vizt.

The Sloop is not to exceed the Burthen of 200 tuns, and is to be Masted with two Masts and Square Sails, in the same manner as Snows are Masted, to be allowed Eighty Men, gun'd with Eight Four Pounders of Six feet long each, and twelve Swivel Guns, to have Seven Ports for Guns, and Fifteen Oar Ports on each side.

To have but One Deck and only a small Cabbin abaft for the Captain, the Length to be by the Range of the Deck from the Rabbitt of the Post, Twelve feet, and the height above the Range of the Deck at the Forepost, Three feet.

The Length of the Fore Castle, from the Rabbitt of the Stem by the Range of the Deck, Eleven feet Eight Inches, and the height above the Range of the Deck at the after part, to be One Foot Nine Inches.

The height of the Wast Three feet and Three Inches, height of the Ports from the Deck, One foot Three Inches. Depth of the Ports, One Foot Nine Inches.

To have a Capstand abaft the Main mast, but that there be no Wooden Awning.

And you are hereby further directed to fix a small Fife Rail, Twenty One feet long abaft, and one afore Fifteen feet long. To have a Square Stern, the Breadth whereof at the upper Rail of the Counter to be Eight feet Four Inches, with a snug Tafferel, and light Thin Quarter pieces set Close to the Side.

To be Built and Equipp'd with Rigging, Furniture and Sails, and in every respect with the greatest Exactness and Care to make her prove a Good Sailing Vessell. To have a Wing Sail to the Main Mast, and to have some Iron Ballast not exceeding Twenty Tuns, part whereof to serve as a Limber Boards, and part to Shift; but all to be so contrived, as to be moved and taken

out, when the Vessell is to be Careened, and you are to send us an Estimate of the Charge of the Hull, Furniture, and Stores: For which this shall be your Warrant.

Dated at the Navy Office The 30th of June 1732:

J. Acworth. J. Pearce. G. Saunder. J. Fawler
To the Respective Officers of his Maj'ts Yard at Portsmouth.

One of the interesting features of this group of eight sloops is their differing appearance one from another, given the precise nature of the warrants as to burthen and fitting out. The Establishments for rated warships similarly avoided a standard draught, but the dimensions were standardised to the most minute level. The conscious decision not to prescribe dimensions for the sloops allowed far more individuality in the vessels designed by each of the shipwrights. Stacey's intention can be seen in the plan of the *Cruizer* II at Fig 13-5. This may have been the most aesthetically pleasing sloop design of our period and warrants close inspection. With this design Stacey had returned to the more boat-like proportions of the early Restoration sloops and his design portrays the highest LBR, making her the slenderest of the eight. Although he also built *Hound* and *Trial* II, he may not have designed them since they were shorter and broader than *Cruizer* II. It is possible that they were designed by the Surveyor, Sir Jacob Acworth.

Using the draughts at the same scale a comparison can be made with *Shark* IV, designed by Joseph Allin at Portsmouth (Fig 13-6). She is shorter, wider and deeper than *Cruizer* II but, more to the point, has a totally different underwater shape with very full fore-sections and a fine run, whereas *Cruizer* II's lines are more symmetrical, which should make her better balanced and probably faster. The other detail of note on the plan at Fig 13-6 is the marked drag aft of her keel. This was not a feature that was all that common at this time – indeed, *Cruizer* II's drag is zero – but it would be used in the latter half of the century, particularly in North America.

Fig 13-5. This plan of *Cruizer* was Stacey's response to the Admiralty order for eight new sloops to the recommended dimensions of the master shipwrights. *Cruizer* was the inspiration for many of these and for two later sloops designed by – or possibly just influenced by the views of – the Surveyor Acworth. This is an iconic design in the history of the sloop. *National Maritime Museum J4723*

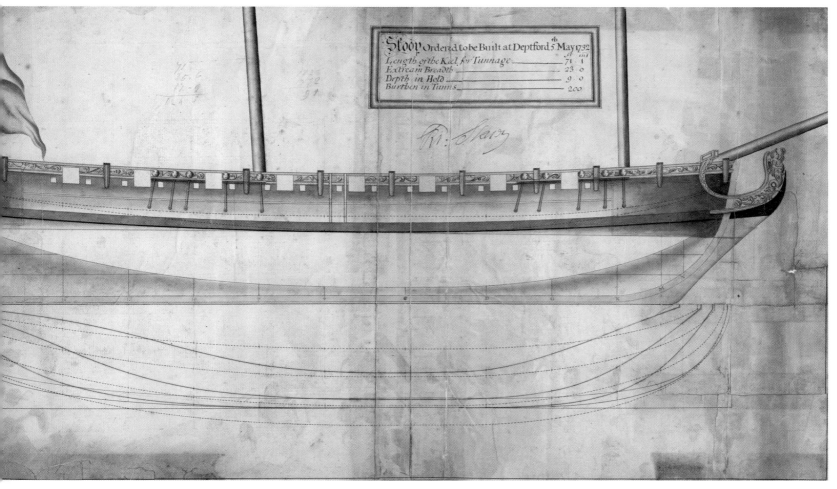

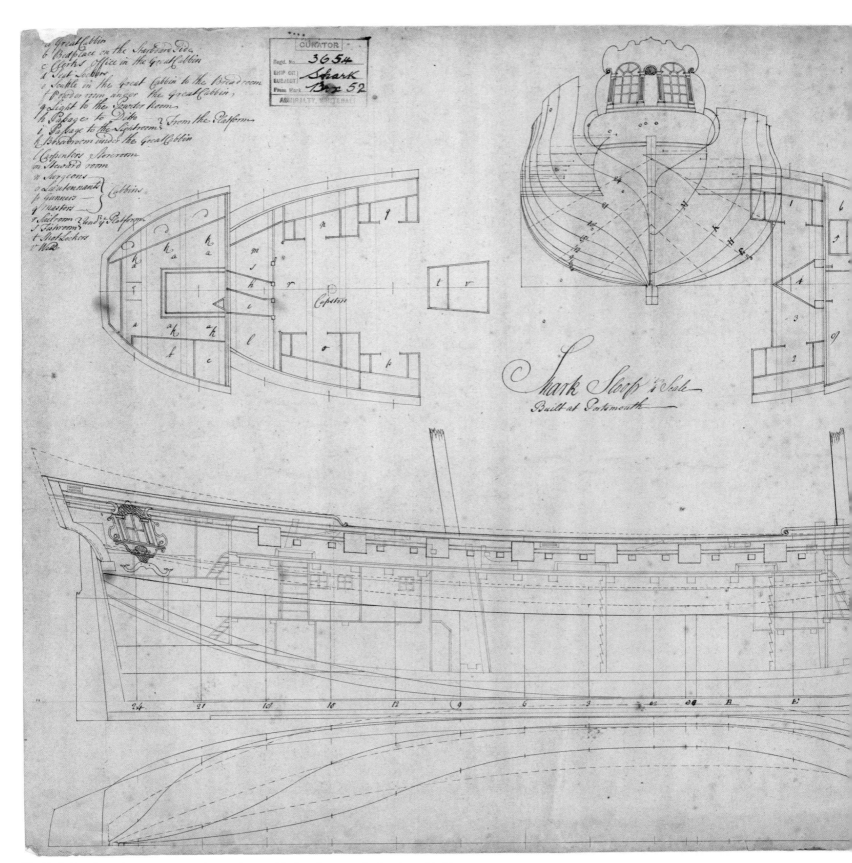

Fig 13-6. One sloop that was very much at variance with the other seven in the class of 1732 was *Shark*. Designed by Joseph Allin junior, master shipwright at Portsmouth, who later became Surveyor of the Navy, she exhibits an unbelievably bluff bow, combined with a relatively fine run aft. The result is an unbalanced hull, yet, despite this, she was a fair sailer but would not lie-to under any sail without attention (see her sailing quality report at Appendix 4). *National Maritime Museum J0219*

Between these two 'extremes' comes *Spy* IV, designed and built at Chatham by Benjamin Rosewell (Fig 13-7). If this plan is placed over that of *Cruizer* II it can be seen that the waterlines are virtually identical, although her sections show slightly more rounded floors and a gentler turn to the bilge. The other most obvious differences are the greater curve of sheer as compared with *Cruizer* II's rather flat one and the fact that both *Spy* IV and *Shark* IV have square sterns as laid down by warrant, whereas *Cruizer* II has a pink stern. This may suggest that the latter's plan is a proposal rather than an 'as built' plan.

Whilst all these sloops were pierced for seven guns a side, they were only allocated eight 3pdrs and 12 x ½pdr swivels (*Shark* IV had 4pdrs, and at one point is recorded as mounting ten). Given some of the engagements they managed, it is a wonder that they survived with such a meagre armament. As 200-ton sloops, it is also surprising that on commissioning they were allocated only 80 men. However, given that the only points of concern in the 1730s were minor difficulties with Spain in the Caribbean and in the Mediterranean and the everlasting problem of the Barbary States, such an armament may have been considered as sufficient in peacetime. There was always the possibility of augmenting the official allocation with more guns, up to a total of 14 – considering that the 113-ton *Jamaica* group carried ten 3pdrs, these larger sloops would certainly have been able to carry the full complement.

Seven of these sloops were given the conventional snow rig which, because of the sensible positioning of the mainmast, was now well balanced. The eighth, *Shark* IV, was allegedly set up with a ketch rig. The warrant, as quoted above, was for snow rig and this is supported by her plan at Fig 13-6, but there is another plan that shows a ketch rig, so there may have been a later amendment to the warrant. Her career is typical of the work of a sloop at this time. She was commissioned at Portsmouth in 1733 and was deployed to the Bahamas, returning home for a great repair and refit at Deptford in 1739. In 1740 she was recommissioned for use in home waters, spending the winter of 1741–1742 in Irish waters. By now the War of the Austrian Succession was underway and France was about to join Spain in the naval campaign against Britain. This renewed the need for convoys, but in this case it was for oceanic deployment rather than coastal as in the earlier War of the Spanish Succession. *Shark* was in the Mediterranean until her return in 1745, the year of the last Jacobite Rebellion, when she was off the coast of Scotland. She was then allowed to go cruising during which time she took two privateers, one French, the other Spanish. Having sailed for North America in 1749 and then to the Leeward Islands in 1750, she returned home in 1752 to be sold in 1755. For a small ship that was continually in use that is not a bad record, given that she only had two significant periods of repair, one in 1739 and the other in 1753.

By contrast, probably the most atypical career for a sloop was that of *Trial* II. Commissioned at Deptford in 1732, she spent her early years in the North Sea and Channel but was then chosen to join Anson's expedition to the Pacific. *Trial* II's experiences on this voyage would test her crew's tenacity to the utmost. The first problem was the breaking of her mainmast on her passage across the Atlantic to the southern coast of Brazil. Towed the remaining distance by the Fourth Rate *Gloucester*, her repairs delayed the squadron by a month. Four days later it broke again and had to be taken out at Port St Julian on the coast of Patagonia. In this desolate spot, it was replaced with a smaller mast, all that could be found. The picture at Fig 13-8 of *Trial* II and the *Centurion*, Anson's flagship, at the entrance to the Straits of Magellan shows, on the left, the shorter main.

The passage around Cape Horn began on 8 March 1741 and the experiences of *Trial* II are well described in the private journal of Philip Saumarez.[12] He had replaced *Trial*'s posted captain, Charles Saunders, who like so many others had fallen ill, and commanded the sloop for the bulk of the passage round the Horn. That the sloop and her crew survived this passage of enormous hollow seas, thick driving snow, exceeding cold and wet and, most dangerous of all, ice and snow clinging to their masts and yards, is almost legendary. Handling sails was a nightmare and often men working on the lower yards were forced under water, so violent was the rolling of the sloop in the hollow and therefore steep and breaking seas.

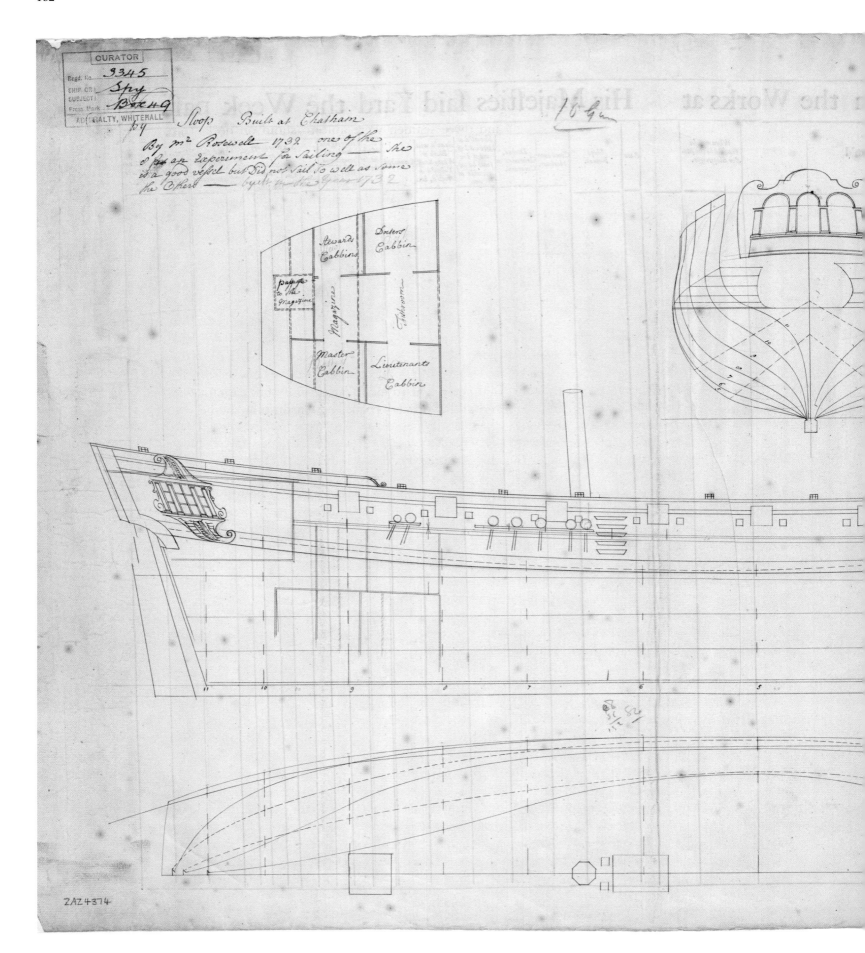

Sloop   Built at Chatham
By Mr Rosewell 1732. one of the
an experiment for sailing —— she
is a good vessel but Did not sail so well as some
the Others —— by the Year 1732

Stewards
Cabbins

Doctors
Cabbin

passage
to the
Magazine

Magazine

Store room

Master
Cabbin

Lieutenants
Cabbin

ZAZ 4374

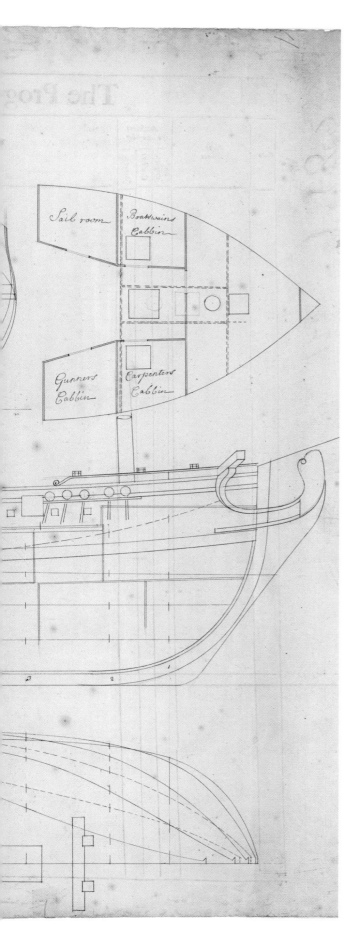

Captain Saunders was returned to *Trial* towards the end of the passage and eventually brought his sloop to her rendezvous with the flagship at the island of Juan Fernandez. As she entered the bay, only her captain, his lieutenant and three seamen were able to stand on deck. Many unburied corpses lay waterlogged on deck when Saumarez and a party of seamen went on board her to manage her anchoring. Apart from *Centurion*, she was the first to reach the island. On 9 September she sailed from the island with the remains of the squadron, in what was described as a doubtful condition. Nevertheless, by the 25th of the month Anson discovered her and the prize she had taken. By now she had lost her main topmast and sprung the main itself. The state of her hull had become critical, her timbers being so strained that her seams could not be caulked. The pumps were manned continuously and there was a danger that she might founder. Reluctantly her captain and all his officers requested Anson that she be abandoned. The coast of southern Chile was to be her last resting place, where she was scuttled on 27 September 1741. It must have been heartbreaking for her crew and there would have been tears in some men's eyes.

By 1739 all the small sloops of the 1720s, including the rebuilds, had either been sold, broken up or wrecked, except for *Otter* III and *Swift* V, who would last until 1741–1742. The Navy's count of sloops stood at fourteen, two from the 1721 'new-build', four from the programme of 1728–1731 and the eight sloops of 1732. The outbreak of the War of Jenkins' Ear afforded the opportunity to take prizes from the Spanish and convert them into temporary

Fig 13-7. HM Sloop *Spy* designed by Benjamin Rosewell, a medium design between *Cruizer* and *Shark* and in many ways foreshadowing the *Merlin* class of the 1740s. *National Maritime Museum J0138*

Fig 13-8. From a near contemporary account and illustration, this sketch by the author shows *Trial* and *Centurion* at the entrance to the Straits of Magellan at the start of Anson's voyage round the World. *Trial* has already been damaged twice. Note her unusual rig occasioned by the lack of spare spars which meant that she had to accept a lower than normal mainmast. This may have saved her during her horrific passage round Cape Horn. Richard Walter, *Anson's Voyage Round the World*.

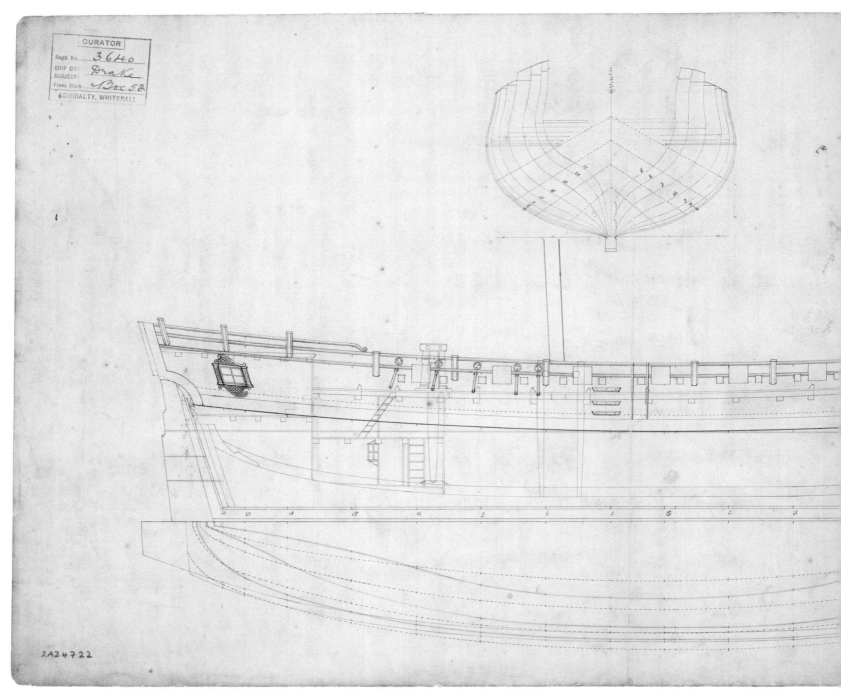

Figs 13-9 and 13-10. A plan for *Swift*, *Hawk* and *Drake* possibly designed by Acworth the Surveyor in 1740. The model is unidentified but is very similar in measurement and design to Acworth's plan. There is a definite harking back to the *Cruizer* design. *National Maritime Museum J0224 and L5773-001*

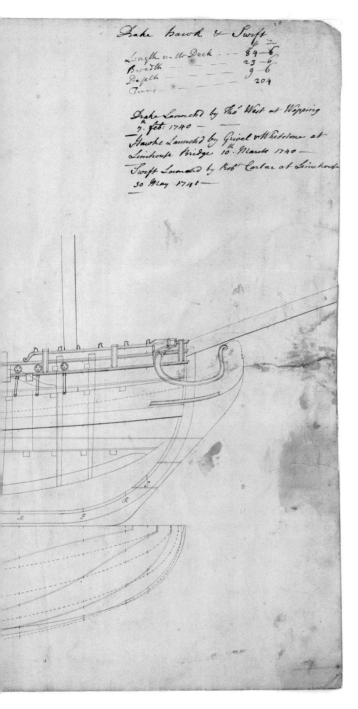

Table 13-1: *DRAKE* AND *GRAMPUS* GROUPS, 1728–1731

Name	*Drake* II	*Spence*	*Grampus*	*Wolf*
Ordered	7-1728	9-1729	4-1731	4-1731
Launched	4-1729	6-1730	10-1731	11-1731
LGD	87ft 0in	87ft 0in	70ft 0in	87ft 0in
LoK	73ft 5in	73ft 5in	56ft 1in	73ft 6in
Beam	23ft 0in	23ft 0in	23ft 2in	25ft 0in
LBR	3.78	3.78	3.03	3.48
Depth in hold[1]	6ft 0in	6ft 0	6ft 0in	6ft 0in
Burthen	207 tons	207 tons	160 tons	244 tons
Guns[2]	8 x 4pdrs + 12 Swivels	8 x 4pdrs + 12 Swivels	8 x 4pdrs + 12 Swivels	8 x 4pdrs + 12 Swivels
Men	100	100	80	100
Rig	Snow	Snow	Snow	Snow
Fate	BU Deptford 1740	Sold Woolwich 1749	Lost Guernsey 1742	Wrecked WI 1741
Builder	Stacey, Deptford	Stacey, Deptford	Hayward, Woolwich	Stacey, Deptford

1 All have two decks. Measurement likely to be from underneath lower deck, to the top of the keelson.

2 *Drake* and *Spence* were designed to have guns on two decks, though in reality this may have not happened.

sloops to support the hard-pressed cadre of British-built sloops, raising the total to twenty. However, this was an insufficient number and the Admiralty were forced to instigate another programme of 200-ton sloops in 1740.

Up to this date the vast majority of the sloop category had been built in Royal Dockyards, but with the emphasis on repairing and building the rated classes for the war with Spain, it was decided that if necessary the building of sloops would be placed out to contract with the merchant yards. This system, that was to last

for the remainder of the eighteenth century and beyond, left the design of the sloops, be they cruisers or bombs, with the Navy Board and the Surveyor, probably supported by the leading master shipwrights. Once agreed on a design, the Navy Board would contract out the building to the commercial yards, mainly on the Thames but occasionally at places such as Harwich,

Fig 13-11. This sail plan is such as might have been used on *Drake* II – essentially an improved snow, but with a brigantine sail lashed to the mast. In the true brigantine rig the main lower mast, and therefore the height of the gaff, would be very much greater. *Author.*

Table 13-2: *CRUIZER* GROUP, 1732

Name	*Cruizer* II	*Hound*	*Trial* II	*Saltash*	*Spy* IV	*Fly* II	*Bonetta* IV	*Shark* IV
Ordered	5-1732	5-1732	7-1732	5-1732	5-1732	5-1732	5-1732	5-1732
Launched	9-1732	9-1732	9-1732	9-1732	8-1732	9-1732	8-1732	9-1732
LGD	87ft 6in	84ft 0in	84ft 0in	85ft 7in	85ft 7in	86ft 6in	81ft 4in	80ft 0in
LoK	71ft 1in	68ft 1in	68ft 1in	69ft 1½in	69ft 5in	69ft 7in	65ft 6in	63ft 0in
Beam	23ft 0in	23ft 6in	23ft 6in	23ft 4in	23ft 4in	23ft 3in	24ft 0in	24ft 6in
LBR	3.80	3.57	3.57	3.67	3.67	3.72	3.38	3.26
Depth in hold	9ft 5in	9ft 6in	9ft 6in	9ft 6in	10ft 6in	10ft 6in	10ft 0in	9ft 11.25in
Burthen	200 tons	200 tons	200 tons	200 tons	201 tons	200 tons	201 tons	201 tons
Guns	8 x 3pdrs + 12 swivels	8 x 3pdrs + 12 swivels	8 x 3pdrs + 12 swivels	8 x 3pdrs + 12 swivels	8 x 3pdrs + 12 swivels	8 x 3pdrs + 12 swivels	8 x 3pdrs + 12 swivels	8 x 4pdrs + 12 swivels
Men	80	80	80	80	80	80	80	80
Rig	Snow	Snow	Snow	Snow	Snow	Snow	Snow	Snow
Fate	Sold Deptford 1745	BU Deptford 1745	Scuttled Pacific 1741	Sold Plymouth 1741	Sold Portsmouth 1745	BU Sheerness 1751	Wrecked WI 1744	Sold Deptford 1755
Builder	Stacey, Deptford	Stacey, Deptford[1]	Stacey, Deptford[1]	Lock Plymouth	Rosewell, Chatham	Ward, Sheerness	Hayward, Woolwich	Allin, Portsmouth

1 Possibly to a design by the Surveyor, Sir Jacob Acworth to Stacey's recommended dimensions and burthen.

Table 13-3: *DRAKE* GROUP AND PURCHASED SLOOP *SALTASH*, 1740–1741

Name	*Drake* III	*Hawk* II	*Swift* VI	*Saltash* II
Ordered	6-1740	8-1740	12-1740	1741 Purchase
Launched	2-1741	3-1741	5-1741	9-1741
LGD	85ft 1½in	84ft 5in	85ft 0in	89ft 0in
LoK	68ft 8½in	68ft 8½in	68ft 8¼in	71ft 3½in
Beam	23ft 9¼in	23ft 8¾in	23ft 7¼in	24ft 1½in
LBR	3.58	3.56	3.60	3.69
Depth in hold	9ft 6in	9ft 6½in	9ft 6½in	24ft 1½in
Burthen	202 tons	206 tons	204 tons	221 tons
Guns	8 (10 from 1744) x 4pdr, 10 swivels	8 (10 from 1744) x 4pdr, 10 swivels	8 (10 from 1744) x 4pdr, 10 swivels	8 x 4pdr, 12 swivels
Men	80, then 100	80, then 100	80, then 100	90
Rig	Snow	Snow	Snow	Snow
Fate	Wrecked 1748	BU 1747	Lost 1756	Burnt 1742
Designer	?Acworth	?Acworth	?Acworth	?Acworth
Builder	Contract	Contract	Contract	Contract

Bursledon on the River Hamble, Gosport and Shoreham. Royal Yards continued to build sloops when time and space were available, as they were a good way of using up offcuts and timbers too small for the rated ships.[13]

The *Drake* group of 1740 were acquired by contract in this way. They all were close to the dimensions and burthen of *Hound* and *Trial* II. These sloops, *Drake* III, *Hawk* and *Swift* VI, were probably designed by the Surveyor Acworth working close to Stacey's recommended dimensions and burthen. Fig 13-9 and Fig 13-10 show that their form, deck arrangement, number of ports and general proportions bear a close resemblance to the earlier sloops of 1732. In 1741 a commercially built sloop of similar tonnage was purchased 'on the stocks' (not to a Navy Board design, but chosen to match the requirements as closely as possible); she was acquired to replace the old *Saltash*, and given her name. Once again these sloops were to have a series of overseas deployments mixed with periods at home. One important change was that in 1744 their armament was formally increased to 10 guns at the larger calibre of 4pdr, although by this date one of them had been wrecked at Gibraltar. This increase is also likely to have been retro-fitted to the remaining sloops of 1732.

The next significant step up for cruising sloops was to come in the following year with the introduction of the 250-ton sloop, but this is a story for the next chapter.

Chapter 14

A MULTI-ROLE CLASS
1728–1749

The two decades after 1728 were to see the sloop of war mature into a distinct multi-role class with an expanding part to play in the security of Britain's coasts and the protection of its interests in the Mediterranean and both West and East Indies. The first decade of this period was one of relative peace, but by the start of the second, in 1739, Britain was once again at war with Spain, and then additionally with France from 1744. As a result, the Navy was overstretched and this may have contributed to the sharp increase in the orders for sloops from 1740 onwards. Fortunately sloops could be built quickly using commercial yards. Another reason for this demand was a change in the nature of maritime warfare, where a plethora of amphibious operations, escorts for commercial traffic and minor skirmishes against all-comers replaced the great battles of the previous century. The threat from privateers

Engagement between the Blast Sloop & 2 Spanish Privateers. 1743.

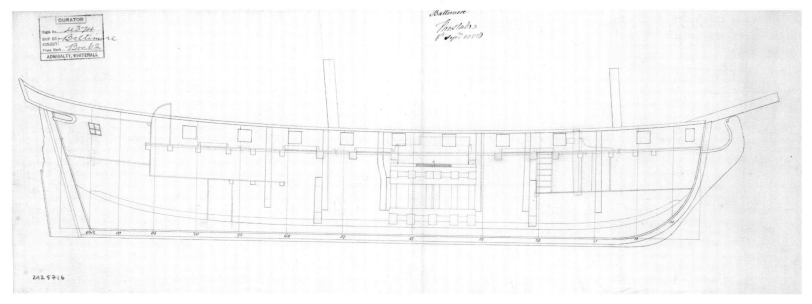

Fig 14-2. The sloop *Baltimore* designed by Lord Baltimore, a member of the Admiralty Board. She was later converted to a bomb vessel with one mortar, which suggests she retained the bilander or 'hollander' rig she was given on commissioning in 1742. *National Maritime Museum J0036*

had diminished, not perhaps in number but certainly in the force or size of the average ship involved. This opened up an increasing opportunity for sloops to be used for assisting in oceanic trade-protection where their speed and weatherliness would help with control, reconnaissance and communication. Their half-sisters, the bomb vessels were also to play their part as cruisers (Fig 14-1).[2]

From the building of the first bomb ketches in 1687, these vessels had always acted as cruising sloops when not required for their speciality. This inter-changeability of role was to be practised with considerable frequency during the period 1730–1763. An examination of pictorial evidence from the late seventeenth century and of ship plans over the first half of the eighteenth century shows that whilst the early bomb vessels had their own distinctive shape, by the 1730s their hulls at least had become close in form to those of their sister cruising sloops. The advantage of a well-shaped hull for the bomb vessel not only made her useful as a cruiser, but also helped her to keep up on passage with a squadron, although her ketch rig could make that difficult in certain conditions of wind and weather. A typical example of this inter-changeability of role can be seen in the career of HM Bomb Sloop *Blast* (Fig 14-1). She was first commissioned as a sloop but a year later she was fitted as a bomb. She was deployed to the West Indies in that role but from her depiction here she appears to be acting as a cruiser. The evidence for this change of role lies in the fact that when she was taken

by these two Spanish xebec privateers she had a crew of at least 80, the complement for a cruising sloop. The evidence for this is that 40 were killed in the fight and as many wounded.[3]

To a lesser extent cruising sloops, and indeed Sixth Rates, could be modified to carry mortars, but for a sloop this was a major undertaking as it would require a transfer from snow to ketch rig unless it carried only one mortar or was already ketch-rigged. This was the case with three 250-ton cruising sloops ordered in the 1740s that were refitted as bombs 16 years later during the Seven Years War. (Fig 14-2)

Other conversions were made. Two *Merlin* class cruising sloop were refitted as fireships in 1762. A bomb sloop, *Furnace*, ordered as such but commissioned as a cruising sloop in 1740, was then refitted with a ship rig for an expedition to find the North West Passage. Later in her career she was refitted for the role for which she was originally ordered, becoming a bomb sloop in 1756 and taking part in the bombardment of Gorée (Senegal, West Africa) and Le Havre during the Seven Years War. Bomb sloops, fireships and temporary conversions for specific expedition will be dealt with later, but this chapter begins with the development of the *Merlin* class cruising sloops.

TWO-MASTED CRUISING SLOOPS

In 1739 the Royal Navy had a total of twenty cruising sloops, six of which were Spanish prizes and were for short-term use only. By 1742 these had all been retired and a small programme of three 200-ton sloops and one commercial purchase was set up to replace them; by the same time seven further British-built sloops had either been broken up, wrecked, lost, scuttled or sold, leaving only ten available for service. War with France was on the horizon, adding to the existing conflict with Spain, so to meet the inevitable demand for small cruisers, the Admiralty set up four building programmes between 1741 and 1743.

The first was for three sloops at 244–249 tons: *Wolf* III, *Otter* IV and *Grampus* II. As in the case of the old *Wolf*, they were designed with two decks. The plan of *Otter* IV at Fig 14-3, when compared to the plans of the *Merlin* class sloops below and those of *Wolf*, *Saltash* and *Cruizer* II in the previous chapter, shows the gradual change in hull design from the long low sloops of the class of 1732 to the more deeply bodied ship-like shapes of 1745. This is not surprising given the fact that in 1732 the main

armament was eight 3pdrs, whilst by 1743 it was between ten and fourteen 6pdrs. The *Wolf* group of 1741 carried fourteen 4pdrs and had a crew of 110 men. All were snow-rigged and all were built by merchant yards to a Navy Board specification and design.

The second programme was again for three sloops that may have varied in shape and rig somewhat. The *Baltimore* at Fig 14-2 above was designed by Lord Baltimore, a man with no obvious naval experience except that of being a Lord of the Admiralty at this time, a post he held for only two years; this was the man King George II said 'thinks he understands everything, but understands nothing.' Unfortunately no lines are available for this odd-looking sloop pierced for 18 guns, but she has a pink stern, though whether this was a feature of the other two, *Saltash* II and *Drake* III is not certain. Her rig, determined in the first place by the Navy

Fig 14-3. HM Sloop *Otter*. Note the shape of the midship frames just above and below the waterline, where the former curve associated with sloop sections has been drawn into a straight vertical line. *National Maritime Museum J0236*

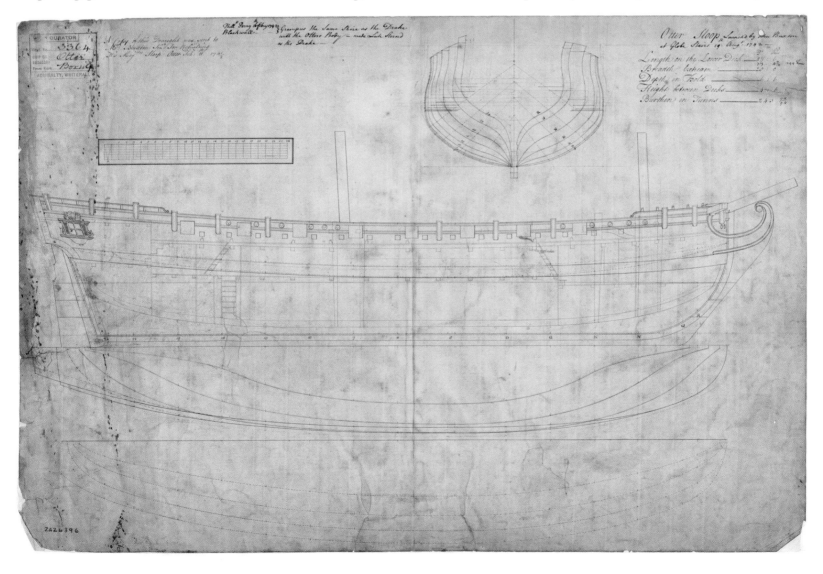

Board, was to have square headsails and a lug main with a square main topsail.[4] This is supported by a note from the officers of Deptford Dockyard supervising her building by Mr West, giving a 'proportion of the masts and yards cast for the new sloop ... that is to be rigged like a Hollands Trader ...' The Harwich packet boats that plied to and from Holland carried this rig.

Her mast and spar dimensions include a crossjack yard on her mainmast, which indicates that her topsail would have been square. This 'bilander' rig was changed in April 1743 when she was fitted at Portsmouth with a conventional snow rig. She would have had this rig at her successful action against a French privateer off the west coast of Scotland on 1 May 1746 and, two days later, with others,

against two French frigates. At this time the 'Young Pretender', Bonnie Prince Charlie, was still in the Outer Hebrides. This sloop also played a part in the development of the bomb sloops and will be referred to again later. Her bilander rig was a bit of a throwback: it had been in use on naval sloops around the turn of the century but had since been replaced, in the 1720s, by the more efficient gaff and boom sail or by the snow rig with its wing sail. The sloop at Fig 14-4 is recognisable as a bilander because she has a lug or bilander main course.

Whilst these sloops may have been different from one another, all three were between 249 and 251 tons and, like the *Wolf* class of 1741, all carried fourteen 4pdrs and 110 men. A fourth sloop, *Ferret* IV, was purchased from her builder in frame and presumably to a similar

Fig 14-4. This painting by John Cleveley the elder illustrates the bilander rig on the mainmast topped by a square sail, giving this vessel a similar rig to the brigantine. The vessel has only five gun ports a side, which taken with the bilander (or hollander) rig may indicate that she is in the packet service. *National Maritime Museum BHC1043*

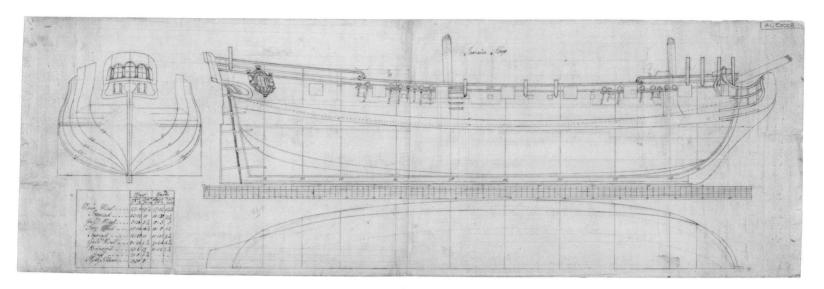

Fig 14-5. HM Sloop *Jamaica* designed by Joseph Allin junior in 1743. This plan includes the mast and yard dimensions. *National Maritime Museum J8579*

overall specification. She was slightly larger at 255 tons and carried fourteen 4pdrs and 110 men.

The third and fourth programmes heralded the start of the *Merlin* class and the introduction of the 6pdr. Until the arrival of the *Swan* class ship-sloops in the 1770s, the *Merlin* class of cruising sloops was the single largest class of vessel acquired by the Royal Navy built to the same specification. These two programmes started in 1743 with one of two 269-ton sloops designed by the Surveyor Sir Jacob Acworth and ordered on 7 July. One month later, the second programme was ordered for four sloops designed by Joseph Allin, three at 273 and one at 267 tons. Two of this order were built by merchant yards and two by Allin himself at Deptford. These were then followed by a programme of nineteen sloops to the Acworth design at a nominal 268 tons.

The evidence that the sloops of the *Merlin* or *Swallow* class were designed by Acworth can be seen from an examination of the plans of the *Jamaica* II, one of Allin's four sloops at Fig 14-5 and of *Falcon* and *Falcon* II by Acworth, both *Merlin* class sloops built by Barnard at Harwich and Alexander at Rotherhithe in 1744 and 1745 respectively (Fig 14-6 and Fig 14-7). Allin's design, whilst it is attractive, is reminiscent of an earlier age, perhaps influenced by the lines of the *Peregrine Galley* on the tulip sections of the hull.[5] On the other hand, the body plan of the *Merlin* class sloops, as shown in the example of *Falcon*, are becoming like those of a small Sixth Rate and have one particular feature not seen heretofore, which is a substantial degree of

verticality – an almost flat area, manifest as a nearly straight line in the sections just above and below the waterline. The view that the *Merlin* class were all to the Acworth design and specification is supported by the fact that they were all contracted to be 268 tons. However, it would be wrong to expect all these sloops to be exactly identical as built; this can be seen from the two examples of *Falcon*.

The original *Falcon* (Fig 14-6), after taking four French privateers in the Channel between March and August 1745, was herself taken by a privateer in the Western Approaches in September but was then re-taken in March 1746. By this time a replacement *Falcon* II (Fig 14-7) had been built, so on re-entering the service *Falcon* I was given the appropriate name *Fortune*. Apart from the obvious difference that one has a pink stern and the other a square, a close examination of the plans reveals that *Falcon* II had a finer run and entry than her predecessor and that her point of maximum beam was near mid-way along her hull, whilst that of *Falcon* I is well forward of midships. Furthermore, a comparison of their sections (placed side by side at Figs 14-8 and 14-9) shows up subtle differences in the floors. Despite this slight variation in the floors, both were allegedly designed by Acworth and both would have been built to the same specification. What they suggest is that by now the Surveyor's office was continually working at the design to improve it on the basis of captains' experiences. It is perhaps no coincidence that the series of detailed Sailing Quality reports, returned to the Surveyor's office, begin around about this time.

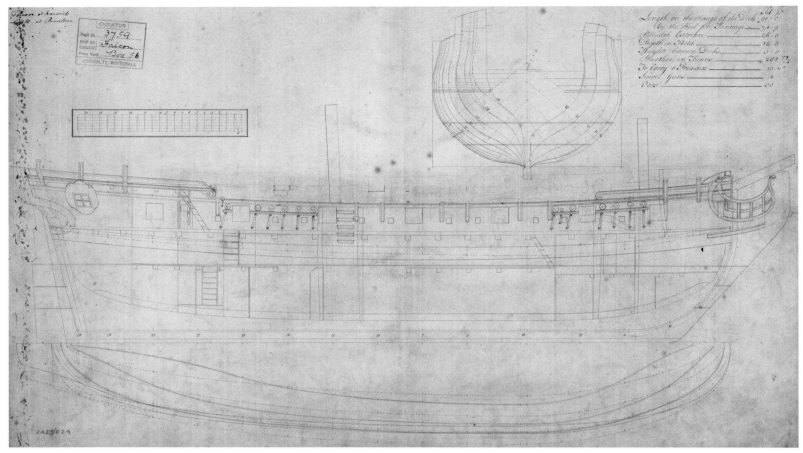

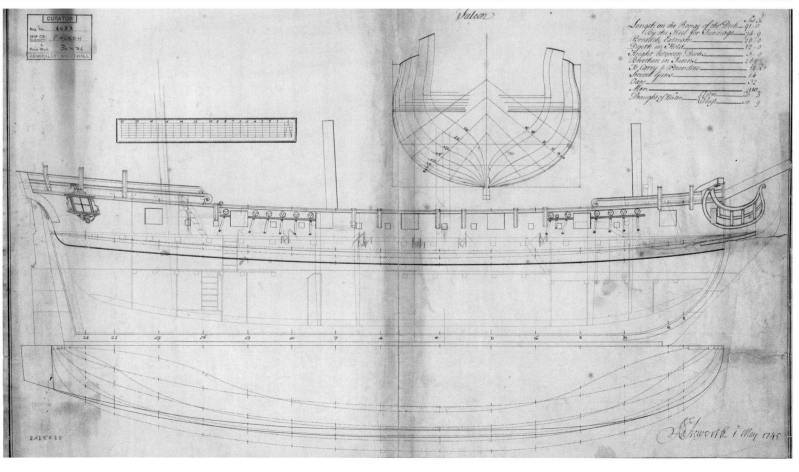

No matter what the design, the members of this class did have the same complement of guns and men. As cruisers they were allocated 110 men and this was only revised (downwards) when any of them was converted to a bomb or fire sloop. Armament for the cruisers was ten and later, at the end of the War in 1748, fourteen 6pdrs; they also carried fourteen ½pdr swivels. The main armament would vary for the conversions detailed below. The common rig was 'snow' but *Falcon* II and (perhaps) *Speedwell* were given the ketch rig which would facilitate a conversion to bomb sloop if required; *Falcon* II was indeed converted in this way. Surprisingly, *Hazard* II was given a brigantine rig for cruising, although this may be attributed to the fact that she was issued with a boom for her 'driver', a much larger and more powerful sail than the traditional wing sail.[6] Despite this she retained the use of a square course, so strictly speaking she was a brig not a brigantine. There were still repeated cases of masts being shortened so it seems that the Surveyor and his master shipwrights were still failing to recognise the danger of too much square canvas on a small ship. Against this there were instances of sloops returning from commissions with an increase to the dimensions of their mast and spars. Much depended on the climatic conditions into which they were deployed and on the individual vessel and her captain and crew.

A significant step in the development of the sloop occurred in 1742 with the first conversion of a sloop to ship rig since the reign of King William III. To recap, ship rig had occasionally been provided for the sloops ordered in 1699 for anti-smuggling work, but the addition of a third mast at that time had much to do with balance, given the difficulty captains were having with their rig. However, to convert a well-balanced snow to ship rig may well have been driven by other considerations, not least that the opposition were using ship rig. Fighting with three masts was preferable to fighting with just two, in terms of retaining manoeuvrability when damaged aloft, and no less than six of the *Merlin* class sloops were converted to ship rig between 1753 and 1755. By this time new-built sloops were being commissioned with ship rig and, in some instances, with a long raised quarterdeck stretching all the way forward to the mainmast. *Saltash* II, launched in 1746, had been the first sloop to be given this deck arrangement, an alteration made to her in 1751 when she was still two-masted. These modifications show the way a dialogue between commanders at sea and members of the Navy Board was beginning to develop the nature of the sloop during the 1750s, but well before the start of the Seven Years War in 1757. Detailed consideration of this rig and deck arrangement will be the subject of later chapters.

Figs 14-6 and 14-7. (Opposite) A comparison of *Falcon* I above and *Falcon* II below shows some interesting variations within the space of one year. Both are shown here set up for snow rig yet *Falcon* II was commissioned with a ketch rig and seems from her plan here to have been considered for ship rig. Note that both have a covered-in forecastle, a feature not seen on sloops since 1722 and that their cutwaters still form a straight line from forefoot to head. *National Maritime Museum J4657 and J4661*

Figs 14-8 and 14-9. These body sections show two rather different hulls as can be seen by the distribution of sections forward and aft of the midship section. *Falcon* I on the left has her midship section well forward, so more sections aft than forward whereas *Falcon* II, with her midsection nearer amidships, has a balance. *Falcon* II also exhibits a slightly fuller body form than *Falcon* I; note the latter's hollow garboards (where the lower futtocks meet the keel), an unusual feature in the sloops of this era. *National Maritime Museum, details from J4657 and J4661*

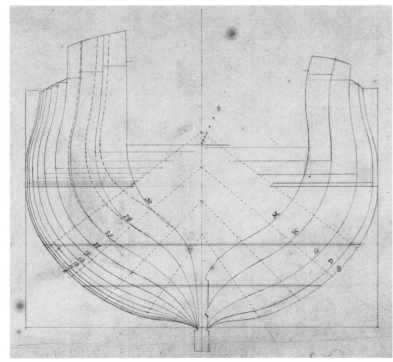

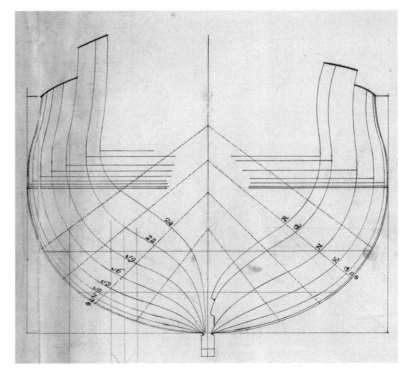

Because there were so many nearly-identical sloops built over the six years from 1741 to 1747, it is more convenient to consider them, not individually, but by class and group; for this purpose any number over five will be called a class.

These robust sloops turned out to be effective, and their ability to take privateers, some of which had a larger armament, spoke well of them, their captains and crew. The sloops listed in the table are those, including the conversions, that were commissioned with two masts from 1742 to 1747. Not listed are the prizes (four)

and the purchases (six) that the Navy acquired between 1744 and 1748. One of the purchased vessels, *Mediator*, was an American sloop in the mercantile sense of the word. She was totally at variance with British naval design policy, having one mast and a hull with great beam, severe deadrise and considerable drag to her keel. She may have been brought in out of curiosity.[7]

It is worth spending a little more time on conversions and fates. Apart from the bomb vessel *Furnace*, which was the first ship-rigged sloop of this period, the remaining conversions took place in the 1750s when there was a major

Table 14-1: CRUISING SLOOP GROUP AND CLASS ORDERS, 1742–1747

Name	*Wolf* Group	*Baltimore* Group	*Swallow* Group (Acworth)	*Hind* Group (Allin)	*Merlin* Class (1744–1746)	Role Conversions (totals)
Number	3	3 + 1 purchase (*Ferret*)	2	4	19	6
Ordered	1741	1742	1743	1743	1744-1746	Bombs: 3 in 1758 FS: 1 in 1755, 2 in 1762
Launched	1742	1742–1743	1744	1744	1744-1746	–
LDG	88ft 0in	88ft 0in	91ft 7in	91ft 3in	91ft 0in by contract	–
LoK	73ft 9in	74ft 0in	74ft 6in	75ft 0in	74ft 9in by contract	–
Beam	25ft 8in	25ft 1in	26ft 2in	25ft 10in	26ft 0in by contract	–
LBR	3.42	3.49	3.50	3.52	3.53	–
Depth in hold	10ft 9in	10ft 6in	6ft 10in to platform	12ft 2in	12ft 0in by contract	–
Burthen	247 tons	250 tons; purchased *Ferret* 255	270 tons	266 tons	269 tons by contract	–
Guns	14 x 4pdrs + 12/14 x swivels	14 x 4pdrs + 12/14 x swivels	10 x 6pdrs + 14 x swivels	10 (14 from 1748) x 6pdrs + 14 swivels	10 (14 from 1748) x 6pdrs + 14 swivels	8 x 4pdrs + 8 swivels for FS, 8 x 4pdrs + 12 swivels as bomb
Men	110	110	110	110 (125 from 1748)	110 (125 from 1748)	60 for bomb, 45 for FS
Rig	All snow	All snow	Both snow	All snow	Majority snow and some ketch	Snow and ketch
Fate	1 wrecked 1748, 1 sold 1763, 1 taken 1744	1 converted 1762, 1 sank 1746, 1 sold 1748, 1 lost 1757	1 wrecked 1744, 1 sold 1748	1 sunk 1747, 1 sold 1767, 1 wrecked 1770, 1 BU 1776	2 sold 1749–1750, 3 sold 1763, 4 sold 1769–1773, 5 converted 1758–1762, 1 wrecked 1746, 1 wrecked 1748, 2 wrecked 1762, 1 taken 1746	1 wrecked 1759, 3 sold 1762, 2 sold 1763
Builder	All contract	All contract	Both contract	2 contract, 2 Allin, Deptford Dyd	All contract	All contract
To bomb	Nil	One	Nil	Nil	2	3 including *Baltimore*
To fireship	Nil	Nil	Nil	Nil	1 in 1755, 1 in 1762 and 1 in 1771	3
To ship rig	Nil	1 (*Ferret* in 1755)	Nil	1 in 1754	1 in 1753, 1 in 1754 and 2 in 1755	6

Note.
Dimensions averaged

move towards this sail plan for both cruising and bomb sloops. Earlier in the 1740s, ship-rigged cruising sloops had been brought into the Royal Navy but these will be covered later. The conversion of a snow to a bomb would require a change of rig unless she carried only one mortar, as was the case with *Baltimore*. Perhaps it was this fact that allowed her to switch role on a regular basis – she saw service as a bomb in 1758–1759 and in 1761–1762 in between stints as a cruising sloop. Three of the *Merlin* class were converted to fireships, two of them changing their names. They would have joined a fleet of vessels taken up from trade and have undergone some extensive internal modification, as would those converting to bombs. The use of a sloop as a fireship is interesting. Two of the three were converted just before the close of the Seven Years War and were not expended then or later. One was converted in 1755 but a year later was re-converted as a pressing tender – a vessel specifically set up to raise men for the Navy, in effect a mobile prison and headquarters of the press gangs. The conversions were mostly made during the Seven Years War to meet urgent current needs.

Reductions took place after each war, with a total of two sloops being sold at the end of the War of the Austrian Succession and seven in the decade after the close of the Seven Years War. The sloop with the longest career was *Grampus*, launched in 1746 and sold in 1780. This points up the fact that these contract-built sloops were soundly built. They lasted well despite hard use in two wars and in the intervening peace, when they would have had the inevitable sloop duties to perform. But perhaps the most important fact is that only three were taken, two of which were recaptured a year later. This, combined with their excellent performance against privateers, suggests that the Admiralty had at long last reached the optimum size and force for the sloop of war for this period.

THE BOMB VESSEL: PURPOSE-BUILT AND SLOOP CONVERSION

After the initial euphoria surrounding the new weapon on its introduction in 1687 and its extensive but unsuccessful employment against the privateering bases in the French Channel ports in the 1690s, there had been a decline in its use during the War of the Spanish

Fig 14-10. A ketch-rigged *Merlin* class sloop. *Author after F H af Chapman*

Succession.[8] Thereafter there were only small-scale deployments in the Baltic and Mediterranean and this was reflected in the fact that Britain built no bomb vessels after 1695, although in 1705 she did rebuild the original *Salamander* of 1687 and in 1718 acquired a Spanish prize for this role. Amazingly, the class of 1695 survived until the 1720s, the last to go being *Basilisk* in 1729, whilst the prize was only broken up in 1734.

The failure to re-equip with this weapon system was due, in part, to disappointment with earlier results but more to the absence of a strategic need in the peaceable 1720s and 1730s. The situation changed in 1729–1730 when a small programme of two vessels was

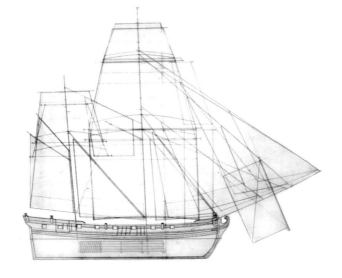

Fig 14-11. This draught shows a sail plan for a Danish ketch-rigged bomb vessel, showing both the sail and spar dimensions of the British 1757 ketch-rigged bombs and the proposed cut-down dimensions for Baltic use. *Based on an original in the Rigsarkivet, Copenhagen*

ordered. Three years before, the mortar had been significantly improved over the earlier model that could be adjusted in direction but not elevation. The advent of a trunnion-mounted mortar in 1726 (Fig 14-12) created new possibilities for use of this weapon at sea, so *Salamander* II and *Terrible* (Fig 14-13) can be regarded as trial horses for the new mortar. But the order for their construction can also be seen in the context of the quasi-war with Spain, nominally settled before they could see action, but renewed hostilities at Gibraltar or in the West Indies remained a distinct possibility.

The design of these new bomb vessels was essentially the same as that of their predecessors, though they had slightly larger dimensions, a head and a different bow profile. They retained the round full-bodied hull, pink stern and ketch rig. Their mortar bays could now be equipped with hatches, for the trunnion mount allowed the mortars to be depressed to horizontal and therefore covered when not in use.[9] Their sheer plan shows that they were pierced for a broadside of seven guns, which suggests that their secondary role of cruising sloop was an important consideration in their design.

This is not surprising since the Navy's experience with the earlier bomb vessels had shown that their use in their primary task was occasional and that it therefore made sense for them to have a good capability in their secondary role of cruising and escort. This was essential

Fig 14-12. A trunnion-mounted mortar, introduced in 1726 and, in an adapted form, fitted to *Salamander* and *Terrible*, on their being equipped as bomb ketches in 1738. They had been first commissioned as cruising sloops in 1730. *Royal Armouries, Tower of London*

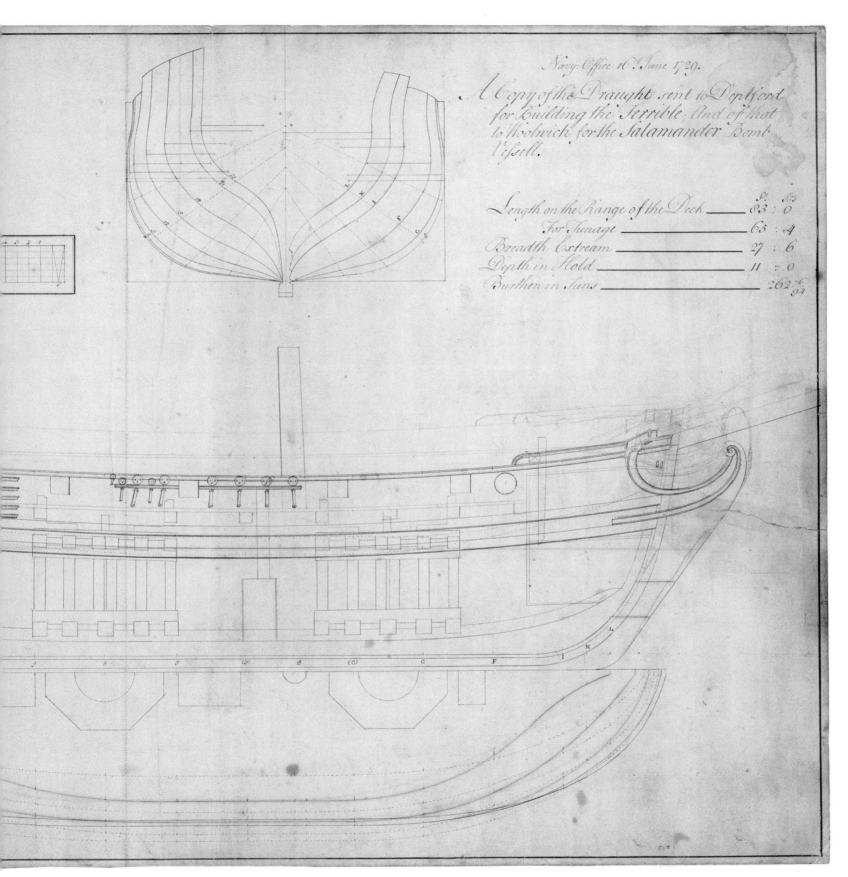

Navy Office 16th June 1729.

*A Copy of the Draught sent to Deptford
for Building the Terrible, And of that
to Woolwich for the Salamander Bomb
Vessell.*

		ft	in
Length on the Range of the Deck		83	0
For Tunnage		65	4
Breadth Extream		27	6
Depth in Hold		11	0
Burthen in Tuns		262 $\frac{76}{94}$	

Fig 14-13. A copy draught dated June 1729 for *Salamander* and *Terrible* of 1728. Note the presence of a windlass and a capstan.
The latter was used in conjunction with a spring onto the mooring cable to adjust the alignment of the vessel in relation to the target.
National Maritime Museum J0314

since the Navy was perennially short of small warships for the host of duties that had to be performed around the coasts and further afield; the average life expectancy of sloop-type vessels was 10–15 years, so much of a bomb's active service would be spent as a cruiser. But unlike their cruising sisters, they did not carry all their guns on the flush gun deck. Two were carried in the after cabin, which extended further forward than those on cruising sloops and whose floor was below the level of the main deck. This was true of most bomb sloops of this period though, as will be seen later, not all were set up in this way.

Salamander II and *Terrible* (Fig 14-13) spent the first five years of their careers as cruising sloops, able to be refitted as a bomb vessel in the space of one to two weeks whilst alongside in a wet dock. They were fitted as bombs in 1738 on the eve of a new war with Spain, which was instigated by Britain. Their overseas deployment was to the Mediterranean, where both were involved in Martin's operations at Naples; here he forced the King of the Two

Sicilies to withdraw from the war literally at gunpoint in the form of naval guns and mortars.[10] *Salamander* was broken up in 1744, still as a bomb, whereas *Terrible* was sold in 1749 having been returned to her initial configuration of cruising sloop.

A pivotal moment in the development of bomb sloops came in 1734 with the ordering of the *Alderney*, initially intended as a cruiser but completed as a bomb. The significance of this vessel lies not in the rig – where the revolution would occur later – but in the shape of her hull. Her design is credited to an amateur, the Duke of Cumberland, better remembered for his exploits on land in the War of the Austrian Succession, but chiefly for his suppression of the 1745 Jacobite rebellion and his pacification of the Scottish Highlands where he was referred to as 'Stinking Billy' (by contrast, in England he was known as 'Sweet William'). However that was all in the future; at this time the teenaged son of King George II was under the tutelage of Sir Jacob Acworth, the Surveyor of the Navy, for whom he supposedly produced a number of

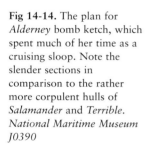

Fig 14-14. The plan for *Alderney* bomb ketch, which spent much of her time as a cruising sloop. Note the slender sections in comparison to the rather more corpulent hulls of *Salamander* and *Terrible*. *National Maritime Museum J0390*

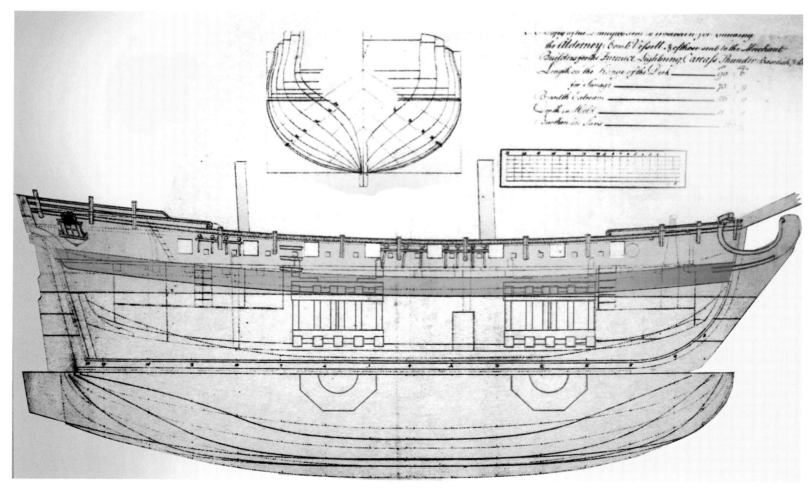

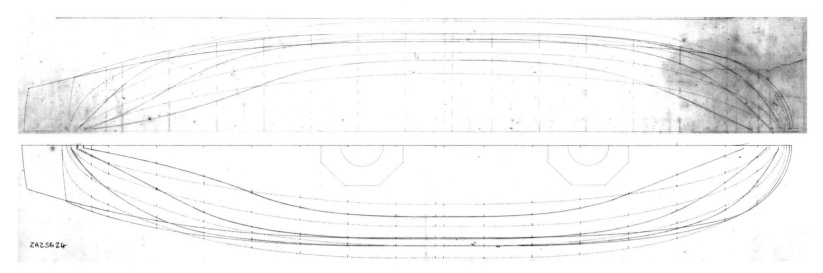

draughts of ships that were actually built. It is extremely unlikely that the boy produced these unaided, or indeed that he really 'designed' them in any meaningful sense. In this case the lines of the *Alderney* are almost identical to those of the *Merlin* class of cruising sloops designed by Acworth nine years later. This becomes evident by comparing Fig 14-14 with 14-6 and 14-7 but noting that the *Merlin* class cruising sloops were slightly finer in their underwater body at the entry and the run since they did not have such a heavy armament and had to be able to chase and run.

The other pointer to the importance of this sloop was the leap in size to 262 tons, which anticipated by nearly a decade the next major increase in sloop dimensions that came with the precursors to the *Merlin* class in 1743. This is partly to do with armament. In 1734 the largest sloops were of 200 tons and carried an armament of only eight 4pdr carriage guns; not until 1741 were they given an increase in armament to fourteen 4pdrs with a corresponding increase in burthen to 246 tons. With the introduction of the 6pdr carriage gun to the cruising sloop, the *Merlin* class sloops had to be beefed-up to cope with the extra burden and for this the use of a hull similar to that of a proven weight carrier was common sense. From this point of view the *Alderney* can be seen as a milestone in the development of both the bomb vessel, in that it gave it a fast sailing hull – unfortunately hampered by a poor sail plan – and also of the cruising sloop, in that it pointed the way for this class to carry an increased armament.

Generally bomb ketches were armed with a 13in mortar abaft the forecastle and a 10in

mortar between the masts, but there were variations. Perhaps the most notable was the use of a 10in howitzer in place of the secondary mortar on *Salamander* II and *Terrible*. A howitzer is a weapon half way between a gun and a mortar and has its trunnions nearer to its centre of mass as with a normal gun. The emplacements for the howitzers may well have been slightly different from those for mortars, but the plan of *Terrible* at Fig 14-13 does not go into this level of detail. Carrying mortars presented problems as, to a lesser extent, did carrying guns. The weight of armament had the effect of raising a ship's centre of gravity, thereby reducing stability and making the vessel what was known as 'crank'.

Alderney was to be the model for all the subsequent bomb ketches until the arrival of the Slade-designed class in 1756. She is of further interest in that, unlike all other models, she did not have a break in her deck from the stem to the sternpost. This supports the view that at the time she was ordered, the Admiralty were highly focused on the multi-role aspect of her forthcoming design.

Two groups, one of six and one of five, followed her during the two ensuing wars between 1739 and 1748. Neither of these groups were considered to be good sea boats and certainly the performance of the bomb vessels in no way matched that of the *Merlin* class sloops, which had a near-identical hull form. The reasons are therefore likely to be found in their ketch rig, which was nowhere near as efficient on all points of sailing as that of a snow. But perhaps the predominant reason was the large weight of armament, mortars and

Fig 14-15. A comparison between the waterlines of *Alderney* of 1734 (below) and *Granado* of 1742 (above) show much similarity. Both were extensively used as cruisers though they may have been less than perfect platforms for mortars. *National Maritime Museum J0387 (Granado) and J0390*

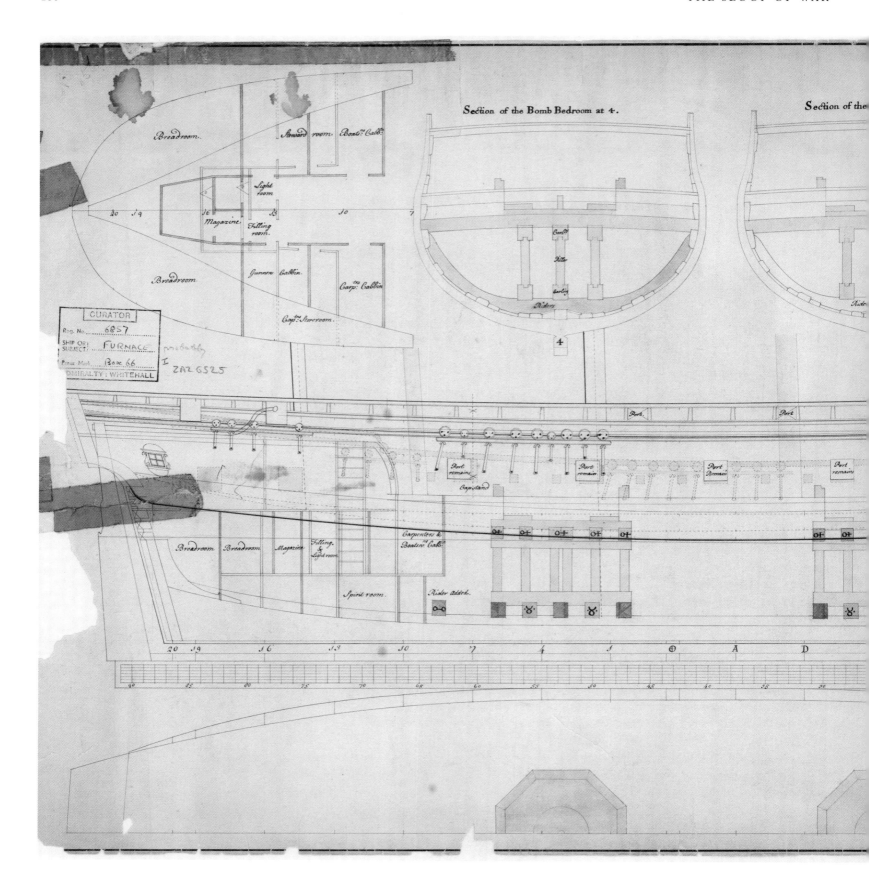

Section of the Bomb Bedroom at 4.

Section of the

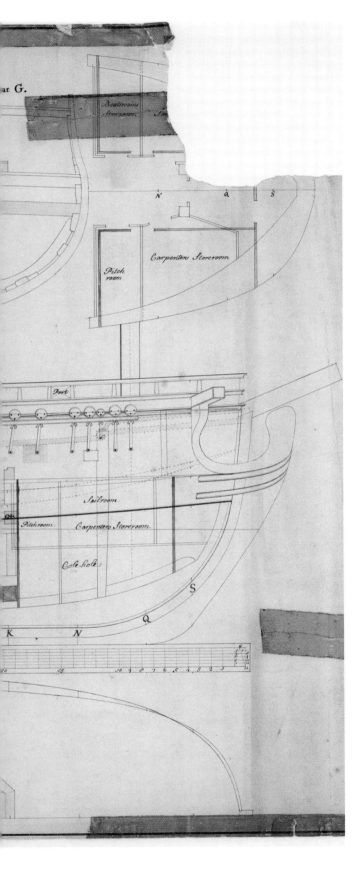

carriage guns, being carried at weather deck level. This issue would not be solved until the Navy started to take delivery of the Slade-designed bomb vessels in 1757, half of which would be ship-rigged. There was only one vessel that was to get a good report from her captain – *Granado* III – which is perplexing since she also had ketch rig. She did have a square stern, but so did others of the *Alderney* class. A comparison of *Alderney*'s entry and run with that of *Granado* III at Fig 14-15 shows an almost identical set of lines. This further shows Acworth's hand as Surveyor behind both designs.

The *Blast* class was the first to enter service, being ordered in March 1740. They were commissioned initially as cruising sloops and were not fitted as bombs until 1741 to support operations against Spanish possessions in the West Indies and possibly South America. By 1742, four were based on Jamaica, one was deployed in 1743 to the Mediterranean and one, *Furnace*, was converted for another classic sloop role: exploration. Her conversion was to raise her topsides and give her ship rig. She was reconverted in 1756.

Whilst on the subject of *Furnace*, it is instructive to look at the work that was done on her internally to fit her to work as a cruising/exploration sloop, because this provides some insight into the work continually being performed by the yards in the endless switching of sloop roles from bomb to cruising and vice-versa. Fig 14-16 shows the full structure for supporting the mortars and for holding their munitions. The mortar beds that lie just below deck level are supported by heavy beams running the full width of the vessel. They can be seen in elevation and cross section in Fig 14-16. They in turn rest on a foundation of substantial transverse timbers that appear to be left in place after conversion; they can be seen in cross section in Fig 14-17 immediately above the keel. The vertical pillars and the fore-and-aft bearers above and below them, together with the storage racks for shells, are removed. It would be reasonable to argue that this would be the same for all other conversions.

In the case of *Furnace*, the conversion would have taken time since she was fitted with a full spar deck over and above her gun deck. She also had to have her masts moved aft and a foremast stepped forward. This was of course unneces-

Figs 14-16 and 14-17. (Left and Overleaf) These two draughts show successive stages in the plans for the conversion of the *Furnace* bomb ketch into a ship-rigged Arctic exploration vessel. In the first the structural work was minimised by retaining the mortar bed structures. However, at the behest of the captain-designate, more substantial modification was eventually agreed, which included the removal of the pillars supporting the mortar beds and the addition of a double capstan in lieu of the windlass to allow the ship to anchor in deep water. *National Maritime Museum J0516 and J0515a*

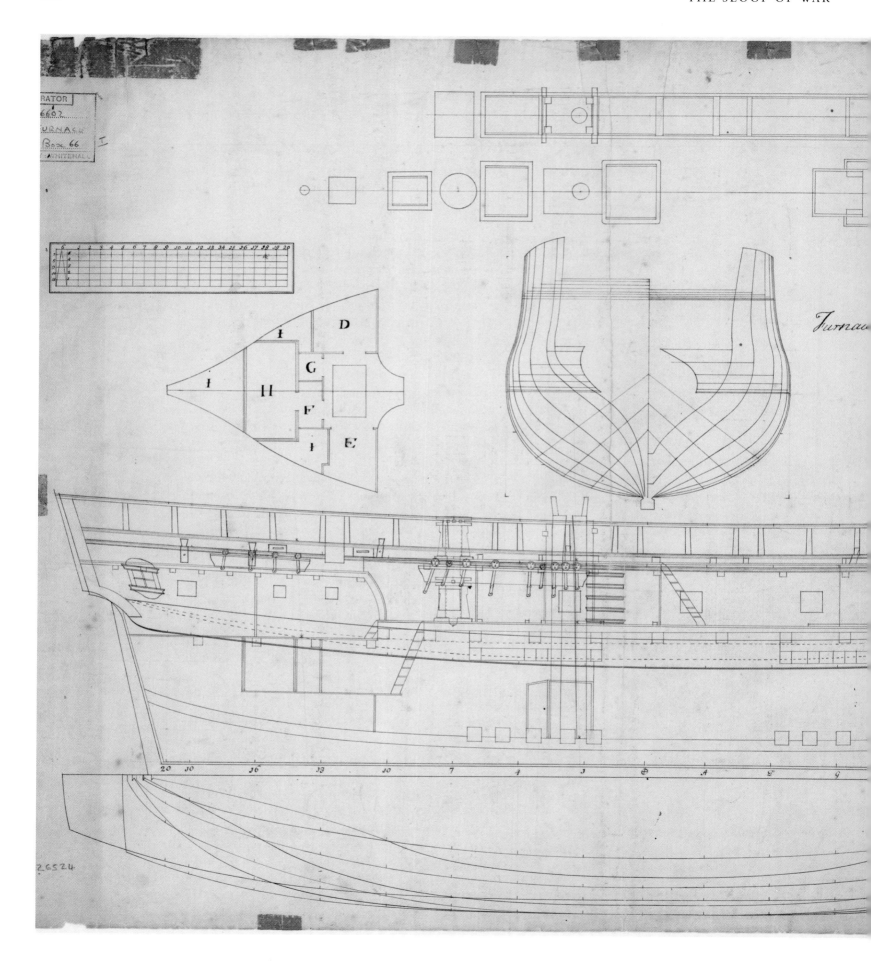

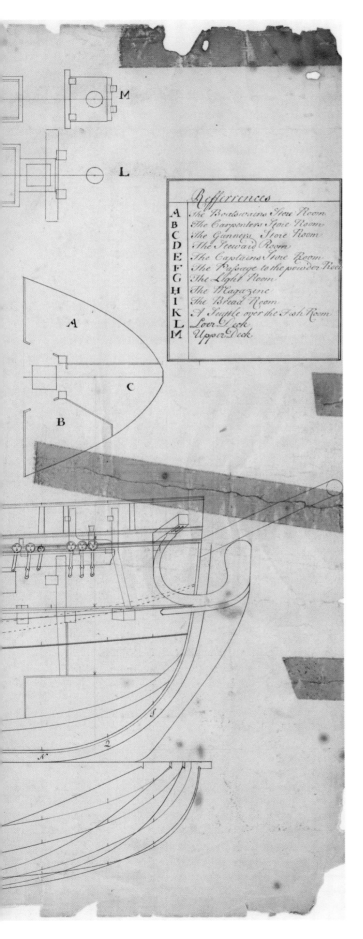

References

A	The Boatswains Store Room
B	The Carpenters Store Room
C	The Gunners Store Room
D	The Steward Room
E	The Captains Store Room
F	The Passage to the powder Room
G	The Light Room
H	The Magazine
I	The Bread Room
K	A Scuttle over the Fish Room
L	Lower Deck
M	Upper Deck

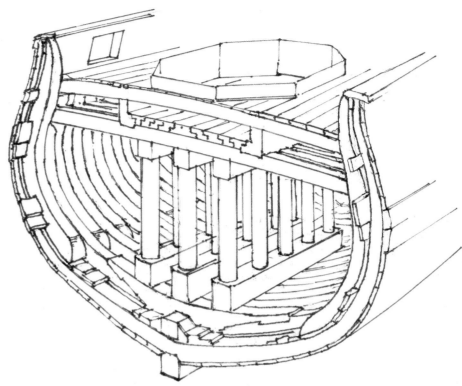

sary when switching from bomb to normal cruising as opposed to polar exploration. Another important point is that conversion could be done afloat and in the space of a few weeks, if not days. This explains in part the reasoning behind the Admiralty's desire to design a vessel that could be quickly switched from role to role to meet operational priorities.

This cross section of the internal works beneath the mortar bed (Fig 14-18) shows how little space is left in its way for crew and stores, the internal frames and double deck beams taking much of the room. These would have been very difficult to move and this suggests that the main timbers would have been left in place when the vessel was recommissioned as a cruising sloop. The bearers and pillars together with any racking would have been much easier to shift.

The *Comet* class, launched in 1741 as an improved *Blast* class, were identical in form with minor deck and internal changes. Obviously the poor sea-keeping ability of the *Blast* class was not an issue at this stage, if it ever was: it may have been accepted as an inevitable compromise to produce a vessel optimised for bombardment. All five of this class were commissioned as bomb vessels. One sailed to the Mediterranean immediately; the

Fig 14-18. A perspective drawing of the hold of a bomb vessel showing the massive structure required to support the mortar beds and to withstand the stresses of firing a non-recoil weapon. The bombs were stowed on racks between the main uprights under the mortar beds. Although the latter might be removed when converted to an exploration role, the heavy framing was necessarily retained, even when employed as a cruiser, which inevitably resulted in poorer sailing qualities than purpose-built sloops of war. *Author*

Fig 14-19. The *Hazard* was classed as a brigantine, probably because her wing/snow sail was converted to a driver with a boom, giving a much larger sail area. However, the proportions of her masts and retained square main course make her a forerunner of the brig. *Author*

was refitted as a sloop. In this guise she was in action with French privateers off the Scottish west coast. Again she was refitted as a bomb between September 1746 and February 1747 and remained in that role until 1754. There is another interesting example of this amazing flexibility. The Admiralty ordered *Serpent* II, operating as a sloop, to be fitted as a bomb in July 1745 but a month later changed this back to sloop, such was the panic about the Jacobite rising in Scotland, a region to which she was immediately deployed.

By the end of the war in 1748 the Admiralty had eight bomb sloops left and they were to sell four of these by 1750. With hindsight this looks ill-judged, but to be fair their hulls may have been worn out. In the 1750s six *Merlin* class sloops, together with the *Baltimore* sloop, were to be added to their number as part of an emergency war programme.

SLOOPS AS FIRESHIPS

Three of the *Merlin* class sloops were converted to fireships: *Viper* in 1755, *Raven* and *Grampus* in 1762 (*Viper* and *Grampus* were appropriately renamed *Lightning* and *Strombolo* on conversion). The switch to the

remainder were converted to sloops then back to bombs and then back to sloops again to meet the current threat. The career of *Terror* II tells the typical story. Built by Greville at Limehouse, she was commissioned as a bomb in March 1742. By July that year she was converted to a cruising sloop, but in December 1743 she reconverted to a bomb and in August 1744 she

Table 14-2: BOMB SLOOP AND CLASS ORDERS, 1728 –1743 Dimensions as designed

Name	*Salamander* Group	*Alderney*	*Blast* Class	*Comet* Class	*Granado*
Number	2	1	6	5	1
Ordered	1729	1734	1740	1741	1741
Launched	1730	1734	1740	1742 as sloop to 1756, then bomb	1742
LDG	83ft 0in	90ft 6in	90ft 6in	91ft 0in	91ft 1in
LoK	65ft 4in	73ft 9in	73ft 6in	75ft 6in	73ft 10½in
Beam	27ft 6in	26ft 0in	26ft 0in	26ft 0in	26ft 2in
LBR	3.01	3.48	3.48	3.50	3.38
Depth in hold	11ft 0in	11ft 0in	11ft 0in	11ft 3in	11ft 4in
Burthen	263 tons	264 tons	265 tons	271 tons	269 tons
Guns as sloop	8 x 4pdrs + 14 swivels	10 x 6pdrs + 14 swivels	10 x 4pdrs + 14swivels	10 x 4pdrs + 14 swivels	10 x 4pdrs + 12 swivels
Guns as bomb	6 x 4pdrs + 8 swivels	6 x 6pdrs + 8 swivels	8 x 4pdrs + 12 swivels	8 x 4pdrs + 8 swivels	8 x 4pdrs + 12 swivels
Mortars	1 x 13in, 1 x 10in howitzer	2 x 13in	1 x 13in, 1 x 10in	1 x 13in, 1 x 10in	2 x 13in then 1 x 13in and 1 x 10in
Men as sloop	80	100	100	100	110
Men as bomb	60	60	60	60	60
Rig	Ketch	Ketch	Ketch	Ketch	Ketch
Fates	1 Sold 1744, 1 sold 1749	Hulked 1742	2 sold 1749–1750, 1 sold 1763, 1 wrecked 1741, 1 taken 1745, 1 lost 1746	1 wrecked 1748, 2 sold 1749, 1 sold 1754, 1 sold 1763	Sold 1763
Builder	Both Dockyard	Dockyard	All contract	All contract	Contract, Harwich

new role required some extensive alterations in the case of these sloops. To begin with they only had one deck whereas a fireship needed two, so an upper deck was built at a point slightly above the level of the rail she would have had as a sloop. The raised quarterdeck was given berthed-up bulwarks and pierced for defensive guns which could no longer be housed in between the decks, a space now stuffed with the combustibles in a specially prepared grid to hold them in position and provide channels for the igniting materials. The lids of the old gun ports were reversed to fall down and outwards to allow a strong draught to enter the vessel at the lower deck, encouraged by apertures cut in the upper deck. Once converted, these vessels floated above their designed waterline so may have sailed fast, which raises a question about the intended tactics of their employment. In the event none were expended and one was converted again to be a vessel for the pressing of men. None of the three were returned to sloop service. Conversion to fireship was generally a one-way move though this did not stop them being used, as an armed vessel, for sloop duties.

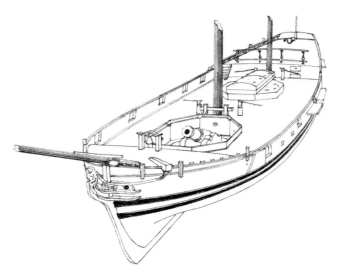

Fig 14-20. A view of the bomb ketch *Granado* of 1742 developed by the author from a model by Bob Lightley. Both the model and the original draught of this vessel are to be found in the National Maritime Museum, ref SLR0331 and J0387.

Fig 14-21. HM Sloop *Grampus* was originally one of the *Merlin* class sloops. She had a notably successful career in the cruising role, her biggest catch being a 16-gun privateer. She was fitted out as a fireship in 1762 but was never 'expended' in that role. This plan shows her conversion to fireship. Note that she has an upper deck laid over her original gun deck. A 'tween deck space was essential to the working of a fireship. *National Maritime Museum J8045*

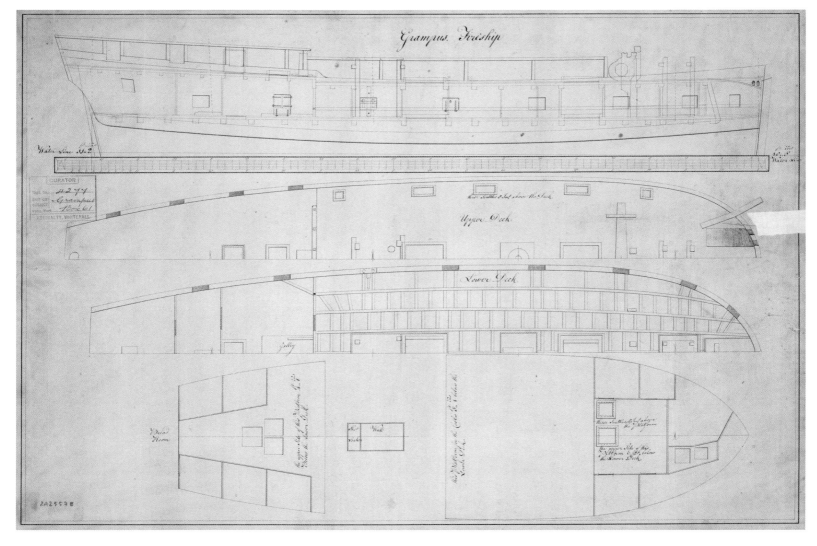

The plan of *Grampus* (later *Strombolo*) at Fig 14-21 gives a good idea of the work required to convert a sloop to a fireship. The ignition position is by a gun port on both sides of the vessel, shown here on the port hand side. Close to this, if not incorporated with it, would be the sally port to allow the crew to escape into their towed tender. The sally port on the starboard side can be seen in the sheer plan above, using the second from aft port cut down to deck level. The centre-line of hatches would assist the apertures cut in the deck in creating a draught; the small square cuts at either end of the waist may be equipped with chimneys to improve the draw. There is no room to work a capstan, which was replaced by a windlass positioned forward on the new upper deck, and hatches provide a clear way down to the platform in the hold for the cables. The amount of work required to refit a cruising sloop as a fireship – and indeed to return it to its original role if that were ever necessary – is substantial compared with the conversion of a bomb sloop, where only the pillars supporting the mortar beds and shell racking had to be removed to provide room for accommodation, stores and a larger crew.

To underline the importance of this period for the sloop of war, it is worth reflecting on the fact that during the seven years from 1741 to 1747 – broadly the span of the War of the Austrian Succession – the Royal Navy acquired 50 cruising sloops and 12 bomb sloops. Including the prizes and purchases built or converted to the role of cruising sloop, this drove up the total to the unprecedented figure of 62 minor warships.

Chapter 15

FRENCH CORVETTE AND PRIVATEER CONSTRUCTION 1734–1763

As pointed out in Chapter 10, in 1696 the word 'corvette' was added to the existing category of 'barque longue'. This grouping then continued until 1746 when the term 'barque longue' was dropped and 'corvette' continued on its own. Thus in the intervening years a barque longue and a corvette were one and the same type of vessel. To recap, an earlier example from around the turn of the century was found in a draught in the Danish Royal Archives (Fig 10-10). It was of a tiny vessel, just over 50ft on deck. From that point on until 1727 the length of a 'barque longue ou corvette' was not to rise to more than about 65ft, but thereafter there was a considerable variation in size and armament until the end of the Seven Years War in 1763.

In terms of building programmes, the years covering the War of the League of Augsburg 1689 –1698 had seen the construction of forty-two of this category, with a further programme of thirteen during the War of the Spanish Succession, 1702–1714. The bulk of these had been built at Dunkirk, whence privateers could fan out to attack commercial traffic along the Dutch coast and the shores of Kent and Sussex. Some went further afield, into the far reaches of the North Sea. This was in strong contrast to the very limited production in the following years. This is understandable since France was exhausted by war and there was no immediate threat from the British or, of greater concern, the Dutch. To put it another way, there was no more opportunity to raid the seaborne trade of those countries.[1] In fact no more corvettes/ *barques longues* were to be launched from Dunkirk after 1708.[2] Two 'large' corvettes were built in 1727–1728 at Le Havre and Toulon, of

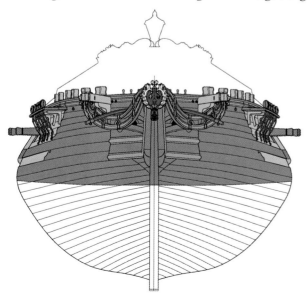
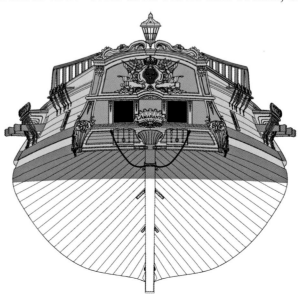

Fig 15-1. The bow and stern designs of *L'Amarante* from a monograph by Gérard Delacroix.

80ft in length and carrying fourteen to sixteen 4pdrs, but the next programme was not until 1734 with the construction of five vessels with lengths varying from 66ft to 79ft, equipped with eight to ten 4pdrs. The burthen of these vessels was 70–90 tons. This makes an interesting comparison with the British 200-ton sloops of the same period, which carried the same armament. The precise rationale for this order is unknown but, unlike the British, the French tended to optimise their corvettes for fleet duties such as scouting and communication. Once an adequate quantity had been reached in this period of peace, there would be little incentive to continue building. In the event, the French would build no further corvettes until they entered the War of the Austrian Succession and again faced Britain in the Channel, the West Indies and the Mediterranean.

During the years of this war the French were to build only six corvettes, whereas the British acquired fifty sloops and twelve bomb ketches, including prizes and purchases, operating them in the cruising and convoy roles. At the beginning of the Seven Years War the French stock of corvettes stood at just two, to which they added fifteen during the course of the war. But again this did not compare with the British who had at its outset a force of forty-two sloops to which they added twenty-four during the war, including nine prizes, some of which are mentioned below. The losses of British-built

sloops during this war amounted to just ten, and most of these were wrecked or foundered in heavy seas.[3] The reason for this is related to Britain's command of the seas and their widespread possessions beyond. In a sense Britain occupied the seas and the oceans and the French used them when they had to. To Britain the sloop formed an important component of its continuing global maritime presence whereas, for the French, the corvette was a fleet asset and therefore did not have the requirement to remain on overseas stations to the same extent as did the British sloop. However, the French and the Spanish were more reliant on the use of privateers, which in some respects made up for their lack of corvettes or other lightly armed warships in the more predatory roles.

Not only did the French Navy place a different emphasis on the roles of its unrated warships, but it allowed for a more relaxed control of the individual designers and shipwrights at this time, whereas the British Surveyor's office tended to centralise design and certainly the establishment of specifications. The variation in the design of French naval corvettes and privateers can be seen in the examples discussed below; the design of privateers, which generally tended to be more extreme, provides further examples. A good starting point for any analysis of French thinking about corvettes are the recorded views of Blaise Ollivier, a key designer and shipwright of this époque.

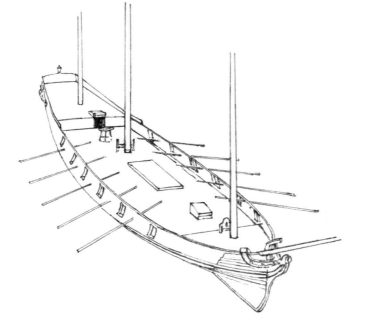

Fig 15-2. Two views of *La Palme* developed by the author from the plan of the ship (Fig 15-3), the sheer and body plans of her sister *L'Amarante*, and a model of *La Palme* published online but without attribution. Both were designed by Blaise Ollivier, one of the most celebrated ship designers of his time. *La Palme* was built by his son at the age of 15!

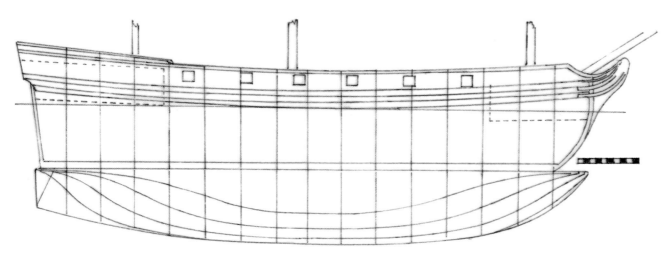

Fig 15-3. A plan of *La Palme*. Note the fine entry and run achieved by nearly vertical stem and sternpost profiles. From Jean Boudriot's monograph *La Corvette*.

In his description of the corvette, Ollivier covers the first half of the eighteenth century and therefore the detail has a wide relevance. He makes the point that the corvette is a small frigate, meaning possibly that it had one flush deck and that it had three masts. This description fits for the middle of the century, when the corvette was beginning to replace the *frégat légère*, but it does not reflect the situation before 1744, when the bulk of this category had only 8 guns and two masts and were more properly called *barques longues*. The increase in armament from 8-10 guns to 10-12 meant that the vessels were built longer and could then use three masts with good effect. In parallel with this Ollivier states that corvettes are between 50ft and 80ft long, but this does not mean that the increase in length is necessarily a progression since one built in 1728 was 80ft on deck and carried 14 guns; another built in 1734 was 66ft on deck and had only 8 guns. The changes in size and armament are not a simple upward progression, which suggests that they were designed for different purposes and situations – not unlike the British alternation between sloops for overseas with 10-14 guns and sloops for anti-smuggling patrols with only 4-8.

Ollivier's description of their deck and cabin arrangement reflects the layout on *La Palme*, built in 1744 by Ollivier's son aged 15 (no doubt carefully supervised by his father).[4] Like the British sloops, most had a slightly raised quarterdeck, but unlike the British they normally had a forecastle raised by 2–3ft. The main deck itself was cut where it met these raised decks and stepped down to provide small cabins fore and aft. The British sloops carried their batteries the length of the weather deck,

with all guns exposed except those in the commander's cabin. The French corvettes – though not the privateers, which had varying arrangements – did not tolerate guns in their cabins, which is why their batteries seem short in relation to the length of the ship. This layout is illustrated in the plan of *La Palme* at Fig 15-3. Below the gun deck these corvettes did not have an orlop deck, the only covered accommodation being the cabins which would include the domestic support for the vessel. Indeed, Ollivier suggested that the crew could 'sleep on the barrels' in the hold! The larger corvettes built from 1757 onwards and armed with sixteen or eighteen 4pdrs (6pdrs from 1762) did have an orlop platform but the space between it and the gun deck was barely five feet. A section at Fig 15-4 illustrates this arrangement, which rather proves the point that the French Navy did not propose to spend long months at sea. The other unusual feature here, and on many projections, is the small space available for the gun's recoil before its carriage would collide with the main hatch coaming. It is also worth noting that there

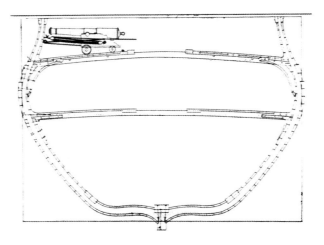

Fig 15-4. The midship cross-section of *La Palme*. These corvettes may appear to be longer and have a greater draught than their British counterparts but this was not so. They were also lighter and ship- as opposed to snow-rigged. They retain the boat-like proportions exemplified in the British sloops of 1732. In contrast to Ollivier's remarks above, *La Palme* does have a lower deck. From Jean Boudriot's monograph *La Corvette*.

are only metal brackets rather than knees supporting the orlop deck, possibly on the basis that it did not have to carry guns.

Turning to the matter of hull design, a marked difference in section will be seen by comparing two draughts of the same date: 1744. On the left, at Fig 15-5, are the sections of the British *Merlin* class sloop capable of carrying fourteen 6pdrs and on the right a corvette, similar to *La Palme*, at Fig 15-6 and armed with twelve 4pdrs. The British hull will have a greater carrying capacity but at the expense of a larger area of wetted surface which, in the days before the copper bottom, would affect speed through the water. The French hull form also demonstrates their favoured shape, of short floors and flat lower futtocks – the so-called 'two-turn bilge' – as opposed to the more rounded forms used in British construction. This sharp form promised speed but at the expense of seakeeping and, potentially, stability. In considering its origins it is well to remember that France had a Mediterranean coast and that French designers would have been well aware, for some time, of the high speed the xebec type could achieve with a similar hull section. This feature of French design was incorporated in a diluted form into the lines of some of the British sloops after 1748, but was not retained in the longer term, as will seen in the next chapter.

The other major difference in hull design concerned lateral resistance. Comparing the sheer plan of the two examples at Fig 15-7, it can be seen that in the French version the designer has drawn out the ends for two reasons: first, it improves lateral resistance, which, together with the proportional greater depth of the French hull (Figs 15-5 and -6) would tend to reduce leeway; and second, it produces a finer entry and run at the middle waterline.

An extreme example of this theory can be seen at Fig 15-8. *Badine* was built at Brest in 1745 by a young assistant shipwright working under the direction of Blaise Ollivier. Only 66ft long on the gun deck, she was armed with six 4pdrs. Quite apart from the unusual stem and stern, she has a totally different underwater section from the larger corvettes, which harks back to the example from 1700 (Fig 10-10). It is, therefore, surprising that she has three masts, particularly as the term *barque longue* was not dropped until the following year, 1746, after which the next corvettes moved up to 84ft long and 12 guns and were in a category now labelled simply 'corvette'.

The French philosophy behind the design of these vessels can be investigated by looking at some of the naval corvettes and privateers produced during the next war, beginning with two captured by the British and taken into the

Figs 15-5 and 15-6. A comparison between the body plans of the *Merlin* class sloops and that of *La Palme*. The latter shows the characteristic French 'two-turn' shape, with hollow garboards, short flat floors, followed by a long almost straight section and a second turn around the waterline and exaggerated tumblehome above. To a greater or lesser degree, these features formed the most common shape of mid-section in French warships up to the size of large frigates for most of the eighteenth century. By contrast, the British preferred more rounded forms, which tended to produce more capacious, stable and sea-kindly hulls, but being fuller, ones which were not as fast. *National Maritime Museum J0146/Author*

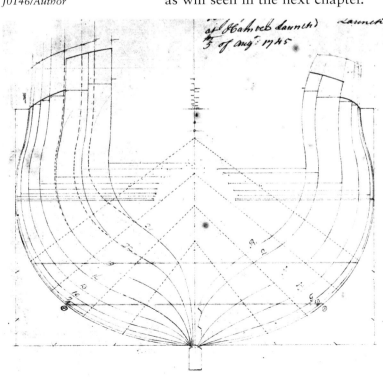

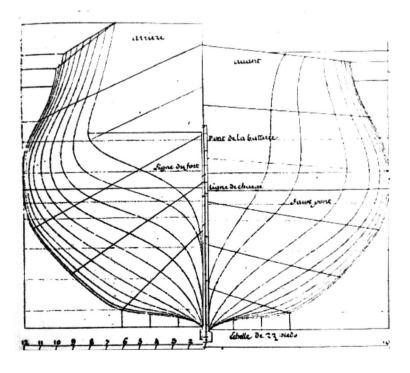

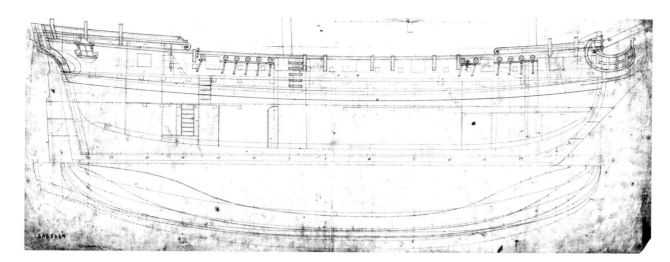

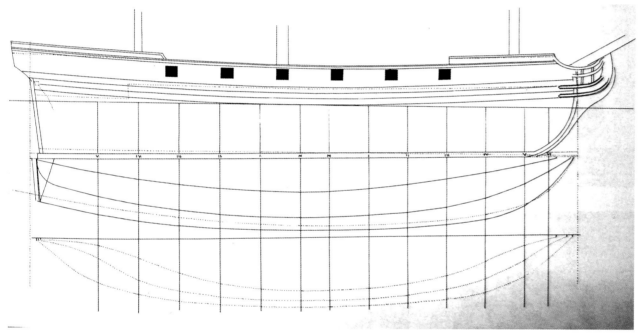

Fig 15-7. A comparison between the sheer plans and waterlines of a *Merlin* class sloop and a French 12-gun corvette with a length on deck of approximately 85ft. The *Merlin* class was slightly larger on deck at 90ft as designed. *National Maritime Museum J0146/Jean Boudriot*

Royal Navy: *Sardoine* built in 1757 and taken in 1761 and *La Guirlande*, also built in 1757 but taken in 1758. Strictly speaking, *La Guirlande* (Fig 15-9) should not be classed as a corvette despite being 110ft long and armed, according to French lists, with sixteen 4pdrs: in fact, the French classified her as a frigate.[5] The Navy Board listed her as having, when taken, eighteen 4pdrs and four 4pdrs, the latter possibly on the quarterdeck, which would seem to tally with the number of ports in the plan made at her survey after capture. She has two masts and seems to be rather different from the normal run of corvettes. Her sheer line is remarkably pronounced and her sections show the steepest deadrise yet encountered, except possibly the *barque longue* at Fig 10-10. She was built at Brest to a Pierre Salinoc design,

which exhibits a greater rake to stem and stern-post than other equivalent vessels at this time. She has a complete lower orlop deck with a headroom of 3–4ft, which may account for her listing as a frigate. Both decks run the full length

Fig 15-8. (Below) This sheer and lines plan for *Badine* of 1745 shows an obsessive use of the plumb stem and stern post. Her sections appear very different to those of her larger 12-gun cousins. From Jean Boudriot's monograph *La Corvette*.

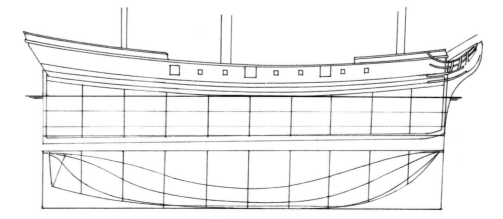

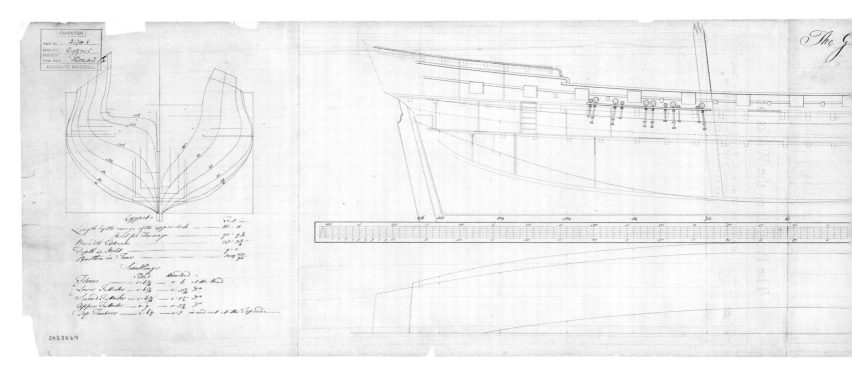

Fig 15-9. The lines of the French 18-gun *La Guirlande* taken off following her capture. Compare these with the model at Fig 15-10 which has been identified as the same ship, albeit after extensive modification! *National Maritime Museum J4161*

of the hull with no steps. There are compartments fore-and-aft on the lower deck, which must have been very cramped. She has a raised forecastle platform parallel to the waterline so protruding above the sheer line at the break – necessary to allow space under it for the forward gun port.

Fig 15-10 shows a model supposedly representing the alteration to *La Guirlande* after she was taken into the Royal Navy as the sloop *Cygnet* in 1757. It is difficult to realise that it is the same ship, so extensive are the modifications, despite the whole refit taking less than two months.[6] Her armament has been reduced to eighteen 6pdrs, giving her more force and using less space. She was also given twelve

swivels though there is no sign of stocks for these on the model. She now has a forecastle, though managing the leading guns would not have been easy. The quarterdeck has been extended to close abaft the mainmast, which has been brought to a vertical position from its previous heavily raked one to make space for the sails of a new mizzen mast. Most interesting

Fig 15-10. Labelled as an 18-gun sloop of about 1760 in the Science Museum's catalogue of sailing ships, this model has been tentatively identified as *Cygnet*, ex-*La Guirlande*. The rigging was completely restored in 1904–5 but the lengths of the masts and spars are probably about 10 per cent too large. The model is described in the Science Museum publication *Sailing Ships*, Part II, by G S Laird Clowes.

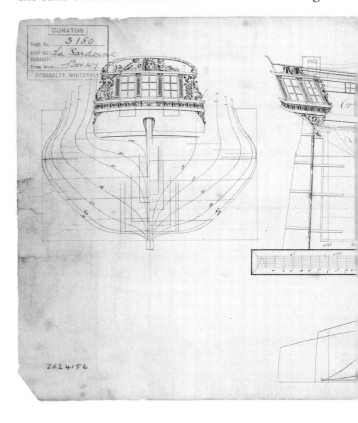

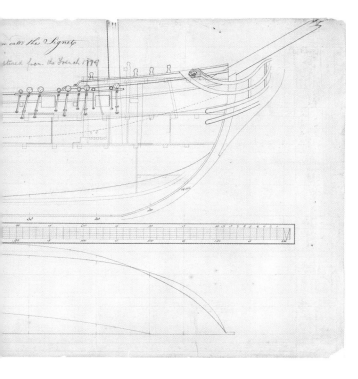

and, after refitting, in North America. She was sold there in 1768. A lot of time and money was spent on this little ship, classed for a while as a frigate, and it was unusual for prizes to remain so long in service after the conclusion of hostilities. A lovely looking ship, she must have proved to be highly effective and with eighteen 6pdrs she and her cousin *Pomona* (Fig 15-13) would have been the most powerful sloops in the Royal Navy until the launch of *Ceres* in 1771, herself built to the draught of *Pomona*.

The next example of a corvette constructed for the French Navy, *Sardoine* (Fig 15-11), was built at Nantes to the design of Jacques-Luc Coulomb. She had four sisters; in fact, the French Navy commissioned nine corvettes designed by Coulomb, most listed as 100ft length on deck. Moreover, his son produced several twenty years later at the time of the American War of Independence. If the corvettes built under the supervision of Blaise Ollivier appear extreme in hull design, they are nothing compared to *Sardoine*, whose sections exhibit an exaggerated version of the earlier designs. *Sardoine* was built thirteen years after *La Palme* and in addition to her highly developed hull, she was about 10ft longer and was pierced for nine guns a side, though armed with only twelve 4pdrs. She was commissioned into the Royal

of all, she has been given a modified head and a substantial gripe. This would be understandable if her rig had not been modified as it would have reduced lee-helm but with a mizzen fore-and-aft sail and square topsail this should not have been necessary.

She had an extensive career in the Royal Navy, serving in the Mediterranean, West Indies

Fig 15-11. Plan made of the French corvette *Sardoine* following her capture in 1761. By British measurement, she was 94ft on deck (9ft longer than *La Palme*) and carried 14 guns. *National Maritime Museum J4452*

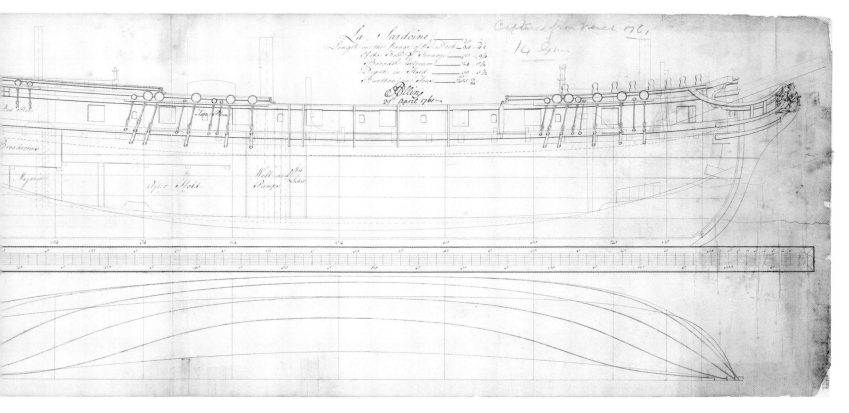

Navy at Portsmouth in 1761 and given an extra pair of 4pdrs.

The waterlines in the half-breadth plan provide a clear view of the remarkably fine ends this vessel, particularly that of the run. Her sheer plan shows the French preference for only a slight degree of rake at bow and stern, but here again there is exaggeration in that her sternpost is actually raked forwards. Like the earlier corvettes, she has a marked degree of tumblehome which may help stability by bringing the weight of the guns closer to the centreline but at the same time it would have made their handling difficult, possibly reducing their rate of fire; it was also less effective at dampening rolling than more 'wall-sided' designs. She is shown with a raised quarterdeck and forecastle on the plan, which is dated April 1761 (*ie* before the prize was formally purchased), so these are probably as captured; the height underneath them is only 5ft aft and 4ft 6in forward. Her tiller and rudder head are also in an exposed position, enhanced by the absence of barricades or rails, generally avoided by the French, who felt such top-hamper added to the windage and damaged the sailing qualities of their smaller ships. In refitting her, the British, with long spells at sea in mind, may have felt the need for additional protection and may have introduced wheel steering. As with *Cygnet*, she served in the Royal Navy until 1768 and served in the West Indies, in home waters and on the North American seaboard.

The vessel at Fig 15-12 was not designed for

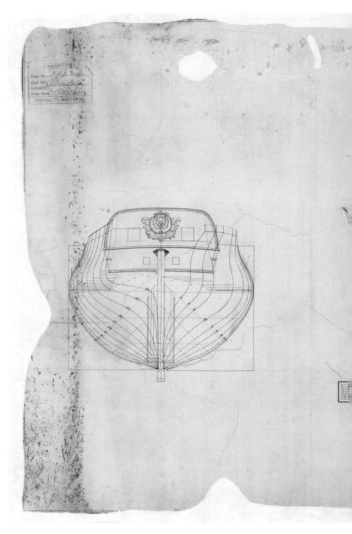

Fig 15-12. *L' Epreuve*, a two-masted French corvette, taken in 1761 which became the model for two ship-rigged sloops, *Vulture* and *Swift* designed by Slade later that year. *National Maritime Museum J4614*

the French Navy, but for a privateering syndicate. However, although she is not formally listed as a corvette, she was acquired by the French Admiralty as such, albeit with only two

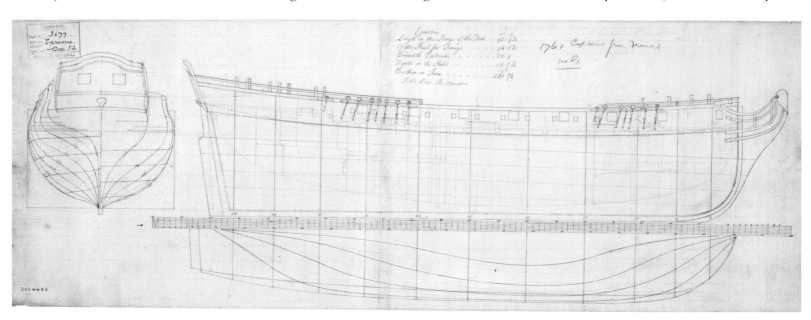

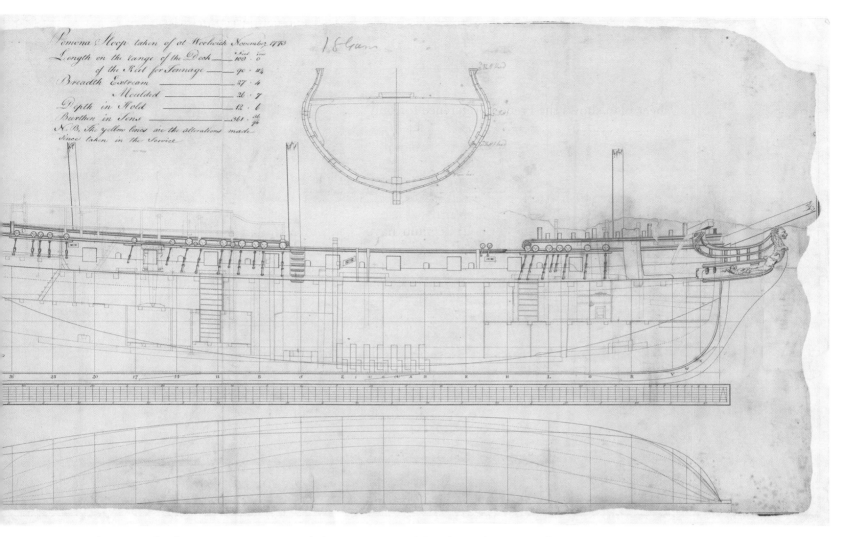

Pomona Sloop taken of at Woolwich November 1763

Length on the range of the Deck_____ 100 . 0
of the Keel for Tonnage _____ 90 . 11¼
Breadth Extream _____ 27 . 4
Moulded _____ 26 . 7
Depth in Hold _____ 12 . 6
Burthen in Tons _____ 561 . 36/94
N.B. The yellow lines are the alterations made
since taken in the Service

masts. She was built at Le Havre and her purchase was completed before her launch in 1759. Originally named *L'Observateur*, she was renamed *L'Epreuve* by the French service, a name retained for her service with the Royal Navy. She is of interest in that she again has a very different hull form as compared with the earlier examples. The design exhibits the steepest deadrise of any vessel here considered since 1650. Sections similar to hers would not come into general use with the Royal Navy, except in experimental vessels, until well into the nineteenth century. The plan also shows the typically French plumb stem and sternpost, although the latter has more rake than it first appears because the hull has a lot of drag aft and the baseline of the plan is the keel and not the waterline.

She has a flush deck but with a small quarter-deck platform raised by just one foot; to all intents and purposes she had a fully exposed gun deck, which would have been perfectly

acceptable for short swift raids into the Channel. Her transom above her counter stern is pierced for two 'chasers', as is her bow, and she has a further seven gun ports on each side of her waist. Although she looks like a smaller vessel than *Sardoine*, she is in fact slightly larger in breadth and burthen. She would have been given either a snow or brigantine rig.

Having been captured in January 1761, she was surveyed, accepted, refitted and recommissioned by June that year. She then served in home waters, before sailing for North America in the following year. She might well have continued to serve had she not foundered on her return passage across the Atlantic in 1764, which may have been Nature's verdict on her extreme hull form. Her hull lines were the inspiration for the 14-gun sloops *Swift* and *Vulture* designed by the Surveyor, Thomas Slade in 1761.[7]

The final example is a vessel that was designed and sailed as a privateer, *Le Chevert*

Fig 15-13. *Le Chevert*, a French ship-rigged privateer, was taken into the Royal Navy in 1761 as *Pomona* where she had a long career. Less extreme in form than others she was a powerfully armed sloop carrying 18 guns. *National Maritime Museum J4554*

Fig 15-14. The sheer plan of the 12-gun corvette *L'Amarante* of 1747, presented here by kind permission of Gérard Delacroix from whose monograph this image is taken.

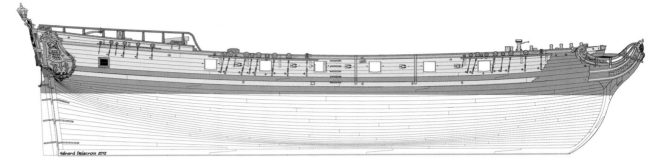

(Fig 15-13). She was large, measuring 108ft on the gun deck and of 364 tons burthen, a size similar to that of *Cygnet* and with sections close to those of that corvette. She was built at Dunkirk and armed with 18 guns. In Royal Navy service these were 6pdrs but whether they were of this calibre when she was a privateer is not known. The designer's intention was that she should have an open flush deck from stem to stern albeit with a short quarterdeck platform raised by no more than two feet. This can be seen from the position of the tiller. It says something for the French privateering seamen and the ship herself that they were able to helm a vessel of this size with a tiller: although they probably employed relieving tackles, the ship must have been beautifully balanced. The plan also illustrates her fine waterlines at the entry and the run. The number of ports on her broadside matches her complement of guns during naval service. There are also two ports for chasers at her stern. British Admiralty proposals for giving her a long raised quarterdeck and wheel steering can be just made out on the plan, along with structural strengthening (riders) within the hull.

As *Pomona*, this corvette/privateer had a long career in the Royal Navy, beginning with a cruising role as part of a squadron based in the Downs. She was then deployed to the north of Ireland in 1763, following a survey that found little fault with her. There she remained until 1773 when she sailed for the Mediterranean for a short spell, returning to Woolwich for a large repair late in that year. Recommissioned there, she sailed for the West Indies in 1775 and was lost at sea with all hands during the hurricane season in the following year. Her lines lived on in the form of the British-built sloop *Ceres* launched in 1771.

There were many captured small craft that were rejected, but those captured vessels taken into the Royal Navy show that the chosen French vessels were well built and that their designs were most acceptable to the British. This was to continue in future wars and it poses the question as to what effect the modern designs developed in France would have upon British small warship design. This will be addressed in the next two chapters, which will examine sloops built following the end of the War of the Austrian Succession and on into the Seven Years War.

It is evident from this brief review that French production of corvettes was far more limited in numbers than their British equivalents and that the control of design was looser in France than in Britain. Nevertheless, the French had given much thought to design and were able to produce some fast hulls with features that would not be fully realised in Britain for another seventy years. Fortunately, the Navy Board were insistent about taking off the lines of the ships that were captured and to an extent this allowed French design concepts to permeate the rather conservative parameters of British design. However, it is important to remember that the Royal Navy's requirements emphasised rather different needs: ships that could keep the sea, with good seakeeping and large stowage capacity, whereas for the French these were less of a priority.

A fitting close to this chapter is the sheer plan belonging to the stern elevation that opened it, the corvette *L'Amarante*, designed and built by Blaise Ollivier and his son at Brest in 1747 (Fig 15-14). This might be seen as illustrating the pinnacle of French corvette design at the middle of the century. What artists they were!

Fig 15-15. Blaise Ollivier.

Chapter 16

THE LAST OF THE SNOW- AND KETCH-RIGGED CRUISING AND BOMB SLOOPS 1749–1761

THE CRUISING SLOOPS

The two decades from 1728 to 1748 were a period of system and commonsense when it came to British sloop design and procurement. Whether for cruising or bomb sloops the intention was to test out a specification with one or two preliminary small-group programmes and then, with the experience gained, build a sizeable class to the same specification. Examples are the *Cruizer* class of 1732, the *Merlin* class of 1743–1745 and the *Blast* class bomb ketches of 1741. The short peace between 1748 and the Seven Years War in 1756 did not see such a calm and rational approach. This could be due to a number of factors, not the least of which was that, at the close of the War of the Austrian Succession in 1748, the Navy List still contained thirty sloops counting cruisers, bombs and prizes, all still capable of several years' service. This meant that, with one exception, sloop building was subject to top-up programmes resulting in runs of two or three vessels built to similar specifications but of differing designs.[1]

Another issue was the impending change of Surveyor. Anson, when he became First Lord of the Admiralty in 1751, was so dissatisfied with current British warship design that radical change was one of his top priorities. He found in Thomas Slade a designer who was prepared to countenance new ideas, including adapting the lines of captured French vessels to the rather different demands of the Royal Navy. At the same time Anson was able to hasten the departure, due to the incumbent's illness, of the current Surveyor, Joseph Allin, an act that removed a rather over-conservative influence on

warship design. Slade's significant contribution to sloop design will be covered later.

There was one recurring theme in the story of sloop procurement. In 1698, following the end of the War of the League of Augsburg, the Admiralty had built eight new sloops to enforce the ban on the smuggling of wool. Vessels for the same purpose were needed again in 1721 after the lingering war with Spain ground to a halt, and it was to be repeated a third time at the end of the War of the Austrian Succession. Accordingly, in January 1749 a competition was arranged for the Surveyor of the Navy and the master shipwrights to send in plans for sloops to be designed to a given specification.[2] This specification included the requirement that the sloops were 'to draw a small draught of water to cruise against smugglers.' Joint winners were the current Surveyor Allin, whose

Fig 16-1. Two 'light' sloops of the *Cruizer* class of 1752–1753, designed by the Surveyor Allin, one with ketch rig, the other with snow rig, sail in company towards the most southerly point of the British mainland, the Lizard. The snow-rigged sloop might have difficulty in setting her spritsail when close-hauled as shown. *Author*

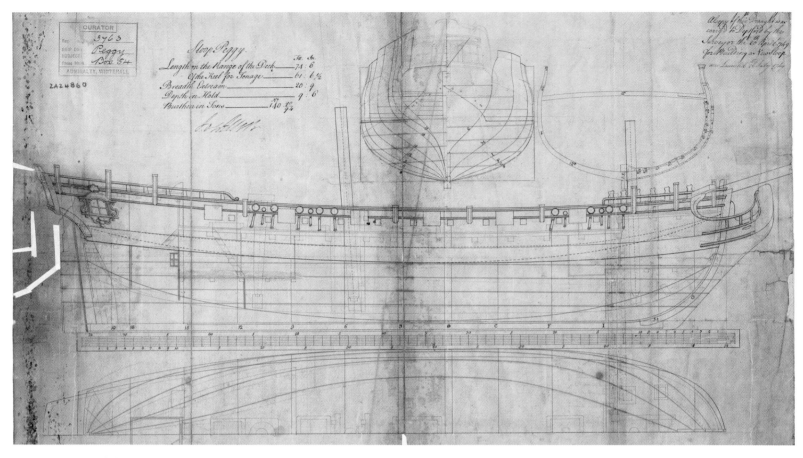

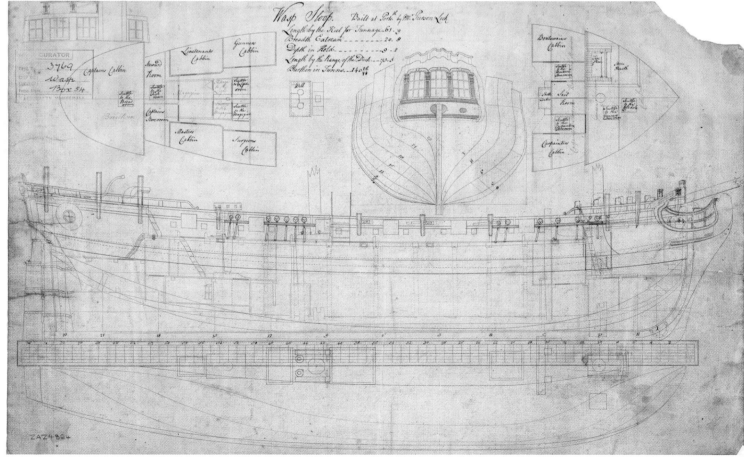

design was to become *Peggy*, and Lock, master shipwright at Portsmouth, who had produced the drawings for *Wasp*. The specification was for a vessel of 140 tons displacement with the dimensions of 74ft 6in on the deck, 61ft 6in on the keel, 22ft 9in breadth and 9ft 6in draught. This gave them a LBR of 3.2; comfortable but not fast. They were to be armed with eight 3pdr guns, although pierced for twelve, to be rigged as snows and manned by a complement of 100. These could be considered light sloops, whereas the *Merlin* class sloops, the bulk of which were still in service, were heavier and far more powerful and not really suited to this policing role.

The competition winners, *Peggy* at Fig 16-2 and *Wasp* at Fig 16-3, may seem similar but the only things they have in common are their dimensions, tonnage, armament and rig; their hulls are not remotely alike. The most obvious difference is in the rake of stem and sternpost. Pierson Lock at Portsmouth follows French practice in giving *Wasp* a plumb stem and stern-post which, as can be seen in Fig 16-3, allows a finer entry and run, whilst Joseph Allin, the Surveyor, influenced by the *Peregrine Galley* and her derivative the *Royal Caroline*, opts for the 'scow' bow and more heavily raked stern-

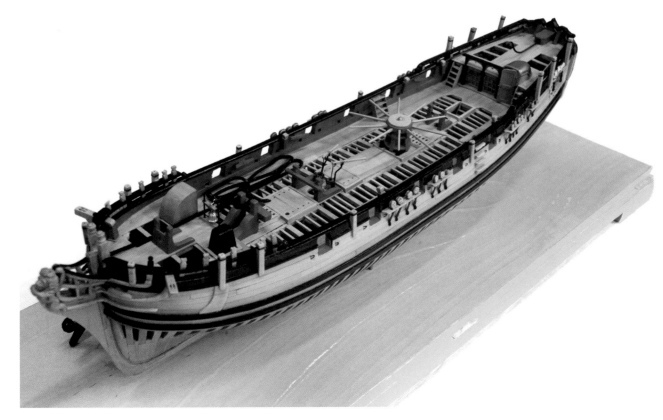

Fig 16-2 and 16-3. (Opposite) The sheer and lines plans of *Peggy* designed by the Surveyor Allin and *Wasp* designed by Pierson Lock, master shipwright at Portsmouth, joint winners of the 1749 competition to produce a light sloop to supress the export of 'uncustomed goods'. *National Maritime Museum J0084 and J0086*

Fig 16-4. (Left and above) Three views of a model of *Fly*, designed by Pierson Lock in 1752. Her similarity to *Wasp* is evident. The model was recently constructed in Navy Board fashion by the late Ken Clarke using plans from the National Maritime Museum.

post.[3] The more subtle difference is in the shape of the body sections, which show in *Wasp* a diluted influence of the French form and in *Peggy* the echo of an earlier age. Of the two, *Wasp* has the better run and entry.

Yet again there was a problem with the rigs of both sloops. The order to build was issued in April 1749; less than four months later *Wasp* was ordered to have her main topmast set abaft the lower main, an order that changed a week later to a requirement that the topmast be capable of stepping both before and abaft the mast. Not content with these arrangements, both sloops had to have further alterations: *Peggy* had both her masts shortened by two feet, indicating a problem of stability; and *Wasp* had her mainmast moved aft at the partners thereby giving it greater rake, suggesting a problem of balance. Looking at the record over the years, clearly the Navy had a recurring difficulty with the rigging of two-masted sloops. This was understandable in the days when they did not have the wing sail abaft the mainmast, but with that in place there should not have been any difficulty in generating a slight weather helm when on the wind. Dissatisfaction with the official rig was to repeat itself yet again with the next pair of sloops, still to the same specification, ordered in July of that year. They were built at Woolwich to an 'Admiralty' design (the exact meaning of this unusual designation is not known) for *Savage* and at Portsmouth to a design by Benjamin Slade for *Hazard*. The alterations for both centred on reducing the height of masts; in the case of *Hazard* by five feet for her lower masts! She was altered to ship rig in 1755.

The problems with smuggling must have persisted, for in January 1752 the Admiralty ordered six new lightly armed sloops of eight 3pdrs. Two, the *Fly* group, were designed by Pierson Lock and four, the *Cruizer* group, by Allin the Surveyor. This is the one point in this period where an initial investigation, the competition of 1749, was used to build a class of six vessels, albeit in two groups. Whilst the vessels within each group were identical in form, the difference between the groups, in terms of hull shape, was marked, although both were again of similar dimensions. The general likeness to his competition-winning *Wasp* can still be seen in *Fly* but unfortunately Lock was

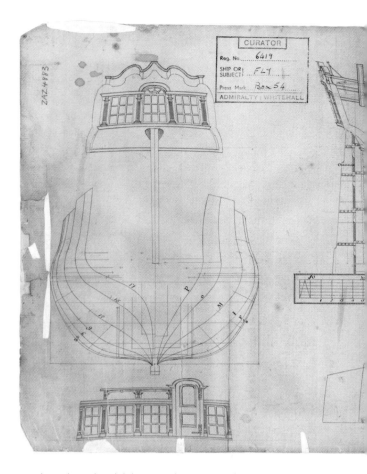

ordered to build her to lines similar to those of the French 74-gun ship *Monarch*. This design had the typical French plumb stem and stern, accompanied by a distinctly different body shape from her British counterparts, with flattish floors and futtocks and with a sharp turn of the bilge and a more marked tumblehome above the waterline. These features can be seen reflected in the shape of *Fly*'s sections. However, she does have a fine entry and run, which is one of the advantages of the plumb stem and sternpost (Fig 16-5). Neither she nor her sister *Ranger* was a success, which is not entirely surprising since the massive scaling-down of a successful larger vessel does not necessarily bestow the advantages of that original ship on the smaller model, particularly when the rig is changed.[4] Neither was ship-rigged, one being a ketch and the other a snow.

The *Cruizer* group, which was the third class with this name, was based on the lines of the *Royal Caroline*. The order was that the *Speedwell* and *Happy* from this group should be rigged as ketches and that *Cruizer* and *Wolf* should be given snow rig. In the event *Cruizer* was converted to ship rig in 1753 shortly after

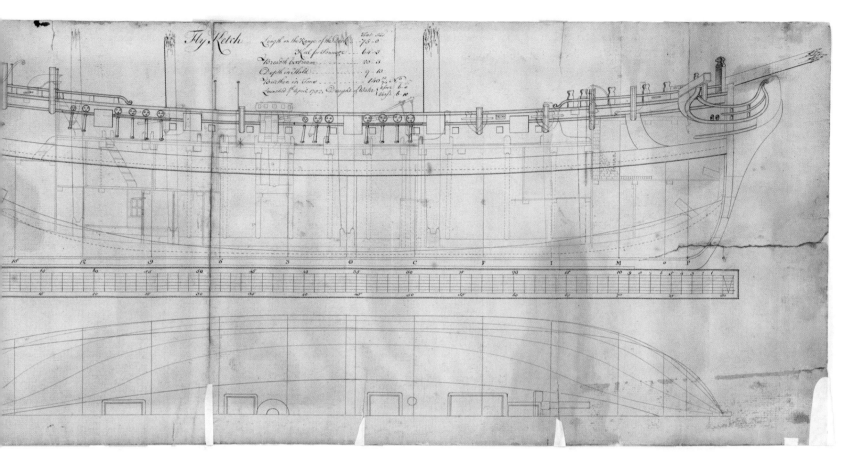

commissioning.[5] The lines of these sloops contrast strongly with those of the *Fly* group. The body sections in both these latter cases are more rounded than those of the *Fly* group and the waterlines of *Cruizer* exhibit the effect of adopting the scow bow and raked transom which tend to preclude the development of fine hollow lines at bow and stern to the degree achievable with a plumb-ended ship (see Fig 15-8). The model at Figs. 16-6 and 16-7, although contemporary, shows an unusual feature in its double wale, which at this time should be a single planked-in wale.[6] The waist is pierced for six guns a side, although on commissioning these groups only carried eight 3pdrs and kept this complement even during the Seven Years War. They also had an allocation of ten swivels. The stocks for these are hard to see on the model since they barely protrude above the rail. Both groups were designed with slightly raised forecastles giving headroom for small cabins in the bow. The short quarterdeck is also raised by about four feet. Access to the captain's cabin below is by an attractive dome-shaped companionway on the port side. The vessels were helmed using a

wheel on the gun deck immediately ahead of the aft cabin bulkhead.[7] There are two oar ports cut between each gun port.

The reconstructions of the lines of *Cruizer* (III) at Fig 16-8 and *Peregrine Galley* at Fig 16-9, serve to show the lineage of the *Cruizer*'s hull design. The *Royal Caroline* was a 1733 rebuild by Richard Stacey of the *Peregrine Galley* launched in 1700. Her lines were then modified by Allin in 1749 to create a new *Royal Caroline*, whose lines in turn were used for the design of the *Cruizer* sloop, so this is essentially a comparison between two ships with 52 years between their designs. The entry and the run of both are nearly identical. The value of the reconstruction is that it provides waterlines – in effect a series of horizontal cuts through the hull – which make obvious the similarity of the hull shape in these two vessels.[8]

As noted above, there were three options for the rig of these light sloops: ketch, snow or ship. The use of ship rig will be discussed in the next chapter; the snow rig (as at Fig 16-10) is already familiar; but the changes to the ketch rig, since the turn of the century, need some brief attention here. Its use had continued in bomb vessels into

Fig 16-5. The sheer and lines plan of HM Sloop *Fly*. Note that despite her small size she still has a raised forecastle but, unlike the *Merlin* class sloops whose gun deck remained flush right up to the stem, *Fly*'s is stepped down to allow for a cabin here (as it does aft under the quarterdeck). The same arrangement applied to the *Cruizer* class sloops of the same period. *National Maritime Museum J0079*

Figs 16-6 and 16-7. Two views of a ketch-rigged version of the *Cruizer* class sloops of 1752–1753. This model is thought to be of *Speedwell. National Maritime Museum D4083-3 and D4083-4*

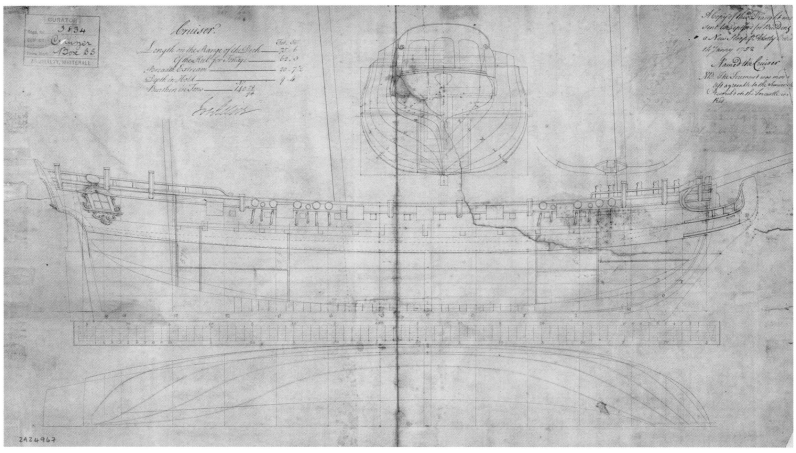

Fig 16-8. The sheer draught of the *Cruizer* of 1752–1753, signed by the Surveyor Allin, who was responsible for the design. This has a light indication of the position for a mizzen mast, which has been highlighted by the author. *Cruizer* was in fact converted to ship rig in 1753, and the addition of a mizzen would most probbaly have forced a reduction in the rake of the mainmast and possibly the foremast as well. *National Maritime Museum J0070*

Fig 16-9. This reconstruction of the lines of *Peregrine Galley* by the author is based on a draught of the ship at the time of her refit and alteration by Richard Stacey in 1733. By that date she was a royal yacht, named *Carolina* after George I's queen, and was then renamed *Royal Caroline*. The buttock–bow lines are derived from the half-breadth plan on the draught NPD1488; they provide a clear indication of why she was such a fast sailer.

the 1740s and would carry on into the 1750s (Fig 16-11). The position of the mainmast had changed with time, moving slightly forward, and now carried a wing sail on its trailing edge. The mizzen now had a smack sail but with no boom holding out its foot. Both masts had topsails and the ability to raise topgallant sails. However, the ketch rig remained unpopular for work with the fleet because on certain points of sailing it could not maintain the necessary speed. Its great advantage in the sloop family was that it facili-

tated the conversion of a cruising sloop into a bomb vessel and vice-versa. The fitting of ketch rig to cruising sloops would end in 1755 with *Hawk*, the last sloop to be designed by the Surveyor Allin and once again based on the lines of the yacht *Royal Caroline*. She did not sail well. For bomb vessels the last group to be ketch-rigged would be launched in 1756. The last cruising sloops to have snow rig were launched in 1761 and were to the design of the *Cruizer* sloop of 1732.

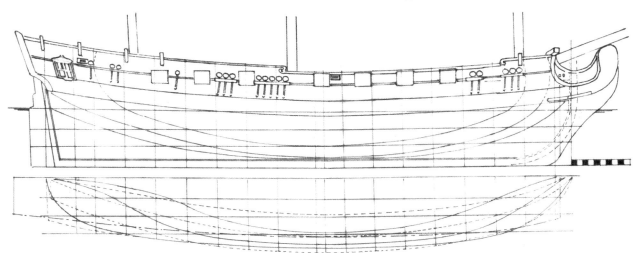

Although these light sloops were ordered as a measure against smuggling, few of them spent their entire careers in this service. The arrival of the next conflict, the Seven Years War, meant that they were co-opted into fleets to provide communications or, more frequently, be used together with rated ships to provide convoy. They were deployed to cruise, at allocated stations in home waters and along the Channel, against French privateers. *Ranger* captured three privateers during the course of the war and *Fly* two. *Fly* was also part of the Belle Isle operation in 1761 (Fig16-12), and captured her two prizes on her way home. After the war these sloops remained at sea around the British coasts and in the Americas, on patrol, providing communications, guarding the fisheries and intercepting smuggling, operations for which they were designed. Some were still on active service during the American War of Independence.

Some insight into the intensive use of these small warships can be gleaned from the log of *Speedwell* (Figs 16-6 and 16-7). She had been brought into Plymouth at the beginning of March 1759, to be fitted for the 'raising of men', after which she went on station to cruise off Lundy Island. She returned to Plymouth and handed over 45 pressed men to HMS *Kingston,* a 60-gun Fourth Rate. Returning to her patrol area, she was caught in gale force winds on 1 June, 32 nautical miles southwest of the Lizard Point, and was making 18in of water each hour. She was forced to turn back for Plymouth where, from 7 to 10 June, a gang of

carpenters worked on her. By 17 July she was in Guadaloupe and by the 25th of that month she was part of a transatlantic convoy of 194 sail leaving for Britain. They sighted land on 28 September, having sounded first on the 22nd at 80 fathoms. On 19 October she was hauled into dock at Sheerness and returned to the Nore by the 27th; by 1 November she was providing convoy to the Tyne. This was quite an achievement, in eight months, for a 140-ton vessel.[9] She was renamed *Spitfire* in 1779, having been converted to a fireship; she was then 27 years old.

In 1755 there was a sharp jump in the size of sloops. The conflict that was to become the Seven Years War was looming and despite the fact that Britain had thirty-one serviceable cruising sloops at the time, a further nine vessels were ordered. These ranged between 220 and 236 tons and except *Hawk*, Allin's last design,

Fig 16-10. (Left) The snow rig applied to a *Cruizer* class sloop. Note the horse (rope) close abaft the mainmast to take the luff of the fore-and-aft wing or snow sail. *Author*

Fig 16-11. (Right) Ketch rig applied to a bomb vessel around 1750. Note the small wing sail set immediately abaft the mainmast. *Author*

Fig 16-12. HM Sloop *Fly* at the Belle Isle operations off the coast of South Brittany in 1761. *Watercolour by the Author*

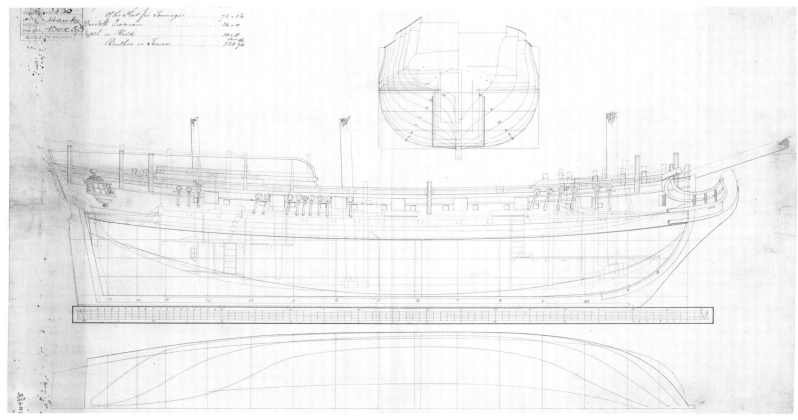

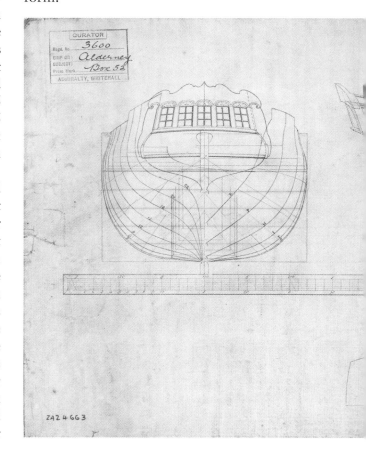

Fig 16-13. (Above) Whilst designed with the intention that she would be rigged as a snow with two masts, in line with contemporary developments, *Hawk* (Allin's last sloop before he retired) was commissioned with ship rig. *National Maritime Museum J4899*

Fig 16-14. (Top right) This plan of *Spy* of the *Bonetta* group was drawn by Slade in 1755, a couple of months before he became Surveyor of the Navy. The influence of the frigate *Lyme* (mentioned on the draught) and hence her French prototype can be seen in these lines. *National Maritime Museum J0226*

Fig 16-15. (Right) Bateley design for the *Alderney* class sloops launched in 1756–1757. These are totally different in form to his later design for at least two of the *Beaver* class ship-rigged sloops (see Chapter 17). The change in design may have been due to the influence of Anson and Slade in using French designs to inform British construction. *National Maritime Museum J4694*

which initially carried eight 3pdrs then ten 4pdrs, all were equipped with the new short-barrelled 6pdr gun by 1761. The two new Surveyors, Slade and Bately, now produced a number of vessels each. Slade designed the *Bonetta* group of three sloops at 220–223 tons followed by the *Hunter* group of two sloops at 223–228 tons. Simultaneously, Bately designed the *Alderney* group of three sloops at 232–236 tons. All these sloops were launched in 1756 with a snow rig, except for *Alderney* and *Stork* which, whilst laid down as snows, were given a ship rig before commissioning.

Whilst *Hawk* (Fig 16-13) was an enlarged version of the *Cruizer* group of 1752, yet having no greater force than these earlier sloops, those designed by Slade were somewhat different in form. Their design originated in a French prize, *Le Tygre*, captured during the War of the Austrian Succession. Two 24-gun frigates were ordered to be built as exact copies in 1747–1748. They were commissioned as the *Unicorn* and *Lyme* and both had a considerable influence on the design of Fifth and Sixth Rates thereafter.[10] Thomas Slade used these lines for the *Bonetta* group (Fig 16-14). In comparison to *Hawk* these sloops had a far better entry and finer run. The sections of *Hawk* show a rather

stolid shape whereas those of the *Bonetta* group, although still rounded, have a slighter form.

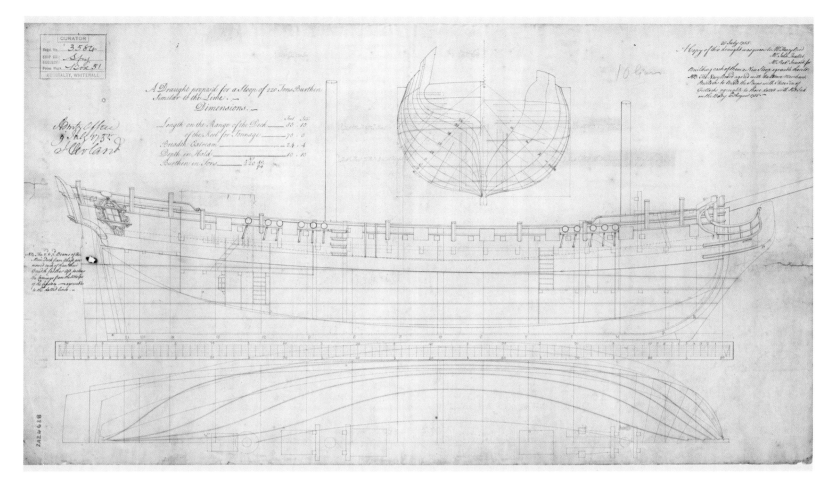

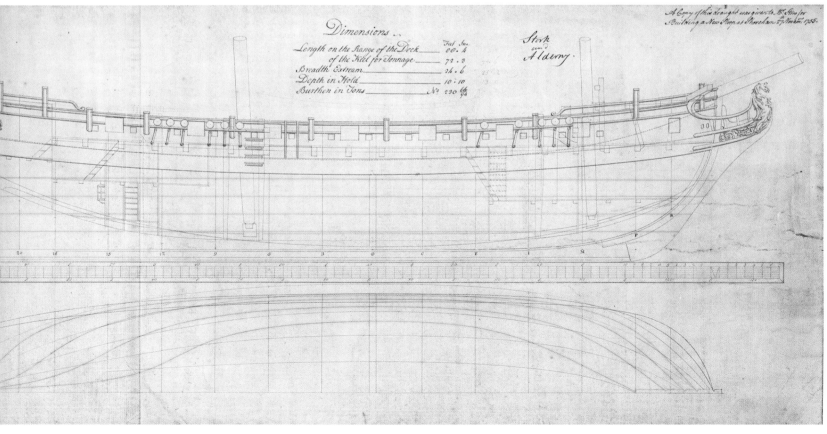

Fig 16-16. A snow-rigged *Cruizer* class sloop of 1752 running – and rolling – before the wind with much reduced sail. *Author*

Fig 16-17. The general arrangement plan of a ketch-rigged bomb vessel of the *Infernal* class; others were ship-rigged, by way of conscious comparative trial. Designed in 1756 the class was not built until 1758 to meet the demands of the Seven Years War. *National Maritime Museum J1443*

extended aft by about 6ft. Both sloops have the deck stepped-down aft to provide a cabin, though in addition *Hawk*'s draught includes as a later modification an unusual raised deck over the last two gun ports (there is the pencil outline of a similar structure on the draught for *Bonetta*); its rationale is a mystery. Both vessels are of the same burthen and share very similar dimensions.

Bately's group of three sloops inclined more to the example of *Hawk* and the royal yacht *Caroline* in terms of body shape; if anything her sections indicate an even fuller form than the other vessels. Like them she has a generous fore-rake at the stem and thus there is no hollowness in any of her waterlines at the bow. Her run is similar to *Hawk*'s. Bately also designed the *Beaver* group of ship-rigged sloops, ordered in 1760 and launched in 1761. They were slightly larger than his two-masted sloops of the *Alderney* group (Fig 16-15). However, his design for *Beaver* was very different from that for *Alderney*, yet one of *Beaver*'s sisters, *Senegal*, was almost identical to this two-masted sloop in hull form, although the lines were scaled up to meet the larger specification.[11] Being ship-rigged, they will be discussed in the next chapter.

Although Bately's *Alderney* group were designed for snow rig, two of them, *Stork* and *Alderney*, were commissioned with ship rig, joining the conversions of the *Merlin* class from the 1740s and the *Cruizer* of 1752–1753 above.

The sloops *Druid* and *Lynx*, ordered in 1760 and launched the following year, were the last snows delivered to the Navy, and even they

These two plans (Fig 16-13 and 16-14) show the differences in the hull shapes of *Hawk* and *Bonetta*, which are most readily appreciated by looking at the body plan sections and the waterlines. Although the waterlines are drawn at different levels for each sloop, a comparison using them and the sections supports the view that *Bonetta* has the finer lines, despite the fact that her LBR is slightly lower than that of *Hawk*. *Bonetta* has a lower above-water profile mainly on account of smaller bulwarks. Both were designed flush-decked to the bow but with a short platform above (what the following century termed a 'topgallant fore-castle'), although *Hawk* later had hers

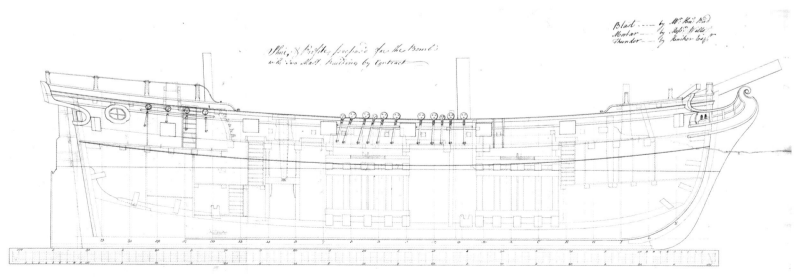

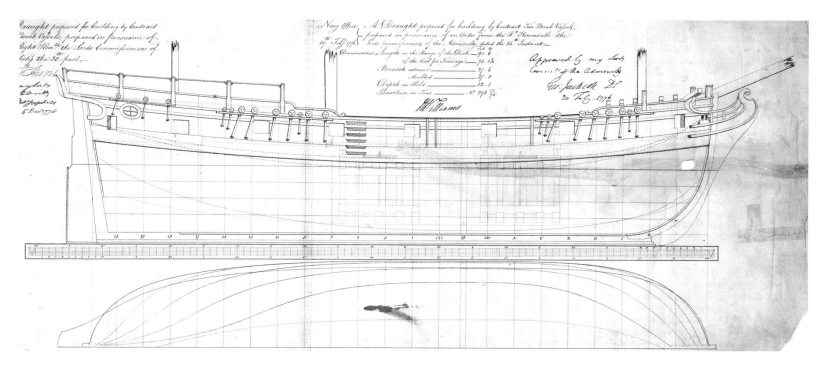

were converted to ship rig early in their careers. Their design was essentially that of Stacey's *Cruizer* class of 1732 with some improvements and additions. It is fitting to close the story of the two-masted sloop on the memory of what was the most attractive of all the sloop classes between 1650 and 1753.

THE LAST KETCH-RIGGED BOMBS

At the end of the War of the Austrian Succession Britain had seven bomb vessels, all ketch-rigged. *Furnace* had been ordered as a bomb ketch in 1740 but commissioned as a cruising sloop in 1741 and was given a ship rig in 1742 for an exploration of the North West Passage; she was operating in the cruising role and was not to be fitted as a bomb until 1756. By that year the stock of this type of vessel had dwindled to three, including *Furnace*. To remedy this, the Admiralty ordered one vessel to be built and rigged as a ketch. This was followed in 1758 by a further order for three more to be ketch-rigged and three to be fitted with ship rig.

The new vessels of the *Infernal* class were designed by the Surveyor, Thomas Slade, and were very different in form from their predecessors. The pink stern at Figs 16-17 and 16-18, which was common on the early bomb ketches but which had largely disappeared during the 1740s, was returned in this design. In fact this new design bears a strong resemblance to the *Salamander* group of 1728. It should be noted

that Fig 16-18 is not one of the original *Infernal* class but is of *Aetna*, a posthumous repeat in 1776 of Slade's earlier class; this now has a ship rig, as was fitted to three of the *Infernal* class. The hull displays a very bluff bow but the run remains reasonably hollow. It is in the body plan that the difference is most noticeable. A comparison between the body plan of the *Alderney* bomb ketch of 1734 at Fig 16-19 (and therefore those of the similar *Blast* and *Comet* classes of the 1740s) and that of the *Infernal/Aetna* class at Fig 16-18, shows how different the hull forms are. The much fuller sections of the 1756 class, almost mercantile in form, come with a minor increase in length of 1ft 0in and an increase in beam of 1ft 6in, increasing the burthen from 261 to 298 tons, a rise of 14 per cent.

Unsurprisingly, their sailing performance was poor, not so much in speed but in weatherliness. These hulls would have been less than ideal for operations in the cruising role where speed and a good ability to sail to windward were important. Nevertheless, they were so employed, two out of the seven being commissioned as sloops with one refitted as a sloop one year after commissioning. This was followed by a mass of sloop/bomb switches in the class until the end of the Seven Years War in 1763, after which most reverted to the cruising role until those that remained were refitted as bombs for the American Revolutionary War.

Fig 16-18. Detail from a general arrangement plan of *Terror*, one of the *Aetna* class. Built in 1776, her design was a repeat of the *Infernal* class of 1758 but with minor modification. All were ship-rigged. *National Maritime Museum J6803*

Figs 16-19 and 16-20. A comparison between the body plans of the *Alderney* of 1734 (top) and the *Infernal* and *Aetna* classes of 1758 and 1776 shows a dramatic reappraisal by Slade of the requirements for a platform capable of carrying and accurately discharging a mortar. *National Maritime Museum, details from J1356 and J6803*

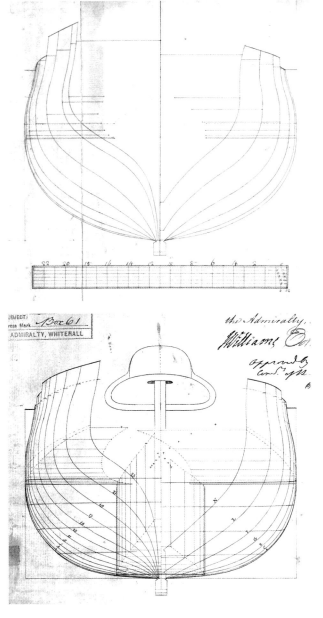

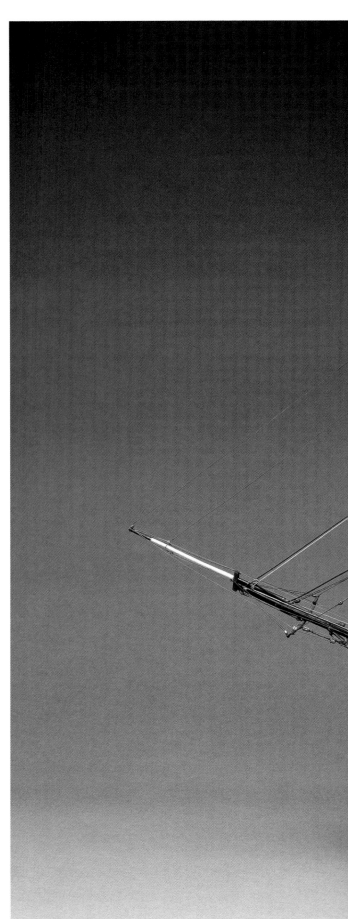

Fig 16-21. (Opposite) This model, in the collection of the National Maritime Museum, represents a ketch-rigged version of the *Cruizer* class of 1752–1753. Others of the class were rigged as snows. The Admiralty required variation in rig to provide comparison in performance. However, both rigs were shortly to be discontinued for naval sloops: in the future sloops of war would be given either a ship rig or, come the 1770s, the new brig rig. *National Maritime Museum D4083-1*

As with their cruising cousins, all these vessels were built in commercial yards. *Infernal*, the prototype was constructed in 1756 at Southampton and commissioned as a sloop in 1757 at Portsmouth. The other six were ordered in September 1758 and launched in the first three months of 1759. *Infernal* was ketch-rigged, as were *Blast, Mortar* and *Thunder*. There was no change in hull form for the three fitted with ship rig.

In 1759, half way through the War, the Navy List contained twelve bomb ketches, one of which was the converted purchase/prize renamed *Racehorse*, and another the converted merchantman *Pelican*. To this was added in 1762 a further three by the conversion of two

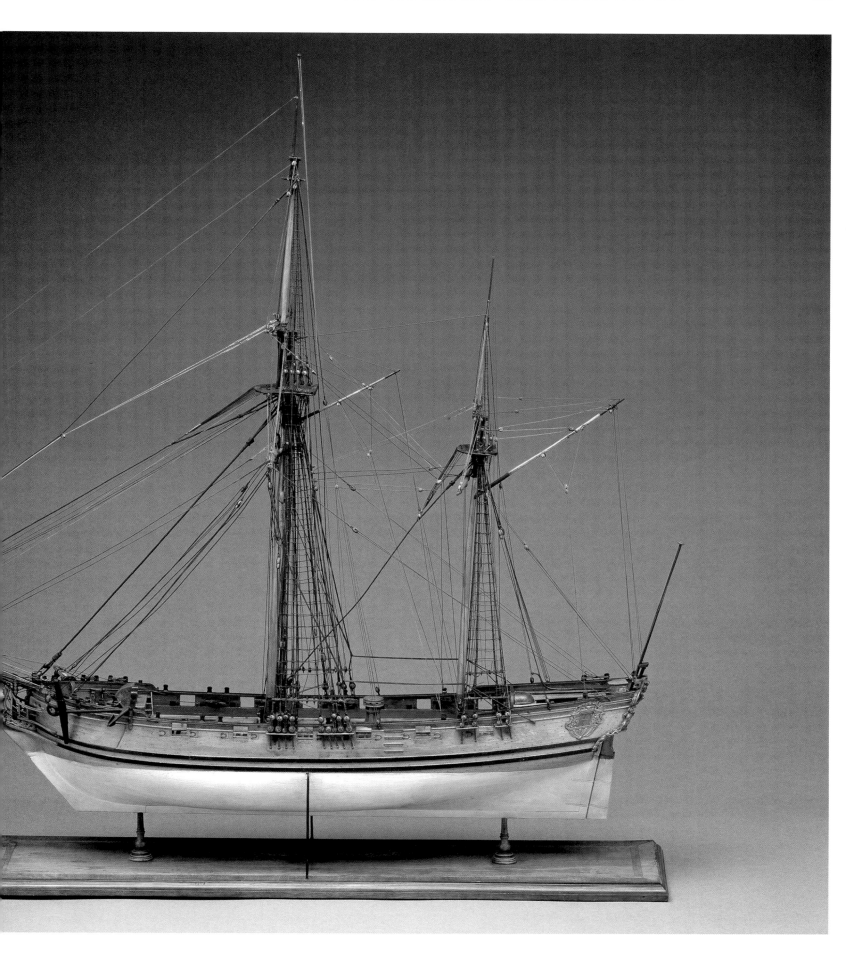

Fig 16-22. The three rigs carried by the four *Cruizer* class sloops of 1752–1753. The dotted lines indicate the possibility that the addition of a mizzen mast to the snow rig forced the use of a boomed-out fore-and-aft mizzen course, since there was comparatively little space to employ a smack sail effectively. *Author*

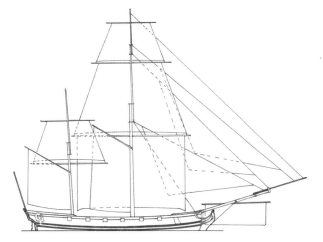

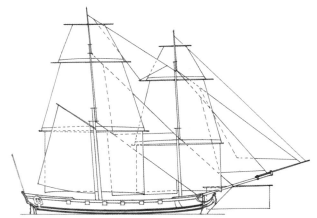

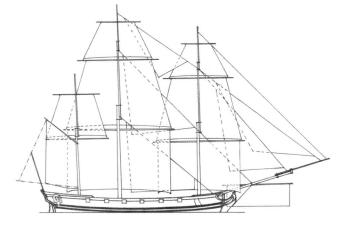

Merlin class sloops and the sloop *Baltimore* from 1740. The latter carried only one mortar and was snow-rigged. The war was noted for the high number of amphibious operations carried out. Apart from the east coast of the Indian subcontinent, where bomb ketches were not deployed, they were used in all the main theatres, but their most concentrated deployments were in the Channel in 1758–1759, which involved attacks with shore bombardment on Le Havre, St Malo, Cherbourg and St Cas, Belle Isle on the Biscay coast in 1761, and the West Indies, particularly against Havana in 1763. With the close of the war in 1763 most were returned to the cruising role. The last-purpose-built ketch-rigged bomb vessel was launched on 15 March 1759.

SNOW- AND KETCH-RIGGED CRUISING AND BOMB SLOOPS, 1749–1761

Table 16-1: 1749 PROGRAMME FOR 140-TON SLOOPS			
Name	*Peggy*	*Wasp*	*Savage*	*Hazard*
Ordered	4-1749	4-1749	7-1749	7-1749
Launched	7-1749	7-1749	3-1750	10-1749
LGD	74ft 6in	73ft 3in	73ft 6in	76ft 3in
LoK	61ft 9in	61ft 6 ½ in	61ft 6in	62ft 8in
Beam	20ft 9in	20ft 8in	21ft 0in	20ft 6in
LBR	3.59	3.54	3.5	3.72
Depth in hold	9ft 6in	9ft 2in	9ft 0in	9ft 4in
Draught	5ft 1in – 7ft 4½in	5ft 3in – 7ft 9in	5ft 1in – 7ft 7in	5ft 5½in – 7ft 2in
Burthen	141 tons	140 tons	144 tons	140 tons
Guns	8 x 3pdr, 10 swivels	8 x 3pdr, 10 swivels	8 x 3pdr, 10 swivels	8 x 3pdr, 10 swivels
Men	50	50	50	50
Rig	Snow	Snow	Snow	Snow
Fate	Wrecked 1770	Sold 1781	Wrecked 1776	Sold 1783
Designer	J Allin (Surveyor)	Pierson Lock	'Admiralty'	Benjamin Slade
Builder	Holland, Deptford	Lock, Portsmouth	Fellows, Woolwich	Lock, Portsmouth

Table 16-2: 1752–1753 PROGRAMME FOR 140-TON SLOOPS

Name	Speedwell	Cruizer	Happy	Wolf
Ordered	1-1752	1-1752	8-1753	8-1753
Launched	10-1752	8-1752	7-1754	5-1754
LGD	75ft 7in	75ft 6in	75ft 6in	75ft 6in
LoK	62ft 4in	62ft 3in	62ft 3in	62ft 3in
Beam	20ft 8½in	20ft 7½in	20ft 7½in	20ft 7½in
LBR	3.63	3.65	3.65	3.65
Depth in hold	9ft 4in	9ft 4in	9ft 4in	9ft 4in
Draught	5ft 9in – 7ft 1in	–	5ft 8in – 7ft 2in	5ft 11in – 7ft 4in
Burthen	142 tons	141 tons	141 tons	141 tons
Guns	8 x 3pdr, 10 swivels	8 x 3pdr, 10 swivels	8 x 3pdr, 10 swivels	8 x 3pdr, 10 swivels
Men	50	50	50	50
Rig	Ketch	Snow, then ship	Ketch	Snow
Fate	Sold 1780	Burnt 1776	Wrecked 1766	Sold 1781
Designer	J Allin (Surveyor)	J Allin (Surveyor)	J Allin (Surveyor)	J Allin (Surveyor)
Builder	Ward/Slade, Chatham	Holland/Fellowes, Deptford	E Allin, Woolwich	Hayes, Chatham

Table 16-3: 1751 PROGRAMME FOR 140-TON SLOOPS

Name	Fly	Ranger
Ordered	1-1752	1-1752
Launched	4-1752	10-1752
LGD	75ft 0in	75ft 0in
LoK	64ft 3in	64ft 1½in
Beam	20ft 3in	20ft 4½in
LBR	3.70	3.67
Depth in hold	9ft 10in	9ft 10in
Draught	6ft 0in – 6ft 10in	5ft 4in – 6ft 9in
Burthen	140 tons	142 tons
Guns	8 x 3pdr, 10 swivels	8 x 3pdr, 10 swivels
Men	50	50
Rig	Ketch	Snow
Fate	Sold 1772	Sold 1783
Designer	Pierson Lock	Pierson Lock
Builder	Lock, Portsmouth	Fellowes/Slade/Hayes, Woolwich

Table 16-4: 1755 PROGRAMME BONETTA AND HUNTER GROUPS 220-TON SLOOPS

Name	Bonetta	Merlin	Spy	Hunter	Viper
Ordered	7-1755	7-1755	7-1755	8-1755	8-1755
Launched	2-1756	3-1756	2-1756	2-1756	3-1756
LGD	86ft 4in	86ft 6½in	85ft 10in	88ft 8in	88ft 7½in
LoK	71ft 4in	70ft 2in	70ft 3in	75ft 11½in	72ft 11½in
Beam	24ft 6in	24ft 5½in	24ft 5in	24ft 3in	24ft 3in
LBR	3.52	3.53	3.51	3.65	3.65
Depth in hold	10ft 10in	10ft 10in	10ft 10in	7ft 0in	7ft 1in
Draught	5ft 8in – 9ft 9in	5ft 1in – 9ft 11in	5ft 3in – 9ft 6in	6ft 6in – 8ft 5in	6ft 6in – 8ft 11in
Burthen	228 tons	223 tons	223 tons	238 tons	228 tons
Guns	10 x 6pdr, 12 swivels	10 x 6pdr, 12 swivels	10 x 6pdr, 12 swivels	10 x 6pdr, 12 swivels	10 x 6pdr, 12 swivels
Men	100	100	100	100	100
Rig	Snow	Snow	Snow	Snow	Snow
Fate	Sold 1776	Burnt 1780	Sold 1773	Sold 1780	Wrecked 1779
Designer	Slade	Slade	Slade	Slade	Slade
Builder	Contract	Contract	Contract	Contract	Contract

Continued overleaf

Table 16-5: 1755 *HAWK* AND *ALDERNEY* GROUPS 220- AND 230-TON SLOOPS

Name	*Hawk*	*Alderney*	*Stork*	*Diligence*
Ordered	7-1755	11-1755	11-1755	2-1756
Launched	4-1756	2-1757	11-1756	7-1756
LGD	88ft 10in	88ft 4in	88ft 7in	88ft 5¾in
LoK	72ft 10in	72ft 3in	72ft 5in	73ft 1in
Beam	24ft 1in	24ft 9in	24ft 7in	24ft 8in
LBR	3.69	3.57	3.60	3.59
Depth in hold	10ft 10½in	10ft 10½in	10ft 10½in	10ft 10in
Draught	6ft 3in – 8ft 10in	–	5ft 9in – 7ft 8in	6ft 1½in – 7ft 4in
Burthen	225 tons	235 tons	233 tons	236 tons
Guns	8 x 3pdr, 10 swivels	10 x 4pdrs, 12 swivels	10 x 4pdrs, 12 swivels	10 x 4pdrs, 12 swivels
Men	80	100	100	100
Rig	Snow	Ship	Ship	Snow
Fate	Sold 1781	Sold 1783	Taken 1758	Sold 1780
Designer	Allin	Bately	Bately	Bately
Builder	Contract	Contract	Contract	Contract

Table 16-6: 1761 PROGRAMME FOR 210-TON SLOOPS

Name	*Druid*	*Lynx*
Ordered	8-1760	8-1760
Launched	2-1761	3-1761
LGD	87ft 6in	87ft 8¼in
LoK	72ft 11in	73ft 4in
Beam	23ft 4½in	23ft 6½in
LBR	3.74	3.72
Depth in hold	9ft 5in	9ft 5¼in
Burthen	212 tons	216 tons
Guns	10 x 4pdr, 12 swivels	10 x 4pdr, 12 swivels
Men	100	100
Rig	Snow, then ship	Snow, then ship
Fate	Sunk as breakwater 1773	Sold 1777
Designer	Stacey in 1732	Stacey in 1732
Builder	Contract	Contract

Table 16-7: 1756 AND 1758 PROGRAMES FOR 298-TON BOMB KETCHES

All Ships

Item	As Bomb	As Cruiser
Mortars	1 x 13in, 1 x 10in	–
Guns	8 x 6pdr, 14 swivels	14 x 6pdr, 14 swivels
Men	60	110
Designer	Slade	Slade
Builder	Contract	Contract

Name	*Infernal*	*Blast*	*Mortar*	*Thunder*	*Carcass*	*Terror*	*Basilisk*
Ordered	10-1756	9-1758	9-1758	9-1758	9-1758	9-1758	9-1758
Launched	7-1757	2-1759	3-1759	3-1759	1-1759	1-1759	2-1759
LGD	91ft 9in	91ft 6in	92ft 0in	91ft 6in	91ft 8in	91ft 6in	91ft 7in
LoK	75ft 0½in	74ft 0in	74ft 8¼in	74ft 1in	74ft 2½in	74ft 1¾in	74ft 4½in
Beam	27ft 9in	27ft 9in	28ft 1in	27ft 8¼in	28ft 0in	27ft 8in	28ft 1in
LBR	3.31	3.29	3.28	3.30	3.27	3.31	3.26
Depth in hold	12ft 1in	12ft 1in	12ft 1¾in	12ft 1in	12ft 1in	12ft 1in	12ft 1½in
Burthen	307 tons	303 tons	313 tons	302 tons	298 tons	302 tons	312 tons
Rig	Ketch	Ketch	Ketch	Ketch	Ship	Ship	Ship
Fate	Sold 1774	Sold 1771	Sold 1774	Sold 1774	Sold 1784	Sold 1774	Taken 1762

Chapter 17

SHIP RIG AND LONG QUARTERDECK
1741–1763

There is pictorial evidence that the application of a third or mizzen mast to two-masted vessels in the Royal Navy began in the last quarter of the seventeenth century. By the turn of the century the captains of the small sloops operating around Ireland were mentioning the use of a mizzen sail in their logs.[1] There is also evidence that some of the brigantines built in the 1690s were equipped with a mizzen mast late on in their careers. The French also had the same practice and called their mizzen sail and the mast the *artimon*, or balancing sail.[2] Thereafter the practice appears to have died until 1741 when the bomb ketch *Furnace* was selected to undertake a voyage to explore the possibility of a North West Passage round the Americas, for which task she would be better ship-rigged.

The choice of a bomb ketch for this sort of work made sense as they were strongly built to cope with the shock of discharging the mortars. Internal reinforcement of their bows was required to withstand the pressure of the ice but their substantial framing gave them a strong defence against lateral pressure. However, their ketch rig was not ideal and hence the conversion to ship rig. Although *Furnace* was laid down as a bomb in April 1740 she was commissioned as a cruising sloop in October of that year. In 1742 the Admiralty ordered that she be given ship rig and at this time her topsides were also raised to provide more accommodation and freeboard, for the better protection of the crew against the elements. The addition of a mizzen mast would have conferred a number of advantages. It would have been an insurance against the loss of a mast in heavy weather, leaving the vessel with at least two masts rather than one. The rig

Fig 17-1. A *Merlin* class sloop converted to ship rig. These sloops were slightly larger than the *Beaver* class ship-rigged sloops of 1760. *Author*

may also have allowed better balance on the wind as well as the option of lying to the wind under the mizzen gaff sail. These considerations should not be forgotten when examining why the Navy began, in the 1740s, to commission commercially built ship-rigged vessels.

The plan of *Furnace* at Fig 17-2 shows in grey her original profile when laid down as a bomb ketch and the modified appearance in thick black line.[3] Refitting her eventually entailed the removal of the mortar bed structures (see Figs 14-16 and 14-17). Examining her original plan also shows that her head has been altered and brought more upright for greater strength.

The conversion of a bomb ketch to a ship-rigged sloop was rare and confined to just the sort of specific challenge outlined above. Aside from this, in broad terms the Navy had four

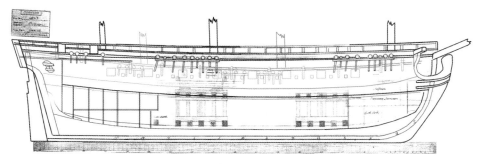

Fig 17-2. A plan showing the *Furnace* bomb vessel of 1742. Her original form is depicted here in grey. Her conversion for exploration required her to have ship rig and a massively increased freeboard in addition to internal structural strengthening, all shown in heavy black line. This image is based on plans from the National Maritime Museum. *John Garnish*

Fig 17-3. (Opposite, top) This Admiralty plan is of a design by a merchant yard for the sloop *Weazle* of 1745. She was bought by the Navy while building, and although designed for snow rig (as shown on the draught) she was commissioned with ship rig. At 300 tons she was big for her time and pierced for 9 guns a side plus a bow-chase port. *National Maritime Museum J4317*

Fig 17-4. (Opposite, bottom) A major landmark in sloop development, the 16-gun *Favourite* was designed by the Surveyor Thomas Slade in 1757. She exhibits a much more powerful form than earlier sloops and is well over 300 tons burthen. She is the first British-built sloop to have a long quarterdeck reaching forward to the mainmast. Her quarterdeck was not armed – that was to come later in the 1770s – although the ship was designed to carry 14 swivels. *National Maritime Museum J4303*

ways of acquiring ship-rigged sloops. First was the option of converting serving snow-rigged sloops to the ship rig. Second was the commissioning of sloops laid down as snows but fitted with three masts before completion, whilst a third was the ordering or purchasing of sloops specifically designed with ship rig. The fourth option was, of course, to take them from the French and Spanish. Taking the second option first, the context of this development was the French entry into the War of the Austrian Succession in 1744, at which time their corvettes were all being given a three-masted rig. In the *Merlin* class of sloops the Royal Navy possessed a good number of well-designed and well-armed vessels, but they were potentially vulnerable in battle, having only two masts.

In 1745–1746 the Navy purchased two sloops from Messrs Taylor and Randall at Rotherhithe on the Thames. They had been laid down as two-masted vessels but as the purchase was made during their construction the Admiralty requested that they be completed with three masts. They were larger at around 310 tons and longer than any of the Admiralty-designed sloops at that time and were well capable of taking a ship rig. The plan of *Weazle* at Fig 17-3 shows her set up for a snow rig, but note that she is pierced for 10 guns a side – the one right forward in the eyes of the ship is a chase port for occasional use, while the aftermost one, in the cabin, may have been more for light and air in the captain's accommodation. In service she only carried sixteen 6pdrs but still had more force than any sloop of the period. She was a remark-ably successful cruiser. After commissioning she took, in the space of one year, seven French privateers and a further two with the help of the British privateer *Lys*. She was also chosen by Admiral Hawke on the conclusion of the second Battle of Finisterre in 1747 to take the news to Jamaica of the approach of an unescorted French convoy, Hawke having destroyed the escort. She

was eventually taken herself, but not until 1779 and then by a 32-gun frigate. Her sister *Porcupine* was also successful and took three privateers in 1747.

Surprisingly, the conversion of two-masted sloops on the stocks did not occur again until 1755 when two of the three *Alderney* group sloops, designed by Surveyor Bately, were ordered to be completed with a ship rig. This must have been a nervous year for the Admiralty with the possibility of another engagement with France imminent, but it was also a period when Anson was First Lord. Anson, through his circumnavigation of 1742, had seen the difficulties experienced by two-masted vessels coping in extreme conditions. He may well have brought his influence to bear on the acquisition of more ship-rigged sloops. This leads naturally to a consideration of the first method of acquiring ship-rigged sloops listed above: conversion in service. This was put into effect over the three years 1753–1755. In the first year two of the *Merlin* class sloops and *Cruizer* of her eponymous class were converted. In the second year another two *Merlin*s were converted and in the third year yet another two *Merlin*s and the sloop *Hazard* received the same

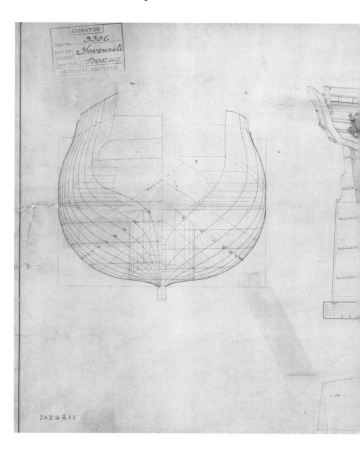

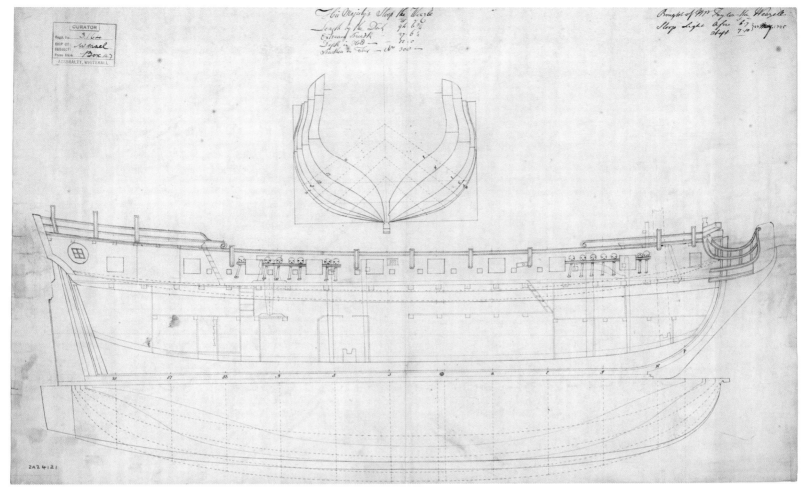

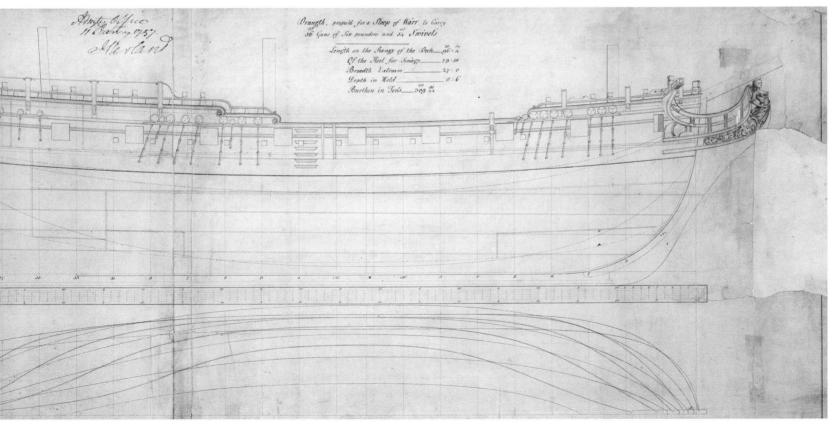

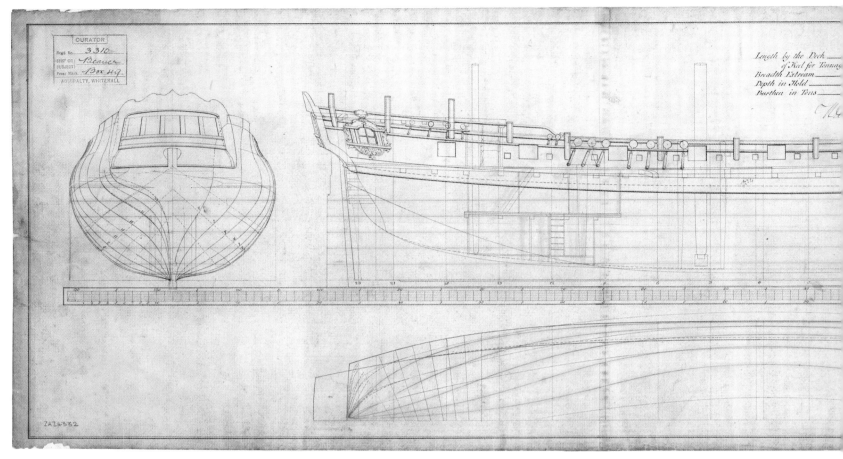

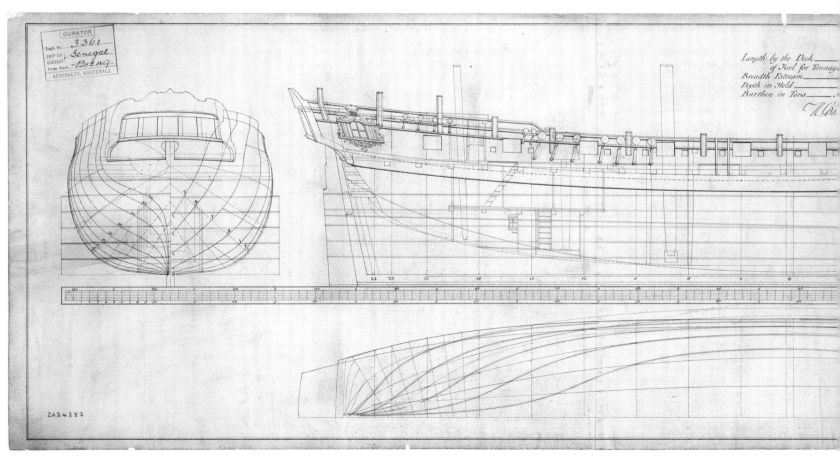

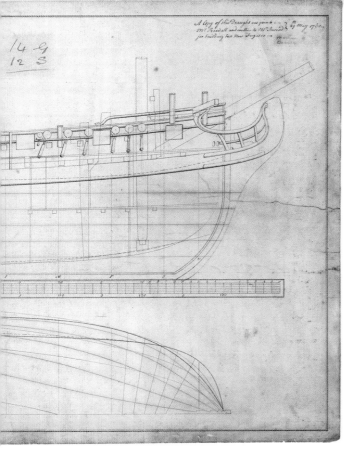

treatment. It is surprising that no more were converted, but the Navy was about to embark on the third method, that of purpose-building ship-rigged sloops.

The *Favourite* class, designed by Slade, were laid down in 1757 as ship-rigged vessels and at first were listed as 'frigates', rightly being returned to the sloop category at the end of the war in 1763. They compared closely to *Weazle* and *Porcupine* in particulars but had a rather different shape. Two were laid down in 1757 and a third with slight modifications was started in 1761. They were armed with sixteen 6pdrs (short model), now the weapon of choice for all sloops. Like *Weazle*, their gun deck ran flush from stem to sternpost without any step, but these later sloops also had an uninterrupted lower deck. They also had an extended raised quarterdeck which, although unarmed at this stage, allowed the crew to handle the sails without interfering with the guns.[4] These sloops were the forerunners of the ship-sloops of the 1770s. They present, in their shape and layout, a splendid compromise between the fast sailing light sloop of the 1730s and one that is built to spend months at sea in all weathers and carry a powerful armament and large crew. Their design draws heavily on that of *Weazle* and like that sloop this group are pierced for 10 guns a side including two bow-chaser ports. Their rig requires little comment since it was a standard ship rig.

Another order for three ship-rigged sloops to a design or designs by Bately was placed with merchant yards in April 1760. An interesting point about this order is that two of the three sloops, for which there are plans, show two sharply contrasting hull forms. That at Fig 17-5 is for *Beaver*, which shows an imaginative hull that reflects French influence; indeed, the Admiralty instructed that her lines should be based on those of *L'Abenakise*, a frigate taken into the Royal Navy as *Aurora*. This ship's lines also influenced the frigate *Lowestoffe* at Fig 17-7 and a number of other designs by Slade.[5] That at Fig 17-6 is for *Senegal*, which is usually listed as a sister to the *Beaver*, the differences in the 'as built' dimensions being well within the tolerances of the time; yet the hull form is very similar to Bately's *Alderney* class sloops of 1755 and hence to the design of the *Peregrine Galley*. These alternative interpretations of the same

Figs 17-5 and 17-6. These two designs of 1760 by Bateley, joint Surveyor of the Navy, were developed from the same specification yet they are totally different in form. *Beaver* above is based on a French model whilst *Senegal* below is close to his earlier two-masted sloop *Alderney* of 1757. *National Maritime Museum J4541 and J4586*

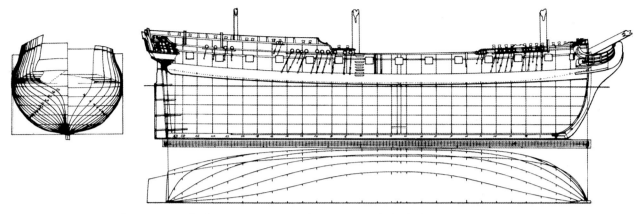

Fig 17-7. A modern drawing of the lines of the 32-gun frigate *Lowestoff*, designed by Slade. The lines were derived from the French prize frigate *L'Abenakise*, which was also the starting point for the hull design of *Beaver*. However, as the Surveyors pointed out to the Admiralty, these could not be simple copies as the Board's orders implied, since the different requirements of sloops and frigates meant a more subtle interpretation of the principles embodied in the French prototype's underwater body.

Fig 17-8. **(Below)** From the painting by Paul Revere, an American patriot of proven equestrian ability, this watercolour by the author shows the three sloops of the *Beaver* class at Boston in 1768 when the British made the first landing of military forces in a prelude to the American War of Independence.

parameters may be part of the experimental nature of design associated with sloops at this time in the Anson-led administration at the Admiralty.

These two sloops were built to the same specification and many of the features are identical, but the position of the masts is different in that *Senegal*'s main and foremast are further aft than *Beaver*'s and *Senegal* has a greater rake to her mizzen mast than *Beaver*. The advantage of a plumb stem and stern are evident in the finer entry and run achieved for *Beaver*; they would also have given her greater lateral resistance. In a match race it is probable that *Beaver* would have the edge over *Senegal* on the wind though off the wind there might be little to choose between them.

Although there is no separate plan of *Martin*, the third sloop in the group, the draught of *Beaver* suggests that it was also to be used for *Martin*; this pair and *Senegal* were substantially different from the *Favourite* class. Whilst they were the same length, they had less beam and

were of slightly less burthen. They did not have a complete lower deck (just platforms fore and aft) nor an extended raised quarterdeck. They were helmed from a wheel located immediately in front of the cabin bulkhead whereas the *Favourite* group had the wheel on the quarterdeck abaft the mast, a space that it shared with the double capstan's upper section. *Beaver* achieved a measure of fame in 1777 when she took the American 14-gun privateer *Oliver Cromwell*.

The final method of acquiring ship-rigged sloops was to capture them from the enemy. The Navy succeeded in taking ten such vessels it regarded as usable, all well-armed and some with eighteen 6pdrs. Four of these have already featured in Chapter 15. Of the ten captured, five

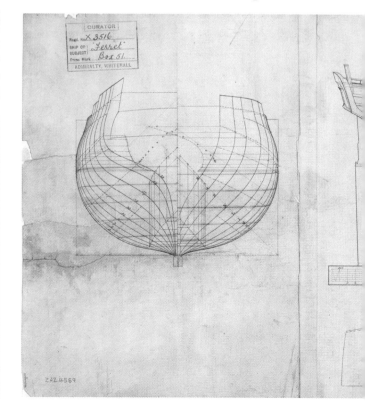

had 14 guns and five had 18. Given that the Navy sustained very few sloop losses, the total at the end of the war for ship-rigged and two-masted sloops was in excess of seventy including bombs and prizes.

The Navy acquired five more ship-rigged sloops before the war's close. One, *Ferret* to a design by Slade, was ordered in 1760.[6] Her general arrangement and lines plan at Fig 17-10 reveal a vessel that is slightly smaller than Slade's earlier *Favourite* group, carrying only fourteen as opposed to sixteen 6pdrs. The other main difference is that she did not have the long quarterdeck like the previous sloops, although her short quarterdeck was extended in 1771. Her dimensions and layout are close to those of the *Beaver* group.

Two of the others were either changes of order whilst under construction or conversions shortly after commissioning. These were *Druid* and *Lynx* built to the old Stacey *Cruizer* design of 1732. Two sloops, *Swift* and *Vulture*, were laid down as ship-rigged sloops to a design by Slade in 1762 and launched early in 1763. These two were based on the lines of *Epreuve*, a privateer taken into the French Navy before being captured by the British. She was two-masted on capture. The position of *Vulture*'s mainmast (Fig 17-11) suggests that she was originally intended

Fig 17-9. A *Beaver* class sloop designed for and commissioned with ship rig. Note the different rig to the mizzen mast compared with that in Fig 17-1. *Author*

for a two-mast rig, and as a result the mizzen has quite a squashed position on the quarterdeck. There is a precedent for this in the conversion of *La Guirlande* into *Cygnet* mentioned in Chapter 15.[7] In *Swift* and *Vulture* the totally different topside detail and internal arrangements compared with the prototype demonstrate that the 'copy' of the French ship is confined to the underwater hull. There is a more substantial and higher quarterdeck and tiller steering has been replaced by a wheel. Some light drawing indicates that thought was given to extending the quarterdeck to just abaft the mainmast.

Against the trend, there was one conversion from three masts to two. Perhaps appropriately,

Fig 17-10. HM Sloop *Ferret*, a design of 1760 by Slade for a ship-rigged sloop. Smaller than *Favourite* and with a short raised quarterdeck, she carried 14 as opposed to *Favourite*'s 16 guns. *National Maritime Museum J5135*

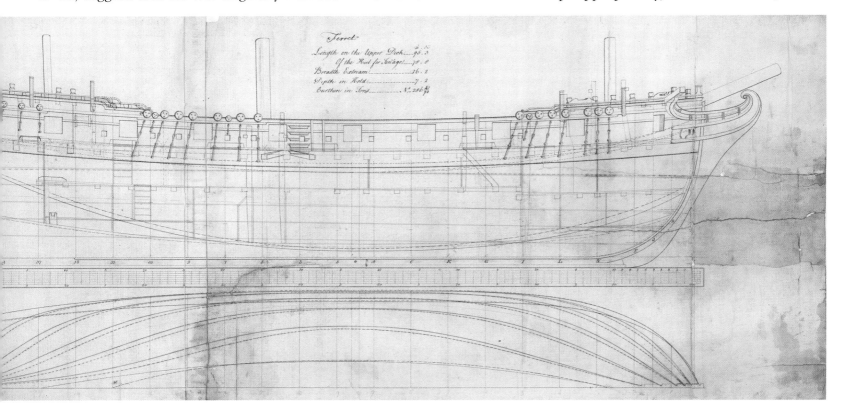

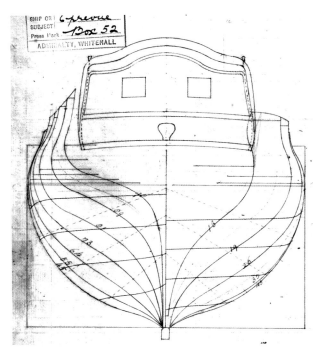

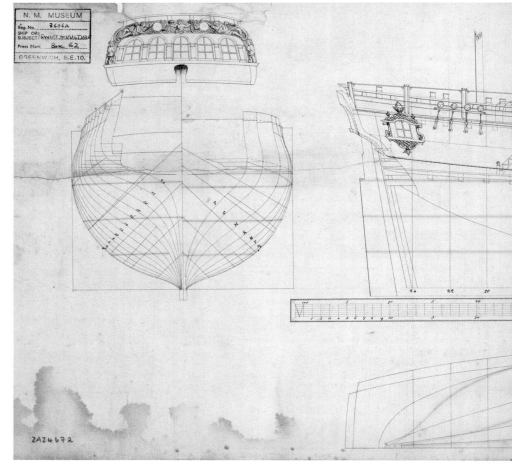

Fig 17-11 and 17-12. A comparison between the body plan of the captured two-masted sloop *L'Epreuve* and the ship-rigged sloops *Vulture* and *Swift* derived from it. The forms of the hulls are virtually identical but the British copy has a forecastle and the same raised deck structure abaft the mainmast seen in *Hawk* (Fig 16-13); she has abandoned the tiller in favour of a wheel for the helmsmen. *National Maritime Museum J4670*

this was the most influential but least typical of all vessels of the sloop family, the final incarnation of the old *Peregrine Galley* of 1700. Rebuilt in 1733, the ship had spent much of her career as a royal yacht, latterly known as the *Royal Caroline*. This role came to an end in 1749 with the launch of a new *Royal Caroline* whereupon the old ship, now 50 years of age, was refitted as

Table 17-1: CONVERSIONS IN SERVICE 14- AND 10-GUN SLOOPS, 1742–1763

Name	Class/Group	Designer	As Ship	Men	Guns	Fate
Raven	*Merlin*	Acworth	1753	125	14 x 6pdr	Sold 1763
Saltash	*Merlin*	Acworth	1753	125	14 x 6pdr	Sold 1763
Cruizer	*Cruizer*	Allin	1753	125	14 x 6pdr	Burnt deliberately 1776
Tavistock	*Merlin*	Acworth	1754	125	14 x 6pdr	Sold 1763
Trial	*Hind*	Allin	1754	125	14 x 6pdr	BU 1776
Hazard	*Hazard*	Slade/Lock	1755	125	14 x 6pdr	Sold 1783
Swallow	*Merlin*	Acworth	1755	125	14 x 6pdr	Sold 1769
Swan	*Merlin*	Acworth	1755	125	14 x 6pdr	Sold 1763
Druid	*Druid*	Stacey	Post 1761	100	10 x 4pdr	Sold 1773
Lynx	*Druid*	Stacey	Post 1761	100	10 x 4pdr	Sold 1777

Table 17-2: CONVERSIONS UNDER CONSTRUCTION 16- AND 10-GUN SLOOPS, 1745–1755

Name	Class/Group	Designer	Ordered as Ship	Men	Guns	Fate
Weazle	Purchased	Taylor & Randall	1745	110/125	16 x 6pdr	Taken 1779
Porcupine	Purchased	Taylor & Randall	1746	110/125	16 x 6pdr	Sold 1763
Stork	*Alderney*	Bately	1756	100	10 x 4pdr	Taken 1758
Alderney	*Alderney*	Bately	1756	100	10 x 4pdr	Sold 1783

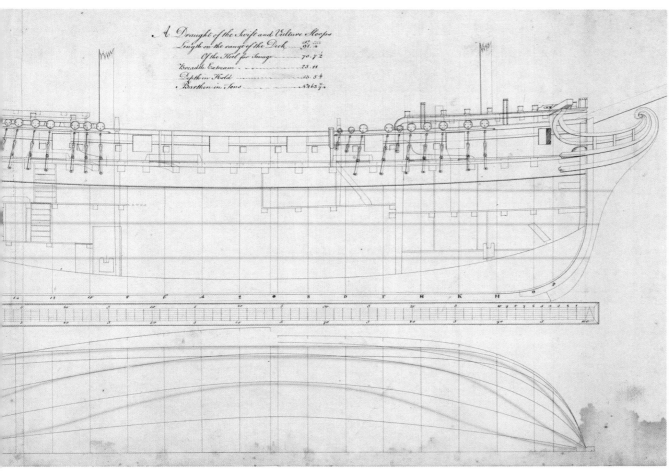

a sloop. She foundered in the western Channel on 28 December 1762, with all hands lost, at the age of 61. She would have been older than any of her crew.

SHIP-RIGGED CRUISING SLOOP ACQUISITION PROGRAMMES, 1742–1763

Besides those enumerated here, there were twenty-nine two-masted cruising sloops at the beginning of the War and twenty-three at the end, six having been converted to other sloop roles. Additionally there were three bomb ketches at the beginning of the war and thirteen at its end, three of which had ship rig. This figure includes three conversions of cruising sloops from the 1740s. Perhaps the most start-ling statistic is that only two ship sloops were lost during the War. Conversely, a high number of sloops were either built, or captured and taken into the Navy during its course. The other, rather depressing, figure is the fact that eight were sold upon the conclusion of the War. However, against a total of 74 sloops including bomb vessels, fireship sloop conversions and prizes, perhaps it does not seem so bad.

Although there were some variations, another interesting comparison is the ratio of men to guns for ship-rigged sloops: those with both fourteen and sixteen 6pdrs had a complement of 125, whilst those with eighteen 6pdrs had 120–130. Those sloops with ten 4pdrs had 100 men. The scaling makes sense except for the 18-gun sloops, which seem to be on the short side; 140 would be the proportional scaling for them.

Table 17-3: PURCHASES WITH SHIP RIG 18- AND 16-GUN SLOOPS, 1757

Name	Class/Group	Designer	Men	Guns	Burthen	Fate
Merlin	Purchase	Randall	130	18 x 6pdr	301 tons	Burnt deliberately 1777
Racehorse	Purchase	Ex-French	120	18 x 6pdr	386 tons	Taken 1778
Pelican	Purchase	Mercantile	80	16 x 4pdr	234 tons	Sold 1763
Roman Emperor	Purchase	Mercantile	100	16 x 6pdrs	272 tons	Sold 1763

Table 17-4: NEW-BUILD 16-GUN SLOOPS 1745/6 AND 1757–1760[1]

Name	Weazle	Porcupine	Favourite	Tamar	Nautilus
Ordered	Purchased 1745	Purchased 1746	1/1757	1/1757	4/1761
Launched	5/1745	9/1746	12/1757	1/1758	5/1762
LDG	94ft 6¾in	94ft 4¼in	96ft 4in	96ft 4in	98ft 0in
LoK	76ft 4½in	76ft 5in	79ft 10in	78ft 9½in	80ft 7½in
Beam	27ft 6¼in	27ft 9½in	27ft 2in	27ft 4in	27ft 4in
LBR	3.44	3.40	3.55	3.52	3.58
Depth in hold	12ft 0in	12ft 0¾in	8ft 6½in[2]	8ft 3½in[2]	12ft 8in[2]
Burthen	308 tons	314 tons	309 tons	313 tons	317 tons
Guns	16 x 6pdr, 14 swivels	16 x 6pdr, 14 swivels	16 x 6pdr, 14 swivels	16 x 6pdr, 14 Swivels	16 x 6pdr, 14 Swivels
Men	110 (125 in 1749)	110 (125 in 1749)	125	125	125
Rig	Ship	Ship	Ship	Ship	Ship
Fate	Taken 1779	Sold 1763	Sold 1784	Taken 1780	Sold 1780
Designer	Taylor and Randall	Taylor and Randall	Slade	Slade	Slade
Builder	Taylor and Randall	Taylor and Randall	Contract	Contract	Contract

1 Weazle and Porcupine are included here again since they were the first ship-rigged sloops acquired by the Royal Navy in the eighteenth century (other than Furnace, a conversion in service, of 1742), and because of the closeness of their details to those of Slade's Favourite group.

2 There is graphic evidence that Favourite and Tamar both had a flush lower deck running from stem to sternpost, whereas the figures here for depth in hold suggest that Nautilus did not.

Table 17-5: NEW-BUILD 14-GUN SLOOPS 1760–1763

Name	Beaver	Martin	Senegal	Ferret	Vulture	Swift
Ordered	4/1760	4/1760	4/1760	4/1760	2/1762	2/1762
Launched	2/1761	2/1761	12/1760	12/1760	1/1763	3/1763
LDG	96ft 7in	96ft 11in	97ft 0in	95ft 6in	91ft 4in	91ft 5in
LoK	79ft 9in	80ft 1in	80ft 8¾in	79ft 4in	73ft 7½in	74ft 3in
Beam	25ft 10in	26ft 0½in	26ft 1in	26ft 8in	26ft 2½in	26ft 2½in
LBR	3.74	3.72	3.71	3.58	3.48	3.49
Depth in hold	12ft 6in	12ft 6in	12ft 5in	12ft 4in	13ft 4½in	13ft 3½in
Burthen	283 tons	289 tons	292 tons[1]	300 tons	269 tons	271 tons
Guns	14 x 6pdrs, 12 swivels	14 x 6pdrs, 12 swivels	14 x 6pdrs, 12 swivels	14 x 6pdrs, 12 swivels	14 x 6pdrs, 12 swivels	14 x 6pdrs, 12 swivels
Men	125	125	125	125	125	125
Rig	Ship	Ship	Ship	Ship	Ship	Ship
Fate	Sold 1783	Sold 1784	Exploded 1780	Foundered 1776	BU 1771	Wrecked 1770
Designer	Bately	Bately	Bately	Slade	Slade (French model)	Slade (French model)
Builder	Contract	Contract	Contract	Contract	Contract	Contract

1 Compare Senegal's burthen with that of Beaver and note the respective body plans at Figs 17-5 and 17-6 for the two vessels.

Table 17-6: SHIP-RIGGED SLOOP NUMBERS DURING SEVEN YEARS WAR

Category	In 1756	Built or Captured	Lost in War	In 1763
Conversion in service, 1749–1755	9	2	1	10
Conversion under construction, 1745–1755	4	0	1	3
Purchased as 18- and 16-gun ship sloops, 1757	0	4	0	4
New-build 16-gun sloops, 1757–1760	0	3	0	3
New-build 14-gun sloops, 1760–1761	0	3	0	3
New-build 14-gun sloops, 1760–1763	0	3	0	3
Prizes taken during War	0	9	0	9
Totals	13	24	2	35

Chapter 18

CONCLUSION

In 1719, a date that can be taken as the nadir for the sloop of war, the Royal Navy had just four cruising sloops and four bomb ketches. At the end of the Seven Years War in 1763, just 44 years later, that number had increased to seventy-four sloops of all types including prizes. What had caused this massive nine-fold increase? It would be too simple to ascribe it just to the intervening wars; to do so would be to ignore the underlying reasons. One direction in which to look is towards the impact of competitive maritime trade.

The War of the Spanish Succession finished in 1714, but Britain still had issues to resolve with Spain. This forced a continuation of the war in the Mediterranean until its conclusion in 1718 with the impressive defeat of the Spanish off Cape Passaro by a British fleet under the command of Admiral Byng (father of the unfortunate admiral executed in 1756 for 'not doing his utmost' to defeat the enemy). In the years following this victory there was no direct threat to the British homeland other than that posed by the possibility of a Jacobite rebellion against the Hanoverian Succession, aided by France and other continental powers. There was, however, the ever-present threat to safe passage across the oceans and this was particularly so in the Caribbean, where a constant watch was required on Spanish activities and on piracy. This demanded alertness at sea and a good intelligence system beyond.

As a maritime power, Britain was a relative newcomer, being the fourth European nation to develop a thriving overseas trade. From the late fifteenth century, the Portuguese and then the Spanish had been the first to establish an overseas trading empire. They were followed by the Dutch Republic in the late sixteenth and seven-teenth centuries. Britain, entering this race last, collided with the Dutch in the latter half of the seventeenth century, but thereafter she gradually extended her interests. During the course of the eighteenth century, Britain succeeded, despite opposition from France and Spain, in working her way into becoming the most powerful maritime trading nation in the world. A trans-oceanic trading empire will normally be accompanied by the establishment of possessions overseas. By 1700 Britain was developing colonies in the West Indies and along the North American coasts, including those of Newfoundland and Canada, alongside those of the Spanish, Dutch and French. Later, during the Seven Years War, she took major steps on the way to securing India and parts of the Far Eastern territories beyond.

A component in the security of these possessions was the sloop; indeed some of the sloops built in 1710–1711 had been acquired specifically for this purpose. Hitherto, the work of the sloop – be it the escort of coastal convoys, fishery protection, enforcing trade bans, the bombardment of French Channel ports, or attendance on the fleet in battle – had centred on the seas around the British Isles. These duties had caused the Admiralty to order a series of craft ranging from small sloops of 60 tons or less for towing ships out of the line of battle (subsequently replaced by a rather more specialist craft, the brigantine), to ketches equipped for shore bombardment and to advice boats – fast, light craft to give early warning of attack and to carry important information.

The stresses of war often forced these small warships to cover each other's work, which suggested the possibility of rationalising the several different classes into one larger type of general ability. At the same time, the changing forms of naval warfare in the first half of the eighteenth century from the set pattern engagement of large fleets, exemplified in the Anglo-Dutch sea-wars of the seventeenth century, to the looser forms of trade protection and amphibious operations, tended to increase the requirement for the sort of flexibility a sloop would need. This nudged designers to look at the possibilities of turning it into a multi-role vessel. These developments, allied to the spread of British overseas possessions and trade, inevitably influenced the growth of the class.

There is another broad development that created the conditions for this growth. Since the defeat of the French Atlantic fleet in 1692, the Allies, that is Britain and the Dutch Republic, had gradually increased their domination of the oceans. This state of affairs takes time to achieve but it is most necessary for the support and safety of maritime trade. Under the aegis of this domination the resulting environment is one in which small warships can have an effect that may be out of all proportion to their size. The ultimate expression of this condition was achieved in the latter half of the nineteenth century when one British gunboat or sloop could, by representing the might of the Royal Navy and the Empire, achieve its local objective without visible support. Another factor was the increasingly ubiquitous nature of naval operations, many of which did not require a massive show of force occasioning large expense, but rather a more suitably adjusted response to match the threat. These opportunities were to increase in the years after our period finishes in 1763, with the impetus coming from the American War of Independence, Britain's growing interest in the Mediterranean and the world-wide expansion of hostilities occasioned by the French Revolutionary War and its successor the Napoleonic War and, in the nineteenth century, the suppression of the slave trade.

Setting aside the strategic value of these small warships, it is worth reflecting on the changing way requirements were expressed to designers and constructors. Many of these demands, particularly in the late seventeenth century, specified what the vessel was supposed to do, such as to work among the sands or to enforce the ban on the illegal export of wool. Later, the orders tended to stress some aspect of the vessel bearing on performance, for example a need for lightness, or an ability to be rowed with oars. In the case of sloops, but not in the case of rated ships which were under the rules of the Establishments, the system of sending specifications to designer/constructors was eventually dropped as the design function became centralised in the Surveyor's office, already part of the Navy Board. Here one or other of the two Surveyors and his team would work on specifications provided by the Admiralty Board; these might be more or less detailed, and since some briefings were delivered verbally, the records are equally patchy. However, the recognisable trend was a move towards a general-purpose capability, exemplified in the sloop *Alderney* of 1734, which was designed to be used either as a bomb vessel or cruising sloop and be readily able to switch role.

One of the key points in this development occurred in 1732, when designers (in practice the master shipwrights at the Royal Dockyards) were asked to give their views as to the optimum size and dimensions of a sloop. This will have caused the members of the Admiralty and the Navy Boards to give careful consideration to what they wanted a sloop to achieve. The outcome at this point appears to have been an emphasis on light construction, an ability to be rowed with oars and on restricted armament, which points to the advice and communication role as the leading one for a sloop at that time. Twelve years later, with the start of another war with France, the direction given by the authorities resulted in a much larger and heavier vessel with twice the weight of firepower. From then on the trend was towards more force and heavier displacement until this forced a split in the class between the ship-sloop for convoy and the protection of trade and the reintroduced two-masted sloop – now rigged as a brig – for reconnaissance and communication. But even then the multi-role aspect was never lost.

It was the prerogative of all captains to have direct access to the Admiralty, which would then pass their requests and comments to the Navy Board for action if the Board Members thought fit. One of the recurring features that this study has discovered is the detailed but helpful criticism of vessels by their captains. From an inspection of their logs, it would

Probably the single most influential vessel in the history of the sloop of war, the *Peregrine Galley*, ended her long career as a royal yacht reconverted to a ship-rigged cruising sloop and renamed *Peregrine*. She was last seen on 28 December 1761 in the Channel en route for the West Indies and is presumed to have foundered in the heavy storm that followed. This is the author's interpretation of her likely final moments.

appear that most of the criticisms were well founded. Sadly, the Navy Board's reaction was not always positive and a number of requests seem to have been turned down unfairly. Nowhere is this more clearly seen than in the reports on rig. The sloop was, until the 1750s, powered by a two-masted sail plan. The Navy Board and the captains out on the sea found considerable difficulty in dealing with the problems this arrangement created, despite some sensible recommendations from the captains. The recurring themes were too high or large a sail plan applied to a hull of limited draught, which led to problems of stability. Two-masted sloops were also continually troubled by a lack of directional stability due to an imbalance in the sail plan which manifested itself in a tendency to carry lee helm. There are repetitive instances of masts being shortened and mainmasts being either repositioned further aft or severely raked in that direction.

There is little evidence that the Navy Board really understood small-ship rigs, from the brigantines and advice boats of the 1690s to the cutters and schooners a century later, but the instinct to standardise led them to draw up sail plans with too little reference to the variations in the vessels carrying these rigs. They were at home with the ship rig which was inherently better balanced and for which there was an enormous corpus of experience on which to base their tables of spar dimensions. Not surprisingly, for sloops the problem was eventually solved by moving to ship rig from 1755.

Later, in the 1770s, when the two-masted sloop staged a comeback, the chosen rig was the more rational brig, for which the Navy Board initially drew on specialist mercantile experience. Yet solutions to these problems need not have taken so long: information was available to the Board in the many letters that captains sent to the Admiralty, particularly in the 1720s. Some recognition of the value of this feedback may have crept into rig design from 1740 onwards since the complaints diminished, and indeed the Board's attempt to achieve some understanding of the problems involved is evident in the sailing quality reports they required of captains. Sadly, many of these reports refer to sloops being 'slack in stays', meaning that tacking was difficult and that would have been due mainly to a poorly designed and positioned two-masted rig.

Another example of a failure to change was the seeming reluctance on the part of the Navy Board to learn from French design and capabilities, although this was modified from the mid-eighteenth century when the Admiralty began to direct that particular designs be based on the lines of captured vessels. There was also a broader conceptual error in not providing vessels that were, in modern terms, fit for purpose. Too often around the turn of the century, a tale of small under-armed vessels being taken by pairs of French privateers of far greater force was reported. This was not to be rectified until the 1740s when the Royal Navy's powerful sloops were beginning to make inroads into the French privateering effort. As far as design is concerned, the force for change in an overtly conservative profession came, not this time from the captains at sea, but from the most senior sea officers appointed to the Navy Board and Admiralty. Sir Cloudesley Shovel was an earlier promoter of improved sailing ability, but the most notable example of influence by a senior officer was the determination of Admiral the Lord Anson, as First Lord of the Admiralty, to appoint Thomas Slade as Surveyor of the Navy. Slade was open-minded enough to take the best from French practice, but his genius was to adapt it for the particular needs of the Royal Navy. The vessels produced as a result of this approach were among the best sailing warships of the century. In sum there was stagnation in the advance of design and capability in the early part of the century, possibly influenced by a government that was keen to avoid war. But this was gradually rectified so that by the late 1750s the Royal Navy's sloops, as well as rated vessels, were capable of delivering decisive results.

This story would not be complete without an acknowledgement of the part that France played in the development of the sloop of war. Its contribution was made in two ways: first by the attack made on British maritime trade, both oceanic and coastal, during all four wars and the British countermeasures that inspired; and second, in the exemplification of an approach to design based on scientific principles. Over the period of 74 years between 1689 and 1763 Britain and France faced each other at sea for no less than 28 years. The two nations, partly through circumstance and partly through will and intention, developed different maritime strategies. The British strove to keep and command the sea; the French chose to use it when the opportunity or need occurred, to trade and to raid. At quite fundamental levels, the warships of the two navies reflect these differing priorities – which is not to say that they had nothing to learn from one another.

It would be fair to say that French privateering operations were at their most ruthless and effective during the wars of Louis XIV. The lower tier of these operations was aimed at coastal trade and the fisheries, much of the onslaught emanating from Dunkirk, and it was therefore of direct concern to the sloops of the Royal Navy. The effectiveness of the French assault forced Britain into ordering emergency war programmes for the rapid production of sloops. Lessons were learnt during engagements in these early wars, in which British sloops were generally out-matched by their French opponents. The areas of concern were sailing ability, size and force, and sheer numbers. These lessons were not forgotten and British sloop design and deployment during the later wars of Louis XV in the middle of the eighteenth century was highly effective against French privateering operations. Perhaps a more subtle contribution came through the capture of French privateers and small naval vessels including their Fifth Rates, *frégats légères* and corvettes, whose forms were taken off and recorded in plans that would be used to inform future British designs. Indeed at the end of our period, sloops were being built whose underwater shapes were virtually direct copies of French models. Much of this was due to the influence of Anson and the ability of Slade.

This book began in 1650 because it was the start of England's serious competition for mastery of the seas, a small part of which was the use of sloop-like vessels to secure inshore passage around her coasts; a century later Britain was on the brink of achieving that goal. During the intervening period the sloop went through the most radical and varied development in its history, providing an interesting and coherent theme. By 1763, the concluding date for this book, the Seven Years War had won Britain her empire, also of no small relevance to the story of the sloop of war. Thereafter, the explosion in the number of sloops would have made this book impossibly large and a rather different story.

From a handful of disparate vessels in 1719, a new and significant warship class had come to fruition. It was the beginnings of the most numerous class of warship ever to exist in the Royal Navy.

NOTES

Abbreviations used in the Notes

TNA. The National Archives, Kew (the rebranded Public Record Office)
NMM. National Maritime Museum, Greenwich, London
NRS. Navy Records Society, London
OED. Oxford English Dictionary

Chapter 1

1. Blanckley wrote the work in the early eighteenth century. Apart from the obvious points in his definition, the implication is that most types of minor warship, no matter what their rig or shape, fell within the broad classification of the word 'sloop'.

2. Very few naval sloops were equipped with just one mast. Although two groups of sloops commissioned in 1710 and 1711 were given a single-mast rig, within four years this had been altered to two masts.

3. The single-mast rig was replaced by the three-masted rig in the fifteenth century. It carried for the most part a six-sail wardrobe: a spritsail on the bowsprit, fore course and fore topsail, main course and main topsail and a lateen mizzen.

4. *Sloops & Shallops*, William A Baker (Barre, Mass 1966), p14: Figure 2. Portugese Barcha, 1430 after Oliveira. Also see his note 32 to Chapter 1. Joao de Oliveira, was a rear admiral in the Portuguese Navy in modern times, who produced a study into the ships used for early exploration.

5. The first sloop in Pepys's list was *Dunkirk*. She was captured from that port in 1656 and would have been similar in form and rig to the Biscay double shallop. *Descriptive Catalogue of the Naval MSS in the Pepysian Library*, Vol 1 (NRS 1903).

6. A small square sail set flying is likely to have been hoisted on its yard, direct from the deck. The yard would be without braces or lifts but some form of control over the sail's clews, such as sheets led through blocks on the extremities of the main yard, would have been necessary. This type of arrangement is only really effective if the vessel is sailing well off the wind.

7. *Fore and Aft Sailing Craft*, Douglas Phillips-Birt (London 1962), pp 83–84 and figure 23, etching possibly by Johannes Saenredam. Another illustration of this rig can be seen in *Old Ship Prints*, E Keble Chatterton (London 1927), p62 and plate 14 (top). Attributed to one of the Visscher family that produced three generations of engravers, it is not clear if what purports to be from the Elizabethan period actually represents a contemporary image. See also p63 and plate 15 'The Capture of Cadiz 1596' – a Dutch line engraving showing an early schooner rig in centre of picture.

8. *Recueil des Veues de tous les differents Bastimens de la Mer Mediterranée et de l'Océan*, J Guéroult du Pas (Paris 1710). A copy can be found in the Bodleian Library, bequeathed by Francis Douce. This work can be viewed online at http://gallica.bnf.fr and is available in a reprint with the slightly modernised title *Bâtiments de la Mer Mediterranée et de l'Océan* (Nice 2004).

9. From the visual evidence available it would appear that the masts were either a simple pole or two poles held together at their doubling by metal bands, the mast being held 'in column' by crosstrees. See Jean Boudriot, *La Créole 1823: Historique de la Corvette 1650-1850* (Paris 1990).

10. One of these was *Fan Fan*, a sloop built by Anthony Deane at Harwich and up-rated to a yacht for Prince Rupert. This meant that she was formally listed as a Sixth Rate because a royal yacht had to be commanded by a captain, the smallest command for which would be a Sixth Rate ship. She appears in a Van de Velde painting now in the Rijksmuseum attending the first rate *Britannia*. M S Robinson, *Van de Velde: A Catalogue of the Paintings of the Elder and Younger*, 2 vols (Greenwich 1990), plate 108.

11. *Descriptive Catalogue of the Naval MSS in the Pepysian Library*, Vol 1 (NRS 1903), p263.

12. The hoy rig is not illustrated here, as it was never used on a sloop. It will be illustrated in the chapter on yachts, which do form part of this history since the hull type and war role of yachts had an influence on the design of the early eighteenth-century sloops.

13. These light sloops were some 60ft long on deck and between 90 and 100 tons burthen. Fore-and-aft rig would have given them a better ability to pursue smugglers in coastal waters.

14. Two Stuart royal yachts were converted to bomb ketches in 1687: *Kitchen* and *Portsmouth*. This was the beginning of English experience with this type of naval weapon system.

15. *Memoires of the Royal Navy 1679-1688*, Samuel Pepys (London 1690), pp102–127. This was reprinted in facsimile by Seaforth Publishing (Barnsley) in 2010.

16. After Pepys had left the Admiralty not only were a group of eight purpose-built fireships ordered, rated as Fifth Rates, but merchantmen were bought in and converted not only into fireships but also into explosion vessels – a sort of floating but guided mine.

17. The last of the original twenty-two Pepysian sloops was *Bonetta*, designed and built by Pett in 1672. She was sold in 1689. A sloop that had been built in the first group of 1667, *Fan Fan*, became a yacht for Prince Rupert in that year and as such was reclassified as a Sixth rate, small though she was. She ended up as a pitch boat in the 1690s, a sad ending to the last of the early Pepysian sloops.

18. HM Sloops *Favourite* and *Tamar* designed by Slade and commissioned in 1757.

Chapter 2

1. *Sloops & Shallops*, William A Baker (Barre, Mass 1966), pxiv. See also p13 where he refers to Aubin's comments on the *barque longue*.

2. Champlain used these boats for his explorations. See Raymond Litalien and Denis Vaugeois, *Champlain: The Birth of French America* (Montreal and Kingston 2004): p102 presents a model of the shallop and p104 a perspective drawing.

3. The wreck was found following the research work of Selma Barkham, a French Canadian, into the Basque whaling industry in Canada in the sixteenth century. Her story, which is an excellent read, is chronicled by Dane Lanken for Air Canada in an article entitled 'Selma Barkham traces our Basque heritage', *En Route* (Air Canada in-flight magazine), Vol 12(5), May 1984, pp46-48, 74, 78.

4. Blaise Ollivier (1701–1746) became the master shipwright at Brest. His dictionary-form *Traité de Construction* is developed from fragments of his writings salvaged from a dockyard fire which burnt all his models and much of his writing. It is therefore difficult to allocate a precise date. He died in 1746 so any year between 1732 and 1740 would be possible. The work was first published in 1980 by Editions ANCRE (Nice). Further to what Blaise Ollivier says, some commentators regard the shallop and the pinnace as being virtually interchangeable. This may well be so in terms of role, but the latter is normally associated with a large square transom, not to be confused with the high small transom of the double shallop. From a naval perspective, the pinnaces were essentially there to serve larger vessels whereas the shallops had their own independent roles. Another confusing feature is that the term pinnace was earlier applied to large ocean-going vessels in their own right: indeed in the navy of Henry VIII there were two of 80 tons.

5. Jean Boudriot, 'Les Barques Longues', *Nautical Research Journal* 27 (1981), p94.

6. Jean Jouve, *Deux Albums des Bâtiments de l'Atlantique et de la Méditerranée*, 1679.

7. See R Morton Nance, *The Mariners' Mirror* Vol II/4 (1912), p362. This is a well illustrated article on the development of the ketch over 300 years.

8. William A Baker, *Colonial Vessels* (Barre, Mass 1962), p115. There is a chapter on Colonial Ketches with much useful information that applies to ketches generally. Captain Boteler, referred to by Baker, was a member of the Virginia Company. He is chiefly remembered as the author of *A Dialogical Discourse* written from 1621 and printed in 1634. He remarks on a number of subjects to do with shipping through six dialogues between an admiral and a captain at sea in which he praises the ketch. Copy in British Library.

9. E W White, *British Fishing-Boats and Coastal Craft, Part II: Descriptive Catalogue and List of Plans*, Science Museum Publication, (London 1952), pp7–8 and plate 1.

10. *Fore and Aft Sailing Craft*, Douglas Phillips-Birt (London 1962), p97.

Chapter 3

1. The Stadtholder was the supreme commander of Dutch forces elected by the individual provinces. The Stadtholderless period came about when the Dutch, having concluded eighty years of war with Spain, formed a republic and for a time dispensed with a Stadtholder. William of Orange, nephew of Charles II and later William III of England, re-took the title following the difficulties of 1672.

2. This was a heroic stand. For details of the capture of Dunkirk see J R Jones, *The Anglo-Dutch Wars of the Seventeenth Century* (London 1996).

3. See Ralph Davis, *The Rise of the English Shipping Industry* (Newton Abbot 1962), p51 and note 6 therein. Also R A Stradling, *The Armada of Flanders* (Cambridge 1992), pp147–150.

4. The King's party had embarked from Scheveling Bay near The Hague on 23 May. The Dukes accompanying him were York and Gloucester, and 'My Lord' was the Earl of Sandwich. The description 'bare' in this passage does not signify that he accompanied the King stark naked, though that might have amused Charles. Rather it indicates that he was unattended by any of his retinue. It was Monk, later the Duke of Albemarle, who had been the chief instigator of the Restoration, believing that in the shambles following the death of Cromwell and later the departure of his son from the office of Protector, legitimate monarchy was the only form of government acceptable to the English public. The brigantine made by Beale would have been an open two-masted vessel, possibly with lug sails and rowed with several oars a side.

5. Contrast this situation with that of the Seven Years War where Crown and Parliament worked together for the common good, allowing the country to reach its full military potential.

6. James had already been offered the position of High Admiral of Spain.

7. The secret treaty of Dover, 1670.

8. This event released pressures within English society that were to result in, amongst other measures, the Test Act where no Roman Catholic could hold an official position. This forced James to resign as Lord High Admiral with consequences for the state of the Navy.

9. Following the strengthened Navigation Act of 1661, an Act was introduced to prevent the Dutch fishing in English coastal waters. They had been selling fish caught in English waters on the English market at very competitive prices. J R Jones, *The Anglo-Dutch Wars of the Seventeenth Century* (London 1996), p144.

10. Cromwell's Protectorate is estimated to have lost between 1000 and 1700 commercial vessels during his disastrous war with Spain (1655–1660). The bulk of these would have been in the coastal waters of the eastern Channel and the southern North Sea. Dunkirk was still a Spanish possession. Ralph Davis, *The Rise of the English Shipping Industry* (Newton Abbot 1962), p51.

11. Although all were grouped as Sixth Rates with less than 20 guns, these ships varied considerably in dimensions and displacement but not in armament. All carried on average 12–14 guns firing 4pdr or 3pdr shot. Draught was between 8ft and 10ft, making them suitable for coastal and some inshore work.

12. One of Anthony Deane's sloops was *Fan Fan*. Officially she was a Sixth Rate since she was completed as a yacht for Prince Rupert, and all yachts were so rated for purposes of officer seniority and pay; but as to design, size and armament she was in effect a sloop and, surprisingly, she had three masts with topsails on fore- and mainmasts.

13. Anthony Deane, who built two of the first group of four sloops at Harwich in the Second War, remarked that they were 'of small draft of water, to clear the sands before this harbour, then much infested with Dutch picaroons'. See L H St C Cary, 'Harwich Dockyard', *The Mariner's Mirror* XIII/2 (1927), p170.

14. Sir Anthony Deane was responsible for designing and building four out of the five Sixth Rates operational in 1672.

15. *Descriptive Catalogue of the Naval MSS in the Pepysian Library*, Vol 2 (NRS 1903), p66.

16. This was a decision that would have appalled anyone trying to run a shipping operation. With the experience of the effect of 'The Dunkirkers' in previous wars, the merchant community knew that to release it would put the security of commercial shipping in the North Sea and eastern Channel in jeopardy.

17. *Fan Fan* was the first sloop launched (1667) and the last to go (1693) when converted to a pitch boat. She must have been very well constructed. She probably outlasted the lady after whom she was named!

Chapter 4

1. There are many details of this replica available, including outline plans from Planaship Maritime Publications, Falmouth, but *Nonsuch* as shown here is substantially different from the accepted form of the ketch in the middle of the seventeenth century. The best information on shape comes from the sketches of Van de Velde the younger of which there are several in the National Maritime Museum's collections. Unfortunately almost all show the vessel in the water so the underwater body remains a mystery.

2. For examples of this type of stern, see *Henry Huddleston Rogers Collection of Ship Models*, the catalogue of the United States Naval Academy Museum (Annapolis Maryland, rev ed 1971), pp5 and 22 covering models 2 and 13 respectively.

3. It is possible that this ketch is the *Deptford*. She was a large 10-gun ketch, built in a naval dockyard by Jonas Shish and was the only ketch in the North Sea at the time of the Anglo-French battles against the Dutch.

4. The gripe is the expression for the bottom few feet of the stem. It is formed between the leading edge of the cutwater and the hull proper. The profile of the stem could be critical to the balance of a ship. Despite the ketch's well-balanced rig, its two large fore-and-aft headsails, when working to windward, could exert considerable pressure sideways. A good gripe (a faired extension forwards of the stem under the waterline) could prevent lee helm, *ie* the tendency of the vessel to turn away from the wind.

5. See Frank L Fox, *The Four Days' Battle of 1666* (Barnsley 2009), pp148-149. Ink painting by Van de Velde the elder.

6. The 'Sound' was the Baltic passage between Sweden and Denmark, through which came those materials essential for English shipping and naval industries. From time to time it was necessary to secure this passage as it could be easily blocked by either country.

7. TNA Adm 2/1745, dated 23 June 1665, James writing to the Navy Board. Despite his wish that 'all possible expedition might be used', only three sloops were built and they towards the end of the war. Open shallops may have been provided in lieu.

8. *Descriptive Catalogue of the Naval MSS in the Pepysian Library*, Vol I (NRS 1903), Register of Ships, pp292–295.

9. For further details on these programmes see Rif Winfield, *British Warships in the Age of Sail, 1603-1714* (Barnsley 2009), pp218–219 and 221–222.

10. Although the Dutch war with Spain had concluded in 1648, Spain still controlled large parts of Flanders, including Dunkirk; hence a link between Dunkirk and the Biscay harbours of Spain existed. *Dunkirk*, the sloop/shallop was probably a large Biscay double shallop. For further details about this vessel see *Sloops & Shallops*, William A Baker (Barre,

Mass 1966), p40. For general background to the situation in the Channel see W L Clowes, *The Royal Navy*, Vol 2 (reprinted London 1996), p137.

11. This drawing has been taken from a painting of *Prince* at the Battle of Sole Bay in 1672 by Van de Velde the younger. In close company with the First Rate are a yacht, a ketch and another small vessel that is identified as *Fan Fan*. She is also listed as being in the Red Squadron as was the *Prince*, leading the Centre Division. The painting is in the Rijksmuseum collection. M S Robinson, *Van de Velde: A Catalogue of the Paintings of the Elder and Younger*, 2 vols (Greenwich 1990), plate 108.

12. See R C Anderson, 'The Rig of the Pepysian Sloops', *The Mariner's Mirror* IX/3 (1923), notes p214.

13. Fig 4-11 is part of the Van de Velde grisaille of the Battle of Schooneveld, 1673 (NMM PAJ3046). Fig 4-12 comes from a sketch by Van de Velde, probably the younger, of 'The Passage of Mary of Modena from Calais to Dover, 21 November to 1 December 1673' (NMM PAJ2537). The small craft left of centre could be regarded as a shallop, but none existed in the Navy at that time so this must be a small sloop, possibly the *Dove* by Shish.

14. For sloops with mizzen sails, see *Sloops & Shallops*, William A Baker (Barre, Mass 1966), p44 and figure 11. The vertical line above the quarterdeck was identified by Baker (p42) as possibly an ensign staff. This is highly unlikely in an English vessel, though this arrangement can be found in small Mediterranean ships, but at p43 he does illustrate a mizzen mast on a sloop 'after Van de Velde'. Another possible explanation might be that the vertical line is a vang from the peak of a gaff and that the lateral lines showing just above the deck represent a boom. But at this date that is highly unlikely.

15. Fig 4-14 is traced from a work by Van de Velde the elder titled 'A Buss and Several Dutch Ships in Light Breeze'. M S Robinson, *Van de Velde: A Catalogue of the Paintings of the Elder and Younger*, 2 vols (Greenwich 1990), Plate 645.

16. This detail is taken from 'A Prospect of the Bay, Towne of St Hillary, Castle Elizabeth and Towre of St Aubin' painted in 1680 by Thomas Phillips as part of a survey of the Channel Islands. This is a very early date for a boomed-out gaff-headed mizzen sail, but Phillips was a military engineer trained in accurate observation.

17. The development of the *barque longue* and corvette is discussed in Chapter 10, so all that needs to be mentioned here is that Dunkirk, after the French acquisition, continued to produce excellent hulls, both handy and fast. See also the captions to the etchings of Guéroult du Pas, and the work of Jean Boudriot quoted in notes 9 of Chapter 1 and 5 of Chapter 2 above.

18. An apt example of this problem was experienced by the sloop *Tulip* of 2 guns. On the East Coast she approached and challenged a Dutchman who responded by firing a 4-gun broadside at her. She was quite incapable of responding in kind so replied with musketry. She was boarded and taken. The unfortunate commander was imprisoned in Holland from whence he wrote to the king. The French subsequently re-took the sloop, returning her to the Royal Navy. *Calendar of State Papers Domestic; Charles II*, for 19 September 1672, p635 in TNA copy.

19. See *Sloops & Shallops*, William A Baker (Barre, Mass 1966), p45.

20. The two models in Figs 4-23 and 4-24 are in the National Maritime Museum collection. The *Mary*, the Dutch-built yacht gifted to Charles II in 1660, is a modern model based on the significant amount of visual evidence available. The other has not been conclusively identified but accords in all details visible with the yacht *Katherine* built by Phineas Pett at Chatham in 1674. The first *Katherine*, built by Peter Pett at Deptford in 1661 would have been similar in all essentials. The vast difference in hull lines between the English and Dutch version is plain to see.

21. David J Hepper, *British Warship Losses in the Age of Sail 1650–1859* (Rotherfield 1994), p11: 17 August 1673.

22. *Fore and Aft Sailing Craft*, Douglas Phillips-Birt (London 1962), p104.

23. Peter Heaton, *Yachting: A History* (London 1955), p47. Chapter 2 of this book has much useful information on the Stuart yachts.

Chapter 5

1. Louis proposed a campaign of 'Reunions', which like the later German unification wars of Bismarck, sought to reclaim territory that was questionably part of France. This provided the excuse to lay claim to parts of the Rhineland as well as territories in Italy and parts of the Spanish Netherlands.

2. See Chapter 2 above for the secret Treaty of Dover between Charles II and Louis XIV, which paved the way for this two-pronged attack on the Dutch Republic.

3. An event that contributed substantially to the preparations between the Dutch and parties in England to replace James II was the birth of a son to Mary of Modena, James's Queen. This displaced William's wife to second in line to the English throne, weakening his legitimate claim.

4. Louis was determined that he should not have an idle king at his court, and had sent an emissary to the viceroy in Ireland, Tyrconnel, a Jacobite sympathiser, to report on the feasibility of an operation to land James to secure that island. See the very detailed study by Edward Powley, *The Naval Side of King William's War* (London 1972), p45.

5. In terms of naval deployment, the 'Straits' implied an area that included not only the western approaches to the straits of Gibraltar between Tangier and Cadiz but also into the western Mediterranean itself. The importance of this area was based on the need to protect Allied trade from the depredations of the Barbary corsairs.

6. Had the landing of James in Ireland been contested by the allies in March, then both the siege of Londonderry and the Battle of the Boyne might have been avoided, allowing William to return to fight his campaign in the Low Countries that much sooner.

7. The prerequisites to a French victory against the Allies were, first, for the French to combine the Toulon fleet with the squadrons in Brest, a small matter of covering 1700 sea miles; and, second, for the Allies to be preoccupied with the protection of their commercial shipping away from the Channel. These two factors gave the French a numerical advantage over the Allies when it came to the confrontation off Beachy Head in 1690. See also Edward Powley, *The Naval Side of King William's War* (London 1972), pp175–186. This passage includes a mention of a *barque longue* used by the French to sail out, into the Bay of Biscay, in fresh winds and at high speed, to make contact with their Toulon fleet bound for Brest.

8. A French engineer invented the bomb vessel in 1682. Two mortars were placed side by side on the upper deck forward, either side of the centreline, firing over the bows. The carrying vessel was a galliot, which had a ketch rig. The first English bomb vessel was commissioned in 1687. These early bomb vessels were like those of France with two mortars abreast forward of the main and leading mast. For an account of these see *Line of Battle*, edited by Robert Gardiner (London 1992), p89; also W L Clowes, *The Royal Navy*, Vol 2 (reprinted London 1996), p328. Two bomb vessels, recorded as fireships in Clowes, were present at Bantry Bay. Both would have been useful to Captain Rooke and General Kirke in their later efforts to relieve Londonderry from siege by James's Irish army.

9. Torrington, who commanded the fleet at the Battle of Beachy Head, is credited with the first use of the phrase a 'fleet in being'. This important concept in naval strategy is based on the premise that an undispersed fleet 'in being' implies a threat which an opponent cannot ignore and which may therefore limit his freedom of action.

10. Scotland represented a real threat to England at this time with some 25,000 Highlanders prepared to flock to James's flag. This threat was to persist until 1745 and had to be accommodated in naval planning.

11. For merchant shipping losses see Ralph Davis, *The Rise of the English Shipping Industry* (Newton Abbot 1962), pp316–317.

12. Admiral Lord Berkeley conducted a series of operations along the North Biscay and Channel coast of France in an attempt to destroy the privateering bases, or at least to discourage their use as such. A large number of bomb vessels were required for this enterprise, which in the event failed to curb the attacks on allied trade.

13. See *Memoires of the Royal Navy 1679-1688*, Samuel Pepys (London 1690), p98.

14. See A T Mahan, *The Influence of Sea Power upon History, 1660 to 1783* (Boston 1890, and many later reprints), p196.

15. For Cruisers and Convoys Act 1708 see John Hely Owen, *War at Sea under Queen Anne 1702–1708* (Cambridge 1938), pp 284–285.

16. See John Hely Owen, *War at Sea under Queen Anne 1702–1708* (Cambridge 1938), pp125 and 222. The latter spells out clearly the lack of small warships for this purpose and points up a continuing failure of the Admiralty to provide the Navy with a sufficiency of small warships.

17. *Model Shipwright* 59 (1987), pp16–22.

Chapter 6

1. These were the round-sterned sloops to which Blanckley was referring. Later sloops exhibited the pink stern but the shape of hull in these cases was sharper than the more rotund seventeenth-century ketches.

2. No details of *Whipster* exist bar her listing by Pepys in his Register of Ships (see Chapter 4, note 8). According to the OED 'whipster' could mean a lively, reckless or mischievous person, or someone wielding a whip to drive animals; both meanings suggest some form of goad or provocation to a potential enemy.

3. The application of the word 'brigantine' specifically to define a type of rig is broadly accepted as occurring within the first twenty years of the eighteenth century. But when it comes to changes in nautical description it is rare for anything to happen suddenly. In the 1690s, brigantines and sloops were beginning to carry lug sails in addition to their 'square' rig equipment. For an example see TNA Adm 1/1466, 2 December 1704, letter from the captain of the *Ferret* sloop.

4. TNA Adm 3/5, 13 February 1691. Having received the draught with the formal order on the 14th, the Navy Board responded four days later with an estimate for the cost of construction and fitting such a craft, Adm 1/2563, 18 February 1691.

5. TNA Adm 106/3920, 1 April 1699.

6. The Mediterranean and the Baltic seas were the habitat of the galley and brigantine. The Russian, Danish and Swedish Navies all made extensive use of hybrid vessels particularly in the shallow seas such as those found in the Finnish archipelago. See R C Anderson, *Oared Fighting Ships* (London 1962), Chapter 11.

7. Harding was one of the Royal Navy's leading shipwrights and was responsible for the design and building of at least one First Rate ship. His views on the fitting out of brigantines would probably have been accepted without question. When it came to replacing the Surveyor Edmund Dummer in 1699, who had been dismissed on suspicion of corruption, subsequently unproven, the top two contenders for the post were Furzer and Harding. Furzer was made Surveyor of the Navy.

   Initially it seems that brigantines were envisaged not as independent cruising commands but as tenders attached to larger warships – in one report of the action at La Hogue *Shark* is referred to as 'the admiral's brigantine' – and Harding's proposed complement of 30 was intended to suffice 'til she be upon service and those wanting may be supplied her out of the ship she serves' (Adm 106/3920, 20 April 1691).

8. The paterero was named after the shot it fired: a stone or stones. Unusually, it was breech-loading with a separate 'chamber' that could be pre-loaded – a leftover from the 'murdering pieces' of an earlier age. It was mounted in a pivoting iron yoke that could be fitted into a wooden stock when required, so was a forerunner of the later ½pdr muzzle-loading 'swivel' gun. Sloops were often given the same number of 'swivels' as carriage guns.

9. See *Sloops & Shallops*, William A Baker (Barre, Mass 1966), p73.

10. See note 3 above and Fig 1-26.

11. In 1696, the brigantine *Post Boy*'s dimensions were given as: 'Breadth from outside to outside 16ft 8½in, Breadth aloft 20ft 8½in', the former being just above the wale and the latter at the rail. Such features rendered brigantines complicated to construct and Fisher Harding petitioned the Navy Board for a piece of plate (traditionally, a piece of silverware that was awarded to a shipwright only on the completion of a major warship) on the grounds that the brigantine was more trouble to build than a Sixth Rate (TNA Adm 106/3290, 24 May 1692).

12. See *Sloops & Shallops*, William A Baker (Barre, Mass 1966), pp43–44.

13. TNA Adm 106/3249, Deal Yard Book, 5 October 1696. The same applied to *Discovery*: Adm 51/3820, 6 June 1702.

14. See L G Carr Laughton, 'HM Brigantine *Dispatch*', *The Mariner's Mirror* VII/4 (1921), p354.

15. The naval manuscripts of Lord Lonsdale, 1680–1700: 'A Distinction of Ships & Vessels as to the manner of Masting and Sailing Common to the English Nation'. The entry next to both brigantines and advice boats reads as follows: '4 Guns, 70 Tuns. With two masts, Square Sailes, & the Maine Yard Sometimes Hung by by ye Thirds.' information from Grant Walker.

16. See TNA Adm 95/15, 8 August 1704. (Comptroller, Misc Stores.) Here are listed "the proportion of stores for the new sloop building at Woolwich". This was *Swift*, a 10-gun sloop designed and built by Surveyor Lee. Amongst the list of stores was listed 'Bilinder', or bilander as it is now spelt.

17. See L G Carr Laughton, 'HM Brigantine *Dispatch*', *The Mariner's Mirror* VII/4 (1921), p354. He does not use her final log (TNA Adm 51/280), which runs from 1709 to 1712 and provides evidence that she was sold with a mizzen mast.

18. TNA Adm 51/601, 14 October 1699.

19. TNA Adm 1/1980, 7 November 1704, from the *Squirrel*, a new 24-gun ship.

20. Among the most historically important models in the Henry Huddleston Rogers Collection are those acquired from the descendants of Charles Sergison, who was Clerk of the Acts (Pepys's old position) from 1690 to 1719. The 'brigantine' is catalogued as HHR 2. The collection is housed at the United States Naval Academy Museum in Annapolis, Maryland.

21. Edmund Dummer had been a promising young master shipwright and an excellent draughtsman in the reign of James II. He rose to become Surveyor of the Navy in August 1692. He formed a view that warships needed to be very strong and the crew well protected. This model demonstrates a stern that is less vulnerable than the more open square sterns and a design that protects the majority of gunners and oarsmen from the elements and incoming shot and ball.

22. In 1694 Dummer supervised the design and construction of some very fast packet ships for the Harwich–Low Countries run. Following his dismissal from the Navy, he set up the first regular transatlantic packet service in 1702. He also designed and built small warships for the Navy as a private contractor in the first decade of the eighteenth century.

23. Frontispiece item 'I' is Ten Advice Boats. The Navy never had as many as ten purpose-built advice boats so this figure must include prizes and other craft co-opted for the work. The volume contains tables for masts and spars but unfortunately the smallest beam covered is 20ft. Reproduction by Gael ECCO Print Editions.

24. TNA Adm 51/601, log of *Merlin*, 3 October to 23 December 1699.

25. TNA Adm 51/601, log of *Merlin*, entries for 19 April and 25 August 1701.

26. TNA Adm 106/3464 of 1712. When *Merlin* was sold items included a horse for the mizzen sheet and a wing sail.

27. TNA Adm 51/123, no date given, but after 9 September 1699 when her captain joined.

28. TNA Adm 1/1592. The type of guns requested would have been falconets, which fire a 2pdr ball.

Chapter 7

1. The smaller Fifth Rate ships of 28 guns were often candidates for modification into fireships. This required extensive internal work to hold the combustibles. Nevertheless there were instances of fireships, like their cousins the bomb vessels, being used in a 'sloop' role. For a full history see Peter Kirsch, *Fireship* (Barnsley 2009).

2. The origin of the name 'Saudadoes' is Portuguese. Its translation can

mean either 'good luck' or 'intense longing'. In the case of Charles II's Portuguese wife Katherine, it is possible that the word implied that she had 'sadness or longing for her homeland'. This was a particularly apt name since this small ship made many visits to Portugal allowing news of her homeland to reach Katherine.

3. Where long quarterdecks were provided, these were inevitably armed by a navy determined to cram on the maximum firepower, often despite the reduction in sailing ability. With a full gun deck and fine lines aft, the addition of more weight on the quarterdeck would not have pleased the designers. Nevertheless, this arrangement was to resurface in the 1770s with the long quarterdeck, ship-rigged sloops.

4. This model of the *Peregrine Galley* is in the National Maritime Museum's reserve collection at Number 1 Smithery in Chatham Historic Dockyard, which is where her frames were lofted before being moved to Sheerness. It is poorly mounted in that it appears that there is considerable drag to the keel. This was not the case and the keel should be seen as being approximately parallel to the waterline. In the NMM catalogue (ref SLR0394) it is described simply as a brigantine, but the evidence for the identification is presented in Robert Gardiner's *The Sailing Frigate* (Barnsley 2012), p22. The model also shows great similarity to the *Caroline* (Fig 7-8), which was master shipwright Richard Stacey's modification of the *Peregrine Galley*.

5. This rig is similar to that of the packet boats, which had to be able to sail to windward.

6. Mast and spar dimensions are laid out in TNA Adm 1/3595 for both her three- and two-masted rigs. The three-masted ship rig is conventional but the two-masted rig when drawn out reveals that she would have been unmanageable if square-rigged. The fore-and-aft options were for the main course either to be set on a heavy standing gaff spar, as was the case of the earlier Stuart yachts, or set as a lug sail. The balance of the rig might well have worked with either of these arrangements, yet because of the extreme forward position of the mainmast it is possible that she would still have carried substantial lee helm: hence the complaints leading to the replacement with ship rig.

7. The St Petersburg model and indeed other early 'schooner' rigs are covered in detail in *The Global Schooner*, Karl Heinz Marquardt (London 2003), pp9–18. Both the rig and the hull of the model are suspect; in fact, the identification of the model does not pre-date the nineteenth century. It is most unlikely that Peregrine Osborne would have given her such a corpulent hull. This would have been totally out of line with his other designs which were, apart from his *Maggot* (a peculiar wasp-waisted design which would have been a nightmare to plank up), aesthetically beautiful. Furthermore, details of a proposed conversion of the *Royal Transport* to a cruiser in 1696 reveal that she had the kind of accommodation typical of a yacht and impossible to reconcile with the layout of the St Petersburg model (TNA Adm 106/3292, 30 November 1696). She must have looked very like the *Peregrine Galley*.

8. Warship construction allowed for fully framed hulls, leaving only small spaces between each individual set of frame-pairs to allow for the inevitable movement in a ship's hull and the expansion and contraction of the wood itself. Planking was completed on the inside of frames, giving the hull a considerable thickness of wood and therefore weight.

9. The length to breadth ratio (LBR) was used as a basic comparator in ship designs, provided the vessels' depth of water was similar. Because it was a ratio, to some degree it obviated the need to take scale into account. It was normally based on the length along the gun deck (LGD) and the maximum beam, normally at that time on the wales.

10. R C Anderson, 'Some Additions to the Brigantine Problem', *The Mariner's Mirror* VIII/2 (1922), p115. In the 1920s Anderson had the Sergison Collection in his care for a time, together with a mass of manuscript material, so he was able to speak with authority on this particular model.

11. See 'Henry Huddleston Rodgers Collection Number 2', a lecture given by Grant Walker, the historian of the model collection, at the US Naval Academy, Annapolis on 25 January 2000. This lecture looks closely at the identity of this small naval vessel.

12. Edmund Dummer became Surveyor of the Navy in 1692, being promoted to this position from Assistant Surveyor to his predecessor Tippets. He had acquired considerable fame in recording and illustrating various projects such as a review of shipping in the Mediterranean, which first brought the French-invented bomb vessel to English attention. He also carried out a detailed examination of England's Channel harbours. His time as Surveyor should be remembered for two main lines of work: his proposals and designs for the commissioning of new dockyards at Portsmouth and Plymouth; and his supervision of the construction of fast packet boats notably from Harwich. Later, following his unfair dismissal from the Navy, he set up a transatlantic service from Falmouth. (Many details can be found on the Falmouth Packet Archives 1688–1850 website www.falmouth.packet.archives.dial.pipex.com) He was also MP for Arundel where *Swift* was built. These facts suggest a connection between Dummer and HHR Model 2.

13. *The Mariner's Mirror* VIII/2 (1922), p115. R C Anderson's identification relates to the model's rig, his suggestion of 'brigantine' implying that the main course must be a fore-and-aft sail, or at least one that can be used in this fashion. The advantage of the lug sail is that good performance can be obtained both downwind and upwind. HHR Model 2, if that model be of *Swift* should at least have a tall buss sail which can be used in this way.

14. *Falconer's Marine Dictionary 1780* (reprinted Newton Abbot 1970), p35. The dictionary points out that the words 'bilander' and 'brigantine' were used in different ways throughout Europe.

Chapter 8

1. There was a proposal in the late eighteenth century that fast sailing fire-ships could be used as a means of forcing a break in the enemy's line-of-battle and thereby creating the opportunity for an envelopment of part of his fleet. It was never put into practice possibly because it could be extremely risky for both sides in a closing engagement, where a division from the attacking squadron would have to follow the fireship through the enemy line. However, a class of small, fast vessels was built in 1780, based on the lines of the French frigate *La Panthère*, taken in the War of the Austrian Succession some forty years earlier. Lord Howe was influential in this revival of interest in the fireship: see Peter Kirsch, *Fireship* (Barnsley 2009), p207.

2. See Edmund Dummer's correspondence with Robert Lee, master shipwright at Chatham, in early 1693 about a new bomb vessel design. The French engineer Fournier, who had been instrumental in the development of the first bombs but was now in William III's service, insisted that such vessels needed mighty strength in their hull scantlings. Dummer disagreed, as did Captain Phillips, the military engineer tasked with preparing the bomb vessels for their first mission, and Captain Phillips 'further says there needs nothing to be fitted for the mortars in the hull as of uncommon strength on the occasion thereof, but what may well be done when they are launched.' (TNA Adm 91/1, 23 February 1693) This is an important point since it means that conversions could be made between cruising and shore bombardment modes without dry-docking the vessel, facilitating its dual purpose.

3. Initially the intention was that the mainstay should remain in position and be a chain rather than a hemp cable since the blast might set it on fire. In Dummer's drawing it would appear that even the chain has been drawn back to the mainmast.

4. Dummer's sumptuously bound manuscript book 'A Voyage into the Mediterranean seas' can be found in the British Library, Kings MS 40. His tour lasted from 1682 until early 1684, and the book was completed in 1685, when Dummer seems to have presented it to the king.

5. To give an idea of the versatility of these craft the tale of *Firedrake* will suffice. She was taken by the French in 1689 in the Channel. They converted her into a *frégat légère* of 22 guns; she was finally hulked in 1713. See Rif Winfield, *British Warships in the Age of Sail 1603–1714* (Barnsley 2009), p231.

6. See Donald McNarry, *Ship Models in Miniature* (Newton Abbot 1975), pp35 and 56.

7. In many ways the Army had more to do with the fitting out of bomb vessels than the Navy; it continued to provide detachments to man the sea mortars until 1844. However, at this period the weapons were provided by a separate 'third service', the Board of Ordnance, who supplied guns to both Army and Navy. The mixed responsibilities were not always helpful to the timely production of vessels fit for service. This was noticeable at the introduction of traversable mortar beds after 1693 when some bombs were equipped with traversing mortars whilst other still had the fixed versions.

8. See Rif Winfield, *British Warships in the Age of Sail 1603–1714* (Barnsley 2009), p231. However, *Firedrake* was equipped with an experimental 'cushee' piece, intended to fire explosive shells on a horizontal trajectory like a conventional gun. This was developed by Captain Leake's father, the name deriving from the *coursier*, the large fixed forward-facing main gun of a galley. Leake may have been one of the few seamen with any incentive to try such a dangerous weapon, so it would be a strong contender to take the credit for the damage caused to the French ship.

9. Dummer's letter of 2 March 1693 suggests a pole foremast 'without a topmast or topsail to step in a case above the forecastle to strike forward upon all occasions, to have a more than ordinary hoist of sail to be taunt [high] but narrow.' (TNA Adm 91/1). Something like this seems to have been adopted at first, but on 24 September 1693 Captain Phillips, the manager of the bomb vessel project, reported that after trials the 'taking down and raising of the fore rigging and mast of the vessel is wholly laid aside being of no advantage but by it being omitted we are in a much better posture of service.' (TNA SP 42/2) He does not give details of how this was achieved, but the two mortars were in fixed side-by-side beds in the French fashion so could theoretically fire either side of the foremast.

10. In commenting on Fournier's design for a bomb ketch, Charles Sergison, Clerk of the Acts to the Navy Board, advised the Admiralty on 21 August 1691 that 'She hath an extreme broad floor whereby we judge she will be leewardly and a short sailer by the wind. Howsoever she may do well in case she be employed near home or in a fair weather sea as it is commonly within the straits [of Gibraltar] but do not think her fit for the British Seas much less for service further abroad lest for want of the good qualities of sailing and working in a sea she should lose company and want a tow.' Quoted from the Sergison papers by David Wray in 'Bomb Vessels, their development and use, Part 1 1682 -1700', *Model Shipwright* 19 (March 1977), pp242–255.

11. For the arguments surrounding the purchase of merchant vessels to convert to bombs and their lists, see Chris Ware, *The Bomb Vessel* (London 1994), pp21–25.

12. Although the damage directly caused by the bomb ketches to the French fleet at Toulon was minor, the French having sunk their vessels to frustrate the English attempts, Sir Cloudesley Shovell and his fleet's continued presence in the area ensured that the time spent by the French ships under the water would be very damaging to them. See John Hely Owen, *War at Sea under Queen Anne 1702–1708* (Cambridge 1938), p191.

13. Two of these, *Julian's Prize* and the *Phoenix*, were commissioned before 1694, in 1690 and 1692.

Chapter 9

1. This antidote was not particularly successful in the face of audacious action by privateer squadron commanders such as Forbin and Du Guay-Trouin. One of the critical problems was the lack of balance in the British convoy squadrons which always had insufficient small warships to fend off the small privateers that sailed in the wake of the larger French ships and fell upon the merchantmen unprotected by the line-of-battle ships engaged with the French main force. See John Hely Owen, *War at Sea under Queen Anne 1702–1708* (Cambridge 1938), pp125–126 and 222.

2. For details of these sloops see Chapter 6.

3. TNA Adm 1/1529, 12 October 1705: a request for two more guns for *Merlin*. In the case of *Bonetta* II, Adm 1/1466 of 6 November 1704, a

request for four falconets in place of four patereroes (swivels); there was also a complaint from this ship that the gun ports were not high enough to allow a decent elevation to the guns, Adm 1/1592 of 1 January 1705.

4. This was the brigantine *Post Boy* II. The first of this name was an advice boat taken by the French and renamed *Le Facteur de Bristol*. She, as a privateer, took *Post Boy* II!

5. See Rif Winfield, *British Warships in the Age of Sail 1603–1714* (Barnsley 2009), p228.

6. Howard I Chapelle, *The Search for Speed under Sail* (New York 1967 & London 1968), p52. Chapelle believed that the *Ferret* class sloops were very similar to a sloop portrayed by Burgis in 'A sloop off Boston light', 1729. This is a dangerous speculation in that the great rake of the foremast in this picture fits better the design of the vessels from Bermuda. It is more likely that the *Ferret* class had a two-part upright mast with a square topsail in the manner of the early Stuart yachts but with a boomed-out main course. However, Chapelle's book has a most useful section on the design requirements for a fast sailing ship (pp35–53).

7. See TNA Adm 2/189, Admiralty Out Letters, 2 August 1710.

8. TNA Adm 51/4377, log of the *Trial* sloop, 30 September 1710 to 7 June 1718. Amongst other details, this log has information on the minor changes to the single-mast rig.

9. TNA Adm 51/1008, log of the *Trial* sloop. Part III deals with the rig after her rebuild in 1719. It would seem that she was given a snow rig with the modification of having a boom for her snow sail to extend it. See TNA Adm 95/16, Navy Board Misc (1718-1730): a reply to the Controller from Portsmouth Officers, 13 July 1719 in which the Portsmouth Dockyard Officers propose to shift her foremast aft by 20in and her mainmast by 14in whilst increasing the length of her boom by one and a half yards, in order to relieve her of excessive weather helm. Even this was not enough as her captain had her masts taken out and converted to brigantine rig at Gibraltar in October that year (Adm 51/1008, 1 October 1719).

10. This reconstruction has followed that of Chapelle, which allows more swivels than the four originally laid down by the Admiralty.

Chapter 10

1. *Falconer's Marine Dictionary 1780* (reprinted Newton Abbot 1970), p184. Falconer incorrectly describes a 'long-boat' as a double chaloupe or *barque longue*. He then adds that it is the largest and strongest boat of any sailing ship, which is correct. There may have been some similarity between a ship's longboat and a double chaloupe, but none between it and a barque-longue. It has to be said that the double chaloupe was generally too large to be carried by any sailing ship at this time.

2. For the complete list see Jean Boudriot, 'Les Barques Longues', *Nautical Research Journal* 27 (1981), p98; or Boudriot, *La Creole 1823: Historique de la Corvette 1650-1850* (Paris 1990). This book contains a history of the development of the corvette and starts with a chapter on the *barque longue*.

3. Jean Boudriot, 'Les Barques Longues', *Nautical Research Journal* 27 (1981), p95.

4. Patrick Villiers, *Les Corsaires du Littoral* (Lille 2000), p214. In the context of this book, the littoral is Dunkirk, Calais and Boulogne. The text is in French. See also *Actes du colloque international Paris, Ecole militaire, 12 June 1987*, anon, 'La Guerre de Course en France de Louis XIV á Napoleon I', p3. From the French: 'The Course started with very small boats. A government order assigned to Dunkirk two small frigates *La Mignone* and *La Trompeuse*, armed with 8 to 12 guns, a double shallop and nine *barques longues*.' This means that all *barques longues* were at that time employed at Dunkirk. The paper quotes Henri Malo, *Les Corsairs Dunkirquois et Jean Bart*, 2 vols (Paris 1913), Vol 2, pp90-97.

5. See J Guéroult du Pas, *Recueil des Veues de tous les differents Bastimens de la Mer Mediterranée et de l'Océan* (Paris 1710), engraving nos 24-26. This work can be viewed online at http://gallica.bnf.fr and is available in a reprint with the slightly modernised title *Bâtiments de la Mer Mediterranée et de l'Océan* (Nice 2004).

6. Guéroult du Pas' representation of figures is unreliable. The figures on the double shallop fit the vessel well; those on the *barque longue* are too large making it appear smaller than it would be in reality.

7. See Boudriot, sources quoted in note 2 above.

8. National Maritime Museum PAH 2532: Battle of Texel (Kijkduin), 11 [OS]/21 August 1673, Fifth Part. This detail from a preliminary sketch by Van de Velde the elder has in the foreground an English sloop, under Dutch colours, with the Biscay rig.

9. See *Encyclopédie des gens du monde*, Vol 7, Part 1 (Strasbourg 1836), pp67– 68. Original copy held by the University of the State of Michigan (Google eBook digitised 2008).

10. See *Falconer's Marine Dictionary 1780* (reprinted Newton Abbot 1970), French section. '*Barque longue* or double chaloupe, a sort of pinnace or large long-boat'. This description does not accord with a miniature warship carrying 4–8 guns. Also in the French section of the Dictionary, a 'corvette' is described as ' sloop of war'. This description is suitable for the late seventeenth and early eighteenth centuries but would not be right for later periods when the corvette was closer to an English 24-gun ship.

11. See Chapter 3 to compare tonnages; but notice the relationship between depth of water and burthen. Those sloops of similar dimensions to a *barque longue* drawing 5ft 9in depth of water, average out at 63.5 tons compared to the *barque longue*'s 36 tons. Burthen was a very crude measurement and should not be confused with displacement. All we can say is that a substantial difference in burthen may indicate a dramatically different hull shape: the smaller the figure the more slender the hull.

12. See note 2 above.

13. This work was set in motion by Texas A&M University together with the French naval historian Jean Boudriot and with access to the town archives at Rochefort. The story of the discovery and its subsequent analysis can be found in *From a Watery Grave* by James E Bruseth and Toni S Turner (College Station, Texas 2005); see Chapter 5.

14. F H Chapman, *Architectura Navalis Mercatoria 1768* (facsimile New York 1967), Plate XXXVIII. The aspects to note are the return of the bilge at the midship section and the hollow entry and run.

    See Rif Winfield, *British Warships in the Age of Sail 1603–1714* (Barnsley 2009), p225 and NMM PAH1865; note the use of this vessel for clandestine operations.

15. Howard I Chapelle, *The Search for Speed under Sail* (New York 1967 & London 1968), p87, Plate 13 shows a plan of the Marblehead schooner which exhibits a marked drag to the keel and a midship section similar to that seen in the plan of the *barque longue*.

16. No such vessel exists in the list of *barques longues* but this is probably because she was not a naval vessel. However a *La Belle* II is listed with a displacement of 50 tons.

17. Construction can be seen in a photograph of the wreck. See pp76-77 in *From a Watery Grave*, by James E Bruseth and Toni S Turner, Texas A&M University Press (College Station, Texas 2005).

18. The flat of the floor is the measurement across the transverse member that lies across the keel and to whose outer limits are attached the futtock frames.

19. The addition of an extra mast for ocean passages was well known. Frequently, ketches were given a foremast for a transatlantic passage thereby becoming pink- as opposed to ketch-rigged.

20. A Jal, *Archéologie Navale* (Paris 1840), p10.

21. *Nautical Research Journal*, Vol 27 (1981), p96.

Chapter 11

1. See Sir George Clarke, *The Later Stuarts* (Oxford, reprinted 1987), pp229–231.

2. Despite the passing of the Act of Settlement in 1701, the Hanoverian succession was by no means assured. See Basil Williams, *The Whig Supremacy* (Oxford, reprinted 1985), pp150–152.

3. In terms of blood James III would have been first in line to the throne. Son of James II and Mary of Modena, his birth was one of the factors leading to William of Orange's descent on Torbay in 1688.

4. For an account of this expedition and the preparations to intercept it see John Hely Owen, *War at Sea under Queen Anne 1702–1708* (Cambridge 1938), pp238–261.

5. For the attempted rebellions of 1719 and 1722 see Basil Williams, *The Whig Supremacy* (Oxford, reprinted 1985), pp173–174 and 182–185.

6. See Basil Williams, *The Whig Supremacy* (Oxford, reprinted 1985), p175.

7. One of the problems facing the British squadron in the Baltic in the late stages of the war was that, as a deep-water force, it could not engage the Russian galley fleets. As Admiral Norris put it, 'Galleys cannot be stopped where ships cannot navigate.' This prompts the question, would sloops like the *Drake* have helped in this setting? The difficulty was that the Russians had a large fleet of galleys and they carried some sizeable guns. Sloops had the shallow draught and the use of oars to help, but above all it did not suit the British to commit themselves to operations among the rocks. Britain had a different job to do in deep water.

8. The Spanish designs on Italy were to reclaim those possessions that had belonged to their empire when they were ruled by the Hapsburg dynasty. Their targets were Sardinia, Naples and Sicily. Although the British, as part of the quadruple alliance against Spain, attempted to prevent this, they were unable to remove the Spaniards from the territories they had occupied despite roundly defeating the Spanish fleet at Cape Passaro in 1718.

9. Piracy had been virtually eradicated from the Caribbean by 1720, but there was ongoing sporadic activity by privateers from all three countries with possessions in that region. This activity would recur again and again during the eighteenth and early nineteenth centuries as an extension of the confrontations on the eastern side of the Atlantic and eventually included the emerging United States of America.

10. Bomb sloops attended the expeditions in 1720, 1721 and 1727 on the expectation that it would be necessary to engage land targets. Only one purpose-built bomb sloop was in the squadron; the others were Sixth Rate ships converted specifically for each expedition. There were no more than a pair on any one expedition.

11. See Rif Winfield, *British Warships in the Age of Sail 1714–1792* (Barnsley 2007), pp272–279 and 294–312.

Chapter 12

1. The fate of the other three was: *Hazard* wrecked Massachusetts Bay 1714; *Jamaica* wrecked Grand Cayman 1715; *Ferret* taken by Spanish 50-gun ship *Arminona* in Cadiz Bay 1718.

2. In 1728 she returned to her original cruising ground of the West Indies.

3. The habit of commissioning an 'old' design of sloop was repeated in 1761 when two sloops, *Druid* and *Lynx*, equivalent to the *Cruizer* class of 1732, were ordered because they were ideal for the job in hand. See Rif Winfield, *British Warships in the Age of Sail 1714–1792* (Barnsley 2007), p311.

4. The captains' logs for the *Trial* (TNA Adm 51/4377, from launch in 1710 to refit in 1719) contain several entries that identify her as having single-mast rig. Those after the refit (Adm 51/1008 Part III, running from May 1719) show the changes to her rig.

   a. Immediately after refit her captain reported getting her mainmast moved aft by 13in and her foremast by 19in (again a lack of understanding within the yards of the relationship between CLR and CoE; see Chapter 1, Management under sail).

   b. On 26 September 1719 the captain reported breaking his fore gaff; so presumably she was schooner-rigged, or had a wing sail abaft her foremast, after her refit.

   c. On 7 October 1719, in the Lisbon river, the captain reported getting out his masts in order to make a brigantine of her.

5. See *Falconer's Marine Dictionary 1780* (reprinted Newton Abbot 1970), p301. There is an explanation here of the process of 'trying', which is a method of managing a ship in severe weather and in a large sea. For this operation a trysail placed behind the fore- or mainmasts could be used to good effect: hence the name of the vertical spar.

6. G S Laird Clowes, *Sailing Ships. Their History and Development*, Vol II (London 1936), p35 and Plate IX: 'A Sloop-of-War (1710-1711)', Cat No 61.

7. TNA Adm 51/1008. There is evidence that the schooner rig may have been intended for use after 1729 for the replacement of the sloop *Spence* I.

8. TNA Adm 3/34, Admiralty Board Minutes, 11 January 1721.

9. TNA Adm 106/3302, 7 October 1731.

10. TNA Adm 3/35, Admiralty Board Minutes, 25 April 1726. This piece has several entries of Admiralty orders to sloops between April and September of that year.

11. TNA Adm 51/961, 4 and 25 October 1721.

12. TNA Adm 106/750, 23 July 1722.

13. TNA Adm 51/660, 31 July. More evidence of lee helm.

14. Accounts of such misbehaviour by sloops and their crews can be read in: C R Benstead, *Shallow Waters* (London 1958), p177; W Page & J H Round (eds), *The Victoria History of the County of Essex*, Vol II (Woodbridge 2008); Hervey Benham, *Once Upon a Tide* (London 1955), p162.

15. TNA Adm 106/757, 23 April 1723, and Adm 91/2, 14 September 1738.

16. TNA Adm 106/3470, 24 January 1729/30.

17. TNA Adm 51/923, Part IV, 22 January 1729/30.

18. NMM POR/A/10, Warrants to Portsmouth Yard, 14 October 1735.

19. TNA Adm 51/216, Part IV, 3 November 1721. Also note that on 16 January 1722 she had taken in six carriage guns and four swivels. Before this she drew 8ft 2in forward and 8ft 4in aft. After loading, she drew 8ft 2in forward and 8ft 9in aft. This would bring her CLR aft giving her more lee helm.

20. There is a variation in the complement of swivel guns. For example Adm 106/743 of 28 November 1721 gives four for *Spy* whilst Adm 106/3466 of 5 October 1721 gives six for *Cruizer*. Some are also credited with eight 4pdrs at various times in their careers.

21. G S Laird Clowes, *Sailing Ships. Their History and Development*, Vol II (London 1936), p50 and Plate XIII: 'Rigged Model of a Naval Schooner (1760-1780)', Cat No 100.

22. TNA Adm 51/4377, 3 December 1711.

23. TNA Adm 3/37, 26 November 1728.

Chapter 13

1. *Drake* has been identified with Model No 2 in the Henry Huddlestone Rogers Collection at the United States Naval Academy, Annapolis. However, her dimensions do not fit.

2. TNA Adm 3/37, Admiralty Minutes, 15 April 1728–22 April 1729. It contains several entries dealing with *Drake* II.

3. TNA Adm 3/38, 29 April 1729–23 June 1730.

4. TNA Adm 106/3301, 5 April 1729. Yard advice was that armament should be 2 x 6pdrs on the lower deck and 4 x 4pdrs on the upper deck.

5. TNA Adm 106/3302, 29 March 1731, reporting on *Drake*'s arrival for breaking up.

6. TNA Adm 106/3470, Clerk of the Survey Out Letters, 24 May 1731.

7. Quoted in a letter from Captain Laws dated 12 January which was enclosed with the warrant of 14 January 1736/7, authorising strong cordage to be issued and an iron horse to be made. NMM POR/A.

8. TNA Adm 106/3305, 22 August 1741.

9. Robert Beatson, *Naval and Military Memoirs of Great Britain from 1727 to 1783* (London 1784), Vol I. The claim for the armament of this vessel is unusually close to that of the *Unicorn* that captured it. There are a number of similar mistakes in Beatson's lists.

10. For a detailed description of these trials, see Howard I Chapelle, *The Search for Speed under Sail* (New York 1967 & London 1968), pp79–80.

11. NMM POR/A/9, Warrants to Portsmouth Yard, 30 June 1732.

12. Leo Heaps, *Log of the Centurion* (London 1973), pp132–134.

13. The first sloops of the Navy, the early Cromwellian ketches, had been designed and built on the East Coast by contract in the 1650s. The oceanic advice boats of 1696/7 were built in Arundel, though probably to a design by the Surveyor. During the War of the Spanish Succession, the building of some small Sixth Rates/sloops had been contracted out because the yards were busy or full.

Chapter 14

1. This painting of *Blast* has been reproduced by the kind permission of the eighteenth Earl of Pembroke and Montgomery and the Trustees of the Wilton House Trust. It shows HM Sloop *Blast* being taken by a couple of large Spanish privateer xebecs off Point Pedro. She was ordered as a bomb in 1740, commissioned as a sloop in 1741 and refitted as a bomb in 1742. Here, in 1745, she is operating as a sloop. Her rig is unusual since, were she designed as a bomb, she would have had a ketch rig. The one shown here is a snow rig without the wing sail abaft the mainmast. Her signature as a bomb is the fact that her after guns are lower than the rest of her battery.

2. In theory the mortar could be carried by any ship. The two Sixth Rates *Seaford* and *Shoreham* were so equipped for the 1727 squadron in the Baltic. This suggests a stopgap move as only the old *Basilisk* remained from 1695. The measure may have prompted the Admiralty to order the building of *Salamander* and *Terrible* in 1729. See David Aldridge, *Admiral Sir John Norris and the British Naval Expeditions to the Baltic Sea 1715–1727* (Lund 2009), p284.

3. See Rif Winfield, *British Warships in the Age of Sail 1714–1792* (Barnsley 2007), p339.

4. TNA Adm 106/3305, Deptford Yard 9th November 1742.

5. Joseph Allin's draughts for the hulls of small vessels have a characteristic curvaceous and full bodied appearance. They seem to be a throwback to the shapes of the *Peregrine Galley* of 1700. This lasted until his retirement from the Navy in 1755. He appears to have been very conservative and as such did not have the support of Anson when the latter rose to be First Lord of the Admiralty. Anson wanted a redesigning of British fighting vessels and he used Allin's illness to hasten his retirement, bringing in his chosen Surveyor Thomas Slade.

6. TNA Adm 106/3308 Deptford Yard Letter Books, 31 July 1749.

7. See Howard I Chapelle, *The Search for Speed under Sail* (New York 1967 & London 1968), pp70–73. A model, sheer plan and sail plan is included.

8. Bomb vessels were used in the siege of Toulon. See John Hely Owen, *War at Sea under Queen Anne 1702–1708* (Cambridge 1938), p169.

9. Chris Ware, *The Bomb Vessel* (London 1994), pp36–37. The model of *Granado* demonstrates clearly the sliding hatches introduced with the *Blast* class bomb ketches. Before their introduction some form of cover would have been applied, but after 1730 the new-style mortars with breech trunnions could be trained down to horizontal, permitting the use of hatches.

10. N A M Roger, *The Command of the Ocean* (London 2004), p240.

Chapter 15

1. *Actes du colloque international Paris, Ecole militaire, 10, 11, 12 June 1987*, anon, 'La Guerre de Course en France de Louis XIV á Napoleon I', Bilan Sommaire de la guerre de course de 1702 a 1815. This table shows that between 1702 and 1713 Dunkirk took 1726 prizes and Calais 1298; Brest was third with 590 and St Malo with 528. Some of the privateers would have been hired from the French Navy.

2. See Jean Boudriot, 'Les Barques Longues', *Nautical Research Journal* 27 (1981), p98. This gives a list of all corvettes/*barques longues* built up to 1744. It disagrees in some details with other lists, but serves to show how few were built following the end of the War of the Spanish Succession.

3. See David J Hepper, *British Warship Losses in the Age of Sail 1650–1859* (Rotherfield 1994), p40 et seq. Ten losses are listed (including the *Pergrine* of 1700), of which three were taken, four foundered and three were either bilged or wrecked. This amounted to about 15 per cent of all sloops available at the beginning of the war and acquired during it, including prizes.

4. Jean Boudriot, *La Creole 1823: Historique de la Corvette 1650-1850*

(Paris 1990), listing corvettes for the 'periode 1re Moitie XVIII Siecle' states in a footnote 'Le Fils Ollivier est a l'epoque age de 15 ans.'

5. Rif Winfield, *British Warships in the Age of Sail 1714–1792* (Barnsley 2007), p276. *La Guirlande* was rated as a frigate by the French despite having only two masts. She may have been considered as a frégat légère because she had a complete lower deck. Given a third mast in British service she would have continued to be rated as a frigate – as were all ship-sloops initially – until reduced quite rightly to sloops after the war.

6. G S Laird Clowes, *Sailing Ships. Their History and Development*, Vol I (London 1932), Plate XXVI. The radical nature of the reconstruction looks unlikely in wartime, but there are documented examples of frigates being similarly transformed.

7. Rif Winfield, *British Warships in the Age of Sail 1714–1792* (Barnsley 2007), p279. *Vulture* and *Swift* were designed by Slade and annotated: 'as nearly as may be conformable to the draught which has been made of HM Sloop *Epreuve*'. Planned for two masts, like the French original, they were completed with three. The close proximity of the mizzen to the mainmast suggests that this was a last-minute thought!

Chapter 16

1. The system for producing a new design before 1743 required the Navy Board to derive a specification from general Admiralty requirements; this would then be passed to the master shipwright at one or more of the Royal Dockyards. This same system was occasionally followed if the construction were to be contracted out to a commercial yard, although for larger ships the merchant builder would be sent an approved draught. The Surveyor of the Navy would confer with the master ship-wrights, who were required to submit draughts and/or models of their proposed design for his scrutiny, criticism and suggested alteration, before final approval. Some insight into the workings of this system can be followed in two surviving volumes of Acworth's correspondence from 1738 onwards (TNA adm 91/2 and 91/3) . It became the habit towards the middle of the eighteenth century for the design work to be centralised in the Surveyor's office. This was of course essential if a large amount of work were to be contracted out, as was the case with sloops. By 1742 the Surveyors in post, Acworth and Allin, were responsible for the majority of sloop designs. But others, notably Pierson Lock at Portsmouth and Benjamin Slade at Plymouth, also contributed to the design portfolios.

2. Admiralty Order of 30 January 1749.

3. *Peggy*'s pedigree starts with a design for a yacht by Peregrine Osborne, the Marquis of Carmarthen, that became the *Peregrine Galley* in 1700. Her rig was covered in Chapter 7, but it is her hull that is of interest here. After spending the War of the Spanish Succession shuttling VIPs to and from the Continent, the ship was chosen to bring George I to Britain following the death of Queen Anne. Returning to the role of yacht, in 1716 she was renamed *Carolina* after the new queen. She was then 'rebuilt' at Deptford in 1732 by master shipwright Richard Stacey, becoming *Royal Caroline*. She was finally refitted as a sloop with the name of *Peregrine* in 1748, making way for a new *Royal Caroline*, designed by Allin in 1749 but heavily influenced by the lines of the earlier yacht. The lines were then replicated in the *Cruizer* class sloops of 1752/3.

4. There is always a difficulty in changing scale when it comes to ships. See Chapter 1, Management under sail, for an explanation as to why sloops, often miniature copies of larger ships, had such difficulty with too much canvas!

5. Conversions of sloops rigged as snows into the ship rig normally entailed leaving the mainmast in its original position. This sometimes produced a rather squashed arrangement abaft the mainmast. Those sloops laid down as snows but commissioned with the ship rig may have had their main in a more central position than would be normal for a snow. Those sloops laid down with ship rig could expect a normal ratio of distances between masts.

6. The plans of the *Cruizer* class and all other sloops of this period indicate one broad wale, whereas the models in the NMM and the Science Museum are both built with the old-fashioned double wale. The plans are probably the more reliable source.

7. The wheeled steering arrangements for these sloops made use of a conventional tiller on the quarterdeck, which was linked to the wheel by an arrangement of blocks and tackles. For an illustration of the system see Ron McCarthy, *Building Plank on Frame Ship Models* (London 1994), p100.

8. Contemporary plans only show waterlines in the horizontal plane. The value of the reconstruction is that it shows the vertical buttock–bow lines. An indication of the potential ease of motion of a vessel through the water is give by the angle at which the quarter beam buttock–bow line crosses the designed surface waterline. See Howard I Chapelle, *The Search for Speed under Sail* (New York 1967 & London 1968), pp35–53.

9. TNA Adm 51/3979, 10 March 1759, et seq.

10. The order for this exact copying was unprecedented at the time and seems to have been the product of direct intervention by Anson, although the *Tygre* was brought to his attention by Benjamin Slade, master shipwright at Plymouth. Although no relationship has been conclusively established with the more famous Surveyor, Thomas Slade, it seems likely that they were of the same family. Thomas certainly shared Benjamin's views on the qualities of the *Tygre*.

11. The ship-rigged sloops are covered in Chapter 17 but the design of *Alderney* (snow) matches that of *Senegal* (ship) of the *Beaver* class. *Beaver*, although built to the same specification as *Senegal*, has a totally different and much improved shape.

Chapter 17

1. See Chapter 6, notes 26 and 27. This was part of the continuing difficulty the Navy was having with the two-masted snow or improved Biscay rig at this time. The solution was either to reposition the mainmast further aft, increase the rake of that mast, apply a wing sail behind the mainmast or, the best solution of all, convert to ship rig.

2. Confusion can occur when reading a French text on rigging in that the word *misaine* is used to identify the foremast and the foresail. The mizzen sail is called the *artimon* and the mizzen mast *le mât d'artimon*. See *Falconer's Marine Dictionary 1780* (reprinted Newton Abbot 1970).

3. See Chapter 14 and Figs 14-15 and 14-16. Three plans are listed under *Furnace* at the NMM. ZAZ5624 or J0390 has been labelled at some stage as *Furnace* but is in fact of *Alderney*, whose lines and dimensions were copied for *Furnace*. Plan ZAZ6525 or J0516, part of which is at Fig 17-2 above, shows the thoughts for conversion, including the arrangement for ship rig, with part of her sheer plan delineated in light pencil work. Plan ZAZ6524 or J0515 shows her converted.

4. The arming of the quarterdeck, other than with swivels did not happen until the arrival of the carronade after 1780, when ship-sloops carried four on this deck, in addition to their armament on the main gun deck of up to 18 short 6pdrs. The powerful, short-range carronade was to become a favourite with the sloop both in its later ship and brig form. Then, provided the sloop could close swiftly with her opponent, she could defeat a larger vessel, but only if it did not also have carronades.

5. The capture of the French Quebec-built frigate *L'Abenakise* in 1757 led to a number of designs based on the lines of this ship. The 32-gun frigate *Lowestoffe* was one example and the 14-gun sloop *Beaver* another. Both the frigate by Slade and the sloop by Bately were ordered in the same year and, not surprisingly looked remarkably alike in hull form.

6. NMM holds a heavily annotated sheer plan of the ship-sloop *Ferret* of 1760. It contains a mine of information, including dimensions, on the sloops of this period. See Charnock collection Ch 31/51 or J8434. Her lines are at ZAZ5132 or J5132. There is also a plan of the internal works at ZAZ4569 or J5135. It is dated 1771 and shows the intention to extend her quarterdeck. This plan also contains mast and yard dimensions.

7. See Chapter 15 and Figs 15-9 and 15-10.

Appendix 1

ALPHABETICAL LIST OF PURPOSE-BUILT AND PRIZE SLOOPS BY NAME, DATES, DESIGNER AND RIG

This list does not include the mass of prizes taken from the Dutch during the three Anglo–Dutch sea-wars, some of which were given traditional sloop names and in some cases the same names as extant English-built sloops. Neither does this list include yachts unless they were employed permanently as sloops. It does include some small Sixth Rates more appropriate to the sloop category. Those purchased while building from merchant yards are included since many of them follow the satisfactory completion of an Admiralty order by the builder concerned. Purchases of completed merchantmen, where circumstances usually forced the Navy Board to be less discriminating, are not included, but the list does cover captured vessels bought–in, when they are listed as prizes rather than purchases.

The symbol † signifies a commercial designer and/or builder. From the 1740s the usual procedure for ordering sloops was that the Surveyor's office produced the design, which would then be contracted out for building. Where this happens the name of the Surveyor is in the Remarks column. In a small number of cases a merchant builder would build to his own design, either as the result of a specific order, or as a speculative venture later purchased by the Admiralty.

Where master shipwrights are the designer and builder, which was the norm up until 1740, there is just one name and no annotation. Where a commercial designer is also the builder there is one annotated name. On rare occasions a sloop might be designed by one master shipwright and built by another. It is possible to find the names of master shipwrights, and even one Surveyor, as commercial contractors. The other feature that becomes evident is that the business of building warships is nepotistic and that succession is through dead men's shoes. Hence the conservative nature of British design and the importance of Anson in correcting this trend by appointing Slade and Bately as joint Surveyors in 1755.

NOTES

Names: Even in official sources spelling of ship names is inconsistent; in this book they are standardised to the most common or the modern form. Sloops which were bomb vessels, purchases or captures are noted as such after their names, but these terms are not treated as part of the name, although in the loose orthography of the time correspondence might refer to, for example, the *Salamander Bomb* or the *Mary Yacht*. However, note the habit of naming some prize ships after their captors, where —'s *Prize* is part of the formal name.

Number: The Royal Navy used its favourite names over and over, and for short-lived sloops this could mean up to seven vessels of the same name just within the period covered by this book. In the table following recurring names are given Roman numerals – I, II, III, etc – in their order of service and the same numbers are quoted after the ship names in the text where there might otherwise be some confusion about which ship is under discussion.

Type, rig: This shows the purpose of the vessel followed by its rig. For the brigantines of the 1690s, no rig is quoted since their sail plans varied considerably during their careers.

Guns: Complement is given as number of carriage guns + swivels. In the case of the *Merlin* class sloops of 1744–1748, the gun complement is the original 10; this was increased to 14 in 1748 for those sloops still in service. Although their immediate predecessors carried 14 carriage guns, they were only 4pdrs as opposed to the 6pdrs of the *Merlin* class, so the *Merlin*s had the heavier broadside.

Name	No	Guns	Burthen	Service Dates	Designer/Builder	Type, rig	Remarks
Advisor prize		8	–	1653–1655	Dutch	–	
Aldborough		10	100	1691–1696	Johnson†	Sloop, ketch	
Alderney bomb	I	6+8	262	1735–1742	Duke of Cumberland	Bomb, ketch	Built by Hayward
Alderney	II	10+12	235	1757–1783	Surveyor/Snook†	Sloop, ship	Bately design; laid down as snow
Badger		10+14	274	1745–1762	Surveyor/Janvrin†	Sloop, snow	Acworth design
Baltimore		14+14	251	1742–1762	Lord Baltimore/West†	Sloop, bilander	As bomb 1758–1759
Basilisk bomb	I	4	164	1695–1729	Surveyor/Redding†	Bomb, ketch	Dummer and master shipwrights
Basilisk bomb	II	8+12	271	1740–1750	Surveyor/Snelgrove†	Bomb, ketch	Acworth design
Basilisk bomb	III	8+14	312	1759–1762	Surveyor/Wells†	Bomb, ship	Slade design
Beaver prize	I	6	–	1656–1658	French	–	Ex-Royalist navy
Beaver prize	II	18+12	334	1756–1760	French	Sloop, ship	Ex-*La Trudaine*
Beaver		14+12	286	1761–1783	Surveyor/Inwood†	Sloop, ship	Bately design
Blackamoor		14	90	1656–1667	Taylor	Sloop, pink	Converted to fireship 1667
Blast bomb	I	4	143	1695–1724	Surveyor/Johnson†	Bomb, ketch	Dummer and master shipwrights
Blast bomb	II	8+12	271	1740–1745	Surveyor/West†	Bomb, ketch	Acworth design
Blast bomb	III	8+14	303	1759–1771	Surveyor/Bird†	Bomb, ketch	Slade design
Bonetta	I	4	57	1673–1687	Pett III	Sloop, Biscay	
Bonetta	II	2+4	66	1699–1712	Miller	Sloop, Biscay	Revenue service
Bonetta	III	4+4	66	1721–1731	Stacey	Sloop, snow	Revenue service
Bonetta	IV	8+12	201	1732–1744	Hayward	Sloop, snow	
Bonetta	V	10+12	228	1756–1776	Surveyor/Bird†	Sloop, snow	Slade design
Brilliant		6	60	1696–1698	French	Sloop, ship	Advice boat
Carcass bomb	I	4	143	1695–1713	Surveyor/Taylor†	Bomb, ketch	Dummer and master shipwrights
Carcass bomb	II	8+12	274	1740–1749	Surveyor/Taylor†	Bomb, ketch	Acworth design
Carcass bomb	III	8+14	309	1759–1784	Surveyor/Wells†	Bomb, ship	Slade design
Cat prize		8	–	1653–1656	Dutch	–	Ex-Dutch
Chatham		4	50	1673–1678	Pett II	Sloop, Biscay	
Chatham Double		4	50	1673 –1683	Pett II	Sloop, Biscay	
Chestnut		8	81	1656–1665	Tippetts	Sloop, pink	
Colchester		8	72	1664–1668	Allin†	Sloop, ketch	
Comet bomb	I	4	143	1695–1706	Surveyor/Johnson†	Bomb, ketch	Dummer and master shipwrights
Comet bomb	II	8+12	280	1742–1749	Surveyor/Taylor†	Bomb, ketch	Acworth design
Cormorant prize		18+14	405	1757–1762	French	Sloop, ship	Ex-*Le Machault*
Cruizer	I	8+4	100	1721–1732	Stacey	Sloop, snow	
Cruizer	II	8+12	200	1732–1745	Stacey	Sloop, snow	
Cruizer	III	8+10	141	1752–1776	Surveyor/Holland	Sloop, snow	Completed by Fellowes; ship rig 1753; Allin design
Cutter		2	46	1673–1673	Deane	Sloop, Biscay	
Cygnet		8	57	1657–1667	Taylor	Sloop, ketch	
Cygnet prize		18+12	386	1758–1768	French	Sloop, ship	Ex-*La Guirlande*
Delight		14	163	1709–1713	Stacey	Sloop, ship	Rated Sixth Rate; completed by Acworth
Deptford	I	–	–	1652–1653	–	–	Shallop
Deptford	II	10	89	1665–1689	Shish	Sloop, ketch	
Deptford's Prize		–	147	1740–1744	Spanish	–	Ex-privateer
Diligence	I	6+2	79	1693–1708	Harding	Brigantine	
Diligence	II	10+12	236	1756–1780	Surveyor/Wells†	Sloop, snow	Bately design
Discovery		6+2	75	1692–1705	Lawrence	Brigantine	
Dispatch	I	6+2	77	1692–1712	Harding	Brigantine	
Dispatch	II	10+14	269	1745–1773	Surveyor/Bartlett†	Sloop, snow	Acworth design
Dolphin		2	60	1673–1673	Shish	Sloop, Biscay	*Continued overleaf*

Name	No	Guns	Burthen	Service Dates	Designer/Builder	Type, rig	Remarks
Dolphin's Prize		12	147	1757–1760	French	Sloop, snow	Privateer ?Marquise de Cavalaire
Dove		4	19	1672 –1683	Shish	Sloop, Biscay	
Drake	I	14	176	1705–1728	Poulter/Allin Snr	Sloop brigantine	
Drake	II	8+12	207	1729–1740	Stacey	Sloop, snow	
Drake	III	10+12	202	1741–1742	Surveyor/West†	Sloop, snow	Contract-built to Acworth design
Drake	IV	14+14	249	1743–1748	Lord Baltimore/Buxton†	Sloop, snow	
Dreadful bomb		4	147	1695–1695	Surveyor/Graves†	Bomb, ketch	
Dreadnought's Prize		12+14	109	1747–1748	French	Sloop, brig	Ex-Le Genereux
Druid		10+12	208	1761–1773	Stacey/Barnard†	Sloop, snow	Design from 1732; later ship rig
Dunkirk prize		–	–	1656–1660	Spanish/Flemish	Sloop, ?Biscay	Ex-Spanish/Flemish
Eagle		10+8	153	1696–1703	Surveyor/Fugar† brigantine	Advice boat, design	Trans-ocean; probably Dummer
Eaglet	I	8	54	1655–1674	Pett/Higgins†	Sloop, ketch	
Eaglet	II	10	95	1691–1693	Shish†	Sloop, ketch	
Emsworth		4	39	1667–1683	Smith†	Sloop, ship	
Epreuve prize		14+10	262	1760–1764	French	Sloop, brig	Privateer L'Observateur taken into French navy and renamed Epreuve
Escorte prize		14+10	225	1757–1768	French	Sloop, ship	Ex-privateer Le Scott
Experiment		4	25	1677–1680	Lawrence Jnr	Brigantine	Listed as a sloop by Pepys
Express		4+6	77	1695–1713	Stigant	Advice boat, brigantine	
Falcon	I	10+14	272	1744–1770	Surveyor/Barnard†	Sloop, snow	Acworth design; French service 1745–1746, then renamed Fortune
Falcon	II	10+14	270	1745–1759	Surveyor/Alexander†	Sloop, snow	Bomb 1758
Favourite		16+14	313	1757–1784	Surveyor/Sparrow†	Sloop, ship	Slade design
Fan Fan		4	34	1666–1692	Deane	Sloop, ship	Listed as Sixth Rate/yacht
Ferret	I	10	128	1704–1706	Dummer†	Sloop brigantine	Contract–build by Ex-Surveyor
Ferret	II	10+4	115	1711–1718	Allin Snr	Sloop, one mast	?Snow rig by 1717
Ferret	III	4+4	67	1721–1731	Hayward	Sloop, snow	Revenue service
Ferret purchase	IV	14+14	256	1743–1757	Bird†	Sloop, snow	Purchased on stocks; ship rig 1755
Ferret	V	14+12	300	1760–1776	Surveyor/Stanton†	Sloop, ship	Slade design
Firedrake bomb	I	12+6	204	1688–1689	Harding	Bomb, ketch	
Firedrake bomb	II	12+6	279	1693–1703	Harding	Bomb, ship	
Firedrake bomb	III	8+12	283	1742–1763	Surveyor/Perry†	Bomb, ketch	Acworth design
Flamborough's Prize		10	115	1757–1763	French	–	Privateer Le General Lally
Fly	I	4+6	73	1694–1695	Stigant	Advice boat, brigantine	
Fly	II	6+2	71	1696–1712	Bagwell	Brigantine	
Fly	III	8+12	200	1732–1751	Ward	Sloop, snow	
Fly	IV	8+10	140	1752–1772	Lock	Sloop, ketch	
Fox		2+4	65	1699–1699	Shortiss	Sloop, Biscay	Revenue service
Furnace bomb	I	4	144	1695–1725	Surveyor/Wells†	Bomb, ketch	Dummer and master shipwrights
Furnace bomb	II	8+12	273	1740–1763	Surveyor/Quallett†	Bomb, ketch	Acworth design; ship rig 1742
Galgo prize		8+12	164	1742–1743	Spanish	–	Ex-privateer
Gibraltar's Prize		14	118	1757–1757	French		Ex-privateer Le Glaneur
Gramont prize		18+?14	324	1757–1762	French	Sloop, ship	Ex-privateer La Comptesse de Gramont
Grampus	I	6+10	160	1731–1742	Hayward	Sloop, snow	
Grampus	II	14+14	249	1743–1744	Surveyor/Perry†	Sloop, snow	Acworth design
Grampus	III	10+14	271	1745–1780	Surveyor/Reed†	Sloop, snow	Fireship 1762 and renamed Strombolo; probably Acworth design

Name	No	Guns	Burthen	Service Dates	Designer/Builder	Type, rig	Remarks
Granado bomb	I	12+6	279	1693–1694	Surveyor/Fowler†	Bomb, ship	Dummer and master shipwrights
Granado bomb	II	4	148	1695–1718	Surveyor/Castle†	Bomb, ketch	Dummer and master shipwrights
Granado bomb	III	8+12	270	1742–1763	Surveyor/Barnard†	Bomb, ketch	Acworth design
Happy	I	6	114	1711–1724–1735	Acworth	Sloop, one mast	Stacey rebuild 1724 with snow rig
Happy	II	8+10	141	1752–1766	Surveyor/E Allin†	Sloop, ketch	Allin Jnr design
Harp		10	94	1691–1693	Frame†	Sloop, ketch	
Hart	I	8	56	1658–1683	Pett	Sloop, ketch	
Hart	II	10	96	1691–1692	Rolfe and Castle†	Sloop, ketch	
Hawk	I	8+4	100	1721–1739	Rosewell	Sloop, snow	
Hawk	II	10+12	206	1741–1747	Surveyor/ Greville†	Sloop, snow	Acworth design
Hawk	III	8+10	225	1756–1781	Surveyor/Batson†	Sloop, ketch	Allin design. Ship rig 1767
Hawke		8	57	1655–1667	Pett /Cooper†	Sloop, ketch	
Hazard	I	6	114	1711–1714	Acworth	Sloop, one mast	
Hazard	II	10+14	273	1744–1749	Surveyor/Buxton†	Sloop, brigantine	Acworth design
Hazard	III	8+10	140	1749–1783	Slade/Lock	Sloop, snow	Revenue service
Hazard's Prize		8+12	101	1756–1759	French	–	Ex-privateer *Le Subtile*
Hind	I	8	56	1656–1667	Pett /Page†	Sloop, ketch	
Hind	II	10	96	1691–1697	Snelgrove†	Sloop, ketch	
Hind	III	12	161	1709–1709	Dummer†	Sloop, ship	Rated as Sixth Rate
Hind	IV	10+14	273	1744–1747	Allin Jnr/Perry†	Sloop, snow	
Hitchingbrooke		10+14	271	1745–1746	Surveyor/Janvrin†	Sloop, snow	Acworth design
Hornet		10+14	272	1745–1770	Surveyor/Quallett†	Sloop, snow	Acworth design
Horsleydown	I	–	–	1651–1652	–	–	–
Horsleydown	II	–	–	1653–1656	–	–	–
Hound	I	4	50	1673–1686	Pett II	Sloop, Biscay	
Hound	II	4+4	83	1700–1714	Miller	Sloop, Biscay	Revenue service
Hound	III	8+12	200	1732–1745	Surveyor/Stacey	Sloop, snow	Stacey-Acworth design
Hound	IV	10+14	267	1745–1773	Surveyor/Stow†	Sloop, snow	Acworth design
Hunter	I	4	46	1673–1683	Deane	Sloop, Biscay	
Hunter	II	10+12	238	1756 –1780	Slade/Stanton†	Sloop, snow	Pink stern; Slade design
Infernal bomb		8+14	298	1757–1774	Surveyor/Bird†	Bomb, ketch	Slade design
Invention		4	28	1673–1683	Deane	Sloop, Biscay	
Intelligence		6+2	75	1696–1700	Lawrence	Brigantine	
Jamaica	I	10+4	114	1710–1715	Allin Snr	Sloop, one mast	
Jamaica	II	10+14	273	1744–1770	Allin Jnr	Sloop, snow	
Jolly		10	168	1709–1714	Dummer†	Sloop, ship	Rated Sixth Rate
Kingfisher		10+14	275	1745–1763	Surveyor/Darley†	Sloop, snow	Acworth design; bomb 1758–1760
Kitchen bomb		8	100	1692–1698	Castle†	Bomb, ketch	Ex-smack-rigged yacht 1670
Lightning bomb		8+12	275	1740–1746	Surveyor/Bird†	Bomb, ketch	Acworth design
Lilly	I	6	64	1657–1667	Callis	Sloop, ketch	
Lilly	II	6	58	1672–1674	Shish	Sloop, Biscay	
Lively		12	126	1709–1712	Wicker†	Sloop, ship	Rated Sixth Rate
Lizard	I	4	39	1673–1674	Shish	Sloop, Biscay	
Lizard	II	10+14	272	1744–1748	Surveyor/Ewer†	Sloop, snow	Acworth design
Lynx		10 +12	216	1761–1777	Stacey/Stanton†	Sloop, snow	1732 design; ship rig later
Mediterranean prize		12	200	1756–1758	French xebec	–	–
Margate		14	163	1709–1712	Surveyor/Allin	Sloop, ship	Rated Sixth Rate
Martin	I	?10	99	1694–1702	Parker†	Sloop, ketch	
Martin	II	14+12	289	1761–1784	Surveyor/Randall†	Sloop, ship	Bately design

Continued overleaf

Name	No	Guns	Burthen	Service Dates	Designer/Builder	Type, rig	Remarks
Mercury		4+6	73	1694–1697	Stigant	Advice boat, brigantine	
Messenger		4+6	73	1694–1701	Waffe	Advice boat, brigantine	
Merlin	I	2+4	66	1699–1712	Furzer	Sloop, Biscay	Revenue service
Merlin	II	10+14	272	1744–1748	Surveyor/Greville†	Sloop, snow	Acworth design
Merlin	III	10+12	223	1756–1780	Surveyor/Quallett†	Sloop, snow	Slade design; renamed *Zephyr* 1757
Merlin	IV	18+14	304	1757–1777	Randall†	Sloop, ship	Purchased on the stocks
Mortar bomb	I	12+6	260	1693–1703	Surveyor/Lee	Bomb, ship	Dummer and master shipwrights
Mortar bomb	II	8+12	280	1743–1749	Surveyor/Perry†	Bomb, ketch	Acworth design
Mortar bomb	III	8+14	313	1759–1774	Surveyor/Wells†	Bomb, ketch	Slade design
Nautilus		16+14	317	1762–1780	Surveyor/Hodgson†	Sloop, ship	Slade design
Nonsuch		8	47	1654–1669	Page†	Sloop, ketch	Sold to Hudson's Bay Company
Otter	I	4+4	83	1700–1702	Miller	Sloop, Biscay	Revenue service; packet 1702
Otter	II	14	167	1709–1713	Surveyor/Smith†	Sloop, ship	Rated Sixth Rate
Otter	III	6+4	91	1721–1742	Stacey	Sloop, snow	
Otter	IV	14+14	247	1742–1763	Surveyor/Buxton†	Sloop, snow	Acworth
Paramour		10	89	1694–1706	Harding	Sloop, pink	Bomb ketch 1702
Peggy		8+10	141	1749–1770	Surveyor/Holland	Sloop, snow	Allin design; Revenue service
Parrot		6	60	1657–1657	Taylor	Sloop, ketch	
Pembroke's Prize		8+12	196	1740–1744	Spanish	–	Ex-armed merchantman
Peregrine prize		8+12	163	1742–1743	Spanish	–	Ex-privateer
Pheasant prize		14+10	292	1761–1761	French	Sloop, ship	Ex-*La Tourterelle*
Pomona prize		18+12	364	1761–1776	French	Sloop, ship	Ex-privateer *Le Chevert*
Porcupine		16+14	314	1746–1763	Taylor and Randall†	Sloop, ship	Purchased on the stocks
Portsmouth prize		4	–	1655–1655	Spanish/Flemish	–	Ex-French prize; retaken by them
Portsmouth	I	10/6	90	1667–1673	Tippetts	Sloop, ketch	Pink (3 masts) 1669
Portsmouth	II	4	42	1667–1672	Tippetts	Sloop, ship	
Portsmouth bomb		Various	143	1689–1703	Pett/Harding	Bomb, ketch	Ex-yacht built 1674
Post Boy	I	4+6	73	1694–1695	Waffe	Advice boat, brigantine	
Post Boy	II	4+6	77	1695–1695	Stigant	Advice boat, brigantine	
Post Boy	III	4+6	76	1696–1702	Harding	Brigantine	
Postillion prize		18+14	365	1757–1763	French	Sloop, ship	Ex-privateer *Le Duc d'Aiguillon*
Prevention		4	46	1672–1683	Deane	Sloop, Biscay	
Prohibition		2+4	69	1699–1702	Harding	Sloop, Biscay	Revenue service
Racehorse prize		18+14	386	1757–1778	French	Sloop, ship	Ex-*Le Marquis de Vaudreuil*
Ranger		8+10	142	1752–1783	Lock/Slade/Hayes	Sloop, snow	
Raven		10+14	273	1745–1763	Surveyor/Blaydes†	Sloop, snow	Acworth design; ship rig 1753
Red Hart prize		6	–	1653–1654	Dutch	Sloop, pink	Dutch prize
Red Horse prize		10	–	1655–1658	Spanish/Flemish	–	
Roe	I	8	56	1656–1670	Pett/Page†	Sloop, ketch	'Made a kitchen' 1661
Roe	II	8	91	1664–1670	Page†	Sloop, ketch	
Roe	III	10	92	1691–1697	Hayden†	Sloop, ketch	
Rose		6	56	1657–1661	Pett	Sloop, ketch	Given to Irish packet service
Rupert's Prize		8+12	142	1741–1743	Spanish	–	
Saint John prize		4	71	1695–1696	French	Sloop, Biscay	Advice boat
Saint Joseph prize		8	–	1696–1699	French	Sloop, Biscay	Advice boat
Salamander bomb	I	10	134	1687–1703–1713	Lee	Bomb, ketch	Rebuilt 1703

Name	No	Guns	Burthen	Service Dates	Designer/Builder	Type, rig	Remarks
Salamander bomb	II	6+8	265	1730–1744	Surveyor/Hayward	Bomb, ketch	
Saltash	I	8+12	200	1732–1741	Pierson Lock	Sloop, snow	
Saltash purchase	II	8+12	221	1741–1742	Bird†	Sloop, snow	Purchased in frame
Saltash	III	14+14	249	1742–1746	Lord Baltimore/Quallett†	Sloop, snow	
Saltash	IV	10+14	270	1746–1763	Surveyor/Quallett†	Sloop, snow	Acworth design
San Antonio prize		4	67	1700–1707	Pirate ship	Sloop, one mast	Service in Caribbean only
Sapphire's Prize		10+10	164	1745–1745	Spanish	Sloop, snow	
Sardoine prize		14+10	256	1751–1768	French	Sloop, ship	Ex-*La Sardoine*
Savage		8+10	144	1750–1776	Surveyor/Lock	Sloop, snow	?Allin design; Revenue service
Saxon prize		16+14	–	1746–1748	French	Sloop, ship	Ex-*La Saxonne* ?corvette
Scarborough		10	94	1691–1693	Frame†	Sloop, ketch	
Scorpion		10+14	276	1745–1762	Surveyor/Wyatt†	Sloop, snow	
Scout Boat		4	38	1695–1703	Stigant	Advice boat, brigantine	
Seahorse		14	162	1709–1711	Surveyor/Yeames†	Sloop, ship	Rated Sixth Rate
Senegal		14+12	292	1760–1780	Surveyor/Bird†	Sloop, ship	Bately design
Serpent bomb	I	12+6	260	1693–1694	Surveyor/Lee	Bomb, ship	Dummer and master shipwrights
Serpent bomb	II	4	140	1695–1703	Surveyor/Lee	Bomb, ketch	Dummer and master shipwrights
Serpent bomb	III	8+12	275	1742–1748	Surveyor/Snelgrove†	Bomb, ketch	Acworth design
Shoreham's Prize		10+18	–	1746–1747	Spanish	Sloop, snow	
Shark	I	6+2	58	1691–1698	Dummer/Harding	Brigantine	Prototype
Shark	II	2+4	66	1699–1709	Miller	Sloop, Biscay	Revenue service
Shark	III	10+4	114	1711–1722–1732	Allin Snr	Sloop, one mast	Stacey rebuild and snow rig 1722
Shark	IV	8+12	201	1732–1755	Allin Jnr	Sloop, ketch	She was rigged as a snow when taken
Sparrow prize		16	–	1653–1659	Dutch	Sloop, pink	
Speedwell	I	10+14	271	1744–1750	Surveyor/Buxton†	Sloop, ?ketch	Acworth design; rig may have been snow
Speedwell	II	8+10	142	1752–1780	Surveyor/Ward/Slade	Sloop, ketch	Allin design; fireship 1770 and renamed *Spitfire*
Spence	I	8+4	114	1723–1730	Stacey	Sloop, snow	
Spence	II	8+12	207	1730–1748	Stacey	Sloop, snow	
Spy	I	4	28	1666–1683	Deane	Sloop, ship	
Spy	II	6+2	78	1693–1706	Lawrence	Brigantine	
Spy	III	4+8	103	1721–1731	Naish	Sloop, snow	
Spy	IV	8+12	201	1732–1745	Rosewell	Sloop, snow	
Spy	V	10+12	223	1756–1773	Surveyor/Inwood†	Sloop, snow	Slade design
Stork		10 +12	233	1756–1758	Surveyor/Stow Bartlett†	Sloop, ship	Bately design; laid down as snow
Swallow	I	6	56	1657–1661	Callis	Sloop, ketch	Given to Irish packet service
Swallow	II	2	68	1672–1673	Shish	Sloop, Biscay	
Swallow	III	2+4	66	1699–1703	Furzer	Sloop, Biscay	Revenue service
Swallow	IV	10+14	272	1744–1744	Surveyor /Buxton†	Sloop, snow	Acworth design
Swallow	V	10+14	278	1745–1769	Surveyor/Bird†	Sloop, snow	Acworth design; ship rig 1755
Swan	I	14	163	1709–1712	Dummer†	Sloop, ship	Rated Sixth Rate; probably Dummer design
Swan	II	10+14	280	1745–1763	Surveyor/Hinks†	Sloop, snow	Acworth design; ship rig 1755
Swift	I	6+2	80	1695–1696	Lee	Brigantine	
Swift	II	10+8	155	1697–1698	Surveyor/Moore†	Advice boat, brigantine	Trans–ocean contract
Swift	III	2+4	66	1699–1702	Waffe	Sloop, Biscay	Revenue service

Continued overleaf

Name	No	Guns	Burthen	Service Dates	Designer/Builder	Type, rig	Remarks
Swift	IV	10	123	1704–1719	Lee	Sloop, snow, later brigantine rig	
Swift	V	6+4	93	1721–1741	Hayward	Sloop, brigantine	
Swift	VI	10+12	204	1741–1756	Surveyor/Carter†	Sloop, snow	Acworth design
Swift	VII	14+12	271	1763–1770	Surveyor/Greaves†	Sloop, ship	Slade design
Talbot		10	94	1691–1694	Taylor†	Sloop, pink	
Tamar		16+14	313	1758–1780	Surveyor/Snooks†	Sloop, ship	Slade design
Tartan prize		4+6	49	1692–1693	French	Advice boat, Biscay	
Tavistock		10+14	269	1745–1763	Surveyor/Darley†	Sloop, snow	Acworth design; renamed *Albany* 1747
Terror bomb	I	4	149	1696–1704	Surveyor/Davis†	Bomb, ketch	Dummer and master shipwrights
Terror bomb	II	8+12	278	1742–1754	Surveyor/Greville†	Bomb, ketch	Acworth design
Terror bomb	III	8+14	302	1759–1774	Surveyor/Barnard†	Bomb, ship	Slade design
Terrible bomb		6+8	263	1730–1749	Surveyor/Stacey	Bomb, ketch	Probably Stacey design
Thunder bomb	I	4	147	1695–1696	Surveyor/Snelgrove†	Bomb, ketch	Dummer and master shipwrights
Thunder bomb	II	6+6	254	1718–1734	Spanish prize	–	–
Thunder bomb	III	8+12	272	1740–1744	Surveyor/E Bird†	Bomb, ketch	Acworth design
Thunder bomb	IV	8+14	302	1759–1774	Surveyor/Henniker†	Bomb, ketch	Slade design
Trial	I	10+4	115	1710–1719–1731	Allin Snr	Sloop, one mast	Rebuilt with snow/schooner rig 1719
Trial	II	8+12	200	1732–1741	Stacey	Sloop, snow	Possible input from Acworth
Trial	III	10+14	272	1744–1776	Allin Jnr	Sloop, snow	
Triumph prize		18	–	1739–1740	Spanish	–	
Tulip		2	22	1672–1673	Shish	Sloop, Biscay	
Viper	I	10+14	271	1746–1762	Surveyor/Durrel†	Sloop, snow	Acworth design; fireship 1755 and renamed *Lightning*
Viper	II	10+12	228	1756–1779	Surveyor/West†	Sloop, snow	Slade design
Vulture	I	4	68	1673–1686#	Shish	Sloop, Biscay	May have been lost in 1678#
Vulture	II	10+14	267	1744–1761	Allin Jnr/Greaves†	Sloop, snow	
Vulture	III	14+12	269	1763–1771	Surveyor/Davis & Bird†	Sloop, ship	Slade design
Wasp		8+10	140	1749–1781	Lock	Sloop, snow	Revenue service
Weazle	I	10	128	1704–1712	Dummer†	Sloop, ?brigantine	Dummer ex-Surveyor
Weazle	II	8+4	102	1721–1732	Hayward	Sloop, snow	
Weazle	III	16+14	308	1745–1779	Taylor and Randall†	Sloop, ship	Purchased on stocks
Whipster		4	64	1672–1683	Shish	Brigantine	
Wivenhoe		8/6	100	1665–1683	Page†	Sloop, ketch	Pink 1669; fireship 1673
Wolf	I	2+4	66	1699–1712	Waffe	Sloop, Biscay	Revenue service
Wolf	II	8+12	244	1731–1741	Stacey	Sloop, snow	
Wolf	III	14+14	246	1742–1748	Surveyor/West†	Sloop, snow	Acworth design
Wolf	IV	8+10	141	1754–1781	Surveyor/Hayes	Sloop, snow	Allin design
Woolwich		4	57	1673–1675	Pett III	Sloop, Biscay	
Wren prize	I	12	–	1653–1657	Dutch	Sloop, pink	
Wren	II	?10	105	1695–1697	Stigant†	Sloop, pink	

Notes

\# Sold by Admiralty Order in 1686 but there is evidence that the crew of *Vulture* petitioned the Navy Board for their losses in a hurricane in 1678.

Appendix 2

A Selection of Mast and Spar Dimensions

Measurements to the nearest ¼ inch

Within the category of sloop, the earliest table of mast and spar dimensions is for the brigantine *Shark* of 1691 (although there is one for the earlier ketch *Deptford*). As her building drew to a close, her constructor Fisher Harding gave his recommendations for dimensions, which were for a galley rig. This rig comprised two short masts with lateen spars on them. It is most unlikely that she was ever so equipped since not only did Harding propose that a two-masted Bermudian rig would be more handy but, from the logs of other brigantines of this period, it is known that they were equipped with lug and square sails. Thus the rigs of the brigantines are largely a matter of speculation, since no definitive records are available as to their spar dimensions as fitted. But there are records for sloops built at the end of this decade and from then on tables are available for most of the groups.

However, one warning is necessary. The rigs of many of the two-masted sloops throughout the period covered by this book, be they ketch, snow or brigantine, were open to adjustment, alteration and conversion, a fact that anyone wishing to make a drawing, painting or model of a particular sloop needs to consider. The majority of tables given below are for individual vessels but their rigging dimensions can be applied to others in their group. However, the example of *Hazard*, a *Merlin* class sloop of the 1740s, is salutary – unlike her sisters, who were in the main snow-rigged, she was set up with brigantine rig. So to rig a sloop accurately, proceed with caution with an eye for the date to be represented!

There are reference books to assist in developing a masting and rigging plan, in particular Steele's *Rigging and Seamanship* and Lees' *The Masting and Rigging of English Ships of War 1625–1860*, but with sloops, which were unrated, the tables these volumes lay down are perforce general and for exact details a visit to the National Archives at Kew or the National Maritime Museum at Greenwich will be necessary.

Beginning with the two-masted snow rig, the first example comes from the sloops that were launched in 1699 to watch the coast for the illegal movement of untaxed goods. They were small and lightly armed.

Table A2-1: PROHIBITION 66-ton sloop 1699. LGD – 58ft 9in; Breadth – 16ft 4in

	MASTS		SPARS	
	Length (Feet – Inches)	Diameter (Inches)	Length (Feet – Inches)	Diameter (Inches)
Main	48	12½	41	10¼
Top	26	6¾	22	5¾
Topgallant	10	3	11	2¾
Fore	44	10½	12	9
Top	23	5½	20	5
Bowsprit	29 – 5	10	8 (spritsail)	6

Reference: The National Archives (hereafter TNA) Adm 106/3292, Deptford Yard letter books, August 1699.

The only slightly questionable feature here is the surprising breadth of the main course. At 41ft it is 2.5 x the vessel's beam, when just over 2.0 would be more normal. Note the early inclusion of a topgallant sail. It is no wonder that captains of these small sloops were continually having difficulty with their sloops being over-canvassed and being liable to capsize if hit by a sudden squall. Two larger sloops were built as part of this programme and it is worth comparing their mast and spar dimensions (Table A2-2) and noting that, apart from the four sloops of 1666, at this early stage and unlike the large programme of sloops built in 1672–1673 which had two masts, these two sloops had ship rig. By the time the surviving smaller sloops of this programme had retired some had mizzen masts.

When *Hound* was sold in 1714 amongst the spars listed were studding sail booms and a flying jib boom (at this time a term that meant a jib boom set 'flying' – not permanently – rather than the extra spar beyond the jib boom as used in the later eighteenth century). In her sail wardrobe were included a main staysail, a main top staysail and a mizzen staysail.

Unfortunately there are no dimensions available for the four sloops built in 1704, but there is a sail inventory for *Ferret*, *Weazle* and *Swift* (Table A2-3). It is clear that although of far greater burthen than the earlier sloops they were all two-masted and had an option of setting square or fore-and-

Table A2-2: HOUND and OTTER 83-ton sloops 1700. LGD – 61ft 1in; Breadth – 17ft 8in

	MASTS		SPARS	
	Length (Feet – Inches)	Diameter (Inches)	Length (Feet – Inches)	Diameter (Inches)
Main	47 – 3	12	36	9
Top	26	6¾	22 – 6	5¾
Topgallant	10	3	11	2¾
Fore	41 – 6	10½	31 – 5	7½
Top	23	5½	20	5
Topgallant	8 – 6	2¾	8 – 6	2½
Mizzen	12	8	10	5
Top	12	3	10	2½
Bowsprit	25 – 8	10½ by calculation	22 (spritsail)	6
Cro'jack	–	–	20	3

Reference: TNA Adm 106/3292, Deptford Yard letter books, April 1700.

aft canvas on the mainmast. A reading of their logs reveals that on occasion they left their lug (not mentioned in the inventory) and bilander sails and yards ashore. This was done particularly in the winter months. In addition to the inventory listed it is known that they also carried a lug main topsail, presumably for use with the lug or bilander main course.

Table A2-3: Sail inventory for FERRET, WEAZLE and SWIFT 1704

Bowsprit	Foremast	Mainmast
Spritsail course – 1	Course – 2	Course – 1
Flying jib – 1	Topsail – 2	Topsail – 1
–	Staysail – 1	Staysail – 1
–	Studding sail – 1	Top staysail – 1
–	Top studding sail – 1	Bilander – 1
–	–	Top bilander – 1
–	–	Wing sail – 1
–	–	Studding sail – 1
–	–	Top studding sail – 1

Reference: TNA Adm 106/594, Navy Board In Letters, Miscellaneous. W (July– December 1704).

Eight Sixth Rates (in effect three-masted sloops; Table A2-4) were built in 1709. All apart from *Lively* had similar dimensions, with a LGD of 76ft 0½in–78ft 4in, a beam of 21ft 10in–22ft 6in and burthen of 160–168 tons.

The sloops of 1710–1711 were all single-masted with a long pole mast (Table A2-5). From the deck it rose up for 78ft, that is 13½ft longer than the sloop's length on the gun deck. It probably had crosstrees to stiffen it above the gaff jaws. By 1715 the mast had been shortened and a fidded topmast added. On commissioning these craft had a long one-piece bowsprit, though they may well have had a jib boom later to take a flying jib as these were already in

Table A2-4: HIND 161-ton small Sixth Rate 1709. LDG – 78ft 4in; Breadth – 21ft 10in

	MASTS		SPARS	
	Length (Feet – Inches)	Diameter (Inches)	Length (Feet – Inches)	Diameter (Inches)
Main	53 – 6	15¼	49	12
Top	32	8¼	30 – 6	7
Topgallant	13 – 6	4	15 – 4	3½
Fore	48	14	43	10½
Top	29	7½	24 – 6	5½
Topgallant	12	3¼	12 – 3	3
Mizzen	47 – 8	10½	46 (lateen)	7½
Top	17 – 8	4¼	16 – 9	3½
Bowsprit	35 – 6	14¼	33	7¼
Top[1]	9 – 8	3¼	16 – 6	3¼
Cro'jack	–	–	32	5½

Reference: TNA Adm 106/3295, Deptford Yard letter books, 6 June 1709.
1 These small ships carried a sprit topmast, an upright small mast at the outer end of their bowsprit. This was most unusual in such small vessels.

service, see above. The bowsprit was just over two-thirds the length of the hull and the main boom was only 10ft shorter than the deck. The fore and aft main course must have been enormous and it is not surprising that these sloops were converted to two-masted rig at the earliest convenient opportunity.

Table A2-5: TRIAL 115-ton sloop 1710. LGD – 64ft 6in; Breadth – 20ft 8in

Dimensions as originally proposed

	MASTS		SPARS	
	Length (Feet – Inches)	Diameter (Inches)	Length (Feet – Inches)	Diameter (Inches)
Main	78, 67 to the shrouds	19	–	–
Boom	–	–	54	11
Gaff	–	–	16 – 6	5¼
Cro'jack	–	–	38	8
Top	–	–	25	4
Bowsprit	44 – 6	14¾	–	–
Sprit Yard	–	–	25	4

Reference: TNA Adm 106/3295, Deptford Yard letter books, 10 August 1710.

Table A2-6 illustrates the change in *Trial*'s rig and shows that sloop rigs were continually being adjusted. She was rebuilt to new dimensions in 1719 (LGD – 76ft; breadth – 21ft 3in) and given two masts. However, the rig on these masts was also to change (1731 dimensions in brackets).

Several sloops were ordered once again in peacetime for revenue duties. There were three groups (two are shown in Table A2-7), each of different tonnage but with similar rig to different dimensions.

Table A2-6: TRIAL 1719 (1733)

	MASTS		SPARS	
	Length (Feet – Inches)	Diameter (Inches)	Length (Feet – Inches)	Diameter (Inches)
Main	70 – 6 (71 – 10)	17½ (18)	49 – 6 (44 – 6)	10½ (10¼)
Top	29 – 6 (30 – 6)	7½ (9½)	25 – 6 (30 – 6)	5½ (6¾)
Topgallant	– (19 – 6)	– (6)	– (22)	– (4)
Fore	51 (55 – 2)	16½ (17½)	44 – 6 (35 – 6)	10½ (8¼)
Top[1]	29 – 6 (20)	9½ (7½)	35 (26)	7½ (6)
Topgallant	15 – 6 (15 – 6)	4½ (5)	21 (19 – 6)	4½ (4)
Main boom	–	–	49 – 6 (50 – 6)	10½ (11¼)
Cro'jack	–	–	35 (–)	7½ (–)
Gaff	–	–	20 (20)	6½ (6)
Jib Boom	– (25 – 6)	– (NYK)	–	–
Bowsprit	33 – 6 (32 – 4)	15 (15)	28 (22)	5½ (4)

Reference: TNA Adm 106/3302 Deptford Yard letter books, 24 June 1731. Retrospective survey.

1 The figure given in brackets for the fore topmast seems unusual, 24–28ft would have been more likely, but this was what was listed officially.

Table A2-7: BONETTA 66-ton sloop 1721.
LGD – 55ft 2in; Breadth – 17ft
CRUIZER 100-ton sloop 1721. LGD – 62ft 0in;
Breadth – 19ft 10in (figures in brackets)

	MASTS[1]		SPARS	
	Length (Feet – Inches)	Diameter (Inches)[2]	Length (Feet – Inches)	Diameter (Inches)
Main	51 – 6 (59 – 6)	– (15½)	36 – 5 (42 – 6)	– (9½)
Top	25 – 6 (29 – 9)	– (9)	27 – 3 (31 – 10½)	– (8)
Fore	45 – 9 (53 – 6½)	– (14)	30 – 5 (35 – 5)	– (8)
Top	21 – 3 (24 – 9½)	– (8¼)	22 – 8 (26 – 6¾)	– (6¾)
Bowsprit	29 – 9 (34 – 8½)	– (13)	22 – 8 (26 – 6¾)	– (6¾)

Reference: TNA Adm 106/3299, Deptford Yard letter books, 21 September 1721 (Cruizer). Bonetta dimensions calculated proportionately from those of Cruizer.

1 These dimensions are for snow rig but with the absence of a gaff spar for the wing sail that would normally be set abaft the main mast. There is a rule (see below) that would allow the calculation for a gaff here.

2 No mast and spar diameters were recorded for Bonetta in the letter books.

From an examination of Otter's sail inventory (a sloop of 90 tons and of similar design) it seems probable that both these sloops would also have been equipped with a jib boom and a gaff-headed wing sail not listed here. Before she retired Cruizer was re-rigged as a ketch. One of her sister sloops, Spy, was at some point in her life rigged as a brigantine and in some cases sloops carried an optional fore-and-aft main course in addition to their square course, which could be either a lug, bilander or a gaff-headed sail with or without boom. The use of these sails would in effect change them from a snow rig to that of a brigantine.

At the end of the 1720s there was a large increase in the size of sloops, with the launching of Drake, Spence, Wolf and Grampus. Drake and Spence were almost identical and both were designed and built by Richard Stacey. Wolf (also built by Stacey) was somewhat larger and Grampus smaller.

Table A2-8: DRAKE 207-ton sloop 1729.
LGD – 87ft; Breadth – 23ft 2in
WOLF 244-ton sloop 1731.
LGD – 87ft; Breadth – 25ft

A record of mast and spar dimensions as commissioned in 1729/1731 (Wolf in brackets)

	MASTS		SPARS	
	Length (Feet – Inches)	Diameter (Inches)	Length (Feet – Inches)	Diameter (Inches)
Main	63 (66)	16¾	42 (49 – 7)	10½
Top	28 – 6 (32 – 6)	9½	28 (34 – 7)	7
Topgallant	9 (polehead) (13 – 6)[1]	N/A	16 (18 – 6)	3½
Fore	50 – 6 (55 – 9)	14	42 (47 – 4)	10½
Top	28 – 6 (31)	9½	28 (35)	7
Topgallant	9 (polehead) (13 – 6)[1]	N/A	16 (?21)	3½
Gaff	–	–	16 (19)	6
Jib Boom	21 (25)	7	–	–
Bowsprit	34 (36)	15	28 (32 – 10)	7

References: TNA Adm 106/3470, Deptford Yard letter books, 6 December 1734 (Drake). Wolf's mast and spar dimensions calculated from her sail dimensions and proportioned to similar sloops.

1 A polehead topmast includes the topgallant section listed here. Crosstrees might be set at the foot of the topgallant section in order to brace it. There is illustrative evidence which shows this custom on earlier vessels. The sail dimensions for Drake and possibly Spence are in Table A2-9 together with those for Wolf in brackets.

The studding sail booms will be 0.55 x the length of the lower yard that carries them and 0.5 x the length of the topsail yard that carries them (see Table A2-16).

The dimensions of the masts and spars of these two sloops can be related to the dimensions of their canvas.

This rig and sail plan would be reasonable, though not exact, for most of the sloops of around 200 tons built between 1729 and 1740. Notable exceptions in this period were Wolf at 244 tons and Grampus at 160 tons; proportional calculations will be required for the latter (see below). Wolf was the same length as Drake but with 2ft extra beam – and breadth was the starting measurement for all mast and spar length calculations at this time. To reflect this, her sail dimensions are in brackets in Table A2-9. Note that no fore topgallant dimensions are given but she may well have had one. The other exception is Shark of 1732, which was ketch-rigged initially (although a sailing quality report of 1748 gives her a snow rig). Booms for enlarged gaff-headed wing sails may have been added during their careers but were definitely not in the mind of Richard Stacey at the time of launch.

Table A2-9: DRAKE 207-ton sloop 1729. LGD – 87ft; Breadth – 23ft 2in WOLF 244-ton sloop 1731. LGD – 87ft; Breadth – 25ft

Sail dimensions as commissioned in 1729 and 1731 (*Wolf* in brackets)

SAIL	*Head (in cloths)*	*Foot (in cloths)*	*Depth (in feet)*
Spritsail Course	14 (15)	14 (15)	10½ (12)
Fore Course	22 (22)	22 (22)	28½ (28½)
Fore Top[1]	12½ (14)	20½ (21)	27 (31½)
Fore Topgallant	8 (–)	12 (–)	9 (–)
Main Course	20 (23)	24 (27)	36 (37½)
Main Top[1]	12½ (14)	20½ (22)	27 (31½)
Main Topgallant	8 (8½)	12 (13½)	9 (13½)
Wing (Gaff-Headed)	8 (10)	17 (18)	37½ luff, 45 leech (36 luff, 45 leech)
Fore Top Staysail	–	13 (13)	33 (33)
Main Staysail	–	14 (16)	33 (34½)
Main Top Staysail	–	15 (16)	39 (39)
Main Studding Sail	6 (8)	10 (8)	39 (43½)
Main Top Studding Sail	4½ (5)	9½ (10)	30 (33)
Flying Jib	–	14 (14 and 13)	42 (52 and 36)

References: TNA Adm 106/3470, Clerk of the Survey out, 24 May 1731 and 5 January 1732

1 Note that the fore and main topsails are identical; the same applies to their spars.

Cloths for these small craft would have had a breadth (seamed or tabled) of 24in. Allowing for the overlap in sewing cloths, together with Steele's recommended 2in slack per yard, a measurement of 22in per cloth would be a fair assumption. As an example here, *Drake*'s main course spar is 42ft. The main course has 20 cloths along its head = 36ft 8in. This allows yardarms of 2ft 8in each side to manage the reefing pennants. Unlike many courses, whose luff/leeches were perpendicular, this one has a foot of 44ft, exceeding its head of 36ft 8in, making the sail broader at the reef band than at the head. It therefore requires a length of yardarm to allow reefing.

Assuming *Wolf* has a fore topgallant sail equivalent to *Drake*'s, the heights of foremast and mainmast canvas on each sloop would be 64ft 6in and 72ft for *Drake* and 69ft 6in and 82ft 6in for *Wolf*. This extra allowance for *Wolf* is a response to her greater beam in that she would have had an inherently more stable form than *Drake*.

In 1732 the Admiralty asked their master shipwrights to specify what they considered to be the ideal sloop dimensions. Arguably, *Cruizer*, designed and built by Stacey was to be the iconic sloop of this period and *Trial*, very similar to *Cruizer* but possibly to lines by the Surveyor Acworth, and again built by Stacey, was to be the one to achieve the greatest fame by her passage of Cape Horn in 1741 as part of Anson's squadron.

Table A2-10: CRUIZER and TRIAL 200-ton sloops 1732. LGD – 84ft; Breadth – 23ft

Mast and spar dimensions (where *Trial* differs from *Cruizer*, dimensions are in brackets)

	MASTS[1]		*SPARS*	
	Length (Feet – Inches)	*Diameter (Inches)*	*Length (Feet – Inches)*	*Diameter (Inches)*
Main[2]	57 + 9 head (56 – 6 + 9 head)	16¾ (17)	48 – 6	11
Top[3]	32 – 6	10	32 – 6	6¾
Topgallant	13 – 6 (polehead)[4]	N/A	18	3¾
Fore	45 – 3 + 9 head (45 + 9 head)	13½	46 – 6	10½
Top[3]	32 – 6	10	32 – 6	6¾
Topgallant	12 – 6 (polehead)[4]	N/A	17	3½
Gaff	–	–	19	5¾
Jib Boom	25 (21)	7½ (7)	–	–
Bowsprit	36	16	32 – 6[3]	6¾

Reference: TNA Adm 106/3302, Deptford Yard letter books, October 1732.

1 Apart from *Shark*, which was ketch-rigged, the other sloops in this class, all built to the same specification, had mast and spar dimensions that differed little from one another.

2 In this table the main is given two dimensions which reveal the length of the head of the mast from where the main shrouds are attached to it, to the mast cap. This provides a useful proportion for applying to dimensions where this detail is not given.

3 Note the identical dimensions for certain spars; this allowed a degree of interchangeability.

4 The polehead here is in effect an extension of the topmast.

The National Maritime Museum has plans and a model of a sloop of 1741 (see Fig 13-9) when three were built to the same specification at just over 200 tons. It is likely that they were designed by the Surveyor Acworth though they bear a

Table A2-11: DRAKE, HAWK and SWIFT 204-ton sloops 1741. LGD – 84ft 6in; Breadth – 23ft 6in

	MASTS		*SPARS*	
	Length (Feet – Inches)	*Diameter (Inches)*	*Length (Feet – Inches)*	*Diameter (Inches)*
Main	65 – 6 (61 – 6)	18½	49	10¾
Top[1]	36 (33)	10	32 – 8	7
Topgallant	13	5	23	4¼
Fore	55 – 6 (54)	16¼	48	10¾
Top[1]	36	10	32 – 8	7
Topgallant	12	4¾	22 – 6	4
Gaff	–	–	21	7¾
Jib Boom	28 – 4	7¾	–	–
Bowsprit	36	16	–	–

Reference: TNA Adm 106/3553, Sheerness Yard letter books, 19 October 1744.

1 Unlike the topgallant masts for *Cruizer* and *Tryall*, which are polehead masts, these are both fidded and this may account for the extra 3ft 6in length in the topmasts. Note that main and fore mast and spar dimensions are identical.

strong likeness to *Cruizer* by Stacey. The mast and spar dimensions for this model are at Table A2-11. However, in 1744 one of the three, *Hawk*, had her masting adjusted. Those figures are in brackets where applicable.

Next to be considered are two larger groups of sloops at about 250 tons. This was a stage on the way to the *Merlin* class sloops, which by 1744 had reached over 270 tons. Each group contained three sloops of varying, albeit close, dimensions. The vessels ranged from 244 to 251 tons. *Baltimore* was the largest at 251 tons. A lengthy and unusual but interesting vessel, she is the example of this intermediate stage. She had been designed by an amateur, Lord Baltimore, probably heavily assisted by the Surveyor, had a pink stern and had a bilander rig. She was converted into a bomb vessel in 1758 with one 13in mortar.

Table A2-12: BALTIMORE 251-ton sloop 1742. LDG – 89ft; Breadth – 25ft 3¼in

| | MASTS | | SPARS | |
	Length (Feet – Inches)	Diameter (Inches)	Length (Feet – Inches)	Diameter (Inches)
Main	76 – 5	19	44 – 6 cro'jack	10½
			55 – 2 lug yard	
Top	37 – 6	11	36 – 9	9
Fore	61 – 3	16	47 – 2	11½
Top	37 – 6	11	36 – 9	9
Topgallant	19	4½	26 – 7	4
Jib Boom	33 – 6	–	–	–
Bowsprit	48 – 2	17½	–	–

Reference: TNA Adm 106/3305, Deptford Yard letter books, 9 November 1742.

The *Merlin* class sloops were developed out of two small preliminary groups, one designed by the Surveyor Acworth and one by the man who was to become joint Surveyor in 1745, Joseph Allin. Acworth's group was extended into the mighty *Merlin* class of 270-ton sloops, which in the main were snow-rigged and varied in size between 268 and 272 tons as completed. Table A2-13 gives the mast and spar dimensions for a 272-ton sloop with figures for a 268-ton sloop in brackets.

Table A2-14 gives the sail dimensions of *Falcon*, which was renamed *Fortune* following her recapture from the French after a short period in their service, by which time she had been replaced in the Royal Navy by another *Falcon*. She was built to the same specification as *Lizard* so her sail plan would have been close to that of her sister. However, with the inevitable changes in masting and rigging to sloops some minor alterations may be necessary: for example, here the cloths at the head of the wing sail appear to make it longer than the gaff to which it is attached.

Table A2-13: LIZARD *Merlin* class sloop 272 tons 1744. LGD – 91ft 3in; Breadth – 26ft 2in

| | MASTS | | SPARS | |
	Length (Feet – Inches)	Diameter (Inches)	Length (Feet – Inches)	Diameter (Inches)
Main	68 – 1	19	51 – 4	11¾
Top[1]	39 – 6	11	33 – 11 (34)	7
Topgallant[1]	16 – 7	5½	24	4¾
Fore	56 – 2	16	49 – 3	11½
Top[1]	39 – 6	11	33 – 11 (34)	7
Topgallant[1]	16 – 7	5½	23 – 5	4¾
Gaff	–	–	20	4
Jib Boom	27	8¼ (8½)	–	–
Bowsprit[1]	39 – 6	16	33 – 11	7

Reference: National Maritime Museum POR/A, Portsmouth Yard, Navy Board Warrants, 31 August 1744.

1 Note the similarity in dimensions.

The studding sail booms will be 0.55 x the length of the lower yard that carries them and 0.5 x the length of the topsail yard that carries them (see Table A2-16).

Table A2-14: FALCON/FORTUNE *Merlin* class sloop 272 tons 1744. LGD – 91ft 3in; Breadth – 26ft 2in

SAIL	Head (in cloths)	Foot (in cloths)	Depth (in feet – inches)
Spritsail Course	17	17	15
Fore Course	25	25	24
Fore Top	15	24	37 – 6
Fore Topgallant	11½	15½	16 – 6
Main Course	26	28	31½
Main Top	16	25	37 – 6
Main Topgallant	11½	16½	16 – 6
Wing (Gaff-Headed)	11	18	31 – 6 at the luff
			39 at the leech
Fore Staysail	–	16	28 – 6
Fore Top Staysail	–	14	36
Main Staysail	–	18	33
Main Top Staysail	–	16	40 – 6
Main Topgallant Staysail	–	14	28 – 6
Main And Fore Top Studding Sails[1]	6	11	40 – 6
Flying Jib	–	16	48

Reference: National Maritime Museum CHA/E/11, Chatham Yard, Navy Board Warrants, 18 January 1754.

1 Had there been an order in the warrant for main and fore studding sails the likely head and foot would have been eight cloths each and the depth 44ft 10in. This can be found from a ratio of 0.66 to length of the mainmast. This figure is achieved by calculating the length of the head of the mast, the distance of the lower yard beneath the top and a suitable height of the sail above deck level (see Chapter 1, Fig 1-7). This can then be compared proportionately with that given for *Wolf*, a sloop with similar mast and spar dimensions.

The pressure of war sometimes prompted the Navy Board to purchase a potential sloop 'on the stocks' – one under construction in a merchant yard, particularly if that builder already had a good reputation for contract-built ships for the Royal Navy. *Weazle* (Table A2-15) was such a sloop, and at 307 tons she was much larger than all the other sloops of the time. She was rigged at Deptford Dockyard in 1745. She was ordered as a snow but completed either just before or after commissioning as a ship. Following his defeat of a large French convoy-escort squadron at the second Battle of Finisterre (1748), Admiral Hawke dispatched her to the West Indies with news of this victory. More importantly, she carried the information that a large unescorted French convoy was making its way thither and was ripe for interception. Her two rigs are detailed below, providing a good example of the many conversions that were being made in the middle of the eighteenth century.

Table A2-15: WEAZLE 308-ton snow- and ship-rigged sloop 1745 and 1749. LGD – 94ft 6¾in; Breadth – 27ft 6¼in (Dimension for ship rig in brackets)

	MASTS		*SPARS*	
	Length (Feet – Inches)	*Diameter (Inches)*	*Length (Feet – Inches)*	*Diameter (Inches)*
Main	68 – 1 (68 – 2)	19 (19½)	51 – 4 (54)	11¾ (13¼)
Top[1]	39 – 6 (39 – 6)	11 (11 – 6)	33 – 11 (38)	7 (8¼)
Topgallant	16 – 7 (18 – 6)	5½ (5¾)	24 (24 – 5)	4¾ (5)
Fore	56 – 2 (56 – 3)	17 (16¼)	49 – 3 (48 – 7)	11½ (12½)
Top[1]	39 – 6 (39 – 6)	11 (11)	33 – 11 (38)	7 (8)
Topgallant	16 – 7 (16 – 6)	5½ (5¼)	23 – 5 (23 – 4)	4¾ (5)
Mizzen	– (45 – 3)	– (10¼)	– (48 lateen)[2]	– (8)
Top	– (24 – 9)	– (5½)	– (23 – 4)	– (5)
Cro'jack	–	–	– (37 – 9)	– (7)
Gaff	–	–	20 (–)[2]	6 (–)
Jib Boom	27 (27)	8 (8¾)	–	–
Bowsprit	39 – 6 (39 – 6)	17 (17½)	33 – 11 (38)[1]	7 (6¾)

Reference: TNA Adm 106/3308, Deptford Yard letter books, 19 July 1750.

1 Note the continuing practice of using the same dimensions for different spars.

2 Lateen spar hence no gaff dimension given for ship rig. This was most unusual on a small ship of this period when a short-headed smack sail would have been more likely. However, for the lateen sail itself there was a tendency to cut off the triangular portion ahead of the mizzen and secure the luff to the mast; presumably the long yard was retained because it was a useful spare spar. The full lateen sail did remain in use on the larger rated ships until later in the century.

Unlike the previous two decades, which saw classes of sloops with similar dimensions, the next period from 1749 to 1763 produced two-masted sloops to many different specifications resulting in a large number of differing dimensions for masts and spars. It is therefore useful to ascertain a few rules to calculate the mast and spar dimensions from key dimensions on the hull where precise figures do not exist; additionally, the Admiralty laid down a scale of diameters for different lengths of spar.

For the period 1745 until the point at which this study ends, the following general proportions can be applied to the mast and spars of sloops whether they be snow-, ketch- or ship-rigged. At the bottom of the table are the lengths for spanker gaffs and booms that could be applied to brigantine-rigged sloops, although there were very few in this period. Unfortunately, in the case of sloops rules were not always followed rigorously or if applied dimensions could always be altered. The only reliable source lies in the yard letters to the Navy Board proposing mast dimensions or relating past and present dimensions. Some of these are quoted above.

Table A2-16: Calculated spar dimensions

Mast lengths	*Ratio*	*Diameter per 3ft length*
Mainmast : maximum beam	2.28	15/16in
Main topmast : mainmast	0.6	9/10in
Main topgallant mast : main topmast	0.49	1in
Foremast : mainmast	0.9	15/16in
Fore topmast : foremast	0.6	9/10in
Fore topgallant mast : fore topmast	0.49	1in
Mizzen mast : mainmast	0.86	8/13in
Mizzen topmast : main topmast	0.7	5/6in
Mizzen topgallant mast : mizzen topmast	0.63	1in
Bowsprit : mainmast	0.63	1 2/9in
Jib boom : bowsprit	0.7	7/8in
Spar lengths	*Ratio*	*Diameter per 3ft length*
Main yard : main mast	0.9	3/4in
Main topsail yard : main yard	0.72	5/8in
Main topgallant yard : main topsail yard	0.5	3/5in
Fore yard : main yard	0.875	3/4in
Fore topsail yard : fore yard	0.72	5/8in
Fore topgallant yard : fore topsail yard	0.5	3/5in
Cro'jack yard : fore topsail yard	1.0	8/13in
Mizzen topsail yard : cro'jack yard	0.75	5/8in
Mizzen topgallant yard : mizzen topsail yard	0.5	3/5in
Trysail gaff : main or mizzen topsail yard	0.63	5/8in
Spritsail yard : fore topsail yard	1.0	5/8in
Spanker boom : main topsail yard	1.0	5/8in
Spanker gaff : driver boom	0.63	5/8in
Main studding sail boom : main yard	0.55	6/10in
Main top studding sail boom : topsail yard	0.5	6/10in
Fore studding sail boom : fore yard	0.55	6/10in
Fore top studding sail boom : topsail yard	0.5	6/10in
Studding sail yards : studding sail booms	0.57	6/10in

Reference: *James Lees,* The Masting and Rigging of English Ships of War 1625–1860 *(London 2nd ed 1984), Appendix 1, p183.*

These proportional diameters and lengths applied to one of the light sloops built by Pierson Lock, master shipwright at Portsmouth in 1752, produce the following calculated dimensions.

Table A2-17: RANGER 140-ton sloop 1752.
LGD – 75ft; Breadth – 20ft 4½in (reconstruction)

	MASTS		SPARS	
	Length (Feet – Inches)	Diameter (Inches)	Length (Feet – Inches)	Diameter (Inches)
Main	46 – 5	14½	41 – 10	10½
Top	27 – 10	8¼	30 – 2	6¼
Topgallant	13 – 8	4½	15 – 1	3
Fore	41 – 9	13	36 – 7	9
Top	25 – 1	7½	26 – 4	5½
Topgallant	12 – 3½	4	13 – 2	2¾
Gaff	–	–	19	4
Jib Boom	20 – 5	6	–	–
Bowsprit	29 – 3	11¾	26 – 4	5½

The first ship-rigged sloops that were actually designed for this rig were launched in 1757 and 1758. *Favourite* and *Tamar* were the work of the Surveyor, Thomas Slade. Their designed burthen was 310 tons with a beam of 27ft 2in. They were followed by other slightly smaller ship-rigged sloops, as for example *Beaver* designed by the joint Surveyor, Bately. She was designed to have a burthen of 283 tons with a beam of 25ft 10in. Steele quotes the mast and spar dimensions for a 300-ton sloop (Table A2-18), which may have been intended to match the large *Swan* class whose prototype was launched in 1767. Therefore these dimensions need to be adjusted slightly for the earlier ship sloops built during the Seven Years War.

Having covered the dimensions for snow-, brigantine-, and ship-rigged sloops, attention now turns to the arrangements for ketch-rigged sloops. Fortunately the second edition of James Lees' *The Masting and Rigging of English Ships of War 1625–1860* has dimensions, taken from an anonymous manuscript of 1685, for an early sloop, *Deptford* (Table A2-19). She was one of the few surviving Restoration ketches and she may be the one drawn by Van de Velde the elder at the Battle of Texel (see Chapter 4, Fig 4-5). Unusually for a ketch, she was built in a royal dockyard by the master shipwright Jonas Shish and this is possibly why her mast and spar dimensions have been preserved. The majority of the other ketches were built in merchant yards, for which very little documentation survives.

The dimensions listed for her might be suitable for the early ketch-rigged bomb ketches, but it is unlikely that they would have had topgallant masts, although these are shown in use on French bomb vessels. The Science Museum model at Chapter 8 (Fig 8-11) does not carry this mast; neither does the *Deptford* as depicted by Van de Velde, and Van de Velde

Table A2-18: STEELE'S 300-ton sloop of about 1770

	MASTS		SPARS	
	Length (Feet – Inches)	Diameter (Inches)	Length (Feet – Inches)	Diameter (Inches)
Main	63	18½	55	12¾
Top	37 – 6	11¼	39 – 6	8¼
Topgallant	18 – 9	6¼	25	5
Fore	56	16½	48 – 5	11¼
Top	33 – 4	11¼	35	7½
Topgallant	16 – 8	5¾	22	4½
Mizzen	48	12	24 – 9 (spanker gaff)[1]	7½
Top	26 – 9	7¾	26 – 4	5½
Topgallant	13	4¼	16 – 6	3¼
Cro'jack	–	–	35	7½
Driver boom	–	–	39 – 6[2]	7½
Jib Boom	27	8	22[3]	4½
Bowsprit	37 – 6	18¾	35	7½

1 This cannot be a square-sail yard because it is too short to take the clews of the topsail above it so it is likely to be a gaff spar for the head of the spanker. The ratio of 2:3 for gaff to spanker boom would seem to be right.
2 Steele credits the spanker boom with a spar of 22ft. This might be an extension that was projected from the spanker boom to accommodate the longer foot of the driver, a bigger sail than the spanker. The driver could also be in the form of a fore-and-aft studding sail and was set from a short yard hoist to the outer end of the gaff with its clew led to the end of the boom extension and its tack to the boom proper; it was suitable for downwind sailing but not for going to windward.
3 The old method for setting a sprit topsail was to raise it on a short sprit topsail mast positioned at the end of the bowsprit, an outlandish arrangement. This was the practice on the small Sixth Rates of 1709 (see above), but by the middle of the eighteenth century the sprit topsail was rigged underneath the jib boom extending forward of the bowsprit. An example of this can be seen at Chapter 14, Fig 14-4.

was known for his accuracy. However, the vessel might have been fitted to rig one in suitable conditions, but even then it would rarely have been used.

Table A2-19: DEPTFORD 89-ton ketch-rigged sloop
1665. LGD – 57ft calculated; Breadth – 18ft

	MASTS		SPARS	
	Length (Feet – Inches)	Diameter (Inches)	Length (Feet – Inches)	Diameter (Inches)
Main	67 – 6	17½	44	11
Top	26	8	24	5½
Topgallant	13	4	12	3
Mizzen	42	8¾	31 (lateen)	5
Top	12	3¾	12	3
Cro'jack	–	–	24	4
Bowsprit	45	15	26	6½
Sprit Topmast	–	–	13[1]	3

1 No dimensions are given for a sprit topmast or jib boom so either the compiler of the list is in error or the sprit topsail yard was set at the outer end of the bowsprit beyond the spritsail yard.

In 1717 William Sutherland published his treatise on shipbuilding, masting and rigging *Britain's Glory or Shipbuilding Unveiled*. In it he included advice on how to mast and spar a ketch, and his principles can be used to reconstruct the masts and spars for the sloop *Cruizer* of 1721. She was originally snow-rigged but at some point in her career she was converted to ketch rig, possibly when she was refitted in 1728.

The starting point is the addition of the extreme beam, 19ft 10in, to the depth in hold, 9ft, making 28ft 10in, which is then multiplied by three to give a height for the combined main and topmast of 86ft 6in. Three-quarters of this, 64ft 10½in (21.62 yards) is for the mainmast including its head, and one-quarter, 21ft 7½in (7.21 yards), for the topmast. The head of the mainmast is found by allowing 4in for every yard of its length, in this case 7ft 2½in. The diameter of the mainmast at the partners, where it passes through the main deck, is found by allowing ¾in to every yard in its length. At the hounds, where the topmast shrouds attach to the mainmast beneath the top or crosstrees, the allowance is three-quarters of that allowed at the partners. The diameter at the heel of the topmast will be that of the mainmast at the hounds and at its head it will be half the diameter of the mainmast at the partners. If a topgallant mast is required it will be ⅔ of the topmast in length with an allowance of 1in to every yard of the mast's length.

The main yard is ⅔ of the mainmast and in diameter it is ⅔in to every yard of its length. The main topsail yard is 5/9 of the main yard with a diameter of 5/7in to a yard. The main topgallant yard is 5/9 of the main topsail yard and with an allowance of 5/7in to every yard of its length.

The mizzen mast is three-quarters of the mainmast length excluding the main topmast; its diameter is 1in to a yard. The mizzen yard (lateen) is 5/7 of the main yard with a diameter of ¾in per yard of its length. Sutherland does not give any dimensions for a mizzen topmast and yard but it would be reasonable to use the same proportions as used on the mainmast.

Table A2-20: CRUIZER 100-ton sloop 1721 as ketch circa 1728. LGD – 62ft; Breadth – 19ft 6in

	MASTS		*SPARS*	
	Length (Feet – Inches)	*Diameter (Inches)*	*Length (Feet – Inches)*	*Diameter (Inches)*
Main	58 – 1½ [1]	14¾ [2]	38 – 9	8½
Top	19 – 4½	11[3]	21 – 6¼	5
Topgallant	12 – 11	4¼	11 – 11½	2¾
Mizzen	43 – 7	14½	27 – 8in	7in
Bowsprit	37 – 2	12½	–	–

1 Includes the head of 6ft 5½in.
2 This dimension is at the partners; at the hounds it will be 11in.
3 This dimension is at its heel; at its head it will be 7¼in.

Table A2-21: GRANADO 267-ton ketch-rigged sloop and bomb vessel 1742. LGD – 91ft 1in; Breadth – 26ft 7in

	MASTS		*SPARS*	
	Length (Feet – Inches)	*Diameter (Inches)*	*Length (Feet – Inches)*	*Diameter (Inches)*
Main	72	24	56	13
Top	60	16	40	8
Topgallant	21	7	22	4¾
Wing Sail Gaff	–	–	18	5
Mizzen	60	16	40 (cro'jack)	8
Top	26	7½	23 – 2	4¾
Topgallant	13	4½	13 – 8	3
Spanker Gaff	–	–	18	4
Spanker Boom	–	–	42 – 8	9
Bowsprit	50	20	40	8
Jib Boom	30 – 6	8½	–	–

The length of the bowsprit is formed by allowing three feet for every foot formed by ⅝, or in some cases 5/7, of the vessel's maximum beam. Its diameter is 1in per yard of its length.

For *Cruizer* this produces the dimensions at Table A2-20.

A later ketch-rigged sloop – and this time a bomb vessel – is the *Granado* (Table A2-21). She was much larger than the ketches above and the position of her main mast was less central. The details of her mast and spar dimensions are recorded by Peter Goodwin in his book on the *Granado* in the Anatomy of the Ship series.

The final example is a light sloop from 1752. In this year six were ordered for the anti-smuggling role, four to a design by the Surveyor Allin and two by Pierson Lock, master shipwright at Portsmouth. The best-known is one of Allin's *Cruizer* class, called *Speedwell* (II) – not to be confused with the earlier *Merlin* class sloop of the same name – of which there is a detailed model in the National Maritime Museum (see Fig 16-6). In this class two were rigged as snows and two as ketches for experimental purposes. One of the snows, *Cruizer*, was subsequently converted to ship rig, which was unusual for a light sloop. All were built in Royal Dockyards, hence the availability of dimensions.

The proportions of the rig for *Speedwell* (Table A2-22) are close to those of *Granado* except in the matter of the gaffs, where *Granado* has the same length of spar for both, whilst *Speedwell*'s mizzen gaff exceeds that of her mainmast gaff. The ketch rig was discontinued after 1752 but the snow rig mutated into the brig rig which was to be the normal sail plan for two-masted sloops until the end of the age of sail.

There are significant differences in the proportions used in the mast and spar dimensions of ketches over this period.

Table A2-22: SPEEDWELL 160-ton ketch-rigged sloop 1752. LGD – 75ft 7in; Breadth – 20ft 8½in

| | MASTS[1] | | SPARS[1] | |
	Length (Feet – Inches)	Diameter (Inches)	Length (Feet – Inches)	Diameter (Inches)
Main	55 – 3 incl 8 – 5 head	18¼	48	11½
Top	36 incl 2 – 8 head	10	34	7½in
Topgallant	19 – 7¼	4¾	22 – 9½in	3¾
Wing Sail Gaff	–	–	17 – 2½	5
Mizzen	43 – 2½ incl 4 – 9¾ head	9½	28 (cro'jack)	5¼
Top	30 incl 8 – 10½ head	5¼	24 – 4¾	3¾
Spanker Gaff	–	–	26	5¾
Bowsprit	38	14	31	5¾
Jib Boom	24	7¼	–	–

1 These dimensions are slightly at variance with those on the Charnock plans at the National Maritime Museum. See Appendix 3, *Speedwell* J8339, Ch 166/63.

The rig underwent considerable change from the time of the Commonwealth to the conclusion of the Seven Years War in 1763. Towards the end of the period the location of the mainmast moved noticeably forward and the proportion of the mainmast to the topmast altered. Early ketches used long mainmasts and short topmasts or even one huge long pole mast. The mainmast in the later ketches was not much longer than the topmast it had to carry and thus it had to have greater diameter per yard of its length than the earlier masts of the seventeenth century.

Appendix 3

A SELECTION OF SLOOP PLANS AND HOW TO MAKE A RUDIMENTARY INTERPRETATION OF THEM

The purpose of a plan or draught was to give a ship-wright the information necessary to transform accurately the designer's intentions into a full-size ship. The lines on the plan were scaled up and drawn out on the floor of a large mould loft, the moulds being full-size formers used as templates to shape the timbers. Therefore many of the small matrices, particularly those that are laid out within the body plan (see below), are there to assist the shipwright in this process of 'lofting'. These lines and curves, whilst of considerable interest, need be of no practical importance to the modelmaker, who can transfer information directly by template, if building to the same scale as the plan, or if not, by using copying techniques, both mechanical and electronic, to reproduce the plan to the desired scale. The initial understanding, and probably the most important, is to be able to visualise the shape of the vessel from the lines placed on the four views usually grouped in what is known as the sheer plan or, traditionally, the sheer draught (Fig A3-1).

The sheer draught contains four views of the hull, starting with a sheer or elevation from the starboard side of the vessel. Below this is a half-breadth plan, which is a view looking down on one half of the hull (usually the port side); the other half is not shown because it is deemed to be a mirror image. The third and fourth views are combined in one body plan, which gives two elevations of the hull: from aft on the left and from forward on the right. As with the half-breadth, this view normally assumes the hull is symmetrical, and therefore portrays the two views using the port side of the hull for each. In this view the keel is deemed to be at right angles to the plan. Fig A3-1 is a plan of the sloop *Spy*, designed and built in 1732 by Benjamin Rosewell, master shipwright at Chatham. This is a simple plan but it shows the essential ingredients that enable the ship to be built.

Looking at the sheer or profile first, the key dimensions here are the length on the lowest full deck or its theoretical extension indicated by the arrows. *Spy* had only one deck, other sloops such as *Wolf* (1741) had two and the lower one was a full deck. This can be referred to in the case of sloops as the length on the gun deck (LGD). It runs from the rabbet

of the stem, vertically above point **B,** to the rabbet of the sternpost, directly above **A.** An alternative description of length then becomes 'between perpendiculars'. The length on the keel runs along the top of the keel from the rabbet of the sternpost at **C** to the point where its upper edge lifts off the horizontal at **D.** The third key dimension is the depth in hold which runs from the top of the deck beam at the lowest point of the deck at **E** down to the top of the floor immediately below at **F.**

There are then a number of fore-and-aft lines drawn on the sheer plan. From the top down, these are the sheer line (1), then the deck line (2), and the line of maximum breadth (3), a dotted line which is also shown on the body plan. The waterlines (4) are a series of parallel lines which are also shown on the half-breadth plan and sometimes on the body plan where they can, but not always, produce a shallow curve. Some explanation is required here to clear any misunderstanding about the relationship of these lines to the keel and to the load waterline. Waterlines are set parallel to and beneath the load waterline. They are not parallel to the keel, unless the keel was intended to be parallel to the load waterline, which it usually was at this time. When it differed from the load waterline, both the load waterline and the other waterlines appear as shallow curves on the body plan. When those lines are straight on the body plan it means that the vessel has been designed so that her load waterline is parallel to the keel. The draughtsman of this sheer view has drawn the waterlines as parallel to the keel but has then produced a load waterline that is not parallel to the keel. Since on the original plan waterlines are not marked on the body plan this does not matter. Those in this doctored plan follow those that have been laid out in the sheer view parallel to the keel. Therefore, in recreating them on the body plan, they appear as straight lines. The 'rising' line (5) joins the outer ends of the floors, the lowest members of the built-up frames.

The sheer plan has stations placed on it, which are drawn down to the half-breadth plan. These stations are also shown on the body plan. They are normally numbered running aft from point **X**, the midship frame, or bend as it was tradition-

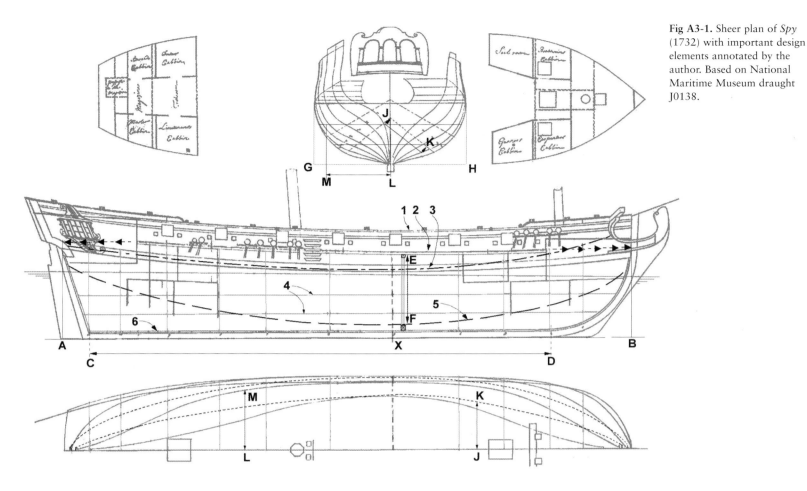

Fig A3-1. Sheer plan of *Spy* (1732) with important design elements annotated by the author. Based on National Maritime Museum draught J0138.

ally called, or lettered, again from point **X**, running forward. The midship station can be shown on both body plans and is sometimes indicated on the sheer profile with a double line. This has not been done on this plan. The double lines filled in with light grey represent a side view of a frame close to the midship frame as an aid to understanding the measurement of the depth in hold.

Turning to the half-breadth plan, it shows in plan view, some of the information on the sheer, namely the waterlines and the stations. It also has dotted lines which are not connected to the dotted line on the sheer plan but are concerned with the dotted diagonal lines on the body plan. These are called fairing or ribband lines and are used to prove that the hull is 'fair' (*ie* of smooth shape with no knuckles or awkward transitions). But they and the water-lines can also be used to establish intermediate transverse stations between those already drawn. The method is best described by using the sheer draught at Fig A3-1. Assume a section is required just aft of the third station from the stem. Its position is determined on the centreline on the half-breadth plan and the distance **J – K** is measured out from that line to the plan view of the fairing line. That measure-ment is then transferred to the body plan running from the centreline along the fairing/ribband line. This then gives a point on an intermediate station. A similar system can be

used on the waterlines. The intermediate station is placed on the half-breadth plan. The distance **L – M** is then measured to the relevant waterline. This measurement is then placed on the body plan and a perpendicular is then extended from its outer end until it reaches the waterline. This represents another point on the intermediate station. This same exercise can be repeated on other fairing lines and waterlines thereby producing a set of points to be joined to create the profile of a bend or frame. This could then be laid out on the loft floor as was done for the main frames/stations. This was supple-mented by the practice, still in use today, of tacking the ribbands (long thin strips of wood) to the main frames as a full-size aid to shaping the intermediate frames.

The final view is the body plan, most of whose informa-tion has already been discussed. It is essentially a pack of cards viewed 'line-ahead' or 'line-astern', where the shape of each card has been backed up with the data required to create that shape. Those data are ingeniously set out in a group of matrices. In the case of Fig A3-1 the body plan contains only one matrix, which lays out the data required to enable a ship-wright to transfer part of the outline of the stations onto a full-scale template. This matrix and others are shown in Fig A3-2. The shape of a station is created by a number of sweeps or arcs and each of these requires a centre point and a radius. The designer sets these out in this example in three tiers. The top tier of radii and centres, one to each station, is labelled **X** and is for the upper breadth line **F** with the line of centres being **A**. In the case of the midship station the arc described is **F – F1**. The next tier is for the lower breadth line using the group of radii **Y** and the relevant centre on the line of centres **B**. The arc thus described is **G – G1**. The lowest tier is for the bottom arc using the radius group **Z** and the required centre on centre line **C**. The midship arc thus described is **H – H1**. This leaves the arc that delineates the shape of the topsides, sometimes known as the timber sweep. Its centre is off the body plan and could be found by extending the upper breadth radius **A – F1** to a point **J**, where it would intersect a horizontal line extended from a point just below the sheer line. The advantage in having a line of centres is that intermediate stations can be drawn using any suitable point on that line. The only other line is that connecting the extremities of the floors at **D**. It is commonly called the rising line and is shown on the sheer or elevation view.

On this plan Rosewell has included the aft and forward platforms together with the cabin arrangements. Often these were on a separate sheet and would detail, in addition to the platforms, the decks and beam structure supporting them. There are other types of structural plan available and these are invaluable if examining a bomb vessel or a conversion for either exploration or for use as a fireship. The detailed information in these plans is largely self-evident and does not require interpretation.

Those wanting a more thorough understanding of this subject can do no better than read a series of articles by David White (then the curator of the ship plans collection at the National Maritime Museum) in the journal *Model Shipwright*, Volumes 46 (1983), pp3–8; 48 (1984), pp 38–44; 50 (1984), pp 120–127; and 51 (1985), pp261–267.

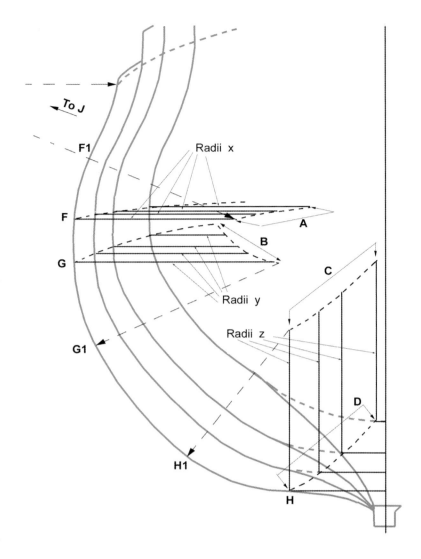

Fig A3-2. Body plan aft showing three matrices for laying off frame stations. *Author*

Plans of sloops in the collection of the National Maritime Museum, Greenwich

This is not a complete list but includes all the most significant plans ranging from 1711 to 1761

Repro ID	Plan number	Sloop's name and plan type	Rig	Career dates	Designer	Remarks
J1356	ZAZ5623	*Alderney*, sheer plan, lines for body only, platforms	Ketch	1734–1741	Duke of Cumberland	Cruiser/bomb
J4694	ZAZ4663	*Alderney/Stork*, sheer plan, internal fitting	Snow/ship	1756–1783	Bately	Compare lines with *Senegal*
J0034	ZAZ5717	*Baltimore*, cross section of mortar bed	Bilander	1742–1762	Lord Baltimore	1 x 13in mortar
J0035	ZAZ5418	*Baltimore*, deck showing mortar bed	Bilander	1742–1762	Lord Baltimore	
J0036	ZAZ5416	*Baltimore*, profile	Bilander	1742–1762	Lord Baltimore	Converted to bomb 1757.
J4541	ZAZ4332	*Beaver*, sheer plan, internal fitting	Ship	1761–1783	Bately	To same spec as *Senegal*
J1443	ZAZ5619	*Blast*, profile and internal fitting only, no lines	Ketch	1759–1771	Slade	Bomb; others were ship rigged
J1444	ZAZ5600	*Blast*, accommodation and structural details	Ketch	1759–1771	Slade	Detailed layout of mortar bays

Repro ID	Plan number	Sloop's name and plan type	Rig	Career dates	Designer	Remarks
J0225	ZAZ4639	*Bonetta/Spy*, platforms and accommodation	Snow	1755–1776	Slade	
J0226	ZAZ4638	*Bonetta/Spy*, sheer plan	*Snow*	1755–1776	Slade	
No scan	NPD0991	*Carolina*, sheer plan, internal fittings. Returned to service as *Peregrine Galley* HM Sloop *Peregrine* in 1749	Ship	1700–1761		Rebuilt and lengthened by Stacey to become royal yacht
J0069	ZAZ4968	*Cruizer*, profile, deck and accommodation	Ship	1752–1763	Allin Jnr	From snow rig in 1753
J4723	ZAZ4721	*Cruizer*, sheer plan	Snow	1732–1745	Stacey	
J0070	ZAZ4967	*Cruize*r, sheer plan and frame detail	Snow	1752–1763	Allin Jnr	
J0223	ZAZ4743	*Drake*, deck and platform layout	Snow	1740–1748	Acworth	Model in NMM Greenwich
J0224	ZAZ4722	*Drake*, sheer plan	Snow	1740–1748	Acworth	
J4614	ZAZ4443	*Epreuve*, sheer plan, internal fitting	Brig	Taken 1760–1764	French prize	Retained French name in RN
J4661	ZAZ5030	*Falcon* (II), sheer plan, internal fitting	Snow	1745–1763	Acworth	Replacement for *Falcon* I, bomb 1758
J4657	ZAZ5029	*Falcon* (later *Fortune*), sheer plan, internal fitting	Snow	1744–1770	Acworth	Taken by French, named *Fortune* on recapture
J4302	ZAZ4212 reverse	*Favourite*, decks platforms quarterdeck, forecastle	Ship	1757–1784	Slade	
J4301	ZAZ4212	*Favourite*, profile, body, internal fitting	Ship	1757–1784	Slade	No waterlines
J4303	ZAZ4211	*Favourite*, sheer plan	Ship	1757–1784	Slade	
J8434	Ch 31/51	*Ferret*, profile and specification	Ship	1760–1776	Slade	Very useful plan with written information
J0218	ZAZ4877	*Ferret*, sheer plan	Cutter	1710–1718	Allin Snr	Single mast
J5132	ZAZ4572	*Ferret*, structure all decks, platforms, accommodation	Ship	1760–1776	Slade	
J5135	ZAZ4569	*Ferret*, sheer plan, internal fitting	Ship	1760–1776	Slade	Includes mast and spar detail, plan made 1771
J0080	ZAZ6617A	*Fly*, accommodation	Ketch	1752–1772	Lock	
J0081	ZAZ4882	*Fly*, lines only	Ketch	1752–1772	Lock	Good body plan
J0079	ZAZ4883	*Fly*, sheer plan	Ketch	1752–1772	Lock	Adjustment of mast positions
J4692	ZAZ4665	*Fly*, sheer plan	Snow	1732–1751	Ward	
J0390	ZAZ5624	*Furnace*, sheer plan, internal fitting	Ketch	1740–1763	Acworth	Cruiser/bomb
J0516	ZAZ6524	*Furnace*, sheer plan, internal fitting	Ship	1741–1763	Acworth	As converted
J0515	ZAZ6525	*Furnace*, structural conversion details	Ship	1741–1763	Acworth	For exploration
J0200	ZAZ5037	*Grampus*, sheer plan	Snow	1746–1780	Acworth	*Merlin* class as fireship 1771
J8047	ZAZ5579	*Grampus/Strombolo*, plan of fittings, upper deck	Ship	1762–1780	Acworth	Includes cabin detail
J8046	ZAZ5578	*Grampus/Strombolo*, profile and internal fittings	Ship	1762–1780	Acworth	As fireship
J8045	ZAZ5577	*Grampus/Strombolo*, sheer plan, internal fitting	Snow/ship	1746/1762–1780	Acworth	Was *Merlin* class; as fireship
J0387	ZAZ5628	*Granado*, sheer plan, internal fitting	Ketch	1742–1763	Acworth	Bomb 2 x mortars
J4161	ZAZ3869	*Guirland/Cygnet*, sheer plan (no waterlines), internal fittings	Brig	Taken 1760–1768	French prize	Brig converted to ship rig with major alteration to stem
J4899	ZAZ4955	*Hawk*, sheer plan, internal fitting	Ketch	1755–1781	Allin Jnr	Ship rigged in 1767
J4900	ZAZ4956	*Hawk*, sheer plan, internal fitting	Ketch	1755–1781	Allin Jnr	Later plan with modifications
J8579	ALC0008	*Jamaica*, sheer plan, no waterlines	Snow	1744–1770	Allin Jnr	Gives mast and spar dimensions
J4808	ZAZ4751	*Lynx*, deck structure. platforms, aft bulkhead	Snow/ship	1761–1777	Stacey 1732	Revived design, but modified
J4807	ZAZ4750	*Lynx*, sheer plan, internal fitting	Snow/ship	1761–1777	Stacey 1732	Revived design, but modified

Continued overleaf

Repro ID	Plan number	Sloop's name and plan type	Rig	Career dates	Designer	Remarks
J4502	ZAZ4318	*Nautilus*, profile of internal fittings	Ship	1762–1780	Slade	Improved *Favourite* class
J4501	ZAZ4317	*Nautilus*, sheer plan, internal fitting	Ship	1762–1780	Slade	Improved *Favourite* class
J0236	ZAZ4396	*Otter*, sheer plan	Snow	1742–1763	Acworth	
J0082	ZAZ4861	*Peggy*, sheer plan	Snow	1749–1770	Allin Jnr	Amended lines
J0083	ZAZ4862	*Peggy*, sheer plan	Snow	1749–1770	Allin Jnr	No waterlines
J0084	ZAZ4860	*Peggy*, sheer plan and cross section frame	Snow	1749–1770	Allin Jnr	Full spec available NMM Masts and spars Ch 4/54 & Ch 5/1
J4804	ZAZ5041	*Peregrina* and *Galgo*, sheer plan, no waterlines. British replacements for two Spanish prizes. Renamed 1744, but plan predates the change of name	Snow	1744–1748	Acworth	Renamed *Merlin* and *Swallow* forming the start of the *Merlin* class, enlarged version of *Otter*
J4556	ZAZ4223	*Pomona*, deck structures, platforms	Ship	Taken 1761–1776	Ex-French *Chevert*	Full spec available TNA
J4554	ZAZ4222	*Pomona*, sheer plan, internal fitting, frame detail	Ship	Taken 1761–1776	Ex-French *Chevert*	Full spec available TNA
J0235	ZAZ4359	*Saltash*, sheer plan	Snow	1732–1741	Lock	
J4452	ZAZ4156	*Sardoine*, sheer plan, internal fitting	Ship	Taken 1761–1768	French prize	Decks on reverse of plan
J0144	ZAZ5038	*Scorpion*, sheer plan, accommodation	Snow	1746–1762	Acworth	*Merlin* class
J4584	ZAZ4389	*Senegal*, platforms and riding bitts	Ship	1761–1780	Bately	
J4586	ZAZ4387	*Senegal*, sheer plan, internal fitting	Ship	1761–1780	Bately	Compare with *Beaver*
J0220	ZAZ4737	*Shark*, full body sections and sheer plan	Ketch	1732–1755	Allin Jnr	
J0219	ZAZ4938	*Shark*, sheer plan, accommodation	Ketch	1732–1755	Allin Jnr	Includes platforms
J0150	ZAZ4842	*Speedwell*, sheer plan	Ketch	1752–1780	Allin Jnr	See *Cruizer* 1752
J8339	Ch 166/63	*Speedwell*, sheer plan, deck structures, platforms stern detail, aft bulkhead	Ketch	1752–1779	Allin Jnr	Mast and spar dimensions on plan, no waterlines
J4688	ZAZ4879	*Spence*, sheer plan, internal fitting, platforms	Snow	1729–1749	Stacey	Note rake of masts and two decks
J0138	ZAZ4374	*Spy*, sheer plan, accommodation	Snow	1732–1745	Rosewall	Internal platforms
J0142	ZAZ5035	*Swallow*, deck and platforms	Snow	1745–1769	Acworth	*Merlin* class
J0141	ZAZ5034	*Swallow*, sheer plan, accommodation	Snow	1745–1769	Acworth	
J0145	ZAZ5040	*Swan*, deck, platforms, beams, accommodation	Snow	1745–1763	Acworth	*Merlin* class
J0146	ZAZ5039	*Swan*, sheer plan	Snow	1745–1763	Acworth	*Merlin* class
J0151	ZAZ4853	*Swift*, sheer plan	Snow	1721–1741	Hayward	
J0314	ZAZ5626	*Terrible*, sheer plan	Ketch	1730–1749	Stacey	Bomb, 2 x mortars
J1445	ZAZ5621	*Terror*, accommodation and structural details	Ship	1759–1774	Slade	Hull as *Blast*
J4669	ZAZ4671	*Vulture*, sheer plan, internal fitting	Ship	1762–1771	Slade	Compare with *Epreuve*
J4670	ZAZ4672	*Vulture/Swift*, sheer plan, internal fitting	Ship	1762–1771	Slade	Later and modified plan
J0086	ZAZ4864	*Wasp*, deck beams, accommodation	Snow	1749–1781	Lock	Best plan
J0087	ZAZ4865	*Wasp*, platforms, deck beams, accommodation	Snow	1749–1781	Lock	
J0088	ZAZ4866	*Wasp*, quarterdeck, forecastle, fore and aft platforms	Snow	1749–1781	Lock	
J0085	ZAZ4863	*Wasp*, sheer plan	Snow	1749–1781	Lock	
J4316	ZAZ4123	*Weazle*, deck structure, accommodation	Ship	1745–1779	Taylor/ Randall	Merchant build/design
J4318	ZAZ4124	*Weazle*, quarter and forecastle decks, platforms	Ship	1745–1779	Taylor/ Randall	Merchant build/design
J4317	ZAZ4121	*Weazle*, sheer plan, internal fitting	Ship	1745–1779	Taylor/ Randall	Merchant build/design
J4219	ZAZ4365	*Wolf*, sheer plan	Snow	1731–1741	Stacey	
J4220	ZAZ4335	*Wolf*, sheer plan, internal fitting	Snow	1741–1741	Acworth	Larger version of 1731 sloop

Appendix 4

PERFORMANCE UNDER SAIL AND SAILING QUALITY REPORTS

Much has already been said about performance under sail particularly in the closing section of Chapter 1. Many may regard performance as simply a matter of how fast a ship will travel under sail or oars but this was certainly not the only concern of the sailing quality reports. Speed is important but behaviour in various conditions of wind, sea state and tide are equally so. Similarly manoeuvrability, particularly for frigates and sloops, can be critical in a single-ship engagement. As has been noted the sloop, especially those specifically designed for cruising were, for their size, possibly the fastest and most manoeuvrable ships of their time, though they often had

difficulty with directional and lateral stability and may not have been entirely easy on the helm.

Sailing quality reports were introduced towards the middle of the eighteenth century in an attempt to analyse and evaluate overall performance, and to pass on to succeeding captains the fruits of earlier experience with specific ships. Within the sloop category there was an ongoing interest in the comparison of sail plans, notably between the ketch and snow rigs, and how these rigs would show in the various questions posed in the reports. The difficulty with these reports was a human one in that instead of creating a separate body to assist captains and inspect and report on

---

BALTIMORE *Bilander Rig 1742–1763. Report Date: August 1743* [*with comments from her 1749 report*]

1. Best sailing draught of water afore and abaft.	9' 4" afore and 9' 6" abaft She has twenty tons of ballast on board [*in a March 1749 report she drew 9' 8" and 9' 10"; this still happens to wooden boats, wet wood being heavier than dry wood*]
2. Lowest gun port cills above the water.	[*Not given: 3' 5" in 1749 therefore possibly 3' 9" in 1743*]
3. How she behaves close hauled and how many knots she runs in a topgallant gale.	If the water is very smooth and all sails set, when clean she goes eight knots and a half as close to the wind as she can lie and she once went nine knots [1749 *no change*]
4. How she behaves close hauled and how many knots she runs in a topsail gale.	8 knots and 8½ if the water be smooth [1749 *no change*]
5. How she steers, stays and wears.	No vessel can steer better or wear or stay quicker
6. How she carries her helm.	Ditto
7. How she carries her helm under reefed topsails.	6, 7and 8 with one reef in, have no experience of her with more [*this entirely misses the point in giving speeds*]
8. How she carries her helm under courses.	Never had occasion to do so
9. Whether she will stay under her courses.	Never tried her
10. Proportion of leeway. [*1 point = 11¼ degrees*]	I never saw any ship or vessel at sea but I got to windward of and fore-reached upon, she makes very little leeway
11. What is her best point of sailing?	Never tried her in all variations – only five days at sea in her – and mostly fine weather and mostly close-hauled. We once had the wind on the beam and she ran 9 knots with a deep laden brig of about 90 tons in tow. She carries her helm about one third a weather commonly [*at this time Baltimore had a bilander rig*]
12. Most before the wind.	No opportunity for trying her [*in 1749: 10 and 11 knots. Rolls deep but easy*]
13. Tries.	No opportunity for trying her [*In 1749: well in each circumstance*]
14. What is she for a roader.	No opportunity for trying her [*In 1749: a good roader*]
15. Careens.	No opportunity for trying her [*in 1749: never careened*]
16. Best sailing trim.	Her best trim is her mainmast raking much aft, her foremast not so much, her topmasts in line with the lower masts and her rigging not too taut

performance, the Admiralty directed that captains should complete these documents themselves, and as a result there is a vast difference in the quality of reporting. There was a rationale to this approach in that the reports were usually written up at the ends of commissions, when captains would have had a reasonably long experience of their sloops. But there is a further problem that reduces the value of the information given, in that the performance of any sailing vessel is attributable to many factors – the vessel's design, the quality of its rig, the state of its bottom and, above all, the competence of its captain and crew. The questionnaire was imprecise in its demand for information, allowing far too much loose description and encouraging a subjective assessment by captains. In addition most of the questions are not amenable to proper measurement. Many invite a subjective response, and are at the mercy of a captain's feelings for his command – usually prejudiced in favour, occasionally downright hostile, but rarely even-handed. Sailing reports, therefore, need to be read with a degree of caution, but they do allow some broad conclusions to be drawn, which will be summarised after examining a selection of the reports.

The questionnaire for the sailing reports was later expanded but for most of the eighteenth century there were 16 questions in total. In the examples reproduced here the original wording has been slightly modernised to clarify the meaning but they are otherwise as recorded. The questions cover the trim of the vessel in the water (1) and (2) and the trim of the masts and sails (16). Considerable emphasis is placed on behaviour and performance close-hauled (ie as close to the wind as the vessel will sail). This is required under two wind strengths, the topgallant gale (3) and the topmast gale (4). Some idea of speed is also required under these conditions. A topgallant gale is one in which a vessel may carry her topgallant sails. In today's parlance this could be considered to be the top end of force 4. The next level of gale upwards was the topsail gale when a vessel could still carry her topsails. All vessels are different in their reaction to the wind, but this level would probably equate to force 7.

The next pressing matter was to find out how well-balanced the vessel was (5). This concerned her responsiveness and manoeuvrability and how she performed in stays, which today we would define as her ability to tack through the wind. The alternative manoeuvre of wearing – that is, heading off down wind and coming up on the opposite tack – was also for comment. How she carried her helm, either as lee helm or weather helm, under normal conditions was required (6) and her ability to steer ('carry her helm') under reefed topsails (7) or just under courses (8) was also needed, as was her ability to tack in these conditions (9).

All sailing ships make leeway: that is, drifting sideways off course, normally due to the pressure of wind on the side of the vessel and her masts, spars and sails. The degree of this effect

---

DRAKE *Snow Rig 1741–1748. Report Date: January 1744*

1. Best sailing draught of water afore and abaft.	Afore 10' 1" Abaft 10' 5" In my opinion whatever draught of water she lies at, she'll go well provided she is kept four inches by the stern. Victualled for 3 months afore 10' 3" abaft 10' 7"
2. Lowest gun port cills above the water.	[*Not given*]
3. How she behaves close hauled and how many knots she runs in a topgallant gale.	Sails well. In regard to a head sea, if they do not press her with too much canvas she is pretty dry and pitches easily and carries her helm weatherly
4. How she behaves close hauled and how many knots she runs in a topsail gale.	Sails very well
5. How she steers, stays and wears.	No vessel can steer, stay and wear quicker
6. How she carries her helm.	[*Not given*]
7. How she carries her helm under reefed topsails.	Behaves well and generally goes about 7 knots [*behaves well = well balanced and easy on the helm*]
8. How she carries her helm under courses.	Likewise and behaves extremely well and goes about 4 and 5 knots
9. Whether she will stay under her courses.	She is a weatherly boat and what ships I have been in company with, have been able to spare them one third of my sail [*meaning that he can keep up with one-third of his sail area not set*]
10. Proportion of leeway. [*1 point = 11¼ degrees*]	As she has such a quick way through the water, it is mine and my officers' opinion that half a point is sufficient [*much the same as a modern cruising yacht!*]
11. What is her best point of sailing?	In general sails well but the best of her going is with the wind a point abaft the beam and then she will run 11 knots
12. Most before the wind.	Between 8 and 9 knots. Rolls deep but easy
13. Tries.	[*Not given*]
14. What is she for a roader.	Rides tolerably easy
15. Careens.	[*Not given*]
16. Best sailing trim.	Iron ballast 20 tons. Her foremast and fore topmast raking a little aft, the main mast and main topmast upright. [*A most unusual trim and may be an error in the writing since all the other sloops were the other way round*]

was required (10). An enquiry is made on the vessel's best point of sailing (11). The answer was inevitably one or two points abaft the beam or sailing large, which today would be described as a broad reach. Downwind performance is noted (12); not just speed but behaviour also. The questionnaire then turns to conduct when the vessel is stationary, or nearly so: this covers behaviour when lying-to under a trysail, *ie* 'how she tries' (13); how she rides at anchor, *ie* 'what is she for a roader' (14); and how easily she can be hauled down for careening (15). The representative tables below are laid out in the question and answer format as in the originals. Author's comments are in [square brackets].

SPY *Snow Rig 1732–1745. Report Date: November 1745*

1. Best sailing draught of water afore and abaft.	Afore 9' 6" Abaft 10' 10" or as much lighter at the same difference as she is able to bear sail
2. Lowest gun port cills above the water.	Being a sloop have no lower deck ports. [*stupid answer*]
3. How she behaves close hauled and how many knots she runs in a topgallant gale.	Large or before it 10 knots in smooth water and upon a wind 7 knots with smooth water
4. How she behaves close hauled and how many knots she runs in a topsail gale.	Large or before it 9 knots and upon a wind 6 knots
5. How she steers, stays and wears.	Steers and wears well and stays well
6. How she carries her helm.	Carries her helm little a weather with all sails set
7. How she carries her helm under reefed topsails.	Large or before it 8 knots and upon a wind 4 or 4½ knots if any sea
8. How she carries her helm under courses.	Upon a wind 3½ knots
9. Whether she will stay under her courses.	Stays well
10. Proportion of leeway. [*1 point = 11¼ degrees*]	Wronged [*ie beat*] most in company when clean. Very weatherly. Leeway two points under her courses
11. What is her best point of sailing?	Her best sailing is large or before the wind and but heavy upon a wind in anything of a sea but in smooth water and light gales of wind is her best sailing and working
12. Most before the wind.	Before it 9½ knots and rolls easy
13. Tries.	Lying-to , or a try, very well under mainsail or wingsail
14. What is she for a roader.	Rides well and is a good roader
15. Careens	Heaves down well
16. Best sailing trim.	Her mainmast and main topmast raking well aft, foremast and fore topmast upright

---

HUNTER *Snow Rig 1756–1780. Report Date: October 1756*

1. Best sailing draught of water afore and abaft.	Afore 11' 3" Abaft 10' 11"
2. Lowest gun port cills above the water.	[*Not given*]
3. How she behaves close hauled and how many knots she runs in a topgallant gale.	Behaves well but carries a lee helm. Runs at 5½ knots [*This may account for the recommendation at Question 1, that she should trim by the head*]
4. How she behaves close hauled and how many knots she runs in a topsail gale.	Behaves well but carries a lee helm. Runs at 4 knots
5. How she steers, stays and wears.	Steers with a lee helm, wears well. Does not stay except the mainsail is set and not then in the case of a head sea
6. How she carries her helm.	[*See questions 3 and 4*]
7. How she carries her helm under reefed topsails.	Will not keep-to, falls off much and carries lee helm. Runs 3½ knots
8. How she carries her helm under courses.	2½ knots makes good weather. Carries a lee helm
9. Whether she will stay under her courses.	No
10. Proportion of leeway. [*1 point = 11¼ degrees*]	Some fishing smacks weathered on us but we fore-reached them
11. What is her best point of sailing?	Stiff gale wind 2 points abaft the beam, runs 8½ to 9 knots. Wind on the beam 6½ knots and carries her helm a little to weather
12. Most before the wind.	8 to 8½ knots. Rolls very easy and makes good weather. The best of her going is with the wind on the quarter
13. Tries.	Lies-to under a mainsail but comes up and falls off 4 points. Will not keep-to under a balanced trysail but falls broad off in the trough of the sea and ships much water
14. What is she for a roader.	A good roader
15. Careens.	Never hove down but in heeling comes down hard being a stiff ship
16. Best sailing trim.	Best trim tried is the foremast right up, mainmast with a small rake aft

FERRET *Snow Rig 1743–1757. Report Date: September 1743* [*commercial design*]

1. Best sailing draught of water afore and abaft.	Afore 10' 10" Abaft 11' 2"
2. Lowest gun port cills above the water.	Lowest port then 5' 5" or more
3. How she behaves close hauled and how many knots she runs in a topgallant gale.	Behaved well and runs 8½ knots
4. How she behaves close hauled and how many knots she runs in a topsail gale.	Behaved well and runs 8 knots
5. How she steers, stays and wears.	Both very well
6. How she carries her helm.	[*Not given*]
7. How she carries her helm under reefed topsails.	Behaves well and runs at 7 knots
8. How she carries her helm under courses.	Behaves well and runs at 3½ knots
9. Whether she will stay under her courses.	[*No occasion, but*] I don't believe she would, unless very smooth water.
10. Proportion of leeway. [*1 point = 11¼ degrees*]	Find that she gathers to windward very much and has done with all ships we have been in company with, especially if it blows hard under her courses or laying- to and makes very little leeway at any time.
11. What is her best point of sailing?	Behaves well in all conditions, but best in a stiff gale, and very well with a head sea. The most she ever ran was 7 knots before a wind, 7½ the wind quartering, 8 upon a bowline [*beating to windward*] and generally carries her helm a little to weather.
12. Most before the wind.	She runs 7 knots and rolls very easy
13. Tries.	Never made trial but believe very well, by reason she goes very dry in a head sea.
14. What is she for a roader.	She will road very well
15. Careens.	She will careen very well
16. Best sailing trim.	Slack rigging

SHARK *Snow Rig 1732–1755 Report Date: June 1748* [*a cod's head–mackerel tail hull; she is listed as being a ketch at launch but this report implies that she was re-rigged as a snow at some stage before it was drawn up*]

1. Best sailing draught of water afore and abaft.	Afore 10' Abaft 12'4" [*this considerable drag to the keel was reckoned to be important to her sailing*] 10 ton shingle ballast exclusive of the iron ballast she always had
2. Lowest gun port cills above the water.	[*Not given*]
3. How she behaves close hauled and how many knots she runs in a topgallant gale.	In smooth water and as much wind as she can bear, and with all her small sails set, 10 knots
4. How she behaves close hauled and how many knots she runs in a topsail gale.	In the like smooth water, the same
5. How she steers, stays and wears.	Extremely well and carries her helm a little to windward of midships and wears and stays very quick.
6. How she carries her helm.	[*Not given, but see above*]
7. How she carries her helm under reefed topsails.	Before the sea has made 9 knots.
8. How she carries her helm under courses.	If she does not head the sea, 7 knots
9. Whether she will stay under her courses.	She will in all weathers, provided you keep her a point or two from the wind just before you go about and keep your bowlines, braces and sheets fast
10. Proportion of leeway. [*1 point = 11¼ degrees*]	She makes twelve degrees of leeway through all varieties of wind
11. What is her best point of sailing?	Extremely well every way, excepting before the wind. In tolerable smooth water and with all sail set and if her way is 3 knots or more she will sail within 4 points of the wind [*45 degrees – not bad!*] she outsails others then the most difference
12. Most before the wind.	Seldom above 10 knots and rolls pretty easy
13. Tries.	She will not lie-to or try under any after sail, but best under a main staysail or a reefed fore-sail and then must be steered all the time otherwise she falls off and comes up 4 or 5 points
14. What is she for a roader.	Indifferent good
15. Careens.	Careens hard
16. Best sailing trim.	The fore ought to stand nearly upright, the head of the mainmast to plumb 10' aft upon the awning, set off from the mast that height the main topmast to plumb abaft the bittacle 2' [*the old term for binnacle*]

FLY Snow Rig 1732–1751. Report Date: August 1748

1. Best sailing draught of water afore and abaft.	Afore 10' 2" Abaft 10' will carry the same sail when 2 inches lighter. [Stowed for] 6 months foreign service drew 10' 8 Afore and 10' 6" Abaft but then was made very deep and made ?[*illegible*] of her way through the water and shipped a great deal of water, it being greatly too much in proportion to her burthen
2. Lowest gun port cills above the water.	[*Not answered*]
3. How she behaves close hauled and how many knots she runs in a topgallant gale.	6 knots
4. How she behaves close hauled and how many knots she runs in a topsail gale.	7 knots
5. How she steers, stays and wears.	Remarkable for easy steerage, wearing and staying, in fact no vessel will work so well
6. How she carries her helm.	[*No answer given*]
7. How she carries her helm under reefed topsails.	8 knots if the water be tolerably smooth
8. How she carries her helm under courses.	5 knots if no great head sea, but if great head sea no more than 3 or 4 knots
9. Whether she will stay under her courses.	She will stay under them if the water be not very rough, and has turned it over the flats under her courses
10. Proportion of leeway. [*1 point = 11¼ degrees*]	In sailing with a fleet upon a wind she has always fore-reached and got to windward. [*Does not really answer the question*]
11. What is her best point of sailing?	Her best sailing is quartering with any sail, but in a stiff gale and head sea she makes little way, pitching much – imagining her foremast being too far forward and having a lean harping and carries a fast helm [*by harping he means the shape at the bow, 'lean' being a way of saying fine-lined; a 'fast helm' suggests that the vessel is very responsive to her rudder*]
12. Most before the wind.	She has several times with reefed topsails gone 10 or 11 knots. Rolls very easy in the trough of the sea, never straining or carrying away any of her masts or rigging, but ships a great deal of water
13. Tries.	She lays to very well under the main sail or if reefed and fore-reaches. Has made less leeway than generally allowed
14. What is she for a roader.	An exceeding good roader
15. Careens.	Careens stiff the first course and will right without the relieving tackle
16. Best sailing trim.	[*Not answered regarding masts*]

HAWK Ketch Rig 1756–1781. Report Date: October 1756 [*fitted with ship rig in 1767, but this report as ketch*]

1. Best sailing draught of water afore and abaft.	Afore 10' 9" Abaft 11' 3"
2. Lowest gun port cills above the water.	3' 3" [*very low for a vessel of this size: 220 tons*]
3. How she behaves close hauled and how many knots she runs in a topgallant gale.	Smooth water 5½ knots
4. How she behaves close hauled and how many knots she runs in a topsail gale.	Smooth water 5½ knots. Close reefed topsails leeway 3 points in a head sea
5. How she steers, stays and wears.	Steers very well, very slack in stays and wears indifferently
6. How she carries her helm.	Carries her helm amidships
7. How she carries her helm under reefed topsails.	Smooth water 4 knots lee helm
8. How she carries her helm under courses.	Smooth water 2½ knots. Under her courses and with a head sea 5 points of leeway and a lee helm
9. Whether she will stay under her courses.	No
10. Proportion of leeway. [*1 point = 11¼ degrees*]	Loaded colliers outwork her by the wind and outsail her large. [*This speaks volumes for the inadequacy of this rig and Allin's poor hull design*]
11. What is her best point of sailing?	[*There does not appear to be one*]
12. Most before the wind.	All sails out steering [*studding*] sails and a fresh gale, 9 knots and rolls very easy
13. Tries.	Have had no opportunity to try her
14. What is she for a roader.	Roads very well
15. Careens.	[*Not given*]
16. Best sailing trim.	All methods having been tried have found no difference.

FAVOURITE *Ship Rig 1757–1784. Report Date: March 1763*

1. Best sailing draught of water afore and abaft.	Afore 13' 9" Abaft 12' 10" [*This is most interesting: she is down by the head which will take her CLR forward, understandable with two-masted rig but not so with ship rig*]
2. Lowest gun port cills above the water.	5' 4" or more
3. How she behaves close hauled and how many knots she runs in a topgallant gale.	6½ or 7 knots in smooth water
4. How she behaves close hauled and how many knots she runs in a topsail gale.	5 or 6 knots, in a head sea 3 or 4 knots
5. How she steers, stays and wears.	She steers tolerably well, stays very well but takes a long time in veering [*veering is turning the head of the vessel away from the wind preparatory to wearing ship; at this time it was synonymous with wearing itself*]
6. How she carries her helm.	[*Not answered*]
7. How she carries her helm under reefed topsails.	In smooth water 6 knots, in a head sea 3½ or 4. [*No comment about her helm or balance!*]
8. How she carries her helm under courses.	3½ or 4 knots in smooth water
9. Whether she will stay under her courses.	She will stay under her courses with a moderate sea [*the question means courses only; even ship-rigged vessels were not always handy in such conditions*]
10. Proportion of leeway. [*1 point = 11¼ degrees*]	As to windward fore-reaches. In company with other men of war she has always remarked to go heavy, but very weatherly under any sail.
11. What is her best point of sailing?	The best of her sailing is with a wind upon the quarter, then the most she ever went was 11 knots and that not often. With the wind upon the beam she had gone 9 and 10 knots. In smooth water she has gone upon a wind 6½ knots. In a great head sea 3 and 3½ is the most. In a strong gale, she carries mostly a weather helm
12. Most before the wind.	10 and 10½ knots she does not roll much
13. Tries.	She lays-to very well either under a reefed mainsail or balanced mizzen and is a remarkably good sea boat
14. What is she for a roader.	Rides very well
15. Careens.	Careens very well
16. Best sailing trim.	[*No answer given*]

MERLIN *Snow Rig 1756–1780. Report Date: November 1756* [*sister ship to* Bonetta *below*]

1. Best sailing draught of water afore and abaft.	Afore 10' 4" Abaft 11' 10" Ballast iron 20 tons Shingle 30 tons
2. Lowest gun port cills above the water.	Midships 4' Abaft 4' 6" [*due to the rise of the sheer line aft*]
3. How she behaves close hauled and how many knots she runs in a topgallant gale.	She goes 7 or 8 knots in smooth water and behaves very well
4. How she behaves close hauled and how many knots she runs in a topsail gale.	She goes 8 or 9 knots in smooth water, is not crank and behaves very well
5. How she steers, stays and wears.	She wears very well, but stays badly for want of after sail
6. How she carries her helm.	In a sea she carries a lee helm. In smooth water and a fresh gale she carries her helm amidships and never carries a-weather for want of after sail
7. How she carries her helm under reefed topsails.	In a first reef topsail and smooth water 7 or 8 knots, in a second reef and smooth water 6 or 7 knots, in a close reef 5 or 6 knots and in anything of a sea carries a lee helm
8. How she carries her helm under courses.	She goes 3 or 4 knots and carries her helm hard a lee
9. Whether she will stay under her courses.	Never tried, but by carrying her helm so much a lee, imagine she will not
10. Proportion of leeway. [*1 point = 11¼ degrees*]	With some ships she fore-reaches and gathers to windward as well as them, with others better; when clean, better than *Ambuscade*, 5th Rate, when she was foul and the *Merlin* clean; better than the *Viper* and *Savage* sloops, *Port Mahon* 24, *Centaur* 24, *Brilliant* and *Maryland Planter* armed ships
11. What is her best point of sailing?	She goes very well through all the variations of the wind, carries a lee helm and goes as above
12. Most before the wind.	11 knots and rolls very much by being over-masted
13. Tries.	Under a mainsail she labours very much by being over-masted
14. What is she for a roader.	She is a very good roader
15. Careens.	Never hove down so don't know how she careens
16. Best sailing trim.	[*Not given*]

BONETTA *Snow Rig 1756–1776. Report Date: March 1757* [*here under ship rig*]

1. Best sailing draught of water afore and abaft.	Afore 10' 2" Abaft 11' 10"
2. Lowest gun port cills above the water.	[*Not given*]
3. How she behaves close hauled and how many knots she runs in a topgallant gale.	Behaves well and runs at 9½ knots
4. How she behaves close hauled and how many knots she runs in a topsail gale.	She runs 8 knots
5. How she steers, stays and wears.	Steers always well, wears in very little room. She stays well in smooth water, but rather slack in stays if against a head sea
6. How she carries her helm.	[*Not given*]
7. How she carries her helm under reefed topsails.	If smooth water 6 knots, against a head sea 5 knots and pitches very deep. If smooth water carries her helm amidships if a head sea a little a-lee.
8. How she carries her helm under courses.	Behaves well, if a head sea, pitches very easy and runs 3½ knots
9. Whether she will stay under her courses.	No
10. Proportion of leeway. [*1 point = 11¼ degrees*]	In a topgallant gale and smooth water: half a point of leeway. Whole topsails and double reef: about a point. Close reef topsails: a point and a half if in a sea. Fore topsail in: two points. Main topsail in: 2¾ points. Try under single reefed main course and mizzen: 5 points. Under mizzen only 6 points
11. What is her best point of sailing?	Sails and behaves well in all circumstances. The wind two points abaft the beam, she will run 11 knots, upon the beam 10. One point before the beam if smooth water 10. If a head sea and stiff gales she pitches deep but very easy and never strains her rigging
12. Most before the wind.	11 knots. Rolls very much if a fresh wind and a sea and ships much water in the waist on each side
13. Tries.	Behaves very well, takes no water and seldom falls off three points under the main course and mizzen. Under mizzen only generally falls off 3 points. [*But see answer at 10 above!*]
14. What is she for a roader.	If at anchor and in a sea, pitches much, but rides very easy by her cables
15. Careens.	Never tried
16. Best sailing trim.	The stays slack, particular the fore topmast stay. The foremast upright and the mainmast and mizzen mast hanging a little aft

FORTUNE *Snow Rig 1744–1770. Report Date: May 1752*

1. Best sailing draught of water afore and abaft.	Afore 12' 4" Abaft 12' 0"
2. Lowest gun port cills above the water.	[*Not given*]
3. How she behaves close hauled and how many knots she runs in a topgallant gale.	Very stiff and weatherly and has gone 7 knots in smooth water
4. How she behaves close hauled and how many knots she runs in a topsail gale.	Very stiff and weatherly and has gone 7 knots in smooth water
5. How she steers, stays and wears.	Wears and stays extremely sure and quick
6. How she carries her helm.	Carries her helm a little to windward
7. How she carries her helm under reefed topsails.	Very weatherly but pitches a good deal in a head sea with fore topsails out
8. How she carries her helm under courses.	Ditto
9. Whether she will stay under her courses.	[*See answer to question 5*]
10. Proportion of leeway. [*1 point = 11¼ degrees*]	Found her to gather very fast to windward in smooth water. Makes little or no leeway but with double reefed topsails and a high sea in proportion she makes a point and a half leeway.
11. What is her best point of sailing?	She has gone 13 knots with the wind upon the quarter
12. Most before the wind.	I have known her go 12 and 13 knots under a foresail
13. Tries.	Extremely easy under a reefed mainsail but comes up in the wind too much with the whole sail out
14. What is she for a roader.	She is a very easy and good roader
15. Careens.	[*Not given*]
16. Best sailing trim.	The main and main topmast to rake a good deal aft, the other masts upright. The rigging well up [*taut*] except the main topmast stays

SWIFT *Snow Rig 1741–1756. Report Date: Undated between 1742 and 1746* [*sister ship to* Drake *above*]

1. Best sailing draught of water afore and abaft.	Draught of water with 3 month provision in, 10' 2". The best for her swimming for sailing is about 14" by the head or an inch more or less [*very different from Drake*] Her quantity of ballast being 40 tons
2. Lowest gun port cills above the water.	3' 10½" having only three months provisions with two months brandy and one month beer
3. How she behaves close hauled and how many knots she runs in a topgallant gale.	On a wind she rolls very deep in a sea but never strains her rigging but is constantly shipping of seas she being very low
4. How she behaves close hauled and how many knots she runs in a topsail gale.	On a wind she rolls very deep in a sea but never strains her rigging but is constantly shipping of seas she being very low. She pitches very easy and scends [*the sudden recovery after pitching precipitately into the hollow between two waves*] very little she being very full abaft underwater, which is the reason of her sailing by the head
5. How she steers, stays and wears.	[*No answer given*]
6. How she carries her helm.	[*Provided her masts are well raked*] she answers her helm well
7. How she carries her helm under reefed topsails.	[*No answer given*]
8. How she carries her helm under courses.	[*No answer given*]
9. Whether she will stay under her courses.	[*No answer given*]
10. Proportion of leeway. [*1 point = 11¼ degrees*]	We find her to be weatherly
11. What is her best point of sailing?	The best of her sailing is with all sails drawing and loves a fresh gale, what trial we have had upon a wind with our convoy
12. Most before the wind.	Had no trial before the wind in a sea, but with very little sail, having always convoys, then she laboured pretty much and shipped a great deal of water
13. Tries.	[*No answer given*]
14. What is she for a roader.	She is a very good roader, never strains her cables we having rid very hard gales of wind in her and ships but very little water over her bows
15. Careens.	[*No answer given*]
16. Best sailing trim.	She requires all her masts to lean a little further aft

If the Admiralty or the Navy Board had chosen to review all the reports on sloops, say, from 1742 to 1756, despite the looseness of the responses, they would have been able to form some broad conclusions about the sailing qualities of these vessels. The salient points would have been as follows:

There are too many cases of sloops carrying lee helm. Those that do not have had their sails trimmed as far aft as possible by the raking of masts, particularly the mainmast.

All sloops have a tendency to roll deep but easy, this because most of them have a gentle turn of the bilge. This is acceptable since to broaden their underwater shape would reduce their speed through the water.

The majority are weatherly and can fore-reach on most other craft.

The pitching of some sloops is excessive and may be due to a number of factors: very fine lines at the bow ('lean harpins'), a fault only remedied by improved design; or to too much weight forward; or to a mast stepped too near the stem.

The early sloops (1732–1741), although they sail well tend to be wet because they are low in the waist. This is to be expected but future designs should be able to avoid this mistake.

The ketch rig does not perform well and should be discontinued as a rig for warships, including bomb vessels.

More attention must be paid to the rig of sloops. In some cases the performance of a good hull is spoilt by a poor sail plan. In particular the amount of canvas available aft needs to be reviewed upwards. This may involve conversion to ship rig or the use of a boomed-out spanker on two-masted sloops.

Staying seems to be achievable for most sloops unless under courses alone and in a head sea, which is likely to be the condition when courses alone are set on a beat. This again points to the inadequacy of sail aft.

Most sloops seem to swim best with a degree of drag to the keel. This was particularly so of the snow *Shark* of 1732. This feature should be evaluated and if found helpful be incorporated into the design of future sloops.

Care must be taken not to overload sloops lest their sailing ability be impaired.

It would appear that most sloops try and ride to their anchors well and that they can be careened easily.

Commercial designers seem to produce some excellent sloops. The practice of buying 'off the stocks' from reliable merchant yards is to be encouraged.

Appendix 5

THE DESIGNERS AND BUILDERS

To compile a list of the builders of sloops is a comparatively easy task but to do the same for the designers is more difficult. For much of the seventeenth century the responsibility for design – that is to say, the decisions on the construction, materials, shape and general layout of a vessel – lay largely with the individual master shipwrights, albeit working to an order or specification passed down by the Navy Board or the Council of State. The same can be said for shipwrights at those commercial yards building naval ketches, in that they were highly experienced in building this type of craft and much was left to their expertise. Correspondence between the Navy Board and the Admiralty in 1691 supports this view (see table below). Following the succession of William and Mary in 1689 there was a change in the 'old order' at the Admiralty and at the Navy Board and this could be regarded as the beginning of a more centralised approach to the design of warships. This was partly due to the arrival of Edmund Dummer as Surveyor in 1692. He had already been working at the Surveyor's office having joined the Surveyor, Sir John Tippets, as Assistant Surveyor in 1689. He pressed for a more rational approach to shipbuilding whereby more aspects of design were to be laid down by the Surveyor's office; indeed, there is evidence that he supplied draughts for ships built by merchant yards, and expected them to be adhered to. This was in effect the first move towards a form of 'establishment'.

In the case of sloops of whatever denomination, from this time onwards there appears to have been a fair degree of discussion between the Navy Board and the master shipwrights as to what was wanted. A good example of this was the debate surrounding the building of the many bomb vessels required at this time to mount an urgent attack on the French Channel harbours. It will be obvious that this period – one in which the Admiralty was under considerable pressure in the wars against France – was one of considerable change in the design process, so that it is not possible, in most cases, to ascribe the responsibility for design in all its forms to any particular post or individual.

At this point the post of Surveyor of the Navy needs some consideration. At the start of this period those appointed to this post had not been master shipwrights earlier in their careers. The first master shipwright appointed to the office was Sir John Tippets, who came to it from Portsmouth in 1672: in other words, this was the first time that a professional shipbuilder had held this post. It must be remembered that the duties of the Surveyor hitherto had encompassed more than just shipbuilding; indeed the whole of the Admiralty estate was his concern and this included dockyards and the survey of the waters around them. Edmund Dummer, when he joined Sir John Tippets in 1689, had previously only been assistant to the master shipwright at Chatham, but before that, under Tippets's patronage, his precocious draughting skills had been in great demand by the Navy Board. It is tempting at this stage to divert into the career of this extraordinarily accomplished man but it is enough to recognise that he was different to others working in this field. Hitherto the art of ship design had been developed from the practical experience of building them. The idea that a design could be derived from mathematics and scientific theory had not yet arrived but it was to be championed by Edward Dummer. He was not entirely successful in achieving his aim, either in this respect or in the centralisation of some aspects of design, but he did make a difference and channelled development in that direction. Sadly, this crusade has lacked subsequent attention partly due to his other outstanding achievements. He is chiefly remembered for his fine work in developing the Royal Dockyards at Portsmouth and Plymouth which made such a contribution to the maintenance of the fleet for the next century and beyond. He was dismissed in 1699 and quickly deployed his outstanding skills to developing packet services, including the first transatlantic service. He had a keen interest in small, fast, well-armed vessels, which influenced the design of sloops of all varieties throughout his short time as Surveyor after 1692. Following his, possibly unfair, dismissal he set up his own yard and continued to build and advise on small warships for the Navy in the early stages of the War of the Spanish Succession. He was succeeded in office by Daniel Furzer who, like Tippets, had been a master shipwright. The choice of a successor to Dummer had been a close one between Furzer and Fisher Harding, the builder of so many sloops. Furzer was to hold the post until 1715 but shared the post from 1706 with William Lee, who had been tasked in 1704 with building a sloop to the same dimensions as those being built by the ex-Surveyor Edmund Dummer. Both Lee and Furzer are likely to have been instrumental in drawing up the specification, including dimensions, for the *Otter* group of four small Sixth Rates built in 1709, though it is possible that Edmund Dummer had some input into this work. Of these, two were launched by master shipwrights and two by commercial yards. All were very close in keel dimension, breadth and burthen, implying that all builders were working to the same specification, if not design. In the following year the Navy bought four more from commercial constructors and it is worth noting that of these, three, including two built by Dummer, bore a remarkable similarity in dimensions and burthen to those that had previously been ordered by the Navy Board. One could be forgiven for suspecting a degree of collusion.

Jacob Acworth replaced Furzer in 1715, Lee having already departed in 1714. Acworth was to hold this post until his death in 1749, being joined by Joseph Allin (the younger) in 1746. In many ways it is a shame that Acworth did not follow Dummer directly for he also took the same stance regarding the centralisation of the design process. Whilst he did not possess the outstanding mathematical and draughting skills of Dummer, he did bring about some notable changes in ship design as in the example of introducing cant frames at the bow producing a far stronger as well as more economical solution to this part of a vessel's anatomy. In 1716 he was instructed to take over the control of the design process for all naval vessels. One wonders if this was at his own suggestion! This was the first time a Surveyor had been asked to take on this responsibility, though Dummer had tried to achieve this earlier, probably without sufficient support from a newly formed Navy Board. Despite this authorisation Acworth had to apply this new responsibility with some circumspection. The most senior master shipwrights jealously guarded their independence and certainly Stacey had been senior to Acworth before the latter's promotion to Surveyor. Therefore, one cannot say that from this point onwards all design was initiated in the Surveyor's office, but its influence grew, with far more oversight, advice and instruction coming from Acworth. This centralised control was even more pervasive in the case of sloops contracted out to merchant builders. This change in process marched in parallel with the gathering shift from a pragmatic and experienced-based approach to shipbuilding to one more influenced by mathematical and scientific theory, a development in which the French were in the lead. This may explain why the Royal Navy was punctilious in taking the lines off many of the French ships it captured.

Radical change in a large organisation is never easy and it has to be said that the knowledge and experience of the master shipwrights was not something that should or could be brushed aside lightly. And so it was with the light sloops built for the prevention of smuggling in 1721–1722. Because they were built by Stacey and Hayward (the two most senior master shipwrights), it is probable that they were also designed by these men. The value of experience accumulated by master shipwrights, at least in relation to sloops, is best shown by considering Richard Stacey's contribution in this field. His experiences in their construction and rebuilding stretched from 1719 to 1725 and possibly because of this he was invited to prepare a design for two much larger sloops: *Drake* launched in 1729 and a new *Spence* launched in 1730. He and Hayward built, and probably designed, two new bomb vessels in 1730. But in addition to this, in 1732 all the shipwrights were invited to offer their opinions as to the ideal dimensions and burthen for a sloop. It was Stacey's recommendations as to dimensions and burthen that were followed when each master shipwright was then invited to submit his own design. From this exercise, six sloops were built by the master shipwrights to their own designs. In Stacey's case, he built three: the *Cruizer* to his own design and two based on her lines but with modifications possibly recommended by Acworth.

The outbreak of the War of Jenkins' Ear in 1739 prompted a demand for more sloops, which was met by placing contracts with commercial yards, and for this it made sense to provide them with a specification and design that had been worked up in the Surveyor's office. By this time that office had a lot of experience of sloop design. Contract-building by commercial yards was a regular wartime practice, since in those circumstances the main task of the Royal Dockyards and their master shipwrights was the repair and maintenance of the extant fleet. Design of these sloops can be attributed to Acworth, but he may have delegated the detailed work to others under his close supervision. He did have a joint Surveyor to share the workload in Joseph Allin, who had been master shipwright at Portsmouth, but this was not until 1746, by which time the *Merlin* class design and that of their cousins the bomb ketches had been settled. The collection of plans at the Maritime Museum in Greenwich demonstrates the gradual shift in form from the sleek sloops of 1732 to the more robust vessels of 1741–1742, culminating in the *Merlin* class of 1744–1746. This shift was most necessary, not least to cope with the much increased weight of armament the sloops had to carry. But perhaps the most delightful postscript to this gradual centralisation of design is the order in 1761 for two sloops to the Richard Stacey design for *Cruizer* of 1732, albeit with some modifications!

It would be wrong to regard design by individual master shipwrights as dead: certainly not in the case of sloops. At the close of the War of the Austrian Succession in 1748 the policy of centralising design for sloops was relaxed, starting with a competition (in 1749) amongst master shipwrights to produce a design for a light sloop. The winners of this competition were Allin, now sole Surveyor, and Pierson Lock, master shipwright at Portsmouth. This led to the building of a group of sloops, some of which followed Allin's work, others that of Lock. But in the wings there was another master shipwright, Thomas Slade, who had come to the notice of Admiral Anson, First Lord of the Admiralty. How this came about is not entirely clear, but Benjamin Slade (probably Thomas's uncle) was master shipwright at Plymouth, where he carried out surveys of many captured French frigates and sloops that so impressed him that he wrote privately to Anson extolling their virtues. He may have taken the opportunity to promote his younger relative's talents at the same time. Certainly, when Allin fell ill in 1755, he was quickly retired by Anson, keen to be rid of his rather conservative influence on ship design, and Thomas Slade was appointed in his place. It was an appointment of genius. Thomas seems to have shared his relative's admiration for some aspects of French design, which he then applied to his own designs for frigates and sloops, and by common consent he went on to become the greatest British ship designer of the age of sail. Once established in office and with the new joint surveyor, William Bately, Slade centralised sloop design once again and, with the approach of the Seven Years War (1757–1763) contracted-out the building of them to merchant yards. It was to remain thus until the end of the war.

To close this preamble a word on specifications and design is necessary. In the mid-seventeenth century many specifications would contain only the barest detail, giving outline dimensions with broad indications of deck layout and cabins, but leaving the hull design of the vessel almost totally in the hands of the master shipwright or merchant builder.

Missing from the historical documentation is any record of the discussions that undoubtedly took place, but by the end of the process both parties had come to an understanding of what was required. For craft like the Commonwealth ketches, greater reliance was placed on the expertise of the commercial builder who specialised in this type. Surviving commercial contracts from the 1690s include a full specification that covers the sizes of every timber (scantlings), how they were to be fixed and the quality of workmanship expected. In Dummer's time as Surveyor, a draught usually accompanied the specification for rated ships, but that seems unlikely for small craft (apart from the brigantines he himself designed). The degree of reliance on the builder can be gauged from the inclusion in the specification of design elements, such as the angle of the stem and the stern post, the size of steps up and down at either end of the deck, the length of quarterdeck and forecastle, the number, size and precise location of gun ports and many other layout details. Ships were regularly checked by Navy Board officials during construction to monitor both progress and quality, and stage payments were dependent on satisfactory adherence to the contract specification. Once design had been centralised in the Surveyor's office, all contracts would be accompanied by a draught.

There follows a list of designers and the sloops of all types they created in approximately chronological order. The rig, if not otherwise noted, would be the two-masted snow or in the seventeenth century the two-masted Biscay rig. Ketches listed as such here had a ketch-shaped hull and ketch rig, so their rig is not detailed here. Bomb vessels were also ketch-rigged except for ship-rigged *Serpent* group of 1693. Their exception is noted in the table. All the others had ketch rig until 1759 when some were then once again given a ship rig.

A list of sloops by designer

(* Master shipwright; † Commercial; • Surveyor)

Designer	Name/launch date	Type	Builder (other than designer)	At	Comment
Robert Page †	Nonsuch 1651	Ketch		Wivenhoe	Purchased to work for the Commonwealth Navy and was a prototype for those that followed
Phineas Pett* and Captain John Taylor*	Eaglet 1655	Ketch	Higgins †	Bermondsey	Commercial builders working to a Pett–Taylor design or more likely a specification
	Hawke 1655	Ketch	Cooper †	Woolwich	
	Roe 1656	Ketch	Robert Page †	Wivenhoe	
	Hind 1656	Ketch	Robert Page †	Wivenhoe	
Captain John Taylor*	Blackamoor 1656	Ketch		Chatham Dyd	Three much larger vessels
	Cygnet 1656	Ketch		Chatham Dyd	
	Parrot 1657	Ketch		Chatham Dyd	
John Tippets*; became Surveyor 1672–1692; knighthood 1688	Chestnut 1665	Ketch		Portsmouth Dyd	Tippets's own designs working to a Navy Board specification
	Portsmouth 1667	Sloop[1]		Portsmouth Dyd	[1] Three masts
Robert Page †	Roe 1670	Ketch		Wivenhoe	
	Wivenhoe 1670	Ketch			
Manley Callis*	Swallow 1657	Ketch		Deptford Dyd	
	Lilly 1657	Ketch			
Christopher Pett*	Rose 1657	Ketch		Woolwich Dyd	
	Hart 1658	Ketch			
John Allin †	Colchester 1664	Ketch		Colchester	
Jonas Shish*	Deptford 1665	Ketch		Deptford Dyd	Most likely to have been to Shish's own designs and based on an order passed through the Navy Board
	Lilly 1672	Sloop			
	Swallow 1672	Sloop			
	Tulip 1672	Sloop			
	Dove 1672	Sloop			
	Whipster 1672	Sloop[2]			[2] Listed as brigantine
	Lizard 1673	Sloop			
	Dolphin 1673	Sloop			
	Vulture 1673	Sloop			
Anthony Deane*	Spy 1666	Sloop[3]		Harwich Dyd	[3] three-masted; remainder two-masted
	Fan Fan 1666	Sloop[3] Yacht[4]		Harwich Dyd	[4] Fan Fan classed as Sixth Rate, being a yacht for Prince Rupert
	Prevention 1673	Sloop		Portsmouth Dyd	
	Cutter 1673	Sloop		Portsmouth Dyd	
	Hunter 1673	Sloop		Portsmouth Dyd	
	Invention 1673	Sloop		Portsmouth Dyd	
John Smith †	Emsworth 1667	Sloop		Emsworth	

(* Master shipwright; † Commercial; • Surveyor)

Designer	Name/launch date	Type	Builder (other than designer)	At	Comment
Sir Phineas Pett II*	Chatham 1673	Sloop		Chatham Dyd	
	Chatham Double 1673	Sloop			
	Hound 1673	Sloop			
Phineas Pett III*	Bonetta 1673	Sloop		Woolwich Dyd	Pett design, but may have been built by his assistant
	Woolwich 1673	Sloop			
Joseph Lawrence	Experiment 1677	Sloop		Greenwich	Son of assistant master shipwright at Woolwich and later to become a master shipwright. This vessel probably to his own design in response to an express order from King Charles; the vessel was to be built 'in imitation of a brigantine'
Master shipwright Joseph Lawrence	Discovery 1692	Brigantine		Woolwich Dyd	Edmund Dummer, Assistant Surveyor at this time, had prepared a draught for these craft the first of which, Shark, was built by master shipwright Fisher Harding (see below). TNA Adm 2/171, 14 February 1691
	Spy 1693	Brigantine			
	Intelligence 1696	Brigantine			
Rolfe and Castle †	Hart 1691	Ketch		Rotherhithe	In 1691 there was correspondence between the Navy Board and the Admiralty regarding these ketches since some of them had been reported as being 'crank' (in modern parlance they were 'tender'), particularly the one built at Aldborough. The correspondence shows that the hull design of these vessels was left to the contractors. The Navy Board's advice was that the ketches' shortcomings may have been due to the shape of their bodies since the dimensions they had issued to the builders had been proved by the success of earlier ketches, notably Deptford and Chestnut. The Board concluded that the fault, if any, lay with the builder. The criticism was probably partial since the captain of Hart extolled her sailing qualities. The Navy Board pointed out that the problems could well be associated with poorly positioned ballast and/or being over-masted. TNA Adm 1/3563, 13 November 1691
Mr John Hayden †	Roe 1691	Ketch		Limehouse	
Mr John Frame †	Harp 1691	Ketch		Scarborough	
	Scarborough 1691	Ketch			
Edward Snelgrove†	Hind 1691	Ketch		Wapping	
John Taylor †	Talbot 1691	Ketch		Rotherhithe	
Jonas Shish †	Eaglet 1691	Ketch		Rotherhithe	
Henry Johnson †	Aldborough 1691	Ketch		Aldborough	
Robert Lee*	Salamander 1687	Bomb/sloop		Chatham Dyd	These prototype bomb vessels were novel in nature and would have been the subject of much discussion between the Navy Board and the master shipwright. There is a substantial body of correspondence on these three-masted bomb vessels (see Chapter 8). Whilst design would have remained with Lee there was considerable input from Edmund Dummer, now the Surveyor, on the rig and from others on the technicalities of mounting mortars
	Serpent 1693	Bomb/sloop			

Continued overleaf

(* Master shipwright; † Commercial; • Surveyor)

Designer	Name/launch date	Type	Builder (other than designer)	At	Comment
Fisher Harding*	Firedrake 1688	Bomb/sloop		Deptford Dyd	Whilst *Firedrake* was purpose-built, *Portsmouth* was a converted yacht, but her conversion would have involved many in the redesign process including engineers and artillery experts
	Portsmouth 1688	Bomb		Deptford Dyd	
	Shark 1691[5]	Brigantine		Deptford Dyd	[5] The draught for *Shark*, the first of the brigantines, was provided by Edmund Dummer (Surveyor 1692–1699). The proposals for her rig came from master shipwright Fisher Harding. The brigantines that followed her had to be redesigned to give them a better grip for towing line-of-battle ships. This meant greater burthen and increased draught. It is not clear whether this redesign work was done by Harding or Dummer but correspondence from Harding indicates that this initiative could well have lain with him
	Dispatch 1692	Brigantine		Deptford Dyd	
	Diligence 1693	Brigantine		Deptford Dyd	
	Firedrake 1693	Bomb		Deptford Dyd	
	Paramour 1694	Pink[6]		Deptford Dyd	
	Post Boy 1696	Brigantine		Deptford Dyd	
	Prohibition 1699[7]	Sloop		Woolwich Dyd	
					[6] This vessel was listed as a pink which indicates that she had the hull of a ketch but with a ship rig. She was used by the astronomer Edmund Halley for long voyages, hence the use of three masts. She was reputed to be 'crank'
					[7] One of a group of eight small sloops required to prevent the passage of illegal goods. Others by different builders
George Fowler †	Granado 1693	Bomb/ sloop	George Fowler	Rotherhithe	Ship rig. See *Serpent* 1693 above
William Stigant*	Fly 1694	Advice boat		Portsmouth Dyd	
	Mercury 1694	Advice boat			
	Express 1695[8]	Advice boat			[8] These two were slightly longer than the boats of 1694
	Post Boy 1695[8]	Advice boat			
	Scout Boat 1695[9]	Advice boat			[9] Small boat for work in Solent
Elias Waffe*	Messenger 1694	Advice boat		Plymouth Dyd	
	Post Boy 1694	Advice boat			
	Swift 1699	Sloop		Portsmouth Dyd	
	Wolf 1699	Sloop			
Mr James Parker †	Martin 1694	Ketch		Southampton	
Mr John Stigant †	Wren 1695	Ketch		Redbridge	
Robert Lee*	Mortar 1693[10]	Bomb/sloop		Chatham Dyd	[10] *Mortar* was one of the ship-rigged bomb/sloops of the *Serpent* 1693 group built under the supervision of the Surveyor Edmund Dummer and others. The second *Serpent* group of 1695 were smaller and ketch-rigged
	Serpent 1695[10]	Bomb/sloop			
	Swift 1695[5]	Brigantine			[5] See above

(* Master shipwright; † Commercial; • Surveyor)

Designer	Name/launch date	Type	Builder (other than designer)	At	Comment
Graves †	*Dreadful* 1695	Bomb/sloop		Limehouse	These bombs were all ketches. Commercial yards would have had good experience of building this type of hull but the reinforcements for bearing the mortars are likely to have been detailed in a Navy Board specification. The Surveyor and others would have supervised this aspect throughout the build
Edward Snelgrove †	*Thunder* 1695	Bomb/sloop		Limehouse	
Robert and John Castle †	*Granado* 1695	Bomb/sloop		Deptford	
John and Richard Wells †	*Furnace* 1695	Bomb/sloop		Bermondsey	
John Taylor †	*Carcass* 1695	Bomb/sloop		Rotherhithe	
Sir Henry Johnson †	*Comet* 1695	Bomb/sloop		Blackwall	
William Redding †	*Basilisk* 1695	Bomb/sloop		Wapping	
Robert Davis †	*Terror* 1696	Bomb/sloop		Limehouse	
Sir Henry Johnson †	*Blast* 1695	Bomb/sloop		Blackwall	
William Bagwell*	*Fly* 1696	Brigantine		Portsmouth Dyd	See design comments above at note [5]
Samuel Miller*	*Shark* 1699	Sloop		Deptford Dyd	[11] Two slightly larger sloops than those of 1699, they carried 4 as opposed to 2 guns. Initially anti-smuggling vessels, they were subsequently used for long-distance advice boat work following the loss of the two purpose-built large advice boats
	Otter 1700[11]	Sloop			
	Hound 1700[11]	Sloop			
Daniel Furzer *	*Merlin* 1699	Sloop		Chatham Dyd	Both completed by master shipwright Robert Shortiss on Furzer's move to Surveyor
	Swallow 1699	Sloop			
Robert Shortiss*	*Fox* 1699	Sloop		Sheerness Dyd	
Edmund Dummer •	*Eagle*	Advice boat	Fugar	Arundel	These two large oceanic advice boats may have been designed by Edward Dummer when he was Surveyor. He was also at that time MP for Arundel!
	Swift	Advice boat	Moore	Arundel	
Edmund Dummer †	*Ferret* 1704	Sloop		Blackwall	These two large sloops (128 tons) were proposed by Edmund Dummer to the Navy Board. A third was built by Master shipwright William Lee to the same dimensions and burthen (see below). The correspondence regarding 'depth in hold' shows that there was an element of competition here. Lee felt Dummer had an advantage with a smaller depth in hold.
	Weazle 1704	Sloop			
	Swan 1709	Sixth Rate			These two small Sixth Rates were closer to sloops in force, dimensions and burthen and are thus included here. These two were not Navy-designed but formed a commercial purchase from Dummer's yard
	Hind 1709	Sixth Rate			

Continued overleaf

(* Master shipwright; † Commercial; • Surveyor)

Designer	Name/launch date	Type	Builder (other than designer)	At	Comment
William Lee*	*Swift* 1704	Sloop		Woolwich Dyd	To same broad specification as Dummer's sloops of the same date. The Board expected that it would be different in form from Dummer's for purpose of comparison
John Poulter *	*Drake* 1705	Sloop	Joseph Allin (elder)*	Woolwich Dyd	John Poulter was master shipwright at Harwich 1706–1709 after which he became master shipwright at Sheerness. This design at 176 tons was the largest yet built and was an unusual one with guns on two decks, a form that was to be repeated by Richard Stacey in a design for two 200-ton sloops in 1729–1730.
Navy design or specification •	*Seahorse* 1709	Sixth Rates	William Yeames †	Ratcliffe (Limehouse)	These four Sixth Rates, included here because they had the force, dimensions and burthen equivalent to a sloop, were built at the same date as those by Dummer above. The Navy Board had ordered three: one, *Delight*, built by Richard Stacey (see below) and two by commercial yards. Subsequently another, *Margate*, was ordered from Master shipwright Joseph Allin (see below). It was then decided to buy four more from commercial contractors, one of whom was Edmund Dummer (see above)
	Otter 1710		Robert Smith †	Rotherhithe	
	Jolly 1709		William Johnson †	Blackwall	
	Lively 1709		John Wicker †	Deptford	
Joseph Allin (elder)*	*Margate* 1709	Sixth Rate		Deptford Dyd	At this point Joseph Allin was one of the most senior master shipwrights. It is therefore likely that the final form of these sloops was left to him, although the as-built dimensions of all, including the contract-built ships, above, suggests a common draught
	Jamaica 1710[12]	Sloop			[12] These four sloops initially were single-masted, although converted later. Two were rebuilt by Richard Stacey in 1719 (*Trial*) and 1723 (*Shark*). It is likely that Allin designed them to meet a Navy Board specification
	Trial 1710[12]	Sloop			
	Ferret 1711[12]	Sloop			
	Shark 1711[12]	Sloop			
Benjamin Rosewell*	*Hawk* 1721	Sloop		Chatham Dyd	
	Spy 1732	Sloop			
John Naish*	*Spy* 1721	Sloop		Portsmouth Dyd	

(* Master shipwright; † Commercial; • Surveyor)

Designer	Name/launch date	Type	Builder (other than designer)	At	Comment
Richard Stacey*	*Delight* 1719	Sixth Rate		Woolwich Dyd	Completed by Acworth
	Trial rebuilt 1719	Sloop		Deptford Dyd	Stacey at Deptford and Hayward at Woolwich
	Bonetta 1721	Sloop			were the two senior master shipwrights at this
	Otter 1721	Sloop			time and they had the lion's share of sloop
	Cruizer 1722	Sloop			design and construction between 1719 and 1732.
	Shark rebuilt 1723	Sloop			Stacey, in particular, benefited from experience
	Happy rebuilt 1725	Sloop			with the rebuilding of the surviving sloops of
	Spence 1725	Sloop			1710–1711
	Drake 1730	Sloop			Most of these sloops were rigged as snows.
	Terrible 1730	Sloop/bomb			*Trial* after rebuilding in 1719 may have been
	Spence 1731	Sloop			rigged for a while as a schooner and was
	Wolf 1731	Sloop			certainly rigged as a brigantine during her
					career
	Cruizer 1732[13]	Sloop			[13] *Cruizer* was one of the sloops in the large
	Hound 1732	Sloop			programme of 1732. Like all the others in
	Trial 1732	Sloop			this group, she followed Stacey's
					recommendations for dimensions and burthen.
					Her design would influence sloop design for
					the next two decades. The design for *Hound* and
					Trial may have come from Surveyor Acworth,
					but both sloops bore a distinct resemblance to
					Stacey's *Cruizer*, albeit with a little more beam
John Hayward*	*Ferret* 1721	Sloop		Woolwich Dyd	
	Swift 1721	Sloop			
	Weazle 1721	Sloop			
	Salamander 1730	Sloop/bomb			
	Grampus 1731	Sloop			
	Bonetta 1732	Sloop			
John Ward*	*Fly* 1732	Sloop		Sheerness Dyd	
Joseph Allin*	*Shark* 1732	Sloop		Portsmouth Dyd	Allin was master shipwright at Portsmouth until 1742 when he moved to Deptford before joining the ageing Acworth as joint Surveyor
	Hind 1744[14]	Sloop	Philemon Perry †	Blackwall	[14] His *Hind* class designs were ordered for
	Vulture 1744[14]	Sloop	John Greaves †	Limehouse	comparison with those of Acworth's *Merlin*
	Jamaica 1744[14]	Sloop		Deptford Dyd	class, the outcome of which was to favour the latter. This led to the building of the largest class of sloops until the arrival of the *Swan* class sloops in the 1760s and 1770s
	Trial 1744[14]	Sloop		Deptford Dyd	

Continued overleaf

(* Master shipwright; † Commercial; • Surveyor)

Designer	Name/launch date	Type	Builder (other than designer)	At	Comment
Joseph Allin •	Peggy 1749[15]	Sloop	John Holland*	Deptford Dyd	[15] Peggy was the joint winner in a competition to find the best design for a light sloop for anti-smuggling work
	Savage 1749	Sloop	Thomas Fellowes*	Woolwich Dyd	
	Speedwell 1752	Sloop	John Ward*, completed by Thomas Slade*	Chatham Dyd	
	Cruizer 1752	Sloop	John Holland*, completed by Thomas Fellowes*	Deptford Dyd	
	Savage 1750	Sloop	Thomas Fellowes*	Woolwich Dyd	
	Happy 1754	Sloop	Edward Allin*	Woolwich Dyd	
	Wolf 1754	Sloop	Adam Hayes*	Chatham Dyd	
	Hawk 1756[16]	Sloop	Robert Batson †	Limehouse	[16] This was the last ship designed by Joseph Allin (the younger). She may have started off as a ketch but given that later in her career she was rigged as a ship it would be more likely for her to have started with snow rig, but see sailing qualities reports in Appendix 4
Jacob Acworth; *	Hazard 1711[17]	Sloop		Woolwich Dyd	[17] These sloops were originally single-masted. As he was one of the most senior master shipwrights at this time, it is likely that Acworth designed them to match a Navy Board specification
	Happy 1711[17]	Sloop		Woolwich Dyd	

(* Master shipwright; † Commercial; • Surveyor)

Designer	Name/launch date	Type	Builder (other than designer)	At	Comment
Jacob Acworth • from 1716	Hound 1732[18]	Sloop	Richard Stacey*	Deptford Dyd	[18] Hound and Trial were almost exact copies of Stacey's Cruizer so the responsibility for design is not clear here. Stacey built them and therefore had the ultimate say in the outcome
	Trial 1732[18, 19]	Sloop		Deptford Dyd	
	Alderney 1734[20]	Sloop/bomb	John Hayward*	Woolwich Dyd	
	Blast 1740[21]	Sloop/bomb	Thomas West †	Deptford	
	Basilisk 1740	Sloop/bomb	Thomas Snelgrove †	Limehouse	[19] This is the famous Trial of Anson's expedition round the world
	Thunder 1740	Sloop/bomb	Elias Bird †	Rotherhithe	[20] Allegedly designed by the teenaged Duke of Cumberland but probably with a lot of assistance from Acworth, who was his tutor. As she was built by a senior master shipwright the responsibility for design may have been shared between Acworth, Hayward and the Duke. There are similarities in her lines with the later bombs and with the Merlin class sloops
	Carcass 1740	Sloop/bomb	James Taylor †	Rotherhithe	
	Lightning 1740	Sloop/bomb	Henry Bird †	Rotherhithe	
	Furnace 1740	Sloop/bomb	John Quallett †	Rotherhithe	
	Drake 1741[22]	Sloop	Thomas West †	Wapping	
	Hawk 1741	Sloop	Greville and Whetstone †	Limehouse	
	Swift 1741	Sloop	Robert Carter †	Limehouse	[21] All the subsequent bombs of this period would have been built to the Surveyor's design, which was a compromise between the more fulsome hull-form of traditional bombs and the sleeker shape of the cruising sloops, permitting these vessels to be used in either role
	Firedrake 1742	Sloop/bomb	Philemon Perry †	Blackwall	
	Mortar 1742	Sloop/bomb	Philemon Perry †	Blackwall	
	Comet 1742	Sloop/bomb	James Taylor †	Rotherhithe	
	Terror 1742	Sloop/bomb	Greville and Whetstone †	Limehouse	
	Serpent 1742	Sloop/bomb	Thomas Snelgrove	Limehouse	[22] These three sloops would have been built to a design from the Surveyor's office. The lines of these sloops show the influence of Stacey's designs of 1732
	Wolf 1742[23]	Sloop	Thomas West †	Deptford	[23] This was an enlarged version of the old Wolf of 1731 by Stacey
	Otter 1742[24]	Sloop	John Buxton (Jnr) †	Rotherhithe	[24] There is some evidence that the design of Peregrina/Merlin (see below) was based on Otter, although the forms are rather different
	Grampus 1743	Sloop	Philemon Perry †	Blackwall	
	Baltimore 1742[25]	Sloop	Thomas West †	Deptford	[25] Apparently this sloop was designed by Lord Baltimore, possibly with assistance from the Surveyor's office. She had a pink stern and a bilander rig
	Saltash 1742	Sloop	John Quallett †	Rotherhithe	
	Drake 1743	Sloop	John Buxton (Jnr) †	Deptford	
	Peregrina later Merlin 1744[26]	Sloop	Greville and Whetstone †	Limehouse	[26] This design was Acworth's proposal for this new class of 270-ton sloops, a design that would have been compared with Allin's Hind class above. The original plan is entitled Peregrina since the vessel was meant to replace a Spanish prize of that name, but she was renamed Merlin well after the plan was made. All sloops listed under this entry are to this design although there were minor alterations in form
	Swallow 1744	Sloop	John Buxton (Jnr) †	Deptford	
	Speedwell 1744[27]	Sloop	John Buxton (Jnr) †	Deptford	[27] Speedwell has been described as a ketch but this may be a confusion with a smaller sloop of the same name built in 1752 and designed by Allin

Continued overleaf

(* Master shipwright; † Commercial; • Surveyor)

Designer	Name/launch date	Type	Builder (other than designer)	At	Comment
	Falcon I 1744[28]	Sloop	John Barnard †	Harwich	[28] Falcon I was captured early in her career and replaced with Falcon II to a similar but not identical design. Falcon I was then recaptured swiftly and renamed Fortune
	Hazard 1744[29]	Sloop	John Buxton (Snr) †	Rotherhithe	
	Lizard 1744	Sloop	Philemon Ewer †	Bursledon	
	Hinchingbrooke 1745	Sloop	Moody Janvrin †	Bursledon	
	Tavistock 1745	Sloop	John Darley †	Gosport	[29] Hazard alone amongst sloops at this time was given a brigantine rig
	Hound 1745	Sloop	Stow and Bartlett †	Shoreham	
	Hornet 1745	Sloop	Chitty and Qualett †	Chichester	
	Raven 1745	Sloop	Hugh Blaydes †	Hull	
	Swan 1745	Sloop	Thomas Hinks †	Chester	
	Badger 1745	Sloop	Moody Janvrin †	Bursledon	
	Falcon II 1745[30]	Sloop	William Alexander †	Rotherhithe	[30] The replacement for Falcon I
	Scorpion 1746	Sloop	Wyatt and Major †	Buckler's Hard	
	Swallow 1745	Sloop	Henry Bird †	Rotherhithe	
	Kingfisher 1745	Sloop	John Darley †	Gosport	
	Dispatch 1745	Sloop	Stow and Bartlett †	Shoreham	
	Viper 1746	Sloop	Tito Durrel †	Poole	
	Grampus 1746	Sloop	John Reed †	Hull	
	Saltash 1746	Sloop	Qualett and Allin †	Rotherhithe	
Henry Bird †	Saltash 1741	Sloop		Deptford	These vessels were purchased whilst they were 'on the stocks', ie during construction. Once launched by the yard they would be fitted out, armed and rigged in one of the Royal Dockyards
Henry Bird †	Ferret 1743	Sloop		Rotherhithe	
Taylor and Randall †	Weazle 1745	Ship-sloop		Rotherhithe	
	Porcupine 1746	Ship-sloop		Rotherhithe	
Randall †	Merlin 1757	Ship-sloop		Rotherhithe	
Pierson Lock*	Saltash 1732	Sloop		Plymouth Dyd	
	Wasp 1749[31]	Sloop		Portsmouth Dyd	[31] Wasp was the joint winner in a competition to find the best design for a light sloop for anti-smuggling work
	Fly 1752[32]	Sloop		Portsmouth Dyd	
	Ranger 1752[32]	Sloop	Thomas Fellowes*[33]	Woolwich Dyd	[32] Fly and Ranger were part of a programme for six light anti-smuggling sloops, half to be ketch-rigged and half with a snow rig. One snow, Cruizer, was later converted to ship rig. Given her small size this is unusual
					[33] At this time there are several instances of master shipwrights building to another's design. In the case of Ranger she was completed by Slade and then Hayes
Benjamin Slade*	Hazard 1749[34]	Sloop		Portsmouth Dyd by Pierson Lock	[34] Benjamin Slade was master shipwright at Plymouth at this time, another example of making use of shipwrights in the design process. On his death in 1750 he was succeeded by Thomas Slade, usually thought to be his nephew

(* Master shipwright; † Commercial; • Surveyor)

Designer	Name/launch date	Type	Builder (other than designer)	At	Comment
Thomas Slade •	Bonetta 1756	Sloop	Henry Bird †	Rotherhithe	
	Merlin 1756	Sloop	John Quallett †	Rotherhithe	
	Spy 1756	Sloop	Robert Inwood †	Rotherhithe	
	Hunter 1756	Sloop	Stanton and Wells †	Rotherhithe	
	Viper 1756	Sloop	Thomas West †	Deptford	
	Favourite 1757[35]	Ship-sloop	Earlsman Sparrow †	Shoreham	[35] The Favourite class were the first sloops
	Infernal 1757[36]	Sloop/bomb	Henry Bird †	Southampton	designed for ship rig, although by this time many
	Tamar 1758	Ship-sloop	John Snooks †	Saltash	of the earlier snows had been converted to this
	Carcass 1759	Sloop/bomb	Stanton and Wells †	Rotherhithe	rig. The other feature of Favourite and Tamar was
	Terror 1759	Sloop/bomb	John Barnard †	Harwich	that Slade had given them a long quarterdeck,
	Basilisk 1759	Sloop/bomb	William Wells †	Harwich	right up to the mainmast
	Blast 1759	Sloop/bomb	Henry Bird †	Southampton	[36] Of this class of seven bomb vessels, four were
	Mortar 1759	Sloop/bomb	William Wells †	Deptford	rigged as ketches and three as ships. From this
	Thunder 1759	Sloop/bomb	Thomas Henniker †	Chatham	point on all purpose-built bomb vessels would be
	Ferret 1760	Ship-sloop	Stanton and Wells †	Rotherhithe	ship-rigged. A number of earlier snows were
					converted to bombs for use in the latter stages of
					the Seven Years War
	Nautilus 1762[37]	Ship-sloop	Thomas Hodgson †	Hull	[37] Unlike her sisters, Nautilus had a short
	Vulture 1763[38]	Ship-sloop	Davis and Bird †	Southampton	quarterdeck
	Swift 1763[38]	Ship-sloop	John Greaves †	Limehouse	[38] Based by Slade on the lines of the ex-French
					privateer L'Observateur. She had been taken into
					the French Navy as Epreuve, a name that she kept
					after capture by the Royal Navy in 1760
William Bately •	Stork 1756	Sloop	Stow and Bartlett †	Shoreham	
	Diligence 1756	Sloop	William Wells †	Deptford	
	Alderney 1757	Sloop	John Snooks †	Saltash	
	Senegal 1760[39]	Ship-sloop	Henry Bird †	Rotherhithe	[39] These sloops were designed by Bately, who
	Beaver 1761[39]	Ship-sloop	Robert Inwood †	Rotherhithe	was instructed to base the hull-form on the lines
	Martin 1761[39]	Ship-sloop	John Randall †	Rotherhithe	of the French frigate L'Abenakise, taken into the
					Royal Navy as Aurora. However, Senegal is of a
					totally different shape with a scow-like forward
					section and a much fuller midship section
Richard Stacey*	Druid 1761[40]	Sloop	Barnard and Turner	Harwich	[40] It is fitting to close with the revival of a design
	Lynx 1761[40]	Sloop	Stanton and Wells	Rotherhithe	from 1732 by a master shipwright who possibly
					contributed more to the development of this class
					of vessel than any other

Appendix 6

ARMING THE SLOOP OF WAR

The arming of a sloop can be examined under two headings: the type of guns carried and the number of those guns. The first is rather simpler than the latter for often sloops were obliged to take what they could get and several, certainly in the late seventeenth century, suffered shortages in their inventory of guns. At this period all guns, whether for land service or naval use, were supplied by the Board of Ordnance, in effect an independent third service. Its personnel were usually military men but the Navy was the bigger customer, and at times this inevitably produced tension if not friction between the parties. The 'joint-service' origins of artillery meant that before the eighteenth century the Navy could not dictate the characteristics of guns for sea service.

Before about 1715 guns were denoted by names rather than the more pragmatic classification by weight of shot that was developed later. The limitations of gunfounding techniques meant that standardisation was almost impossible, so

the tolerances accepted in dimensions and weight of shot for any particular type of gun were very loose by modern standards. Furthermore, guns existed in variant forms: either intentionally shortened versions called 'cutts' or specially strengthened ones described as 'fortified'. (There was the additional complication of whether the guns were made of brass or iron, although the only sloop-size vessels carrying brass guns would be the royal yachts.) Because of these factors, each gun type covered a broad spectrum of variations, so the sources do not necessarily agree on the data they quote for each type. In practice, while the vessel's design specification might cite a weapon of a particular type and median weight, sloops often received the nearest available, and this might not even result in a homogeneous battery in terms of gun lengths and weights. There are a few Board of Ordnance records that list the precise armament of ships at a particular point in time, but they are rare. As with the details of rigging, the best way to be sure of the arming of a sloop,

Characteristics of guns carried by sloops

Name	Approximate dates of service in sloops	Weight of shot	Weight	Length and comments
Patereroes	1650–1712	Grape shot	1½cwt	3ft, breech-loading
Swivel guns	1712–1815	½lb and grape shot	1½cwt	3ft, muzzle-loading
Robinet	1650–1689	¾lb	1cwt in land service, 2½cwt in sea service	5ft land service, less for sea service, (so a shorter and heavier weapon)
Falconet	1650–1712	1¼–1½lb	1¾cwt in land service, 3½–4½cwt in sea service	6ft in sea service; however, logs indicate that lengths of 5ft could be obtained
Falcon	1650–1712	2½–3lb	5cwt (560lb) in land service, 600–800lb in sea service	7ft in length; however, there were few sloops that could have accommodated this length so the naval weapon was probably a 'cutt'
3-pounder, sea service only	1690–1760	3lb	4–9cwt	4½–6ft
Minion	1655-1715	4lb	10cwt in land service, 4–9cwt in sea service	4-7ft in land and sea service
4-pounder, sea service only	1715–1800	4lb	11–12cwt	5½–6ft
Saker, sea service only	1656–1700	5lb	For ketches, 7–10cwt	For ketches, 6–7ft
6-pounder, sea service only	1744–1815	6lb	16–24cwt	6-9ft. The short 6-pounder was introduced in 1755
9-pounder or demi-culverin, sea service only	1656–1683	9lb	For ketches, 11–13cwt	For ketches 6–7ft

particularly up until the death of Queen Anne, is by examining the captains' logs, which often note changes to proposed armaments and mid-career alterations due to the strategic situation or to captains' demands for more firepower. Below is a table which will act as a rough guide to the type of guns employed by sloops over the period of this book.

There are some seemingly odd figures in this table which need clarification. All guns and cannon should ideally have a fixed internal length related to the size of their bore. The diameter of the bore is the weapon's calibre. The lengths quoted in official lists obviously relate to the overall length of the weapons. In a cannon for land service, the barrel length does not matter, but in sea service it does as space is at a premium (ideally, the gun should be short enough to allow reloading inside the gun port but long enough so that muzzle flash does not threaten the ship's side – this latter depending on the type of ship and where the gun was to be mounted). The barrel could be cut down or, more likely, be cast shorter, and such guns were referred to as 'cutts'. The disadvantage was that it reduced the power of the weapon for any given charge. Taking the example of the 6-pounders as carried by sloops after 1744, they were shortened (or new

'short' weapons were issued) in 1755 and then used by sloops until the end of the century and beyond. If specifically designed as a 'short' weapon, it could have its weight of metal increased to permit a larger charge to be used to overcome the shortness of the barrel. A short barrel could not throw a shot as far as a long one size for size because the ball would leave the barrel before achieving peak velocity. The important point is that the variation in weight and length of these weapons is not surprising since they had to be tailored to suit the ships that would carry and fire them.

The type and number of guns carried are listed in the main text but for an overview the official allocations are set out below. Care should be taken not to confuse the number of gun ports shown in plans with the number of guns actually carried. For example, the *Cruizer* class of 1732 were ordered to be pierced for 14 but were only allocated 8 guns (though they had a large complement of swivel guns). In the seventeenth century there was the additional complication of different peace and war complements of both men and guns, but sloops tended to have so few guns that they were rarely affected. Please note that in dealing with groups and classes the table inevitably averages the burthen and gives only an outline date or period for launchings.

Gun establishments for sloops

Type/class (number of vessels)	Approx burthen (tons)	Dates launched	Pierced for (broadside + bow-chase)	Carriage guns	Number	Swivels
Ketches: *Nonsuch* and the *Eaglet* group (6)	55	1654–1656	8	Minions	6–8	Not given
Ketches (2)	90	1656	8	Demi-culverins and sakers	6 and 8	Not given
Ketches: *Cygnet* group (6)	55	1657	8	Minions	6–8	Not given
Ketches (5)	90	1664–1665	10	Sakers	8-10	Not given
Sloops (4)	28–43	1666–1667	4	?Falcons	4	Not given
Sloops (17)	19–68	1672–1673	2–4	?Falcons	2-4	Not given
Bomb *Salamander*	134	1687 ?	14	Minions	8	Not given
				Falconets	2	
Bomb *Firedrake*	203	1688	Not given	Minions	8	6 patereroes
				Falcons	4	
Bomb *Portsmouth*	142	1688	Not given	Minions	8	Not given
				Falcons	2	
Ketch: *Hart* group (8)	96	1691	10	?Sakers	10	Not given
Brigantines: *Shark* group (5)	77 (*Shark* 58)	1691	6	3pdr and falconets, possibly as swivels	6	2 See left
Bomb *Kitchen*	100	1692	Not given	?Minions	8	Not given
Bomb vessels: *Serpent* group (4)	270	1693	14	Sakers	12	6 patereroes
Advice boats (4)	73	1694	Not given	Minions	4	6 patereroes
Ketches (3)	95	1694–1695	Not given	?Sakers	10	
Bomb vessels: *Serpent* class (10)	150	1695–1696	Not given	Sakers	12	6 patereroes
Advice boats (3)	77 (*Scout Boat* 38)	1695–1696	6	Minions	6, *Scout Boat* 4	6 patereroes
Brigantines (4)	75	1695–1696	Not given	3pdr	6	2

Type/class (number of vessels)	Approx tons	Dates launched	Pierced for (broadside + bow-chase)	Carriage guns	Number	Swivels
Advice boats (2)	153	1696	14	3pdr	10	8
Sloops: *Bonetta* group (8)	65	1699	2	Falconets	2	4 patereroes
Sloops: *Hound* group (2)	83	1699	4	Falconets	4	4 patereroes
Bomb *Salamander* as rebuilt	122	1703	Not given	Not given	4	Not given
Sloops: *Ferret* group (3)	126	1704	Not given	As built: minions & falconets	8+2	Not given
				Later: 3pdr	12	
Sloop: *Drake*	176	1705	Not given	3pdr	14 on two decks	Not given
Sloops/Sixth Rates: *Otter* group (4)	162	1709	Not given	Minions	14	Not given
Sloops/Sixth Rates: purchased (4)	162	1709	Not given	*Hind* & *Swan*: 4pdr	12	Not given
				Jolly: 4pdr	10	
				Lively: 3pdr	12	
Sloops: *Jamaica* and *Hazard* groups (6)	114	1710–1711	12	As built: 3pdr	10	4
				Later: 3pdr & 4pdr	2+8	
Sloop: *Trial* as rebuilt	142	1719	12	3pdr	10	4
				As rebuilt: 3pdr & 4pdr	2+8	
Sloops: *Bonetta* group (2)	60	1721	Not given	3pdr	4	4
Sloops: *Otter* group (2)	90	1721	8	3pdr	6–4	4
Sloops: *Cruizer* group (4)	100	1721	12	4pdr	8–6	4
Sloops: rebuilt from *Jamaica* and *Hazard* groups above (2)	124 and 114	1723–1725	12	3pdr	10	4
Sloop: *Spence*	114	1723	12	3pdr	8	4
Bomb vessels: *Salamander* class (2)	263	1730	10	As sloop 4pdr	8	As sloop 14
				As bomb 4pdr	6	As bomb 6
Sloops: *Drake* class (2)	200	1729–1730	14	4pdr	8	12
Sloops: *Grampus* and *Trial*	160 and 244	1731	12 and 14	3pdr	6 and 8	10 and 12
Sloops: *Cruizer* class (8)	200	1732	14	3pdr (4pdr in *Shark*)	8	12
Bomb: *Alderney*	264	1734	16 + 2	As sloop 6pdr	10	14
				As bomb 6pdr	6	8
Bomb vessels: *Basilisk* and *Comet* classes (12)	270	1740–1742	16–14	As sloop 4pdr	10	As sloop 14
				As bomb 4pdr	8	As bomb 8
Sloops: *Drake* class (3)	200	1741	14	4pdr	8 (10 in 1744)	12
Sloop: *Saltash* purchased	220	1742	Not given	4pdr	8	12
Sloops: *Wolf* and *Baltimore* classes (6)	250	1742–1743	16	4pdr	14	14
Sloop: *Ferret* purchased	255	1743	Not given but possibly 16	4pdr	14	14
Sloops: *Merlin* and *Hind* classes (25)	270	1744–1746	14	6pdr	10 (14 in 1748)	14
Ship-sloops: *Weazle* and *Porcupine* purchased	310	1745 –1746	18 + 2	6pdr	16	14
Sloops: *Wasp* group (4)	140	1749–1750	12	3pdr	10	10
Sloops: *Fly* and *Cruizer* classes (6)	140	1752	12	3pdr	8	10
Sloop: *Hawk*	220	1756	14 + 2	3pdr (4pdr in 1761)	8 then 10	10
Sloops: *Bonetta* and *Hunter* classes (5)	220	1756	14 + 2	6pdr (short)	10	12
Sloops: *Alderney* class (3)	235	1756	14 + 2	4pdr	10	12
Ship-sloops: *Favourite* class (3)	310	1757–1762	18 + 2	6pdr (short)	16	14
Ship-sloop: *Merlin* purchased	304	1757	18 + 2	6pdr (short)	18	14
Ship-sloops: *Ferret* and *Beaver* classes (4)	290	1760–1761	16 + 2	6pdr (short)	14	12
Sloops: *Druid* class (2)	210	1761	14	4pdr	10	12
Ship-sloops: *Swift* class (2)	270	1763	14 + 2	6pdr (short)	14	12

BIBLIOGRAPHY

Aldrich, David Dennis, *Admiral Sir John Norris and the British Naval Expeditions to the Baltic Sea 1715-1727*, Nordic Academic Press, 2009

Anderson, Dr R C, *Oared Fighting Ships*, Percival Marshall, London, 1962

Anderson, Dr R C, *Seventeenth-Century Rigging: a Handbook for Model-Makers*, Percival Marshall & Co Ltd, 1955

Baker, William A, *Sloops & Shallops*, Barre Publishing Co, Massachusetts, 1966

Baker, William A, *Colonial Vessels: Some Seventeenth Century Ship Designs*, Barre Publishing Co, Massachusetts, 1962

Benham, Harvey, *Once Upon a Tide*, George G Harrap, London, 1955

Biddlecombe, George, *The Art of Rigging*, Dover Publications Inc, New York, 1990

Black, Jeremy, *Naval Power: A History of Warfare and the Sea from 1500*, Palgrave Macmillan, Basingstoke, 2009

Boudriot, Jean, *La Belle: Cavalier de La Salle – The 1684 Expedition*, Collections Archeologie Navale Française, Les Editions ANCRE, Nice, 2012

Boudriot, Jean, *Corvette La Creole*, J Boudriot Publications, Paris, 1990

Bromley, J S, *Corsairs and Navies 1660-1760*, The Hambledon Press, London, 1987

Bruseth, James E & Turner, Toni S, *From a Watery Grave: The Discovery and Excavation of La Salle's Shipwreck, La Belle*, Texas A & M University Press, College Station, 2005

Chapelle, Howard I, *The History of the American Sailing Navy*, W W Norton Co Inc, New York, 1949

Chapelle, Howard I, *The Search for Speed under Sail*, W W Norton Co Inc; published in the United Kingdom by Allen & Unwin Ltd, London, 1967

Clark, Sir George, The *Later Stuarts 1660–1714* (2nd edition), Oxford University Press, Oxford, 1987

Cockett, F B, *Peter Monamy 1681–1749 and his circle*, The Antique Collectors Club Ltd, Woodbridge, 2000

Colledge, J J, & Warlow, Ben, *Ships of the Royal Navy*, Casemate, USA, 2010

Corbett, Julian S, *Some Principles of Maritime Strategy*, Filiquarian Publishing on demand. Original publication London 1911

Cordingly, David, *The Art of the Van de Veldes*, National Maritime Museum, London, 1982

Dalton, Tony, *British Royal Yachts*, Halsgrove, Tiverton, 2002

Davies, J D, *Pepys's Navy*, Seaforth Publishing, Barnsley, 2008

Davis, Ralph, *English Merchant Shipping and Anglo-Dutch Rivalry in the 17th Century*, National Maritime Museum, HMSO, London, 1975

Davis, Ralph, *The Rise of the English Shipping History in the 17th and 18th Centuries*, David and Charles, Newton Abbot, 1972

de La Roncière, Ch & Clerc-Rampal, G, *Histoire de la Marine Française*, Librairie Larousse, Paris, 1934

Dull, Jonathan R, *The French Navy and the Seven Years War*, University of Nebraska Press, Lincoln and London, 2005

Falconer, William, *Falconer's Marine Dictionary (1780)*, David & Charles Ltd, Newton Abbot, 1970

Ferreiro, Larrie D, *Ships and Science: The Birth of Naval Architecture in the Scientific Revolution 1600-1800*, The MIT Press, Cambridge, Massachusetts, 2010

Fox, Frank L, *The Four Days' Battle of 1666*, Seaforth Publishing, Barnsley, 2009

Froude, James Anthony, *English Seamen in the Sixteenth Century*, Longmans, Green & Co, London & Bombay, 1901

Gardiner, Robert and Lavery, Brian (eds), *The Line of Battle: The Sailing Warship 1650–1840*, Conway Maritime Press, London, 1992

Gardiner, Robert, *The First Frigates: 9-pounder and 12-pounder Frigates, 1748–1815*, Conway Maritime Press, London, 1992

Goodwin, Peter, *The 20-Gun Ship Blandford*, Conway Maritime Press, London, 1988

Goodwin, Peter, *The Bomb Vessel Granado 1742*, Conway Maritime Press, London, 1989

Goodwin, Peter, *The Construction and Fitting of the Sailing Man of War 1650–1850*, Conway Maritime Press, London, 1987

Greene, Jack P & Morgan, Philip D, *Atlantic History: A Critical Appraisal*, Oxford University Press, Oxford, 2009

Harding, Richard, *Seapower and Naval Warfare 1650–1830*, UCL Press Ltd, London, 1999

Harland, John, Illustrated by Myers, Mark, *Seamanship in the Age of Sail*, Conway Maritime Press, London, 1984

Harris, Daniel G, *F H Chapman: The First Naval Architect and His Work*, Conway Maritime Press, London, 1989

Heaps, Leo, *Log of the Centurion, based on the original papers of Captain Philip Saumarez on board HMS Centurion, Lord Anson's flagship, during his circumnavigation 1740–44*, Hart-Davis MacGibbon, London, 1973

Heaton, Peter, *Yachting – A History*, B T Batsford, London, 1955

Hepper, David J, *British Warship Losses in the Age of Sail 1650–1859*, Jean Boudriot Publications, Rotherfield, 1994

Hill, J R (ed), *The Oxford Illustrated History of the Royal Navy*, Oxford University Press, Oxford, 1995

Hogg, Ian & Batchelor, John, *Naval Gun*, Blandford Press, Poole, 1978

Howard, Dr Frank, *Sailing Ships of War 1400–1860*, Conway Maritime Press, London, 1979

Jenkins, E H, *A History of the French Navy*, Macdonald and Janes, London, 1973

Jones, J R, *The Anglo-Dutch Wars of the 17th Century*, Longman Group, London, 1996

Keble Chatterton, E, *Old Ship Prints*, Spring Books, London, 1965

King, Cecil, *H.M.S.: His Majesty's Ships and Their Forbears*, The Studio Publications, London, 1940

Kirsch, Peter, *Fireship: The Terror Weapon of the Age of Sail*, Seaforth Publishing, Barnsley, 2009

Laird Clowes, G S, *Sailing Ships: Their History and Development*,

Part 1 Historical Notes, HMSO, London, 1962. (Based on the Science Museum collection)

Laird Clowes, G S, *Sailing Ships: Their History and Development, Part 2 Catalogue of Exhibits, with Descriptive Notes*, HMSO, 1952. (Based on the Science Museum collection)

Laird Clowes, Sir William, *The Royal Navy, Vol 2*, reprint Chatham Publishing, London, 1996

Landstrom, Bjorn, *The Ship*, Allen and Unwin, London, 1961

Lavery, Brian and Stephens, Simon, *Ship Models: Their purpose and development from 1650 to the present*, Zwemmer, London, 1995

Lavery, Brian (ed), *Deane's Doctrine of Naval Architecture, 1670*, Conway Maritime Press, London, 1981

Lavery, Brian, *The Arming and Fitting of English Ships of War 1600–1815*, Conway Maritime Press, London, 1995

Lees, James, *The Masting and Rigging of English Ships of War 1625-1860*, Conway Maritime Press, London, 1979

Little, Benorsen, *Pirate Hunting*, Potomac Books Inc, Virginia, 2010

Lyon, David, *The Sailing Navy List*, Conway Maritime Press, London, 1993

Macintyre, Donald, *The Privateers*, Paul Elek, London, 1975

Mahan, A T, *The Influence of Seapower upon History 1660-1783*, reprint Dover Publications Inc, New York, 1987

Marquardt, Karl Heinz, *The Global Schooner: Origins, Development, Design and Construction 1695–1845)*, Conway Maritime Press, London, 2003

Marquardt, Karl Heinz, *Eighteenth-century Rigs & Rigging*, Conway Maritime Press, London, 1992

McKay, John & Colman, Ron, *The 24-Gun Frigate Pandora 1779*, Conway Maritime Press, London, 1992

McKee, Eric, *Working Boats of Britain*, Conway Maritime Press, London, 1983

Mehl, Hans, *Naval Guns: 500 years of Ship and Coastal Artillery*, Chatham Publishing, London, 2002

Munday, John, *Naval Cannon*, Shire Album No 186, Shire Publications Ltd, Princes Risborough, 1998

National Maritime Museum, *The Art of the Van de Veldes*, The National Maritime Museum, 1982

Norman, Charles Boswell, *The Corsairs of France ... with portraits and a map*, Sampson Low, Marston, Searle & Rivington, London, 1887. Reprinted by Amazon on demand from British Library copy

Owen, John Hely, *War at Sea under Queen Anne 1702-1708*, Cambridge University Press, Cambridge, 1938. Print on demand edition, Cambridge, 2010

Padfield, Peter, *Maritime Supremacy and the Opening of the Western Mind: Naval Campaigns that shaped the Modern World 1588-1782*, John Murray, London, 1999

Pepys, Samuel, *Memoirs of the Royal Navy 1690*, reprint Naval Institute Press, Maryland and Seaforth Publishing, Barnsley, 2010

Pepys, Samuel (Latham, Robert & Matthews, William, eds), *The Diary of Samuel Pepys*, 11 vols, Collins, London, 1970–1983

Peterssen, Lennarth, *Rigging Period Ship Models*, Chatham Publishing, London, 2000

Phillips-Birt, Douglas, *Fore and Aft Sailing Craft and the Development of the Modern Yacht*, Seeley Service, London, 1962

Pocock, Tom, *Battle for Empire: the very first world war 1756-63*, Michael O'Mara Books Ltd, London, 1998

Powley, Edward B, *The Naval Side of King William's War*, John Baker, London, 1972

Ritsema, Alex, *Pirates and Privateers from the Low Countries 1500–1810*, Published by the Author, 2008

Rodger, N A M and Cock, Randolph, *A Guide to the Naval Records in the National Archives of the UK*, University of London, School of Advanced Study, Institute of Historical Research, 2008

Rodger, N A M, *The Command of the Ocean: A Naval History of Britain, 1649–1815)*, Allen Lane, London, Books, 2004

Salisbury, W & Anderson, R C, *A Treatise on Shipbuilding and A Treatise on Rigging written about 1620–1625*, The Society of Nautical Research, London, 1958

Stradling, R A, *The Armada of Flanders: Spanish Maritime Policy and European War, 1568-1668*, Cambridge University Press, Cambridge, 1992

Sutherland, William, *The Ship-Builder's Assistant*, Ecco Collections Online and on demand

Sutherland, William, *Britain's Glory or Ship-Building Unveil'd*, Ecco Print Editions, reproduction from The British Library copy

Tredrea, John and Sozaev, Eduard, *Russian Warships in the Age of Sail 1696 – 1860 (Design, Construction, Careers and Fates)*, Seaforth Publishing, 2010

Tunstall, Brian, Naval *Warfare in the Age of Sail (the Evolution of Fighting Tactics 1650-1815)*, Conway Maritime Press, 1990

United States Naval Academy Museum, *Henry Huddleston Rogers' Collection of Ship Models*, The Naval Institute Press, 1971

Waite, A H, *National Maritime Museum Catalogue of Ship Models Part 1, Ships of the Western Tradition to 1815*, Undated loose-leaf binder, HMSO

Wallersdin, Immanuel, *The Modern World-System II (Mercantilism and the Consolidation of the European World-Economy, 1600-1750)*, Academic Press, Inc, New York, 1980

Ware, Chris, *The Bomb Vessel (Shore Bombardment Ships of the Age of Sail)*, Conway Maritime Press, 1994

White, E W, *British Fishing-Boats and Coastal Craft, Part I: Historical Survey*, HMSO. 1957 (Based on the Science Museum Collection).

White, E W, *British Fishing-Boats and Coastal Craft, Part 2: Descriptive Catalogue and List of Plans*, HMSO, 1952 (Based on the Science Museum Collection).

Wilcox, L A, *Mr Pepys' Navy*, G Bell and Sons, London, 1966

Williams, Basil, *The Whig Supremacy 1714–1760 (2nd edition)*, Oxford University Press, Oxford, 1985

Willis, Sam, *Fighting at Sea in the Eighteenth Century: The Art of Sailing Warfare*, The Boydell Press, Woodbridge, 2008

Winfield, Rif, *British Warships in the Age of Sail 1603–1714*, Seaforth Publishing, Barnsley, 2009

Winfield, Rif, *British Warships in the Age of Sail 1714–1792*, Seaforth Publishing, Barnsley, 2007

Woodman, Richard, *The History of the Ship*, Conway Maritime Press, London, 2005

Xabier Agothe & Jose Lopez, Bertan Series No 23, *Gure Itsasontziak, Gipuzkoako Foru Aldundia Disputacion Foral de Gipuzkoa*, A publication by the Albaola Association at Pasaia in Northern Spain. Written in Basque but with an English translation

INDEX